Y0-BRL-995

» «

CONTENTS

» «

iii

Contents

iv

Contents

Contents

Contents

ACKNOWLEDGMENTS

》《

"The Meanings of Work." A portion of the introduction to Part I appears in a slightly altered form in *The Journal of Psychiatric Treatment and Evaluation*.

Chapter 1

James O'Toole, et al. "Work in America." From *Work in America*, edited by James O'Toole. Report of a Special Task Force to the Secretary of Health, Education, and Welfare. The MIT Press, 1973. Reprinted by permission of the author.

Mortimer J. Adler, "Work, Education, and Leisure." From *Relating Work and Education*, edited by Dyckman W. Vermilye. Copyright © 1977 by Jossey-Bass, Inc. Reprinted by permission.

E. F. Schumacher, "Good Work." From *Relating Work and Education*, edited by Dyckman W. Vermilye. Copyright © 1977 by Jossey-Bass, Inc. Reprinted by permission.

Daniel Yankelovich, "The Meaning of Work," in The American Assembly, *The Worker and the Job: Coping with Change*, edited by Jerome M. Rosow, pp. 19–47. Copyright © 1974 by The American Assembly, Columbia University. Reprinted by permission. All rights reserved.

Chapter 2

"Samuel Lipson: Bread and Water." Reprinted by permission of the publisher from *American Labor: The Twentieth Century*, edited by Jerold S. Auerbach. Copyright © 1969 by Bobbs-Merrill Company.

Studs Terkel, "Steelworker: Mike Lefevre." From *Working: People Talk About What They Do All Day and How They Feel About What They Do*, by Studs Terkel. Copyright © 1974 by Studs Terkel. Reprinted by permission of Pantheon Books, a division of Random House, Inc.

John R. Coleman, "Blue-Collar Journal: A College President's Sabbatical." Abridged from pp. 24, 28–29, 39–40, 49, 59, 183–184, 219–225, 242–243 in *Blue-Collar Journal: A College President's Sabbatical*, by John R. Coleman (J. B. Lippincott Company). Copyright © 1974 by John R. Coleman. Reprinted by permission of Harper and Row, Publishers, Inc.

Göran Palm, "The Flight from Work." Adapted from *The Flight from Work*, by Göran Palm. Copyright © 1977 by Cambridge University Press. By permission of the publisher.

Chapter 3

Thomas Dublin, "Women, Work, and Protest: The Early Lowell Mills. . . ." Adapted from "Women, Work, and Protest in the Early Lowell Mills: 'The Oppressing Hand of Avarice Would Enslave Us,' " by Thomas Dublin, *Labor History*, volume 16 (Winter 1975), pp. 99–116. Copyright © 1975 by *Labor History*. Reprinted by permission of the publisher.

Acknowledgments

Carl Sandburg, 10 lines from "Mill Doors." From *Chicago Poems*, by Carl Sandburg, copyright 1916 by Holt, Rinehart & Winston, Inc.; copyright 1944 by Carl Sandburg. Reprinted by permission of Harcourt Brace Jovanovich, Inc.

Barbara Wertheimer, "Women's Wages, Women's Work." From *We Were There: The Story of Working Women in America*, by Barbara Mayer Wertheimer. Copyright © 1977 by Barbara Mayer Wertheimer. Reprinted by permission of Pantheon Books, a Division of Random House, Inc.

Agnes Nestor, "Birth of a Labor Organizer." Reprinted by permission of Rosalyn Baxandall, from *America's Working Women*, edited by Rosalyn Baxandall, Linda Gordon, and Susan Reverby, Random House, 1976, pp. 288–291.

Augusta Clawson, "Shipyard Diary of a Woman Welder." Reprinted by permission of Rosalyn Baxandall, from *America's Working Women*, edited by Rosalyn Baxandall, Linda Gordon, and Susan Reverby, Random House, 1976, pp. 288–296.

Terry Wetherby, "Butcher: Nancy Kaye Andersen." From the book *Conversations: Working Women Talk About Doing a Man's Job*, by Terry Wetherby. Copyright 1979. Published by Les Femmes Publishing, 231 Adrian Road, Millbrae, CA 94030.

Chapter 4

Studs Terkel, "Editor: Nora Watson." From *Working: People Talk About What They Do All Day and How They Feel About What They Do*, by Studs Terkel. Copyright © 1974 by Studs Terkel. Reprinted by permission of Pantheon Books, a Division of Random House, Inc.

J. Patrick Wright, "Loyalty—Team Play—The System." From *On a Clear Day You Can See General Motors*, Grosse Pointe, Michigan: Wright Enterprises, 1979, pp. 32–48. Copyright 1979 by J. Patrick Wright. Reprinted by permission.

David W. Ewing, "Freedom Inside the Organization." Adapted from "The Black Hole in American Rights" from *Freedom Inside the Organization*, by David Ewing. Copyright © 1977 by David Ewing. Reprinted by permission of the publisher, E. P. Dutton.

Jacques Barzun, "The Professions Under Siege." Copyright © 1978 By *Harper's* Magazine. All rights reserved. Reprinted from the October 1978 issue by special permission.

Earl Shorris, "Dividends." From *Harper's*, March 1981, pp. 71–72 (excerpted from *The Oppressed Middle: Politics of Middle Management*, Anchor Press/Doubleday, 1981). Copyright 1981 by Earl Shorris. Reprinted by permission of the author.

Chapter 5

Daniel T. Rodgers, "Work Ideals and the Industrial Invasion." Reprinted from *The Work Ethic in Industrial America, 1850–1920*, by Daniel T. Rodgers by permission of The University of Chicago Press. Copyright © 1974, 1978 by the University of Chicago Press. All rights reserved. Published 1978.

Russell Sage, "Ambitious to Rise in Life—But Never by Luck!" From *Talks with Great Workers*, edited by Orison Switt Marden, 1901.

Daniel J. Boorstin, "Time Becomes Fungible: Packaging the Unit of Work." From *The Americans: The Democratic Experience*, by Daniel J. Boorstin. Copyright © 1973 by Daniel J. Boorstin. Reprinted by permission of Random House, Inc.

Chapter 6

Amitai Etzioni, "Opting Out: The Waning of the Work Ethic." From *Psychology Today*, July 1977, p. 18. Copyright © 1977 by Amitai Etzioni. Reprinted by permission of the author.

Graham L. Staines and Pamela O'Connor, "Conflicts Among Work, Leisure, and Family Roles." From *Monthly Labor Review*, August 1980.

Michael Maccoby and Katherine A. Terzi, "What Happened to the Work Ethic?" U.S. Congress Joint Economic Committee, Special Study on Economic Change, Vol. 1, 1980.

J. Richard Hackman and Greg R. Oldham, "Work Redesign: People and Their Work." From Hackman/Oldham, *Work Redesign*, © 1980, Addison-Wesley Publishing Company, Inc., Chapter 1, pages 3–20. Reprinted with permission.

Acknowledgments

Bill Billiter, "Workaholics Do More but Accomplish Less." Copyright 1981, Los Angeles Times. Reprinted by permission.

Robert Townsend, "Up the Organization—People." From *Up The Organization*, by Robert Townsend. Copyright © 1970 by Robert Townsend. Reprinted by permission of Random House, Inc.

Chapter 7

Richard N. Bolles, "The Three Boxes of Life." Adapted from Chapter 1 of *The Three Boxes of Life and How to Get Out of Them*, by Richard Bolles, Ten Speed Press, 1978, pp. 5–25. Copyright © 1978 by Richard N. Bolles. Reprinted with permission.

Sue Kaufman, "Diary of a Mad Housewife." From *Diary of a Mad Housewife*, by Sue Kaufman. Copyright © 1967 by Sue Kaufman. Reprinted by permission of Random House, Inc.

Emily Greenspan, "Work Begins at 35." © 1979/1980 by The New York Times Company. Reprinted by permission.

Solomon Arbeiter, "Mid-Life Career Change: A Concept in Search of Reality," Excerpted from "Mid-Life Career Change: A Concept in Search of Reality," *AAHE Bulletin*, (Washington, D.C.: American Association for Higher Education), October 1979. Reprinted by permission.

Donald B. Miller, "Personal Growth and Vitality Inventory." From *The Personal Vitality Workbook*, by Donald B. Miller. Copyright © 1977 by Addison-Wesley. Reprinted by permission.

Chapter 8

Louise Kapp Howe, "Salesworker." Reprinted by permission of G. P. Putnam's Sons from *Pink Collar Workers*, by Louise Kapp Howe. Copyright © 1977 by Louise Kapp Howe.

Joan E. Crowley, Teresa E. Levitan, and Robert P. Quinn, "Seven Deadly Half-Truths About Women." Reprinted from *Psychology Today*. Copyright © 1973 by Ziff-Davis Publishing Company. By permission of the publisher.

Carl Hoffman and John Shelton Reed, "Sex Discrimination? The XYZ Affair." Reprinted with permission of the authors from *The Public Interest*, no. 62 (Winter 1981). © 1981 by National Affairs, Inc.

"Leading Occupations of Women." From *America's Working Women: A Documentary History—1600 to the Present*, edited by Rosalyn Baxandall, Linda Gordon, and Susan Reverby. Copyright © 1976 by Rosalyn Baxandall, Linda Gordon, and Susan Reverby. Reprinted by permission of Random House, Inc.

Isabel V. Sawhill, "Perspectives on Women and Work in America." From *Work and the Quality of Life*, edited by James O'Toole. Copyright © 1974 by The Massachusetts Institute of Technology, Cambridge, Massachusetts. Reprinted by permission of The MIT Press. All rights reserved.

Rosabeth Moss Kanter, "Secretaries." Excerpted from: *Men and Women of the Corporation*, by Rosabeth Moss Kanter, pp. 69–88, 101–103. © 1977 by Rosabeth Moss Kanter. Published by Basic Books, Inc., New York. Reprinted by permission.

Chapter 9

Caryl Rivers, Rosalind Barnett, and Grace Baruch, "He Works, She Works: Does the Marriage Work?" Reprinted by permission of G. P. Putnam's Sons from *Beyond Sugar and Spice*, by Caryl Rivers, Rosalind Barnett, and Grace Baruch. Copyright © 1979 by Caryl Rivers, Rosalind Barnett, and Grace Baruch.

Nancy Seifer, "Working Class Women: Departure from Tradition." From *Absent From the Majority: Working Class Women in America*, by Nancy Seifer. Copyright © 1973 by the American Jewish Committee. Reprinted by permission of the Institute on Pluralism and Group Identity of the American Jewish Committee.

Rosabeth Moss Kanter, "Jobs and Families: Impact of Working Roles on Family Life." From *Children Today*, March–April 1978. Reprinted with permission of the Smithsonian Institution, 6th Annual Symposium on Families, June 1977.

Acknowledgments

Betty Friedan, "Feminism Takes a New Turn." © 1979/80 by The New York Times Company. Reprinted by permission.

Chapter 10

Fred Best, "Flexible Life Scheduling." From *Flexible Life Scheduling*, by Fred Best. Copyright © 1980 by Praeger Publishers. Reprinted by permission from Praeger Publishers.

Allan R. Cohen and Herman Gadon, "Flexible Working Hours." From Cohen/Gadon, *Alternative Work Schedules: Integrating Individual and Organizational Needs*, © 1978, Addison-Wesley Publishing Company, Inc., Chapter 3, pages 33–48. Reprinted with permission.

Barney Olmsted, "Job Sharing: A New Way to Work." Copyright February, 1977. Reprinted with permission from *Personnel Journal*, Costa Mesa, California. All rights reserved.

John L. Zalusky, "Alternative Work Schedules." From the *College and University Personnel Association Journal*, Volume 28, Number 3, Summer 1977, pp. 53–56. Copyright © 1977 by the College and University Personnel Association. Reprinted by permission.

Chapter 11

Richard E. Walton, "Teaching an Old Dog Food New Tricks." Reprinted with permission from *The Wharton Magazine*, Vol. 2, no. 2, © 1978 by The Wharton School of the University of Pennsylvania.

Robert H. Guest, "Quality of Work Life—Learning from Tarrytown." Reprinted by permission of the *Harvard Business Review*. Excerpts from "Quality of Work Life—Learning from Tarrytown" by Robert H. Guest (July–August 1979). Copyright © 1977 by the President and Fellows of Harvard College; all rights reserved.

Robert Schrank, "How to Relieve Worker Boredom." Reprinted from *Psychology Today*. Copyright © 1978 by Ziff-Davis Publishing Company.

Robert Goldmann, "Six Automobile Workers in Sweden." Reprinted from *American Workers Abroad*, edited by Robert Schrank, by permission of The MIT Press, Cambridge, Massachusetts. Copyright © 1979 by The Massachusetts Institute of Technology. All rights reserved.

Ted Mills, "Human Resources and the Unions." Reprinted by permission of the *Harvard Business Review*. Excerpts from "Human Resources: Why the New Concern" by Ted Mills (March–April 1975). Copyright © 1975 by the President and Fellows of Harvard College; all rights reserved.

Chapter 12

Robert Zager, "Managing Guaranteed Employment." Reprinted by permission of the *Harvard Business Review*. Excerpts from "Managing Guaranteed Employment" by Robert Zager (May–June 1978). Copyright © 1978 by the President and Fellows of Harvard College; all rights reserved.

David W. Ewing and Pamela Banks, "Participative Management at Work: An Interview with John F. Donnelly." Reprinted by permission of the *Harvard Business Review*. Excerpts from "Participative Management at Work," an interview with John Donnelly (January–February 1977). Copyright © 1977 by the President and Fellows of Harvard College; all rights reserved.

Paul Bernstein, "Advanced Democratization." Published by permission of Transaction, Inc. from *Workplace Democratization: Its Internal Dynamics*, by Paul Bernstein. Copyright © 1976 by Transaction, Inc. Reprinted by permission.

Daniel Zwerdling, "IGP: Democracy at Work." Excerpted from *Workplace Democracy*, by Daniel Zwerdling. Copyright © 1980 by Daniel Zwerdling. Published by Harper & Row, 1980. Reprinted with permission of the author.

Acknowledgments

Chapter 13

Harrry Maurer, "Not Working." From *Not Working*, by Harry Maurer. Copyright © 1971 by Harry Maurer. Reprinted by permission of Holt, Rinehart and Winston, Publishers.

Elliot Liebow, "Men and Jobs." From *Tally's Corner*, by Elliot Liebow. Copyright © 1967 by Little, Brown and Company (Inc.). Reprinted by permission.

Willard Wirtz, "No Man's—or Women's—Land." Reprinted from *The Boundless Resource: A Prospectus for an education-Work Policy*, 1975. Courtesy of National Institute for Work and Learning.

Chapter 14

Elliot Liebow, "The Human Costs of Unemployment." Originally titled "No Man Can Live with the Terrible Knowledge That He Is Not Needed." © 1970 by The New York Times Company. Reprinted by permission.

Daniel P. Moynihan, "The Problem of Dependency." From *The Politics of a Guaranteed Income*, by Daniel P. Moynihan. Copyright © 1973 by Daniel P. Moynihan. Reprinted by permission of Random House, Inc.

Martin Feldstein, "The Economics of the New Unemployment." Excerpts reprinted with permission of the author from *The Public Interest*, no. 33 (Fall 1973). © 1973 by National Affairs, Inc.

Chapter 15

Bernard E. Anderson, "Minorities and Work." From *Work in America: The Decade Ahead*, edited by Clark Kerr and Jerome M. Rosow. © 1979 by Litton Educational Publishing, Inc. Reprinted by permission of Van Nostrand Reinhold Company.

Colin Norman, "The New Industrial Revolution: How Microelectronics May Change the workplace." From *The Futurist*, February 1981. Reprinted by permission of *The Futurist*, published by the World Future Society, 4916 St. Elmo Avenue, Washington D.C. 20014.

Warren Bennis, "The Decline of Bureaucracy and Organizations of the Future." Published by permission of Transaction, Inc. from *Transaction* magazine, copyright ©, July 1965 by Transaction, Inc.

James O'Toole and August Ralston, "Exploring Trends and Events That Might Mold the Future of Work." Original material written for the book.

»«

PREFACE

»«

────────────────────────── **W**──────────────────
orking: Changes and Choices is the
fifteenth in a series of books developed for Courses by Newspaper (CbN).
Originated and administered by University Extension, University of
California, San Diego, Courses by Newspaper has been preparing materials for the nation's newspapers and for nontraditional college-level
courses since 1973. The project has been funded since its inception primarily by the National Endowment for the Humanities.

The program features a fifteen-part series of articles written by some of
the nation's leading experts, who address an audience of millions through
the pages of approximately 450 participating newspapers. Interested readers can pursue the subjects further in this book of readings and in an
accompanying study guide. In addition, approximately 300 colleges and
universities offer college credit for a course based on these materials, and
many community organizations sponsor public forums and discussion
groups on CbN themes.

This volume supplements the fifteen newspaper articles written especially for the fifteenth Course by Newspaper, "Working: Changes and
Choices," offered for the first time in fall 1981.

Courses by Newspaper would not have been possible without the cooperation of hundreds of newspaper editors and publishers, who contributed
valuable space to bring the newspaper series to their readers, and the
faculties and administrations of the participating colleges and universities, who made credit available on a nationwide basis. We wish to thank
them here.

We would also like to acknowledge those individuals who contributed to
the development of this course. The authors of the newspaper articles—
Fred Best, Joseph Raphael Blasi, Richard N. Bolles, Robert Coles, Thomas
Dublin, David W. Ewing, J. Richard Hackman, Edward E. Lawler III, Barbara B. Lazarus, Elliot Liebow, Michael Maccoby, Daniel T. Rodgers, Isabel

V. Sawhill, Robert Schrank, Lester C. Thurow, and William Foote Whyte—contributed valuable suggestions for this anthology and for the bibliographies that appear at the end of this volume. In addition, the National Board and the CbN Faculty Committee made important contributions to the conception of the course, as did Henry Clark, whose thoughtful paper on the humanistic aspects of working was instrumental in the formative stages of our planning.

Deserving special mention at the University of California, San Diego, are Paul D. Saltman, who served as the first academic coordinator in 1973 and has guided the project as chair of the Faculty Committee, and Mary L. Walshok, Dean of University Extension and an authority on working women, who was a valuable resource in the development of the course content. Special thanks also go to George A. Colburn, Project Director of Courses by Newspaper, and to the other members of the CbN staff— Yvonne Hancher, Stephanie Giel, Beverly Barry, Sally Cirrito, Susan Graff, Sharon McDaniel, Gwen Bargsten, and Yvonne Rounds—who have played crucial roles in developing and administering the program.

Finally, we wish to express our gratitude to our funding agency, the National Endowment for the Humanities, for its generous support. The Endowment is a federal agency created in 1965 to support education, research, and public activities in the humanities.

Although Courses by Newspaper is a project of the University of California, San Diego, and is supported by the National Endowment for the Humanities, the views expressed in course materials are those of the authors only and do not necessarily reflect those of the funding agency or of the University of California.

J.L.S.

» «

INTRODUCTION

» «

Twenty years ago, a book on work would not have been at all like the one you are now reading. Until recently, most books and courses about work or workers were designed to train specialists: managers, industrial engineers, organizational psychologists, and others who were concerned with maximizing worker effort and productivity. It was all very simple and "scientific" in those good old days. For example, industrial engineers would teach students how to undertake "time and motion studies" to find the "one best way" to organize jobs. The goal was to find just the right spot for workers to stand and just the right place for their tools and supplies, and to calculate precisely just how many nuts and bolts they should screw together in a typical hour.

The psychologists who were concerned about what makes workers work had their own brand of certainty. Depending on the school of thought to which they belonged, they would tell their students that (1) all workers need to be loved (therefore managers should be more caring) or (2) all workers seek self-fulfillment (therefore managers should organize jobs to help them find it); or, (3) all workers seek security (therefore managers should give it to them); or (4) managerial leadership style is what counts (and good leaders are not born but made through training). An exhaustive list of all the psychological schools of thought about worker motivation would run for several pages. I shall spare you.

There is a lot less certainty about work and workers today. None of the contemporary authors in this volume assumes anything monolithic (hence, simplistic) about the 100 million workers in the United States and their jobs. Today, unlike the past, experts on workplace issues do not believe in a single, unchanging work ethic. They do not believe that all workers seek and need the same things from work. They do not believe that there is one best way to organize jobs. Indeed, except in a historical or pejorative context, the word "science" is not used in this book. Unlike a scientific inquiry, our study of work and workers is not designed to establish "laws" of work organization or to predict the behavior of workers. Rather, we seek better understanding of the complex, nonpredictable human institution that engages nearly a third of the time of our lives. Hence, our focus is on two concepts that would have made workplace scholars terribly uncomfortable twenty years ago: Changes and Choices.

It is constantly evident in these pages that work is not static and that workers are not unchanging. There has been a radical shift in the kinds of jobs most people do. Early in this century, the typical American worked for Old McDonald on his farm; today, she is likely to be serving up Quarter Pounders at McDonald's. A scant two decades ago, the typical American was engaged in making things in factories or on construction sites; today, he is more likely to be found typing in an office, taking blood samples in a hospital, processing data in a government bureau, or teaching courses in a community education center. In less than a century, then, the American economy has undergone two fundamental transitions: (1) from an agricultural base to an industrial base, and (2) from an industrial base to one in which the provision of services and information dominates.

Workers have changed, too. In 1960 a third of the workforce was female; today about 42 percent of all American workers are women. In 1960 only 9.5 percent of American workers had completed four or more years of college; today the figure is about 19 percent. Compared to twenty years ago, the typical American worker is less likely to be a member of a union, more likely to be a part-time employee, less likely to be working after age 65, more likely to have changed jobs in the last year, and more likely to be enrolled in continuing education after work.

In the past, one might have been able to take a figurative snapshot of American work and workers, hang it on the wall, and assume that the picture would still be a reasonably accurate illustration a decade later. Today one would need one of these newfangled video-discs to catch the dynamic reality of worklife. The laser technology would allow us to make a moving picture, capturing some scenes from different angles (even letting us see the back of the image). The new technology would allow us to record the fact that various parts of the picture are moving at different speeds and to present a highly individualized, interactive portrait—a changing and special one, even, for each worker.

Of course, some things at work do remain constant: the primary purpose of the activity still is to provide the goods and services society needs at the price it is willing to pay; in exchange for their time, workers still receive pay in order that they may buy the things they need and want. But even here there are elements of change. Because of rising affluence, those primary purposes are not quite as all-consuming for all workers as they were in the past. In the last decade there has been an increasing emphasis—particularly among younger workers—on the secondary purposes of work: as a source of individual identity and self-esteem; as a source of attachment to the human community; as a reason for living in a world increasingly devoid of religious, familial, or cultural ties; and, as a source of interest, excitement, and pleasure. These are some of the changes that we will be exploring.

Choices? The picture here is even more complex. American workers undeniably have more choice about when, where, how, and with whom they will work than ever before. But is all this choice a blessing or a curse? That question is the source of more than a bit of controversy. On the one hand, it is a sure sign of progress when more and more people have more and more control over their lives. A society that offers increasing choice to increasing numbers of its citizens is one that is becoming ever-more free, democratic, and egalitarian.

On the other hand, a society that offers cafeteria-type choices of life-styles, careers, working conditions, and uses of one's time also is likely to be marked by anxiety, tension, instability, and conflict. Choice creates discontent. Nothing is more difficult or frustrating than having to choose between two desirable things. We feel cheated if we cannot have both, like the teenager who sits in misery through an exciting baseball game because he is missing a good movie on television at home. Never mind that our parents often did not have any choice at all; we have come to *expect* choice. We even feel we are entitled to it—even if choosing is not always a pleasant process (sometimes we must choose between two *un*desirable alternatives).

Here are some of the tough choices about work that America and Americans face:

• Women and men often must choose between work roles and family roles.

• Students must choose between job training that will get them quick access to a high-paying entry-level job and a long-term investment in higher education that may or may not lead to a professional career.

• Adults often must choose between staying in a secure but boring job or taking the risk of mid-career retooling for more interesting work.

• Unions must choose between bargaining for higher wages or moderating their demands so as not to price their members out of world competition.

• Managers must choose between retaining their traditional power and prerogatives or sharing decision-making powers with workers in the hope of increasing productivity.

• Americans have to choose whether they want to work harder to retain their high standard of living or put less time and effort into work to pursue leisure or "the quality of life."

• Americans have to choose whether to retain millions of people on welfare or make the difficult changes needed to find productive jobs for these people.

• Americans will have to choose whether it is better to automate jobs in order to increase productivity to meet foreign competition or to resist automation in order to keep everyone fully employed (but, perhaps, poorer).

These are short-hand descriptions of just some of the extremely complex choices about work that individuals, organizations, and society face. The purpose of the readings that follow is not to find answers to such questions, but to increase our understanding of the genesis of the changes occurring at work and the potential consequences of the choices we face. Like the subject matter we are addressing, sometimes our inquiry will be fun, and sometimes it will be plain hard work. But in the end, I trust you will be able to look back with satisfaction at a job well done! Let's get to work . . .

James O'Toole

THE MEANINGS OF WORK

》《

Our first task is to define the word "work." This will not be an easy job because even the experts mean different things when they use the word. For example, each of the seventy-odd authors in this book defines the word—and, hence, the activity of work itself—in a slightly different way. The numerous synonyms for work in the English language give subtle clues about the many conscious and unconscious ways in which work is viewed. Think of the different and vivid images that come to mind when one uses one of the following words instead of work: labor, employment, industry, toil, travail, enterprise, sweat of one's brow, grind, drudgery, slavery, handiwork, craftsmanship, elbow grease, task, occupation, profession, exertion — and more than a few others that can't be printed in a textbook!

Unlike us, Eskimos apparently have no word at all in their language for work. This is not because work is unimportant to them, but because, for the Eskimo, all life is work; all of life's activities consist of the necessity of providing food, clothing, and shelter. In fact, for most of mankind, for most of history, work was as it is for the Eskimo today: an inescapable, all-consuming activity.

In modern times, labor has often been thought of, like disease and death, as man's punishment for his disobedience to God. In Genesis, the Lord said to Adam: "Cursed is the ground for thy sake; in toil shalt thou eat of it all the days of thy life. . . . In the sweat of thy face, shalt thou eat bread, till thou return into the ground." This painful view of work was not limited to the Judeo-Christian tradition. In classical Greece, work was also seen as unalloyed drudgery. Aristotle believed that man's only salvation was through automation, in which "every instrument could accomplish its own work," leaving man free for the higher calling of using leisure creatively.

The Roman emperor Marcus Aurelius was one of the first Western philosophers to find a purpose, even nobility, in work:

1

In the morning when thou risest unwilling, let this thought be present—I am rising to the work of a human being. Why, then, am I dissatisfied if I am going to do the things for which I exist and for which I was brought into the world? Or have I been made for this, to lie in the the bed-clothes and keep myself warm? But this is more pleasant. Dost thou exist, then, to take thy pleasure and not at all for action and exertion?

According to some historians, work not only had a purpose, but it was instrumental in creating civilization. They suggest that it was the need for men to work together that led the human race out of barbarism. Karl Wittfogel, for example, theorizes that primitive irrigation projects required the first coordinated human activity that extended beyond the family or the tribe. These collective engineering feats demanded an organizational hierarchy that eventually led to government. Although such speculations cannot be proven, most anthropologists believe that the functional differentiation of individuals in work activities was the initial basis for such systems of social stratification as class, caste, and slavery. Even religious hierarchies may have originated in work activities—the "high priest" was often the director of the earliest mass work projects. During the Roman empire, such systems ossified and, for many centuries to follow, class standing was hereditary throughout most of Europe.

Most experts agree that the division of labor is a prime determinant of the structure of a society. That is, the social pecking order is based mainly on the kinds of work people do. This division of labor ultimately leads not only to specialization among carpenters, farmers, and priests, but also to sub-specialization within each such occupation. Such specialization, though natural in the animal kingdom, was rare in human affairs until the eighteenth century. In 1776, the world was amazed by Adam Smith's description of a pin factory in which it took eighteen distinct operations to make the finished product. Smith was also the first to call attention to the fact that extreme specialization is potentially harmful to the psyche:

> In the progress of the division of labor, the employment of far greater part of those who live by labor . . . comes to be confined to a few very simple operations, frequently one or two. . . . The man whose whole life is spent on performing a few simple operations . . . has no occasion to exert his understanding or to exercise his invention . . . . He naturally loses, therefore, the habit of such exertion, and generally becomes as stupid and ignorant as it is possible for a human creature to become.

Smith, like Aristotle before him, was expressing concern for what is called today the quality of working life—or job satisfaction, in the popular press.

2

But in contrast to Aristotle, Smith believed that technology was the ultimate source of drudgery and not the potential savior that would free man from Adam's curse.

Significantly, these two conflicting views of technology have not, to this day, been resolved. To E. F. Schumacher (Chapter 1) and many environmentalists, technological progress often appears dangerous and inhumane. By contrast, most economists and industrialists believe that technology is the driving force of human betterment. Even in Smith's time, there was controversy about the two faces of technology: on the one hand, it was seen as improving the standard of living of society in general; on the other hand, it was seen as debasing the lives of the workers who manned the machines of industry. For example, Richard Arkwright's water frame, a spinning machine that helped revolutionize the textile industry, exhibited these two contradictory characteristics. Economist Robert Heilbroner details the negative side-effects of Arkwright's incredibly efficient invention:

> But having constructed his machine he found it was not so easy to staff it. Local labor could not keep up with the "regular celerity" of the process—wagework was still generally despised and many a capitalist found his new-built factory burned to the ground out of sheer blind malice. Arkwright was forced to turn to children, "their small fingers being active." Furthermore, since they were unused to the independent life of farming or crafts, children adapted themselves more readily to the discipline of factory life.

At about this same time, Josiah Wedgwood was having similar difficulties introducing the laborers in his pottery works "to a novel form of discipline that ran contrary to centuries of independence." According to historian Melvin Kranzberg:

> It was a constant test of Wedgwood's ingenuity to enforce six hours' punctual and constant attendance upon his workers, to get them to avoid waste, and to keep from drinking on the job and taking unauthorized "holidays." Because he was a busy man involved in all tasks of running an enterprise and could not stand over his workers and control their movements, he had to develop a hierarchy of supervisors and managers.

To this managerial revolution, Eli Whitney added the "American system" in the early 1880s. The mass production and assembly of many identical parts was brought to its logical conclusion by Henry Ford with his famous—or infamous—assembly line. Kranzberg points out that between 1912 and 1913 Ford reduced the time needed to assemble a car chassis from twelve-and-a-half *hours* to ninety-three *minutes*.

3

Although these new methods increased productivity, they also transformed further the nature and organization of work—and thereby its meaning to individuals. The skill level in Ford's plants was reduced to the point where, in comparative hindsight, Adam Smith's pin makers look like skilled generalists. At the same time, Ford's revolution also changed the structure of the labor force—reducing the number of manual workers needed and increasing the white-collar support staff of managers, supervisors, accountants, engineers, and secretaries.

The mass production techniques introduced during the first quarter of this century also spawned the industrial engineer, the most successful (and notorious) of whom was Frederick Winslow Taylor (Chapter 5). As the father of scientific management, Taylor developed books full of techniques designed to get the maximum production out of each worker. Today, we are apt to laugh at the Chaplinesque consequences of Taylor's famous time and motion studies (Taylor would measure the worker's every movement, and time his every activity with a stopwatch, in order to find the "one best way" to do a given job). But we should recognize that Taylor's descendants are still at work today in many American industrial settings—and in factories around the world. Taylorism is particularly popular in the Soviet Union—Taylor was one of the few Americans Stalin truly admired.

Nonetheless, Taylor's contribution has been distorted by his friends and foes alike. In fact, his motives were altruistic (at least by the standards of 1915, the year in which he died). He wanted to reduce the laborious efforts of workers and to help them earn more money. After his death, his disciples and the bosses who employed them quickly forgot Taylor's motives and simply used scientific management to wring the last ounce of effort out of workers—often without concomitant monetary rewards.

It is significant that Taylor's experimental subjects had been impoverished, uneducated immigrants who were desperate for *any* job. For it was soon found that native-born Americans would not submit to Taylor's robot-like programming. Even first generation Americans were too well-fed, too well-educated, and had too high expectations to submit to the constant supervision required by Taylorism. If managers treated them the way Taylor treated their fathers, they were likely to talk back, quit, or join a union. Mostly they did the latter.

The Psychology of Work

Enter the psychologist. We are inclined to forget that America had a productivity problem during the Roaring Twenties. Apparently, it is always difficult to get people to work hard when they are experiencing rising affluence. To meet this problem, the brass of the telephone company called on Elton Mayo of the Harvard Business School to conduct a series of experiments at the Hawthorne plant of Western Electric in Illinois. These experiments led to the replacement of Taylorism with the human relations school of management in many—but far from all—U.S. industries. The

4

Hawthorne experiments "proved" that worker productivity would increase if management showed that it cared. Because of these successful experiments, psychologists became permanent fixtures in American workplaces.

The next psychologist to have a lasting effect on the workplace was Abraham Maslow. In the 1940s, Maslow theorized that all human beings have the same hierarchical order of needs and, as each level of need is fulfilled, the next level becomes salient. These needs start at the bottom of the hierarchy with such basic physiological requirements as food and shelter, followed on subsequent rungs by safety, security, friendship, and—at the top of the ladder—the crowning human achievement, "self-actualization" (realizing one's full potential). Not unreasonably, psychologists such as Frederick Herzberg in the 1970s argued that, since American workers were in general safe, secure, and affluent, they must then be searching for self-fulfillment through creative and challenging work.

Now, for the first time in forty years, psychologists have fallen out of favor in American industry. Part of the reason is an understandable reaction by abused managers to the excesses of the therapy-group era. Many businessmen today would like to drown humanistic psychologists in their hot tubs. But even the more conservative industrial psychologists who were never influenced by C. J. Jung or Carl Rodgers are not as influential as they once were. These individuals undercut much of their own credibility by insisting that the study of human behavior was a science, and that human behavior was, ultimately, as predictable as natural phenomena. (Ironically, these psychologists were climbing on the scientific bandwagon at about the time physicists, chemists, and astronomers were getting some humility and admitting that there were a great many things about nature that they could neither explain nor predict.) Psychologists claimed that patterns of worker attitudes, values, satisfactions, and behavior were universal—or at least common to all men and women in the advanced, industrial societies. Moreover, these patterns were said to be not only measurable through survey research instruments, but also predictable.

This hubris has proved to be quite embarrassing for psychologists in the field of organizational behavior. They had their Maslovian under-pinnings knocked out from under them in the mid-1970s with the realization that the hierarchy of human needs was not universal. It was shown during that time, for example, that there were affluent, educated people who were quite content with job security and had no detectable desire to move on toward self-actualization.

The most common source of error in this regard was to draw conclusions about worker needs and desires from aggregate survey data. But when the information was broken down and analyzed in the mid-1970s, it was discovered that worker attitudes and values varied greatly according to such characteristics as age, sex, race, occupation, income, place of residence (that is, urban or rural area), and educational attainment. One of the most

striking discoveries was that the work values of the large Baby Boom generation (born between 1946 and 1960) are markedly different from the
values of preceding generations. While the values of many people in this
generation come close to replicating the pattern hypothesized by Maslow,
not all of the young people share the universal hierarchy, and some appear
to seek security as much as their parents.

Psychologist Daniel Yankelovich (Chapter 1) and others have identified a
"psychology of entitlement," or a rising consciousness of individual rights
in America, particularly among young workers. Things that were once
privileges to be earned are today assumed to be the rights of a citizen, or
rights that adhere automatically to employment. In this latter category is a
host of new rights including health care, cost of living allowances, vested
pensions, maternity benefits, and educational tuition remission.

Yankelovich has found a distinct difference in attitudes toward entitlements between the Baby Boom generation and their parents (whom we'll
call Depression Kids). The under thirty-fives, as distinct from their parents,
are most concerned about purely social and psychological rights. For
example, young workers feel they are entitled to a voice in the decisions
that affect their jobs. Older workers, in contrast, tend to stress purely
economic rights, such as pensions, job security, and the like.

For purposes of clarity, Yankelovich divides the workforce into two
broad but distinct categories:

1. *Traditionalists*, the shrinking 56 percent majority of workers who are
   still motivated by money, status, and security. Included in this category are the older, blue-collar workers for whom work is a habit; the
   older "silent majority" white-collar workers with conservative values
   and life-styles; and a small number of young "go-getters" who have
   traditional goals and life-styles (Jaycees, for example).
2. *Nontraditionalists*, the growing 44 percent of the workforce, almost all
   of whom are under thirty-five. This category includes the "turned-
   off," hedonistic, poorly educated, working-class and poverty youths,
   who do not share the culture of the majority. But most attention is
   paid—perhaps unfairly—to the larger category of highly educated,
   bright, creative underemployed young people who have turned to
   leisure and nonwork avocations for the challenge and fulfillment they
   cannot find at work. Yankelovich found that only 21 percent of the
   nontraditionalists state that work means more to them than leisure.
   The nontraditionalists' strongest demand for change in working conditions is more time away from the job. In fact, University of Michigan
   researchers have recently found that one-half of employed Americans
   report that they have problems with the inflexibility of their working
   schedules, and that the demands of work leave them with inadequate
   time for leisure activities (see Chapter 6). One-third of these workers
   report that inconvenient or excessive working hours interfere with

their family life. In a separate study, Fred Best of the California Department of Employment found that 70 percent of American workers would be willing to give up 2 percent *or more* of their income for less time at work.

Good Work, Bad Work

. . . And so the meanings of work have changed over the millennia. In the words of sociologist C. Wright Mills:

> Work may be a mere source of livelihood, or the most significant part of one's inner life; it may be experienced as expiation, or as exuberant expression of self; as bounden duty, or as the development of man's universal nature. Neither love nor hatred of work is inherent in man, or inherent in any given line of work. For work has no intrinsic meaning.

Whether work has an intrinsic meaning or not, there is no doubt that meanings can be given to the activity, meanings that shape the activity and change its relationship to leisure.

In Chapter 1, "Toward a Definition of Work," a clear distinction is made by all four authors between good work and bad work. Good work provides a sense of mastery; it is closely related to the notion of craftsmanship. As Mortimer Adler points out, good work is work we would do even if we were not paid. Carpenters, skilled repairers, sculptors, teachers, entrepreneurs, writers, and almost every worker who has a nonroutine task requiring some mental or manual skill will have experienced the exhilarating feeling that Swedish author Göran Palm describes:

> When I sit at home writing I usually think that time passes too quickly. I seldom look at my watch because my work absorbs me. But if I do look at the time I hope it is earlier than it really is. . . . As a rule, it is later.

However, for many people in routine work or manual labor, the situation is different. If work is bad, time drags. The problem for these people is to get their working hours over with as quickly as they can. But when they look at their watches, it is almost always earlier than they hoped.

Bad work is work that can better be done by animals or machines. There is no creativity in it, no opportunity for a sense of mastery. E. F. Schumacher points out that such work is inhumane. It destroys the dignity of workers; it demeans them.

The selection by Studs Terkel in Chapter 2, "What Work Means to a Blue-Collar Worker," gives weight to these views. The blue-collar worker Terkel interviews finds nothing ennobling about dirty work. In fact, none of the authors finds any intrinsic human value in bad work. They would all seem to agree with C. Wright Mills.

What almost all our authors *do* find is an attempt by people in bad jobs to interject some meaning into the eight hours in which they labor. According to Schumacher and to Lipson, Terkel, Coleman, Dublin, and Nestor (Chapters 2 and 3), blue-collar men and women cope with unrewarding work by creating a sense of community. If the task itself is meaningless, meaning can at least be attached to the social interaction with fellow workers. People form bonds with their co-workers that are, if anything, stronger than the bonds with neighbors and other friends. If these workers face a day of dirty work, the promise of being with friends helps to get them out of bed and onto the job. As Robert Schrank later points out (Chapter 11), "schmoozing" is a prime source of job satisfaction for blue-collar workers. Consequently, if the noise or the pace of work makes it impossible to schmooze with fellow workers (as on an auto assembly line), then bad work can become intolerable. Agnes Nestor gives a nice account of the role of schmoozing among women stitchers and sewers in turn-of-the-century Chicago, and the selection by Coleman shows that things have not changed all that much.

Chapter 3, "Blue-Collar Women," makes it apparent that, traditionally, women have had more than their share of dirty work. Even today, there are more women than men on assembly lines (more assembly-line work involves putting together small and microscopic parts than big, heavy car parts). It was always said that women are better suited for such tasks. Although today probably no one believes that women are genetically more tolerant of routine work, it is true that historically they were more willing than men to tolerate it. Why? Social conditioning, perhaps. Another factor was that, traditionally, a man's sense of identity and self-esteem was tied directly to his job; a woman derived hers from her role as wife and mother. Consequently, women were less likely to feel demeaned by dull and undemanding work—they were mothers first, and laborers second. Today, because women are about as likely as men to take their identity from their jobs, employers are starting to find that they, too, aren't "naturally suited" to assembly-line work.

Prestige, Pay—and Problems

We sometimes forget that even people in so-called glamorous jobs are workers, too. True, their jobs come closer to the definitions of "good work" provided in Chapter 1, but doctors, lawyers, engineers, and corporate executives do not always find the satisfactions that they seek in work. Although their jobs are characterized by autonomy, high pay, and social prestige, they also provide a large share of stress, responsibility, and exposure to critical scrutiny by others. As Jacques Barzun shows in Chapter 4, "Professionals and Managers Are Workers, Too," doctors are constantly in the public eye; the mistakes they make—unlike those made by blue-collar workers—are *public* mistakes that can result in malpractice suits, professional censure, and criticism in the press.

Perhaps the worst aspect of high-level occupations for many people is the way they limit off-the-job freedom. Even in his off hours, John Coleman (Chapter 2) writes that he was always "on duty" as a college president. Similarly, doctors are seldom completely off duty. They can't "leave their work at the office" and completely forget about their patients in their off hours. Worse, as Robert Townsend and J. Patrick Wright (Chapter 4) illustrate, executives must conform to the politics, life-styles, and prevailing norms of behavior of their corporations. Where blue-collar workers can wear beards, act grumpy toward their supervisors and co-workers, associate with whomever they please, and pass the hat for the Socialist Workers' Party during off hours, corporate executives and even many lower-level white-collar workers have none of these freedoms.

Indeed, as David Ewing writes, a demand for more political, social, and personal freedom is being voiced by white-collar workers across America. Ewing argues that it is an anomaly of American life that it is characterized by democracy, freedom, and civil liberties off the job, while life at work is neither democratic nor free; it is not protected by the Bill of Rights. As Earl Shorris brilliantly demonstrates in the concluding article of this section, many middle managers have only one freedom: the right to quit.

This review of the meanings of work to blue- and white-collar workers raises an intriguing question: If work is so unpleasant, what explains the fact that America has traditionally been a nation of hard workers? Are we now losing that tradition? Are our attitudes toward work changing? These and other questions are explored in the next part of the book.

1

》《

TOWARD
A DEFINITION
OF WORK

》《

Lewis Hine/International Museum of Photography at George Eastman House

» James O'Toole, et al «

Work in America

» «

According to the authors of the government-sponsored report, Work in America, *work is something more than "paid employment"—it is "an activity that provides something of value for other people." In addition to the economic functions of work, satisfying jobs are those that provide individuals with a sense of mastery, identity, and self-esteem.*

It is both humbling and true that scientists are unable, in the final analysis, to distinguish all the characteristics of humans from those of other animals. But many social scientists will agree that among those activities most peculiar to humans, work probably defines man with the greatest certainty. To the archaeologist digging under the equatorial sun for remains of the earliest man, the nearby presence of primitive tools is his surest sign that the skull fragment he finds is that of a human ancestor, and not that of an ape.

Why is man a worker? First of all, of course, man works to sustain physical life — to provide food, clothing, and shelter. But clearly work is central to our lives for other reasons as well. According to Freud, work provides us with a sense of reality; to Elton Mayo, work is a bind to community; to Marx, its function is primarily economic. Theologians are interested in work's moral dimensions; sociologists see it as a determinant of status, and some contemporary critics say that it is simply the best way of filling up a lot of time. To the ancient Greeks, who had slaves to do it, work was a curse. The Hebrews saw work as punishment. The early Christians found work for profit offensive, but by the time of St. Thomas Aquinas, work was being praised as a natural right and a duty — a source of grace along with learning and contemplation. During the Reformation, work became the only way of serving God. Luther pronounced that conscientious performance of one's labor was man's highest duty. Later interpretations of Calvinistic doctrine gave religious sanction to worldly wealth and achievement. This belief, when wedded to Social Darwinism and laissez-faire liberalism, became the foundation for what we call the Protestant ethic. Marx, however, took the concept of work and put it in an even more central position in life: freed from capitalist exploitation, work would become a joy as workers improved the material environment around them.

Clearly, work responds to something profound and basic in human nature. Therefore, much depends on how we define work, what we conceive work to be, what we want work to be, and whether we successfully uncover its meaning and purpose. Our conceptions (and misconceptions) of ourselves, the wisdom with which public policy is formulated on a range of issues, and the rationality with which private and public resources are allocated are influenced greatly by the degree to which we penetrate the complex nature of work.

Because work . . . plays a pervasive and powerful role in the psychological, social, and economic aspects of our lives, it has been called a basic or central institution. As such, it influences, and is influenced by, other basic institutions — family, community (particularly as a political entity), and schools — as well as peripheral institutions. Work, then, provides one institutional perspective — but a broad one — from which to view these interrelationships that affect ourselves and our society.

Toward a Definition of Work

We measure that which we can measure, and this often means that a rich and complex phenomenon is reduced to one dimension, which then becomes prominent and eclipses the other dimensions. This is particularly true of "work," which is often defined as "paid employment." The definition conforms with one readily measurable aspect of work but utterly ignores its profound personal and social aspects and often leads to a distorted view of society.

Using housework as an example, we can see the absurdity of defining work as "paid employment." A housewife, according to this definition, does not work. But if a husband must replace her services — with a housekeeper, cook, baby-sitter — these replacements become workers, and the husband has added to the Gross National Product the many thousands of dollars the replacements are paid. It is, therefore, an inconsistency of our definition of work that leads us to say that a woman who cares for her own children is not working, but if she takes a job looking after the children of others, she is working.

Viewing work in terms of pay alone has also produced a synonymity of "pay" and "worth," so that higher-paid individuals are thought by many to have greater personal worth than those receiving less pay. At the bottom of this scale, a person without pay becomes "worthless." The confusion of pay with worth is a result of historical events and traditions apparently rooted in the distinction between "noble" and "ignoble" tasks. History might have been otherwise, and garbage men, for example, in recognition of their contribution to health, might have been accorded monetary rewards similar to those received by physicians. Certainly, it takes little reflection to conclude that, except in crude economic terms, no one is worth nothing, nor is anyone worth a hundred times more than another merely because he is paid a hundred times as much.

We can come closer to a multi-dimensional definition of work if we

13

define it as "an activity that produces something of value for other people." This definition broadens the scope of what we call work and places it within a social context. It also implies that there is a purpose to work. We know that the housewife is *really* working, whether she is paid or not; she is being productive for other people. Substituting the children a woman cares for does not change the nature of her work, only the "others" for whom she is productive. And voluntary tasks are certainly work, although they are not remunerated. Some people at various stages of their lives may be productive only for themselves, a possible definition of leisure.

The Functions of Work

The economic purposes of work are obvious and require little comment. Work is the means by which we provide the goods and services needed and desired by ourselves and our society. Through the economic rewards of work, we obtain immediate gratification of transient wants, physical assets for enduring satisfactions, and liquid assets for deferrable gratifications. For most of the history of mankind, and for a large part of humanity today, the economic meaning of work is paramount.

Work also serves a number of other social purposes. The workplace has always been a place to meet people, converse, and form friendships. In traditional societies, where children are wont to follow in their parents' footsteps, the assumption of responsibility by the children for one task and then another prepares them for their economic and social roles as adults. Finally, the type of work performed has always conferred a social status on the worker and the worker's family. In industrial America, the father's occupation has been the major determinant of status, which in turn has determined the family's class standing, where they lived, where the children went to school, and with whom the family associated — in short, the life style and life chances of all the family members. (The emerging new role of women in our society may cause class standing to be co-determined by the husband's *and* wife's occupations.)

The economic and societal importance of work has dominated thought about its meaning, and justifiably so: a function of work for any society is to produce and distribute goods and services, to transform "raw nature" into that which serves our needs and desires. Far less attention has been paid to the personal meaning of work, yet it is clear from recent research that work plays a crucial and perhaps unparalleled psychological role in the formation of self-esteem, identity, and a sense of order.

Work contributes to self-esteem in two ways. The first is that, through the inescapable awareness of one's efficacy and competence in dealing with the objects of work, a person acquires a sense of mastery over both himself and his environment. The second derives from the view, stated earlier, that an individual is working when he is engaging in activities that

14

produce something valued by other people. That is, the job tells the worker day in and day out that he has something to offer. Not to have a job is not to have something that is valued by one's fellow human beings. Alternatively, to be working is to have evidence that one is needed by others. One of these components of self-esteem (mastery) is, therefore, internally derived through the presence or absence of challenge in work. The other component (how others value one's contributions) is externally derived. The person with high self-esteem may be defined as one who has a high estimate of his value and finds that the social estimate agrees.

The workplace generally, then, is one of the major foci of personal evaluation. It is where one finds out whether he is "making the grade"; it is where one's esteem is constantly on the line, and where every effort will be made to avoid reduction in self-evaluation and its attending sense of failure. If an individual cannot live up to the expectations he has of himself, and if his personal goals are not reasonably obtainable, then his self-esteem, and with it his relations with others, are likely to be impaired.

Doing well or poorly, being a success or failure at work, is all too easily transformed into a measure of being a valuable or worthless human being, as Erich Fromm writes:

> Since modern man experiences himself both as the seller and as the commodity to be sold on the market, his self-esteem depends on conditions beyond his control. If he is successful, he is valuable; if he is not, he is worthless.

When it is said that work should be "meaningful," what is meant is that it should contribute to self-esteem, to the sense of fulfillment through the mastering of one's self and one's environment, and to the sense that one is valued by society. The fundamental question the individual worker asks is "What am I doing that *really* matters?"

When work becomes merely automatic behavior, instead of being *homo faber*, the worker is *animal laborens*. Among workers who describe themselves as "just laborers," self-esteem is so deflated that the distinction between the human as worker and animal as laborer is blurred. . . .

Work is a powerful force in shaping a person's sense of identity. We find that most, if not all, working people tend to describe themselves in terms of the work groups or organizations to which they belong. The question, "Who are you?" often solicits an organizationally related response, such as "I work for IBM," or "I'm a Stanford professor." Occupational role is usually a part of this response for all classes: "I'm a steelworker," or "I'm a lawyer." In short: "People tend to 'become what they do.' "

Several highly significant effects result from work-related identification: welfare recipients become "nobodies"; the retired suffer a crucial loss of identity; and people in low-status jobs either cannot find anything in their work from which to derive an identity or they reject the identity forced on them. Even those who voluntarily leave an organization for self-employment experience difficulties with identity — compounded by the confusion of others. . . .

Basic to all work appears to be the human desire to impose order, or structure, on the world. The opposite of work is not leisure or free time; it is being victimized by some kind of disorder which, at its extreme, is chaos. It means being unable to plan or to predict. And it is precisely in the relation between the desire for order and its achievement that work provides the sense of mastery so important to self-esteem. The closer one's piece of the world conforms with one's structural plans, the greater the satisfaction of work. And it follows that one of the greatest sources of dissatisfaction in work results from the inability to make one's own sense of order prevail — the assembly line is the best (or worst) example of an imposed, and, for most workers, unacceptable structure.

These observations have been verified a number of times in investigations of mass and protracted unemployment. Loss of work during the Depression was found to produce chronic disorganization in the lives of parents and children, as documented in several studies of the 1930's. Cynicism, loss of self-confidence, resentment, and hostility toward the Federal Government, helplessness, and isolation are all experienced during such difficult periods. According to Charles Winick,

> Inasmuch as work has such a profound role in establishing a person's life space, emotional tone, family situation, object relations, and where and how he will live, either the absence of work or participation in marginal work often makes it likely that he will develop a pervasive *atonie*.

Atonie is a condition of deracination — a feeling of rootlessness, lifelessness, and dissociation — a word which in the original Greek meant a string that does not vibrate, that has lost its vitality.

Besides lending vitality to existence, work helps establish the regularity of life, its basic rhythms and cyclical patterns of day, week, month, and year. Without work, time patterns become confused. One recalls the drifting in T.S. Eliot's "The Wasteland":

What shall I do. . . . What shall we do tomorrow?
What shall we ever do?

When duration of employment has been prolonged, unemployed workers progress from optimism through pessimism to fatalism. Attitudes toward the future and toward the community and home deteriorate. . . .

Many of the studies revealing the disorganizing effects of unemployment during the Depression have found echoes in recent "ghetto ethnographies." Such studies as Liebow's *Tally's Corner* show these effects to be as much a function of unemployment and marginal employment *per se* as of economic catastrophe. This is so because to be denied work is to be denied far more than the things that paid work buys; it is to be denied the ability to define and respect one's self.

It is illusory to believe that if people were given sufficient funds most of them would stop working and become useless idlers. A recent economic analysis shows that as people increase their earnings and acquire wealth they do not tend to decrease the time and energy that they invest in work. In another study, when a cross section of Americans were asked if they would continue working even if they inherited enough to live comfortably without working, 80% said they would keep on working (even though only 9% said they would do so because they enjoyed the work they were doing). Some people may not want to take specific jobs — primarily because of the effects on their self-esteem — but working, "engaging in activities that produce things valued by other people," is a necessity of life for most people. . . .

Some of the most compelling evidence about the centrality of the functions of work in life comes from the recent efforts of women to fill what some interpret as a void in their lives with the sense of identity derived from work. . . .

It must be realized that although *work* is central to the lives of most people, there is a small minority for whom a *job* is purely a means to a livelihood. To them a job is an activity that they would gladly forgo if a more acceptable option for putting bread on their table were available. What little evidence there is on this point indicates that for most such individuals the kinds of jobs that they see open to them do little to provide the self-esteem, identity, or mastery that are the requisites for satisfying work. These individuals turn to other activities (music, hobbies, sports, crime) and other institutions (family, church, community) to find the psychological rewards that they do not find in their jobs. In effect, these activities, for these people, become their real work. This unusual phenomenon helps to explain the small amount of job withdrawal that occurs among welfare recipients [and the fact that] welfare mothers may choose the personally fulfilling work of raising their children to the alternative of a low-level, unchallenging job — the only kind available to them. . . .

» Mortimer J. Adler «

Work, Education, and Leisure

» «

Mortimer J. Adler, editor of the Encyclopaedia Britannica, *is one of the few contemporary philosophers to address the issues of work that historically engaged the world's greatest thinkers from Aristotle through Karl Marx. Adler illustrates that there are many kinds of work, ranging from pure drudgery at one extreme to work we would do even if we were not paid for it at the other. At the latter end of the spectrum, he points out, the distinctions between work and leisure tend to blur. Leisure, like good work, is a creative activity, unlike playing or idling, which just kill time. In an ideal world, people would be educated so that they could spend their time in good creative work and leisure to the full extent of their native talents—and drudgery would be left to machines.*

We are going to consider first the distinction between work and leisure; second, the relation of education to both work and leisure; and, finally, the relation of all three—education, work, and leisure—to the living of a good human life.

We begin with the distinction between *work* and *leisure*. Both of those words name activities: working and leisuring. The word *leisure* should never be used as an adjective, modifying time. We should never say *leisure time* when what we mean is *free time*. Nor should the word *leisure* ever be used as a synonym for another form of activity: play, recreation, or amusement. Like play, leisuring is one of the ways men do and should fill their free time—time not consumed by compulsory activities, by activities necessary for life itself or for obtaining a livelihood.

But, unlike play and like work, leisuring is a serious activity that results in products of value to the individual and to society. The Greek word for *leisure* was *schole*—the word from which we derive *school*. Its basic meaning was learning or human growth.

There are four questions to be answered in distinguishing different forms or categories of human activity. First, is the activity compulsory or optional? It is compulsory, if necessary for staying live, for living, if not for living well. Second, if optional, is it morally desirable? Morally obligatory? Not just for living, but for living well? Third, what purpose does it serve? What goods or values does it achieve for ourselves, for others, or for society? Finally, how is the activity related to the result it achieves and to the agent producing the results? Is the result immanent or transitive, or both? Is the result intrinsic or inherent to the activity, or is it a consequence of the activity?

Before we ask these questions about working and leisuring, let me apply them to two other forms or categories of activity to make the analysis clear—sleeping and playing. I would like to use the term *sleep* to cover all forms of biologically necessary activity, not just slumbering, but eating and cleansing and exercising, as well as slumbering.

Sleep in this sense is compulsory, necessary for life itself. The good result it achieves is bodily health and vigor. That result is a consequence of the activity, not inherent in it, and it is almost wholly immanent. It is a good that remains in the agent, not something external to him. Play, on the other hand, which covers all forms of recreation and amusement, is optional, not compulsory, not necessary for life itself. It may be regarded as desirable for a good life, but only within certain limits, not unlimitedly. And it is not morally obligatory. The good result it achieves is pleasure, and that result is inherent in the activity itself, not a consequence of it. In fact, playing is the only form of activity that has a good result that is inherent in the activity itself and also immanent in the agent or actor, not transitive.

Still considering sleep and play, we can observe a few additional points that will be helpful to us when we come to consider working and leisuring. A particular activity may belong to both categories. For example, eating or drinking merely for the pleasure inherent in the process may be compared with eating or drinking solely for the sustenance derived therefrom. When eating or drinking, which in its primary or pure form belongs to the category of biologically necessary activity, is thus transformed into another category, we should note this transformation by calling it "playful eating or drinking." Similarly, swimming for the sake of one's health, under doctor's orders, may be compared with swimming for the sake of the pleasure inherent in the process. Here we have swimming as play versus therapeutic swimming—swimming in the category of sleep, serving the purpose of health.

A given activity, in addition, may of course fall under both of these distinct categories at the same time. It may be an admixture of both, in varying proportions.

One further characteristic of the two forms or categories of activity we have been considering is this: Although both achieve good results, those results are entirely immanent—a good that benefits the agent or actor, his health, his enjoyment of pleasure. In sharp contrast, the two forms of activity to which we now turn, working and leisuring, usually result in extrinsic commodities: marketable goods or services. As we shall see, the results they produce may be both transitive and immanent—a product external to the agent and a result remaining in the agent.

In the light of these preliminary clarifications, let us now examine working and leisuring. It is of the utmost importance to note two distinct considerations that affect our understanding of how work and leisure are related. One is whether the activity engaged in involves extrinsic compensation needed by the individual because it is necessary for him to earn a living—to obtain the means of subsistence. Unlike play, which is always optional, work is compulsory. But unlike sleep, which is compulsory for all, work is compulsory only for those who do not have independent incomes and so must earn their livelihood.

The other consideration concerns the character of the activity itself as it affects the person doing it. If the activity engaged in for subsistence benefits the worker, improving him in one respect or another, then it has the aspect of leisure. If, however, the activity does not benefit the individual and, far from improving him, may cause his deterioration, then it has the aspect of drudgery.

Work for subsistence may consist in pure drudgery or may be entirely leisure work, or it may involve admixtures of both aspects in varying degrees. In other words, there is a spectrum of work for subsistence, with pure drudgery at one extreme and pure leisure work at the other and with admixtures of both components in between.

This leads us to still one further consideration with regard to work and leisure. One and the same activity may be performed solely for the benefit it confers on the person doing it, for extrinsic compensation, or for its self-rewarding quality. When, for example, composing music, doing scientific research, or teaching is done as a creative activity and without any extrinsic compensation, let us call that activity a *leisure pursuit*. But when that kind of activity is engaged in not only for the inherent reward or benefit it confers on the agent but also for the extrinsic compensation that it earns, let us call it *leisure work*.

Thus we see that the leisuring may enter human life in three ways:

1. As an uncompensated leisure pursuit.

2. As pure leisure work, to which some compensation is also attached.

3. As an aspect of work for subsistence in which some element of drudgery is also involved.

Work that earns an extrinsic compensation does so by producing marketable commodities—goods or services. These may take the form of economic goods and services—the various forms of wealth. Or they may consist of the goods of civilization—contributions to knowledge, artistic productions, political or religious activities, and so on.

Since work is by definition an extrinsically compensated activity, work always produces a transitive result, a marketable commodity, regardless of whether the immanent result of the work (its effect on the worker) makes it pure drudgery, pure leisure work, or some admixture of the two.

In contrast, leisure pursuits, which are not work, have an immanent result only—the beneficial effect on the person engaging in them, the improvement of his mind or his character.

The quality of the activity may be exactly the same whether it is a self-rewarding, uncompensated leisure pursuit or whether it is extrinsically compensated leisure work. The reason for calling the same activity a *leisure pursuit*, on the one hand, and *leisure work*, on the other, is that in the one case the activity is engaged in solely for its immanent result, the moral or intellectual growth or improvement of the individual, whereas in the other case there is an additional purpose, the earning of a livelihood.

The confusion of play and leisure (or playing and leisuring) occurs because some leisuring, in the form of leisure pursuits, is, like play, purely optional—something we do in the time that is not occupied by sleep and work. When the activity that is a leisure pursuit for some is leisure work for others, it is not likely to be confused with play.

Before I attempt to summarize the spectrum of work from pure drudgery at one extreme to pure, but compensated, leisuring at the other, let me ask you to consider two questions. What is the character of those activities in which no one would willingly engage unless he could not earn a living in any other way? I think the answer is that such activity is drudgery, sheer toil—activity that carries no intrinsic reward for the person engaging in it, because it is mechanical, repetitive, stultifying, totally noncreative.

On the other hand, what is the character of the activities in which everyone should enage if he did not have to do a stroke of work to earn a living and if he recognized that he was morally obligated to occupy his free time with optional activities other than purely playful ones? Imagine a man whose whole time is free after eight hours of sleep, eight hours of biological activity, with sixteen hours of free time. Can he play for sixteen hours a day? If not and if he does not have to earn a living, what does he do with that time? The answer must be, it seems to me, the pursuits of leisure—all of them creative rather than mechanical and repetitive activities, all of them resulting in some form of learning, personal growth, or self-improvement.

Among those who have to earn a livelihood by work, the most fortunate individuals are those who can do so by pure leisure work, the kind of activity that would be a leisure pursuit if it were uncompensated, if no compensation were needed. Not quite so fortunate but nevertheless happily circumstanced are those who can earn a living by work that has a large component of leisure in it and very little drudgery. The least fortunate are those who earn their living either by work that has a large component of drudgery in it, or is nothing but drudgery, and results in their deterioration rather than in their self-improvement.

Let me now recapitulate all these points by describing the spectrum of work, from drudgery at one extreme to pure leisure work at the other.

At one extreme are those tasks or jobs that no one would ever engage in for a moment except to earn a living and in which one engages under the dire necessity of having no other alternative way of getting the means of subsistence, except by theft or charity. These are all mechanical, repetitive activities, involving no mental or creative input, and so they are stultifying to the person engaged in them, detrimental to the mind and body of the worker. These are all tasks that one hopes might be completely done by machines and not by men—and by automated machines, largely unattended by men. Karl Marx in the *Communist Manifesto* was completely right in describing such work as activity that improves or enhances the materials worked on (the raw materials turned into saleable products), but which at the same time degrades or deteriorates, both in body and mind, the condition of the worker.

At the opposite extreme are those tasks or undertakings for which a person may be in fact compensated, but in which a person would engage even if he did not have to do anything at all in order to earn a living. They are such activities as: all forms of artistic work; all forms of scientific research or philosophical thought; all forms of political or religious activity (engagement in the work of the state or of the church, or of society generally); and all forms of truly professional activity, such as teaching, healing, nursing, and engineering. What characterizes all these activities is that:

• Engaging in them is self-rewarding in the sense that the individual learns or grows—improves as a human being—by doing them.

• They are all creative, involving intellectual inputs that are not routine or repetitive. They are the very opposite of mechanical activities.

• They are essentially work rather than play because they may be done for compensation and because they may be done without any intrinsic pleasure in doing them; they may be tiring or fatiguing, as tiring or fatiguing as other forms of work.

• Like all other forms of work, they may be productive of goods valuable to others and even marketable, as well as of goods that enhance the person and life of the individual who engages in such work.

In between the extremes of work that is pure drudgery and that therefore should be eliminated from human life and work that is compensated leisuring are many degrees and modes of admixtures.

Many tasks or jobs that men engage in for compensation because they have to earn a living involve admixtures of repetitive chores (drudgery) and creative input (leisuring). Obviously, the larger the creative input and the fewer the chores, the better the work is for the human being doing it, regardless of the amount of money that is compensation for doing it. Some persons wisely choose lower emoluments because they want a job that is intrinsically more rewarding.

One further observation should be added concerning the spectrum of subsistence work from pure drudgery at one extreme to compensated leisuring at the other. It is sometimes unfortunately the case that persons engage in activities that have the character of leisuring but do so for the wrong reason—just for the extrinsic compensation involved. For example, the teacher who does not learn anything in the course of teaching, and teaches only to earn a living, has transformed leisuring into drudgery. The same thing holds for all the creative arts and the learned professions. One can think of lawyers or physicians, even of writers and musicians, who turn leisuring into nothing but compensated drudgery.

The opposite transformations seldom, if ever, occur. An activity that is nothing but drudgery (because it is mechanical, repetitive, and so on) rarely gets turned into something like leisuring. Higher or better activities can be debased and deformed, but the lowest forms of activity can seldom, if ever, be elevated.

The moral ideal that emerges from this analysis can be simply stated. It concerns the role of compensated leisure work and uncompensated leisure pursuits in the accomplishment of a good human life. For those who need to work in order to earn a living, that work should, so far as possible, involve some degree of compensated leisuring and should never be pure drudgery. And in relation to the individual's talents and capacities, the subsistence work he engages in is better for him as a human being in proportion as it involves fewer chores or less drudgery and more creative leisuring. For all, whether they need to work for a living or not, and especially for those who earn their living by work that does not involve a large component of leisuring, a larger proportion of the individual's free time should be spent in leisure pursuits or activities than in the various forms of play or recreation.

While play and leisuring—the two main fillers of free time—are neither biologically nor economically necessary, they are both morally desirable. I would go further and say that, from the point of view of the human potential, leisuring is morally obligatory. One cannot discharge one's obligation to make a good human life for one's self without engaging in the pursuits of leisure.

The educational significance of this understanding of the spectrum of work and of leisure pursuits beyond any need for extrinsic compensation, in relation to the good life, can be simply summarized. In 1817, Thomas Jefferson recommended to the legislature of Virginia that all children be given three years of free public schooling, after which those destined for labor should be separated from those destined for leisure learning, the former to be sent to the shops and the farms and the latter to colleges of education. Today, everyone who not only is committed to but also understands the democratic ideal should agree that all children are destined for leisure, whether or not they have to work in order to earn a living.

Hence the controlling objective of formal and informal education in a democratic society—education before school, in school, after school, on the job, and off the job—can be stated as follows: Prepare and school the young—liberally, not vocationally—so they can earn a living by doing work that has as large a component of leisuring in it as they are capable of by their talents and native endowments. School them in such a way that they can use as much of their free time as possible for the pursuits of leisure. And provide all citizens, during the years in which they are engaged in subsistence work and after they have retired from it, with continuing formal and informal facilities for learning and self-education, since learning is the very essence of leisuring.

Let me add to this one final comment. The ideal of the educated man at the end of the twentieth century differs sharply from the aristocratic ideal of the past, which more or less prevailed from the time of the ancient Greeks to the end of the nineteenth century. That aristocratic ideal is no longer viable or applicable in our industrial democracy, where universal citizenship is accompanied by universal schooling and where everyone, not just the fortunate few, is entitled to think of the ideal of becoming an educated human being as a condition that he or she can attain. The old aristocratic ideal was stated in terms of intellectual content—things known, skills possessed—and, as so stated, was open only to the few. We must replace that ideal with one more appropriate to our kind of society and our commitment to the education of all or at least to helping all to become educated.

Let me restate the ideal. An educated person is one who can and does work creatively and who uses what free time he or she has for the pursuits of leisure, each according to his or her native talents and capacities. The ideal, as thus restated, is, in my judgment, a viable one in our society, one that is applicable to all, except the few in asylums of one kind or another. It is an objective that the educational and economic institutions of a democratic society should aim at and should be able to serve effectively.

And no one shall work for money, and no one shall work for fame,
But each for the joy of working.
—Rudyard Kipling, When Earth's Last Picture is Painted

» E.F. Schumacher «

Good Work

» «

*E. F. Schumacher was a humanist who opposed large-scale technology and mass
production. He favored producing things in small-scale enterprises with what he
called "nonviolent" technologies. These simple technologies would preserve the
dignity of humans and the quality of the environment. To Schumacher, good work
was closely related to the concept of living a good life; good work gives workers an
opportunity to utilize and develop their capacities and to help them overcome their
egocentricity by joining with others in a common task. Schumacher calls our
attention to the products of work. Good work must, he argues, be work that
produces things of quality.*

To understand the meaning of
"good work" and "education for good work," we must first face such
age-old questions as "What is man?" "Where does he come from?" and
"What is the purpose of his life?" Today such questions are called "prescientific" and there is no attempt to answer them. If they are indeed "prescientific," this can only mean that science is not of essential importance for
the conduct of human life. Good answers to such "prescientific" questions
are of infinitely greater importance.

Some time ago I visited Leningrad and did some sightseeing in that
beautiful city. At one point, I consulted a map to find out where I was. I
could see several enormous churches, yet there was no sign of them on my
map. An interpreter came to help me and said, "We don't show churches
on our maps." I pointed to some other churches, which were clearly indicated. "These are museums," he replied. "We don't show living churches
on our maps."

It then occurred to me that this was not the first time I had been given a
map that failed to show many of the things I could see right in front of my
eyes. All through my so-called education at schools and universities I had
been given maps of life and of knowledge that bore few traces of many of
the things I considered of the greatest possible importance to the conduct
of my life. For many years my perplexity was complete, and no interpreter
came along to help me. It remained complete until I ceased to suspect the
sanity of my perceptions and began instead to suspect the soundness of
the maps.

Our ancestors did ask and did answer questions like "What is man?" and
"What is the purpose of human life on earth?" But the maps I was

given—and nothing seems to have changed since then—advised me that virtually all our ancestors, until quite recently, were rather pathetic illusionists who conducted their lives on the basis of irrational beliefs and absurd superstitions. Even illustrious scientists such as Johann Kepler and Isacc Newton spent most of their time and energy on theological studies of "non-existing" things. None of it was to be taken seriously today, except of course as a museum piece.

I was taught all this and many similar things at school, although not so plainly and frankly. After all, ancestors had to be treated with respect: They could not help their backwardness; they tried hard and sometimes even got quite near the truth in a haphazard sort of way. Their preoccupation with questions of meaning and purpose, with religious and metaphysical questions, was just one of many signs of their underdevelopment. There is, of course, a degree of interest in religion today, which legitimatizes some of the beliefs of earlier times. It is still permissible, on suitable occasions, to refer to God the Creator, although every educated person knows that there is no real God, certainly not one capable of creating anything, and that the things around us came into existence by a process of mindless evolution—that is, by chance and natural selection.

Modern education insists that only such things as can be proved to exist should be taught. "If in doubt, leave it out." The question of what constitutes proof is, however, a very subtle and difficult one. Would it not be wiser to invert the principle and say, "If in doubt, show it prominently"? After all, matters that are beyond doubt are, in a sense, dead; they do not constitute a challenge to the living. If I limited myself to knowledge that I can consider true beyond doubt, I minimize the risk of error, but I also maximize the risk of missing out on what may be the most important and most rewarding things in life. Thomas Aquinas, following Aristotle, taught that "the slenderest knowledge that may be obtained of the highest things is more desirable than the most certain knowledge obtained of lesser things."

Western civilization, like all great civilizations, was built on this scale of values. But since Descartes it has turned the scale upside down and declares that the pursuit of knowledge of the highest things is a waste of time and "prescientific," and that nothing is worth knowing unless it can be known with certainty. "Those who seek the direct road to truth," said Descartes, "should not bother with any object of which they cannot have a certainty equal to the demonstrations of arithmetic and geometry." That is, we should study only those objects "to the sure and indubitable knowledge of which our mental powers seem to be adequate." The Cartesian revolution has led Western civilization into a total rejection of "the slenderest knowledge that may be obtained of the highest things" and a total fixation on scientific knowledge of the lower things. As a result, questions like "What should I do with my life?" cannot really be answered any more.

26

To ask them is considered a lapse into prescientific modes of thinking, something long abandoned by well-educated modern people.

What, then, is the meaning of "education" or of "good work" when nothing counts except that which can be precisely stated, measured, counted, or weighed? Neither mathematics nor geometry, neither physics nor chemistry can entertain qualitative motive like "good" or "bad," "higher" or "lower." These disciplines can entertain only *quantitative* notions of "more" or "less." It is easy to distinguish between "less education" and "more education," and between "less work" and "more work," but how can we make a *qualitative* evaluation of education or of work? This, we are told, would be purely subjective; it could not be *proved*; it would be anybody's guess, since it cannot be measured and made objective.

The Cartesian revolution has removed the vertical dimension from our map of knowledge. Only the horizontal dimensions are left. Science provides excellent guidance through this flatland. It can do everything except lead us out of the dark wood of a meaningless, purposeless, "accidental" existence. Modern science answers the question "What is man?" with such inspiring phrases as "a cosmic accident," or "a rather unsuccessful product of mindless evolution or natural selection," or "a naked ape." It is not surprising that it has no answer to the question of what this absurd, accidental product of mindless forces is supposed to do with itself—that is to say, what it should do with its *mind*.

In these circumstances, what could be the purpose of education? In Western civilization, as in all other great civilizations, the purpose used to be to lead people out of the dark wood of meaninglessness, purposelessness, drift, and indulgence, up a mountain where the truth that makes you free can be gained. This was the traditional wisdom of all people in all parts of the world. We modern people, who reject traditional wisdom and deny the existence of the vertical dimension of the spirit, also, like our forefathers, desire nothing more than somehow to be able to rise above the humdrum state of our present life. We hope to do so by growing rich, moving around at ever-increasing speed, traveling to the moon and into space, but whatever we do in these respects, we cannot rise above our own humdrum, petty, egotistical selves. Education may help us to become richer quicker and to travel further faster, but everything remains as meaningless as before. As long as we remain entrapped in the metaphysics represented by the Cartesian revolution, education can be nothing but a training that enables people to establish themselves more comfortably— the body, not the soul—in the dark wood of meaningless existence.

In other words, as long as we arrogantly persist in dismissing traditional wisdom as "prescientific," and therefore not to be taken seriously, fit only for the museum, there is no basis for any form of education other than "training for worldly success." Education for good work is quite impossible. For how could we possibly distinguish good work from bad work if human life on Earth has no meaning, no purpose? The word *good* presupposes an aim—good for what? Good for making money? Good for promotion? Good for fame or power? These things can also be attained through work that, from another point of view, would be considered very bad work. Without traditional wisdom, no answer can be found.

Traditional wisdom derives all its answers from a knowledge of the tasks and purposes of human life on earth. The human being's first task is to learn from society and tradition and to find its temporary happiness by following directions from outside. The second task is to interiorize this knowledge, sift it, sort it out, keep the good, and jettison the bad. This process may be called *individuation,* or becoming self-directed. The third task, which cannot be tackled until the first two tasks are accomplished, is dying to oneself, to one's likes and dislikes, to all one's egocentric preoccupations. For this task, a person needs the very best help he can find. To the extent that he succeeds, he ceases to be directed from outside, and he also ceases to be self-directed. He has gained freedom or, one might say, he is God-directed. If he is a Christian, that is precisely what he would hope to be able to say.

If these are the tasks that face each human being, we can say that "good" is what helps me and others along on this journey of liberation. I am called on to "love my neighbor as myself," but I cannot love him at all, except sensually or sentimentally, unless I love myself enough to embark on the good work of personal development. I cannot love and help my neighbor as long as I have to say, with St. Paul: "My own behavior baffles me. For I find myself not doing what I really want to do but doing what I really loathe." In order to become capable of doing good work for my neighbor as well as for myself, I am called upon to love God—that is, strenuously and patiently to keep my mind stretching towards the highest things, to levels of being above my own. Only there is goodness to be found. This is the answer given by traditional wisdom, that is to say, by the metaphysics that has given rise to all the great civilizations of humanity. From this wisdom, we can derive all the guidance we need.

What are a human being's greatest needs? In our spiritual lives, we are primarily and inescapably concerned with values. In our social lives, we are primarily and inescapably concerned with people and also with other sentient creatures. As individuals, our greatest need is self-development.

Accordingly, as anyone can confirm from experience, there are three things healthy people most need to do, and education ought to prepare them for these: first, to act as spiritual beings—that is to say, to act in accordance with their moral impulses; second, to act as neighbors—that is to say, to render service to their fellows; and third, to act as persons, as autonomous centers of power and responsibility—that is to say, to be creatively engaged, using and developing the gifts that have been laid into them. These are the human being's three fundamental needs, and in their fulfillment lies happiness. In their unfulfillment lies frustration and un-happiness.

In a subtle way, which ought to be studied, modern society has made it increasingly difficult or even impossible for most of the people, most of the time, to meet these needs. And education, including higher education, seems to know little about them. Strange to say, most people do not even know what their needs are. For reasons well known to traditional wisdom, human beings are insufficiently "programmed." Even when fully grown, they do not move and act with the surefootedness of animals. They hesitate, doubt, change their minds, run hither and thither, uncertain not simply of how to get what they want, but uncertain, above all, of what they want.

If education is unable to teach them what they want, is it of any use? Questions like "What shall I do with my life?" or "What must I do to be saved?" relate to ends, not merely to means. To such questions, it does not help to say, "Tell me precisely what you want, and I shall teach you how to get it." The whole point is that I do not know what I want. Maybe all I want is to be happy. But the answer, "Tell me what you need for happiness, and I shall then be able to advise you what to do," again, will not do, because I do not know what I need for happiness. Perhaps someone says, "For happiness you need the truth that makes you free." But can the educator tell me what *is* the truth that makes us free? Can he tell me where to find it, guide me to it, or at least point out the direction in which I have to proceed? Maybe I feel that good work is what I am really longing for. Who can tell me what good work is and when work is good?

Traditional wisdom teaches that the function of work is at least threefold: to give workers a chance to utilize and develop their faculties; to enable them to overcome their inborn egocentricity by joining with other people in a common task; and to bring forth the goods and services needed by all of us for a decent existence. Now, I think all this needs to be *taught*.

Until quite recently, I heard it said everywhere that the real task of education was not education for work, but education for leisure. Maybe this extraordinary idea has now been abandoned. Fancy telling young and eager souls, "Now, what I really want you to envisage is how to kill time when you have nothing useful to do." As our ancestors have known (and as it has been expressed by Thomas Aquinas), there can be no joy of life without joy of work. This is a statement worth pondering. Laziness, they also knew, is sadness of the soul. This, too, is worth pondering. A nineteenth-century thinker said something to this effect: "Watch out—if you get too many useful machines, you will get too many useless people." Another statement worth pondering.

The question is raised: "How do we prepare young people for the future world of work?" And the first answer, I think, must be: we should prepare them to be able to distinguish between good work and bad work and encourage them not to accept the latter. That is to say, they should be encouraged to reject meaningless, boring, stultifying or nerve-wracking work where man (or woman) is made the servant of a machine or a system. They should be taught that work is the joy of life and is needed for our development but that meaningless work is an abomination.

A sensitive British worker wrote: "It is probably wrong to expect factories to be other than they are. After all, they are built to house machines, not men. Inside a factory, it soon becomes obvious that steel brought to life by electricity takes precedence over flesh and blood. The onus is on the machines to such an extent that they appear to assume the human attributes of those who work them. Machines have become as much like people as people have become like machines. They pulsate with life, while man becomes a robot. There is a premonition of man losing control, an awareness of doom." This worker has been conditioned not even to expect good work. He has been conditioned to believe that man is nothing but a somewhat complex physiochemical system, nothing but a product of mindless evolution. So he may suffer when machines become like men and men become like machines, but he cannot really be surprised nor expect anything else.

It is interesting to note that the modern world of work takes a lot of care that the worker's body should not accidentally or otherwise be damaged. If it is damaged, the worker can claim compensation. But what of his soul and his spirit? If his work damages them, by reducing him to a robot, that is just too bad. Materialistic metaphysics, or the metaphysics of the doctrine of mindless evolution, does not attribute reality to anything but the physical body. Why then bother about the safety or health of such nebulous, unreal things as soul or spirit? Anyone who says the worker needs work for the development of his soul sounds like a fanciful dreamer.

In depriving work of any higher purpose, we reduce it to the level of "unpleasant necessity." At this level there is no use talking about good work, unless we mean *less* work. What is the point of making something perfect, when it is easier and cheaper to make something imperfect? Ananda Coomaraswamy used to say, "Industry without art is brutality," because it damages the soul and spirit of the worker. He could say this because his metaphysics is very different from that of the modern world. He also said, "It is not as if the artist were a special kind of man; every man is a special kind of artist." This is the metaphysics of good work.

How, then, could there be education for good work? First of all, we should have to alter the metaphysical basis from which we proceed. If we continue to teach that the human being is nothing but the outcome of a mindless, meaningless, and purposeless process of evolution, a process of selection for survival—that is to say, the outcome of nothing but utilitarianism—we can come only to a utilitarian idea of work, an idea that work is nothing but a more or less unpleasant necessity, and the less there *mindless evolution*

is of it, the better. Our ancestors knew about good work, but we cannot learn from them if we continue to regard them with friendly contempt, or if we continue to treat traditional wisdom as a tissue of superstitious poetry, or if we continue to take materialistic scientism as the one and only measure of progress. The best scientists know that science deals only with small, isolated systems, showing how they work, and provides no basis whatever for comprehensive metaphysical doctrines such as the doctrine of mindless evolution. But we nevertheless still teach the young that the modern theory of evolution is a part of science and that it leaves no room for divine guidance or design. We thus wantonly create a conflict between science and religion that causes untold confusion.

Education for good work could then proceed to a systematic study of traditional wisdom, where answers are to be found to questions about the purpose and meaning of life. It would emerge that there is indeed a goal to be reached and that there are many paths to the goal. The goal can be called "perfection"—"Be ye therefore perfect as your father in heaven is perfect"—or "the kingdom," "salvation," "nirvana," "liberation," or "enlightenment." And the path to the goal is good work. "Work out your salvation with diligence." "He who has been given much, of him much will be demanded." In short, life is a kind of school, and in this school nothing counts but good work—work that ennobles the product as it ennobles the producer.

In the process of doing good work, the ego of the worker disappears. As he frees himself from his ego, the divine element in him becomes active. None of this makes sense if we proceed from the basic presuppositions of materialistic scientism. How can the product of mindless evolution—whose abilities are only those selected by blind nature for their utilitarian value in the universal struggle for survival—free itself from its ego, the center of its will to survive? What a nonsensical proposition!

ego

The world of work created by modern metaphysics is a dreary place. Can higher education prepare people for it? How do you prepare people for a kind of serfdom? What human qualities are required for becoming efficient servants of machines, systems, or bureaucracies? The world of work of today is the product of a hundred years of "*de*skilling"—why take the trouble to let people acquire the skills of craftsmanship when all that is wanted is the patience of machine minder? The only skills worth acquiring are those which the system demands, and they are worthless outside the system. They have no survival value outside the system and therefore do not even confer the spirit of self-reliance. What does a machine minder do when, let us say, an energy shortage stops the machine? Or a computer programmer, without a computer?

Maybe higher education could be designed to lead to a world of work that is different from the one we have today. But this cannot be as long as higher education clings to the metaphysics of materialistic scientism and the doctrine of mindless evolution. Figs cannot grow on thistles. Good work cannot grow out of such metaphysics. To try to make it grow on such a basis can do nothing but increase the prevailing confusion. The most urgent need of our time is the need for a metaphysical reconstruction, a supreme effort to bring clarity and cohesion into our deepest convictions with regard to such questions as "What is man?" "Where does he come from?" and "What is the purpose of his life?"

The master word [work] is the open sesame to every portal, the great equalizer in the world, the true philosopher's stone which transmutes all the base metal of humanity into gold.
—Harvey Cushing, *Life of Sir William Osler*

» Daniel Yankelovich «

The Meaning of Work

» «

Psychologist Daniel Yankelovich has spent the better part of the last decade measuring the changing work and social values of young Americans. He uses data from polls he has taken of college-age youth to show that there has been a not-too-subtle shift in the American work ethic. Better educated, more affluent Americans are less willing than their parents to tolerate routine, unchallenging work just to put bread on their tables. Young workers demand meaningful work and a say in decision-making on the job. Indeed, Yankelovich says that young people now feel entitled to many of the things that their parents once saw as privileges: pensions, medical care, and even job satisfaction.

"**A**mericans know more about how to make a living than how to live." Although Thoreau made his astute observation on American life more than a century ago, by and large it remains valid today.

Looking Up from the Grindstone

We still organize our lives around the struggle to make a living. We place our economic institutions at the center of the society because they create the jobs and produce the growth that keeps the economy rolling. We also organize family life around the job: family responsibilities are parceled out to make it as handy as possible for the male head of the household to be the economic provider, while the wife picks up most of the residual chores. Where we live, how well we live, whom we see socially, how we pattern our daily routines, how we educate our children—all of these facets of our lives are dominated by the work we do to make a living.

Many of these social arrangements are now changing. Under the impact of [women's liberation] the rigid division of labor in the family is beginning to break down. People are growing balky on the job: they seem less willing than in the past to endure hardships for the sake of making a living. Some unions are now stressing noneconomic issues at the bargaining table. Many people are seeking jobs that may pay less well but offer a more agreeable life style. And even the high value we place on economic growth as the main goal of our society is cast in doubt. . . .

We are living through a period of vast cultural change, the essence of which lies in the transformation of work values and the work ethic. Indeed, so central is the work ethic to American culture that if its meaning shifts,

33

the character of our society will shift along with it. Conversely, if our general cultural outlook undergoes a reorientation, then the changed meanings of work will probably emerge as the salient expression of the country's new social philosophy. . . .

Contemporary Meaning of the Work Ethic   The present-day work ethic in America is rooted in [the] Protestant tradition. A study on basic American life values carried out by Daniel Yankelovich, Inc. in the mid 1960s showed that a majority of the adult population at that time associated four cultural themes with work. These themes link work with peoples' life values and form essential parts of what we mean by the American work ethic:

The "Good Provider" Theme—The breadwinner—the man who provides for his family—is the real man.

Here is the link between making a living and the society's definition of masculinity. Masculinity has little to do with sexual prowess or physical strength or aggressiveness or a virile appearance. For almost 80 percent of the adult population to be a man in our society has meant being a good provider for the family. The concept of masculinity here at issue also conveys overtones of adulthood, responsibility, intensity of loving care for others.

The Independence Theme—To make a living by working is to "stand on one's own two feet" and avoid dependence on others. Work equals autonomy. To work and be paid for it means one has gained—and earned — freedom and independence.

The Success Theme—"Hard work always pays off." Hard work leads to success, its form dependent on one's abilities, background, and level of education. For the majority, the "payoff" comes in the form of a home of one's own, an ever rising standard of living, and a solid position in the community.

The Self-respect Theme—Hard work of any type has dignity whether it be menial or exalted. A man's inherent worth is reflected in the act of working. To work hard at something and to do it well: a person can feel good about himself if he keeps faith with this precept.

Manhood, responsibility, economic security, independence, freedom, self-respect, success in life, self-esteem, dignity—this is the moral stuff from which the daily life of people is shaped. We often underestimate the potency of moral issues in people's lives, giving more attention to the practical and pleasure-seeking sides of life. But most lives are as immersed in a sea of morality as fish are immersed in water: morality surrounds us. It is the element we breathe. It is rarely noticed—except if it is polluted or absent. From this substratum of moral values grows such diverse phenomena as the traditional American resistance to nonpunitive welfare legislation (because it suggests that not working is morally acceptable), and the deterioration of morale caused by prolonged unemployment, apart from its economic consequences (because of the threat to self-respect and self-esteem). Pay for housework has become a demand of great symbolic significance to the women's movement, one implication of the work ethic being that work for which one is *not* paid connotes second class citizenship—whether it be that of the housewife or the volunteer.

We begin to see how deeply embedded the work ethic is in general cultural values, and why changes in the culture necessarily color the role and meaning of work.

New Cultural Trends

Let us examine some of the new cultural trends that are gradually transforming the work ethic. They are interrelated, each reinforcing the other. For purposes of analysis they can be identified separately. Among the most important are: the changing meaning of success in America; lessening fears of economic insecurity; a weakening of the rigid division of effort between the sexes; a growing "psychology of entitlement" leading to the creation of new social rights; and spreading disillusionment with the cult of efficiency.

The Changing Meaning of Success   Throughout most of the post World War II era, Americans shaped their ideas of success around money, occupational status, possessions, and the social mobility of their children. . . .

The [same] components of success . . .   still count [today]. Certainly, Americans are drawn to money for its practical uses and also to signify to themselves and others that they have achieved a niche in the world. Yet an increasing number of people are coming to feel that there is such a thing as enough money. And this is new. Few scoff at money or reject the opportunity to enhance their standard of living, but people are no longer as ready to make sacrifices for this kind of success as they were in the past. The crucial question has become: "What do I have to give up for the money?" These days, a "big earner" who has settled for an unpleasant life-style is no longer considered more successful than someone with less money who has created an agreeable life-style for himself. There are, of course, millions of people who adhere to older views of success as defined exclusively in terms of money, but the trend is moving away from them.

Similar considerations hold for the other elements of success. Many studies in the sociological literature show that people find it easy to rank jobs by the degrees of prestige that adhere to types of occupation. Yet the status of doctors, scientists, lawyers, and business executives has begun to lose some of its lustre—especially if achieving occupational success involves sacrifice and unpleasantness. The prestige of the business executive, for example, has plummeted in recent years. A 1973 study carried out by the Opinion Research Company shows the public ranking of the professions in terms of prestige in the following order: Physician (66 percent),

Scientist (59 percent), Lawyer (44 percent), Minister (44 percent), Engineer (40 percent, Architect (40 percent), U.S. Congressman (39 percent), Banker (33 percent), Accountant (29 percent), Businessman (20 percent).

Material possessions, too, have begun to lose some of their connotations of success. This is not to say that Americans have lost their taste for material goods. We still surround ourselves with appliances, television sets, charcoal grills, power lawnmowers, snowmobiles, and the other assorted gear associated with American life. And the love affair with the automobile continues unabated. But it has changed its character. The ownership of a huge, gas-guzzling, boat-like car is no longer the crowning symbol of having arrived in the world. Few people these days celebrate each move up the hierarchy of success by the size and make of automobile they own.

Perhaps most significantly, the trend is away from postponing self-gratification in order to insure the upward mobility of one's children. . . . I am not saying that parents are no longer willing to make sacrifices for their children. . . . But they no longer regard vicarious living through their children as a proper substitute for success in their own lives. They feel they have their own lives to live, and do not need to live through their children. . . .

What has taken its place? New ideas about success revolve around various forms of self-fulfillment. The emphasis now is on the self and its unrealized "potential," a self that cries out for expression, satisfaction, actualization. If the key motif of the past was "keeping up with the Joneses," today it is "I have my own life to live—let Jones shift for himself." The new consciousness about the self does not destroy the older definition of success as money and occupational status. But it diminishes the relative importance of "goods" to the individual. They have, as it were, to move over to make way for the newcomer. Money, possessions, a good position—these can and do become instruments of self-expression. But in the process, a subtle but far-reaching transformation takes place. They become means, rather than ends in themselves. And, most significantly, they are not the only means available but must compete with other less materialistic means of self-fulfillment such as being closer to nature, finding new ways to be "creative," spending more time with friends. . . .

Reduced Fear of Economic Insecurity   Less general in its effect on the culture, but equally fraught with significance for the work ethic, is a greatly reduced fear of economic insecurity. Vast segments of the public have grown less fearful that economic catastrophe will strike without warning and render them destitute. Of course, inflation disturbs people and causes them to be distressed about making ends meet. But people today are less afraid of losing their jobs, facing a poverty-stricken old age, or finding themselves in a situation where they are unable to cope economically. . . .

Economic security has not become less important to people. For most, economic security continues to dominate their lives. But today people take some economic security for granted. If they are working, the future prospect that they might be unable to make a living seems curiously unreal.

For many generations an unspoken consensus prevailed in the country, so widespread and universally accepted that there has been no need to make it explicit: the consensus held that economic security is so important and so difficult to insure that no sacrifice is too great for the sake of preserving it. This silent assumption has dominated our national life. Its unchallenged acceptance has given our society its distinctive character, shaping common goals, and pervading the political and economic life of the nation. For example, if an industrial plant was spewing pollutants into a nearby waterway and the community objected, all the plant manager would have to say was, "That will mean we'll have to lay off a few hundred men," and typically the community would back off from its demands.

In the past few years, the consensus has begun to collapse. A majority of adults . . . state that they continue to place economic security above all other goals, but a substantial . . . minority say that they are now prepared to take certain risks with their own and the nation's economic security for the sake of enhancing the quality of life. We are not surprised to find that the majority still adheres to the old view; what is striking is that so large a minority has adopted this new and far-reaching value-orientation.

One consequence of the lessened fear of economic insecurity is a growing willingness to take unprecedented risks. This confidence pertains both to personal life and to national policy. People are seeking to realize new values relating to the preservation of the environment, to self-enhancement and, as we shall shortly discuss, to the quality of working life.

3. **Economic Division of Labor Between the Sexes**   . . . One consequence of the reduced fear of economic insecurity has been a concomitant lessening in the fear and guilt experienced by people when they take a more casual attitude toward their role obligations in marriage. The iron economic discipline that maintained the rigidity of the sex roles in the past has weakened. Under the impact of the women's liberation movement a far greater flexibility has marked the relationship between the sexes. . . .

While most people reject an interchange of roles between men and women, they are very much in favor of an easier, more flexible division of effort. Gradually, year by year, they are accepting a more informal, less fixed separation of obligations, expectations, and responsibilities. A majority of families today feel that it is perfectly all right for men to participate in shopping and in cleaning the home, and more than three out of ten families look with favor on men participating in daily meal preparation. Conversely, the idea of women working for purposes of self-fulfillment rather than economic motives gains wider acceptance all the time. And, in fact, women are pouring into the work force in unprecedented numbers—and at a faster rate than men. (Women now constitute almost 40 percent of the total work force.) These labor participation rates tell us nothing about the psychological reasons for work. It is here that the real change is taking place. Women have always worked for economic reasons, but now, superimposed on the economic motive, is the powerful psychological force of self-realization. Its effects are changing work values almost as much as they are changing the nature of the family.

The Psychology of Entitlement A fourth category of cultural change is a spreading psychology of entitlement, the growth of a broad new agenda of "social rights." This is the psychological process whereby a person's wants or desires become converted into a set of presumed rights.

> From "I would like to have a secure retirement," to "I have the right to a secure retirement."
>
> From "If I could afford it, I would have the best medical care," to "I have the right to the best medical care whether I can afford it or not."
>
> From "My job would mean more to me if I had more to say about how things are run," to "I have the right to take part in decisions that affect my job."
>
> From "I'd like to have a job that gives me pleasure and satisfaction, rather than just something I do to make a living," to "I have a right to work on something that lets me do a good job and gives me pleasure."
>
> From "I hope we will be able to afford to send our children to college," to "Our children have as much right to a higher education as anybody else."
>
> From "I hope that this breakfast cereal is fresh," to "I have the right to know when it was made and how long it will stay fresh." . . .

The concept of social rights has always exerted a strong force in our society, but in recent years a number of new insititutional forms have sprung up that immensely shorten the time span between the individual's sense of entitlement and political action. . . .

As individual desires and privileges become converted into rights, the marketplace—the forum for expressing desires—is gradually being constricted by the political process and by regulative and legislative mechanisms for enforcing rights. It is this process more than any other that accounts for the moving line of demarcation between the public sector and the private sector which, as Daniel Bell has observed working from a different source of data, is one of the hallmarks of an emerging post-industrial society.

fate of western societies — everything based on rationality.

5. The Adversary Culture Challenges the Cult of Efficiency   Max Weber, a founder of modern sociology, believed that the master key to the fate of Western industrial societies lay in the implacable unfolding of the process of "rationalization." By rationalization Weber meant a broader version of what a modern plant manager tries to do when he "rationalizes" his production line, i.e., organizes it so that he can produce the most products at the greatest speed for the least amount at the lowest cost, with all the standardization and controls that this process implies. Weber predicted that in modern industrial society the process of rationalization and bureaucratization would not remain confined to the domains of business and government. He foresaw rationalization spreading to areas as diverse as music, religion, economics, law, and politics. All of our large institutions, he observed, tend toward inexorable systematization. In the rationalized society that results, relations among men become ruled by how useful people are in performing their utilitarian function. People, in effect, *become* the roles they play in carrying out the functions of the society. Institutions grow ever more organized in order to contribute more efficiently to the whole. And a false sense of progress, to which we attribute the highest of moral purposes, accompanies the entire process of growth piled upon growth, system on system.

Max Weber

Weber identified the psychological motive for rationalization as the passion for mastering the environment. He predicted that we would pay a high price in human satisfaction with every step we took toward perfecting the process of rationalization. He also noted that one consequence of increasing efficiency would be to strip life of all mystery and charm. Above all, he feared that the process would extend beyond the regulation of man's economic and political activities to stifle his private and personal life. . . .

In the past few years, . . . the average American [has begun to] wonder whether too great a concern with efficiency and rationalization is not robbing his life, just as Weber suspected it would, of the excitement, adventure, mystery, romance, and pleasure for which he yearns—especially if he is a young American. To be sure, people are annoyed when the telephone does not work or their automobile mechanic does not know what he is doing. Nonetheless, they are beginning to suspect the merits of values centering on efficiency, planning, and organization of time.

Life Values and Their Effect on Work Values

We have been examining five forms of cultural change: emerging new definitions of success; a dwindling fear of economic insecurity; more flexible man-wife role relations; a spreading psychology of entitlement; and the growth in the adversary culture of a serious challenge to the cult of efficiency. These changes, and not others, have been selected out of the vast sweep of social transformations in our society because: (a) they represent cultural as distinct from . . . *structural* changes . . . (b) they are important enough to merit special attention; and, (c) they are either slowly eating away at the work ethic or are likely to do so in the foreseeable future. Let us now examine how these social changes affect work values.

The important question of whether or not Americans are satisfied with their work is presently bogged down in a heated but fruitless controversy. On the one side are those observers of the work scene who cite public opinion polls to prove that the overriding majority of Americans are satisfied with their work. The other side, represented by many sociologists, industrial psychologists, journalists, and other observers, point to a variety of statistics, observations, and studies that show a rising tide of disaffection in the work force.

Which side is correct? Well . . . both are. Each party to the controversy has fastened onto a different facet of a complex, multifaceted problem. The seeming contradiction between them is more apparent than real. It can probably be resolved—and a useful perspective gained—by keeping three variables in mind: the age of the worker, the expectations he (or she) brings to the job, and the difference between the economic and psychological satisfactions people seek from their work.

Economic Satisfactions The key economic satisfactions people look for from their jobs are a good salary, the prospects for a secure retirement, and job security. Significantly, most people today who are employed full-time feel that these economic needs are now being met by their jobs, more or less satisfactorily. This feeling, more than any other, creates a climate of social stability that was lacking in the 1930s when the country faced what then appeared to be the insoluble problem of mass unemployment. This is a point of cardinal importance. If we are to retain perspective on changes in the work ethic, we must always bear in mind that most people who work for a living do so mainly for economic reasons and that the large majority of them feel that their economic expectations are met by their current jobs. . . .

The two most disaffected groups of working people in the country are people under 25, both men and women, and blacks of all ages. The reasons for their discontent are sharply different. Typically, blacks are unhappy because their basic economic demands are not being met. Young white men and women, although they too are concerned with economics, are restive because they are tuned into the psychological benefits of work—and they do not feel they are being fulfilled.

Psychological Benefits There are three psychological benefits people would like to gain from their work. One is the opportunity to advance to more interesting, varied, and satisfying work that also pays better and wins more recognition than their current job. This is, of course, a traditional work desire with an economic as well as a psychological component. But the psychological side of the job mobility demand is gradually growing more important.

The desire to do a good job at whatever one is doing—a part of the traditional work ethic—is a second psychological gratification sought by people. This is an even more universal desire than job mobility and is expressed by people of all ages, levels of education, sex, and race. This desire is . . . not created by employers by means of their systems of rewards and punishments. It is a deeply rooted need that people bring with them to their work, and as such is one of the country's greatest strengths. . . .

The third category of psychological need is comparatively new, at least in the sense that it is rapidly spreading to more and more people. This is the yearning to find self-fulfillment through "meaningful work." By meaningful work people usually mean: (1) work in which they can become involved, committed, and interested; (2) work that challenges them to the utmost of their capabilities; and (3) participation in decision making. A growing number of young people each year say that they are prepared to trade off salary and other economic benefits in exchange for meaningful, self-fulfilling work, i.e., work that offers them more than money.

It should be stressed that nearly everyone would like to enjoy both types of benefits from their jobs—economic and psychological. Almost all now expect the economic benefits—increasingly as a matter of right. But only the younger people feel they are *entitled* to some of the psychological benefits as a right rather than as a matter of luck or special effort on their part. . . .

Just a few years ago, the country was reduced to near panic by what seemed to be the wholesale alienation of college youth. Now we find an almost classic formula for accommodation and adaptation. The research findings . . . show that the new definitions of success appeal hugely to college students. . . .

Summary

The present impact of the five cultural trends we have been examining is not evenly distributed. The three groups most directly affected are the college-educated; the young people who lack a college education; and women. For the majority of our college-educated youth, and a growing majority at that, the future effects of these trends seem likely to strengthen the social order. . . . there is a good fit between what these young people want and what the occupational structure of the country requires and is prepared to give in return. For noncollege youth, however, the future is fraught with instability. The work motivations of these young people are being undercut by a myriad of cultural and economic changes. Unless the large employing institutions of the country grasp what is happening and respond intelligently, the negative impact on the economy and on our future social stability may be quite uncomfortable.

The new cultural values are drawing women into the work force in unprecedented numbers and many of them bring a serious career orientation with them. This tendency is, perhaps, the most dramatic cultural trend in the country today. One unanticipated side effect of women's success in the workplace may be to threaten an old social accommodation among men. This, like many other traditions, has some repugnant features but also serves a complex social need that will not be easy to replace if the old values disappear.

Perhaps the best way to summarize these various trends and counter-trends is to forecast what changes are likely to occur in the work ethic as defined at the beginning of [the article]. Four principal themes were associated with the work ethic as of the mid 1960s. One is the link between work and psychological independence, especially between *paid* work and autonomy. This link is likely to grow even stronger in the future. In the past, it has been tied mainly to the male adult. In the future, it will be developed increasingly as an entitlement, a social right, appropriate to women as well as men, and to youth as well as the middle-aged.

A second theme, long associated with the work ethic, that of the good provider, will probably change in the future. The change may be slow since there is deep resistance to the idea that traditional sex-linked roles should be abandoned totally. Though gradual, this shift is already in motion: sex-linked roles in marriage are becoming far more flexible, especially among our college-educated young people.

The idea that all jobs possess an inherent dignity, however menial, as long as the work is "honest work" is the third theme. Here, I suspect, we will see rapid change in the future as the psychological satisfactions demanded from work increase in intensity. For better or worse, dignity will adhere to work that the individual can define to himself as "meaningful." Since the definition of meaningfulness is largely subjective, there is no necessary relationship between low status jobs and lack of dignity. The Harvard graduate who chooses to become a farmer or carpenter or forest ranger is still a rarity. But as rigid status stratifications lose some of their iron grip on the society, and as the vagaries of individual self-fulfillment find new forms of expression, we may see the occupational structure lose as much of its hierarchical character as has the General Motors line of cars.

The most far-reaching transformations are likely to occur in the fourth theme, the idea that "hard work always pays off." In the past, the payoff for hard work has come in the form of the extrinsic rewards of money and job security. In the future, as new ideas of success take hold, the definition of what success in work means will also change. There will be far more stress on the quality of working life, with the psychological qualification of work being given as much weight as the economic. The incentives to work hard, if they are to prove effective, will have to include a self-fulfillment payoff as well as a monetary one.

The following schematic summarizes the likely impact of present cultural trends on the work ethic:

Future Impact of Cultural Trends on the Work Ethic

Work Ethic in 1960s	Changes in Work Ethic in 1970s
Paid work means autonomy.	Meaning will intensify and spread, especially to women.
The working male is the good provider, the real man.	Slow erosion of this meaning with unknown but far-reaching consequences.
All work has inherent dignity.	Only "meaningful" work has inherent dignity.
Hard work always pays off.	Rapid erosion of this meaning, because of the changing nature of the payoff.

Ours has been a society with its nose held close to the grindstone. Even today most people are preoccupied with making a living and little else. Gradually, and with increasing momentum, Americans are growing restless with the day-to-day routines of dull jobs and drab housekeeping. They are beginning to look up from the grindstone.

The workplace has long been dominated by the rule of the carrot and the stick—as if we were a nation of donkeys. But the carrot—the lure of material well-being as defined by money and possessions—is subtly losing its savor. And the stick—once a brutal club labeled "economic insecurity"—has thinned down to a flaccid bundle of twigs.

We do not know what will happen in the workplace of tomorrow under the influence of the new cultural trends. But one thing is sure: it is not likely to resemble the old grindstone so familiar to those of us who grew up stuck to it.

2

»«

WHAT WORK MEANS TO A TO A BLUE-COLLAR WORKER

»«

© 1974 Yale Joel

» Samuel Lipson «

Bread
and
Water

» «

This excerpt from a 1912 congressional hearing reminds us how the issues of blue-collar work have changed over this century, partly as the result of union organization, partly from governmental legislation, and partly as the result of education. In this poignant interview, Samuel Lipson, the textile worker testifying to Congressman Berger, is concerned with issues of bare survival: food, clothing, and shelter. This congressional investigation of working conditions was prompted by a strike in the Lawrence, Massachusetts, textile mills, where more than 20,000 persons joined the picket lines, attracting nationwide attention.

MR. BERGER. Why did you go on a strike?

MR. LIPSON. I went out on strike because I was unable to make a living for my family.

MR. BERGER. How much wages were you receiving?

MR. LIPSON. My average wage, or the average wage of my trade, is from $9 to $10 a week.

MR. BERGER. What kind of work do you do?

MR. LIPSON. I am a weaver.

MR. BERGER. You are a skilled workman?

MR. LIPSON. Yes, sir; for years.

MR. BERGER. You have have been a skilled workman for years and your wages average from $9 to $10 per week?

MR. LIPSON. Yes, sir; that was the average.

MR. BERGER. How many children do you have?

MR. LIPSON. I have four children and a wife.

MR. BERGER. You support a wife and four children from a weekly wage averaging from $9 to $10 per week and you are a skilled workman. Did you have steady work?

MR. LIPSON. Usually the work was steady, but there was times when I used to make from $3 to $4 and $5 per week. We have had to live on $3 per week. We lived on bread and water. . . .

MR. BERGER. How much rent do you pay?

MR. LIPSON. I pay $2.50.

MR. BERGER. Per week?

MR. LIPSON. Yes, sir.

MR. BERGER. You pay $2.50 per week for rent out of $10 weekly wages?

MR. LIPSON. Yes, sir. You asked me whether I supported my family out of $10 per week. Of course we do not use butter at the present time; we use a kind of molasses; we are trying to fool our stomachs with it.

MR. BERGER. It is a bad thing to fool your stomach.

MR. LIPSON. We know that, but we can not help it. When we go to the store without any money, the storekeeper tells us that he can not sell us anything without the money.

MR. BERGER. How much were you reduced by reason of the recent cut in the wages?

MR. LIPSON. From 50 to 65 to 75 cents per week.

MR. BERGER. How much does a loaf of bread cost in Lawrence?

MR. LIPSON. Twelve cents; that is what I pay.

MR. BERGER. The reduction in your wages, according to this, took away five loaves of bread from you every week?

MR. LIPSON. Yes, sir. When we go into the store now with a dollar and get a peck of potatoes and a few other things, we have no change left out of that dollar. Of course we are living according to what we get.

MR. BERGER. Living in Washington, I can appreciate that. How many months in the year were you employed?

MR. LIPSON. I was employed the year through. The company keeps us in the mills no matter whether there is work or not, and sometimes we only go home with $3 or $4 in our envelopes.

MR. BERGER. Do you do piecework?

MR. LIPSON. Yes, sir.

MR. BERGER. What can you tell us about the speeding-up system in the Lawrence mills?

MR. LIPSON. The speeding-up system is according to the premium.

MR. BERGER. They have premiums, also? That is interesting. Kindly give the committee a description of the premium system at Lawrence, Mass.

MR. LIPSON. The premiums are not alike in all the mills. In some mills they start with $35 and some small change. They get 5 percent more; and if they come up to it they get 5 percent more in the month. In other mills, where the machinery runs faster, they are started, say, at $39 per month, and they add 5 percent per month. When it happens to the weaver to make $44 per month, that means he is getting 10 percent, but the majority of them do not get 10 percent. It is a heavy month when they get 10 percent. The loom operatives also get premiums. When a section makes up a certain amount of cloth, they get a certain premium. Therefore they have us to speed up the machinery. If a man can not come up to it he gets fired out. Sometimes one is sick, and sometimes our stomach is empty, because our pay does not always last to the end of the month. When we come to that, we wish it was Saturday, because we usually get our pay on Saturday, but we stay in the mills just the same. They stay there, sick at the loom.

MR. BERGER. What is the effect, then, of the premium system on the weaker workingman — on the man who can not work as fast as the others?

MR. LIPSON. The effect upon him is that he is working less. There is no work for him. He has no work; they do not employ him. . . .

MR. BERGER. You are a member of the strike committee, are you not?

MR. LIPSON. Yes, sir.

MR. BERGER. Tell us the immediate cause of the strike.

MR. LIPSON. The workers in the American Woolen Co.'s mills had meetings and discussed the question of what can we do to make a living. It was unbearable. In one of our meetings we decided to see the agent of the mill, and one committee went up to see the agent of the mill, and he told them to go back to their machines; he did not want to give them any answer at all. At another one of the mills they were absolutely turned down, and in the Washington mill they were told to go to Boston and see the president of the American Woolen Co., Mr. Wood. When they told us to do that, we sent a special delivery letter to Mr. Wood, telling him about how it is in Lawrence. We expected to get an answer, because it was a special delivery letter, and we are waiting for that answer still. Well, they were trying to make up two hours, and they tried to speed up the machinery in order to make us do 56 hours work in 54 hours time, and try to cut off the pay at the same time. The question was whether we could make a living. Well, they cut down the wages after they speeded up the machinery, and as they were trying still to speed up the machinery and trying to cut down the wages, we thought we would have to starve.

MR. BERGER. Do you mean to convey by your statement that you were required to do 56 hours work in 54 hours time, because a law was recently passed in Massachusetts cutting down the hours of labor to 54 per week?

MR. LIPSON. Yes, sir.

MR. BERGER. Were you working 56 hours before that new act was passed?

MR. LIPSON. Yes, sir.

MR. BERGER. What effect did this have on the strike?

MR. LIPSON. The people were complaining that it was impossible for them to bear their sufferings any longer, in so many ways.

MR. BERGER. Do you mean that they were required to furnish as much product in 54 hours as in 56 hours?

MR. LIPSON. Yes, sir.

MR. BERGER. And then suffer a cut in wages besides?

MR. LIPSON. Yes, sir.

MR. BERGER. How many nationalities are there represented among the workers at Lawrence?

MR. LIPSON. Sixteen nationalities. . . .

MR. BERGER. How many of the workers of Lawrence are women and children? How many are men?

MR. LIPSON.   I cannot tell you about how many, but I can tell you that the majority of them are women and children, and as we are speeding up, these children are doing more work. If they cannot do the work, they are fired out. They must do the work that goes from one machine to another, and they must prepare the work for us. If they do not speed up, they are fired out.

MR. BERGER.   Do you mean that the children are discharged?

MR. LIPSON.   Yes, sir.

MR. BERGER.   If the children do not speed up, they lose their places in the mills?

MR. LIPSON.   Yes, sir; and the women who are used in the same place are pushed out sometimes and the children take their places.

MR. BERGER.   Do they have any accidents in the factory?

MR. LIPSON.   Yes, sir.

MR. BERGER.   Give a few instances of accidents.

MR. LIPSON.   There is a girl over there, Camella Teoli, and everyone present can see her. She is an Italian girl, but also speaks English. She started to work in the spinning department, on a machine that is a long one, with three or four different sides. The machine was speeded up and was running with such speed that her hair was caught and her scalp was cut by the machine. Her scalp was torn down, as you see. She was there working for the American Woolen Co. two years ago, and she is still under the treatment of a physician and at work at the same time, because the family consists of seven and she is the oldest. She is 16 years old; her father works in the mill and gets $7 per week. Of course, her parents have no money to have a trial with the company.

MR. BERGER.   She has not sued the company?

MR. LIPSON.   No, sir. That happened two years ago, and she is working to keep up the family. They are poor and she and the father are working to keep up the family. The youngest is a little older than a year.

MR. BERGER.   She would not stand much chance in a lawsuit against the American Woolen Co. The American Woolen Co. is a powerful concern.

MR. LIPSON.   Yes, sir; that is true.

MR. BERGER.   What are the demands of the strikers now?

MR. LIPSON.   The demands are 15 percent increase in wages, based on 54 hours work per week, and double pay for overtime. The reason I wish to call your attention to the demand for 15 percent increase is this: These people work sometimes only two or three days in a week. Her father works only three days in a week, and has $2.88 per week for the family, and they absolutely live on bread and water. If you would look at the other children, you would see that they look like skeletons. . . .

MR. BERGER.   What reception did the strikers get from the mill owners?

MR. LIPSON. I told you before.

MR. BERGER.   I want to know whether you got any other answer. You said

Mr. Wood did not answer your letter, and that the foreman simply told the committee to go back to your machines.

MR. LIPSON.   Yes, sir. They said if we did not like it to get out.

MR. BERGER.   Well, you failed to tell us that before, and it is important.

MR. LIPSON.   We are so used to it that I did not mention it. To you these things are new, but to us it is an old story.

No man is born into the world whose work
Is not born with him; there is always work,
And tools to work withal, for those who will;
And blessèd are the horny hands of toil!
　　　　　　—James Russell Lowell, *A Glance Behind the Curtain,*

» Studs Terkel «

Steelworker: Mike Lefevre

» «

Terkel, media personality and author, took his tape recorder around the country and interviewed average Americans about what work means to them. Among them was a steelworker whom Terkel calls Mike Lefevre. Unlike Samuel Lipson, Lefevre is not concerned with survival. But Terkel's interview illustrates what many social observers had long suspected: Many of America's well-paid blue-collar workers are in a constant struggle to retain their dignity in boring, undemanding, and even demeaning jobs.

It is a two-flat dwelling, *somewhere in Cicero, on the outskirts of Chicago. He is thirty-seven. He works in a steel mill. On occasion, his wife Carol works as a waitress in a neighborhood restaurant; otherwise, she is at home, caring for their two small children, a girl and a boy.*

I'm a dying breed. A laborer. Strictly muscle work . . . pick it up, put it down, pick it up, put it down. We handle between forty and fifty thousand pounds of steel a day. (Laughs) I know this is hard to believe—from four hundred pounds to three- and four-pound pieces. It's dying.

You can't take pride any more. You remember when a guy could point to a house he built, how many logs he stacked. He built it and he was proud of it. . . .

It's hard to take pride in a bridge you're never gonna cross, in a door you're never gonna open. You're mass-producing things and you never see the end result of it. (Muses) I worked for a trucker one time. And I got this tiny satisfaction when I loaded a truck. At least I could see the truck depart loaded. In a steel mill, forget it. You don't see where nothing goes.

I got chewed out by my foreman once. He said, "Mike, you're a good worker but you have a bad attitude." My attitude is that I don't get excited about my job. I do my work but I don't say whoopee-doo. The day I get excited about my job is the day I go to a head shrinker. How are you gonna get excited about pullin' steel? How are you gonna get excited when you're tired and want to sit down?

It's not just the work. Somebody built the pyramids. Somebody's going to build something. Pyramids, Empire State Building—these things just don't happen. There's hard work behind it. I would like to see a building, say, the Empire State, I would like to see on one side of it a foot-wide strip from top to bottom with the name of every bricklayer, the name of every electrician, with all the names. So when a guy walked by, he could take his son and say, "See, that's me over there on the forty-fifth floor. I put the steel beam in." Picasso can point to a painting. What can I point to? A writer can point to a book. Everybody should have something to point to.

It's the not-recognition by other people. To say a woman is *just* a housewife is degrading, right? Okay. *Just* a housewife. It's also degrading to say *just* a laborer. The difference is that a man goes out and maybe gets smashed. . . .

If you can't improve yourself, you improve your posterity. Otherwise life isn't worth nothing. You might as well go back to the cave and stay there. . . .

You're doing this manual labor and you know that technology can do it. (Laughs.) Let's face it, a machine can do the work of a man; otherwise they wouldn't have space probes. Why can we send a rocket ship that's unmanned and yet send a man in a steel mill to do a mule's work?

Automation? Depends how it's applied. It frightens me if it puts me out on the street. It doesn't frighten me if it shortens my work week. You read that little thing: what are you going to do when this computer replaces you? Blow up computers. (Laughs.) Really. Blow up computers. I'll be goddamned if a computer is gonna eat before I do! I want milk for my kids and beer for me. Machines can either liberate man or enslave 'im, because they're pretty neutral. It's man who has the bias to put the thing one place or another.

If I had a twenty-hour workweek, I'd get to know my kids better, my wife better. Some kid invited me to go on a college campus. On a Saturday. It was summertime. Hell, if I have a choice of taking my wife and kids to a picnic or going to a college campus, it's gonna be the picnic. But if I worked a twenty-hour week, I could go do both. Don't you think with that extra twenty hours people could really expand? Who's to say? There are some people in factories just by force of circumstance. I'm just like the colored people. Potential Einsteins don't have to be white. They could be in cotton fields, they could be in factories.

The twenty-hour week is a possibility today. The intellectuals, they always say there are potential Lord Byrons, Walt Whitmans, Roosevelts, Picassos working in construction or steel mills or factories. But I don't think they believe it. . . .

It isn't that the average working guy is dumb. He's tired, that's all. I picked up a book on chess one time. That thing laid in the drawer for two or three weeks, you're too tired. During the weekends you want to take your kids out. You don't want to sit there and the kid comes up: "Daddy, can I go to the park?" You got your nose in a book? Forget it.

I know a guy fifty-seven years old. Know what he tells me? "Mike, I'm old and tired *all* the time." The first thing happens at work: when the arms start moving, the brain stops. I punch in about ten minutes to seven in the morning. I say hello to a couple of guys I like, I kid around with them. . . .

I put on my hard hat, change into my safety shoes, put on my safety glasses, go to the bonderizer. It's the thing I work on. They rake the metal, they wash it, they dip it in a paint solution, and we take it off. Put it on, take it off, put it on, take it off, put it on, take if off. . . .

I say hello to everybody but my boss. At seven it starts. My arms get tired about the first half-hour. After that, they don't get tired any more until maybe the last half-hour at the end of the day. I work from seven to three thirty. My arms are tired at seven thirty and they're tired at three o'clock. I hope to God I never get broke in, because I always want my arms to be tired at seven thirty and three o'clock. (Laughs.) 'Cause that's when I know that there's a beginning and there's an end. That I'm not brain-washed. In between, I don't even try to think. . . .

Somebody has to do this work. If my kid ever goes to college, I just want him to have a little respect, to realize that his dad is one of those some-bodies. . . .

I went out drinking with one guy, oh, a long time ago. A college boy. He was working where I work now. . . .

He saw a book in my back pocket one time and he was amazed. He . . . said, "You read?" I said, "What do you mean, I read?" He said, "All these dummies read the sports pages around here. What are you doing with a book?" I got pissed off at the kid right away. I said, "What do you mean, all these dummies? Don't knock a man who's paying somebody else's way through college." He was a nineteen-year-old effete snob.

Yet you want your kid to be an effete snob?
Yes. I want my kid to look at me and say, "Dad, you're a nice guy, but you're a fuckin' dummy." Hell yes, I want my kid to tell me that he's not gonna be like me . . .

If I were hiring people to work, I'd try naturally to pay them a decent wage. I'd try to find out their first names, their last names, keep the company as small as possible, so I could personalize the whole thing. All I would ask a man is a handshake, see you in the morning. No applications, nothing. I wouldn't be interested in the guy's past. Nobody ever checks the pedigree on a mule, do they? But they do on a man. Can you picture walking up to a mule and saying, "I'd like to know who his grand-daddy was?"

I'd like to run a combination bookstore and tavern. (Laughs.) I would like to have a place where college kids came and a steelworker could sit down and talk. Where a workingman could not be ashamed of Walt Whitman and where a college professor could not be ashamed that he painted his house over the weekend.

If a carpenter built a cabin for poets, I think the least the poets owe the carpenter is just three or four one-liners on the wall. A little plaque: Though we labor with our minds, this place we can relax in was built by someone who can work with his hands. And his work is as noble as ours. I think the poet owes something to the guy who builds the cabin for him.

I don't think of Monday. You know what I'm thinking about on Sunday night? Next Sunday. If you work real hard, you think of a perpetual vacation. Not perpetual sleep . . . What do I think of on a Sunday night? Lord, I wish . . . I could do something else for a living.

I don't know who the guy is who said there is nothing sweeter than an unfinished symphony. Like an unfinished painting and an unfinished poem. If he creates this thing one day—let's say, Michelangelo's Sistine Chapel. It took him a long time to do this, this beautiful work of art. But what if he had to create this Sistine Chapel a thousand times a year? Don't you think that would even dull Michelangelo's mind? Or if da Vinci had to draw his anatomical charts thirty, forty, fifty, sixty, eighty, ninety, a hundred times a day? Don't you think that would even bore da Vinci?

Way back, you spoke of the guys who built the pyramids, not the Pharaohs, the unknowns. You put yourself in their category?

Yes. I want my signature on 'em, too. Sometimes, out of pure meanness, when I make something, I put a little dent in it. I like to do something to make it really unique. Hit it with a hammer. . . . I'd like to make my imprint. My dodo bird. A mistake, *mine.* Let's say the whole building is nothing but red bricks. I'd like to have just the black one or the white one or the purple one. . . .

This is gonna sound square, but my kid is my imprint. He's my freedom. There's a line in one of Hemingway's books. I think it's from *For Whom the Bell Tolls.* They're behind the enemy lines, somewhere in Spain, and she's pregnant. She wants to stay with him. He tells her no. He says, "if you die, I die," knowing he's gonna die. But if you go, I go. Know what I mean? The mystics call it the brass bowl. Continuum. You know what I mean? This is why I work. Every time I see a young guy walk by with a shirt and tie and dressed up real sharp, I'm lookin' at my kid, you know? That's it.

Consider the history of labor in a country [U.S.A.] in which, spiritually speaking, there are no workers, only candidates for the hand of the boss's daughter.
—James Baldwin, *The Fire Next Time*

» *John R. Coleman* «

Blue-Collar Journal: A College President's Sabbatical

» «

In middle age, John R. Coleman, President of Haverford College, "dropped out."
He left his secure, antiseptic, upper-middle-class world to work as a laborer and
garbageman. An economist by training, Coleman is a humanist by instinct. The
work he did was hard and dirty, but in it he not only found what drives American
blue-collar workers to endure poorly esteemed and often dehumanizing work, he
also found a new source of dignity for himself.

Construction Worker

Saturday, February 17   In the work I do as college president, there are
only two tasks that require doing the same thing over and over again for
any sustained period of time. One is shaking hands at commencement and
parents' day (a happy task); the other is signing thank-you notes to alumni
contributors (a very happy task). But both the lines of people waiting to be
greeted and the pile of notes waiting to be signed have definite ending
points: I know when I'll be done with them. The ditch today didn't seem to
have an end. As fast as I cleaned up one foot of it, the backhoe made at
least one more foot of it ahead.

The soil was uniform in its reddish color, and each load looked almost
exactly like the one before. Now and then there was a rock in it, which
made for a bit of variety, particularly in the effort it took to get the load
shoulder high. For the rest, there was almost no break in the morning's
routine. . . .

Eventually I was ordered to shovel asphalt and clay with two men from
the group of eight laborers hired from the contract agency in Atlanta. These
men are the equivalent in manual occupations of the Kelly Girls in office
work. I asked one of them how these agencies work.

"Simple. It's about the same way they buy and sell cows. You get there about five-thirty or six in the morning and sit on one of their bare benches until a call comes. The guy who runs it says, 'O.K., you — and you — and you.' He crowds the gangs for two or three jobs into the back of an old panel truck — no windows, no heat. Then some young punk drives us out to the jobs, drops us off, gets a receipt for us, and disappears. If he's any good, he finds out when to pick us up again. If he isn't, we just wait. We do what we're told for the day. Then it's back into the truck, except it smells more by then, and back to the hiring hall. We get paid each night — and if we're smart we get drunk right after. Same thing the next day. You never know what you'll be doing. And nobody gives a shit anyway."

He thought they were getting $1.50 an hour, but he wasn't sure. He had no idea what the agency got. Their shoveling showed the low pay, low esteem, and low morale in their work. With a new boss every day of their lives, they saw no gain in impressing any one of them with a burst of energy. Now that I was working beside two of them, I couldn't decide whether to slow down to their pace as a way of getting along with them or to keep up the morning's pace as a way of getting along with Gus [the construction crew boss]. As a result, I think I went back and forth from slow to fast and puzzled everyone in turn.

No one had mentioned anything about quitting time. I assumed now that it would be 4:00, making this an eight-hour day. But that hour came and went without any signal from Gus. So did 5:00. My shovel was fully a part of me now, just like my legs and arms. Most of what we had to show for the day was already buried beneath the ground. The trench was gone and so was the pipe. Only the newly raked ground would tell a passerby that we had done a job there.

It was 6:00 when Gus called it a day. . . .

Wednesday, February 21   I was happy driving to work this morning. The muscles were no longer as sore as before, I knew some of the men I'd be working with for the day, and I felt that I was beginning to fit in with the crew. At the diner where I had breakfast once again, I felt that I was fully a part of the blue-collar world. Two gas station attendants, a schoolbus driver, and the short-order cook knew mine was a familiar face and said hello. I was proud of the fact that I would probably work more hours and use up more physical energy that day than most of the others with whom I ate eggs and toast.

Whatever pride I felt lasted through the morning, even though there was not much work to do. This particular project is almost complete. We will soon move to a site somewhere southwest of the city. What remains to be done here is mainly cleaning up. I spent the morning, therefore, raking the dirt on a slope beneath which our sewer lay. It is part of Gus's contract that the land is left clean and level after the pipes are laid. The sun was warm on the slope. I made more of the raking than was necessary, perhaps, but it did fill the time while Gus was away. I was content. . . .

My job didn't have much status or pay, but it had a sense of immediate utility and also of peace.

That afternoon killed that feeling completely. We did nothing. Almost six hours of nothing. That turned out to be harder than anything I had yet done, even though we were being paid. . . .

The boredom of the day got to all of us. I had heard each of [the] men complain about the heavy work we had done earlier this week. I saw now that that was a different kind of complaint. What I had heard before was as much a boast as a gripe; it was a reminder to ourselves of how much we could do when pushed. Today's moaning was the real thing, a call to be spared from doing nothing. Perhaps it is true, as some writers have said, that the work ethic in America is on the decline. Yet, on the basis of what I have seen on this one job, I cannot agree. These men go on acting as if they want to work when they are at work and to play when they are at play. Just don't mix up the parts of our lives, they ask.

Monday, February 26   It doesn't take long to get used to the shifts into this new world. I scarcely give a thought now to the fact that I have no idea what I am going to be asked to do on any day, that I never hear why we are doing what we are doing, and that my opinion is certainly never sought on any matter concerning the job. I come here when I'm told, do what I'm told, eat when I'm told, and go home when I'm told. For the moment, that feels just fine. . . .

Sandwich and Salad Man

Tuesday, March 27   One of the waitresses I find hard to take asked me at one point today, "Are you the boy who cuts the lemons?"

"I'm the man who does," I replied.

"Well, there are none cut." There wasn't a hint that she heard my point.

Dana, who has cooked here for twelve years or so, heard that exchange.

"It's no use, Jack," he said when she was gone. "If she doesn't know now, she never will." There was a trace of a smile on his face, but it was a sad look all the same.

In that moment, I learned the full thrust of those billboard ads of a few years ago that said, "BOY. Drop out of school and that's what they'll call you the rest of your life." I had read those ads before with a certain feeling of pride; education matters, they said, and that gave a lift to my field. Today I saw them saying something else. They were untrue in part; it turns out that you'll get called "boy" if you do work that others don't respect even if you have a Ph.D. It isn't education that counts, but the job in which you land. And the ads spoke too of a sad resignation about the world. They assumed that some people just won't learn respect for others, so you should adapt yourself to them. Don't try to change them. Get the right job and they won't call *you* boy any more. They'll save it for the next man. . . .

Trash Collector

Saturday, April 7 We hauled trash for a solid four hours without a break of any sort except for about five minutes when we stopped at one street's end to talk. I suppose I may have walked further than this before, perhaps in climbs on Mount Katahdin in Maine and Mount Assiniboine in Canada, or perhaps on route marches in the wartime officers' training corps at the University of Toronto. I have carried as heavy loads as these for short times and briefly carried heavier ones in Atlanta five weeks ago. But the combination of distance and weight today was a record for me.

There was every incentive to work fast. The time was ours. If we moved slowly, we hurt only ourselves. If we moved quickly, we cut our day and still got our pay. The swiftness with which Steve [my partner] moved was contagious too. I caught glimpses of him moving from yard to yard across the street, and I wanted to keep up with him. I succeeded only because he moved the truck in addition to cleaning his side of the street. I still felt that I was moving fast for me.

My shoulder called out for mercy each time I put another full barrel on it, and my legs occasionally shook as I started out to the street. But all the rest of me said, "Go, trashman, go."

I could not have guessed in advance that there would be exhilaration in this. . . . It will be hard to explain that I finally learned the joy of competitive sports on a garbage run in Maryland.

Dump. Lift. Walk. Dump. Lift. Walk. The hours went by with speed.

Saturday meant that most adults were at home on the route. So were school-age children. I thought this might mean more talk back and forth as I made the rounds today. There were many people outdoors, tending to their spring yard chores. Most of them looked friendly enough. While I wouldn't have time to talk at length, there was time to exchange the greetings that go with civilized ways.

That is where I got my shock.

I said hello in quite a few yards before the message sank in that this wasn't the thing to do. Occasionally, I got a straight man-to-man or woman-to-man reply from someone who looked me in the eye, smiled, and asked either "How are you?" or "Isn't this a nice day?" I felt human then. But most often the response was either nothing at all, a look of surprise that I had spoken and used a familiar tongue, or an overly sweet hello.

Both men and women gave me the silent or staring treatment. A woman in housecoat and curlers putting her last tidbit of slops into the pail was startled as I came around the corner of her house. At the sound of my greeting, she gathered her housecoat tightly about her and moved quickly indoors. I heard the lock click. In a way I was flattered by that, even though I had nothing more than picking up her trash on my mind. . . . A man playing ball with his two young sons looked over in response to my voice,

stared without a change of face, and then calmly threw the next ball to one of the boys. And so it went in almost every yard. . . .

The sweet treatment came from women alone. From the way they replied and asked after my health, I knew that at the day's end when they listed the nice things they had done, there would be a place on the list for "I spoke to the trashman today."

I shouldn't have been so caught by surprise. I had read Robert Coles's *The South Goes North* and had been moved by his interview with the Boston garbage collector who said: "I could see the ten- or twelve-year-old kids do one of three things: they'd snicker, or they'd look at you as though you're a freak or something, or they'd feel sorry for you — on their faces it was written the pity they'd have. Well, I didn't want their pity, and I still don't." But reading those things was different from having them happen to me.

Steve spoke spontaneously about these things on the long ride to the dump.

"The way most people look at you you'd think a trashman was a goddamn monster. Say hello and they stare at you in surprise. They don't know we're human. They think that we can carry any load at all, and that we should carry whatever they put out. . . .

"Most of them don't think of you as a person. I want to tell them, 'Look, I come as clean as you do,' but it wouldn't help. I don't tell anyone I'm a trashman. I say I'm a truck driver. My family knows, but my in-laws don't. If someone comes right out and asks, 'Do you drive for a trash company?' I say yes. I figure we're doing a service that people need, like a policeman or a fireman. I'm not ashamed of it, but I don't go around boasting about it either. . . ."

I thought on Thursday night that I might stick at this job for only two days. I was planning to look for something else in tomorrow's want ads, perhaps one of those landscaping jobs. Tonight I feel different.

In these weeks away, I have worked at two jobs which I liked and from which I learned, in Atlanta and Boston. Now I was on one that a man could scarcely say he liked or learned much from except about people and himself. One trek back to the truck with the trash is about like the next one. But I'm going to stay. The exercise is great. The lifting gets easier with every load, even if the left shoulder stays sore. I become faster and neater as time goes by. I'm outdoors in clean air. And, contrary to what people think, I don't get dirty on the job. (I was far dirtier in Atlanta.)

I'm resolved too to go on saying hello in backyards. It can't hurt, and it still feels right. Frankly, I'm proud. I'm doing an essential task, "like a policeman or a fireman." I left this country a little cleaner than I found it this morning. Not many people can say that tonight. . . .

Sunday, April 8 I've been interested in watching for the defenses which trashmen build against those who look down on them. I have met men this week who simply close up into themselves once they are on the route, get the job done, and get out of those neighborhoods as fast as they can. I doubt that they even return a greeting in the few cases where the householder extends that courtesy first.

I have heard men in the garage talk among themselves about what's wrong with people who need someone else to kick around. A black man put it best: "Those motherfuckers think I'm coming after their jobs and that I'm going to make them take mine. They're sick." So it is that the scorn gets turned around.

I have listened too to those among us who go that extra mile in asserting pride in themselves. One man spoke of how insulted he was by the woman who said, perhaps with only kindly intent, "Those dresses in the can aren't really very old. Wouldn't you like to take them to your wife?" "Hell," he told us, "my wife won't touch even a new dress unless it costs at least fifteen bucks."

I saw pride asserted in a different way today. Steve had never spoken to me explicitly about how I was to leave the area around the cans where I dumped. But he made his point more effectively than any lecture could do. He showed me a photo that a housewife had given him of the mess left by one of his helpers earlier last week; his anger that one of his men would do the job that badly was plain to see. He has been on this route eighteen months, and, whatever those on the route think of him, he knows how the job should be done. I know that I took extra pains after seeing that picture. I didn't pick up what the family had strewn about before I came; I don't think Steve did either. But I chased most of what the wind blew away from me as I worked.

I have no idea how many Steves there are on garbage routes today. The one I know may not stay there much longer. He talks either of studying accounting some day or of driving an over-the-road trailer truck. "I know a guy with a really good deal. He makes two overnight runs to South Carolina and makes a pile doing that. And he's home every night of the week but two." Maybe neither of those dreams will come true. But he is likely to do something where he gets as much credit as he gives.

John Gardner has said that a society which lauds its philosophers, whether good or bad, and scorns its plumbers is in for trouble. "Neither its pipes nor its theories will hold water," he warns. He might have gone a step further and called for respect for both our economists and our refuse men; otherwise they'll both leave trash behind.

I am the people—the mob—the crowd—the mass.
Do you know that all the great work of the world is done
through me?

> —Carl Sandburg, *I Am the People, the Mob*

» Göran Palm «

The Flight from Work

» «

"Thank God, it's Friday," the famous last words of the workweek, are more than a joke to most blue- and white-collar employees in routine jobs, says Swedish author and poet Göran Palm. He believes that most workers, if given the choice, wouldn't work at all. Unlike professional, managerial, and technical workers, the majority of people don't have exciting careers; rather they have unchanging, routine drudgery. Like John Coleman, Palm gained this understanding of the workers' situation by leaving his intellectual world to become one of them—in this case in one of Sweden's largest firms, the LM Ericsson telephone company. What is fascinating about Palm's thesis is that the world he is describing is the Swedish welfare state where workers are among the world's best paid. These people work only for the money that allows them to enjoy life off the job.

Working hours—if we take those as the first example—are not the same for everyone at LM Ericsson. The managers have flexible working hours. The ordinary office employees have fixed working hours. The workers in the Low Block punch their cards 12 minutes before the workers in the High Block, who in turn punch their cards earlier than anyone in the office sector. The shift workers clock in earliest and latest of all, depending on whether they have the morning or the afternoon shift.

But what is most important of all is that the working hours are *experienced* in very different ways on the various levels into which the company is divided.

When I sit at home writing I usually think that time passes too quickly. I seldom look at my watch because my work absorbs me. But if I do look at the time, I hope that it is earlier than it really is. Almost always! If it is later, I become nervous. If it is earlier, I grow hopeful. As a rule, it is later. Stretching out the time to cover what has to be done is a constant problem.

I should imagine that most of the managers at LM experience working hours in much the same way. As do many salaried employees caught up in their careers, administrators who love administering, engineers who must soon complete a major project, dutiful supervisors, hurried cashiers, skilled workers who are in demand, as well as all employees at all levels who enjoy doing the work they do—and such people can be found in the most surprising places. Even amongst semi-skilled workers.

Whether it be due to stress or to joy, they all find that time goes too quickly at work.

But for the vast majority of workshop and office workers, the situation is quite different. Their problem seems to be to get their working hours over as quickly as possible. It sometimes happened that I myself forgot the time at LM. . . . But, for the most part, I often looked at my watch. And when I looked at my watch I hoped it would be later than it was. Almost always! As a rule, it was earlier. Sometimes the hands crept around. Some days they seemed almost to stand still.

And this was by no means peculiar to my watch. Those who sat so that they had a wall clock in view claimed that it was like being subjected to a mild form of torture. Even the second hand terrorized them. During the final minutes before each break the hands moved in slow motion. But as soon as the bell rang, they rushed round like mad. . . .

Most of those who worked near me seemed to agree that the best working days were those when time passed quickly and that time passed particularly quickly when there was a lot to do. Not *too much* to do, which frequently happens in piece-rate work. "You get out of step both with time and with yourself then," Otto [my coworker] said. "Moderation is best.". . .

Nevertheless, I wonder if Otto and all those who agree with him realize what they are saying. They are saying that the most important thing in work is that the working day should end as quickly as possible. They are saying that the occupation which they have at hand, the work which they have here and now, is seldom good enough and must be put to flight in one way or another. They are saying that time, the time they spend at work, is there to be whiled away.

Minute by minute, day by day, year by year.

The Sacred Future

When the present is not good enough, one puts one's trust in the future. In doing this, one must find as much as possible to look forward to and to long for so that the present does not overwhelm one. At eight o'clock in the morning, for example, one begins to look forward to the nine o'clock break. At ten o'clock one begins to look forward to the lunch break. At two o'clock one begins to look forward to the afternoon coffee break. After coffee, one begins to look forward to the bell which rings to mark the end of the working day.

Soon, looking forward to small things like these becomes a habit. . . .

Since this habit of looking to the future is such a sensitive matter for a great number of people, it is dealt with in innumerable brutal jokes on the shop floor and, in all likelihood, in many of the office corridors too. . . .

"Holiday? You mean those rainy weeks in July when you get eaten alive by mosquitoes?"

"Thank God that bloody camping is over for this year.". . .

These jokes sometimes come from the privileged minority of workers who do not need to take out insurance on the future—and that is why they are brutal. After various transfers or training courses, they may have found something which most people can only dream about, a job which they find so stimulating that time passes by itself. Or else they belong to that rare breed who simply enjoy work, no matter what it is or how much one is paid for it. . . .

But most of those who joke about the sacred future belong to the group which counts the minutes most eagerly until the breaks, the days until the weekends, the months until the summer holidays, and the years until new jobs. That is, so to speak, why they joke. . . .

But there are also those who adopt a more methodical approach when they stake out the sacred future.

One of my workmates did not permit himself to go and make a telephone call home until he had punched out his job card. Another did not permit himself to buy a mug of chocolate at the dispenser until he had soldered a unit. A third did not permit himself to sit down and rest until he had screwed all of the guide plates into position on his rack. For my own part, I decided at an early stage that I would not smoke more than once an hour, starting at seven o'clock. In this way, I set up nine foolproof future beacons, evenly distributed over the entire working day, bright enough to begin to twinkle strongly by twenty to the hour. And this happened nine times each working day.

They talk of the dignity of work. Bosh. The dignity is in leisure.

—Herman Melville

Even trivial events can be provided with an enticing shimmer in this way—something which is not without importance when one is completely or partly paid by the hour and has few other fixed points to break up the monotony of the work itself.

Things are different for the large majority of workers, who are employed on a piece-work basis only. For them, this hysterical dreaming of the future is, so to speak, built into the system itself. The carrot with its promises of constantly increasing earnings hangs in front of them as a never-ending reminder of the brightness of the future and the inadequacy of the present. . . .

The atmosphere of pursuit and competition which surrounds all piece-work seems to invite semi-masochistic devices of the most neurotic type. Many workers who are tormented by the payment-by-results system are also afraid that time would pass much more slowly if they were on a monthly salary.

How innocent a part do all these conjurations play in excluding the present from life and putting work to flight? How innocent, how indispensable, how destructive are they? The answer to this seems to depend on what is at stake.

When temporary workers like myself glance at our watches and count the days, we are doing nothing more serious than what National Servicemen do when they mark off the time left to demob. We have something else ahead of us all the time. Another job, another life, *and we know that both of them are within our reach*. We toss one or two years of our lives into the kitty at LM and then withdraw. But many of the others will almost certainly spend all of their working lives at Midsommarkransen. Or at some other of the Group's factories in Sweden if the work at Midsommarkransen is transferred elsewhere. If they have been working for LM for ten years or more they seldom make any changes. What do they have to look forward to apart from the fact that it will soon be Friday again for the thousandth time?

A better job? Their prospects are reduced for each year they remain where they are.

A win on the football pool? Their prospects are even smaller there.

Wage increase? If they are over 45 they are more likely to get a wage reduction.

Further education? They should have thought of that earlier.

Reschooling? This future prospect seldom holds any enticing shimmer.

Retirement? Yes, many look forward to their retirement. Once they have celebrated their 50th birthday, retirement day is all that remains. And yet there are quite a few who fear that retirement will be the threshold to an empty room, a room where "that bloody job" will be replaced by something even worse—idle loneliness. When *these* faithful toilers in the vineyard wish that the working day would come to an end as quickly as possible, there is nothing innocent in their wish. They have far too much at stake for that. Their entire working lives usually lie in the kitty. And when retirement approaches, it turns out that many of them want to stay on as long as they can, despite all—despite all!

As a rule, those who are younger satisfy themselves with shorter future perspectives and more modest stakes. But those who are younger are often cheated of their rewards when the longed-for future changes into the present. . . .

Hour after hour, [they] look forward to the moment when the bell will ring so that they can finally do whatever they want to do, and year after year the older hourly-wage earners look forward to the approach of their 65th birthday so that they, too, can do whatever they want to do—and the thought of everything they can do then helps both the younger and the older workers to keep their spirits up during the course of their work. But

63

in order to be able to afford to do whatever they want to do and, at the same time, in order to pass the period of waiting, they are often forced to work so hard that when the gates are finally opened they are seldom capable of doing as they wish any longer.

When they finally have both time and money, they no longer have the energy required. They go home and fall asleep in front of the television set instead. . . .

And yet, when the present in the form of the working day and the working week remains a darkness which must be banished, the hopes which are linked to the weekend and the holidays are often so escalated that reality seldom lives up to them. The closer the free time comes, the more these expectations are mingled with anxiety. . . .

If one takes a closer look at the sacred future, it shrinks and disappoints many of its worshippers. When the future becomes the present, it frequently turns out to be as grey as an ordinary working day.

And yet it never loses its sacredness. . . .

Work was like cats were supposed to be: if you disliked and feared it and tried to keep out of its way, it knew at once and sought you out and jumped on your lap and climbed all over you to show how much it loved you. Please God, he thought, don't let me die in harness.

—Kingsley Amis, *Take a Girl Like You*

There is, of course, a limit to the number of disappointments a wage-earner's dreams of the future can stand. And there is a certain turnover on the stock exchange of the future at LM. Those who have staked considerable amounts on discotheques, football pools, Saturday drinking bouts, or holiday trips for a number of years gradually begin to invest in more gilt-edged future securities instead. When they set their sights on building a house or a boat, when they study for upper-secondary school qualifications, when they devote themselves to associations, or save money for a longer leave of absence, they frequently count on passing their leisure time in a more meaningful manner for several years. Or, at least, their disappointments will be more widely spaced out.

What seldom happens, on the other hand, is that disappointed future-dreamers address themselves to the present on the shop floor so as to try to extract some of the meaning and joy, which their free time so often cheats them of, from the reality around them. It is, after all, there, at work, that they spend by far the greater part of their waking lives. It is, after all, there, at work, that they are forced to expend most of their energy.

They never arrive at their leisure time thoroughly rested in the way they arrive at work.

But the working day and the working week seem to have been rejected from the beginning as quite impossible investment objects from the point of view of joy and meaning. Instead, the working day and the working week emerge as a sort of enormous, unchangeably gloomy burden of enforced dead time which one should push ahead of one and get rid of as soon as the "bell of freedom" rings. Work does not seem to contain any enticing future.

Down on the lowest reaches of [the] shop floor, this manner of experiencing time seems to be so generally accepted that few regard it as destructive. "The best working days" are those which come to an end in the quickest, easiest way. . . .

"Work is something which just has to be done."

"That's the way it is."

Most of those who do semi-skilled work, machine supervision, transport work, or store work—and this comprises by far the greatest majority of shop workers in the LM Group, particularly in the rural factories—seem to be relegated to such a low level of demand that they expect nothing more of the work they do here and now than that it finance their leisure time in the most painless way possible. As long as the sun drags itself across the sky at a reasonably acceptable pace, as long as the taximeter ticks, they are more or less satisfied. Perhaps they pin a few expectations on some of their needs, perhaps they pin a few expectations on the breaks.

But they seem to pin no expectations whatesoever on the actual work. . . .

It seems so self-evident to most of these employees that the working day is there to be passed as quickly as possible that they seldom even think of the fact that *it could be* different. . . .

But the very fact that this way of experiencing working hours is common entails a pretty crushing judgment on those who have organized and distributed the jobs at LM. And not only at LM. They have organized these tasks in such a way that those who have to carry them out do not feel satisfied until the tasks have come to an end, i.e., when the bell rings. They have organized these tasks in such a way that those who have to carry them out concentrate on getting through them as quickly as possible so that they can go home.

Every day at 6 minutes past four the Low Block employees rush as one man to clock out. Every day at 18 minutes past four, the High Block employees rush as one man to clock out. Everyone seems to want to shake the dust of LM from their feet as fast as possible, and no one ever tries to halt the flow by calling: We have only one life! What sort of madness is it to kill time instead of filling it with meaning? Not a single day can ever be relived!

Instead, each one of them searches silently and feverishly after his or her clock card.

When I say each individual, I am not forgetting that the workshop sector also contains those who devote themselves to their work and sometimes enjoy their work so much that the clock almost seems to race ahead. I have already mentioned the skilled workers, but numerous exceptions can also be found among the rank and file. . . .

[But the] high rate of absence and rapid employee turnover do not exactly indicate that most workers are satisfied with the working conditions which are offered to them. An increased aversion to over-time, an increased tendency to apply for early retirement pension, and sudden, long sick leaves due to "nerve trouble" do not indicate this either. Silent and expensive protest actions of this type do not even indicate that most employees are mainly interested in money. After all, most of them earn less when they are ill, when they permit themselves to be retired early, when they refuse over-time, or when they frequently change jobs.

Nevertheless, most seem to find it so important to flee from work that they are even willing to sacrifice earnings in order to do so at regular intervals.

3

»«

BLUE-COLLAR WOMEN

»«

From the film, *The Life and Times of Rosie the Riveter*, © 1980, Clarity Productions

» Thomas Dublin «

Women, Work, and Protest: The Early Lowell Mills

» «

Thomas Dublin, a history professor at the University of California, San Diego, describes the working lives of women who labored an average of seventy-three hours a week in the textile mills of Lowell, Massachusetts, from 1823 to 1850. Most of these women were native-born Americans between the ages of fifteen and thirty; they were the first generation to leave farms for jobs in industry. Dublin describes the transformation of these independent daughters of freemen into an organized industrial community struggling for fair wages and a 10-hour workday. This selection documents how the industrial revolution created a working class among American women.

In the years before 1850 the textile mills of Lowell, Massachusetts, were a celebrated economic and cultural attraction. Foreign visitors invariably included them on their American tours. Interest was prompted by the massive scale of these mills, the astonishing productivity of the power-driven machinery, and the fact that women comprised most of the work force. Visitors were struck by the newness of both mills and city, as well as by the culture of the female operatives. The scene stood in sharp contrast to the gloomy mill towns of the English industrial revolution.

Lowell, was, in fact, an impressive accomplishment. In 1820, there had been no city at all — only a dozen family farms along the Merrimack River in East Chelmsford. In 1821, however, a group of Boston capitalists purchased land and water rights along the river and a nearby canal, and began to build a major textile manufacturing center. Opening two years later, the first factory employed Yankee women recruited from the nearby countryside. Additional mills were constructed until, by 1840, ten textile corporations with thirty-two mills valued at more than ten million dollars lined the banks of the river and nearby canals. Adjacent to the mills were rows of company boardinghouses and tenements which accommodated most of the eight thousand factory operatives.

As Lowell expanded and became the nation's largest textile manufacturing center, the experiences of women operatives changed as well. The increasing number of firms in Lowell and in the other mill towns brought the pressure of competition. Overproduction became a problem and the prices of finished cloth decreased. The high profits of the early years declined and so, too, did conditions for the mill operatives. Wages were reduced and the pace of work within the mills was stepped up. Women operatives did not accept these changes without protest. In 1834 and 1836 they went on strike to protest wage cuts, and between 1843 and 1848 they mounted petition campaigns aimed at reducing the hours of labor in the mills.

These labor protests in early Lowell contribute to our understanding of the response of workers to the growth of industrial capitalism in the first half of the nineteenth century. They indicate the importance of values and attitudes dating back to an earlier period and also the transformation of these values in a new setting.

The major factor in the rise of a new consciousness among operatives in Lowell was the development of a close-knit community among women working in the mills. The structure of work and the nature of housing contributed to the growth of this community. The existence of community among women, in turn, was an important element in the repeated labor protests of the period. . . .

The mutual dependence among women in early Lowell was rooted in the structure of mill work itself. Newcomers to the mills were particularly dependent on their fellow operatives, but even experienced hands relied on one another for considerable support.

New operatives generally found their first experiences difficult, even harrowing, though they may have already done much hand-spinning and weaving in their own homes. . . .

The textile corporations made provisions to ease the adjustment of new operatives. Newcomers were not immediately expected to fit into the mill's regular work routine. They were at first assigned work as sparehands and were paid a daily wage independent of the quantity of work they turned out. As a sparehand, the newcomer worked with an experienced hand who instructed her in the intricacies of the job. . . .After the passage of some weeks or months, when she could handle the normal complement of machinery—two looms for weavers during the 1830s—and when a regular operative departed, leaving an opening, the sparehand moved into a regular job. . . .

In addition to the integration of sparehands, informal sharing of work often went on among regular operatives. A woman would occasionally take off a half or full day from work either to enjoy a brief vacation or to recover from illness, and fellow operatives would each take an extra loom or side of spindles so that she might continue to earn wages during her absence. Women were generally paid on a piece rate basis, their wages being determined by the total output of the machinery they tended during the payroll period. With friends helping out during her absence, making sure that her looms kept running, an operative could earn almost a full wage even though she was not physically present. Such informal work-sharing was another way in which mutual dependence developed among women operatives during their working hours.

Living conditions also contributed to the development of community among female operatives. Most women working in the Lowell mills of these years were housed in company boarding houses. In July 1836, for example, more than 73 percent of females employed by the Hamilton Company resided in company housing adjacent to the mills. Almost three-fourths of them, therefore, lived and worked with each other. Furthermore, the work schedule was such that women had little opportunity to interact with those not living in company dwellings. They worked, in these years, an average of 73 hours a week. Their work day ended at 7:00 or 7:30 P.M., and in the hours between supper and the 10:00 curfew imposed by management on residents of company boarding houses, there was little time to spend with friends living "off the corporation."

Women in the boarding houses lived in close quarters, a factor that also played a role in the growth of community. A typical boarding house accommodated twenty-five young women, generally crowded four to eight in a bedroom. There was little possibility of privacy within the dwelling, and pressure to conform to group standards was very strong . . . . The community of operatives which developed in the mills . . . carried over into life at home as well. . . .

Upon entering the boarding house, the newcomer came under pressure to conform with the standards of the community of operatives. . . . Over time they dropped the peculiar "twang" in their speech which so amused experienced hands. Similarly, they purchased clothing more in keeping with urban than rural styles. It was an unusual and strong-willed individual who could work and live among her fellow operatives and not conform, at least outwardly, to the customs and values of this larger community.

The boarding houses were the centers of social life for women operatives after their long days in the mills. There they ate their meals, rested, talked, sewed, wrote letters, read books and magazines. From among fellow workers and boarders they found friends who accompanied them to shops, to Lyceum lectures, to church and church-sponsored events. On Sundays or holidays, they often took walks along the canals or out into the nearby countryside. The community of women operatives, in sum, developed in a setting where women worked and lived together, twenty-four hours a day. . . .

Group pressure to conform, so important to the community of women in early Lowell, played a significant role in the collective response of women to changing conditions in the mills.

70

In addition to the structure of work and housing in Lowell, a third factor, the homogeneity of the mill workforce, contributed to the development of community among female operatives. In this period, the mill workforce was homogeneous in terms of sex, nativity, and age. Payroll and other records of the Hamilton Company reveal that more than 85 percent of those employed in July, 1836, were women and that over 96 percent were native-born. Furthermore, over 80 percent of the female workforce were between the ages of 15 and 30; and only 10 percent were under 14 or over 40.

Workforce homogeneity takes on particular significance in the context of work structure and the nature of worker housing. These three factors combined meant that women operatives had little interaction with men during their daily lives. Men and women did not perform the same work in the mills, and generally did not even labor in the same rooms. Men worked in the initial picking and carding processes, in the repair shop, and on the watchforce, and filled all supervisory positions in the mills. Women held all sparehand and regular operative jobs in drawing, speeding, spinning, weaving, and dressing. A typical room in the mill employed eighty women tending machinery, with two men overseeing the work and two boys assisting them. Women had little contact with men other than their supervisors in the course of the working day. After work, women returned to their boarding houses, where once again there were few men. Women, then, worked and lived in a predominantly female setting.

The labor of women in the house, certainly, enables men to produce more wealth than they otherwise could; and in this way, women are economic factors in society. But so are horses.
—Charlotte Perkins Gilman, *Women and Economics*

Ethnically the workforce was also homogeneous. Immigrants formed only 3.4 percent of those employed at Hamilton in July, 1836. In addition, they comprised only 3 percent of residents in Hamilton Company housing. The community of women operatives was composed of women of New England stock drawn from the hill-country farms surrounding Lowell. Consequently, when experienced hands made fun of the speech and dress of newcomers, it was understood that they, too, had been "rusty" or "rustic" upon first coming to Lowell. This common background was another element shared by women workers in early Lowell.

The work structure, the workers' housing, and workforce homogeneity were the major elements which contributed to the growth of community among Lowell's women operatives. To best understand the larger implications of community, it is necessary to examine the labor protests of this period. For in these struggles, the new values and attitudes which developed in the community of women operatives are most visible.

In February, 1834, 800 of Lowell's women operatives "turned-out"—

went on strike—to protest a proposed reduction in their wages. They marched to numerous mills in an effort to induce others to join them, and, at an outdoor rally, they petitioned others to "discontinue their labors until terms of reconciliation are made." Their petition concluded:

> Resolved, That we will not go back into the mills to work unless our wages are continued . . . as they have been.

> Resolved, That none of us will go back, unless they receive us all as one.

> Resolved, That if any have not money enough to carry them home, they shall be supplied.

The strike proved to be brief and failed to reverse the proposed wage reductions. Turning-out on a Friday, the striking women were paid their back wages on Saturday, and by the middle of the next week had returned to work or left town. Within a week of the turn-out, the mills were running near capacity.

This first strike in Lowell is important not because it failed or succeeded, but simply because it took place. In an era in which women had to overcome opposition simply to work in the mills, it is remarkable that they would further overstep the accepted middle-class bounds of female propriety by participating in a public protest. The agents of the textile mills certainly considered the turn-out unfeminine. . . .

Mill agents assumed an attitude of benevolent paternalism toward their female operatives, and found it particularly disturbing that the women paid such little heed to their advice. The strikers were not merely unfeminine, they were ungrateful as well.

Such attitudes notwithstanding, women chose to turn-out. They did so for two principal reasons. First, the wage cuts undermined the sense of dignity and social equality, which was an important element in their Yankee heritage. Second, these wage cuts were seen as an attack on their economic independence. . . .

Connecting their turn-out with the efforts of their "Patriotic Ancestors" to secure independence from England, they interpreted the wage cuts as an effort to "enslave" them—to deprive them of their independent status as "daughters of freemen."

Though very general and rhetorical, the statement of these women does suggest their sense of self, of their own worth and dignity. Elsewhere, they expressed the conviction that they were the social equals of the overseers, indeed of the mill owners themselves. The wage cuts, however, struck at this assertion of social equality. These reductions made it clear that the operatives were subordinate to their employers, rather than equal partners in a contract binding on both parties. By turning-out, the women emphatically denied that they were subordinates; but by returning to work the next

72

week, they demonstrated that in economic terms they were no match for their corporate superiors. . . .

While the women's traditional conception of themselves as independent daughters of freemen played a major role in the turn-out, this factor acting alone would not necessarily have triggered the 1834 strike. It would have led women as individuals to quit work and return to their rural homes. But the turn-out was a collective protest. When it was announced that wage reductions were being considered, women began to hold meetings in the mills during meal breaks in order to assess tactical possibilities. Their turn-out began at one mill when the agent discharged a woman who had presided at such a meeting. Their procession through the streets passed by other mills, expressing a conscious effort to enlist as much support as possible for their cause. At a mass meeting, the women drew up a resolution which insisted that none be discharged for their participation in the turn-out. This strike, then, was a collective response to the proposed wage cuts—made possible because women had come to form a "community" of operatives in the mill, rather than simply a group of individual workers. The existence of such a tightknit community turned individual opposition to the wage cuts into a collective protest.

In October, 1836, women again went on strike. This second turn-out was similar to the first in several respects. Its immediate cause was also a wage reduction; marches and a large outdoor rally were organized; again, like the earlier protest, the basic goal was not achieved: the corporations refused to restore wages and operatives either left Lowell or returned to work at the new rates.

Despite these surface similarities between the turn-outs, there were some real differences. One involved scale: over 1500 operatives turned out in 1836, compared to only 800 earlier. Moreover, the second strike lasted much longer than the first. In 1834 operatives stayed out for only a few days; in 1836, the mills ran far below capacity for several months. . . .

Differences between the two turn-outs were not limited to the increased scale and duration of the later one. Women displayed a much higher degree of organization in 1836 than earlier. To coordinate strike activities, they formed a Factory Girls' Association. According to one historian, membership in the short-lived association reached 2500 at its height. . . .

In their organization of a Factory Girls' Association and in their efforts to shut down the mills, the female operatives revealed that they had been changed by their industrial experience. Increasingly, they acted not simply as "daughters of freemen" offended by the impositions of the textile corporations, but also as industrial workers intent on improving their position within the mills. . . .

In contrast to the protests of the previous decade, the [later] struggles now were primarily political. Women did not turn-out in the 1840s; rather, they mounted annual petition campaigns calling on the State legislature to limit the hours of labor within the mills. These campaigns reached their

73

height in 1845 and 1846, when 2,000 and 5,000 operatives, respectively, signed petitions. Unable to curb the wage cuts or the speed-up and stretch-out imposed by mill owners, operatives sought to mitigate the consequences of these changes by reducing the length of the working day. Having been defeated earlier in economic struggles, they now sought to achieve their new goal through political action. The Ten Hour Movement, seen in these terms, was a logical outgrowth of the unsuccessful turn-outs of the previous decade. Like the earlier struggles, the Ten Hour Movement was an assertion of the dignity of operatives and an attempt to maintain that dignity under the changing conditions of industrial capitalism.

The growth of relatively permanent labor organizations and institutions among women was a distinguishing feature of the Ten Hour Movement of the 1840s. The Lowell Female Labor Reform Association was organized in 1845 by women operatives. It became Lowell's leading labor organization over the next three years, organizing the city's female operatives and helping to set up branches in other mill towns. The Association was affiliated with the New England Workingmen's Association and sent delegates to its meetings. It acted in concert with similar male groups and yet maintained its own autonomy. Women elected their own officers, held their own meetings, testified before a state legislative committee, and published a series of "Factory Tracts" which exposed conditions within the mills and argued for the ten-hour day. . . .

Another aspect of the Ten Hour Movement which distinguished it from the earlier labor struggles in Lowell was that it involved both men and women. At the same time that women in Lowell formed the Female Labor Reform Association, a male mechanics' and laborers' association was also organized. Both groups worked to secure the passage of legislation setting ten hours as the length of the working day. Both groups circulated petitions to this end, and when the legislative committee came to Lowell to hear testimony, both men and women testified in favor of the ten-hour day.

The two groups, then, worked together, and each made an important contribution to the movement in Lowell. Women had the numbers, comprising as they did over 80 percent of the mill workforce. Men, on the other hand, had the votes, and since the Ten Hour Movement was a political struggle, they played a crucial part. . . .

Although co-ordinating their efforts with those of working men, women operatives organized independently within the Ten Hour Movement. For instance, in 1845 two important petitions were sent from Lowell to the State legislature. Almost 90 percent of the signers of one petition were females, and more than two-thirds of the signers of the second were males. Clearly the separation of men and women in their daily lives were reflected in the Ten Hour petitions of these years. . . .

The women's Ten Hour Movement, like the earlier turn-outs, was based in part on the participants' sense of their own worth and dignity as daughters of freemen. At the same time, however, it indicated the growth of a new consciousness. It reflected a mounting feeling of community among women operatives and a realization that their interests and those of their employers were not identical, that they had to rely on themselves and not on corporate benevolence to achieve a reduction in the hours of labor. One women, in an open letter to a state legislator, expressed this rejection of middle-class paternalism: "Bad as is the condition of so many women, it would be much worse if they had nothing but your boasted protection to rely upon; but they have at last learnt the lesson which a bitter experience teaches, that not to those who style themselves their 'natural protectors' are they to look for the needful help, but to the strong and resolute of their own sex." Such an attitude, underlying the self-organizing of women in the ten-hour petition campaigns, was clearly the product of the industrial experience in Lowell.

Both the early turn-outs and the Ten Hour Movement were, as noted above, in large measure dependent upon the existence of a close-knit community of women operatives. Such a community was based on the work structure, the nature of worker housing, and workforce homogeneity. Women were drawn together by the initial job training of newcomers, by the informal work sharing among experienced hands, by living in company boarding houses, [and] by sharing religious, educational, and social activities in their leisure hours. Working and living in a new and alien setting, they came to rely upon one another for friendship and support. Understandably, a community feeling developed among them.

This evolving community as well as the common cultural traditions which Yankee women carried into Lowell were major elements that governed their response to changing mill conditions. The pre-industrial tradition of independence and self-respect made them particularly sensitive to management labor policies. The sense of community enabled them to transform their individual opposition to wage cuts and to the increasing pace of work into public protest. In these labor struggles women operatives expressed a new consciousness of their rights both as workers and as women. Such a consciousness, like the community of women itself, was one product of Lowell's industrial revolution.

The experiences of Lowell women before 1850 present a fascinating picture of the contradictory impact of industrial capitalism. Repeated labor protests reveal that female operatives felt the demands of mill employment to be oppressive. At the same time, however, the mills provided women with work outside the home and family, thereby offering them an unprecedented independence. That they came to challenge employer paternalism was a direct consequence of the increasing opportunities offered them in these years. The Lowell mills both exploited and liberated women in ways unknown to the pre-industrial political economy.

» *Barbara Mayer Wertheimer* «

Women's Wages, Women's Work

» «

By the turn of the century, much of the dirty work in American industry was being done by women. In factories, mills, and sweatshops, women often labored long hours in inhumane, unsafe, and unhealthy working conditions. This was the barbarous condition in England that Charles Dickens made infamous. In America, conditions were only a little better, as described in this selection by Barbara Wertheimer, director of Cornell University's Working Women's Program for Research and Education. Industrial life for women was made slightly more tolerable on this side of the Atlantic, however, by more responsive state and federal laws, and by a system of greater upward social mobility. As bad as the situation was, fewer daughters in America than in England followed their mothers into the dark satanic mills.

> You never come back.
> I say good-bye when I see you going in the doors,
> The hopeless open doors that call and wait
> And take you then for — how many cents a day?
> How many cents for the sleepy eyes and fingers?
>
> I say good-bye because I know they tap your wrists,
> In the dark, in the silence, day by day,
> And all the blood of you drop by drop,
> And you are old before you are young.
>   You never come back.
>   —Carl Sandburg, "Mill Doors"

At the turn of the century, one-half of America lived in cities. Except in the crowded tenement sections of the biggest of these, such as New York and Chicago, women still cultivated vegetable patches, raised rabbits and chickens in their back yards, and canned much of the food their families ate during the winter months. Many supplemented family incomes by taking in boarders. In 1890 the United States Bureau of Labor found that this was true for one in every five working-class families. For some families, it constituted the entire income. . . .

Sewing, another home occupation for women, might involve dressmaking, mending, or making over worn-out, outgrown, or outmoded garments. Especially in the cities, women brought work home from garment factories, or made cigars, artificial flowers, and caps, often in tenement sweatshops. They also took in laundry. While the 1890 census found more than 200,000 laundresses, mostly black women who often worked in their employers' homes, it neglected to count the many women who provided laundry service to boarders on an individual basis.

The same census reported 1.2 million women in domestic service as *census* housekeepers, office cleaning women, maids, cooks, or hotel chambermaids. Most were young and single and worked as live-in help, earning from $2 to $5 for a workweek one-and-a-half times as long as that of a factory worker. Half were foreign-born or had parents who were. One in four was black.

By 1900, one-fifth of America's 25 million women were in the work force. At least half of all workers in textile mills and tobacco factories were women, while in the garment industries they outnumbered the men. Women worked in the shoe industry, in food processing and canning, and in heavy industries such as foundries and tin-plate mills. In every case, they held "women's jobs," for the most part unskilled, offering little chance to learn a trade or move up the job or pay ladder. Even where women held jobs requiring considerable skill, such as coremaking in foundries, which took two years to learn, they earned just one-half the wages of non-union men doing the same work and one-third those of union men. . . .

Women had entered the burgeoning electrical industry, doing not only routine work such as winding coils but also heavy work such as splitting mica. They shaped bolts and screws, braided and twisted cable in the cablemaking companies (at a starting wage of 50 cents a day), and worked in hinge factories and enameling plants. In tin-plate mills, women and boys performed unskilled work as "openers." They wore gloves with a heavy lead piece in the palm, with which they took hold of a sheet of welded plates, beat it on the ground to separate the parts, and then made an opening. Forcibly tearing the plates apart, they held part of the sheet down with one knee while they tore the metal with the other.

Factory women, like women in domestic service, tended to be single and young. Three out of four were under twenty-five years of age, and fewer than one in twenty were married (though one in twelve domestic workers were married women). They were almost always white, for few black women — or men — were accepted for factory jobs. Three-fourths were either foreign-born themselves or had foreign-born parents.

This was the era in which reformers, settlement-house workers, and journalists began to expose the inhumanity of tenement sweatshops and factory work, particularly the conditions under which women and children were so often employed. In 1893 Helen Campbell wrote, in *Women Wage-Earners*, of the conditions turned up by the Massachusetts Bureau of Labor.

They had found

> employees packed "like sardines in a box"; thirty-five persons, for
> example, in a small attic without ventilation of any kind. Some
> were in . . . basements where dampness was added to cold and
> bad air. . . . In one case girls were working in "little pens all
> shelved over. . . . There are no conveniences for women; and men
> and women use the same closets, wash-basins, and drinking cups,
> etc." . . . In another a water-closet in the center of the room filled
> it with a sickening stench. . . .

. . . In 1888 the United States Bureau of Labor issued a report on women
wage earners in 22 cities and 343 firms. In each city it found wages
low. . . .

According to a 1905 survey, women's wages averaged $5.25 a week,
from which most paid at least $2.25 for board and lodging, if single, and
with which many women tried to support families. Often they did not earn
even this amount. If they had worked steadily over the year, their average
wages would have totaled $273.00, but industries where women worked
seldom provided a full year's employment. Although men averaged yearly
earnings of $440.00, almost twice those of women workers, even this did
not come close to the figure of $800.00 that was considered the minimum a
family of four needed to maintain itself.

Women in the Steam Laundries

> How would you like to iron a shirt a minute? Think of standing at a
> mangle just above the washroom with the hot steam pouring up
> through the floor for 10, 12, 14, and sometimes 17 hours a day!
> Sometimes the floors are made of cement and then it seems as
> though one were standing on hot coals, and the workers are drip-
> ping with perspiration. Perhaps you have complained about the
> chemicals used in the washing of your clothes, which cause them
> to wear out quickly, but what do you suppose is the effect of these
> chemicals upon the workers? They are . . . breathing air laden with
> particles of soda, ammonia, and other chemicals! . . .

Investigations turned up not only low wages and workweeks 78 hours
long, but found that women were fired for refusing to perform overtime at
no pay. Illinois factory inspector Florence Kelley reported women fainting
at their work: "Girls have been removed from the laundry to the hospital
suffering exhaustion after working sixteen, eighteen, and even twenty
hours in heat and dampness in ill-ventilated laundries "

In San Francisco in 1900, laundry workers "lived in," each laundry providing board and lodging for its employees. . . .

These laundry workers earned no more than $8.10 in cash wages each month, in addition to their room and board. Those who lived at home could expect from $17.50 to $25.00 a month. So many letters of complaint were received by newspapers and by the California State Labor Commissioner about conditions in these laundries that the state decided to investigate. Inspectors found violations of the law forbidding work after 10:00 P.M., with women often on the job until 2:00 in the morning. As a result a new ordinance was passed forbidding work after 7:00 at night.

By this time laundry workers had realized that no law would be enforced unless they themselves got together to demand it. Three hundred women applied to the Laundry Workers International Union for a charter. Although the men in the laundries did not want women in their union, to its credit the parent International Union insisted that the women be admitted. . . .

In 1907 the union presented new demands for the 8-hour day and higher wages. When the owners refused, 1,100 workers from fourteen laundries walked out. The union was able to hold out for eleven weeks, supporting its members, and reached a compromise settlement that brought workers the 51-hour week, to be reduced gradually until the 8-hour day was in place by April of 1910. . . . By 1912 the San Francisco laundry workers had brought up wages by 30 percent, installed safety measures in the plants, and organized all the city's steam laundries. Few unions in such a low-wage, unskilled industry had ever lasted so long or accomplished so much.

Elizabeth Butler, who studied the steam laundries of Pittsburgh in 1907, found that 2,185 of the 2,402 workers were women. Wages in the steam laundries had risen after the turn of the century, because employers in Pittsburgh competed for labor, even trying to steal workers from each other. But the work was physically hard and unhealthy. Steam from huge vats that boiled all day long rose from the washrooms in the basement to the floor above. There was no relief from the steam, for the windows had to remain closed against the soot from the city's iron and steel mills, which would soil the clothes even before they were out of the tubs.

Poor drainage in the basements meant flooding, so that workers stood in water all day long. While the men ran the washing machines, the women hand-washed items too delicate to put in the vats. Basement work paid $1 for a 10-hour day. Although this was higher than in some trades, the work was so unhealthy and respiratory disease so common that women preferred almost any other work and came to the laundries as a last resort.

Mangle operators also worked in unbearable heat for $3.00 to $3.50 a week. "Shakers" took the wet clothes as they were brought from the washroom and shook them out to be fed into the mangle. . . . Wet sheets and towels made this heavy work. In fact, women did not last long in laundry work, perhaps two to four years. Mangles were dangerous machines even when the inadequate guards were installed, which they frequently were not. After an exhausting day of work, women easily caught fingers, hands, and even arms in the machinery. Ironers' and pressers' work carried an additional hazard: the heavy irons were gasheated. In England this gas had been found so dangerous that ventilation standards were prescribed by law, but in the United States in the early 1900's no such laws covered laundries.

Men and women competed for the elite laundry jobs, sorting and checking. Men who held these jobs earned $12 to $20 dollars a week; women earned $5 to $12 for performing exactly the same work.

Canning Moves to the Factory

One of the new and often dangerous industries which offered increasing employment for women in the early years of the new century was that of canning and food processing. Because the industry was seasonal, manufacturers were able to get exemptions from hours limitations for their workers. From the start, women made up over half the work force in canning. . . .

Most cannery workers were young women sixteen to twenty years old. While men in the factories did the cooking, the women prepared the raw vegetables and fruits, washed, filled, and labeled bottles, and cut and labeled the tin cans. . . . Women averaged no more than $3.50 to $4.00 a week for six 11-hour days that stretched to 14 hours or more during the rush season. . . .

One of the most vivid descriptions of conditions in the canning and bottling industry was given by Mother Jones (Mary Harris Jones), United Mine Workers organizer and a legend in herself. During the 1905-1911 period, when she was not on the organizing payroll of the Mine Workers, she often worked in different industries to help support herself, and in 1910 spent two months alongside women who washed bottles in a Milwaukee brewery. In the *Miner's Magazine* she reported the conditions she found:

> Condemned to slave daily in the wash-room in wet shoes and wet clothes, surrounded with foul-mouthed, brutal foremen . . . the poor girls work in the vile smell of sour beer, lifting cases of empty and full bottles weighing from 100 to 150 pounds, in their wet shoes and rags, for they cannot buy clothes on the pittance doled out to them. . . . Rheumatism is one of the chronic ailments and is closely followed by consumption. . . . The foreman even regulates the time [the girls] may stay in the toilet room, and in the event of overstaying it gives the foreman an opportunity for indecent and foul language. Should the patient slave forget herself and take offense, it will cost her the job. And after all, bad as it is, it is all that she knows how to do. To deprive her of the job means less crusts and worse rags. . . . Many of the girls have no home nor parents and are forced to feed and clothe and shelter themselves . . . on $3.00 per week. . . .

Bindery Women

Women in bookbinding in the early 1900s provided a sharp contrast to the average factory worker. They were for the most part American-born and were better educated. Of the 14,000 bookbinders reported by the United States Census in 1900, just over half were women. They did not compete for jobs in the industry with the men, who completed a four-year apprenticeship, while the women performed only the less skilled work. Although no rule prevented women from serving such apprenticeships, they were never offered them.

The International Brotherhood of Bookbinders formed in 1892, and by 1910 had 130 affiliated locals, of which 24 included both men and women members. Twenty-five percent of all women bookbinders were unionized. By and large, the women organized separately. The most famous of their locals, Women Bookbinders Local 43 of New York City, is still in existence. This unusual local began with 50 members in 1895 and grew to have 1,400 by 1910. Women from its ranks who served as elected officers developed effective collective bargaining machinery, established the six-day, forty-eight-hour week, preferential hiring for union members, and time-and-a-half pay after fifty-four hours if overtime was required. . . .

Mary Van Kleeck, who studied and wrote about a number of women's occupations for the Russell Sage Foundation, tried to determine the source of the strength of the bindery women. She decided their success was due to the way the local kept track of each member to ensure that union women were the first hired in union shops, ahead of any non-union workers; in effect, the local served as a hiring hall. In addition, all permanent workers had to join Local 43 after two weeks on the job; the women had achieved a "union shop." Van Kleeck found that all the women seemed to share a pride in the union's victories, and those she spoke with wanted to be sure she understood that they had done it for themselves, without much help or cooperation from the men. Even employers she interviewed confirmed that the women deserved full credit for the wages and working conditions they had achieved.

Women in Packingtown

Upton Sinclair, in his novel *The Jungle,* brought conditions in the Chicago stockyards and packing plants to the attention of the public. He writes of Marija, a young woman who had been fired from her job painting cans in a meat-packing plant because of union activity. She spent four weeks and half the fifth combing the packing plants without finding any job. . . .

> When she first came to Packingtown, Marija would have scorned such work as this. She was in another canning factory, and her work was to cut up the diseased cattle. . . . She was shut up in one of the rooms where the people seldom saw the daylight; beneath

her were the chilling rooms, where the meat was frozen, and above her were the cooking rooms; and so she stood on an ice-cold floor, while her head was often so hot she could scarcely breathe. Trimming beef off the bones by the hundredweight, while standing up from early morning to late at night, with heavy boots on and the floor always damp and full of puddles, liable to be thrown out of work indefinitely because of a slackening in the trade, liable again to be kept overtime in rush seasons, and be worked till she trembled in every nerve and lost her grip on her slimy knife, and gave herself a poisoned wound — that was the new life that unfolded itself before Marija. But because Marija was a human horse she merely laughed and went at it; it would enable her to pay her board again, and keep the family going.

The Jungle produced such an outcry from the public that a major investigation into the food-packing industry resulted — but the outrage was over the unsanitary and diseased food that was being sold to the public, not the dangerous, inhuman conditions under which it was produced. The investigation was followed by the passage of federal legislation calling for meat inspection, a host of safeguards, and the labeling of food and drugs. These were all inadequately enforced, and life continued in Packgingtown as before.

It was left to the workers themselves to organize . . .

Women first struck over repeated cuts in the piece rate. Maggie Condon, one of the fastest packinghouse workers, noticed that whenever her take-home pay went above a certain amount, her rate was cut, and that the rate cut went all down the line. This meant that the slowest workers suffered for the speed of the fastest. The fast workers began to organize, holding back on their production to protect their fellow workers. Hannah O'Day, who had been packing meat since she was eleven years old but was not one of the fast workers, joined the group. They did not take long to decide that they needed a union. However, they got no encouragement from the men, not even when Hannah O'Day raised her red handkerchief on a stick, motioned the women to follow her, and led hundreds of women out on a spontaneous strike. The women won nothing, but managed to stay together by forming a club, called the Maud Gonne Club after an Irish patriot. But the club might never have evolved into a union if Maggie Condon had not read a newspaper account of a talk given by Mary McDowell, head of the University of Chicago Settlement House, which was located right near the stockyard. McDowell had described the terrible conditions of the women working in the packing plants. Condon and O'Day, feeling that here at least was someone who understood, began a series of discussions with her that came to include other women from the plant. Out of these grew Local 183, which in 1903 was finally granted a charter by the Amalgamated Meatcutters and Butcher Workmen. . . .

In 1904 a general strike of packinghouse workers occurred, with the women supporting the men who had walked out. This strike was a major defeat, and Local 183 went down with the men. Hannah O'Day had believed firmly that "we ought to organize for them that comes after us," but it would be a long time before packinghouse workers could regroup and rebuild their union.

However, women workers had made some progress. Although few were union members, more than a dozen unions now admitted women and most no longer segregated them by sex. Shoeworkers and waitresses, bookbinders, garment, tobacco, and laundry workers, women in textile mills, and glove sewers were beginning to organize. Gradually unions were coming to see the importance of including women workers.

Where Black Women Worked

Almost no black women were eligible for union membership . . . since they were seldom permitted to work in skilled occupations that organized. They were concentrated in Southern agricultural and domestic service jobs, in laundries, and in tobacco factories, particularly in tobacco stripping.

There were tobacco strippers in the North, too, but it was often a home industry. Elizabeth Butler, in her study of women in the Pittsburgh trades, describes the tenements in which women worked:

> The only source of air was a narrow door leading by a flight of steps up to the street. A tiny slit of a window at the far end was close barred, and two-thirds of the cubic space in the room was occupied by bales of tobacco and cases of stripped stock. Pools of muddy water stood on the earth floor, and the air was foul beyond endurance.

Of the 523 tenement tobacco strippers in Pittsburgh whom Butler found, all but 18 were women earning from 60 cents to $1.00 a day working piece rate. There was no union to help them, for the Tobacco Workers International Union, founded in 1895, did not — or could not — organize home workers, isolated from each other, poor, and often frightened. It is worth noting, however, that the two largest locals of this international union were the one in Detroit, where women outnumbered men by more than two to one, and the one in Richmond, Virginia, where 236 men and 131 women, all black, maintained a successful union.

Where black women did work in mills, it was at the heavy labor jobs or as janitresses, not at the machines. In the South, the only jobs they could get were those white workers refused to do, while white workers went into the cotton mills. Poor as the wages and working conditions in these mills were, white workers struck thirty-one times between 1882 and 1900, not to organize unions, but to keep black workers from being hired to work on machines.

After the Civil War many black women worked in the fields alongside the men, just as they had done as slaves. . . . Those who could manage it headed North — by 1910 some 400,000 of them had moved to Northern cities. There they found domestic service open to them and little else. Though the 1890 census reported 11,846 black women working as seamstresses and 7,586 more as dressmakers, many black seamstresses were hired to fill a servant's role.

The first entry of black women into factory sewing was usually as scabs in labor disputes. A study done in 1900 showed that in New York City's leading industry for women, dressmaking, only 813 black women were employed out of a total of 37,514 women in this trade. The same study revealed the degree to which unemployment attended black men when they moved North, for 25 percent of all married black women were found in New York's work force, as compared with only 5 percent of married white women.

In an 1899 study of black workers in another major city, Philadelphia, W.E.B. Du Bois [found that] . . . men's wages averaged from $2.61 a week for a bellboy to $8.58 a week for a coachman, while women's earnings ranged from $2.00 weekly for an errand girl to $4.06 for a janitress. Cook and laundress were the only other occupations that averaged $4.00 a week or a few cents more. He found black women employed as dressmakers and seamstresses, errand girls, children's nurses, chambermaids, waitresses, ladies' maids, laundresses, cooks, janitresses, undertakers, and general workers. The highest wages Du Bois recorded for a black woman were those of a child's nurse and a cook, who earned $10.00 a week. Black people lost their jobs more rapidly than white, paid more for housing of poor quality, had to take insults and accept poor service, and watched their children grow up in the face of constant discrimination.

Although light-skinned black women had an easier time finding skilled employment, they were fired as soon as it was learned that they were not white. Du Bois found that one out of every ten domestic workers had some high school education and was qualified to hold a more skilled job — but could find none. A few black women managed to enter professions such as nursing, teaching, social work, medicine, journalism, or the law. Since almost all professions were barred to them, it took tremendous energy, talent, and courage to achieve a professional education and then to break into the field itself. . . .

Until World War I, black women moved slowly into factory jobs. Some entered the garment industry, some the packing plants in the Chicago stockyards; some worked in crab picking, others in canning factories; and there was almost always employment for them in the growing number of steam laundries. In the South, tobacco and cigarette factories employed black women in the least desirable jobs. Few black women could get office or sales jobs or work for the telephone company. Only during World War I did opportunities to work in industry open for black women, although rarely at the same jobs and almost never side-by-side with white women.

» Agnes Nestor «

Birth of a Labor Organizer

» «

Agnes Nestor was vice-president of the International Glove Workers Union and president of the Chicago Women's Trade Union League. In this selection, she points out some of the pressures of the <u>piecework system</u> as she describes the working conditions of the women who sewed and stitched gloves in a Chicago factory at the beginning of this century. The women had long been outraged because they had to pay for the power to run their sewing machines, as well as pay for their own needles and machine oil. When the company tried to subdivide their work—possibly reducing their rate of pay—they went on strike in what was a rather spontaneous expression of frustration. In the process, Nestor found herself spokeswoman for the group and, without forethought, a union organizer for life.

O ur machines were on long tables in large rooms, and we operators sat on both sides of the tables. At last I was where I had longed to be, and here I worked for ten years. I was earning fairly good pay for those times, and I was happy. We would mark out the quantity of our work and keep account of our earnings. I still have that little book in which I kept my accounts. It is interesting to see how I gradually increased my weekly pay.

To drown the monotony of work, we used to sing. This was allowed because the foreman could see that the rhythm kept us going at high speed. We sang *A Bicycle Built for Two* and other popular songs.

Before we began to sing we used to talk very loudly so as to be heard above the roar of the machines. We knew we must not stop our work just to hear what someone was saying; to stop work even for a minute meant a reduction in pay.

We did want to do a little talking, though. In order not to lose time by it, we worked out a plan. We all chipped in and bought a dollar alarm clock which we hung on the wall. We figured that we could do a dozen pairs of gloves in an hour. That meant five minutes for a pair. As we worked we could watch the clock to see if we were on schedule. If we saw ourselves falling behind, we could rush to catch up with our own time. No one was watching us or pushing us for production. It was our strategem for getting the most out of the piecework system. We wanted to earn as much as we possibly could.

But, though we all seemed happy at first, gradually it dawned dimly within us that we were not beating the piecework system; it was beating us. There were always "pacemakers," a few girls who could work faster than the rest, and they were the ones to get the new work before the price was set.* Their rate of work had to be the rate for all of us, if we were to earn a decent wage. It kept us tensed to continual hurry.

Also, there were some unjust practices, outgrowths from another era, which nettled us because they whittled away at our weekly pay. We were charged fifty cents a week for the power furnished our machines. At first we were tolerant of the charge and called it "our machine rent." But after a time that check-off of fifty cents from our weekly pay made us indignant.

We were obliged, besides, to buy our own needles. If you broke one, you were charged for a new one to replace it. We had, also, to buy our own machine oil. It was expensive; and to make matters worse, we had to go to certain out-of-the-way places to obtain it.

But this was not all. Every time a new foreman came in, he demonstrated his authority by inaugurating a new set of petty rules which seemed designed merely to irritate us. One such rule was that no girl must leave her own sewing room at noon to eat lunch with a girl in another room. My sister Mary had now come into the factory, and we were in the habit of grouping at lunch time with friends from other departments. But even two sisters from different departments were not permitted to eat lunch together. Mary was in a different department at the time, and this regulation seemed too ridiculous to be borne. Consequently, whenever the foreman had left the room at noon, we went where we pleased to eat our lunch. Sometimes he spied on us and ordered us "Back where you belong!"

In the face of all this, any new method which the company sought to put into effect and disturb our work routine seemed to inflame the deep indignation already burning inside us. Thus, when a procedure was suggested for subdividing our work, so that each operator would do a smaller part of each glove, and thus perhaps increase the overall production—but also increase the monotony of the work, and perhaps also decrease our rate of pay—we began to think of fighting back.

The management evidently heard the rumblings of a threatened revolt. Our department was the "glove-closers." A representative of the company sent for a group from another department, the "banders," asking them to give this new method of subdividing the work a trial and promising an adjustment if the workers' earnings were found to be reduced. The group agreed to try out the new method; but when they got back to their depart-

---

Ed. note: The price changed at random and often varied from day to day.

86

ment and told the banders about it, the banders revolted, refused to work the new way on trial, and walked out.

We of our department felt that we should be loyal to the girls who had walked out, and we told the foreman that if the company tried to put new girls in the places of the banders, we would walk out, too!

We had taken a bold step. Almost with spontaneity we had acted in support of one another. Now we all felt tremulous, vulnerable, exposed. With no regular organization, without even a qualified spokesman, how long would such unified action last? If anyone ever needed the protection of a firm organization, I for one at that moment felt keenly that we certainly did.

The glove-cutters, all men, had a union which had existed for about a year. The girl who sat next to me told me about it. She had a boyfriend in this union, but she was always careful not to let anyone hear her talk about it because in those days unions were taboo. She said that the cutters—all men—had talked of trying to get the girls to join the union and had wanted to approach our plant to suggest it, but that some of the members had said, "You'll never get those girls to join a union. They'll stand for anything up there!"

The banders had been smart. They had walked out on Saturday. One of their number decided to get publicity about their grievances and she gave the newspapers the full story about their strike.

The Chicago Federation of Labor was having a meeting that day, and the glove-cutters from our shop had special delegates there. A labor reporter went to these delegates asking for details about the walkout of the banders. It was the first the delegates had heard of the matter. But, learning that the banders of their own factory had struck, they decided to try to get all the girls to join the union.

On Monday the president of the union tried to arrange a meeting with our group. But it was too late. During the week end, the boss had decided to abandon the new system. Workers had been sent word to come back and everything would be all right, that they could work as before. We felt that now we had a certain power and were delighted over what seemed to us a moral victory. Monday morning found us back at work.

All was not settled, however. On Monday the glove-cutters' union rented a hall within a block of the factory. As we came out from work that afternoon, members of the glove-cutters' union met us telling us to go to a union meeting at this hall.

Israel Solon was one of these men. Sometimes, if a girl hesitated about going to the hall, he would urge:

"Don't be afraid of the boss; protect yourself! Go to the union meeting!"

I was only too anxious to go and did not care who saw me. It seemed legitimate to protect one's self from unjust rules. I went without hesitation.

The meeting was a great success; workers packed the hall, and many non-members signed for membership. The work of organizing continued for three evenings, until most of the shop had been persuaded to join.

Toward the end of the week, there was a disturbance in the cutting department. It leaked through to us that a cutter had been discharged and that the cutters were organizing a protest strike. We were young and inexperienced in union procedure; and, as I look back now, I see that because of that lack of experience, and because we were newly organized and therefore anxious to use our new organization, we did a rash thing. We started a strike movement in protest at the discharge of the cutter and also for the redress of our own grievances. We even celebrated the event with a birthday party for one of our girls and had a feast with lemon cream pie at lunch time. During the feast we formulated our plan. We decided it would be cowardly to walk out at noon. We would wait until the whistle blew for us to resume work, and then, as the power started up on the machines, we would begin our exodus.

Somehow the foreman got wind of our plan. We were forming a line when reinforcements from the foremen's division scattered around the room ordering us to go back to our places. We began to chant: "We are not going to pay rent for our machines!" We repeated it over and over, for that was our chief grievance. . . .

We walked out. We did not use the near-by stairs but walked through the next room in order that the girls there might see us leaving. The girls there were busily at work quite unconscious of our strike movement. I knew that our cause was lost unless we got those girls to join us. When we got out to the street, I told my companions that all was lost unless we could get those others to walk out too. We lined up across the street shouting "Come on out!" and calling out the names of some of the girls. We kept this up until a few did obey us. Gradually others followed until the shop was almost emptied. Then we paraded to the hall on Leavitt Street for the meeting with the union leaders.

At the meeting we were called upon to state our demands. We gave them: no more machine rent; no paying for needles; free machine oil; union shop; raises for the cutters who were paid the lowest wages. . . .

Evidently the union officers thought I was a ringleader, for when the committee was appointed to represent our group, my name was called. When Mary heard it, she said:

"Why did they put Agnes on? She can't talk!"

This seems amusing to me now; also to certain of my friends who were present at that meeting, for they assure me that I have been talking ever since. . . .

We joined the picket line again and held meetings every day and evening in the hall the cutters had rented. How important we felt! Speakers sent to our evening meetings were furnished by the Chicago Federation of Labor Organization Committee headed by John Fitzpatrick. One evening they sent Sophie Becker of the Boot and Shoe Workers Union, the only woman on the organization committee. I am afraid that I was a great hero-worshipper in those days! I was so thrilled with her speech that as she left the hall I leaned over just to touch her. Then I leaned back satisfied because I had got that close to her.

All this was happening at the same time that streetcar conductors were being discharged because it became known that they were forming a union. Some of the conductors, as they passed our picket line, would throw us handsful of buttons which read: ORGANIZE. I'M WITH YOU!

We wore those buttons on our coats, and when we boarded the cars we would watch the expression on each conductor's face to find out whether or not he had joined the union. . . .

The second week of our strike began. About the middle of the week, we girls on the picket line each received a letter from the company urging us to come back to work and promising that if we reported upon receipt of the letter our old places would be restored to us, that there would be no more machine rent or "power charge," as they called it, that needles would be furnished at cost, that machine oil would be furnished free, and that the cutters would receive a dollar a week raise. But no mention was made of our demand for a union shop.

We talked it all over with misgivings, lest some of the girls be misled by these promises. Without a company recognition of our union, we might all be lured back to work, the more progressive and outspoken of us discharged one by one, and all the old practices put back in force, perhaps even more tightly than ever. Such things had happened before. Our safety and our future, we knew, lay in our union. We decided not to return to work just yet. Meanwhile we doubled our picket line, determined that none of our group should falter.

We had hoped to get all the girls in the factory into our union, but we had had trouble with the girls of the kid glove department. Only a few of these "aristocrats" had ventured to walk out with us. The rest had remained aloof. Like the gloves they made, the kid glove makers felt that they were superior to the rest of us and used to refer haughtily to the rest of us as the "horsehide girls."

During one of the last days of our strike, one of these kid glove girls passed along our picket line on her way to work. We told her that she wasn't going in; we formed a circle around her and took her to the streetcar a block away and waited to see that she went home. We stood waiting for the car beside a long water trough where teamsters watered their horses. One girl who was holding tightly to the kid glove maker threatened, "Before I let go of you, I will duck you in that water trough." It was only an idle threat; of course she did not intend doing it.

Newspapermen were on hand trying to get stories about the strike. Luke Grant, a veteran labor reporter, was watching as we put the girl on the streetcar.

Next morning a front-page story appeared headlined, "STRIKERS DUCK GIRL IN WATER TROUGH." Other newspapers carried the same fiction and played it up for several days, some even with cartoons of the fictitious event. . . .

Perhaps because of this newspaper publicity—and Luke Grant always insisted that his story won the day for us—or perhaps because it looked as though we girls would refuse forever to return to work unless all our demands were met, the management agreed to our union shop and to the redress of all our grievances. We went back to work the following Monday with, as we said, "flying colors." Our union shop, we felt, was our most important gain.

The women who do the most work get the least money, and the women who have the most money do the least work.
—Charlotte Perkins Gilman, *Women and Economics*

» *Augusta Clawson* «

Shipyard Diary of a Woman Welder

» «

During World War II, American women worked on airplane assembly lines, in munitions factories, and in shipyards, taking jobs that were vacated by the men who had been mobilized to fight the Japanese and Germans. "Rosie the Riveter" became as much a part of American folklore as "G.I. Joe." This first-person account by one such woman conveys a good sense of how millions of American women, without experience and without training, quickly and efficiently assumed the skilled and semi-skilled blue-collar jobs of their husbands, fathers, brothers, and sons. When the men returned, most of these women returned to work in their homes. There was little lasting effect on the work roles of women as the result of this wartime experience.

But a parallel story, not told here, did have a lasting legacy: black Americans came from the rural South to the industrial North, Midwest, and West Coast to work beside America's many white Rosies. Many of these black men and women lost their jobs, too, when the white soldiers returned from war. But, instead of returning to the South, these people stayed, joining a growing black urban lower class that is still fighting today for a toe hold in the labor market (see Part Four).

Back to work and more welding. I "dis-improved" as rapidly after lunch as I had improved during the morning. One girl stopped to ask, "How you doin'?" and watched me critically. "Here, let me show you, you're holding it too far away." So she took over, but she couldn't maintain the arc at all. She got up disgusted, said, "I can't do it—my hand shakes so since I been sick," and I took over again. But she was right. I held it closer and welded on and on and on. . . .

The redheaded mother of seven was terribly upset. Her boy got his papers yesterday, and she hadn't slept all night. First thing this morning she had to take her test and was as jittery as could be. I wonder if this is the sort of thing that people glibly call "the emotional instability of women" without investigating first to find its cause! A mother has a right to be at less than her calmest when her eldest son is leaving to join the Army. But

91

this woman, in the midst of all her worry, had room for concern about me. She came running up. "Say, my eldest boy leaves tomorrow. You can come and live with us if you like." I hesitated, reflecting that it would be difficult to record my daily impressions without risking her suspicion that I might have an ulterior motive for taking this job. So I temporized. "You're a brick to suggest it, but you can't spare a room for me when you still have six children in the house." She looked puzzled. "A room?" she said. "Why, I don't know—maybe I could fix you up a room." Then she shrugged her bewilderment away. "No, I mean just come and live with us." That's what I call hospitality. . . .

We were called to another safety lecture—good sound advice on Eye Safety . . . . Only Chile has a higher accident rate than the United States. Last year the shipyard had fairly heavy absenteeism, but this year they hope to build an extra ship on the decrease in absenteeism. He cautioned us about creating hazards by wearing the wrong kind of clothing, and told us not to wear watches or rings. After it was over, Missouri was bothered about her wedding ring. It hadn't been off in fourteen years. She was willing to take it off, but only if necessary.

The lecturer brought up the rumor that arc welding causes sterility among women. He said that this was untrue, and quoted an authoritative source to prove its falsity. . . . Actually, welders had *more* children than other people. "No, thanks," said the first girl; "I don't like that either!"

The Big Swede is a real pal. She had not forgotten the patch for my overall trouser leg. She had cut a piece from an old pair of her husband's, scrubbed it to get the oil out, and brought it to me with a needle stuck in the center and a coil of black thread ready for action. "Here," she said, "I knew you wouldn't have things handy in a hotel room. Now you mend that hole before you catch your foot in it and fall.". . .

I, who hates heights, climbed stair after stair after stair till I thought I must be close to the sun. I stopped on the top deck. I, who hate confined spaces, went through narrow corridors, stumbling my way over rubber-coated leads—dozens of them, scores of them, even hundreds of them. I went into a room about four feet by ten where two shipfitters, a shipfitter's helper, a chipper, and I all worked. I welded in the poop deck lying on the floor while another welder spattered sparks from the ceiling and chippers like giant woodpeckers shattered our eardrums. I, who've taken welding, and have sat at a bench welding flat and vertical plates, was told to weld braces along a baseboard below a door opening. On these a heavy steel door was braced while it was hung to a fine degree of accuracy. I welded more braces along the side, and along the top. I did overhead welding, horizontal, flat, vertical. I welded around curved hinges which were placed so close to the side wall that I had to bend my rod in a curve to get it in. I made some good welds and some frightful ones. But now a door in the poop deck of an oil tanker is hanging, four feet by six of solid steel, by *my* welds. Pretty exciting! . . .

Poor Texas had to work all afternoon in double bottom. She said she couldn't stand; she couldn't even sit up straight. She rested somewhat on a narrow pipe and did production. She was not very happy about it. It's funny the way we all dodge production. There isn't such a great difference between the techniques of tacking and doing production welding, but there is in the responsibility. When we tack we know a production welder will weld over the tack, and any gaps will be filled by him (or her). But when we do production we know ours is the final responsibility. . . .

I talked with Joanne, a very attractive brunette who had previously been a waitress in Atlantic City. She came West when her husband came on for a job. She, like the other waitresses, preferred welding because you "don't have to take so much from the public.". . .

I had a good taste of summer today, and I am convinced that it is going to take backbone for welders to stick to their jobs through the summer months. It is harder on them than on any of the other workers—their leathers are so hot and heavy, they get more of the fumes, and their hoods become instruments of torture. There were times today when I'd have to stop in the middle of a tack and push my hood back just to get a breath of fresh air. It grows unbearably hot under the hood, my glasses fog and blur my vision, and the only thing to do is to stop.

For almost an hour I tacked on in spite of the fact that there was no blower in the room. Then I took Texas's advice and decided "no blower, no welder." . . . My work was in the poop deck where the last crew had put brackets in place *upside down*. The burner had to burn off six of them completely. For me, this meant climbing halfway up the wall and tacking them in place with horizontal, vertical, and overhead tacks. One's position is often so precarious at such an angle that it is hard to maintain a steady arc. Add to this that often I could not stand straight nor kneel. The result was that trying to hold a position halfway between would start some contrary nerve quivering so that my hand would carry out the "jiggle" and affect the weld. Yet the job confirmed my strong conviction—I have stated it before—what exhausts the woman welder is not the work, nor the heat, nor the demands upon physical strength. It is the apprehension that arises from inadequate skill and consequent lack of confidence; and this *can* be overcome by the right kind of training. I've mastered tacking now, so that no kind bothers me. I know I can do it if my machine is correctly set, and I have learned enough of the vagaries of machines to be able to set them. And so, in spite of the discomforts of climbing, heavy equipment, and heat, I enjoyed the work today because I *could do it*. . . .

The drinking fountains are a godsend in such weather as this. The water is always cold. Often I hesitate to leave work long enough for a drink, since if a tack is needed the shipfitters have to stop work until it is done. But I think we are all getting to be more sensible about realizing that once in a while we have to stop, even if work waits for a moment. So midway in the morning I told my men, "Guess I have to have a drink," and off I went. All

93

the time that I was tacking, three or four shipfitters would be sitting down waiting for me to finish. Several weeks ago this would have given me a hurried feeling; I'd have rushed the work, done it less well, and been more tired. I've learned now to work a steady pace and to ignore the fact that anyone is waiting. It relieves the strain and the work really gets done faster. There is a lot in this game in learning to relax *on* the job as well as *between* jobs.

》 *Terry Wetherby* 《

Doing a "Man's Job"

》《

Beginning in the 1960s, many daughters of the women who were forced by necessity to take blue-collar jobs during World War II began voluntarily to enter the skilled trades. Today, women are not only riveters and welders, but butchers, carpenters, truck drivers, and auto assembly-line workers, too. As indicated in the following interview by a woman who is herself a welder as well as a writer, blue-collar women have more opportunities than their mothers, but they are still not fully accepted by the men with whom they work.

After only a month as an Alpha *Beta supermarket bagger, Nancy Andersen was selected to be a butcher. Andersen, then nineteen, took the opportunity and "didn't know what" she was getting into. She entered a world of razor-sharp knives, slicers, and hamburger mixers as big as stoves—a world where the temperature is constantly fixed at 51 degrees Fahrenheit and all her peers are men.*

At the time of this interview, Andersen lived at home with her parents in Penngrove, California, a town of 300 people, "one gas station, two bars, and one grocery." Andersen had been with Alpha Beta a little more than a year.

I'm a journeyman meatcutter at Alpha Beta in Santa Rosa. I break and process meat—pork, veal, lamb, beef, fish and poultry—breaking it down from whole carcass into steaks and roasts. Processing is just breaking into certain cuts of beef—your rounds, your chucks, and the different varieties. Then you're steaking things into counter form. . . .

Physically, your work must be hard.
Yeah, it's hard. But no harder for me than it is for a lot of the guys. Your lifting is hard mainly. Your boxes of pork rinds weigh about 75, sometimes 80 pounds. And you're expected to lift.

Did you find this difficult at first?
Oh yeah! [Laughs.] But eventually you just get so you can handle it. You learn how to pick things up. Most of the guys are really cooperative and everybody works together. You're never working alone, except at night.

How did you become a meatcutter?
I worked in Alpha Beta first as a courtesy clerk— a bagger. Then the store supervisor asked me if I'd be interested in taking the job; there was an opening.

What did they ask you?
They felt that I was qualified for the job. I worked a little harder and had a little more initiative than other people did, I guess. I was willing.

There are fields opening. And companies are under pressure to get women into these kind of jobs. Some women haven't been successful. I think a lot of the guys have made it hard for them. A lot of guys feel that women are taking jobs away from men that have families. I'm single and I'm making as much as guys that support families with four kids. . . .

Was there opposition to your becoming a meatcutter?
When Gregg, the store supervisor, said he wanted me to be a meatcutter, everybody said, "Oh. *No way!*" They said it was really crazy and that sort of thing. But it wasn't. . . .

You get familiar with all of the machinery at first . . . the saws, the grinding machines, the weights. You learn to wrap meat. A lot of the meatcutters today were wrappers.

I had had no experience at all. So it was kind of rough when I started out.

Did you like meatcutting at first?
I've *always* liked it. I like physical work. I've been raised around horses all my life, so I've been outdoors and I've never enjoyed working in an office.

During the first month, I made hamburger and wrapped and did very little cutting. You have to get used to the saws and that sort of thing. It takes a long time. You're afraid . . . [Laughs.] Meat's slick! And the saws are *fast*.

You were afraid?
Oh *yeah!* The knives are sharp. You have to learn to sharpen your own knives, to use a steel. You get knicks and cuts.

What are the occupational hazards?
Losing your *fingers*. I've known people who have lost fingers. The year that I went to school, there were two guys who lost fingers out of about 20 or 25 people. . . .

96

The cold

What was the most difficult adjustment for you when you began meat-cutting?
I *never* thought I'd get used to the cold. The shop is kept at 51 or 52 degrees all the time. Some butchers never get used to it, and they've been in the business for 30 years. Now I'm used to it and I love it.

When I first worked I wore long underwear every day. [Laughs.] I wore my gloves in the cooler, my coat and everything. Now it isn't anything for me to go in there, because I guess your body adjusts to that.

Butchers get arthritis. A lot of them get frost-bite too. You take inventory in the freezer, and sometimes it's pretty cold. The health department wants your grinder in the cooler which is really cold. [Laughs.] The cooler is where your meat is kept at a certain temperature in the 30s or 40s. You really get cold—that hamburger's *cold!* . . .

Men have problems with jobs too, just like women do. If women only knew that, I think it would help them succeed, if they really want to do it.

How did you become a member of the butcher's union?
You had a thirty-day period. You worked in the shop, and they saw how you could get along and how you liked it. I got along *fine*.

What is your attitude toward the union?
I think it's good for me. I believe in the union, and I attend the meetings. It's a good thing.

They keep everybody in line. We've had problems in our shop, and certain members haven't been able to work in the shop because of the *rules* of the union. And it is a strong union. It's by the book, and that's *good*. The members *are* kept in line.

We *do* get a lot of money, and I think most of us work for it. [Her union initiation fee was 166 dollars. Dues are sixteen dollars a month.]

What is your salary?
I make $286 a week. That's for a forty-hour week. You make two dollars night premium. That's two dollars more for the evening if you work after seven o'clock at night or before seven in the morning. . . .

What is your typical day?
One day you work 2 to 11 and the next day you work 8 to 5. I wear a smock, an apron over that, and then a hardhat.

Usually you'll just start right in on the block. You'll start boning, cutting steaks, cutting up chickens, bagging chickens. The head of the shop would be telling me what to do, or if he's not there then the second man would be running the shop. Everybody else is journeyman cutter.

You just cut till you go home. You help people at the counter, you load the counter, and you set up displays. We have contests throughout the company for our displays.

In Santa Rosa, I bone twelve or thirteen (beef) rounds a night. They weigh about 65 pounds a piece. And that's a *lot* of boning. . . .

Are you stronger than most women?
That's where I have an advantage over a lot of girls. I'm just built a little bigger. I'm about five feet five and weigh about 135 pounds. I'm built strong.

Most guys can just pick things up and throw things around, and they never really hesitate, where me . . . I would draw back. The guy I worked with first and learned a lot from weighed about 200 pounds and was about five foot nine inches tall. [Laughs.] And it was easy for *him* to say, "Well! Do it this way!" It didn't matter how he lifted it anyway, because he was so *big!* [Laughs.] It wasn't so easy for me. Eventually I learned to lift so it was easy and didn't hurt my back. Lift with your knees and not with your back.

Your speed is really important. I think this is a drawback for women, because when I lifted things, I wasn't as fast. You always have to push. Competition—there *is* competition.

Were there times when you thought about quitting?
Oh yeah. When I thought I was never going to *learn.* To handle a knife is like learning to write. Cutting's an art, definitely. And the lifting was hard to learn, even though my father was a carpenter and we worked with him a lot. . . .

Do you regard meatcutting as a fulfilling occupation?
Many times I go home and know that I *really* did the job well and that I'm doing what I've wanted to do for so long. It doesn't pay off all the time. I might go home really tired with my hands all cramped up from boning, but I love it. . . .

Have you had **any** *problems with co-workers because you're a woman?*
The people I worked with never made it a woman in a man's job. I was expected to do the things that a man did. And I *did.* I'm in a shop now where the situation isn't quite the same. Before, I was working for a guy that expected me to do *everything* everybody else did. The work was the work. My boss never thought I can do it, but I had the drive. I took it upon myself to say every night when I went home, "That's alright! I'll be there one day and you may be working for *me!*" And it helped.

If you really want to do anything, I've always felt that you can do it. I've had a great opportunity and I intend to make a future of my work. . . .

But I think that there's no reason that a woman should be a burden to males working in the same shop. If she *can't* pull the weight, I think she should get out.

The work is hard, and you can't make anybody else's job any harder than yours is. It's important for a woman who doesn't feel she can handle it to get out— in *any* job.

4

》《

PROFESSIONALS AND MANAGERS ARE WORKERS, TOO

》《

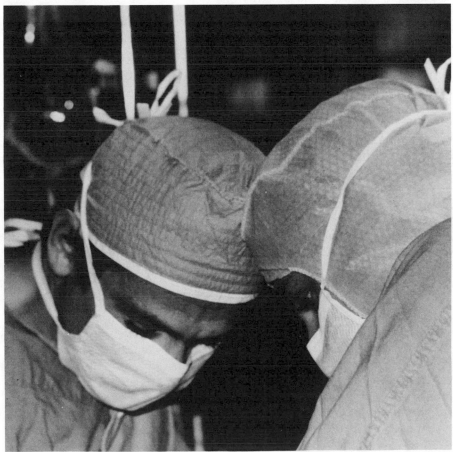

Leonard Rhodes/Photophile

» Studs Terkel «
Editor: Nora Watson
» «

Nora Watson is a pseudonym for a technical writer, one of countless "average"
Americans interviewed by Studs Terkel. Watson calls our attention to the fact that
not all high-level (professional, technical, and managerial) jobs are good jobs. No
doubt, she speaks for many American workers who feel, as she does, that they have
jobs that are too small for their spirits.

Jobs are not big enough for people.
It's not just the assembly line worker whose job is too small for his spirit,
you know? A job like mine, if you really put your spirit into it, you would
sabotage immediately. You don't dare. So you absent your spirit from it.
My mind has been so divorced from my job, except as a source of income,
it's really absurd.

As I work in the business world, I am more and more shocked. You
throw yourself into things because you feel that important questions—
self-discipline, goals, a meaning of your life—are carried out in your *work*.
You invest a job with a lot of values that the society doesn't allow you to
put into a job. You find yourself like a pacemaker that's gone crazy or
something. You want it to be a million things that it's not and you want to
give it a million parts of yourself that nobody else wants there. So you end
up wrecking the curve or else settling down and conforming. I'm really in a
funny place right now. I'm so calm about what I'm doing and what's
coming . . .

> *She is twenty-eight. She is a staff writer for an institution*
> *publishing health care literature. Previously she had worked as an*
> *editor for a corporation publishing national magazines.*
> *She came from a small mountain town in western Pennsylvania.*
> *"My father was a preacher. I didn't like what he was doing, but it*
> *was his vocation. That was the good part of it. It wasn't just: go to*
> *work in the morning and punch a time clock. It was a profession of*
> **himself.** *I expected work to be like that. All my life, I planned to be*
> *a teacher. It wasn't until late in college, my senior year, that I*

realized what the public school system was like. A little town in the
mountains is one thing . . ."

I paper the walls of my office with posters and bring in flowers, bring in
an FM radio, bring down my favorite ceramic lamp. I'm the only person in
the whole damn building with a desk facing the window instead of the
door. I just turn myself around from all that I can. I ration my time so that
I'll spend two hours working for the Institution and the rest of the time I'll
browse. (Laughs.)

I function better if they leave me alone more. My boss will come in and
say, "I know you're overloaded, but would you mind getting this done, it's
urgent. I need it in three weeks." I can do it in two hours. So I put it on the
back burner and produce it on time. When I first went there, I came in early
and stayed late. I read everything I could on the subject at hand. I would
work a project to the wall and get it really done right, and then ask for
more. I found out I was wrecking the curve, I was out of line.

The people, just as capable as I and just as ready to produce, had realized
it was pointless, and had cut back. Everyone, consciously or unconsciously, was rationing his time. Playing cards at lunch time for three
hours, going sun bathing, or less obvious ways of blowing it. I realized:
Okay, the road to ruin is doing a good job. The amazing, absurd thing was
that once I decided to stop doing a good job, people recognized a kind of
authority in me. Now I'm just moving ahead like blazes.

I have my own office. I have a secretary. If I want a book case, I get a
book case. If I want a file, I get a file. If I want to stay home, I stay home. If I
want to go shopping, I go shopping. This is the first comfortable job I've
ever had in my life and it is absolutely despicable.

I've been a waitress and done secretarial work. I knew, in those cases, I
wasn't going to work at near capacity. It's one thing to work to your limits
as a waitress because you end up with a bad back. It's another thing to
work to your limits doing writing and editing because you end up with a
sharper mind. It's a joy. Here, of all places, where I had expected to put the
energy and enthusiasm and the gifts that I may have to work—it isn't
happening. They expect less than you can offer. Token labor. What writing
you do is writing to order. When I go for a job interview—I must leave this
place!—I say, "Sure, I can bring you samples, but the ones I'm proud of are
the ones the Institution never published."

It's so demeaning to be there and not be challenged. It's humiliation,
because I feel I'm being forced into doing something I would never do of
my own free will—which is simply waste itself. It's really not a Puritan
hang-up. It's not that I want to be persecuted. It's simply that I know I'm
vegetating and being paid to do exactly that. It's possible for me to sit here
and read my books. But then you walk out with no sense of satisfaction,
with no sense of legitimacy! I'm being had. Somebody has bought the right

to you for eight hours a day. The manner in which they use you is completely at their discretion. You know what I mean?

I feel like I'm being pimped for and it's not my style. The level of bitterness in this department is stunning. They take days off quite a bit. They don't show up. They don't even call in. They've adjusted a lot better than I have. They see the Institution as a free ride as long as it lasts. I don't want to be party to it, so I've gone my own way. It's like being on welfare. Not that that's a shameful thing. It's the surprise of this enforced idleness. It makes you feel not at home with yourself. I'm furious. It's a feeling that I will not be humiliated. I will not be dis-used.

For all that was bad about my father's vocation, he showed me it was possible to fuse your life to your work. His home was also his work. A parish is no different from an office, because it's the whole countryside. There's nothing I would enjoy more than a job that was so meaningful to me that I brought it home. . . .

I'm coming to a less moralistic attitude toward work. I know very few people who feel secure with their right just to be—or comfortable. Just you being you and me being me with my mini-talents may be enough. Maybe just making a career of being and finding out what that's about is enough. I don't think I have a calling—at this moment—except to be me. But nobody pays you for being you, so I'm at the Institution—for the moment. . . .

When you ask most people who they are, they define themselves by their jobs. "I'm a doctor." "I'm a radio announcer." "I'm a carpenter." If somebody asks me, I say, "I'm Nora Watson." At certain points in time I do things for a living. Right now I'm working for the Institution. But not for long. I'd be lying to you if I told you I wasn't scared.

I have a few options. Given the market, I'm going to take the best job I can find. I really tried to play the game by the rules, and I think it's a hundred percent unadulterated bullshit. So I'm not likely to go back downtown and say, "Here I am. I'm very good, hire me."

You recognize yourself as a marginal person. As a person who can give only minimal assent to anything that is going on in this society: "I'm glad the electricity works." That's about it. What you have to find is your own niche that will allow you to keep feeding and clothing and sheltering yourself without getting downtown. (Laughs.) Because that's death. That's really where death is.

» J. Patrick Wright «

Loyalty—Team Play— The System

» «

John Z. De Lorean was clearly on his way to becoming president of General Motors when he suddenly and unexpectedly resigned from the corporation. His story, as told to J. Patrick Wright, was published in On A Clear Day You Can See General Motors; *it not only documents De Lorean's reasons for quitting a $650,000-a-year job, but also offers a fascinating insider's view of the culture of G.M.'s "14th floor" executive suite. De Lorean says he quit because he believed that G.M.'s top managers were socially irresponsible, unconcerned with the welfare of employees, short-sighted, and too busy listening to each other to hear what American consumers wanted and needed in their cars. In this excerpt, De Lorean describes several highly amusing instances of "brown-nosing" among G.M.'s top brass. He claims that promotions at G.M. often came more as a reward for loyalty than for merit. Team play was stressed to such an extent that, were someone to suggest building a safe, nonpolluting, fuel-efficient car, he would have been accused of heresy.*

"Goddamnit! I served my time picking up my bosses at the airport. Now you guys are going to do this for me."

—Pete Estes to John De Lorean.

Choosing among executives for promotion is a difficult task at best, but one which is vital to the success of a business. If two people vying for the same job are equal in talent and performance, and one is a friend, I will most likely choose the friend. That's human nature. If the other, however, is obviously more accomplished than my friend, the job would go to him or her. The point is that merit always surpasses friendship in matters that pertain to business promotion. This was not always the case in General Motors. . . .

As I grew in General Motors it became apparent that objective criteria were not always used to evaluate an executive's performance. Many times the work record of a man who was promoted was far inferior to the records of others around him who were not promoted. It was quite obvious that something different than job performance was being used to rate these men.

That something different was a very subjective criterion which encom-

103

passed style, appearance, personality and, most importantly, personal loyalty to the man (or men) who was the promoter, and to the system which brought this all about. There were rules of this fraternity of management at GM. Those pledges willing to obey the rules were promoted. In the vernacular, they were the company's "team players." Those who didn't fit into the mold of a manager, who didn't adhere to the rules because they thought they were silly, generally weren't promoted. "He's not a team player," was the frequent, and many times only, objection to an executive in line for promotion. It didn't mean he was doing a poor job. It meant he didn't fit neatly into a stereotype of style, appearance and manner. He didn't display blind loyalty to the system of management, to the man or men doing the promoting. He rocked the boat. He took unpopular stands on products or policy which contradicted the prevailing attitude of top management.

At General Motors, good appearance meant conservative dress . . . Only blue or black suits were tolerated then [1956]. I remember thinking that was silly. But in those days I followed the rules closely.

Style and personality in the corporate mold mean simply that a GM executive is a low-profile executive. What is to be most memorable about the corporation today is the letters G and M, and not the people behind the letters. A General Motors man rarely says anything in public that adds the least bit of color or personality to those letters G and M. He identifies his success with the corporate success. And that success is measured in dollars earned per share. This system is best documented in its results. . . .

If your appearance, style and personality were consistent with the corporate stereotype, you were well on your way to being a "loyal" employee. But loyalty demanded more. It often demanded personal fealty, actual subservience to the boss. You learned loyalty as you learned the business. Loyalty was talked about openly. It was part of team play. Pete Estes often talked about the need for "loyalty to your boss." He demanded it. He got it.

My introduction to "loyalty" was as assistant chief engineer at Pontiac. The division was staging a "ride and drive" program in San Francisco. . . . There were about ten engineers in San Francisco for the four-day test.

I was showering in a motel near San Francisco International Airport the morning of the first day out there when the bathroom door flew open practically taking the hinges off in one jerk. I was shocked by the noise and I threw open the shower curtain and saw Estes who was chief engineer at Pontiac and my boss. The spitting image of Tennessee Ernie Ford, Estes was usually happy and pleasant. This time, however, he was red-faced and mad. "Why the hell wasn't someone out to meet me at the airport this morning? You knew I was coming, but nobody was there. Goddamnit, I served my time picking up my bosses at the airport. Now you guys are going to do this for me," he barked.

The thought had never even crossed my mind until then. I figured we were just supposed to get out to the West Coast on our own and be on time for the ride and drive session. I quickly became aware, however, that the pecking order at GM, as at many major U.S. companies, demanded that inferiors on the corporate ladder cater to their superiors. It was called "brown-nosing" a professor in college, KMAing (kiss-my-assing) when it was done by a supplier to a customer, and "loyalty" when it was done inside GM. As a rule, bosses were to be met at the airports by their charges. The bigger the boss at General Motors, the bigger the retinue waiting at the airport terminal. . . .

The greatest shows of force were reserved for the chairman of the board. On a trip he would often take several top executives with him, even if they had no worthwhile purpose in accompanying him. When he got to his destination, it would seem as if half of the area's GM employees were there to greet him—local sales managers of the car divisions, top plant people, chauffeurs. It was expected and demanded.

I discouraged the practice at Chevrolet. I often told our regional and zone office people that unless we had specific business to discuss, I would rather have them working on the job than meeting me at the airport. . . .

My personal feelings are that time spent traipsing after the boss is unproductive and wasteful of executive talent and ability. I didn't quarrel with the show of importance but rather with the system that made such fawning an essential part of the underling's job. It created an obvious servant-master relationship between the bossed and the boss. When the tally sheets were reviewed for promotions, as much credit was given to an executive's "form" as to his actual performance. It was like picking a suit of clothes because of its style without examining the quality of the cloth. In the end, the real corporation—the shareholders—suffered. . . .

The practice of fawning over the boss gave birth to all kinds of ridiculous practices. One was the use of a secret network in the corporation to find out the likes, dislikes and idiosyncrasies of the boss. The information was usually passed on from one secretary to another. It was used by underlings to please their superiors. Display their loyalty. . . .

This network of intelligence served up information which provided the most outlandish example of "loyalty" that I have ever heard of inside General Motors or out. And I heard it several times. It involved a Chevrolet sales official at a rather low level of management for this feat extraordinaire. It showed how deep in GM management the loyalty system ran.

In preparing for the sales official's trip to this particular city, the Chevrolet zone sales people learned from Detroit that the boss liked to have a refrigerator full of cold beer, sandwiches, and fruit, in his room to snack on at night before going to bed. They lined up a suite in one of the city's better hotels, rented a refrigerator and ordered the food and beer. However, the door to the suite was too small to accommodate the icebox. The hotel apparently nixed a plan to rip out the door and part of the adjoining wall. So the quick-thinking zone sales people hired a crane and operator, put them on the roof of the hotel, knocked out a set of windows in the suite, and lowered and shoved the refrigerator into the room through this gaping hole.

That night the Chevrolet executive wolfed down cold cut sandwiches, beer and fresh fruit, no doubt thinking, "What a great bunch of people we have in this zone." The next day he was off to another city and most likely another refrigerator, while back in the city of his departure the zone people were once again dismantling hotel windows and removing the refrigerator by crane. It was the most expensive midnight snack ever eaten by a GM executive.

While loyal employees attended the boss's personal needs with care and dispatch, they attended his corporate decisions with unwavering support, even if they thought the decisions were wrong. This was business loyalty. It not only capitalized on a natural inclination to support the man at the top. It made it mandatory.

This practice as I knew it flourished under Frederic G. Donner, who was chairman of the board of General Motors from 1958–1967. . . .

To Donner business came ahead of anything else. And business to him meant business his way. He would rarely tolerate views opposed to his. He refused to rediscuss previous decisions, even in the light of new information. "We already decided that!" he would snap. And that was the end of any attempt to reopen old business.

The Peter Principle: *In a Hierarchy Every Employee Tends to Rise to his Level of Incompetence.*

Work is accomplished by those employees who have not yet reached their level of incompetence.
—Dr. Laurence J. Peter and Raymond Hull, *The Peter Principle*

With such closed-mindedness at the top, a guiding precept of management soon developed. "Thou shalt not contradict the boss." Ideas in this kind of a system flowed from the top down, and not in the reverse direction. The man on top, whether he was a plant manager, department head or divisional general manager, was the final word. Each executive in turn supported the decisions of his boss right up the ladder. The chairman, of course, in this system had the final say on everything unless he parcelled out power to those around him. . . . The system stayed on even though Donner retired in 1967. . . .

This system quickly shut top management off from the real world because it surrounded itself in many cases with "yes" men. There soon became no real vehicle for adequate outside input. Lower executives, eager to please the boss and rise up the corporate ladder, worked hard to learn what he wanted or how he thought on a particular subject. They then either fed the boss exactly what he wanted to know, or they modified their own proposals to suit his preferences.

Original ideas were often sacrificed in deference to what the boss wanted. Committee meetings no longer were forums for open discourse, but rather either soliloquies by the top man, or conversations between a few top men with the rest of the meeting looking on. . . . When they did offer a comment, in many cases it was just to paraphrase what had already been said by one of the top guys.

Terrell was the master of the paraphrase, although he was by no means the only practitioner. He often parrotted the views of Chairman Gerstenberg with unabashed rapidity. So often did he do this that the practice became a joke. Divisional general managers and their staffs entertained each other over lunch with various impressions of Terrell paraphrasing Gerstenberg in an Administrative Committee meeting. The dialogue would go something like this:

> Gerstenberg: "Goddamnit. We cannot afford any new models next year because of the cost of this federally mandated equipment. There is no goddamn money left for styling changes. That's the biggest problem we face."
>
> Terrell, after waiting about 10 minutes: "Dick, goddamnit. We've just got to face up to the fact that our number one problem is the cost of this federally mandated equipment. This stuff costs so much that we just don't have any money left for styling our new cars. That's our biggest problem."
>
> Gerstenberg: "You're goddamn right, Dick. That's a good point."

It was humorous to witness and replay at lunch, but it was sad to realize that executives could build credibility in this way. . . .

Terrell was by no means alone. Many Fourteenth Floor executives operated in similar ways. What they did to the Donners, Roches, Gerstenbergs, and Coles of the corporation, the divisional general managers often did to them. Simply regurgitated to the boss his own ideas. These lower managers were identified as the young turks of the corporation. They were loyal employees. They knew exactly where the power resided at the top. They were more than willing to play up to that power and rise in the company in the process. When the boss said "jump," they never asked "why," only "how high."

A system which puts emphasis on form, style and unwavering support for the decisions of the boss, almost always loses its perspective about an executive's business competence. Even if the man in power is a competent businessman, but adheres to the system, the chances of his successors' being equally competent are reduced because they are graded not on how they perform as businessmen but on how they perform as system-men. Once they get into power, they don't tamper with the system which promoted them. So a built-in method of perpetuating an imperfect management system is established. This is what I feel has happened at General Motors. . . .

Not only is the system perpetuating itself, but in the act of perpetuating itself the system has fostered several destructive practices which are harmful to executive morale. They developed from the psychological need, as I see it, of less competent managers to affirm in their own minds a logical right to their positions, even though the basis for their promotions was illogical by any business-performance standard. Once in a position of power, a manager who was promoted by the system is insecure because, consciously or not, he knows that it was something other than his ability to manage and his knowledge of the business that put him in his position. . .

Donner, as chairman, wanted to affirm for all that he was the boss. He went about this through a system of calculated promotions of "loyal" employees and management by intimidation.

From him developed what I call "promotion of the unobvious choice." This means promoting someone who was not regarded as a contender for the post. Doing so not only puts "your man" in position, but it earns for you his undying loyalty because he owes his corporate life to you. The "unobvious choice" is a devoted follower of the system who has nothing noteworthy in his background to mark him as a promotable executive. He often is surrounded by team players who are more qualified for the promotion. . . .

There were and are men in positions of power at GM who do not know the business they are running. Many were not good businessmen in the areas with which they are familiar. "Promotion of the unobvious choice" has put some of them into their positions. Others simply played the loyalty system game so well they just moved up the corporate ladder every few years. What developed in some cases is "management by crony" . . .

Insecure, an executive often resorts to defense mechanisms to affirm psychologically his position. Intimidation is a favorite tool, and once again the art of management by intimidation as I know it at GM began with Frederic Donner. He was the master intimidator and often reverted to gimmicks to show his power.

One time in an Administrative Committee meeting he asked the head of GM Truck & Coach Division:

"How many buses did you build last month?"

The executive replied: "Approximately three thousand" or a rounded figure like that. It was an approximation.

Donner scowled and snapped back something like: "Last month you built three thousand, one hundred and eighty-seven vehicles." Whatever the figure was, it was precise.

It was obvious to most of us in the meeting that Donner had just looked it up since the precise figure wasn't all that important. But the fact that he would rattle off the exact production figure in such an authoritarian, arro-

108

gant manner told us just one thing, that Donner was trying to make the point, "Look how I know this goddamn business, people! Look what a mind I have!"

The Donner memory game is not new to GM or American business. But it is a management cheap shot. . . .

Donner had his corporate imitators. Roger Kyes learned the art of intimidation at the master's knee. . . .

Kyes, to my way of thinking, was the consummate corporate bully. A man unfortunately given frighteningly bad looks, he used his features to his advantage. He once referred to himself as "one mean, ugly sonofabitch." At six-feet four, he was an imposing figure of a man with a harsh and foggy voice and penetrating look that made executives wilt.

He was a hatchet man in the corporation and relished the job just as he relished a similar duty while he was assistant secretary of defense in the Eisenhower Administration. . . . One of his duties was to tell has-been executives that they were going to take early retirement. He bullied more than a couple of men into taking early retirement. If one rebelled, he'd gather a case against the executive, break the results to him and then give him the option of being fired or taking early retirement. . . . In some of these cases, it was publicly announced that this or that executive was taking early retirement for health reasons. The word around the corporation was, "When Kyes tells you that you're sick, you're sick."

He threatened me with firing often when I ran Pontiac and Chevrolet. The threats were made in private when he objected to something I did which wasn't the way he wanted it done. One time, though, he threatened me in public, and I fought back.

All the divisions were ordered to cut back on personnel. We were given specific areas in which to cut back. Included in my order was the dismissal of a handful of test drivers for Chevrolet Engineering at the GM Tech Center. It seemed like a ridiculous directive because we would still have to have the testing done. But we would have to go outside of the company to get it done and end up spending a helluva lot more money. So I practiced that old corporate trick of foot dragging. I didn't fire the drivers. A review of the cutback program was being conducted at an Administrative Committee meeting. I was asked about the dismissal of the test drivers and answered something innocuous like: "I'm working on it."

Suddenly Kyes boomed back: "If you can't fire those goddamn guys, then we will get somebody who can. If you can't do it, you don't know how the hell to do your job."

The words stung like arrowheads. I was thoroughly embarrassed at the dressing down in front of my superiors and peers. I was livid and started to yell back at him but stopped short and held my peace. After the meeting . . . I stormed down the hall into Kyes' office.

"You sonofabitch! If you embarrass me with a tirade like that again, I'll knock you on your ass. Right in front of everybody."

He turned white and rattled off something about wanting to impress me with the importance of his orders. That was the end of it. He never confronted me in such a manner again in public. But his craggy visage haunted me until he retired from GM in 1971. Sadly for Kyes, his usefulness to the company waned in his last couple of years. He was taken out of active management at the age of 63 and made an assistant to the president until age 64 when he ironically took an early retirement. It may have been a case of Roger Kyes telling Roger Kyes he was sick. He died a year later.

I use Roger Kyes as an example not to desecrate his memory but rather to point out the adverse influence he had on my career at General Motors. He embodied many facets of a man made by the GM system. He was a team player. Loyal to his superiors and the system—to a fault.

» David W. Ewing «

Freedom Inside the Organization

» «

It is a curious fact that the rights guaranteed in the U.S. Constitution extend to every aspect of our lives but one: our jobs. Paradoxically, such basic freedoms as speech, assembly, due process, and other rights are not guaranteed in the workplace. David Ewing, an executive editor of the Harvard Business Review, *argues that many companies have little respect for free expression, conscience, privacy, or other civil liberties of employees. Employees are expected to be loyal, regardless of the legal or ethical implications of their actions. Ewing argues that it is time for a bill of rights for the workplace. Constitutionalism on the job would erase the contradiction of freedom in the community and totalitarianism at work.*

For nearly two centuries Americans have enjoyed freedom of press, speech, and assembly, due process of law, privacy, freedom of conscience, and other important rights—in their homes, churches, political forums, and social and cultural life. But Americans have not enjoyed these civil liberties in most companies, government agencies, and other organizations where they work. Once a U.S. citizen steps through the plant or office door at 9 A.M., he or she is nearly rightless until 5 P.M., Monday through Friday. The employee continues to have political freedoms, of course, but these are not the significant ones now. While at work, the important relationships are with bosses, associates, and subordinates. Inequalities in dealing with these people are what really count for an employee.

To this generalization there are important exceptions. In some organizations, generous managements have seen fit to assure free speech, privacy, due process, and other concerns as privileges. But there is no guarantee the privileges will survive the next change of chief executive. As former Attorney General Ramsey Clark once said in a speech, "A right is not what

111

A right — not something someone gives to you; it's what no one can take from you.

someone gives you; it's what no one can take from you." Defined in this manner, rights are rare in business and public organizations.

Rightlessness is most conspicuous for employees who do not belong to unions—for most engineers, scientists, technicians, accountants, sales people, secretaries, managers, administrative assistants, and people in related categories. These nonunionized employees make up the great majority of nongovernment workers—about 50 million of the 72 million total . . . .

Union members are not much better off, as a rule. [There are] some significant exceptions, where union Robin Hoods bounded to the aid of employees penalized for speaking out or resisting an unethical directive. But in general the unions seem to have been far more interested in the material conditions of work life—pay, hours, safety, cleanliness, seniority—than in civil liberties. In fact, these powerful bureaucracies seem to be not much different from the corporate organizations they joust with, as far as employee rights are concerned.

What about government? Here there is a little more light but not much. A series of federal court decisions beginning in 1968 appears to have removed the gag from many public employees, but as yet few civil servants have paid much attention to these decisions on speech, or even know about them. As for such other rights as privacy, due process, and conscience, government employees are in the same ghetto as corporate employees . . . .

What about other types of organizations, such as colleges and universities, professional firms, research agencies, and health organizations? In general, they seem to follow the same practices as business and government. In a few progressive organizations privileges are enjoyed—the autocracy is benevolent. But the organization is still an autocracy.

In effect, therefore, U.S. society is a paradox. The Constitution and Bill of Rights light up the sky over political campaigners, legislators, civic leaders, families, church people, and artists. But not so over employees. The employee sector of our civil liberties universe is more like a black hole, with rights so compacted, so imploded by the gravitational forces of legal tradition, that, like the giant black stars in the physical universe, light can scarcely escape.

Perhaps the most ironic thing is that only in recent years have Americans made many noises about this paradox. It is as if we took it for granted and assumed there was no alternative. . . .

To put the situation in focus, let us make a brief review of rights in the workplace.

Speech In many private and public organizations there is a well-oiled machinery for providing relief to an employee who is discharged because of his or her race, religion, or sex. But we have no mechanisms for granting similar relief to an employee who is discharged for exercising the right of

112

free speech. The law states that all employers "may dismiss their employees at will . . . for good cause, for no cause, or even for cause morally wrong, without being thereby guilty of legal wrong."

[handwritten margin note: no free speech at work.]

Of course, discharge is only the extreme weapon; many steps short of discharge may work well enough—loss of a raise in pay, demotion, assignment to the boondocks, or perhaps simply a cutback of normal and expected benefits. . . .

So well-established is the idea that any criticism of the company is "ratting" or "finking" that some companies hang out written prohibitions for all to see. . . .

Except for organizations where there are union newspapers and journals, there is no freedom of press in American organizations. In the corporate earth, here and there an underground press survives. . . . [But] the circulation of underground journals has been low, their publication frequency sporadic, and their editorial quality seedy. . . .

Conscientious Objection   There is very little protection in industry for employees who object to carrying out immoral, unethical, or illegal orders from their superiors. If the employee doesn't like what he or she is asked to do, the remedy is to pack up and leave. . . . [But] resignation may mean having to uproot one's family and move to a strange city in another state. Or it may mean, for an employee in the semifinals of a career, or for an employee with a specialized competence, not being able to find another suitable job anywhere.

In 1970 Shirley Zinman served as a secretary in a Philadelphia employment agency called LIB Services. One day she was instructed by her bosses to record all telephone conversations she might have with prospective clients. This was to be done for "training purposes," she was told, although the callers were not to be told that their words were being taped. The office manager would monitor the conversations on an extension in her office. Ms. Zinman refused to play along with this game, not only because it was unethical, in her view, but illegal as well—the telephone company's regulations forbade such unannounced telephone recordings.

Congress shall make no law . . . abridging the freedom of speech or of the press, or the right of the people peaceably to assemble, and to petition the government for a redress of grievances.

—First Amendment to the Constitution of the United States

So Ms. Zinman had to resign. She sought unemployment compensation. The state unemployment pay board refused her application. It reasoned that her resignation was not "compelling and necessitous." With the help of attorneys from the American Civil Liberties Union, she appealed her case to the Pennsylvania Commonwealth Court. In a ruling hailed by civil rights leaders, the court in 1973 reversed the pay board and held that Ms. Zinman was entitled to unemployment compensation because her objection to the unethical directive was indeed a "compelling" reason to quit her job.

What this interesting case leaves unsaid is as important as what it does say: Resignation continues to be the accepted response for the objecting employee . . . . Within the organization itself, an employee is expected to sit at the feet of the boss's conscience.

Security and Privacy When employees are in their homes, before and after working hours, they enjoy well-established rights to privacy and to protection from arbitrary search and seizure of their papers and possessions. But no such rights protect them in the average company, government agency, or other organization; their superiors need only the flimsiest pretext to search their lockers, desks, and files. The boss can rummage through an employee's letters, memoranda, and tapes looking for evidence that (let us say) he or she is about to "rat" on the company. . . .

It doesn't matter that employees may be right about the facts, or that it may be the superiors, not the employees, who are disloyal to the stockholders. In one of his verses for "The Watergate Mother Goose," published in the *Chicago Tribune*, Bob Cromie expressed the management rationale as follows:

> I do not like thee, Dr. Fell,
> But why this is I cannot tell;
> Meanwhile, to erase those smiles,
> We plan to rummage thru your files.

Choice of Outside Activities and Associations In practice, most business employees enjoy no right to work after hours for the political, social, and community organizations of their choice. To be sure, in many companies an enlightened management will encourage as much diversity of choice in outside activities as employees can make. As noted earlier, however, this is an indulgence which can disappear any time, for most states do not mandate such rights, and even in those that do, the rights are poorly protected. . . .

Ironically, however, a company cannot discriminate against people whose politics it dislikes when it *hires* them. It has to wait a few days before it can exercise its prerogatives.

In the federal government, freedom of choice of outside activities seems to be well recognized.

Due Process "Accidents will occur in the best-regulated families," said Mr. Micawber in *David Copperfield*. Similarly, accidents of administration occur even in the best-managed companies, with neurotic, inept, or distracted supervisors inflicting needless harm on subordinates. Many a subordinate who goes to such a boss to protest would be well-advised to keep one foot in the stirrups, for he is likely to be shown to the open country for his efforts.

This generalization does not hold for civil service employees in the federal government, who can resort to a grievance process. Nor does it hold for unionized companies, which also have grievance procedures. But it holds for *most* other organizations . . . .

The absence of a right to due process is especially painful because it is the second element of constitutionalism in organizations. . . . Employee constitutionalism consists of a set of clearly defined rights, and a means of protecting employees from discharge, demotion, or other penalities imposed when they assert their rights. . . .

Autocracy—Rare, Medium, or Well Done?

Although many corporations and public agencies could be despotic if they chose to be, they are not. No law compels the managements to provide a fair and equitable environment, but many do that anyway, for reasons of their own. . . .

Nonetheless, observation suggests that numerous employers have little respect for free expression, conscience, privacy, and other civil rights of employees. In many organizations the dominant reality is "management by fear." For all practical purposes, employees are required to be as obedient to their superiors, regardless of ethical and legal considerations, as are workers in totalitarian countries. An employee who is victimized by a boss is free only to take a cue from Shakespeare and "trouble deaf Heaven with my bootless cries." . . .

Without minimizing the great and solid gains achieved by the unions, equal employment opportunity officials, occupational safety officials, and enlightened managements, let there be no doubt that much goes on which violates the average American's sense of justice and fair play. The only question is whether such violations characterize 40 percent, 60 percent, or some other proportion of organization life.

This conclusion stands even if generous allowances are made for the exigencies of efficient work and production. No realist will argue that companies, government bureaus, and other public agencies should be run democratically. There must be discipline. There must be control. There must be scope for quick and arbitrary judgments by decision makers. Otherwise there can be no efficiency, there can be little employee satisfaction with a job well done, and the impact on the cost of goods and services would be staggering. . . .

In drawing the line in an organization, it is necessary to do the same thing we do in judging what is fair in community and political life; that is, try to put conflicting desires and interests in some sort of creative balance.

The prospects and consequences of employee constitutionalism depend on how we understand a series of issues that are open to debate:

1. *Can important new employee rights be justified legally and socially?* Working conditions in industry, government, education, and other fields are good in the United States. The common law, which is the foundation of employer prerogatives, has been built on centuries of experience. Moreover, there has been a long-term tendency toward improvement. Therefore, would we do better to leave well enough alone?

2. *Can employee rights be justified economically—are they too costly?* Productivity in the business sector is high; in public organizations it may not be so high, but it still compares favorably with that in the rest of the world. Conceivably, constitutionalism could endanger the efficiency of organizations. To be realistic, what can we learn from the experience of organizations that have recognized one form or another of employee rights?

3. *If new rights are justified, what rights?* We might settle just for a few more rights in specific areas, such as protection for the employee who reports a violation in safety standards, as provided under Occupational Safety and Health Administration legislation. Or we might simply establish minimum rights for certain types of employees—for example, outlawing industry-wide "blacklisting" of a chemist or engineer who has resigned or been fired. At the other extreme, we might seek to establish the right to criticize publicly any and all decisions made by management; we might support an elaborate and formal process of review for all grievances; we might urge sweeping guarantees of privacy on the premises; and so on.

These are the possibilities. What should we try to achieve?

4. *How are employee rights to be enforced?* The whole concern with rights is meaningless if there are no realistic, practical ways of enforcing them. Some observers feel that the movement might founder on this question, for there are numerous subtle ways that an employer can retaliate against a dissident employee—ways that are most difficult to anticipate in legislation or prove in court with "hard" evidence.

Some possible methods of enforcement have already been used in a few organizations. Would they work on a larger scale? Other possibilities are judge-inspired changes in the common law, with courts providing remedies for penalized employees. Still other possibilities are anticipated in legislation already proposed. Might some of these approaches have practical value?

* * *

What Action Is Needed?

What can companies, government agencies, universities, and other organizations do to make constitutionalism—that is, a bill of rights plus adequate means of enforcement—a reality in the workplace?

On their own initiative, without any official prods and threats from outside, they can create bills of rights for their employees. They can set up mechanisms for enforcement such as . . . informal courts, arbitration, ombudspeople, employee boards, "hot lines," and other devices already tested and proved by one leading organization or another. . . .

If enough companies and agencies voluntarily take strong steps in this direction, the need will be met with a minimum of legislative and legal bloodshed. Let us hope they do. But the *if* is a big one, and so we must consider other kinds of actions as well.

The state and federal courts can stand the common-law rules of employee rightlessness on their head. . . . There now may be a strong possibility that the state courts or the federal courts, or perhaps both, will make major new decisions in favor of employee speech, conscience, privacy, due process, and other needed rights. . . .

But we must not hope for too much from any court system. Judges cannot legislate; they can only decide one question at a time, and even then only when an employee can get enough help from the American Civil Liberties Union, a trade union, friends, or some other source to fight his case from bench to bench. . . .

Another route to constitutionalism might be for state legislatures to pass laws upholding employee rights, perhaps even requiring companies incorporated in the state to enact bills of rights. It is not too much to hope that some states will move in this way . . . some already have done so in connection with employee rights to buy products and with wiretapping.

Even clear statements of public policy by state legislatures, with no attempt actually to control behavior in organizations, could be significant. For instance, the legislators might declare that it is in the public interest for employees to be able to speak out with impunity about illegal actions being taken by their organizations, to engage in outside activities of their choice, and/or to have certain basic rights of privacy. Such statements would give many a state court the basis to justify broadening employee rights in judicial interpretations. . . .

There are several forceful measures that the U.S. Congress could take to further the employee rights movement. . . . If [Congress] goes all the way and legislates bills of rights for employees in federal agencies, the results would be significant. . . . If these more than a million employees became entitled to constitutionalism, the country would be well on its way.

As for employees of most large companies, Congress could put them under the umbrella of constitutionalism by enacting new statutes. Also . . . Congress could introduce federal chartering of corporations. In order to obtain a federal charter entitling it to engage in interstate commerce or take government contracts, a corporation could be required to enact a bill of rights for its employees and institute suitable means of enforcing the rights.

What about a constitutional amendment? This is the most ambitious proposal. . . . Employee rights would be a particularly fitting subject for a constitutional amendment since they represent a fresh extension of principles in the Bill of Rights. . . .

Because the constitutional road is so direct and visible, it is likely to catalyze opposition more than any other approach would. But it is also the fairest way to achieve employee rights, and in the end it may prove the most satisfactory for all concerned.

People Versus Their Organizations

American institutions everywhere are getting low marks from the public for credibility and performance. These poor ratings appear in survey after survey. Curiously, organizations have come to be seen as something apart from the people who staff them. Those who work in business, government, and the professions do not denigrate themselves. But organizations have become "they," and individuals have become "we," and so it has become possible to berate private and public organizations as if they were lives unto themselves—Species O . . .

Why has a division developed between "we" the people and "they" our organizations? Many good explanations might be advanced, and the one offered here is only one, but it is significant. We have seen that a serious value conflict exists between organizational life and private life. From kindergarten through high school, from boy scouts and girl scouts to senior citizens groups, from church meetings to town meetings, we are taught respect for discipline and hard work, yes, but also esteem for individual choice, privacy, the expression of conscience, variety of viewpoint. Liberty is part of the American way, we tell ourselves, and, as James Bryant Conant once said, "Liberty like charity must begin at home."

But when we report to work at the average company, public agency, or large professional firm, we find a big exception. As employees we are now supposed to forget some of the values emphasized at home and in school. We are supposed to leave those esteemed rights outside, like cars in the parking lot. We are supposed to concentrate on discipline and to specialize in know-how, as if such needs could not mix with personal rights. . . .

By "Americanizing" our organizations we may produce no magic increases in productivity and performance, though the experience of the few rights-leading companies suggests that gains will indeed be made. But by erasing a subtle division in our culture which makes us rights-holders at home and in the community but puppets in the plant and office, we could reduce an important cause of ambivalence in our outlook. We could become more whole. The American genius has been to seek to bring the halves together—property-holders and non-property-holders, immigrants and native born, North and South, black and white, male and female, liberals and conservatives. Whenever the effort succeeded, the country as a whole succeeded. It is time to begin erasing the division that afflicts some 85 million people and their families—totalitarianism at work versus freedom in the community.

value conflicts vs
O – values
people's values

》 Jacques Barzun 《

The Professions Under Siege

》《

Jacques Barzun is Professor Emeritus at Columbia University, where his has long been one of the clearest voices regarding the role of the humanities in everyday life. In this selection, he argues that the public has turned suspicious, even hostile, toward the once venerated professions. Doctors, lawyers, scientists, academics, and accountants have suffered a rash of charges of dishonesty, incompetence, and malpractice. For example, seeking "a second opinion" is no longer viewed as disrespectful of one's doctor. Lawyers are blamed for the litigiousness (and inefficiency) of society. Students sue teachers for failing to have taught them to read and write. Part of the problem is a general distrust of authority in an egalitarian society. Another part of the problem has been the tendency of some professionals to view their work not as "a calling" but just as a job like any other. At the same time, almost every occupation from cosmetologist to nutritionist has been transmuted into a "profession." For a variety of reasons, then, the prestige and authority of the once sacred vocations have been profaned.

Something new has happened when the heads of two of the three branches of our government publicly attack two of the leading professions. The President [Carter] has called down the lawyers and the doctors in turn; the Chief Justice has twice criticized the men of law. But the feelings behind these acts of censure are not new; they have agitated the public and the press for a decade or more, and it is evident to all that the learned professions are not the splendid companies, held in awe and respect, that they once were.

The doctors, formerly worshiped as omniscient Good Samaritans, are now seen as profiteers, often of doubtful competence. Lawyers have never been popular, but they did seem the defenders of private and civil rights in time of need. Now they are thought neglectful and extortionate, when not actually dishonest. The poor academics, who won sudden prestige in the war years because they knew so much about so much that was useful, lost it all by their fecklessness in the troubles of 1965–68. As for the scientists, demigods since Darwin, they became objects of suspicion after Hiroshima. Their work was amoral; they dabbled in either treason or warmongering, and in any case their view of the universe was probably at the root of the modern malaise. Latest on the carpet, the austere, unfathomable accountant is being shown up as a master of misrepresentation, a cordon bleu at cooking the books. With his fall, the idea of "the professional man" is near to being swallowed up in contempt. For if the engineers seem to escape, it is because the public never sees them.

This comprehensive resentment against the visible professions does not spring wholly from experience, though facts at second hand or in print are not lacking. Part of the animus comes from the general unrest and impatience with authority in the Western world, coupled with the belief that anything long established is probably corrupt.

But to judge a profession rightly is not easy at a distance, and indignation on some immediate ground usually lacks perspective. For example, the medical profession has been under especially heavy fire; clearly, one reason is its formerly undisputed preeminence: The disillusion is proportionate. Until lately, doctors in this country were revered as in an earlier day only the clergy could hope to be. The physician simply displaced the clergyman when Western man shifted his allegiance from religion to science and technology and when medicine could show that it, too, was scientific. Such facts tell us something about the status of any profession; it goes up and down like the stock market, in response to things other than net worth.

Vulnerable Institutions

More than a century ago, Oliver Wendell Holmes—the great Holmes, father of the Justice, and a remarkably original physician—noticed this effect of culture on medical practices themselves: "The truth is that medicine, professedly founded on observation, is as sensitive to outside influences, political, religious, philosophical, imaginative, as is the barometer to the changes of atmospheric density." This conditioning is ignored, usually, both by those inside a profession and by those outside.

A profession is an institution, and as such it cuts a figure in public that may or may not match the prevailing habits and merits of the practitioners. The insiders genuinely believe in that figure; they live by it in more ways than one, and they can hardly help thinking of The Profession as going on forever in the same glorious way, altering itself only as it improves performance by new skill. Then, suddenly, it comes to grief through the outsiders' dissatisfaction, expressed in various unpleasant ways. Physicians have seen their brethren buffeted by malpractice suits, charged and convicted of fraud in handling federal and local health moneys; accused of mismanaging hospitals and clinics both medically and financially. With the mistrust has come the belief that doctors care only for money and make too much; that they cover up one another's homicidal mistakes; and that their

120

lobbying as a closed corporation is holding back the advent of a much improved national health.

The parallel grievances about lawyers include, besides exorbitant fees, total disregard of the interests of society, mutual protection through the bar associations' connivance at error and fraud, and calculated deception of the public through the use of purposely mystifying language.

As for teachers in school and college, the grumbling is still diffuse, in part because the work they do or bungle is not observable case by case and is not paid for directly. Academic incompetence, indifference, misdirection of effort may be known or suspected, as they widely are today, but clear-cut instances of malpractice are hard to prove, and so far the few lawsuits against schools generally have failed.

The rights and wrongs of the charges will continue to be argued—as they should be—but what is of greater moment to the nation is the present state of disaffection from what used to be considered not only the best brains in the country, but also the most dedicated and self-sacrificing. . . .

Long ago, Bernard Shaw . . . charged, "Every profession . . . is a conspiracy against the laity." The epigram should not be dismissed as a joke or a needless exaggeration. The only overemphasis is in the word *conspiracy*, which implies a secret purpose to overreach the public. Yet it is that very imputation of making the most of closely held secrets that becomes the common man's idea of a profession when it begins to lose the public's faith and regard. And there lies the danger. For the obvious next idea that occurs to the aroused critics is to demand strong supervision from outside. . . .

To go in pain or anxiety and ask for expert help with a bludgeon up one's sleeve has something so topsy-turvy about it that the scene would be high comedy if issues of life and well-being were not involved. Better relations between layman and professional than we now seem to enjoy can hardly be brought about in mutual suspicion and hostility. Nor can there be improvement through collective bargaining. The essence of those relations is individual, from which it follows that some clearer idea of what a profession is must once again become common property among insiders and outsiders both.

Physician, heal thyself.

—New Testament

According to Dr. Abraham Flexner, the famous critic and reformer of medical education fifty years ago, to be medically trained implies "the possession of certain portions of many sciences arranged and organized with a distinct practical purpose in view. That is what makes it a 'profession.' " The key words here are: "a distinct practical purpose in view," for which "special training is required." Since the laity, by definition, has no such purposes and lacks special training, a profession is necessarily a

121

monopoly. In modern societies this monopoly is made legal by a license to practice; but the professions have always managed to form a guild, a trade union, claiming the exclusive right to practice the art. . . . But between monopoly and conspiracy the line of demarcation is hard to fix and easy to step over.

The upshot is that a profession is by nature a vulnerable institution. It makes claims; it demands unique privileges; and it has to perform. But "it" of course does not exist as a single entity; it is a dozen or a few hundred or many thousands of individuals, who differ as widely as all other human beings, yet who, as professionals, are expected to act in a standard manner and to be invariably successful in their art. At this point one might conclude that a profession was not merely vulnerable but naturally unstable, a scheme beyond human strength to live up to.

Nonetheless, professionals of all kinds have existed for thousands of years, and it is this apparent continuity that gives them the illusion of immortality. What every professional should bear in mind is the distinction between a profession and a function. The function may well be eternal; but the profession, which is the cluster of practices and relationships arising from the function at a given time and place, can be destroyed—or can destroy itself—very rapidly. The priest-physician is gone, like the priest-astrologer—two plausible combinations of roles. The town crier has disappeared. The broadcaster of news and advertising carries out the same function in a totally different form. . . .

Even the professions that look ancient and continuous have radically changed, and not solely in the materials of their respective arts. . . .

These changes, both external and intrinsic, are linked to the influences that Oliver Wendell Holmes listed, and it would seem reasonable that in a time of public suspicion and outcry, the many professions would examine themselves in the light of these influences—political, social, religious, and philosophical. This should be done not just through the associations' committees, which are likely to deal in whitewash, but individually and silently, which is the only way to reawaken a sense of fact narcotized by habit.

To do so with honesty and lucidity, it is important to look back through time to the professional life as such, and to begin by saying that the ancestral jokes that ridicule the stereotypes of each calling can be disregarded: the clergyman is holier-than-thou and hypocritical; the professor is dry-as-dust and lives in an ivory tower—lucky man!; the lawyer thrives on complicating simple things and drags out the case to swallow up the estate in costs. These clichés go back thousands of years. . . .

Complaints only express the public's desire for workmanship and accountability; and obviously, the more advanced the profession, the less the public can judge of either.

But, however stupidly put, these demands by the laity should remind all professionals of the permanent clash of cross-purposes between even the best practitioner and his customer. In teaching, the professor's tendency is to expound the truth in all the particulars of interest to him. The student wants to be interested in another sense, besides learning what will get him past the examination and certified for his line of work. In the law, it is true, both client and advocate want to win, but the lawyer is trained to exercise caution amid confusion and often takes pleasure in a nice point of law. Both attitudes then seem to the client a pretext for additional expense of time and money. In medicine also, the case may claim the physician's absorption in the disease rather than in the patient, who will judge his comfort neglected or even his life endangered for the sake, presumably, of medicine in the abstract.

The Rule of Diversity

This tension of opposites is inevitable; its ever-present reality should be a constant warning to the professional. It is his duty to reduce the difference as far as possible, and in any case not imagine that the human being he is serving ought to be grateful for whatever he gets. . . . The profession does not exist for itself, as a game, or as a field of free, uncommitted activity, such as pure science, philosophy, art, or mathematics.

Three faces wears the doctor: when first sought
An angel's; and a god's cure half-wrought;
But when, the cure complete, he seeks his fee,
The devil looks less terrible than he.

—Anon.

In this regard, a rereading of Molière's comedies about doctors and other professionals yields a healthy lesson. The plays show how, in order to daunt the patient, the doctors of the time dressed in black robes and pointed hats and talked a barbarous Latin, in which they argued whether the patient was suffering or dying according to the rules of the faculty. The treatment that followed was an automatic routine. From other sources we learn that in Molière's day there were about 100 doctors in Paris and only four new ones admitted each year." . . .

All this, no doubt, sounds remote from present-day practice, but in times of troubles one can profit from parallels. Traits connected with monopoly practice recur in altered guise. More than one modern specialist has in effect asked a patient: "Have you got *my* disease?"—which is not far from the Molière model of making the customer fit the rules. As for automatic treatment, what of the temptation to prescribe the current antibiotic, formerly the sulfa drugs? The present complaint that surgery is resorted to too readily and too often needlessly again suggests treatment without forethought. . . .

In these and other ways, the professions exhibit their fatal tendency toward routine. Routine relieves the mind of the effort of thought, and it is

123

protected by the secret and the monopoly of the art. . . .

Today, diversity is the rule among physicians and other professionals. Their training, work arrangements, and reserves of mental and ethical strength vary widely. The tendency of an egalitarian age to turn every occupation into a profession has complicated the substance of ethics. What is right or wrong for a journalist, a marriage counselor, an optometrist—all now under distrustful scrutiny? Like their elder guilds, these new mysteries get little support from outside their numbers. Especially in cities, the public cannot readily tell the competent from the incompetent; there is no local opinion, and the mutual judgment of laity and professionals that used to be exercised easily within a small community is a thing of the past. The professional does not know how the client lives, whether he is honest and conscientious, and what he can understand. This information has relevance beyond the single case, for in the present outcry against the professions one must not forget the repeated proofs that the public, too, can be charged with corruption: shoplifting, bilking, padding accounts, cheating employers or examiners or the government are no longer specialties in the hands of dedicated crooks; they have become ecumenical avocations. And equally important—as is true of the high-school graduate claiming entrance to college—words, titles, grades, symbols, and diplomas no longer mean what they say.

This confusion, moreover, is occurring at a moment when the nation wants a huge supply of first-class services evenly distributed. Leaving aside the question of costs, there is little chance that the requisite number of able and devoted professionals can be found. Here again we must stop and think what a profession *as institution* is for. It is to turn people who are *not* born teachers, born builders, born advocates, or born healers into a good imitation of the real thing. Easier said than done. . . . It is not true that with increasing numbers of people you get a proportional number of every sort of talent. Many other opportunities disperse and absorb that talent; and even apart from this fact, the supply is unpredictable. The country cannot say that now it has four times as many writers of the first rank as it had 100 years ago.

Criticism from Without and Within

As a whole, every profession is always horribly average, mediocre. By definition it cannot be anything else. But the public expectation aims much higher than mediocrity, so that in a time of reckoning, when the laity is hot about its rights, general dismay and recrimination are inevitable. What is more, although any art should be judged by its best results, a democratic nation, bent on equality in all things, is sure to judge a profession by its worst exemplars. That is the condition we are in now.

Consider the malpractice suits. From one point of view it is just that a patient—or his heirs—should recover damages for careless or ignorant treatment. From another point of view it is absurd that after the best professional efforts failure should be a cause of complaint. Yet a customer cannot tell whether he has had the best. He always judges by gross results—kill or cure—and wants the reasons plain. On such points the public intelligence is weak. Certain groups have voiced demands that show they expect from the professions nothing less than divination and infallibility. . . .

The subtleties of the predicament are even clearer in education, where the failure to "educate" a particular student is evident in the student, yet assigning blame is beyond human wit. Nor can our modern system follow the example of the old-time college president who said to the indignant parent: "Madam, we guarantee results—or we return the boy."

It is because of these intricacies behind the gross results—a cure, a good education, winning the lawsuit—that for centuries it has seemed best to let the professions police themselves. The assumption is that inside the shop merit and demerit are correctly judged. That is by and large true. . . .

Through their own routines, [government] regulatory agencies lag behind the facts. They also protect featherbedding, prevent innovation, and give inspectors a power that may invite and spread corruption.

But this generally true verdict is incomplete. The regulation of business came about because business did not regulate itself. It exploited labor and the buyer, under the motto "The public be damned." An alert professional today has the uneasy feeling that the professions are at the juncture where the same motto, unspoken on their part, is being imputed to them by a public ready to clamor for regulation.

There are other signs of a gradual demoting of the professions to the level of ordinary trades and businesses. The right of lawyers and physicans to advertise, so as to reintroduce money competition and break down the "standard practices," is being granted. Architects are being allowed to act as contractors. Teachers have been unionized. Laymen demand the right to sit on various professional bodies, on boards of trustees, and wherever "community representation" may be argued for, on the ground that internal management is unable to serve the public fairly without supervision. The great force of government money works to the same end, for bureaucracy follows the funds and while directing their use is bound to control the user. And where government does not intrude, unionism will.

Such moves, whether viewed as threats or as reforms, signify one thing: the modern professions have enjoyed their monopoly for so long that they have forgotten that it is a privilege given in exchange for a public benefit. . . .

Forgetting the great principle of reciprocity will ruin any profession. The scientists felt a touch of the menace when they too loudly claimed complete autonomy from social judgment. Nor can the workaday professions be saved when only a faithful remnant performs well and behaves ethically. An institution exists for use, not to be an object of wonder.

It may be, of course, that we are witnessing the evolution some have predicted—the drive toward a society collectivized through and through, that is, in which groups interlock in mutual control; the theory being that no individual *or* group can be trusted. That would mean the death of the very idea of a profession, which so far has been synonymous with a blend of individual and group self-governance.

The message for the professions today is that their one hope of survival with anything like their present freedoms is the recovery of mental and moral force. No profession can live and flourish on just one of the two. For its "practical purpose" it requires the best knowledge and its effective use. But since that purpose is to transfer the good of that knowledge from the possessor to another person, the moral element necessarily comes into play. *Moral* here does not mean merely honest; it refers to the nature of any encounter between two human beings. . . . Such practices as experiments on poor patients, or operations by young residents while the patient thinks he is in the hands of the great surgeon, seem clear-cut matters that find their parallels in teaching and in the law. But more subtle situations arise from group practice, in any profession, where the client may be tossed about among several hands, having to reestablish his identity and need, losing confidence all the while, and in the end knowing that responsible attention has been denied him. . . .

No doubt the codes now in force (through hardly the Hippocratic oath, so moving and yet so ineffectual) can benefit from thorough revision. But what the professions need in their present predicament is, first, the will to police themselves with no fraternal hand, with no thought of public relations. . . .

Policing, being negative, is not enough. It will not effect moral regeneration, which can come about only when the members of a group feel once more confident that ethical behavior *is* desirable, widely practiced, approved, and admired. After a marked decline, it can only be a slow growth and only one force can start it on its way, the force of moral and intellectual leadership. What all the professions need today is critics from inside, men who know what the conditions are, and also the arguments and excuses, and in a full sweep over the field can offer their fellow practitioners a new vision of the profession as an institution.

For each profession, details such as these will have to be spelled out, for in human affairs the great and perpetual shortage is that of imagination. . . . When the problem is a failure of competence and morality, nothing will solve it but the work of an individual mind and conscience, aided of course by the many scattered men of talent and good will who are only waiting for a lead. Without some such heroic effort, we professionals shall all go down—appropriately—as non-heroes together.

❯❯ *Earl Shorris* ❮❮

Dividends: Little Man, What Now?

❯❯ ❮❮

Although they may be held in higher esteem than blue-collar workers, white-collar workers can have meaningless jobs, too. Being a cog in the machinery of a bureaucracy is no more fun than being a cog in an industrial process, as Earl Shorris illustrates in this beautiful vignette from his book The Oppressed Middle: Politics of Middle Management. *How would the office manager Shorris depicts feel about working in the office described by Daniel Zwerdling in Chapter 12?*

> *Receiving bread from us, they will see clearly that we take the bread made*
> *by their hands from them, to give it to them, without any miracle.*
> —Dostoyevsky, "The Grand Inquisitor"

He and his wife had always lived alone. They were proud people to whom punctilio was important. Their cat was Siamese; its box was always clean and deodorized. He never wore the same suit on consecutive days; she pressed the other suit between wearings. They attended the opera eight times each year; she preferred the French, he preferred the Italians, they were united in their dislike of the Germans. Each year at Christmas she worked as a clerk in a famous and expensive leather goods store; it was their rule to use her earnings solely for gifts, for each other, for his secretary, for her nephews, for his aunt, and for his brother who was confined to a hospital in Ohio.

She cooked for him with great pleasure and attention. Every night they each had one glass of wine with dinner. They bought wine by the gallon and decanted it into crystal bottles that had been left to them by her mother. Wrong for the wine, he said. But right for the wine drinkers, she said. For summer they had a small house near the seashore, which had also been left to them by her mother. They rented out the house during the hottest part of summer, saving for themselves only the first three weeks in September. The tenants always made them unhappy, leaving behind a trail of nicks, scratches, chips, and stains, and failing to tend the garden properly. Of their three weeks at the seashore two were always spent returning the house and garden to their original and proper condition. He had a talent for carpentry and painting, she prided herself on her green thumb. To have such work performed by hired help, they agreed, diminished the pleasures of living by the sea.

Children earned no esteem from them. Early in their protracted courting they had found to their mutual delight that neither of them wished to raise a pack of nasty brats. Furthermore, the low opinion they held of children extended to parents, nursemaids, schoolteachers, babysitters, and purveyors of real and metaphorical pap. He thought it very witty of her to have said that the trouble with children is that they sour the wine.

In his work he had long ago earned a reputation for intolerance. As manager of the office he was, he believed, required to rage with equal vehemence over thefts, spots on the carpeting, broken furniture or machines, computer failures, tardiness, recalcitrance, disrespect, indiscreet modes of dress, and dubious expense accounts. Yet he considered himself a good and generous Christian. When a freckled black girl came to him to ask his advice about an unwanted pregnancy, he paid for an abortion out of his own pocket. When one of the boys in the mail room, a middle-aged, slightly retarded man, told him tearfully of a fire that had destroyed his two-room apartment and all his furnishings, he permitted the mail room boy to purchase certain items of worn office furniture at the scrap price. He never failed to give people ample time, with pay, to attend to illnesses and deaths, nor had he ever chastised a woman for failing to come to work during the first day of her menstrual period. As a result, he considered certain people owed him more loyalty, and therefore more nearly perfect performance, than the rest, and he was therefore more intolerant of their failings.

His superiors, as he called them, constantly disappointed him. They were men of little style or taste, aggressive, opportunistic, avaricious. He thought some of them less than adequate to their tasks and a few of them nothing less than benighted. Business as such held very little interest for him. He did not follow sales reports or stock market prices. He had certain responsibilities, which he exercised with care and concern for costs and appearances. Production, marketing, sales, finance, personnel, procurement, international were all the same to him, all equally uninteresting.

He did, however, have some special feeling for the chief executive officer, a man with a full red face and thick white hair, a figure, the office manager said. It was the chief executive officer who had for some years borne the cultural responsibilities of the company: a seat on the board of the opera, fund raiser for the symphony, patron of the ballet. How many times the chief executive officer, forced to be out of the city on business, had sent his tickets to the office manager! How generous! How considerate of the value of the seats!

During twenty-five years with the company the office manager's salary had not risen greatly. Because of the rate of inflation, his income after taxes had actually fallen over the past several years; yet he did not complain. It was not necessary to be rich to be cultured, he told his wife. In fact, had he earned a great deal of money, they might have become bourgeois; money had that effect on many people of quality. He had observed it more than once, hadn't she? Even so, the economies forced upon them were irritating; they could no longer buy art books or eat endive; the quality of the wine they drank was not what it had been—they took risks on Italian wineries, experimented with unknown vintages; he worried that the lapels of his suit coats were just a bit too narrow; she sensed that everyone, particularly her husband, noticed the faint marks left by lowered hemlines; and their underwear had begun to gray.

They needed more money, she said. Perhaps she should consider full-time employment. How often they had called from the leather goods store to ask her to accept a full-time position! Wasn't this the proper time to accept the offer?

He thought not. They would reward him at the office, he said. The chief executive officer was a cultured man, he was not unjust or unthinking. While the world was going to hell in a handbasket, there were still men of quality, companies of quality; he was fortunate enough to have cast his lot with such a company. At any time their problems would be solved. Meanwhile, the triennial increase in their rent could be accommodated easily enough; they had only to rent the summer house for two more weeks, taking their own holiday later, when the summer people had gone and the air was truly brisk and refreshing.

We are not poor, he reminded her, merely a bit on our uppers, and only in the most temporary way.

An envelope arrived for him in the company mail. It was marked CONFIDENTIAL and PERSONAL. Inside it, he found a notice of his inclusion in the stock-owner program. He was to receive ten shares of stock initially and then have the opportunity to purchase additional stock on a one-for-one basis: for each share he purchased, the company would purchase one for him. The record of stock dividends was included in the envelope. Over the last twenty years the company had never failed to pay a dividend. In the chart of stock prices he noticed that the stock had split four times since the company had first gone public.

He suffered an epiphany. It was suddenly clear to him that one who owned shares of stock in the company was more likely to profit by his labors than he. But why? They did not work. Ownership of such a well-managed company was hardly a risk. It was entirely unjust that they should be paid so much while he labored for a steadily declining salary, while his standard of living fell year after year, while his wife, a woman of quality, considered accepting a salesclerk's position full time.

And who were these persons who profited by his labor? Speculators! Jews, mafiosi, union crooks, oil-rich illiterates from Texas, Arabs, Germans, Japanese, trash of every variety.

He took a piece of stationery from his desk, not notepaper or a memo form but the best stationery, the rag bond, and wrote a brief letter to the chief executive officer:

Dear Sir:

It has come to my attention that the earnings of my labors over these twenty-five years past have, for the most part, been paid out to persons who have no interest in the firm, no connection with our operations, and no loyalty to our goals or products. These stock owners, who are, in actuality, mere speculators, have no right to the fruits of my labor.

Unless this situation is remedied post haste, I must submit my resignation effective immediately. I await your reply.

Shortly before five that afternoon the director of personnel telephoned the office manager, asking that he return his building pass, company credit cards, keys, and so on. I'm sorry you're leaving, the director of personnel said, because you would have been entitled to early retirement in only two years.

The office manager said, I shall put the items you require into the company mail immediately. As to your regrets, I can do without them, thank you.

The office manager packed his personal belongings, which were few, into his old leather briefcase and left the office promptly at five. There was no one to whom he felt he owed a farewell. On his way home he went out of his way to pass by the elegant leather goods store in which his wife worked during the Christmas season. It really was a lovely place, he noted, filled with rich browns and maroons, smelling of expensive leather, patronized solely by persons of quality.

II

» «

CHANGING ATTITUDES TOWARD WORK AND CAREERS

» «

Until recently, there were widely shared assumptions about what is "natural" in the world of work. It was natural for the sons of the middle classes to go to college and later pursue professional or managerial careers, and for the daughters to stay home and rear children (or, if they worked, it was only natural for them to be secretaries or teachers). It was natural for the sons and daughters of the working classes to follow their parents into factories or onto construction sites. It was natural for people to spend their lives on one job. It was natural (if you were a middle-class man) to spend the first five years of life in play, the next sixteen in school, the next forty-five at work, and whatever was left at the end in retirement. And it was natural to work eight hours a day, five days a week, fifty weeks a year.

Now, Americans of both sexes and of every age, race, class, and occupation seem to be questioning these basic assumptions about what is natural in the institutions of work and careers. In Chapter 7, "The Changing Notion of a Career," Richard Bolles questions the appropriateness of dividing life into the three discrete and sequential boxes of education, work and leisure; and Emily Greenspan questions the fairness of excluding women from the workforce after they have had children. Several authors in Chapter 6, "The Work Ethic Today," even question that most basic of assumptions, that people naturally want to work. In fact, a budding "leisure ethic" seems to be challenging the traditional work ethic.

The traditional assumptions of managers that certain workers—women, minorities, and immigrants—were "naturally" suited for routine jobs has been especially challenged. After much trial and error, social scientists have found that job needs and desires are not clearly related to sex, race, or any of the other characteristics that managers once relied on when assigning work roles. As Hackman and Oldham point out in Chapter 6, each worker has different job needs and desires, which change over his or her career. The things people look for from their jobs are influenced by their experience, educational attainment, age, personality, and a zillion un-knowns. Some people do seem to like routine work. Others prefer routine work at those times when they have other responsibilities and don't want to be bothered with the psychological demands of a more complex job. The secret to job satisfaction is to achieve the proper fit between a worker's special needs and wants and the special characteristics of each job. Many of the articles in Chapters 6 and 7 discuss the importance of making that fit and suggest some ways for better matching workers to jobs. (This theme is picked up again in Chapter 9, "Work and the Family," and Chapter 10, "Alternative Work Patterns.")

If each worker is different, does that mean we can't generalize about the work ethic? Does everybody have his or her own individualized work ethic? Perhaps. But various philosophies about work have influenced the way American workers, in general, feel about their jobs. In Chapter 5, "Roots of the American Work Ethic," we see how the American frontier, Christianity, the Horatio Alger myth, and scientific management all subtly influenced the way workers feel about work and how they experience it on the job.

Whether a worker is poor or affluent also will significantly affect the meaning he or she attaches to work. As authors Yankelovich (in Chapter 1) and Etzioni (in Chapter 6) illustrate, today's affluent, educated workers see work differently than did their less fortunate parents. For example, younger, better educated Americans tend to feel they are underemployed; about a third of the workforce believes that they bring more to their jobs in the way of skills, training, and education than their jobs permit them to use. According to Yankelovich, young workers want "meaningful" work, which means work in which they can become involved, committed, and interested, work that challenges them to the utmost of their capabilities, and work in which they can participate in decision making. But, as the article by Maccoby and Terzi in Chapter 6 shows, young workers are not finding jobs with these characteristics. Perhaps this is why there is the flight from work that Etzioni and Palm describe. Surveys undertaken at the University of Michigan, summarized by Staines and O'Connor, find that a growing demand for more time away from work was one of the major changes in work values in the 1970s.

How can we put all these facts together? Perhaps Mortimer Adler gave us the clue back in Chapter 1. He shows that there is little difference to the individual between good work and leisure—both are creative activities that offer a sense of mastery, identity, and self-esteem. If this is so, could it be that young Americans are turning to leisure activities for the essential human needs that they feel are not being fulfilled on their jobs? If so, does this mean that the work ethic has changed? Does this mean America has a crisis in its workplaces? Not only do the selections in these three chapters raise difficult questions, but they also defy us to offer simple answers.

5

»«

ROOTS OF THE AMERICAN WORK ETHIC

»«

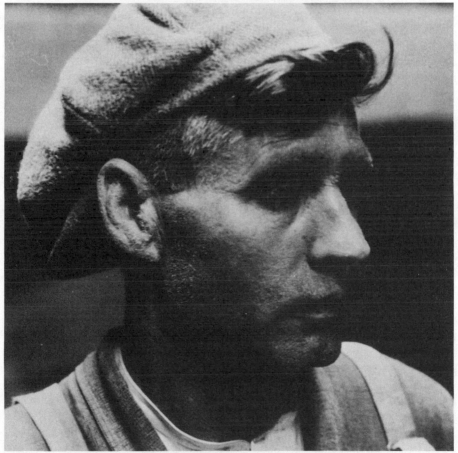

Lewis Hine/International Museum of Photography at George Eastman House

» Daniel T. Rodgers «

Work Ideals and the Industrial Invasion

» «

The work ethic has been a part of our cultural heritage for so long that it is easy to forget that a far older Western tradition extolled the virtues of leisure. The ancient Greeks and Romans, whose civilization depended on slave labor, wrote of a golden age when men, like the gods, did not have to work. The Christian tradition, too, pictured paradise as "a land of milk and honey," and Augustine wrote of the "eternal leisure" of heaven. America itself was, at first, portrayed as a Garden of Eden, a land of such abundance that the natives did not have to toil but simply gathered the riches that nature provided. This myth was slow to die in the southern colonies. But in the North, as historian Daniel T. Rodgers points out in the following selection, the settlers came prepared to establish, through hard work, a godly civilization in the wilderness.

> *Works and days were offered us, and we chose work.*
> —Ralph Waldo Emerson, "Works and Days" (1857)

Unlike the first new world adventurers, the settlers of Puritan New England and Quaker Pennsylvania came with no hopes for prelapsarian ease. They were laborers for their Lord, straighteners of crooked places, engaged in a task filled with hardship, deprivation, and toil. . . . Such men came ready, if not eager, to work in the sweat of their faces and to see, as William Penn wrote, "what sobriety and industry can do in a wilderness against heat, cold, wants, and dangers." They chose to call America a wilderness because it fit the countervision in their minds' eye that the moral life was a matter of hard work and hard-bitten determination. Out of the American Eden they fashioned a land preoccupied with toil.

During the first half of the nineteenth century, when Europeans began to come in numbers to inspect the new American nation, they marveled at the extent of the transformation. . . . "In the United States," Tocqueville wrote, "a wealthy man thinks that he owes it to public opinion to devote his leisure to some kind of industrial or commercial pursuit or to public business. He would think himself in bad repute if he employed his life solely in living." . . . It was not the pace of work in America that inspired responses like this so much as its universality, its bewilderingly exalted status, the force of the idea itself. . . .

Ultimately Penn and Hooker and their heirs assaulted the paradise myths themselves, redrawing their moral to suit their revaluation of toil. Like the Puritans before them, nineteenth-century moralists agreed that Adam had worked in Eden or, if not, that his idleness had been all the worse for him. Over and over again, to anyone who would listen, they insisted that work was not a curse, whatever the hints in the Genesis story. Nor was it merely a painful means to moral health and redeeming grace. Labor was a blessing: not "a burden or a bare necessity . . . [but] a privilege, a glory, and a delight."

In the end, even heaven itself—Augustine's "perpetual sabbath"—fell before the onslaught. . . . "Surely there must be work to do in heaven,/ Since work is the best thing on earth we know," the mill girl turned poet, Lucy Larcom, wrote toward the end of the century. New York's flamboyant evangelist DeWitt Talmage claimed more confidently that heaven was "the busiest place in the universe." Shunting aside generations of mythmaking, the moralists succeeded in writing the gospel of work not only on the land but on paradise itself. "God sent you not into this world as into a Play-house, but a Work-house," ran a Puritan reminder. It was, in fact, a choice Northerners made for themselves.

Blessed is he who has found his work; let him ask no other blessedness.

—Thomas Carlyle, *Past and Present*

In our day we know that perplexing decision as the "work ethic." It is a simplified label, as inviting to abuse as it is convenient, but it points to an important truth: for the elevation of work over leisure involved not an isolated choice but an ethos that permeated life and manners. It reared its head in the nineteenth and early twentieth centuries in countless warnings against the wiles of idleness and the protean disguises of the idler. It gave a special reverberation to the word "duty" and set an infectious model of active, conscientious doing. Theodore Roosevelt caught its tenor in his thundering insistence that only the strenuous life was worth living, that "nothing in this world is worth having or worth doing unless it means effort, pain, difficulty." That conviction was by no means Roosevelt's alone. The doctrine of the industrious life pervaded churches and children's storybooks, editorial columns and the stump rhetoric of politics. Not least, it transformed the processes of work themselves, energizing, mechanizing, and systematizing them in ways that made those who cared most about the worth of toil at once immensely proud and profoundly uneasy. But in another sense the phrase is misleading, for the work ethic as it stood in the middle of the nineteenth century, at the threshold of industrialization, was not a single conviction but a complex of ideas with roots and branches.

The taproot, as Max Weber suggested long ago, was the Protestant Reformation. Universalizing the obligation to work and methodizing time, the Reformers set in motion convictions that were to reverberate with enormous consequences through American history. At the heart of Protestantism's revaluation of work was the doctrine of the calling, the faith that God had called everyone to some productive vocation, to toil there for the common good and His greater glory. . . . In the end faith, not labor, saved, of course; the Reformers never confused the secular vocation with a believer's primary, spiritual calling. But Protestantism extended and spiritualized toil and turned usefulness into a sacrament. Zwingli's benediction put the point succinctly: "In the things of this life, the laborer is most like to God." . . . But Weber was certainly right in his claim that Puritanism tried to "penetrate . . . [the] daily routine of life with its methodicalness." Puritans methodized the English calendar, throwing out the irregular carnival of saints' days and replacing it with the clocklike rhythm of the weekly Sabbath, when men were to be as tireless and unbending in their rest as they had been during the week at their labors. In the same manner, Puritanism saturated its believers with an acute sense of the dangers of idleness, enjoining them to guard against the misspence of time and to improve the passing moments, each of which, in the end, had to be accounted for in heaven. This was an asceticism of a novel sort, worldly and systematic, looking forward to the time-and-profit calculus of industrial life rather than backward to the flesh-denying torments of the desert hermits. Joined with the doctrine of the calling, it demanded not only that all men work but that they work in a profoundly new way: regularly, conscientiously, and diligently. . . .

Yet the nineteenth-century work ethic was not simply the Protestant ethic in modern dress. In the first place, by the middle of the nineteenth century a good deal of secularization had taken place. The old ideas never completely died out, but gradually the term "calling" faded from common speech and with it the idea that in work one labored in the first instance for the glory of God. Increasingly the moralists talked instead of usefulness. Benjamin Franklin helped set the new tone in his tireless string of maxims and projects for the public good, and by the era of the American Revolution political writing was saturated with the idea of public usefulness, the common weal filling the place the Reformers had given to God. The legacy persisted well into the nineteenth century. . . .

Not only did immense projects seem to wait at every hand, but with rising conviction, economists, editors, and preachers insisted that a failure to meet them, a slackening of the pace, would send the nation skidding into poverty and decay. The Victorian concern with scarcity, with the economic necessity of constant doing, was evident well before Darwin's *Origin of Species* made its full impact in America. . . .

Scarcity gradually nudged out the common good, just as the ideal of public usefulness had all but nudged out God. Where Puritans had been called to their vocations, nineteenth-century Americans were told that in a world of pressing material demands it was one's social duty to produce.

Working also held one back from the sink of idleness. Despite the gradual dropping away of the theological superstructure of Puritanism, the ascetic injunctions of the Protestant ethic retained and multiplied their force in the mid-nineteenth century. Looking back on her New England childhood years in the 1830s, Lucy Larcom remembered growing up "penetrated through every fibre of thought with the idea that idleness is a disgrace. It was taught with the alphabet and the spelling-book; it was enforced by precept and example, at home and abroad; and it is to be confessed that it did sometimes haunt the childish imagination almost mercilessly." . . .For those who saw their world as beset with temptations and dangers, the sanitizing effects of constant labor offered at once a social panacea and a personal refuge.

The doctrine of usefulness and an intense, nervous fear of idleness were both indirect legacies of the Reformation. The other two ingredients of the mid-nineteenth-century work ethic—the dream of success and a faith in work as a creative act—had other roots and implications. By diligence a man could improve his lot; as the proverbs had it, he could stand before kings. The hope had seeped early into Puritanism, overturning the initially static implications of the "calling." Benjamin Franklin had condensed it into the kind of aphorisms that stuck in one's head and helped shape the axioms of a culture. But none of this was a match for the massive outflow of literature that the nineteenth century produced on behalf of the argument that work was the highroad to independence, wealth, and status. This is a country of "self-made men," where from the humblest beginnings a man with "merit and industry" could rise to the top, Calvin Colton announced in 1844 at the beginning of the flood. Endless repetition—in conduct guides, boys' storybooks, handbooks of business advice, and magazine fillers—ingrained the idea as one of the century's most firmly held commonplaces. In the fluid American economy, hard work, self-control, and dogged persistence were the certain escalators of success. . . .

Finally, it was urged, through work men impressed something of themselves on the material world. "A small Poet every Worker is," Carlyle wrote. Emerson seconded the idea: "Labor: a man coins himself into his labor; turns his day, his strength, his thoughts, his affection into some product which remains a visible sign of his power." Craft traditions, the legacy of the Renaissance artist-craftsmen, and romanticism all converged on the theme, often with extravagant results. . . .

Obviously there were tensions within this set of ideas. Work was a creative act and a means of self-repression, a social obligation that paid off in private rewards. The ingredients of the work ethic were not held together by the logical consistency of their premises. The clearest of the tensions lay between the idea of work as ascetic exercise and work as art. The one looked toward system, discipline, and the emerging factory order; the other toward spontaneity, self-expression, and a narrowing of the gulf between work and play. The latter, creative ideal was clearly the weaker of the two in the nineteenth century. . . .

There was a second, nagging contradiction between the ideals of duty and of success—between the appeal to the dignity of all labor, even the humblest, and the equally universal counsel to work one's way as quickly as possible out of manual toil. Manual workers felt the full force of the contradiction and complained repeatedly of the disjuncture between the grandiloquent rhetoric and the practical disrepute of their occupations. . . . [Nevertheless] the disparate strands all came together to reaffirm the central premise of the work ethic: that work was the core of the moral life. Work made men useful in a world of economic scarcity; it staved off the doubts and temptations that preyed on idleness; it opened the way to deserved wealth and status; it allowed one to put the impress of mind and skill on the material world. At the advent of the factory system, few of the keepers of the Northern moral conscience did not, in some measure, believe in them all. . . .

There was a sociology to the work ethic as well as an amalgam of ideas. Praise of work in the mid-nineteenth century was strongest among the middling, largely Protestant, property-owning classes: farmers, merchants, ministers and professional men, independent craftsmen, and nascent industrialists. . . .

On both ends of the social scale one can readily find other ethics and other styles of life. . . . In early nineteenth-century America, it is clear that many urban laborers did their best to punctuate work and play in the irregular, clock-defying pattern that is far older than the Protestant ethic. Gambling, rioting, generous drinking habits, and a good deal of boisterous, elbow-shoving, Sabbath-defying amusement played an important part in urban working-class life. . . . Among the very rich, too, the ideal of industriousness met with resistance. . . . Conspicuous leisure was everywhere the identifying mark of the aristocrat, his bastion against the moralistic assaults of the middle classes; and in this regard the North was no exception.

Work was the gospel of the bourgeoisie, above all, of the Protestant bourgeoisie, but it was not for that reason simply a subcultural peculiarity. In the American North, as nowhere else in the Western European orbit, the middle classes set the tone and standards for society as a whole. They did so through their hold over the strategic institutions of economics and culture. Business enterprise was theirs. So were the Protestant churches and

138

the myriad agencies of moral reformation they spawned in the nineteenth century to care for the poor, educate the ignorant, and hold the wayward to the path of virtue. So were the institutions of learning: the schools and the colleges, the nation's publishing houses, and the major journals of opinion. It was in the last, in particular, that the ideals of middle-class Protestant respectability were debated, codified, and—with the conservative power of print—preserved. . . . I have called this interlocking set of persons the "moralists," keepers of their countrymen's moral conscience. They were not the only Northerners who felt keenly about ethics, but, given the institutional structure of their society, their opinions carried uncommon weight and influence. . . .

None of the ingredients of the work ethic were unique to America. . . . But nowhere else than in the American North, with its truncated social structure, was resistance to these claims so limited. The result was an odd creation: a class and sectarian dogma that was at the same time as close to an article of popular faith as the region afforded.

Exactly how busy is a diligent man? It was only after the factories had overrun economic life that Northern industrialists set out to answer that question with any precision and to graft onto their countrymen the time obsession characteristic of modern industrial societies. The work ethic in its mid-nineteenth-century form did not entail a particular pace of activity so much as a manner of thinking, a moral preoccupation with labor. Moreover, the ideas that came together in praise of work took shape and flourished in an era when, by modern standards, time moved at a haphazard gait. . . . It was not until the Civil War that the characteristic arbiters of industrial time—cheap, mass-produced pocket watches—began to pour out of the American Watch Company plant at Waltham. . . .

Not only time but work moved in irregular, often leisurely rhythms in preindustrial America. . . . Farming, the dominant colonial occupation, oscillated between bouts of intense labor and the short, much slower days of winter and was punctuated by country recreations—fishing, horse racing, visiting, and tavern-going—that even in Puritan New England were as much a part of rural life as the aching toil of planting and harvesting. In the same manner, the typical colonial workshop, with its three or four journeymen and apprentices, went through cycles of activity and probably was rarely busy day in and day out. By the early nineteenth century the tempo of economic life had increased perceptibly. In the East, many rural families now filled in the slack periods of farming by turning materials put out to them by nearby wholesale merchants into boot and shoe uppers, woven cloth goods, straw hats, and a variety of other products. The stores and workshops of Jacksonian America were bigger and considerably more bustling than their colonial counterparts. But weather, changes in demand and availability of materials, and poor communication and transportation facilities still conspired to interrupt the steadiness of work. . . . In a world

139

remote from the time clock and the efficiency expert, the work ethic was not a certain rate of busyness but a way of thinking.

Yet the strength of mid-nineteenth-century work ideals was exactly in their mesh with the bustling, irregular economy of the antebellum North. In this regard two characteristics of the antebellum economy were acutely important: its expansive energy and its limited industrial technology. The first is difficult to exaggerate. In the early nineteenth century the North underwent a startling transformation from an essentially agricultural to a commercial economy. . . .

But, for all the aggressive innovation of the age, as late as 1850 the centers of manufacturing remained the home and the workshop. . . .

The cotton textile industry was the great exception. Barn-sized, water-powered spinning mills had begun to appear in southern New England as early as the 1790s. It was the founding of Lowell, Massachusetts, in the early 1820s, however, that marked the real beginning of the new industrial order in America. Lowell was the first of the large-scale mill towns, an unprecedented assemblage of machines, bosses, and operatives. Within a decade there were nineteen textile mills in operation in the city, employing an army of 5,000 factory hands. . . . The cotton mills were the first and archetypal factories, set off by their size, discipline, and thorough mechanization. Dwarfing most other enterprises, the largest mid-nineteenth-century textile mills employed a thousand or more workers, operatives for the most part, tied to the power looms and spinning machinery they tended and hemmed in by rigid sets of factory rules. Less dramatically, a few other industries moved in the direction of the cotton mills. . . . [But] outside the textile centers, the home, farm, and workshop still ruled the early nineteenth-century economy. . . .

This was an economy in the earliest stages of industrialization—expansive yet simple—and it went hand in hand with the intellectual legacies to fashion the mid-nineteenth-century work ethic. The economic matrix reinforced old assumptions about work, stirred up new ones, and held them all together in a way logic could not. Expansion fueled the command to be up and doing and helped turn the ideal of usefulness out of the religious and political spheres and make it an economic obligation. . . .

Expansion likewise took the hope of upward mobility and screwed it to a new pitch. In a world that seemed to have jumped the old restraining ruts—where a Cornelius Vanderbilt could ride the new transportation systems to a fortune, and a skillful Yankee carpenter such as Thomas Rogers could become one of the nation's leading locomotive manufacturers—the dream of success was hardly to be escaped. . . . [But] if growth fueled dreams of success, the sudden collapses and paralyses ingrained the lessons of scarcity, heightened anxieties over the disorders of commercial and urban life, and added to the Victorian nervousness. In all, it was a paradoxical society—booming yet fragile, engaged in the march of progress yet adrift in flux, inspiring expansive hope even as it reinforced the fears that encouraged the ascetic, nerve-numbing discipline of diligence. On all counts, even in its contradictions, it helped reinforce the primacy of work.

Finally, the economy of the antebellum North was one in which a certain measure of independence and creativity could be taken for granted. . . . But, in the face of an enormous enthusiasm for technology, little of this penetrated far into the consciousness of middle-class Northerners. They thought their society what it seemed to be: a land of bustling farms and workshops where work told; where indeed it was the core of living.

When men are employed, they are best contented; for on the days they worked they were good-natured and cheerful, and, with the consciousness of having done a good day's work, they spent the evening jollily.

—Benjamin Franklin, *Autobiography*

In the second half of the nineteenth century the factory system invaded the antebellum farm and shop economy, overturning not only the familiar patterns of work but the ways Northerners had been accustomed to think of their labor. The speed of the transition to the factory economy varied widely from industry to industry and from place to place. It was an uneven movement—felt not as a shock, as it has often been described, but as a series of shivers, greatest in years of major labor unrest when the nation suddenly reckoned up the extent of change. But in the end the factory system challenged each of the certainties upon which the work ethic had rested and unsettled the easy equation of work and morality in the minds of many perceptive Americans.

At times and in places, moreover, the transition to the factory economy took place with wrenching, unsettling speed. The shoe industry was for most nineteenth-century Americans the preeminent example of the rate at which the new could obliterate the old. As late as the 1840s the typical New England shoe shop was a 10′ x 10′ cottage housing a handful of skilled workers who made shoes by time-honored hand methods according to their personal, often eccentric, notions of size and fit. Some subdivision of tasks set in during that decade under the pressures of the merchants who controlled the trade, but the real revolution in shoemaking came in the 1860s with a rash of inventions, beginning with a sewing machine capable of stitching soles to uppers. Aggressive subdivision of labor, mechanization, and factory building quickly followed. By the 1870s, the shoemaking cottages were empty, and the men who had once been shoemakers now found themselves factory machine operators: beaters, binders, bottomers, buffers, burnishers, channellers, crimpers, cutters, dressers, edge setters, and so on through some thirty or forty subdivided occupations. . . .

Size, discipline, and displacement of skill characterized the factories. The physical growth of the workplace was evident at every hand. . . . By 1916

141

the McCormick plant [at Chicago] had grown to 15,000 workers; and in that year the payroll at the Ford Motor Company works at Highland Park reached 33,000. Workshops of the size that had characterized the antebellum economy, employing a handful or a score of workers, persisted amid these immense establishments. But they employed a smaller and smaller fraction of the workers. By 1919, in the Northern states between the Mississippi River and the Atlantic Ocean, three-fourths of all wage earners in manufacturing worked in factories of more than 100 employees, and 30 percent in the giants of more than 1,000.

In plants of this size, the informality of the small workshop was an inevitable casualty. . . . By the 1890s . . . gates were common around factories, supplemented by the exacting eye of the first factory time clocks. Inside the plants the baronial foremen, who had commonly hired, fired, and cajoled the necessary labor out of their workers on their own whim and responsibility, slowly disappeared. In their place the larger factories evolved tighter, more systematic, and more centralized schemes of management. By 1920 personnel departments, rational and precise cost accounting, central planning offices, and production and efficiency engineers had become fixtures of the new factory bureaucracies. . . .

By the same token, skills disappeared in the new factories. Whether owing to such a simple device as the cigar mold—a wooden frame that enabled an untrained worker to bunch cigar tobacco—or the complex, automatic tools of the machine shop, the factories made obsolete a host of carefully preserved hand trades. Tailoring, cabinetmaking, barrel making, felt-hat making, and pottery making all gave way before new inventions and the specialization of labor. The clothing and slaughtering industries were particularly conspicuous examples of the relentless subdivison of tasks. . . . Nowhere did the pursuit of efficiency go on more aggressively than in the automobile industry, where the jobs were relentlessly morseled before being chained to the assembly line. . . .

The factories made skills as well as destroyed them. Mule spinners in the textile factories and heaters and rollers in the steel mills worked at highly skilled, factory-created jobs. But the drive toward ever-greater efficiency made every skilled job precarious. . . . Despite occasional compensations, all factory jobs increasingly converged toward the semiskilled; the typical factory hand became a machine operator or fractionated workman, toiling at a single bit of the manufacturing process.

How extensive the new modes of work actually were was a matter of some debate. In 1860, one-fifth of the gainfully occupied population of the Northern states worked in what the census defined as a manufacturing establishment; by 1919, when the correlation between factory and "manufacturing establishment" was considerably closer, the proportion had grown to about a third. But the new forms of toil affected not only manufacturing workers but spread out from the factories as well. In the late 1870s, large-scale production methods invaded agriculture in the wake of the rapid mechanization of farm tools. . . . The transformation of coal mining in the early twentieth century was more complete. Between about 1900 and 1910, coal-cutting machinery and subdivision of labor began to enter the bituminous coal mines of the Middle West, remaking the operations and shoving out the hand miners who had once worked at the pit faces virtually as autonomous subcontractors. About the same time the efficiency experts began to turn their attention to the huge new clerical forces employed by firms like Sears and Roebuck. Arrayed behind banks of desks, strictly supervised, paid at times like industrial workers on piecework, many of the new clerical workers differed from factory hands only in status and neatness—just as the big, turn-of-the-century department stores employing several thousand saleswomen and cash girls differed little from fair-sized industrial establishments. In 1850 the job of a clerk or a farmer had been worlds away from that of a mill hand, but slowly, perceptibly, all work grew more and more like factory work.

What industrialization offered in return was a fantastic increase in output. The constantly growing flood of goods impressed and bewildered Northerners. . . . Between 1860 and 1920, the nation's population a little more than tripled, but the volume of manufactured goods produced increased somewhere between twelve- and fourteenfold. . . . By the turn of the century the United States had pushed past all other nations in industrial production. By 1910 it had outstripped its nearest rival, Germany, by nearly two to one.

All work, even cotton-spinning, is noble; work is alone noble. . . . A life of ease is not for any man, nor for any god.
—Thomas Carlyle, *Past and Present*

This avalanche of factory-produced goods might have been expected to flow neatly into greater general well-being, but it did not. By the 1880s many businessmen had begun to worry that there were too many factories for the economy to absorb. . . . Intellectually, too, the phenomenon of more goods than the market could absorb was deeply troubling. Production had long been the chief of the economic virtues, impossible to take to excess. But if the industrial cornucopia could easily spew out far more goods than the nation was able to buy, what then was the place of work?

This was only one of the questions the invasion of the factories posed to those who cared deeply about work. The whole issue was a maze of paradoxes. The industrial economy was in large part a creature of the intense regional faith in the worth of labor. The work ethic helped impell the restless personal energies of the Northern manufacturers, blessed their enterprises with a sense of mission, and gave them a transcendent sanction. It helped anesthetize employers to the eleven- and twelve-hour days they imposed on their workers and the pace at which the factories drove them. The work ethic provided the language of calculation, system, and diligence into which the efficiency engineers poured their new and stricter meanings, turning the new plants into matchless hives of industriousness. But if the factories were creatures of middle-class work ideals, they devoured those ideals as well. In disturbing ways, the transformation of labor undercut virtually all the mid-nineteenth-century assumptions about the moral preeminence of work.

Industrialization upset the certainty that hard work would bring economic success. Whatever the life chances of a farmer or shop hand had been in the early years of the century, it became troublingly clear that the semiskilled laborer, caught in the anonymity of a late-nineteenth-century textile factory or steel mill, was trapped in his circumstances—that no amount of sheer hard work would open the way to self-employment or wealth. Still more rudely, the factory system overturned the equation of work and art. Amid the subdivided and monotonous tasks, the speed, and the discipline of a box factory or an automobile plant, where was the room for mind or for the impress of individual creativity? Even the successes of the industrial transformation unsettled ideas and values. As the factories poured forth an ever-larger volume of goods into the homes of the middle class, the ascetic legacies of the Protestant ethic slowly and steadily eroded, giving way to a noisy gospel of play and, at the fringes of middle-class thought, to a cultivation of a life free of effort itself. As industrialization shook the idea of the permanence of scarcity, as the measure of economic health turned from how much a society produced to how equitably and conscientiously it consumed, it became harder and harder to insist that compulsive activity, work, and usefulness were the highest goals of life.

The moralists did not perceive these troubling questions all at once. When they did there were always the ancient maxims to fall back on. Work, they continued to insist, was what man was made to do—the foundation of happiness, the condition of existence since the days of Adam's husbandry in the garden. But industrialization could not be stopped from wedging into the preserve of ethics. And as the economy was transformed a deeply rooted set of presumptions cracked and shifted.

» Russell Sage «

Ambitious to Rise in Life—Never by Luck

» «

Of all the self-help and success stories of the late nineteenth century, the fictional "rags-to-riches" tales of Horatio Alger are probably the best known. Sometimes life not only imitates art, but outdoes it, as in the extraordinary career of millionaire financier Russell Sage (1816-1906). Not even Alger willed himself to the level of success Sage achieved, nor was Alger quite so glib about the secret of success. "The essentials of success, in my opinion," Sage proclaimed, "are just three: honesty, industry, and economy." In this 1898 interview (which initially appeared in a magazine appropriately called Success), *Sage not only extolled the virtues of hard work, he also expressed the unmitigated confidence of the age that "any young man, amid existing opportunities, has a chance of becoming a millionaire."*

I have come to ask you to tell me the story of your life," I said, "for I am sure it must be of great interest."

Mr. Sage smiled. "I don't kow about its being of interest. It is very simple and commonplace to me. You know I began as a grocery clerk in a country town. That is a very humble beginning, I'm sure. I received a dollar a week for working from early morning until late at night, but I was well satisfied with my lot because I knew that it was bound to lead to better things. So I worked my very best, and saved my wages, which were slowly increased as I went along, and finally I had enough money to start a little store for myself. When I was twenty-one years old I had a store of my own, and I made a success of it."

"But how did you happen to come to New York?" I asked.

"Oh, I was ambitious," laughed Mr. Sage. "Like most boys, I thought there was no other place like a city for success, and I finally sold my country store when I was still very young, and came to New York. I started in as office boy, at very low wages, and from that day on I worked myself up and up, until I finally became a financier on my own account. It took a long time, though. It was not all accomplished in a day; though when I came to New York I expected to be rich in two or three years. I was very much like other boys, you see. They all expect to get rich in a day."

"But some of them never get rich," I said.

"Well, it's their own fault if they do not succeed," said the financier. "Surely, every one has as good a chance as I had. I don't think there could be a poorer opportunity for a boy to rise. The trouble is that most of them are not very anxious to rise. If they find themselves wealthy some morning they are glad, of course; but they are not willing to work, and make themselves rich."

"Some say that it is all luck," I ventured to suggest.

"Oh, pshaw!" said Mr. Sage, with great disgust. "There's no such thing as luck. I'm sure there was none of it about my career. I know just how I earned every penny, and the reason for it, and I never got anything I didn't work for. I never knew any one to obtain lasting wealth without lots of hard work."

"Do you think there are as good opportunities for getting rich today as there were thirty years ago, or when you made your start, Mr. Sage?"

"Undoubtedly. I think there are even greater opportunities, for new industries are being established all the time, and there are broader fields to work in. But then, the old fields of business are not overworked, by any means. I always say that there is room for good men anywhere and at anytime. I don't think there can ever be too many of them. It is true that there are many applicants for every place in New York, but if I were unable to get a place in an Eastern city I should go West, for there are great opportunities there for every one."

In an English ship, they say, it is poor grub, poor pay, and easy work; in an American ship, good grub, good pay, and hard work. And this is applicable to the working populations of both countries.

—Jack London, *The People of the Abyss*

"People say, though, that the West is not what it is supposed to be," I remarked.

"Yes, there are always pessimists," said Mr. Sage. "The people who say the West has no opportunities are the same persons who used to call it foolish for any young man to come to New York. When I decided to come here, I was told on every side that I would regret my action; but I never have. Some people never see opportunities in anything, and they never get along. I did not see any very great opportunity ahead of me when I came to New York, but I knew that if I had a chance I could make one. I knew that there are always openings for energetic, hard-working fellows, and I was right."

"Of course, you believe that strict honesty is essential to success, Mr. Sage? I've heard many people say that honesty doesn't pay, especially in Wall Street."

"That is a foolish question," said the financier. "It is absurd to imagine that it pays to be dishonest, whatever your business or profession. Do you suppose if I had been dishonest in any dealings when I started out, that I would be worth anything today?"

"What do you think of the chances for country boys in a great city like New York today, Mr. Sage?"

"I think they are as great as ever. Employers are on the lookout for bright young men, and I believe that they would prefer that they come from the country, provided there is no danger of their becoming dissipated. I think that is the only thing men have against country fellows, and there are many things in their favor. I think an earnest, ambitious, hard-working boy from the country has a splendid chance of becoming somebody. There are much greater opportunities for him to exercise his good qualities, and the reward of his enterprise is much larger. The same energetic labor that would make a man worth twenty-five thousand dollars in a small town would be very likely to make him worth a hundred thousand or so in a great city, and all on account of the wider field."

success

"What, Mr. Sage, are the essentials of success?"

"The essentials of success, in my opinion, are just three: honesty, industry, and economy. Any young man, amid existing opportunities, has a chance of becoming a millionaire."

"To what do you owe your wonderful vitality?" I asked. Mr. Sage smiled, before answering me.

"I never smoke, I never drink any liquors, I retire early, and get up early, and take care of myself in every possible way," he said. "Don't you think I ought to be healthy? I have always taken care of myself, and I think I've proved that hard work is not bad for one's health. In fact, I think that work is the best thing I know of for improving a man's constitution, for it makes a good appetite, and encourages digestion. It is not work that ruins so many men. It's the wine they drink, and the late hours they keep, and their general dissipation. I expect to be at my desk for many years to come, and just because I've taken good care of myself.

"You ask me why I don't stop work. I'll do it if you will answer me one question: 'What else can I do that will do as much good and keep me as well?' Well, you can't answer it; nobody can."

There is no substitute for hard work.
                                                —Thomas Alva Edison, *Life*

» *Daniel J. Boorstin* «

Time Becomes Fungible: Packaging the Unit of Work

» «

In this selection, Librarian of Congress Daniel Boorstin recounts the story of the man who probably had the greatest single influence on the conditions of work in America. Frederick W. Taylor was the father of "scientific management." More than anyone else, Taylor is responsible for introducing the notion of industrial efficiency into America's lexicon of values. It was Taylor's idea to break down every job into its component parts, then time each of these to find the "one best way" of performing it. Ironically, this man who was responsible for turning American workers into robots was himself a humanist who believed he was advancing the welfare of workers with his "time and motion" studies. Taylor's influence has been nearly universal. Henry Ford incorporated his ideas into the assembly line; labor unions used his ideas to classify jobs according to wage/skill levels; and large businesses chose to make only items that could be mass produced, thus affecting the types and quality of American goods. Curiously, Taylor was one of the few Americans admired by the Soviet dictator Joseph Stalin. Indeed, this quintessential American's legacy is probably greater today in Eastern Europe than in America.

L ost time," said *Poor Richard's Almanac*, "is never found again." The work ethic was based on the notion that each working moment was unique and irrecoverable. There were morning hours and evening hours, and there was something different about the labor of each man. Each brought his own shovel to the coal yard, and shoveled in his own peculiar way, and any one man's shoveling was apt to be very different from another's. And somehow it seemed that this was not only right and proper, but inevitable. Man was the only measure of man. Life was a series of unrelivable, unrepeatable episodes. Time was a procession of unique moments— each was now and never again. The past was what had gone beyond recall.

148

In twentieth-century America even this old truism would cease to be true. For time became "fungible," a series of closely measured, interchangeable units. Time was no longer a stream and had become a production line.

Clocks and watches were scarce in the United States until the mid-nineteenth century. If every unit of time was vague and imprecise, then, of course, a unit of work could not be measured by the time it required. The contours of the work unit were necessarily uncertain so long as work hours were bounded by daylight and darkness. . . .

Only [around 1900] when Americans could afford to buy watches and clocks and had found ways to make them in unprecedented numbers did they begin to wear wristwatches and to measure their lives in minutes.

"Efficiency," an American gospel in the twentieth century, meant packaging work into units of time. In a nation where labor was often scarce and always costly, efficiency was measured less by "quality" or "competency" than by the speed with which an acceptable job was accomplished. Time entered into every calculation. An effective America was a speedy America. Time became a series of homogeneous—precisely measured and precisely repeatable—units. The working day was no longer measured by daylight, and electric lights kept factories going "round the clock." Refrigeration and central heating and air conditioning had begun to abolish nature's seasons. One unit of work time became more like another.

And there were special American incentives to mark off and record standard work-time units. Mass production was standardized production. Patterns for making parts of uniform shape and size were only a beginning. The American System of Manufacturing had required progress in the measurement of all kinds of units and in the making of units to a standard. Henry Ford added the techniques of flowing production. And after Ford, mass production also meant assembly-line production, which required removing all uncertainty about the duration of each task. Now the job was brought to the man. In order to keep up production it was essential that each man's task be timed so that the line could be kept flowing and not a moment would be wasted. The speed of the assembly line, which now meant the speed of production, depended on the speed with which the slowest task could be done. All this meant timing.

Frederick W. Taylor, the Apostle of the American Gospel of Efficiency, was the first man to proclaim these truths with dogmatic clarity. His life and character embodied the dilemmas of modern America. On the one hand he preached an almost inhuman obsession with things, a single-minded concern for efficiency—for producing more and better and cheaper things. "In the past," Taylor wrote in *The Principles of Scientific Management* in 1911, "the man has been first; in the future the system must be first." Yet, on the other hand, he preached a sentimental, sometimes passionate concern for

149

the fulfillment of each individual man and for a loving harmony among men. He was troubled to see men stunted by what William James called "the habit of inferiority to your full self." To Taylor, an inefficient man was like "a bird that can sing and won't sing." . . . Was there, somehow, a necessary contradiction between the fulfillment of a man's individuality and the fulfillment of his productive possibilities? In America, where man's productive energies were unleashed as never before, the question would be tested. . . .

By the work one knows the workman.

—Jean de la Fontaine

Taylor seemed untroubled by these contradictions of purpose and feelings, for he possessed an evangelical belief in the healing, harmonizing power of efficiency. His panacea was the greater production and diffusion of things. "The one element more than any other," Taylor observed, "which differentiates civilized from uncivilized countries—prosperous from poverty-stricken peoples—is that the average man in the one is five or six times as productive as the other." This was his gospel:

> Scientific management involves a complete mental revolution on the part of the workingman. . . . And it involves the equally complete mental revolution on the part of those on the management's side. . . . in the past a great part of the thought and interest . . . has been centered on what may be called the proper division of the surplus resulting from their joint efforts. . . . The great revolution that takes place . . . under scientific management is that both sides take their eyes off the division of the surplus as the all-important matter, and together turn their attention toward increasing the size of the surplus until this surplus becomes so large that it is unnecessary to quarrel over how it shall be divided.

Taylor therefore opposed labor unions. Had they not been made superfluous by his God, a harmonious and efficient God, the God of Productivity?. . .

Taylor's most important (and unpatentable) invention was a new system for organizing *all* factories. What Taylor called the principles of scientific management in 1911 aimed to reshape the very concept of work. Taylor's essential idea was to do for the work unit what Eli Whitney, and his predecessors and successors, had done for the material unit in the American system of manufacturing. Taylor broke down every operation in a factory into the simplest tasks, then timed each to find the most economical way of performing it.

Time was Taylor's ruling dimension, the stopwatch his essential tool. When Taylor went to work for the Bethlehem Steel Company in 1898, he undertook a series of experiments "to find out how quickly the various kinds of work that went into the shop ought to be done." Taylor's prescription for a proper time study was:

First. Find, say, 10 to 15 different men (preferably in as many separate establishments and different parts of the country) who are especially skillful in doing the particular work to be analyzed.

Second. Study the exact series of elementary operations or motions which each of these men uses in doing the work which is being investigated, as well as the implements each man uses.

Third. Study with a stop watch the time required to make each of these elementary movements and then select the quickest way of doing each element of work.

Fourth. Eliminate all false movements, slow movements, and useless movements.

Fifth. After doing away with all unnecessary movements, collect into one series the quickest and best movements, as well as the best implements.

This new method, involving that series of motions which can be made quickest and best, is then substituted in place of the 10 or 15 inferior series which were formerly in use.

Taylor and his staff spent five months gathering this kind of data at Bethlehem on the best way of shoveling.

The "science of shoveling" (the butt of his opponents' jokes), which was the result of Taylor's research, became his classic example of the promise of scientific management. In 1912, before a special committee of the House of Representatives, he suggested that if he actually could make a science of shoveling, there was nothing in the world he could not make a science of. Taylor recounted his experience at the Bethlehem Steel plant. On his arrival there he had found that each laborer brought his own shovel to the yard and used the same shovel to move all sorts of material. "We would see a first-class shoveler go from shoveling rice coal with a load of 3½ pounds to the shovel to handling ore from the Messaba Range, with 38 pounds to the shovel. Now, is 3½ pounds the proper shovel load or is 38 pounds the proper shovel load? They cannot both be right. Under scientific management the answer to this question is not a matter of anyone's opinion; it is a question for accurate, careful, scientific investigation."

Nothing is so certain as that the evils of idleness can be shaken off by hard work.

—Seneca, *Epistles*

After gathering data on the tonnage of each kind of material handled at Bethlehem by each man each day, Taylor had designed his own shovels and supplied them to the men. He then noted the result as he changed the length of the handle. He found, for example, that by cutting off the handle so that the shoveler picked up 34 (indead of 38) pounds in each shovel-load of ore, he could increase the shoveler's daily handling from a total of 25 to 35 tons. Taylor continued to cut off the shovel handle until he found that at 21½ pounds per load, the men were doing their largest day's work. By pursuing this kind of study, he found that the best results in the plant as a whole were obtained when there were fifteen different kinds of shovels, each one for moving a different kind of material—ranging from small flat shovels for handling ore up to immense scoops for handling rice coal, and forks for handling coke. And he had also defined the proper technique for the use of each of these tools. . . . Taylor sent his team about the plant instructing the laborers in the science of shoveling.

After three and a half years, as a result of Taylor's new science, 140 men were doing the work formerly done by 600. The cost of handling material was cut in half, and the shovelers still employed were receiving a 60 percent increase in wages.

What Taylor did for shoveling, he and his disciples were soon attempting to accomplish for all the other operations in hundreds of factories over the nation. Under the name of "scientific management," time-study men were breaking down jobs into their components, timing each component, and designing the best way to do each one. Factory work had been atomized into precisely separated and precisely timed tasks. "The work of every workman is fully planned out by the management at least one day in advance, and each man receives in most cases complete written instructions, describing in detail the task which he is to accomplish, as well as the means to be used in doing the work." Taylor's disciples went still further in atomizing the factory's operation, in describing elementary human movements, and in measuring split seconds. . . .

One of the most energetic of those who joined in Taylor's work was Frank Gilbreth, whose elaborate efforts to organize an efficient household with his numerous children made him the hero of the best-selling book and the popular movie *Cheaper by the Dozen* (1948). Gilbreth, who had worked as a bricklayer, collaborated with his wife in a three-year time-and-motion study of bricklaying. Gilbreth then reported to Taylor his shocking discoveries of waste: "My God . . . that is nothing short of barbarous. Think of it! Here I am a man weighing over 250 pounds, and every time I stoop down to pick up a brick I lower 250 pounds of weight down two feet so as to pick up a brick weighing 4 pounds, and then raise my 250 pounds of weight up again, and all of this to lift up a brick weighing 4 pounds. Think of this waste of effort. It is monstrous." Gilbreth and his wife spent a year and a half trying to cut out that motion. When they had finished they had perfected a method for laying bricks which required only five motions per brick, in place of the previous eighteen motions. Out of this the Gilbreths developed their own new science of "motion economy." It included, among others, the principle that two hands should not be idle at the same instant except during rest periods, that motions of the arms should be in opposite and symmetrical directions. Each elementary motion they called a *therblig* (Gilbreth spelled backwards). After Frank Gilbreth's death, Lillian Gilbreth wrote several books showing how these notions could be applied to running a household.

"Scientific management" became a synonym for good housekeeping in the industrial world. . . . Taylor's concept of time study and his notion of the elementary task were soon incorporated in the calculations both of manufacturers and of labor unions. By mid-century, General Motors, in its contracts with its workers, had divided the hour into six-minute periods, had fragmented the work to fit the periods, and the worker was being paid by the number of tenths of an hour that he worked. The United States Steel Corporation contract with the C.I.O. on May 8, 1946, defined a "fair days' work" as "that amount of work that can be produced by a qualified employee when working at a normal pace . . . a normal pace is equivalent to a man walking, without load, on smooth, level ground at a rate of three miles per hour." In their wage-rationalization program the next year, they described 1,150 jobs within 152 classifications. The Aluminum Company of America spent three and a half years and a half-million dollars developing a formula to rationalize and classify 56,000 jobs.

In the nineteenth century, European visitors had noted the initiative and intelligence and freedom from routine which they said helped explain the higher American standard of living. But now Taylor warned American workers against the old-fashioned virtue of "initiative." The workman who was required to do his job in the one "right" way, he said, was no more being inhibited than was the surgeon who was instructed in the one best way to perform an appendectomy. Most of what passed for "initiative," Taylor insisted, was really nothing but waste: the futile rule-of-thumb efforts of the ignorant to reinvent old ways. If the worker was paid by the tenth of an hour for performing his task precisely as prescribed, then he would have no need and little opportunity for initiative. And the fractioning of work by the new calculus of scientific management would make the meaning and the value of the factory-worker's exertions harder than ever for the worker himself to understand.

Those rule-of-thumb ways of doing things which were anathema to Taylor had at least given a man on the job the feeling that he was doing what he should. To abolish the rule of thumb in factory work would excise a part of every worker's emotional investment and personal satisfaction. Could a worker now fail to feel that he was doing somebody else's job, or a job dictated by the machine? Rule of thumb was personal rule. Scientific management, which made the worker into a labor unit and judged his effectiveness by his ability to keep the technology flowing, had made the worker himself into an interchangeable part.

Scientific management had its effect, too, not only on *how* anything was produced but also on *what*. Items to be manufactured were designed and selected for production according to how quickly and economically they could be produced. In place of the naïve consumer, the "scientific" system now made its own demands. Was this a price for the limitless productivity which the American system of manufacturing promised? Was this the end of America's brilliant new techniques for "conserving" human resources?

The full pathos and the subtle contradictions in the new American effort to make the most of men could not long remain hidden. It was revealed in a famous experiment by Elton Mayo at the Hawthorne Works of the Western Electric Company in Chicago in the 1930's. For thirteen weeks six girls employed in assembling telephones were studied. Every possible variable was noted and calculated: the heat and the light in the workroom, the amount of sleep they had the night before, or two nights before. For the purposes of the study, one variable at a time was changed and the results noted, but no individual variable proved to be the controlling factor. Regardless of what the experimenters changed in the work situation, the productivity of these six girls rose and continued to rise. Mayo's shrewd conclusion was that the real explanation was the experiment itself—the show of concern for the particular workers, together with the esprit it gave them as a working team. A moral of Mayo's study, of course, was that no physical improvement in scientific management could overwhelm the feelings that living men and women had about their work and their relation to it.

Before long this discovery itself became the basis of another new doctrine in the quest for greater productivity. If workers produced more when they felt that the employer was interested in them as individuals, then the most efficient means must be found for giving workers the impression that the employer was interested. And here was another step in what the sociologist Daniel Bell calls the movement "from authority to manipulation as a means of exercising dominion." Scientific management brought in its wake as a catalyst, or perhaps even as an antidote, a "science of human relations," with the novel profession of personnel management. But this science, too, while ostensibly designed to take fuller account of man's humanity, was destined (in Elton Mayo's phrase) to become "a new method of human control."

6
»«
THE
WORK ETHIC
TODAY
»«

Lewis Hine/International Museum of Photography at George Eastman House

» Amitai Etzioni «

Opting Out: The Waning of the Work Ethic

» «

Amitai Etzioni, a former presidential advisor and Columbia professor, now does public policy research at Georgetown University. He argues that Americans don't want to work as much as they once did. Like the Swedes described by Göran Palm (Chapter 2), Americans are characterized as "fleeing from work." Etzioni argues that trends in early retirement, part-time work, and labor force participation all point to a decline in the willingness to work.

The idea of "vacation time"—weeks, a month, set aside for one's idle pursuits—is actually a part of the Protestant work ethic that used to dominate our society. Webster defines vacation as a "respite or a time of respite from something: *intermission.*" That which is vacated is the norm, the pattern of discipline and work (or its equivalent, say in full-time studying). However, millions of Americans no longer subscribe to the work ethic and are unwilling to wait for July or August, or the summer, to have a vacation. They have repatterned their lives to "vacate" the whole year from the routine of full-time labor, the discipline of work.

There are many ways this is achieved—by working part time only; by choosing a second career, often less well paying but more flexible in its work demands than the discarded one; by delaying entering the labor force (especially by studying longer), and, above all, by retiring earlier. Public attention, meantime, has focused on those older Americans who *wish* to work but are *forced* to retire. Legislators have drafted bills to outlaw mandatory retirement. Firing a person because of his or her age is increasingly recognized as a form of discrimination. The notion that people who retire earlier die earlier because they feel no longer needed, is often cited when the issue arises.

Hidden by this quite justified concern with forced retirement of those who wish and are able to work are the millions of Americans who are not in the labor force because to one degree or another they do not wish to work.

Consider what has been happening with males between the ages of 55 and 64, a group traditionally expected to work, and fight retirement. Over the last years, members of this age group have retired in record numbers. The ranks grew from 13.1 percent of the labor force in 1950 to 17 percent in 1970 (at 0.19 percent a year). By 1975 their proportion increased to 24.2 percent (or an average annual increase of 1.04 percent), a rate five times faster.

While the proportion of women from age 55 to 64 not in the labor force has *decreased* from 73 percent in 1950 to 57 percent in 1970, they too join the early-retirement wave over the following five years: 59 percent of them were not in the labor force in 1975 (both figures for men and women *exclude* those unemployed but actively seeking employment).

Some of those not in the labor force are in ill health; some gave up looking for work; but a two and a half times increase (as of 1950) in men who do not work and a more than 20 percent in the proportion of women—a total of 8.3 million Americans—cannot be accounted for by these factors. Health conditions have improved, not worsened in the era, and underemployment has increased only marginally. A significant pro-portion of Americans aged 55 to 64—there seem to be no exact figures—*choose* not to work, at least not actively seek those jobs open to them. They choose, in effect, to trade income (and later higher pensions) for an earlier recasting of life to make more room for leisure, study, public life, or some combination thereof—indeed, to make some nonwork activity their central life interest.

While there is no hard evidence that most of the millions involved are neither plagued by guilt, nor die younger because they find no mission in life-after-work, the fact that the average life expectancy continues to rise, despite few recent breakthroughs in medicine, suggests indirectly that quite possibly millions of those Americans are embracing a new ethos. They increasingly feel that what used to be called nonproductive pursuits are quite legitimate patterns of living. That having more time for leisure, each other, sex, education, culture, politics, is as good as working 10 more years, or better. That you can't take it with you, and hence, you may as well spend your savings now, enjoy your life now, even if this may mean you will have less to spend later or may run out of money one day.

Those who remain on or around the campus after graduation; who choose less lucrative but more actualizing second careers; who no longer take their briefcases home, are making America less of a work-hard society and one more concerned with the quality of living. The increasing result is a society with less interest in periods of vacation and more in fulfillment all year round.

I didn't want to work. It was as simple as that. I distrusted work, disliked it. I thought it was a very bad thing that the human race had invented for itself.

—Agatha Christie, *Endless Night*

» **Graham L. Staines and Pamela O'Connor** «

Conflicts Among Work, Leisure, and Family Roles

» «

The University of Michigan's Survey Research Center has recently undertaken a series of controversial surveys of American working conditions. They have found a persistent concern with the soft, "quality of life" issues that trade unionists, industrial engineers, and labor economists have traditionally dismissed as unimportant or, at best, important only to upper-middle-class intellectuals. In fact, according to the Michigan surveys, middle-aged blue-collar workers are somewhat less interested in job quality issues than are young workers, professionals, managers, and the college educated. Nonetheless, the Michigan researchers have documented many important, undeniable trends, including the growing problem of underemployment: About one-third of all American workers in the most recent survey (1977) report that their skills, training, and education are underutilized on their jobs. In addition, more than half the respondents complained about a lack of control over their work schedules and job assignments. Overall, there was a "slight but significant" drop in job satisfaction between 1973 and 1977. The following article, based on the 1977 survey, analyzes one specific aspect of job satisfaction: the extent to which jobs and free time interfere with each other. The researchers conclude that the demand for more leisure is growing in the United States, particularly among those workers who are experiencing increased conflicts between work and family roles.

Workers in the 1977 Quality of Employment Survey were asked, "How much do your job and your free time activities interfere with each other?" A third of the 1,515 workers reported that conflict between work and free time activities occurred "a lot" or "somewhat."

When asked "In what ways do they interfere with each other?" these workers most frequently mentioned excessive amounts of work which prevented them from spending enough time in other activities. The second most common complaint involved work schedules that interfered with leisure. "Other" time conflicts ranked third and reports that work makes the worker too tired or too irritated to engage in leisure activities were fourth.

Demographic subgroups of workers reported different types of conflict between work and leisure. Men, who on average work more hours than women, were significantly more likely than women to report excessive amounts of work. Older workers (45 years and over) were significantly less likely than younger workers to report excessive amounts of work, scheduling conflicts, or spillover from work of fatigue and irritation. Married workers were more likely than unmarried workers to report excessive amounts of work, but were less likely to report scheduling conflicts. Parental responsibility was positively and significantly associated with reports of excessive amounts of work, but not with reports of the other types of interference. Workers with a high school diploma cited spillover of fatigue and irritation more frequently than did workers in other educational categories, but education was not related to the other types of interference. Workers in managerial and administrative occupations were the group most likely to complain of excessive work, whereas service workers were the group most inclined to mention scheduling conflicts.

Factors Associated with Conflict

Conflict between work and leisure clearly appears related to the demographic characteristics of the worker and to various dimensions of work, leisure, and family roles. Table 1 summarizes the findings for the degree of conflict associated with demographic factors. The "mean" in the table is the average value of response to the question: "How much do your job and your free time activities interfere with each other?" Degrees of interference were scored from 1 to 4 points, with "not at all" equaling 1 point and "a lot" equaling 4 points.

Working men reported significantly more conflict between work and leisure than did working women, as did younger workers (under age 45), compared with older workers. The degree of interference was not related to marital status but was positively and significantly related to level of parental responsibilities: parents of children under age 6 were more likely to report conflict, followed by parents of school-age children, and then workers with no children at home. Moreover, workers with a college degree or above reported significantly more conflict than did those with less education. Among the major occupational groups, workers in managerial and administrative occupations registered the highest level of conflict.

A number of work-related items were significantly related to work-leisure conflict. (See Table 2.) As expected, amount of time spent on the job was positively and significantly related to interference. Another significant factor was shift assignment: workers on afternoon or night shifts reported the highest levels of interference; those on day shifts reported the lowest level; and those on rotating shifts or other irregular patterns registered scores in between.

The significance that workers assign to their work role was assessed by asking the following two questions: "How often do you think about your job when you're busy doing something else? Often, sometimes, rarely, never" (role perseveration); and "How much do you agree or disagree that the most important things that happen to you involve your job? Strongly agree, agree, disagree, strongly disagree" (role importance). Role perseveration was significantly and positively related to interference, but role importance was not. Interference produced a significantly negative relationship with satisfaction with work. . . .

Table 1. Reported conflict between work and leisure, by selected demographic characteristics

Characteristic	Mean[1]
Sex	
Men	2.26[2]
Women	2.10[2]
Age	
Under 30 years	2.29[2]
30–44 years	2.29[2]
45 years and older	2.02[2]
Marital status	
Married	2.23[3]
Not married	2.13[3]
Parental status	
No children	2.13[2]
Youngest child 6–17 years	2.22[2]
Youngest child under 6 years	2.34[2]
Education	
Less than high school diploma	2.05[2]
High school diploma	2.21[2]
Some college	2.20[2]
College degree or more	2.39[2]
Occupation	
Professional and technical	2.21[2]
Managerial and administrative	2.41[2]
Sales and clerical	2.02[2]
Crafts	2.15[2]
Operatives	2.39[2]
Service	2.07[2]

[1]The mean is the average value of response to the question: "How much do your job and your free time activities interfere with each other?" Degrees of interference were scored from 1 to 4 points with "not at all" equaling 1 and "a lot" equaling 4. Levels of significance indicate the presence of significant differences among subgroup means (based on analysis of variance).
[2]Significant at .01.
[3]Not significant.

In addition, the significance of leisure (role perseveration, role importance) was positively and significantly associated with work-leisure conflict, whereas satisfaction with leisure produced a significantly negative association. . . .

In sum, reports of work-leisure conflict tend to be positively associated with involvement in all major roles of life (work, leisure, family), regardless of whether involvement is measured in behavioral (variety of activities, time allocated) or attitudinal (significance assigned to role) terms. Exception: conflict is negatively related to time spent on leisure during a workday. In addition, such conflict is consistently associated with low satisfaction with each of the major roles of life.

Table 2. Reported conflict between work and leisure, by selected work-related items

Item	Mean[1]
Time on the job:[2]	
6.9 hours or less	2.05[3]
7.0–7.9 hours	2.13[3]
8.0 hours	2.12[3]
8.1-9.9 hours	2.25[3]
10 hours or more	2.47[3]
Shift[4]	
Day	2.12[3]
Afternoon	2.57[3]
Night	2.51[3]
Rotating	2.20[3]
Other	2.31[3]
Role perseveration	
Never	2.04[3]
Rarely	2.21[3]
Sometimes	2.14[3]
Often	2.36[3]
Role importance	
Disagree	2.17[5]
Agree	2.23[5]
Strongly agree	2.30[5]
Satisfaction with work	
Not at all or not too	2.62[3]
Somewhat	2.30[3]
Very	2.02[3]

[1]See table 1, footnote 1
[2]Time spent working on a workday was assessed using the question "During the average week, how many hours do you work, not counting the time you take off for meals?" For each worker, the number of hours worked per week was then divided by the number of days worked to yield an average number of hours worked per day.
[3]Significant at .01.
[4]Day or regular shift starts between 4 a.m. and 12 noon, afternoon shift starts between 12 noon and 8 p.m., and night shift starts between 8 p.m. and 4 a.m.
[5]Not significant.

» Michael Maccoby and Katherine A. Terzi «

What Happened to the Work Ethic?

» «

Survey findings about worker discontent and the increasing demand for leisure have led many business people as well as social scientists to question what is happening to the work ethic. In the following selection, Michael Maccoby and Katherine Terzi, of the Program on Technology, Work, and Character, relate the changing work ethic to the changing American character. According to the authors, there have been four major work ethics in American history: the Protestant ethic, the craft ethic, the entrepreneurial ethic, and the career ethic. Today, these four ethics coexist to varying degrees, but they are all being eroded by changes in technology and in our social and economic systems. The authors caution that unless business, union, and government leaders support a new work ethic of self-fulfillment, our society is in danger of losing its motivation to work.

What Is the Work Ethic?

In exploring American history, we can discern four definitions of the work ethic that represent changing socio-economic periods, and a changing American character. (At any time, there is probably a mix of ethics, with more than one existing side by side, but with one dominant.) The four are: (1) The Protestant ethic; (2) the craft ethic; (3) the entrepreneurial ethic; and (4) the career ethic.

At the present, a fifth ethic, a self-development ethic is emerging; the work ethic in America is changing, but it has changed before.

The Protestant Ethic and the Craft Ethic   The Protestant ethic in America grew out of Calvinistic and Quaker individualism and asceticism. To some extent, this religious imperative to work at a calling for the glory of God was later secularized in the craft ethic of Benjamin Franklin which served as the ideal for generations of Americans. . . .

Unlike the Puritans, Franklin's craftsman no longer works for God's glory, but for himself. "In the affairs of this world, men are saved not by faith, but by the want of it," states Franklin, and he concludes: "God helps those who help themselves.". . .

162

The essence of the work ethic, for a nation in which 80 percent of the work force was self-employed (mainly as farmers and craftsmen) is Franklin's resolve:

> To apply myself industriously to whatever business I take in hand, and not divert my mind from my business by any foolish project of growing suddenly rich.

The Entrepreneurial Ethic In the beginning of the 19th century, a new spirit of the frontier and the industrial revolution began to infuse the Nation's business. A combination of gambling and building, of egalitarianism and ambition emerged in the America of Andrew Jackson. . . .

The frontier offered dreams, hopes and opportunities for the ambitious. The new entrepreneur had lost the craftsman's traits of caution and moderation. . . . Americans wanted to live well, and they were natural businessmen. After the Civil War, the acceleration of the industrial revolution, exploitation of technology and resources favored the rise of a new social character, new ideals, and a new version of the work ethic. . . .

The first new entrepreneurs were merchants, not manufacturers, and the entrepreneurial ethic first emerged in a commercial rather than an industrial context. Then the creation and use of productive technology outgrew the reach of single individuals or groups of craftsmen. The entrepreneurs were able to organize and control the craftsmen. Through the division of labor and organized skills they were able to employ unskilled farm labor and the immigrants from Europe.

As Benjamin Franklin expressed the craft ethic, so the heroes of Horatio Alger exemplified the entrepreneurial ethic for Americans. They became the models for success in a society increasingly dominated by rapidly growing business, and full of immigrants seeking employment. In contrast to the conservative, self-contained, and taciturn craftsmen, like Poor Richard, Alger's heroes, like Ragged Dick, are smart talking, tricky, entrepreneurial, and liberal spenders with a taste for elegance. They are poor, but tough and honest, neither mean nor lazy. . . . Nonfictitious "Horatio Alger" type success stories include Andrew Carnegie, John D. Rockefeller and craftsmen-entrepreneurs like Thomas Edison, Henry Ford, and George Eastman. Small businessmen also identified with these entrepreneurial strivings. However, as the frontier closed, the trend continued toward larger and more powerful business—with many small enterprises becoming less feasible, particularly where large technological systems had been built. . . .

The entrepreneurial ethic, the idea that a person with the right attitude can make it on his own, became a justification for inequality and an answer to those who complained about submitting to the discipline of organizations. Auto workers interviewed by Eli Chinoy as late as the early 1950's dreamed of opening up their own gas stations or garages. Yet, during the

163

period 1800 to 1970 the number of self-employed in America fell from 80 to 8 percent of the work force.

This trend implies that it is harder and harder for an individual entrepreneur to prosper. . . . Character traits that formerly served a certain type of independent small businessman in the market are no longer useful in competing with large corporations. The willingness to work long hours and keep the store open on Sundays and holidays used to contribute to success. But what is the use of such sacrifice and durability when large chains such as Safeway decide to remain open on Sundays? In addition, the small businessman must be able to handle increasingly costly and complicated government regulations. In this market, self-employment becomes a realistic possibility only for the brilliant entrepreneur, not for the average American whose work future more often centers in a large organization.

Although the self-employed are still, on the average, more satisfied with work, than wage earners, an increasing percentage of the self-employed perceive disadvantages to self-employment in excessive responsibility, long hours, and economic insecurity, as compared to a career in organizations.

The Career Ethic As the economic system changed and with it the traits necessary for success, the entrepreneurial ethic no longer expressed the strivings of many of the most talented and highly motivated individuals. At the same time, new technological systems required increased division of labor and complex organizational hierarchies. Success in the large organization depended on administrative rather than entrepreneurial skills. Business schools began to train managerial technicians with a new managerial—career ethic, replacing the entrepreneurial ethic. Rather than hoping to establish their own businesses, these people sought jobs in the large organizations in business, government and the non-profit sector. Their goal was to move up in the organization toward increased responsibility and organizational status. In the 1950's the career ethic seemed confined to management; in the 1970's, it appears to some observers as the work ethic for labor, as well.

The career ethic implies technology that is less craft like, and more dependent on codified and systematized knowledge which can be applied somewhat independently of a specific organizational context. In entrepreneurial business, cumulative experience pays off, whereas in organizations using new and changing technology, theoretical knowledge becomes more significant than experience, especially experience within a particular organization.

This ethic belongs especially to "the new class" of professionals and technicians who make their living by their ability to solve problems, to apply the latest information, and to manage.

As more young people enter the work force with high school and college education, aspirations for careers emerge in traditionally blue collar workers. These people expect the workplace to be a meritocracy: anyone who demonstrates the indicated skills and abilities should be able to rise in the organization. Talent and hard work should earn success and promotion. . . .

Those with the credentials who do not move up fast enough feel cheated. Those who fail to make the grade become resentful and turned off to work. . . .

Each work ethic implies a different social character, different satisfactions and dissatisfactions at work, and a different critique of society. The Protestant ethic implies a character driven to work, consciously to show membership in the elect, unconsciously to overcome any doubts about faith. The Puritan worked for the glory of God, and his own salvation, and reward in heaven. His goal was a community of the elect needing neither kings nor bishops, and he would not tolerate unethical and undisciplined behavior.

The craft ethic implies a hoarding-productive character oriented to saving and self-sufficiency, to independence and self-control, and to rewards on earth. The craftsman is most satisfied by work which he controls, with standards he sets . . . . The craftsman's critique is of bosses, either entrepreneurs or company men, who tell him what to do, and threaten his independence. He distrusts bigness and power, even in the face of a technology grown too large to have been created or controlled by individuals.

The entrepreneur implies a bold, risk-taking character, with an orientation toward exploiting opportunities and using people. The entrepreneur is most satisfied by the opportunity to build his own business. Some entrepreneurs are satisfied with economic independence; others seek wealth and are motivated by the gambling spirit. The entrepreneur's critique is of a society that strangles free enterprise and individual initiative. He is critical of bureaucracy, red tape and regulation, and of people who choose security ahead of adventure. He dislikes unions which he feels destroy his relationship with employees.

You can't eat for eight hours a day nor drink for eight hours a day nor make love for eight hours a day—all you can do for eight hours is work. Which is the reason why man makes himself and everybody else so miserable and unhappy.
—William Faulkner

The career ethic implies an other-directed, ambitious, marketing character. Such an individual is most satisfied by work which gives him the chance to get ahead, to develop himself in a way which fits the requirements of career, to become a more attractive package, worth more in the market. . . . The careerist expects fair play in his assigned role, and wants to know the rules of the game, what is expected of him and what he will receive in return. He criticizes a system which blocks him, which leaves him "stuck" in dead end jobs, powerless to move ahead or develop himself. The career ethic challenges both unionism and paternalism with their emphasis on seniority and loyalty because moving ahead to the careerist is based on winning a game with rules in which the best triumph.

More than the other types, the career ethic thus involves a critique of the whole organization and its principles. This critique can call for changes in the organization of work, to increase fairness in promotions, and to provide opportunities for learning and development. The careerist may recognize that to enjoy greater freedom to make decisions, he must move up the ladder. Failure to do so may also mean loss of respect from others and self-respect.

On a deeper level, many successful careerists suffer from anxiety, guilt and depression. They are anxious about constantly being judged and evaluated and worried about saying or doing the wrong thing. . . .

The extent of self-alienation resulting from the career ethic has driven many individuals to question its value. Even some who have reached the top criticize the costs of careerism in family life and the underdevelopment of the emotions.

Recent surveys indicate that a concern with both life outside of work and intrinsic aspects of work is challenging the career ethic. Jerome M. Rosow reports that only 21 percent of workers say that their work is more important than leisure activities. . . .

Surveys by both Yankelovich and the University of Michigan indicate that a large percentage of Americans want work that is "challenging" and/or allows the opportunity for "self-expression" and "growth." This seems to contradict the flight from work to leisure activities, unless a reason for turning away from work is the lack of opportunity for growth, or people wanting challenge, but not so much as to make work all absorbing.

Yankelovich believes that the work ethic is being challenged by what he calls a "self-fulfillment" ethic. A growing number of people, especially the younger, more educated and affluent are concerned with personal growth and enjoyment of life both at work and leisure. When these strivings take priority over considerations of career, large organizations which count on the career ethic are in trouble. . . .

Is there a fifth work ethic of self-fulfillment or self-development? Does it imply a change in the American character? Is it adaptive to changing technology and work? Before considering the meaning and implications of "self-fulfillment" in the context of change in technology and the socioeconomic system, we shall examine the evidence of whether Americans are less motivated to work today than in the past.

Laziness may appear attractive, but work gives satisfaction.
—Anne Frank, *The Diary of a Young Girl*

166

Is There Less Motivation to Work?

Are Americans less motivated to work now? . . .

Objective Indicators . . .Objective indicators do not form a conclusive pattern supporting the hypothesis of a decline in motivation, but there is evidence from cases that when leadership understands and respects the goals and values of different employees, productivity increases.

Although unscheduled absences have until recently been on the rise, this may have been due to more liberal personnel policies rather than to a change in work attitudes. Strikes over working conditions have increased, but they cover a wide spectrum of issues making generalizations difficult. . . .

The Commitment to Work For most people the issue is not: Do I still want to work? as much as: Does my job turn me off? Surveys show a consistently strong affirmation of the value of work for three-quarters of the population. When asked if they would continue to work even if they could live comfortably for the rest of their lives without working, most people choose to work. This holds constant throughout several surveys from 1969 to 1978. . . .

The labor force continues to grow at an increasing rate, as many people not previously employed, in particular women and the old, try to enter the world of paid jobs. . . . The demand for paid jobs is not likely to let up soon. Syndicated columnist Ellen Goodman reported a particularly striking statistic from a national survey aiming to assess future educational needs: In 1973–74 only 3 out of 100 (3 percent) 17-year-old girls claimed "housewife" as their number one career choice. Clearly, they intended to take a job rather than stay home. . . .

If we accept the premise that Americans still believe in the value of work well done and most want the chance to work, how can we understand indications of dissatisfaction? The first explanation is that while working remains important, other arenas of life—leisure, family—are also gaining in importance. The second explanation, now explored, concerns dissatisfaction, not with work *per se*, but with the actual jobs that people hold and the nature of supervision. . . .

There is evidence to suggest some jobs are less satisfying despite a still high motivation to work. One item on the University of Michigan survey supports this view. When asked: "If you were free to go into any type of job you wanted, what would your choice be?", the results were:

	1969	1973	1977
The job he or she now has	49.2%	43.7%	38.1%
Retire and not work at all	6.3	4.6	1.9
Prefer some other job to the job he or she now has	44.4	51.7	60.0[1]

[1]15.6 percent increase.

Here we see a striking shift with implications for motivation to work. Of those questioned by the Gallup poll [in 1973,] 50 percent said they "could accomplish more each day if they tried." Those dissatisfied with their jobs tended to say they could do more if they tried. The Harris Poll [in 1972] asked whether people would be "very willing to work harder under certain conditions." Between 46 percent to 64 percent were willing to work harder, depending on the reward. Pay came out ahead (64 percent) but was closely followed by "more to say about the kind of work you do and how you do it" (61 percent); additional schooling or training (59 percent); and being able to work more independently (58 percent).

There is little agreement on the relationship among attitudes, productivity, and other economic indicators. In many workplaces, individuals do not share ideas for improving productivity because they lack the confidence that they will be listened to, or will share equitably in productivity gains.

Studies also indicate a growing crisis of legitimacy, confidence, trust, authority: A crisis of leadership. While reaffirming the importance of work to individual well-being, most people no longer expect to be rewarded equitably, according to their efforts. Between 1967 and 1975 the number of students who believed "Hard work always pays off" was nearly reversed, from 69 percent agreeing in 1967 to 75 percent saying "no" in 1975. . . . This finding suggests that a key belief which is consistent with both the traditional craft ethic and the career ethic is dissolving. . . .

Job Satisfaction—Demographic Differences . . . Who is most dissatisfied? Who is most satisfied? Whose attitudes are changing most? Do we know why?

There is general agreement that the most dissatisfied sectors of the labor force are young (under 30), black, and low income (under $10,000.). The most satisfied are older (over 50), in professional/managerial occupations or self-employed. . . .

Declines in job satisfaction, however, are reported across-the-board for most sectors of the labor force. Demographic differences show some trends, but many researchers consider that they are "not generally the best indicators of job satisfaction." How else can the differences between groups of people be understood? Few studies are available which focus on understanding differences in job satisfaction based on character and culture. Yet many reports allude to such differences. Descriptions of a "new breed" of worker, the "new narcissism," the "me generation" all refer to a change in the American character. There is evidence of such an attitudinal change emerging, from the career ethic to the self-fulfillment, self-development ethic.

No work ethic fits all Americans, but most Americans are motivated to work. For some, work is an expression of religious belief. For some, it is craftsmanship. Some are driven by entrepreneurial dreams. Some strive to climb the corporate ladder to success or at least to a position of status.

Some seek a form of self-fulfillment through service.

A large number of individuals who are motivated to work are dissatisfied with employment that blocks their strivings for self-fulfillment, and which does not fit their work ethic. The frustrated craftsman forced into monotonous work may become angry and careless. The hard-working careerist stuck in a dead-end job which allows neither learning nor promotion may become bitter. Many of those who feel bored and powerless at work lose interest and look for satisfactions outside. These can be either self-developing activities: child rearing, community service, gardening, crafts, sports; or they may be activities that support an escapist, consumer attitude, encouraged by T.V. images of enjoyment. The evidence from studies indicates, however, that unfulfilling work stimulates escapist leisure, rather than self-developing ones, and that it is difficult to develop and maintain an active attitude to life when one is continually turned off at work. This issue of human productivity is not limited to the workplace. Rather it is an issue of national character and national vitality. Unless leadership in business, government, and unions understands what motivates people, the worst rather than the best in a changing national character will emerge.

Conclusion: The Changing American Character

To understand the changes in the American character, that have caused increased dissatisfaction with work, two broad interrelated historical currents need to be examined.

One current is the transformation of traditional rural to modern urban values based on innovations in technology, increased education and the disappearance of a sense of independence rooted in self-employment and the entrepreneurial ethic. The other is the decline of patriarchal authority, based on new demands for human rights and the changed role of women including equality in the workplace. These are, of course, trends. Some people, especially in rural areas, are still rooted in the older patterns; and different social character types (e.g., craftsman and careerist) express these changes differently, but they affect everyone.

One of the most significant social changes in America in this century has been the migration from farms and small towns to the cities. Traditional rural values included fundamentalist religious belief and an ascetic ethic of self-sacrifice either for personal salvation or for family welfare. . . . The unity of family and religious community is no longer necessary for survival. The majority today must adapt to a different reality of large organizations, where success depends on technical or professional competence and the ability to cooperate with different types of people. Although Americans are still more religious than many West Europeans, the modern urban individual is more skeptical about religion and beliefs that separate people than his rural counterpart, and more oriented to self-fulfillment rather than to God or family. Technological advances have lessened the need for hard physical work and stimulated new desires for entertainment. Technology for the home as well as telecommunications and personal transportation have freed women from housework and isolation in the household. Education has encouraged more people to aspire to higher status. Freed somewhat by technology and affluence from the tyranny of necessity, individuals of all classes have broken old taboos and chased experiences that in the past were the exclusive property of the rich. . . . Such factors have undermined the main mechanisms of the traditional, "up-tight," hoarding character. The negative traits of the new character are narcissistic modes of self-fulfullment, self-centeredness, greediness, and lack of concern for others. The positive traits are increased concern and personal responsibility for self-development and personal health, freedom to learn and experiment.

The disappearance of self-employment is in large measure a result of the demise of the family farm and the small town services that supported it; and the growth of corporate forms of organization, aided by innovations in telecommunication and data processing. . . . Increasingly, the sense of independence is rooted in technical, professional, and managerial skills, rather than ownership of a farm or a business. The negative traits that have resulted are those of careerist self marketing, the need to sell oneself, to become an attractive package at the expense of integrity. The positive traits are those of flexibility and tolerance, and the need to understand and cooperate with strangers.

The decline in patriarchy has resulted from urban values, from a science and information based technology, and from many challenges to the domination of the father and the boss. . . .

For organizations, the negative side of this trend has been the crisis of authority. Lacking respect for traditional bosses and institutions, employees become cynical, rebellious and experts at beating the system. The positive side is a critical and questioning attitude; the wish for mutual respect; and the desire to be cooperatively involved in an organization run on principles of equity and concern for individual development.

The rebellious spirit can either undermine authority or transform the authority structure. How will this transformation take place? One approach has been in the establishment, through collective bargaining, of Union-Management Cooperative Projects chartered to reorganize work in Bolivar, Tennessee (Harman-UAW) and Springfield, Ohio (City Management-AFSCME). They have required managers able to act as resources rather than bosses.

These projects and others have demonstrated that the primary tasks of leadership at work are to understand different attitudes, different strivings for self-fulfillment, and to establish operating principles that build trust, facilitate cooperation, and explain the significance of the individual's role in the common purpose. . . .

This is a generation prepared to communicate, and be responsive to reasonable explanations. Leadership will bring out the best in the emerging American character only by welcoming the positive aspects of that character: the needs for equity, involvement, personal development—including life-long learning at work. Experience in projects to improve work in both industry and government indicates that only a small minority of workers has a negative character structure that is immune to organization based on ethical principles and the resulting peer pressure to cooperate. New forms of organization become a necessity in an era of limits when concern for the common good must temper the career ethic. . . .

If leadership in business, unions and government does not help to establish a new work ethic of self-development and service by appealing to the positive elements in the American character, it is likely that the traditional work ethics will be replaced by a negative search for "self-fulfillment." This ambiguous ethic can mean either greedy cravings to have more for oneself, or it can mean demands for employment that serves both personal growth and social welfare. It can mean development of one's authentic interests in the arts, sciences, and professions; or it can mean a drive to win at any price. As long as there is a failure to distinguish ethically based self-development from other modes of self-development, and as long as there is a failure to organize work to support what is most productive in the American character, the new ethic may contribute to undermining the motivation to work.

» J. Richard Hackman and Greg R. Oldham «

Work Redesign: People and Their Work

» «

Business school professors J. Richard Hackman of Yale University and Greg R. Oldham of the University of Illinois caution us about how we should interpret the data on job dissatisfaction presented in the preceding selections. They argue that survey responses to such simple questions as "Are you satisfied with your job?" obscure more facts than they reveal. Workers could mean a variety of things when they say they are satisfied. The real question is, satisfied compared to what? Compared to the job my father had? Compared to the job I aspired to in my youth? Compared to how good this job could be with just a few changes? Compared to how bad this job could be if the foreman didn't happen to be a nice guy? The authors suggest that, rather than focusing on such simplistic notions as job satisfaction, we can better understand worker attitudes by focusing on the "fit" between people and their jobs. Although Hackman and Oldham believe there is probably no "crisis" in job-person relationships, there is a tremendous opportunity to make workers happier and workplaces more productive by improving the "fit" for the millions of workers whose skills and abilities are currently underutilized.

Ralph Chattick is a 44-year-old worker in a metal fabrication shop on the south side of Chicago. He grew up in the same neighborhood where he now lives, and has worked for the same company since graduating from high school many years ago. His job is to cut sheets of metal according to specification, with good accuracy and little waste. Ralph's work goes to another section, where various types of metal assemblies are constructed.

Ralph doesn't work very hard at his job, and he doesn't have to. He knows how to get through a workday without getting too tired and without attracting any special attention from his foreman. Indeed, one might infer from observing Ralph at work that he and his foreman have an agreement of sorts—perhaps best characterized as a truce—which specifies that if Ralph does a reasonable amount of work of reasonable accuracy, the foreman will leave him alone. The pay Ralph gets is adequate, and if asked on a survey whether or not he was "satisfied with his job," Ralph would say, without much thought, "yes." He is not angry, he's not looking for a better job (although he'd like more pay), and he's not much interested in how well the company does. Ralph gets along. He knows his place, it's reasonably comfortable, and he stays there.

The top management of the company where Ralph works is concerned. Productivity is down, customers are complaining about the quality of the products, and the organization seems to be stagnating. An organization development consultant has been contacted, and the president of the company is considering contracting with the consultant for a program to improve the quality of organizational management. The program being contemplated will involve a thorough diagnosis of the managerial styles of all top- and middle-level managers, a study of interlevel and interdepartmental relationships, and an analysis of how the design of the organization itself fits with the imperatives of its technology and its environment. Based on the results of this diagnostic work, a change program may be undertaken to revitalize the management of the organization and, it is hoped, eventually to improve the productivity and profitability of the company.

Will the program, if undertaken with vigor and commitment, achieve its goals? Perhaps. But if improved productivity is among the goals of the program, it will at some time have to touch Ralph and his co-workers— because they are the ones *who do the productive work of the company*. . . .

[Perhaps] <u>one of the major influences on organizational productivity is *the quality of the relationship between people who do the work and the jobs they perform*</u>. If there is a good "fit" between people and their jobs, such that productive work is a personally rewarding experience, then there may be little for managment to do to foster high motivation and satisfaction—other than support the healthy person-job relationship that exists. But if that fit is faulty, such that hard and productive work leads mainly to personal discomfort and distress, then there may be little that management *can* do to engender high productivity and satisfying work experiences. . . .

A Crisis in Person-Job Relationships?

Just how satisfactory are person-job relationships in contemporary organizations? Are most people prospering in their work, or at least as comfortable with their jobs as Ralph seems to be? Or are most employees chafing in jobs that are grossly inappropriate for their personal needs, skills, and aspirations?

There is a good deal of controversy about the matter. Some commentators argue with vigor that we are currently in the midst of a major "work ethic crisis" that portends revolutionary changes in how work will be designed and managed in the future. Others respond that the purported "crisis" is much more in the minds of those who herald its arrival than in the hearts of those who perform the productive work of society. That there is a great deal of commentary and controversy about the quality of person-job relationships is clear. But *is* there a crisis?

Yes Consider the following statement, which opens a book by Harold Sheppard and Neal Herrick titled *Where Have All the Robots Gone?*

> In today's highly regimented, increasingly automated, and deeply impersonal industrial society, the human being who has found fulfilling work is indeed among the blessed. But more and more workers—and every day this is more apparent—are becoming disenchanted with the boring, repetitive tasks set by a merciless assembly line or by bureaucracy. They feel they have been herded into economic and social cul-de-sacs. . . .

A similar theme is used by Studs Terkel to introduce his book *Working*, in which the thoughts and feelings of workers from many occupations and classes are reflected:

> This book, being about work, is, by its very nature, about violence—to the spirit as well as to the body. It is about ulcers as well as accidents, about shouting matches as well as fistfights, about nervous breakdowns as well as kicking the dog around. It is, above all (or beneath all), about daily humiliations. To survive the day is triumph enough for the walking wounded among the great many of us. . . .
>
> For the many, there is a hardly concealed discontent. The blue-collar blues is no more bitterly sung than the white-collar moan. "I'm a machine," says the spot-welder. "I'm caged," says the bank teller, and echoes the hotel clerk. "I'm a mule," says the steelworker. "A monkey can do what I do," says the receptionist. "I'm less than a farm implement," says the migrant worker. "I'm an object," says the high-fashion model. Blue collar and white call upon the identical phrase: "I'm a robot." . . .

By the mid-1970s, numerous statistical data had accumulated to support the expressed concerns. In 1976, for example, roughly 80 million hours *per week* were lost to absenteeism. Productive output per employee hour decreased in two-thirds of the industries included in the Bureau of Labor Statistics's 1974 report on industrial productivity. . . . Turnover rates, averaging 1.2 percent per month in the early 1960s, more than doubled by the end of the decade. . . .

How are we to account for such changes in employee behavior and attitude? Those who perceive that we are in the midst of a work ethic crisis tend to argue along the following lines. No less than a revolution in the

174

way productive work is done in the United States has occurred in this century, they suggest. In the last several decades, organizations have increased the role of technology and automation in attaining organizational objectives, and have dramatically expanded the number of jobs that are specialized, simplified, standardized, and routinized. Moreover, organizations themselves have become larger and more bureaucratic in how they function. As a consequence there have been great increases in the use of managerial and statistical controls to guide and enforce the day-to-day activities of organization members. . . .

As organizations increased in efficiency early in this century, workers demanded (and, through unionization, got) an increased share of the economic benefits that were being generated. Moreover, through taxation, another portion of these benefits was channeled into programs and activities aimed at increasing the personal and social welfare of the populace. People become more affluent, the number of years of schooling obtained by young people dramatically increased, and the hopes and expectations of the present generation of workers about what life—and work—would hold for them took a quantum jump upwards. . . .

In sum, even as work organizations have continued to get bigger, more mechanistic, more controlling of individual behavior, and more task-specialized, the people who work in those organizations have become more highly educated, more desirous of "intrinsic" work satisfactions, and perhaps less willing to accept routine and monotonous work as their legitimate lot in life. According to this line of reasoning, we may now have arrived at a point where the way most organizations function is in severe conflict with the talents and aspirations of most of the people who work in them. Such conflict manifests itself in increased alienation from work and in decreased organizational effectiveness. . . . Ways of structuring jobs and managing organizations that worked early in this century, it is argued, cannot work now because the people who populate contemporary organizations simply will not put up with them.

Ralph Chattick? A temporary casualty of poorly designed work. Living evidence that simplified, routinized work is neither effective nor humane. Yet while work stamped out the spark of Ralph's humanity, reversal is possible. Expand Ralph's job, make it challenging, manage him as a person rather than a machine part, and he will surprise management (and, perhaps, himself) with a level of motivated, productive work of which he now seems incapable. And he will move from a state of personal stagnation to growth in the bargain.

Yes, profound alterations in the design and management of work are required. And the benefits of those changes will be well worth the cost and effort required to bring them about.

No   Other observers argue that there is no real "crisis" in the world of work—that instead the reports of worker discontent and demands for

175

personally fulfilling work activities have been wildly exaggerated by journalists and social scientists. The work ethic crisis, it is argued, is more manufactured than real, and represents a serious misapprehension of the needs and satisfactions of those individuals who are seen as most troubled by dissatisfying work.

Considerable evidence can be marshalled in support of this view—some anecdotal, some systematic and scientific. Perhaps most widely publicized is the project sponsored by the Ford Foundation to test whether or not U.S. automobile workers would find satisfaction and fulfillment working on highly complex and challenging team assembly jobs in a Swedish automobile plant. Six Detroit auto workers spent a month working as engine assemblers in a Saab plant—and at the end of the month five of the six reported that they preferred the traditional U.S. assembly line. As one worker put it: "If I've got to bust my ass to be meaningful, forget it; I'd rather be monotonous." . . .

[Some] researchers and critics also have cast doubt on the popular notion that people who work on routine and repetitive tasks inevitably experience psychological or emotional distress as a consequence. . . .

Those who doubt the existence of a crisis in job satisfaction conclude . . . that the "crisis" can be observed only if one looks through the eyes of journalists and behavioral scientists who have a vested interest in seeing it. . . .

Data from a 1973 survey by the Survey Research Center of the University of Michigan would seem to support this position.* While blue-collar workers reported less overall job satisfaction than did white-collar workers, questions about what was the most *important* to blue- versus white-collar workers suggested that "interesting work" is not nearly as important to the blue-collar workers as more bread-and-butter matters such as job security and pay. . . . And, by implication, when changes are contemplated to improve the quality of worklife of blue-collar workers, perhaps they should focus on the items highest on the "importance" list of these workers— rather than on changes intended to make jobs more interesting and challenging.

A crisis in job satisfaction? An explosion of blue-collar blues? No. Most people are satisfied with their work. And when they are not, the reasons have more to do with basic issues such as pay and job security than with any unfilled aspirations for interesting and challenging work assignments. Ralph Chattick is a perfect example: he is paid well, his supervisor treats him fairly, and (most importantly) he is not asking to have his job changed. When he says he is satisfied we should believe him. If we really want to be helpful to Ralph and improve his "quality of worklife," then let's focus our changes on the things *he* wants (like a higher salary) rather than on something that journalists or behavioral scientists *think* he should want.

---

*The results of the [more] recent Survey Research Center survey, however, provide some evidence of a decline in job satisfaction.

Some Facts About People and Work

Both the argument for and the argument against a crisis in job satisfaction can be persuasive, and one can argue either side of the question forcefully and with ample supporting data. . . . Yet there are certain facts about people and about work which, if understood, would make discussions about the "crisis" a little less polemic and a little more thoughtful than typically has been the case. These facts, moreover, offer some guidance about how person-job relationships might best be managed in contemporary organizations. . . .

Fact One: Many People Are Underutilized and Underchallenged at Work. These people, whom [James] O'Toole calls the "reserve army of the under-employed," have more to offer their employers than those employers seek, and they have personal needs and aspirations that cannot be satisfied by the work they do. It seems to us indisputable that numerous jobs in the bowels of organizations have become increasingly simplified and routinized in the course of the last century, even as the workers who populate those jobs have become generally better educated and more ambitious in their expectations about what life will hold for them.

The result is a poor fit between large numbers of people and the work they do . . . [because the person is too much for the job rather than because the job is too much for the person]. The fact is that there are millions of individuals in this society for whom work is neither a challenge nor a personally fulfilling part of life.

Fact Two: People Are More Adaptable Than We Realize. When they absolutely must do so, people show an enormous capacity to adapt to their environments. . . . The same is true for work.

This plasticity often goes unrecognized by those who argue loudly on one or the other side of the "work ethic" debate. Part of the reason is that it is very hard to see adaptation happening, except when the environment changes dramatically and suddenly. . . . It is very hard to figure out what is happening (or what has happened) to a person at work if you look only once.

With this in mind, let us review the case of Ralph Chattick, but this time with some additional information about how his life and career developed. We will discover that Ralph, like the rest of us, is a pretty adaptable person.

Ralph did very well in high school, and thought seriously about the possibility of going on to college. . . . But ultimately the limitations of family finances, and Ralph's inability to obtain a large enough scholarship, decreed that he would go to work directly after graduation.

When he took up employment in the metal fabrication shop (where he still works) he retained his dream of saving money and of applying once again to college in a few years. His first job was as a helper to a metal cutter, and he rather enjoyed it. . . . After two years he was promoted to a

177

position in a cutting department where he worked mostly without supervision, and from what he heard from his foreman he was performing quite well.

But soon he mastered the job, and work became a fairly predictable routine. Ralph began to get bored. He had some money saved, and he once again raised in his mind the possibility of applying to college. However, he also wanted to get married and start a family, and it was clear to Ralph that doing one precluded doing the other. He eventually decided to go ahead with marriage (it was not a hard choice), to use his modest savings to set up house, and after his personal life settled down to do something to improve his situation at work.

Ralph's initial attempts to better his life at work took place within his own company. When he asked about the possibility of promotion, he was told that he might eventually become a foreman, . . . but that promotion would be some years down the road. . . . A career in higher management was unlikely because he did not have any college work. A transfer to another department was possible, he learned, but he would have to wait his turn. . . .

As his restlessness and frustration increased, Ralph looked around for a job in a different company. Unfortunately, unemployment was high at the time, and there were few good jobs open. The only ones that struck him as really attractive required college, experience, or technical skills that Ralph did not have.

At about this point in Ralph's life, in his mid-twenties, he faced a choice of lifetime significance. On the one hand, he could keep looking for a job that he would find fulfilling, and keep fighting the constraints he experienced at work. Or he could accept his job and his organization as his lot in life, and begin the process of adjusting to it. It was a major choice, one of the most important Ralph would make about his work career. But he did not experience it that way. Instead, it was a series of smaller choices, none of which seemed monumental at the time: not to borrow money to go to school; to quit looking at the want ads in the paper; not to spend so much time with those of his workmates who were always complaining about the job and scheming about how to make things different for themselves.

Gradually, the summed effects of those small choices began to show themselves. Ralph's feelings of restlessness dropped. He developed an "understanding" with his supervisor, and devised ways of getting through a typical workday without being bothered too much by the monotony of the work. His productivity settled into a predictable pattern: not too little, not too much, and not to worry too much about quality and waste. Ralph's expectations about what work should mean to a person changed from what they were when he started with the company, and his aspirations about his work career became less ambitious. Increasingly, he became more interested in his wages and what they could buy, and (for the first time) he began to notice how his retirement plan funds were accumulating. Had the possibility of changing organizations come up in later years (it never did), Ralph probably would have decided against such a move because he would have lost substantial retirement benefits. . . .

The great majority [of those who started work with Ralph] took the same route Ralph did, and adapted to what they experienced as the inevitability of it all.

When we have to, most of us do. Not to do so would open us to continual feelings of dissatisfaction and distress, which we're well-motivated to avoid. So we adapt: some of us to challenging, exciting jobs, others of us to a pretty routine state of affairs.

When someone, be it a manager or a social scientist, observes us working comfortably at our job, the temptation is to attribute our attitudes and our behavior to "the way we are" as individuals. More often, however, what the observer sees and hears is the way we have *become*. Our work experiences, what happens to us day in and day out over the years, change us in profound ways. . . . Those who would take what we say and how we act on the job today as reflecting fixed traits of "personality" severely underestimate the profound long-term effects of adaptation processes.

Fact Three: Self-Reports of Job Satisfaction Are Suspect. Precisely because we adapt to our work environment, it is hard to interpret self-reports of how "satisfied" people are with their work, or how "motivated" they feel to perform well. If we had asked Ralph if he was satisfied with his job when he first started to work, his answer would have been a clear "yes." He was involved, he was learning new and interesting things, and he had a vision of an attractive future. If we had asked him a few years later, as he was trying to find ways to get out of a job he experienced as nonchallenging and monotonous, his answer would have been a resounding "no." And hear him now:

> *Are you satisfied with your work?*
> Yes, I guess so.
>
> *Would you keep working if you won a million dollars in the lottery?*
> Sure. *(Why?)* Well, you have to do something to fill the day, don't you? I don't know what I'd do if I didn't work.
>
> *Do you work hard on your job?*
> I do my job. You can ask them if I work hard enough.
>
> *Is it important to you to do a good job?*
> Like I said, I do my job.
>
> *But is it important to you personally?*
> Look, I earn what I'm paid, okay? Some here don't, but I do. They pay me to cut metal, and I cut it. If they don't like the way I do it, they can tell me and I'll change. But it's their ball game, not mine.

Ralph is telling us that he is basically satisfied with his work. But . . . obviously all is not well with Ralph; some signs are present in the above interview excerpt, and our knowledge of Ralph's personal and job history make us even more dubious about the validity of his "yes" to our question. . . .

[But] to answer other than affirmatively would raise for Ralph the specter that *he has been a bad chooser in his life.* . . . So the easiest response, and also one that seems honest, is to say "sure, I guess I'm satisfied with my job."

For these and other (more methodological) reasons, short-answer responses to job satisfaction questions, especially among people who have some tenure in their jobs, are suspect. . . . Alternatively, we might look beyond questions of satisfaction for other indicators that all is (or is not) well in the person-job relationship. Productivity, work quality, absence and turnover rates, degree of utilization of employee talent, and overt signs of high commitment to (or alienation from) the work may be useful in this regard. . . .

Fact Four: *Change Often Will Be Resisted, Even When It Is a Good Idea.* Listen again to Ralph, as the possibility of change is raised:

Is there any way in which you'd like to see your job changed?
Sure, more money.

Any other ways?
Sometimes the boss gets on my back, but I guess that's not too much of a hassle. The tools are okay. Sometimes they tell you to do things one way and then bitch that you didn't do it a different way; that's bad. (Pause) The job itself is a bore, that's for sure.

What if they gave you a job where instead of just cutting metal you did the whole assembly. Would you like that?
They'd never do that.

But what if they did?
(Pause) No, that wouldn't really make sense. It's set up pretty good now. Things are okay the way they are. I come in here, do my job, and go home with my skin still on. You start rocking the boat, no telling what's going to develop.

Would you like to be a foreman?
(Laugh) That's a hassle I don't need. Leave that to the other guys. There's a couple of them I'd like to see canned, though.

Why should Ralph resist change—indeed, resist the very *thought* of change? There are at least three good reasons. First, even opening the question resurrects the anxieties that were long ago put away when Ralph made his peace with the job. Second, change raises the possibility that

Ralph will have to learn some new ropes, when no new ropes have been learned for years. And third, Ralph may have a very real and understandable concern about change wrecking the rather comfortable style of work he has developed. . . .

Is change worth such risk and possible pain? To Ralph at age 20, yes, without question. Now, no, also without question.

If change agents are genuinely interested in Ralph's well-being and have genuine respect for his feelings and beliefs, should they leave him in peace and search for an organization where the employees are more eager for what they have to offer? Or should they work intensively with Ralph (and others of similar views), in hopes of helping him work through his concerns and anxieties and eventually alter his views about the desirability of more complex and challenging work? Or, perhaps, should the agents charge ahead with change in any case, on the grounds that Ralph feels the way he does largely because of what the organization did to him by keeping him on a routine, monotonous job—and that the change can reverse what has been an unfortunate set of organizational experiences?

Such questions have no easy answers. . . . In any application of work redesign there will be differences among people in their readiness for job change and in their desire for it. Sometimes it will be a 20-year-old who will be as uncomfortable with the prospect of change as Ralph is, and sometimes it will be the 44-year-old who is ready and eager for change. But there will always be individual differences among people in their attitude toward change, and a well-designed change program will always have to deal with them.

One More Time: Is There a Crisis?

The question has no clear answer, given the degree to which people adapt to their work, the caution with which answers to job satisfaction surveys must be interpreted, and the variation among people in their readiness for and attitudes toward change. What *is* clear is that the person-job relationship is key in understanding both organizational productivity and the quality of employees' work experiences. Moreover, there appears to be plenty of room for improving the fit between people and their jobs: there are literally millions of people in tens of thousands of organizations who are neither giving as much to their work as they might, nor getting as much from it as they need.

Jobs that underutilize people are just as inefficient as computers that underutilize their memories or assembly lines that run too slowly. And jobs that provide people with insufficient opportunities to satisfy important personal needs at work can be just as debilitating as a marriage that goes sour or a school that fails to educate. That some people adapt to a bad job (as they adapt to a bad marriage) by emotionally withdrawing from it and seeking need satisfactions elsewhere is no consolation.

Is there a national crisis in job satisfaction? It is probably the wrong question. A better question, perhaps, is how organizations can be designed, staffed, and managed so that employees are simultaneously utilized and satisfied to the fullest extent possible, with neither the goals of the organization nor the personal needs of the employees dominating the other. In other words, how can we achieve a "fit" between persons and their jobs that fosters *both* high work productivity and a high-quality organizational experience for the people who do the work?

》 Bill Billiter 《

Workaholics Do More but Accomplish Less

》 《

In some instances, hard work has become a caricature of the virtues embodied in the behavior of Russell Sage. Many professional workers who are called "workaholics" apparently produce more of a show than legitimate output on the job.

They spend untold hours at work, as their marriages crumble, their children become alienated and their friendships, if any, wither away.

They suffer high levels of stress and a high incidence of heart attacks. They say they love their work, but they really don't.

And despite their slavish hours of work, they are inefficient and ineffective contributors to any business or group effort.

They are the workaholics.

This is the picture that has emerged from a 14-year study soon to be published by Dr. Charles Garfield, a psychologist on the staff of the University of California, San Francisco, Medical School.

Garfield, working with his Berkeley-based, nonprofit Optimal Performance Center, launched a nationwide study in 1967 to find out why some people are very successful workers and others are not.

Garfield labeled the highly successful, highly beneficial workers "optimal performers." He used the familiar term "workaholics" to describe another group, one that his study found does not include optimal performers.

In an interview, Garfield described some parts of his study.

"What we wanted to do in the study of high-level performance was to study what work styles are most productive, and we studied a number," he said.

Garfield said that although "the workaholic's style is pretty much revered in our culture . . . it turned out not to be the group that makes the major contribution" in any group, profession or business.

Here are Garfield's assessments of workaholics:

"They are addicted to work, not results. They are not necessarily aware of the fact that they don't make the major impact (in their group or business), although they sometimes see themselves as making the major impact.

"They tend to be motivated more by fear and loss of status than by high level motivation and creative contribution.

"They tend also, as times goes on, to be more and more reluctant to take the risks within the organization necessary for positive, creative outcome.

"The career trajectories of workaholics are very, very predictable. They tend to burst on the scene, be labeled 'up and coming,' a real contributor. They rise quickly on the basis of their initial contribution, and then they tend to level off and end up managing the details of their careers.

"That (leveling off of their careers) very frequently happens when workaholics are in their mid-30s to mid-40s, and that's precisely the point where the incidence of cardiovascular disease, especially heart attacks, psychosomatic disorders, alcoholism, drug abuse and marital conflict all start merging on the workaholic."

Don't Enjoy Their Work

"Workaholics are high on every major index of stress. Their incidence of coronary heart disease is very high.

"Workaholics don't enjoy their work, even though they protest madly that they do. The question you can usually ask yourself is: 'What are they running from? What are they trying to avoid as a consequence of staying at work rather than going somewhere else?'

"Workaholics tend to decimate their personal and professional relationships. Their divorce rate is among the highest in the nation. The classic profile of the male workaholic is someone whose wife, if he still has one, will say: 'John has no real friends. I'm his only friend.' "

By contrast to the workaholic, Garfield's study found the "optimal performer" to have "warm, outgoing relations and a good collaborative sense, both personally and professionally. They surround themselves with people who are highly competent and whom they can freely delegate to. They are masters at delegating."

Garfield said the study also found the following about optimal performers:

"They don't work for work's sake. They work in order to achieve results. They tend to be lower than the norm on all stress indexes."

I do not believe a man can ever leave his business. He ought to think of it by day and dream of it by night.

—Henry Ford

» Robert Townsend «

Up the Organization—People

» «

Robert Townsend was the man who made Avis, the car rental firm, "try harder."
Through a mix of splashy advertising and sound management, he transformed Avis
from a tiny company to number two in its industry. In his irreverent book, Up the
Organization *(which he jokingly called "a guerilla guide" to changing organiza-*
tions), Townsend summarized his managerial philosophy. In this selection, he para-
phrases, in his inimitable words, the scholarly concepts "Theory X and Theory Y"
of Douglas McGregor, and Abraham Maslow's "hierarchy of human needs." The
theories of these two psychologists were used by humanists in the 1950s and 1960s
as counterweights to the philosophy of Frederick W. Taylor (see Chapter 4).

There's nothing fundamentally wrong with our country except that the leaders of all our major organizations are operating on the wrong assumptions.* We're in this mess because for the last two hundred years we've been using the Catholic Church and Caesar's legions as our patterns for creating organizations. And until the last forty or fifty years it made sense. The average churchgoer, soldier, and factory worker was uneducated and dependent on orders from above. And authority carried considerable weight because disobedience brought the death penalty or its equivalent.†

From the behavior of people in these early industrial organizations we arrived at the following assumptions,‡ on which all modern organizations are still operating:

1. People hate work.
2. They have to be driven and threatened with punishment to get them to work toward organizational objectives.

---

*By all the evidence, the other industrialized countries are as bad off, but no worse; their major institutions are operated on the same silly assumptions.

†Dismissal and blacklisting brought starvation to an industrial worker; excommunication brought the spiritual equivalent of death to a churchgoer.

‡Douglas McGregor called these three assumptions "Theory X." Organizations that run on these premises—the hierarchies—are Theory X outfits.

3. They like security, aren't ambitious, want to be told what to do, dislike responsibility.

You don't think we are operating on these assumptions? Consider:

1. Office hours nine to five for everybody except the fattest cats at the top. Just a giant cheap time clock. (Are we buying brains or hours?)

2. Unilateral promotions. For more money and a bigger title I'm expected to jump at the chance of moving my family to New York City. I run away from the friends and a life style in Denver that have made me and my family happy and effective. (Organization comes first; individuals must sacrifice themselves to its demands.)

3. Hundreds of millions of dollars are spent annually "communicating" with employees. The message always boils down to: "Work hard, obey orders. We'll take care of you." (That message is obsolete by fifty years and wasn't very promising then.)

Back off a minute. Let's pretend we know everything man knows about human nature and its present condition here, but nothing about man's organizations and the assumptions on which they're based. These things* we know about man:

1. He's a wanting animal.

2. His behavior is determined by unsatisfied needs that he wants to satisfy.

3. His needs form a value hierarchy that is internal, not external:

    (a) body (I can't breathe.)

    (b) safety (How can I protect myself from . . .?)

    (c) social (I want to belong.)

    (d) ego (1. Gee, I'm terrific. 2. Aren't I? Yes.)

    (e) development (Gee, I'm better than I was last year.)

Man is totally motivated by each level of need in order—until that level is satisfied. If he hasn't slept in three days he's totally motivated by a need for sleep. After he has slept, eaten, drunk, is safe, and has acceptance in a group, he is no longer motivated by those three levels of needs. (McGregor's examples: The only time you think of air is when you are deprived of it; man lives by bread alone when there is no bread.)

We know that these first three need levels are pretty well satisfied† in America's work force today. So we would expect man's organizations to be designed to feed the ego and development needs. But there's the whole problem. The result of our outmoded organizations is that we're still acting as if people were uneducated peasants. Much of the work done today would be more suitable for young children or mental defectives.

And look at the rewards we're offering our people today: higher wages,

---

*McGregor again.

†This [selection] does not come to grips with the problem of America's 20 million poor: it deals with the 80 million psychiatric cases who do have jobs.

medical benefits, vacations, pensions, profit sharing, bowling and baseball teams. *Not one can be enjoyed on the job.* You've got to leave work, get sick, or retire first. No wonder people aren't having fun on the job. So what are the valid assumptions for present-day circumstances? McGregor called them "Theory Y":

1. People *don't* hate work. It's as natural as rest or play.

2. They don't *have* to be forced or threatened. If they commit themselves to mutual objectives, they'll drive themselves more effectively than you can drive them.

3. But they'll commit themselves only to the extent they can see ways of satisfying their ego and development needs (remember the others are pretty well satisfied and are no longer prime drives).

All you have to do is look around you to see that modern organizations are only getting people to use about 20 percent—the lower fifth—of their capacities. And the painful part is that God didn't design the human animal to function at 20 percent. At that pace it develops enough malfunctions to cause a permanent shortage of psychoanalysts and hospital beds.

Since 1952 I've been stumbling around building and running primitive "Theory Y" departments, divisions, and finally one whole "Theory Y" company: Avis. In 1962 after thirteen years Avis had never made a profit.* Three years later the company had grown internally (not by acquisitions) from $30 million sales to $75 million sales, and had made successive annual profits of $1 million, $3 million, and $5 million. If I had anything to do with this, I ascribe it all to my application of Theory Y. And a faltering, stumbling, groping, mistake-ridden application it was.

You want proof? I can't give it to you. But let me tell you a story. When I became head of Avis I was assured that no one at headquarters was any good, and that my first job was to start recruiting a whole new team. Three years later, Hal Geneen, the President of ITT (which had just acquired Avis), after meeting everybody and listening to them in action for a day, said, "I've never seen such depth of management; why I've already spotted three chief executive officers!" You guessed it. Same people. I'd brought in only two new people, a lawyer and an accountant.

Bill Bernbach used to say about advertising effectiveness: "Ninety percent of the battle is what you say and 10 percent is what medium you say it in." The same thing is true of people. Why spend all that money and time on the *selection* of people when the people you've got are breaking down from under-use.

Get to know your people. What they do well, what they enjoy doing, what their weaknesses and strengths are, and what they want and need to get from their job. And then try to create an organization around your people, not jam your people into those organization-chart rectangles. The only excuse for organization is to maximize the chance that each one,

---

*Except one year when they jiggled their depreciation rates.

working with others, will get for growth in his job. You can't motivate people. That door is locked from the inside. You *can* create a climate in which most of your people will motivate themselves to help the company reach its objectives. Like it or not, the only practical act is to adopt Theory Y assumptions and get going.

It isn't easy, but what you're really trying to do is come between a man and his family. You want him to enjoy his work so much he comes in on Saturday instead of playing golf or cutting the grass.

7
»«
CHANGING NOTIONS OF A CAREER
»«

Michael Abramson/Liaison Photo Agency, Inc.

» Richard N. Bolles «

The Three Boxes of Life

» «

Mid-career change became a hot topic of conversation among middle-aged Americans in the 1970s. It seemed everyone was changing jobs—housewives, teachers, even clergymen. Especially clergymen, as it turned out. So many men of the cloth (there weren't many women ministers then) were turning in their clerical collars that one of them, Protestant minister Richard Bolles, wrote a book to guide them through the difficult transition to secular careers. His book, **What Color is Your Parachute?,** *became an overnight best seller when thousands of men and women who were never in the clergy discovered that it was the ideal "how to" book for them, too. In Bolles' latest book, he argues that Americans have unnaturally segmented their lives, reserving youth for education, middle age for work, and old age for leisure. In this selection, he explains why we should get out of these age-segregated boxes and pursue education, work, and leisure continuously throughout our lives.*

At times in my life I have felt really boxed in. Apparently you have too. No way to turn. Nowhere to escape to. Really in a box. As we grow older, however, we learn how to cope with that feeling. That's one of the benefits of growing up. We become not so afraid of the little boxes anymore. All that remains then is to learn how to deal with the Big Boxes of life—I mean, the *really* big ones. The ones called: EDUCATION, WORK, and RETIREMENT.

To be sure, these are not normally called "boxes." Lying out on some hillside, on a warm summer day, with our arms behind our head as we contemplate the sky and the mysteries of life, we are more likely to think of them as "periods" of life. Our whole life, we tell ourselves, is divided into three periods. The first period is that of "Getting an Education." The second period is that of "Going to Work, and earning a living." While the third and last period is that of "Living in Retirement." Thus, our total lifespan on Earth looks—in theory—something like this:

The World of Education	The World of Work	The World of Retirement

In point of fact, of course, it ends up looking quite differently from this. First of all, the segments or periods on either end—namely, Education and Retirement—have been getting longer and longer. That is to say, a lot of people are delaying their entrance into the World of Work until a later and later age, as they pursue more and more Education; and, a lot of people are retiring much earlier than they used to, sometimes at age 50. So, the periods begin to look more like this, overall:

The World of Education	The World of Work	The World of Retirement

Secondly, these periods have become more and more isolated from each other. Life in each period seems to be conducted by those in charge without much consciousness of—never mind, preparation for—life in the next period. Despite all the talk about "career education," for example, a survey of graduating high school seniors in one U.S. school district revealed that 63% felt they had received little or no training in school which would help them find a job. Likewise, those coming to the end of their time in the World of Work feel they have been given little or no help by that world, in preparing for Retirement. The most that the average organization does is to offer a pension plan, as a sort of bribe to keep an employee working for that particular organization. And often, despite recent legislation, the employee finds that this bribe fails to materialize, when the chips are down and Retirement is almost within grasp. So, these three periods—in their isolation from one another—end up looking (or feeling) like three boxes:

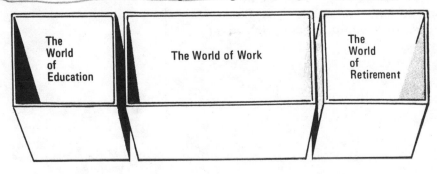

The box-like nature of these three phases of our lives is further accentuated by what it is that happens to us, timewise, in each one. If we look, for example, at the time devoted to "getting an Education," the cultural expectation is that while we are in the first box (from age five through 18, 22 or whatever) the major portion of our time will be devoted to that task.

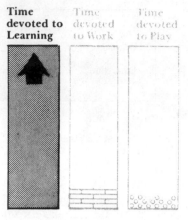

in The First Box of Life

While we are in the second box, however, the cultural expectation is that only a relatively small proportion of our time will be devoted to formal education—and that, mostly to upgrade our work skills or to prepare us for a change in career.

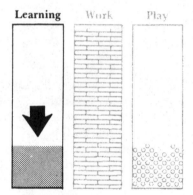

in The Second Box of Life

And when we enter the third box (usually between ages 50 and 68) it is assumed that we will devote little time to formal schooling thereafter, since clearly our brain has atrophied by then!

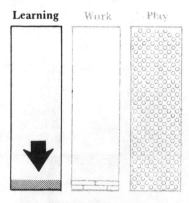

in The Third Box of Life

Turning now to look at the question of how much time we devote in each box to "Working," "holding down a job," or to "formal achievement for pay," we see a very similar imbalance. The cultural expectation is that while we are in the first box, a comparatively small proportion of our time will be devoted to Working—just enough, in fact, to help underwrite our expenses in connection with "getting an Education."

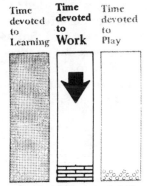

The First Box of Life

And if we complain that the time devoted to Working, while we are in this first box, seems disproportionately small to say the least, the response we customarily receive is that of The Postponement Principle. Namely, "You may not be able to work as much as you like, right now. But just be patient, and after you get out of school you'll be able to work yourself to death."

Sure enough, it turns out to be as was predicted. In the second box the largest proportion of our time is indeed devoted to working—more than making up for the deprivation we felt earlier.

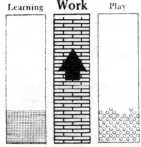

The Second Box of Life

When we get to the third box, however, the cultural expectation is that we will get out of the job market—since clearly our needs, in retirement, are expected to turn modest; the younger bodies now need the jobs that we hold.

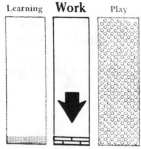

The Third Box of Life

193

Well, what is left? Clearly, the time devoted to Leisure or Recreation. In the first box, we are told that we should not expect to have a lot of time for Leisure. Just enough to recharge our batteries, as it were, in order that we may be ready to go back to our studies.

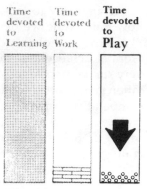

The First Box of Life

In the second box, we are again told that we should not expect to have a lot of time for Leisure. Just enough to recharge our batteries in order that we may be ready to go back to work. And if we feel, by this time, like complaining about the disproportionately small amount of our time which Leisure commands, The Postponement Principle is once more invoked—"You may not be able to play as much as you would like, right now; but just be patient. Once you retire, you will be able to play yourself to death." Which turns out to be true, sometimes in an ironic sense. For we read of couple who waited for forty years to take that trip to Bermuda, or whatever, and then one of them has a fatal heart attack on the eve of their departure.

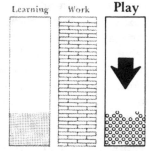

The Second Box of Life

But—leaving such rare occurrences aside —most of us can count on an inordinate amount of time being devoted to Leisure, Play, or Recreation during the time that we are in the third box of life.

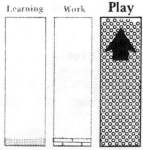

The Third Box of Life

194

What all of this adds up to, is an imbalance between the time spent on Learning, the time spent on Working, and the time spent on Play, in all three boxes of life. And it is precisely this which helps make them into boxes.

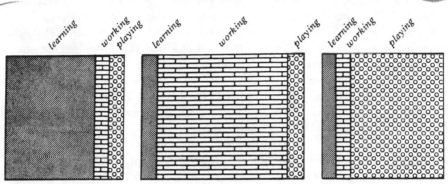

The World of Education   The World of Work   The World of Retirement

What we could all envision is a quite different way of doing this: one in which there was more of an equitable balance between Learning, Working and Playing in *each* of the three boxes. Thus, they would end up looking more like this:

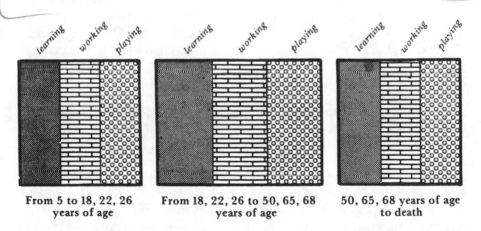

From 5 to 18, 22, 26   From 18, 22, 26 to 50, 65, 68   50, 65, 68 years of age
years of age   years of age   to death

How you can go about building this better balance in your own life is precisely what life/work planning . . . is all about. . . .

What's Happening?

First, however, we need to notice another characteristic of these three periods in our life, which turns them into boxes. This is the fact that there are different issues, perplexities or problems in life that we all have to

195

wrestle with. And that these issues have a kind of logical order in which we tackle them. I believe this can best be illustrated with the aid of a fantasy. Imagine that tonight you go to sleep in your own familiar bed, in your own familiar room. Tomorrow morning, you awaken. You are still in your own bed, but to your absolute astonishment you and your bed have been transported into the middle of some mysterious jungle. All around you, ferns and tall trees, exotic-looking flowers, mysterious sounds, and sunlight filtering down through the trees. Now, what kinds of issues, perplexities, or problems do you have to work through? Well, the first issue—or family of issues—that you would have to work your way through, it seems to me, is one which we might entitle: WHAT'S HAPPENING? You know the kind of questions that would naturally occur to you, right off the bat: Where am I? How did I get here? What on earth is happening? Is this truly a jungle? What kind of jungle is it? Are there dangerous beasts or people here? What kind of food and drink is available? And so forth. Your absolute first need would be to settle this question of WHAT'S HAPPENING—or, at least, to get a kind of temporary "fix" on it. Until that happens, the question would preoccupy your attention, and you would be pretty well immobilized, and thus prevented from doing anything else.

Survival

When you had, at least for the time being, gotten enough of an answer to satisfy you, you would then be able to take your attention off this issue, and go on to the next one. That would be, in the very nature of the case, one which we might entitle: SURVIVAL. Granted I have some elementary idea about what's happening, what's going to happen to me? Am I going to make it, or not? These are the kinds of questions that would just naturally occur to you. SURVIVAL, like its predecessor WHAT'S HAPPENING, would turn out to be not simply one issue, but a whole family of issues. There would be the issue of *physical* survival: is there food and water? Can I survive the weather, and any hostile environments? And so forth. Then there would be the issue of *emotional* survival: there's a whole different role for me here, than the one I am accustomed to. Have I got what it takes to survive all this emotionally? Or will I become a basket-case? Along with this, there would be *spiritual* survival: I've always believed myself to be a certain kind of person, with certain kinds of values and things I believe in; will this experience so change me, that I won't even recognize myself any longer? Or not? If you were not in the jungle, but in the midst of some sort of civilization, you would also have the issue of *financial* survival. Thus SURVIVAL ends up being this whole family of issues, and while such members of the family as spiritual survival may not be terribly urgent, other members of that family—such as physical survival—would immediately rivet your attention. Until you had some kind of resolution of your worry about it, in at least a temporary sort of way, it would be about all that you could think about.

Meaning or Mission

When you had solved the issue of SURVIVAL to your immediate satisfaction at least, you would then be ready to deal with the next family of issues. And that, it seems to me, is one which we might call: MEANING OR MISSION. Once you were assured that you had some idea of what is happening, and that you were going to survive, then of course you would have to decide what you were going to do with your time. It appears that there are four answers which people come up with, in everyday life—and, I suppose, in the jungle:

1. "All that is important, about the use of my time, is that I manage to keep busy." If this is your answer to the issue of MEANING OR MISSION, in the jungle, then you will probably say, "I'll wake up each morning and figure out what I'm going to do that day. That's as far ahead as I intend to plan." Of course, you may—in time—turn to another answer:

busyness

2. "It isn't enough just to keep busy. I want to enjoy what I'm keeping busy with; so I'm going to determine what kinds of things I enjoy." If this is your preferred answer to the issue of MEANING OR MISSION, . . . your goal would be to give maximum time to those activities—frivolous or essential—which you particularly enjoy, and minimum time to those activities you did not enjoy. This answer to the issue of MEANING OR MISSION might satisfy you for some time. Then again, it might not. In which case, you would search for another answer.

enjoyment

Synonyms and Related Words for *Meaning or Mission*	My Goal My Target My Purpose	My Objective My Plan My Aim	My Intention My Design My Ambition

3. "It isn't enough to just enjoy myself; I want to have some meaning to my life, and I want my activities to furnish that meaning." Tracing out what this means there in the jungle, you might decide to give time and thought to those questions about existence which have puzzled all thinking men and women for centuries . . . Were you not in the jungle, you might decide to find meaning by helping other people, someway, somehow. In any event, you would have moved beyond "busy" and "enjoy" to the deeper issue of "meaning." And whatever, for you, made your life meaningful, would determine how you used your time.

meaning

4. There yet remains however, one still deeper answer to the issue of MEANING OR MISSION. That is to find, beyond meaning, some ultimate goal or mission for your life, that drives you on with a kind of sacrificial, burning passion. It is the kind of mission that drove Pasteur, Schweitzer, Einstein, and many lesser names. It is the kind of drive that—in any or every profession—distinguishes some men and women from the rest of the "common herd." So, in the jungle of our fantasy, you might decide . . . to become the most innovative architect and builder of tree-huts in the history of the world, finding some whole new principle of design and of materials. Or whatever.

mission

Effectiveness

Well, whatever principle you use to determine the use of your time—busyness, enjoyment, meaning, or mission—you are still wrestling with this family of issues regarding what you choose to do, once "what's happening" and "survival" are no longer preoccupying you. Only when you have solved this question of MEANING OR MISSION, is your attention sufficiently freed up to notice and deal with the next family of issues—namely, that of EFFECTIVENESS. This is the whole question of "Am I preoccupying myself with the sorts of activities that I really want to be doing, or ought to be doing? And, if so, am I doing those activities in the most effective, efficient, and competent manner possible? Am I building this tree-hut in the best manner possible, for me? Should I be building this tree-hut at all; or is there some better use I could find for my time? That sort of question. We might call this the issue of Evaluation and Re-evaluation, except that Evaluation is so often interpreted these days as something that *others* do for you (or to you). Effectiveness, however, is essentially a self-actuated, self-directed form of questioning. It springs out of a desire to improve your performance, of a particular task; and to improve the way in which you are working toward your goals.

The Pyramid of Issues

What's Happening; Survival; Meaning or Mission; and Effectiveness—these seem to me to be the four major *families* of issues that you would have to wrestle with, in a jungle. They also seem to me to be the four major families of issues that people are wrestling with, everywhere. And at any stage of their lives. . . .

I think that . . . the pyramid is the most appealing [way to represent these families of issues]. "Pyramid" implies that, even as the ancient Egyptians built theirs from the bottom up, so you (and I) must work through these issues, from the bottom up, step by step, level by level. "The Pyramid of Issues" even *sounds* nice . . . .

So, the pyramid it will be— . . . albeit dressed up a little bit three-dimensionally, as follows:

THE PYRAMID OF ISSUES

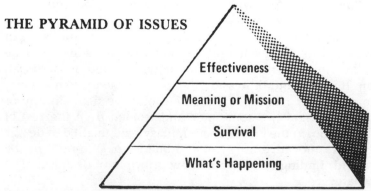

Effectiveness

Meaning or Mission

Survival

What's Happening

Incidentally, it has been suggested that there ought to be a fourth level added at the bottom of this pyramid—an even more basic one, entitled something like "Drifting." This, in order to take into account those people who will not even wrestle with the issue of "What's Happening"; they just don't seem to care. Upon reflection, however, it seems that "drifting" is not in itself an issue, let alone a family of issues, but rather *a way* of dealing with the issues already on the pyramid. Or a way of non-dealing. Two other ways of dealing with these issues might be defined: namely, *superficially* or *in depth*. Thus, a complete picture of the pyramid would come out looking something like this:

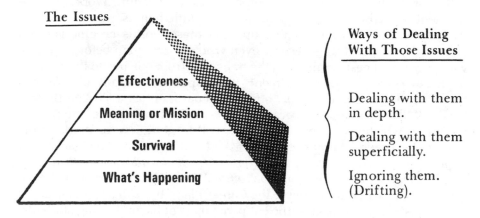

The Issues

Effectiveness

Meaning or Mission

Survival

What's Happening

Ways of Dealing
With Those Issues

Dealing with them
in depth.

Dealing with them
superficially.

Ignoring them.
(Drifting).

Boxes and Pyramids

Now, as I said earlier, this pyramid seems to me to represent the four major families of issues we have to wrestle with, at *any* stage in our lives. The answers we discover, say during the time that we are in the first box of life (the World of Education), will generally serve us during the rest of the time we are in that box. But when we go out into the World of Work, it soon becomes clear that the answers which served us so well while we were in the first box, no longer apply. We have to, as it were, work our way up the pyramid all over again. What's Happening in the World of Work is entirely different from What's Happening in the World of Education. How you survive in the World of Work is also quite different.

When the time comes for us to move into the World of Retirement, once more we have to work our way up the pyramid all over again. For the World of Retirement *is* a whole new world. Thus, in essence, we have to work our way up the pyramid of issues three different times—three *major* times, anyway. This fact, alone, does not help to turn these three periods of our life into boxes. For if everyone who taught in the World of Education or administered that world were conscious of the fact that the place where their students are going, after they leave that world, is precisely to the World of Work where the Pyramid of Issues will require quite new answers; and if every educator consequently concluded that *part* of the task of Education is to acquaint students with those answers, then the pyramid would not (in and of itself) turn these periods of life into boxes.

Or again, if every employer in the World of Work were extremely sensitive to the fact that people in that world—employee and employer alike—are going to go, next, into the World of Retirement, where the Pyramid of Issues will need to be wrestled with, all over again; and if every employer consequently concluded that it was part of his or her task to help prepare people for that experience, ahead of time, then once more the pyramid would not—in and of itself—isolate one box from another.

It is precisely because each period or world (Education, Work, and Retirement) is a whole new ballgame, *and* very little help is given to prepare us for the next ballgame coming up, that these worlds become isolated from each other and thus become even worse boxes, than before. All that we are given (at best) to aid us in the transition from one box to the next is *a single* advisor, office or department. It is supposed to do it all. We may therefore think of that advisor, office or department as a "Token Bridge-keeper." "Bridge-keeper," because they stand (alone) at the entrance to the bridge which leads from one box or world (Education, or Work) to the next. And "Token," because they are asked to do a monumental task *which ought to be the concern of everyone who "runs" that world, rather than being shifted off onto the shoulders of one small office.* When that task proves to be too monumental, when for example the Career Planning & Placement office at college just can't "place" a sufficient percentage of its graduating students, you would suppose that the whole philosophy of "Token Bridge-keeper" would be subjected at last to long-overdue examination. Not so. Rather, it is customarily assumed by the college that something is wrong with that particular placement or career planning director. So he or she is fired (thus becoming "Scapegoat Bridge-keeper"), and a new Token is elected to this Mission Impossible.

The same situation obtains, of course, in the World of Work, except that there the Token Bridge-keeper is the Personnel Director, or the Personnel Department. Now, of course, some of you will object that you know some sterling exception to all of the foregoing: some college or some organization within industry, that takes very seriously the next world into which its students or employees will be going, and does everything possible to help them before the time. I know such exceptions, too. The problem is, they *are* exceptions. In general, the boxes remain. Looking, overall, somewhat as the figure on page 201 indicates:

Not forgetting the imbalance within each box, noted earlier, between time devoted to Learning, and time devoted to Working, and time devoted to Playing.

They *are* boxes. We *are* in them. And the problem that faces us all is: *how* to get out of them.

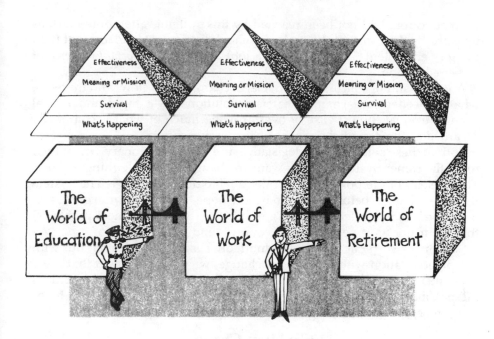

Systemic Answers

How do you stop Education, Work, and Retirement from becoming three boxes? Generally speaking, the proposed solutions have tended to divide into two separate families, as it were. The first is one we might call The Systemic Family. This stresses the fact that the three boxes of life are essentially too formidable and too overwhelming for any one individual to deal with; therefore, it is the whole system which must be changed. The conclusion normally drawn from this is that therefore we must press for mammoth legislative change, or mammoth institutional change, in the whole way that Education, or Government/Industry, or Retirement is conducted. This solution involves a vast amount of public education, information-dissemination, lobbying or other forms of pressure, and so forth. This sort of change, if it does come about, is slow, but certainly legal. Or perhaps I should say, legal but certainly slow. I think, for example, of the most widely-heralded and publicized systemic attempt to unify education and work, in this country, which the U.S. Office of Education has called "career education." This effort to impact the estrangement between education and work in all fifty states has been ongoing now for a number of years, with all the leadership the federal government could possibly give it. Yet in a survey commissioned and conducted between June 1975 and May 1976, assessing the status of this systemic effort to change things, the American Institutes for Research of Palo Alto, California (which did the survey) revealed that only 3% of the nation's students were in school districts with broadly-implemented career education programs. Moreover,

201

even educators had not been reached by this systemic attempt (so far), as revealed by the fact that the nation's school districts rated Placement (i.e., the former students' ability to find a job) as *the least important outcome* of career education.

Another kind of conclusion is that legal change is too slow, and therefore what is needed is a change that is revolutionary—a rapid and radical change, even at the expense of overthrowing much of what is commonly regarded as the essential social structure of our society.

Both of these solutions, the legislative and the revolutionary, are at their roots the same: Systemic. They want to change the whole thing at once. They dispair of the power of the individual to do it alone. It is The System that must change, before there can be any hope. That is the *credo* of most of the reformers in modern history; and it is the solution (to most problems) that the majority of people in our country tend to subscribe to.

Sometimes systemic change is admittedly absolutely essential. But with our preoccupation with this kind of change, we must not forget that there is another possibility—complementary to the first, if less popular. This is the possibility of giving the individual person some tools by which he or she can begin now to change the system *at least as if affects his or her life.*

Individual Change

If, for example, Education, Work and Retirement have become three boxes of life, we can work on legislative and institutional ways of changing the whole system. *And, at the same time,* we can try giving individuals some tools, to see if he or she can at least change the box-like nature of Education, Work, and Retirement, *for his or her own life.*

In its most primitive motivation, this Individual Change solution is a kind of "every person for themselves" theory. It is as though an ocean liner had become impaled upon some reefs, and everyone were running for the lifeboats, heedless of what happened to the rest of the passengers. However, in its most mature motivation, this Individual Change approach is itself a theory and form of Systemic Change. If enough individuals were to change, it argues, then the system would have to change. Or, if enough individuals were to change, then willy nilly the system itself would already be changed.

In comparatively recent history, the best example—perhaps—is that of the so-called Vietnam peace movement. It began with a few individual voices being raised on some of our nation's college campuses. In time, as these individuals persuaded others, the movement became a kind of juggernaut. Eventually it was so powerful that a President of the United States—associated in people's minds with that unpopular war—found he could not be re-elected, in all probability. Thus, what began as individual change became, in the end, systemic.

But we do not have to appeal to history, in order to establish how systemic change may thus begin by changing a few individuals. A theoretical foundation may equally be found in biology, by appealing to the human body. There we see first one individual cell change, and then another. And then another. Eventually, however, as a consequence of these individual cell changes, the whole body is constitutionally different from what it was when it began.

Handy Guide to Public Policy Proposers and Their Proposals

	View of Present and Future	Proposals for Future
Ideological Positions		
Horrified Humanist	A slim chance of surviving our chaos and obsolescence.	Sweeping reforms, world government, national planning.
Languishing Liberal	Troubled times.	More money and programs; racial integration.
Middling Moderate	No thoughts: cross-pressured.	Various platitudes to avoid offending other policy proposers.
Counteracting Conservative	Crime, centralization, and crumbling civilization.	Law, order, soap, haircuts, Truth and Morality.
Rabid Rightist	It's getting *Red*der all the time.	Wave flags and stockpile arms (public and private).
Primitive Populist	Domination by pointy-headed pseudo-intellectuals.	Throw briefcases in Potomac, restore common sense.
Passionate Pacifist	A garrison state.	A peaceable kingdom.
Radical Romantic	A cancered civilization.	Small experimental communities.
Rumbling Revolutionary	A repressive, racist, imperialist, capitalist, establishment.	Confront and destroy The System (other details worked out later).
Apocalyptic Apostle	Armageddon coming to a sinful world.	Be saved.
Role-Related Positions		
Urgent Urbanist	Decline and fall of cities.	More funds and programs sidestepping states.
Emphatic Ecologist	Decline and fall of everything else.	Control contaminators and restore nature.
Boiling Black Man	Here a pig, there a pig, everywhere a pig pig.	Black everything.
Status-Seeking Sibling Sender	Crisis in our schools and colleges.	More funds and programs, tax deductions.
Multi-Megamuscled Militarist	Growing Chinese and/or Russian capabilities.	More National Security regardless of national security.

Handy Guide to Public Policy Proposers and Their Proposals *(cont.)*

	View of Present and Future	Proposals for Future
Technocrat-on-the-Take	No thoughts; not within scope of specialty.	Well-funded studies and use of arcane models.
Sincerely Sorry Scientist	Profligate technology.	Think of alternative futures and their consequences.
Bullied Budget-Binder	Up-tight.	Making this year's budget and getting more for next year.
Tortured Taxpayer	Growing gaps between income, aspirations, and expenditures.	Cut Cut Cut Cut Cut Cut Cut Cut Cut.
Stultified Student	Entrapment in *their* world.	Inner and interpersonal exploration, and other relevant learning.
Contracting Conglomerator	Cybernation, diversification, and internationalization.	Withering of the state.
Hi-throttle Highwayman	Paving the nation.	Re-paving the nation.
Frustrated Feminist	Futility, frivolity, and frigidaires.	Fun-filled fulfillment.
Star-Struck Spaceman	Up, up, and away.	Science must not be impeded.
Bonded Bureaucrat	Six years to go until retirement.	Longer coffee breaks.

Source: Michael Marien, Educational Policy Research Center, Syracuse University Research Corporation. Reprinted with permission from Public Administration Review, Volume XXX, No. 2, March/April 1970. Bi-monthly publication of the American Society for Public Administration, 1225 Connecticut Avenue, N.W., Washington, D.C. 20036.

» Emily Greenspan «

Work Begins at Thirty-five

» «

Author Emily Greenspan reviews the problems and rewards of becoming a career woman at thirty-five. The majority of such women work out of economic necessity, not for self-fulfillment. Many are displaced homemakers. But many of this increasing number of women not only lack the skills to find and hold a good job, they also find that the psychology of being a homemaker has left them fearfully unassertive, dependent, and without sufficient self-confidence to succeed in the bruising job market.

Making a transition from homemaker to career woman means that employers as well as family and friends must cope with a new woman; their successes in overcoming many of the obstacles presented by the transition are evidence of the adaptability of American culture to radical change.

> *Women, like me, after a certain number of years of Fulfilling themselves in domestic necessities, are supposed to leave the seclusion of the lair and re-enter The Greater World, where they're supposed to snap to and get with it right away. They're supposed to go back to a job they once had and left, or never having had a job, get a job . . . they can go back to school and get a Ph.D., they can open an art gallery or an antique store . . . it doesn't matter what, as long as it's Action. Which, of course, is the reverse of this paralysis I'm in. And as soon as I pull myself out of it, things will fall into line and get better, maybe better than they've ever been before.*
> —Sue Kaufman, *Diary of a Mad Housewife*

These are the women who played by the rules—scrubbing kitchen floors and children's faces, neatly folding their identity in with their husband's laundry, serving milk and cookies in the afternoon and *boeuf bourguignon* at night. They got married to stay married—not anticipating divorce or the illness, unemployment or death of a husband, an itch for self-fulfillment or a floundering economy. And now they are in transition.

205

Many college women today have already chosen a career by the time they graduate and are facing their own set of conflicts about marriage and childbirth. In contrast, the middle-aged homemaker who enters or re-enters the work force is not only thrown into an arena that favors malleable young men and women with a "future," but in many cases, she must reorganize her personality and incorporate "assertive career woman" into "supportive wife and mother." It is not only a change for her, but she is also asking her husband, children, friends and relatives to adjust to her new life. In the last decade, more than three million women between the ages of 35 and 54 from all classes and ethnic groups have gotten jobs at a variety of different levels—many for the first time, others returning after years (or even decades) of homemaking. What is causing this mass influx of older women into the working world and how does their entry or re-entry affect their self-image and their family relationships?

A 1980 Roper poll, commissioned by Virginia Slims, found that the primary reason women work is for money—only 14 percent said they worked for self-fulfillment. While middle-class, married women work to maintain the family's standard of living, to help finance their children's educations or simply to avoid the empty-nest syndrome, displaced homemakers—women who are divorced or widowed after years of being supported by their husbands—feel a more pressing need. As one divorced mother of three puts it, "I don't feel any need to prove myself—just to eat."

Regardless of class, women who have been financially dependent on their husbands are beginning to realize that they may be only a marriage certificate away from economic peril. One of every three currently married women will eventually divorce—and only 14 percent of divorced women are granted alimony. Women currently outlive men by eight to ten years; therefore almost all married women will one day be widows. A 1979 study by the United States Department of Labor Women's Bureau conservatively estimated that there are at least four million displaced homemakers in America and most do not qualify for CETA (Comprehensive Employment and Training Act), welfare or unemployment benefits. The Federal allotment to Displaced Homemaker Programs in 1980 was $5 million—which averages a mere 80 cents per person. . . .

Many women who have derived their sense of self from their husbands rarely ponder life after divorce. "Today, any woman with her eyes open can see she's not necessarily going to be taken care of for her whole life," Barbara Bergmann, professor of economics at the University of Maryland says in Lucia Mouat's book, *Back to Business*. "There's a significant chance that sometime she'll be out on her ear in a cold world."

Blondell Scott did find herself out on her ear. After 17 years of marriage, she says, her husband walked out on her and their two young daughters. "It hit me so hard I didn't know how I felt for a while," Mrs. Scott recalled in an interview. "I made up my mind that nothing was gonna keep me down. But when I went out looking for a job I had no sense of direction. No doors were opening. I felt like I was on the verge of a nervous breakdown. Then I heard about the Displaced Homemaker Program, and they helped me get my résumé together. They sent me to the Federation of Employment and Guidance Centers, which got me my present job." Mrs. Scott now works in the order department of a paint company, and after only 10 months, she is up for a promotion and a raise. . . .

"Women going through divorce are emotionally wiped out," explains Doris L. Sassower, a matrimonial lawyer. "Many feel 'dumped' by their husbands at their worst psychological moment. They are scared of growing old, of being abandoned, then, suddenly, of imminent economic disaster. Often, these women tell me they feel like 'garbage'—and these are the women many of our judges say 'should learn to be self-sufficient,' as they award them limited alimony, if any. Sadly, older women are the fastest growing poverty group in America."

After traumatic events such as death, illness, unemployment or divorce, women are not only faced with the mechanics of jobhunting, but also with re-evaluating their goals and values. Accustomed to putting the needs of their children and husbands first, they now must decide what is best for *them*. . . .

Over and over women heard in voices of tradition and Freudian sophistication that they could desire no greater destiny than to glory in their own femininity [and] to pity the neurotic, unfeminine, unhappy women who wanted to be poets or physicians or presidents.

—Betty Friedan

Take economic necessity; add the difficulty in making these perceptive transformations; fold in rusty or outmoded job skills, little or no job experience and lack of contacts or familarity with today's job market; garnish with employers who are unwilling to credit previous work experience or volunteer activities as evidence of future potential; simmer with age and sex discrimination, and you have a recipe for today's re-entering homemaker. And she is often willing to settle for low-skilled, low-paying, traditionally female jobs that afford minimal opportunity for advancement and maximal stress. . . .

The main reason returning women tend to have low expectations is not ignorance, but fear. A study by the Yale University School of Medicine found that 40 percent of American women looking for a paying job after years of homemaking suffered from symptoms of stress and depression. These symptoms occurred so frequently that they warranted names like "job hunter's stomach" and "interview insomnia." Stress is caused by contradictory pulls, and in the re-entering woman this often takes the form of a struggle between the desire to achieve and the fear of competition.

Many homemakers have powerful needs that simply are not being met at home. According to Dr. Anke Ehrhardt, associate professor of clinical psychology at Columbia University College of Physicians and Surgeons, married women have higher depression rates than single, divorced or widowed women. "Being married seems to have a detrimental effect on some women and a protective effect on men," she said at a conference last year. "The homemaker's role is particularly stressful if it is the only role. Several studies show that working married women cope better with stress."

Other women find motherhood more satisfying, but, as their children grow older, it is no longer an all-absorbing task. Pat Ferrari, a slim, energetic, 38-year-old lawyer, says, "Although I thoroughly enjoy my children, there was a lot of dead time when I was just sitting on the bench in the playground. And while I went all out trying to be a perfect mother for my first child, by the time the fifth came along, I had a better idea of what was required. It dawned on me that I wanted to do something else, and after a year and a half of pondering what to do and how to arrange it, I applied to law school." Her children, however, remained a major concern, and so, after graduation, she worked for four years as a part-time attorney. She also hired a full-time housekeeper. "My husband and I are fortunate that we earn enough to afford a housekeeper," she says. "It enables us to avoid the difficulties faced by working couples who don't make as much as we do." Her household help is even more necessary today, because Mrs. Ferrari took a very demanding, full-time job last year.

"At whatever age a woman knows incontrovertibly that she will never have another child," says Gail Sheehy in her book, *Passages*, "an intriguing phenomenon has been observed. . . . Whatever pursuit a woman decides to follow, she pours more of herself into it than she ever did when the option of reproducing was available." Instead of slowing down, middle-aged women are speeding up, and they are making significant contributions in all fields.

Yet, while women may feel an itch to work outside the home, they are often afraid to scratch it. In the February 1980 issue of the Harvard Educational Review, Georgia Sassen, former director of field studies at Hampshire College in Amherst, Mass., argues that the climate of competition arouses the anxiety, not the fear of success, as Matina Horner, now president of Radcliffe, proposed in the late 1960's. Citing recent studies where sex differences in performance levels showed up only for competitive tasks, Miss Sassen concludes that women find it difficult to commit themselves to competitive success because of their interpretation of social situations. They focus on preserving relationships rather than the rules, and view moral dilemmas in terms of responsibilities rather than rights.

So, although many doors are opening for the re-entering woman, it takes an enormous amount of strength and dedication to cross the thresholds. And women often abandon the effort in frustration, retreating instead to the familiar four walls of their kitchens. But home is not the sanctuary it once was. As the societal pendulum has swung the other way, conferring status on those with paid employment, homemakers who are satisfied with their situations require a certain motivation simply to resist the pressure to get a job. . . . At cocktail parties they become defensive or apologetic when confessions of their wife-and-mother status are greeted with long silences. "Housewife—I hate that word," Jeanne Goldman, wife of a psychiatrist, snaps indignantly. "I'm married to my husband, not my house."

But for those who do go back to work, the rewards frequently outweigh the difficulties. In the Yale survey, a follow-up four months later showed that almost all of the former homemakers had found jobs and that their depressions had lifted. And many women find that even the perimeter of baby's playpen can be a fertile training area. Rena Bartos, a senior vice president and director of communications development for J. Walter Thompson, the world's largest advertising agency, re-entered advertising when her son was 12 years old. "When I first came back to professional life, I found that Dr. Spock worked beautifully in the advertising business. His advice about handling a 3-year-old's temper tantrum is just fine for dealing with account executives: If you're calm, if you're consistent, if you don't change your story, your message will get through."

Instant acceptance of the older woman, however, is rare. A period of adjustment is often necessary for the employer and fellow employees as well as the former homemaker. "Mature women entering at the same level as college graduates may feel out of phase," says Cynthia Epstein, a professor of sociology at Queens College and at the City University of New York's Graduate Center. "And while employers know how to treat junior recruits, they sometimes become confused when dealing with an older woman. But employers soon find that the mature woman usually brings real commitment and a sense of gratitude, whereas many younger people feel they're entitled to a good job."

Some employers actually prefer the mature woman, knowing that she is not there to catch a husband and probably will not leave to have children. Moreover, child care is rarely a problem, since her children are often old enough to take care of themselves. They also appreciate her emotional stability, loyalty, low absenteeism and ability to get along with other people. . . .

Maxine Wineapple and Sally Skidmore work together directing New Options, a counseling service for re-entering women. "As homemakers," says Mrs. Skidmore, "women don't get praise and recognition for day-to-day repetitive tasks. When they get into the working world, they get a lot more feedback. After years of defining themselves in terms of others, they get a better sense of who they are, and they learn a new respect for the business world."

For the past four years, Marilyn Tucker has been a stockbroker at Merrill Lynch, Pierce, Fenner & Smith Inc. in White Plains, N.Y., her first paid employment after 16 years of being a wife, mother and community volunteer. Armed with a college economics degree, experience in managing the family's financial portfolio, an intense desire to succeed and a gracious manner, she took her place among two other women and 38 men. "From the beginning," she says, "I felt that this was very much a man's world. There isn't a casual association between men and women in an office like this. But on the professional level, there's a lot of mutual respect. We can share our triumphs and disappointments and accept one another's criticism and advice."

The transition was relatively easy for Mrs. Tucker, but for many women, it is much more difficult. According to Dr. Kenneth Greenspan, director of the Center for Stress-Related Disorders at New York's Columbia Presbyterian Medical Center, "Whatever personal traits the individual has will be accentuated when he or she is nervous. The woman who has been a good homemaker—neat and perfectionistic—will become more rigid in the workplace, working harder and more diligently, when she should be observing and learning more."

At home, too, she must adjust by learning to compromise. Unfortunately, instead of working out new arrangements, many women are reticent about requesting change, feeling guilty that they have grown restless in the traditional role of motherhood or suspecting that an unwritten clause not to be troublesome was included in their marriage vows. Yet, inevitably, in the attempt to do everything, nothing is done well; and in the attempt not to make waves, resentment builds to a tidal wave of vituperation.

"Members of the family may give lip service to a woman's desire to return to work, but inwardly may not be pleased about the cost to them," says Dr. Epstein of Queens College. "This disenchantment is often played out indirectly. Instead of coming out and discussing their ambivalence, it surfaces in irrelevancies.". . .

For many women a successful transition from homemaker to career woman depends upon one critical factor: a supportive husband. The degree to which a husband stands behind his spouse is partly dependent on his attitude toward the role of a wife and the extent to which maintenance of that role serves him professionally or emotionally. A husband who has internalized the traditional role of a wife from his parents' marriage—and his own—may develop a list of fears as long as his wife's: fear that she will make more money and fear that she will neglect the housework, the children and, more important, the marriage.

Even men who intellectually understand the need for women to have careers and feel pride in their wife's work may chafe emotionally under the yoke of new responsibilities. In her book, *Breaking Out of the Middle-Age Trap*, Leslie Aldridge Westoff describes Marvin, a 49-year-old securities analyst, father of two teen-age sons—and husband of a restaurant manager whose job often takes her away from home. "I get almost schizophrenic about it," he says, referring to his wife's frequent absences. "How can I possibly resent her having a whole other life, when for our whole married life, I have had one?" But almost immediately, Marvin the shopper, launderer and lonesome husband adds, "I get ticked off having all this burden put on my shoulders because my dilettante wife wants to indulge herself in what seems like mere pastime to me. When I feel that way, I can't quite bring myself to recognize that this is really a serious endeavor for her.". . .

Yet, he has grown closer to his sons, is happy that his wife enjoys her work and is more aware than ever of the tedium of her prior existence.

Diverging life cycles can also create conflict. The woman who returns to work after a 20-year hiatus is recognizing her potential at a time when her husband is looking forward to winding down—traveling more with his wife or serving as a mentor to a younger work associate.

One area in which a change in attitudes toward sex roles occurs extremely slowly is in the upper echelons of the corporate world. In a survey of executive officers of Fortune 500 companies and their wives, Maryanne Vandervelde, a psychotherapist in Mercer Island, Wash., and author of *The Changing Life of the Corporate Wife*, found that 85 percent of the husbands—and 70 percent of the wives—said that their attitudes about corporate wives had not changed during the last few years. They considered the issue mainly from the viewpoint of money and convenience—corporate wives provide untold hours and effort entertaining and being entertained, and their support and flexibility allow the executive husband more time and energy to ascend the corporate ladder.

Dr. Ralph Hyatt, a clinical psychologist in Philadelphia, recently ran a series of workshops with highly educated professionals and their wives who were contemplating returning to work. "The premise of the workshop was that since the husbands had more work experience, they'd give their wives the support they needed," says Dr. Hyatt. "Instead, what I found was that many husbands focused on financial issues—the fact that unless their wives made a certain salary, they wouldn't get a tax break."

Those husbands who are flexible enough to allow for change often benefit from the results. A working wife can ease their responsibility of being the sole breadwinner, providing them with the opportunity to change careers. In addition, since leaving the home during the day allows the wife to attain a more distanced perspective, she often returns with a new appreciation for her marriage and family. And as she develops a wider range of interests and greater self-confidence, she becomes a more stimulating companion and enlarges the couple's circle of friends. . . .

Although many women fear the impact of their working on their children's development, studies show that children of working mothers tend to be self-reliant, to have fewer self-doubts and to be as well-adjusted socially as children whose mothers stay home full time. . . .

While there have always been exceptional women to serve as role models, for the first time such women are commonly found in the home. The older working woman is providing a career-role model for her daughters and the model of a working woman for her sons—a model the next generation will emulate as they seek to combine marriage and career. The changing attitude was aptly illustrated by the button that Pat and Bob Ferrari's 15-year-old daughter Lisa made to celebrate her school's Career Week: "Kiss Me! My Parents are Lawyers." Or by the 4-year-old girl who announced on the "Today" show, "I want to be married by the time I'm 20 and have a lot of kids . . . and I want to be President."

Today, women are re-entering the labor force three to four years after childbirth. Their career and marriage cycles and goals are significantly different from those of their mothers. But it is the older women who have paved the way. Raised with one set of aspirations and adopting another, they were caught in a transition of values. Many have bucked a system that is, in all ways, antithetical to the life cycle and style of a nurturer, and have overcome formidable internal and external obstacles to develop a new sense of self-confidence and self-respect through working. "Probably the greatest untapped resource that we have in this country," says Bruce Gelb, an executive vice president of Bristol-Myers Company, "is the woman over 35. She has the maturity; she has the experience; she has discovered her own identity, and she is rediscovering her very real potential."

» Solomon Arbeiter «

Mid-Life Career Change: A Concept in Search of Reality

» «

If nothing else, this selection is proof of the proposition that there are two sides to every issue. Solomon Arbeiter and some colleagues at the College Board recently completed a survey of Americans' attitudes toward career change. As a result of this study he argues that mid-career changes are not occurring in significant numbers and that it is unlikely that the environment of the 1980s will be conducive to mid-career change. In short, Arbeiter skeptically pours cold water on the beliefs and wishes of a significant number of middle-aged Americans.

American society, increasingly middle-aged, has become infatuated with the concept of mid-life career change. Gail Sheehy, who popularized the idea of mid-life developmental stages (*Passages: Predictable Crises of Adult Life*), asks whether there is

> still any need to question, "Why a second career?" The simple fact that people are living longer in better physical condition than ever before makes commitment to a single forty-year career almost predestinate stagnation. Added to that is the accelerated rate of technological change that makes almost any set of skills subject to obsolescence. We are becoming accustomed to the idea of serial marriages. It will be progress when we come to think of serial careers, not as signifying failure, but as a realistic way to prolong vitality.

In an introduction to an excellent synthesis on research about mid-life redirection, Anthony Pascal of the RAND Corporation writes that he and his colleagues "suspected that the next stage in the progress of social policy in wealthy industrialized states might well encompass the granting of second chances to adults wishing to change their careers." Educational researchers such as K. Patricia Cross, Cyril Houle, and Richard Peterson have written extensively about a "lifelong learning society" wherein each individual continually needs the benefits of education to further occupational change or other forms of self-renewal.

But is there really an underlying ferment among middle-aged Americans for career change? Maybe there *should be*. Maybe we'd all be happier if mid-life career change became the great self-fulfilling hypothesis of the 1980s. But at present it appears that mid-life career change is more theory than fact. Moreover, considering the conditions which limit and enhance mid-career change, actual mid-career changes can be expected to decline in the 1980s.

The Facts on Career Mobility

The career mobility rate of employed Americans is quite modest, has remained virtually unchanged during a recent seven-year period and decreases significantly with increasing age—particularly as one enters the years defined as mid-life or mid-career. In the data which follow, I have equated occupational change with career change, and not included job change, which normally means transferral of a similar work role and career to a different employer. . . .

These [current] data . . . indicate a steady decline in occupational change after 35 and, additionally, the continuation of a clear trend toward career and occupational stability with increasing age. These data would indicate a strong divergence from the popular wisdom promulgated in recent years that as Americans enter mid-life they reassess and re-evaluate their work situations—and engage in significant career changes. Further, mid-life career change has been held by many to be increasing . . . [but this idea] does not appear to be supported by [the] data. . . .

The RAND researchers reviewed data and reports from social scientists and statisticians and their ". . . first discovery in reviewing various contributions that touch on the question of adult vocational redirection was that, for people in their middle years, there is not a great deal of the kind of voluntary occupational change we have labeled mid-life redirection." On the contrary, the researchers who reviewed "The voluminous literature on job discontent and career aspiration . . . found that, first, surprisingly few people, usually less than 20 percent, directly express dissatisfaction with their work. Even 57 percent of unskilled workers state they would prefer doing the same thing if given a second chance."

The RAND findings on overall worker satisfaction are supported by a synthesis of papers presented at the Second Annual Conference on Major Transitions in the Human Life Course. The author of the conference summary reported on the U.S. Department of Labor's National Longitudinal Survey, which indicated that "the work situation of the middle-aged male has been generally favorable in recent years." Men interviewed in these studies "Had on average 'moved up the occupational ladder during the course of their careers and regarded their current occupations as the best they have ever had.' '' It is a truism to observe that not all employees are satisfied with their occupation or career. However, it is equally true that the literature fails to reveal any increase in discontent during mid-life— even one of modest proportions. What most researchers have reported is a career tranquility which accrues with middle-age. And this is supported by the data on labor mobility.

The data from studies on labor mobility confirm the[se] reviews. The rates of geographic mobility of labor are highest for young adults (ages 18 to 25) and begin a steep decline at age thirty. As analyzed by [E.M.] Hoover, "the most conspicuous differences in migration rates are those experienced by the individual (male) in passing through successive stages of a lifetime. . . . The rate rises suddenly when he is ready to look for a job or choose a college, and remains high until after he is married and has children of his own. As his stake in his job and community grows, and as his and his family's local ties develop, he becomes less and less likely to move. His mobility recovers somewhat at the stage when all of his children are on their own. . . ." Although Hoover refers to males, the migration rate for employed females is strikingly similar. Age is clearly related to mobility, with mid-life ushering in a steep and consistent decline in migration rates. . . .

This study is supported by more recent data on general mobility collected by the Bureau of Labor Statistics [in 1978]. The disparity between household movers and non-movers increases proportionately with age after 25. Obviously, some families and individuals relocate for non-occupational purposes. However, most moves are job and career related, and it remains true for this recent time period that the proportion of movers decreases as individuals grow older. . . .

The data from a recent career counseling study also supports the peaking of career interest in the mid-twenties and a decline by the late thirties. In a [recent] survey . . ., inquiry was made of a random sample of adult Americans as to whether they were interested in a job or career change. A significant percentage of Americans (36 percent) indicated an interest in finding out more about potential jobs and careers and then expressed a possible interest in job and/or career change. However, within this category of Americans in career transition, the only significant demographic differences between Americans seeking to change jobs and careers and those *not* in career transition was age. The percentage . . . not in transition exceeds the percentage of those in career transition for the first time at the 40–44 age range—and consistently increases its margin with increasing age. Past the age of 40, an overwhelming majority of Americans not only do not consider themselves in career transition, but do not even wish to obtain information or counseling on career opportunities.

The trend of the [available] data . . . is rather clear. There is a strong tendency to seek career and job security with advancing age and this tendency has been consistent over time. The mid-life period, rather than being one of change, appears to solidify the chronological move toward stability. The data appear to indicate an acceptance of one's career by mid-life adults rather than an agonizing reappraisal of one's work-life and the undertaking of a career change or redirection.

There are, of course, divergent views. However, the major changes which other analysts have "seen," turn out, upon inspection, to be changes *within closely allied* categories of occupations. These are not *major* career changes. . . .

Future Trends

To look to the future, it is desirable to list the factors that foster career change and those which militate against a career shift. It might then be possible to isolate particular trends which will grow stronger during the decade of the 1980s and offer some guidance as to the direction which mid-life career mobility might assume.

A list of some conditions which facilitate career changes and some which serve to maintain occupational stability are given [opposite]. These are not intended to be exhaustive listings, but illustrative.

As we scan the two lists, it may be observed that certain factors in both categories will have a tendency to grow stronger. Among those which facilitate career shift would be the increasing number of underemployed Americans. As indicated by the occupational forecasts, most jobs developed in the 1980s will not require a four-year college degree and there will be "a potential supply that is greater than potential requirements for college graduates beginning in the late 1970s in jobs traditionally held by these workers." In addition, there will be a higher proportion of women in the workforce, many of whom will be strongly career oriented. Finally, there will be a modest increase in clerical workers in the 1980s and this group contains a high proportion of occupation changers. However, the conditions which foster an occupational shift appear to be relatively modest when viewed against the factors which militate against such career changes.

Most economic reports indicate that America will encounter stable or minimal economic growth during the decade of the 1980s. Our condition of wealth vis-à-vis the rest of the world will decline, and the increasing cost of energy will hold industrial growth stable. More importantly, the large shift of the workforce will be into the mid-life years. The same cohort that competed vigorously for space in our colleges in the 1950s and 1960s will compete for the better managerial, white-collar and blue-collar positions during the 1980s—and this competition will occur in the face of longer working lives for top and middle managers in their late fifties and sixties. This tight job market for mid-lifers will not be conducive to mid-career shifting, but rather to the maintenance and securing of one's attained position and status.

Other social trends will also lead to a narrowing of mid-life career

Conditions Which Facilitate Mid-career Change
• Full employment (more job openings—greater overall job and oc-cupational mobility).
• A high proportion of workers in categories with strong career mobility (farmers, clerical workers, and laborers have the highest rate of occupational mobility).
• Underemployment of workers (trained individuals working in lower-skill jobs are more likely to be job and career mobile).
• A younger workforce (workers in their twenties are the most highly mobile).
• A high proportion of women in the workforce (women are newer to the workforce and, even in middle age, display the career traits of younger workers).

Conditions Which Limit Mid-career Change
• A society which is predominantly middle-aged (workers over 35 have the lowest job and career mobility rates).
• A work force with a high proportion of white collar and profes-sional employees (careers in which a high level of education and certification is required have low turnover rate).
• Slow industrial and business growth (a stable economy has lower rates of career and job transition).
• A high proportion of workers with an investment in pension plans (the importance of retirement plans in financial planning dis-courages job change).
• A high proportion of workers fearful of job discrimination (older workers, minority workers, and women continue to face a difficult employment situation and this tends to decrease their job and career mobility rate).

change. A major occupational shift has been from farm work to operative, laborer, and other categories. This will decrease substantially for two reasons: A decline in the number of farm workers to 1.6 percent of the workforce by 1985 (from 7.9 percent in 1960) and a concurrent decrease in operatives (to 15.1 from 17.3 percent) and nonfarm laborers (4.4 percent from 5.7 percent). This decrease in "spaces" for occupational mobility among lesser-trained workers may also limit some of the recent downward mobility of college-trained workers into the farming and craftsman ranks; there simply will not be as much "room at the bottom."

Conversely, those occupational categories which have the lowest amount of career changers will increase in size, i.e., the white collar and professional groups. . . . As the number of professional and technical workers is expected to increase to 17 million by 1985 (as compared to 7.2

million in 1960) and constitute 16.8 percent of the workforce (as compared to 11.0 percent in 1960) . . . we may expect this trend to exacerbate the decline of mid-life career mobility fostered by a slow economy and a large mid-life cohort in the 1980s.

Implications for Education

What, then, are some of the implications for the learning society in general and educational institutions in particular? . . .

In viewing the trends which resonate between career mobility, stability and educational needs, it would appear that a sound direction for educational institutions would be to position themselves to best serve the avocational and leisure needs of mid-life adults. The risks attendant upon a mid-life career change for the individual appear to be increasing, and if men and women will be required to work in the same occupation for a longer time, then a great deal of their effort and attention will be turned toward hobbies and recreation. This is not to imply that schools and colleges need abandon their traditional liberal arts or professional training, but rather that they tailor course offerings to the "freedom of selection" mentality of Americans who have been credentialized and will be seeking intellectual stimulation. The captive audience will be replaced by an "education buyer," and course packaging will be as important as content. The 1980s will challenge many of our institutions, but none more than our schools and colleges.

» *Donald B. Miller* «

Personal Growth and Vitality Inventory

» «

Too few employers help their employees plan their own careers. One that does is IBM. In 1974 they published a "Personal Growth and Vitality Inventory," excerpted below, intended to help workers understand how they feel about their current work and analyze what they should be doing in the future. The underlying theory is that those who know who they are and how they feel about work should be better prepared to make career choices. There are no right or wrong answers to the questions in the inventory, and some of the questions may not be appropriate for all workers. The questions in bold type should be answered first, before looking at the follow-up probing questions. According to Donald Miller, author of the questionnaire, analysis of answers should focus on the difference between what you feel your job is and what it should be. For example, if a job interferes with your growth, ask why. The idea is to identify what and how to change in order to improve the way your job is working for you.

This is a [selection] of questions for people who work. The questions are designed to help you, the reader, assess how you feel about your growth and your vitality. Personal analysis is a starting point to help you focus on the opportunities for growth. Questions are assembled on the thesis that if we know who we are and how we feel we are better able to make choices, set goals, and live an effective satisfying life. The questions reflect the belief that work is central to our lives and that we can redesign work to improve our personal payout—*satisfactions*. . . .

Your analysis of your answers should primarily focus on the difference between what is and what you feel would be right. For example, if your answer to the second question in growth is that the job helped you grow—ask why. Ask too how it could be made to be more growth oriented. If, on the other hand, your answer was that the job interfered with your growth then ask what should be changed for that interference to stop. An important point of view, therefore, is to identify what and how to change to improve the way your job and your life are working for you. . . .

Growth

What is growth? On first impression it is getting bigger or gaining more of something. Surely our knowledge, our skills, and our bodies can get bigger. A more subtle aspect of growth may refer to reordering of priorities, values or concepts without any apparent change in size or any accumulation. Growth can be change in capacity to do. A reordering of priorities could allow you to appreciate something new.

What growth is for you is a matter of perspective. Perspective is built on experiences, education, and expectations. These questions are designed to help you explore your concept of growth and see if it is working for you.

1. How have you grown in the past year? (circle applicable letter)

	Very Much	Some	Very Little	Not at All	Deteriorated
In skills and knowledge	A	B	C	D	F
In self-understanding	A	B	C	D	F
In personal relations	A	B	C	D	F
In job responsibility	A	B	C	D	F
In income	A	B	C	D	F
In status	A	B	C	D	F
In physical fitness	A	B	C	D	F

Reflect on the ratings of growth.

2. How did the job help or hinder your growth? Did your job assignments contribute to new learning or simply use knowledge you already possessed? Did the job stimulate new study? Did you make new contacts as a result of your work? Did you start new activities or enlarge your fields of interest? Did you spend enough time on the tasks to really become proficient?

3. How did your manager's relationship with you and your work affect growth? Did appraisal by your manager encourage growth and learning? Do you and your manager see growth in the same way? Has managerial counsel been helpful? Did you get feedback from your manager on your growth?

4. How do you personally rank the importance of the following items which may relate to growth? How do you feel the company (management) ranks these items?

Utmost importance	(1)	**Little importance**	(4)
Considerable importance	(2)	**No importance**	(5)
Some importance	(3)		

	Your Importance	Company Importance
Promotion to the next level (advancement)	☐	☐
Meeting deadlines (productivity or accomplishment)	☐	☐
Being on a winning team	☐	☐
Opportunity for intellectual exchange	☐	☐
Salary increases	☐	☐
Being asked to contribute or help	☐	☐
Personal development of independent capability	☐	☐
Gaining knowledge through formal study	☐	☐
Informal self-directed reading and learning	☐	☐
On-the-job learning (a chance to do something new)	☐	☐
Challenge in your work	☐	☐
Freedom to direct your activity (make decisions)	☐	☐

5. How did activities or interests outside the job affect your growth in the past year? Did these activities expand your areas of interest? Did these activities supplement or substitute for growth that you feel should take place on the job?

6. Is your rate of growth as fast as in the past? Does it seem to be gaining or declining now? Why? What would influence the rate and kind of growth? Should you make changes or are there changes the organization should make to increase your rate of growth?

7. Is growth important to you? Do you want to grow? How? What are your growth goals for this year, for the next five, etc.? Are these new goals, or have you had them for some time? Have you expressed these goals to others such as your manager, or your family? What kind of feedback have you gotten from discussing these goals?

Summary of Growth
   • Growth is (very important) (moderately important) (not very important) to me at this time. I feel I am (losing ground) (not growing at all) (growing at a moderate rate) (growing rapidly).
   • My job is (greatly helping) (helping) (provides a moderate part of) (has nothing to do with) (hindering) my growth.
   • My rate of growth is (too slow) (about right) (too fast).

Learning

An aspect of growth is learning. Learning may be related to increased knowledge, to current and future work, to hobbies, to supplemental activities, or to human relations. Learning results from a test of reality. It is both experiential and cognitive or intellectual. In western culture we have tended, until recently, to play down experiential and emphasize intellectual learning. Balanced growth probably means continued learning on all fronts, though certainly not at the same rate or with equal emphasis. Some learning is the result of unplanned activity and other learning is the result of our plans. Some is self-motivated and some learning is externally stimulated. Learning pace and intensity, as well as form, varies between individuals and with motivation and phase of life for a given individual. An aspect of learning is unlearning when you set aside a piece of previous knowledge for new information which works better.

1. How has your learning progressed in the following areas over the last year? (Circle the applicable letter)

	Very Much	Some	Very Little	Not At All	Deteriorated
On your job	A	B	C	D	F
In your hobbies	A	B	C	D	F
In self-understanding	A	B	C	D	F
In understanding others	A	B	C	D	F
In your specialty or field	A	B	C	D	F

Reflect on the ratings of learning.

2. What do you know about your learning habits? Do you learn best in concentrated bursts or spread out over time? Is your learning stimulated by the class or group environment? What kind of interaction with others aids your learning?

3. Did you enjoy school? Did your enjoyment change from grade school to high school or college? Do you enjoy company-sponsored study courses and seminars? Do you study something regularly? Have your patterns of study changed over time? How?

4. Are you motivated to learn now? If so, how can this best be carried out? Can you see a way to integrate learning with your job? Or, by contrast, is your motivation to learn in a direction away from the job? Are you doing something about your desire to learn?

5. What are your reading habits? Have you read in your field, in related fields, in other areas within the last six months? How much reading do you do? What affects your reading pattern?

6. Which of your five senses is your prime learning route? How has this affected your patterns of learning? Are you setting up learning situations to capitalize on this knowledge?

7. How about unlearning? Is your knowledge or past experience blocking new learning? Can you let go of experience or knowledge which is no longer useful or appropriate? What do you know about your unlearning? Is it easy? How do you do it?

8. Is the company providing the facilities necessary for learning? Are there courses or activities which you need that are not available? How does the convenience (i.e., proximity and low cost) affect your taking of courses or other formal study activities? Do you prefer to learn in company courses or with people outside the company?

9. Is your primary desire for learning outside the job? With respect to hobbies? With respect to areas of interest that might relate to future jobs? Have you enrolled or are you planning to enroll in courses which relate to hobbies or new interests outside work?

10. Do you take the time to document your accomplishments and communicate them? Do you analyze what you did and how you can learn as a result? Do you perceive the company as wanting this analysis, or just the results?

Summary of Learning

• My learning has (stopped) (slowed) (stayed the same) (increased) over the past year.

• I am (not motivated) (moderately motivated) (strongly motivated) to engage in new formal learning and study now.

• My job provides (no chance) (moderate opportunity) (a good opportunity) to learn.

Interests

Interests are the activities through which we seek values. For example, those who put a high value on monetary worth put a priority on interests which yield income. Someone putting a high value on esthetics develops interests in art. Interests form the basis of several approaches to career selection. Breadth and depth of interests as well as the expansion to new areas is closely related to personal vitality. Acquisition of new interests provides a clue as to whether change and growth are in progress.

1. What is your most recent new interest? When did you develop this interest? Why? What did you do as a result? Is it related to your job? Does it have the potential of leading to a new job or career?

2. What is your field or fields of expertise and knowledge? Have you deepened your understanding in these areas recently? How do you describe your prime job interest? What is your secondary job interest? How do job interests relate to your outside interests?

3. What is your range of interests? List them and then indicate how long you have had them. How have they changed over time? Have they narrowed or expanded? Have you dropped and added interests? Why? Do you want to change them or add to them now?

4. Does the company environment provide opportunity for you to discuss and develop your areas of interest? Do your associates listen to your interests? Does the company listen to your interests?

Summary of Interests

• I believe my interests are (narrow) (moderately broad) (very broad).

• My interests are (compatible with) (complementary to) (not in line with) my job.

• I am (satisfied with) (not attentive to) (need to expand) my interests.

• My desires for expanding interests are (not related to) (related to) (to change) my job.

I don't like work—no man does—but I like what is in work—the chance to find yourself. Your own reality—for yourself, not for others—what no other man can ever know.
—Joseph Conrad, *Heart of Darkness*

Utilization

Whether or not we are using our talents is an important aspect of vitality and growth. Utilization is necessary for positive feedback which leads to further learning and growth. Utilization varies with the opportunity to apply capability and knowledge as well as your motivation to do so. It is highly probable that none of us utilizes more than a portion of our talents in any one pursuit. We often compensate for non-utilization at work by the development of an outside activity which does give vent to an interest, skill or knowledge. A way to encourage your own growth is to expand the utilization of your skills and abilities.

1. What portion of your knowledge is required for your assignment or job? How has this changed over time? Is it important to you to utilize your knowledge on your job? Do you feel your current job uses an appropriate proportion? What can you do to change this proportion within the job you now have? Would a change of jobs be required to change this proportion? What could your manager or the company do to help you change this proportion?

2. What portion of your skills is being utilized on your job assignment? How has this changed over time? Is this an appropriate proportion? Can it be increased in this job or by a change of job? If it should change, can you or your manager initiate the change?

224

3. Are you pushed by your job? Do you establish the pressure on your job? Do you create activity schedules and direction? Do you feel you have appropriate control over your work pressure? Would change in the pressure improve your utilization?

4. What are the key demands in your job? Do these meet your expectations? If not, can you change them? How have they changed over time or with phase of activity?

5. How do you feel about the amount of work you have? Is it about right, too much, or too little? Does it vary or follow some cyclical pattern?

6. How do you feel about the amount of challenge in your work? What factors create challenge for you? Can you define challenge in terms of probability of failure, or a chance of success?

Summary of Utilization
  • I feel my job (is not related to) (underutilizes) (utilizes) (really stretches) my capabilities.
  • Change in utilization is (key) (not key) to improving my growth and vitality.
  • I expect my job will (continue to) (not continue to) (increasingly) utilize my capabilities over the next few years.
  • My job provides (about right) (poor) proportions of work quantity to work quality. I feel I (do not need) (need much) increased challenge.

Self-Concept

One's self-concept is the picture or image used in relating to others and to activities. People tend to choose occupations which reflect their self-image. Balance between the accepted image for a role and your self-image would tend to make that role feel like it fits.

Part of the search for vitality and self-renewal starts with understanding of self, analysis of life style and understanding your personal philosophy of life. While this subject may normally be considered outside of the scope of the employee-employer relationship, the "whole person" does influence that relationship.

Here are some questions designed to help with this aspect. These questions may be the most personal and most searching and you may not want to share the answers. That feeling or not sharing is okay.

1. Write at least ten completions of the statement; I am a . . . (i.e., traits— good listener, procrastinator, quiet person, creative person).

2. List the roles you play (i.e., engineer, father, teacher, etc.). Then try to rank them on the basis of importance to you.

225

3. The proportion of our energy we use on different aspects of our life may reveal interests, biases, or problems. Estimate the portion of your total energy that you spend on the following aspects of your life.

	Energy percentage I use	Energy percentage I'd like to use
Relations with family	_____	_____
Relations with manager	_____	_____
Job performance	_____	_____
Hobbies	_____	_____
Study and reading	_____	_____
Worry	_____	_____
Private personal activities	_____	_____
Physical enhancement	_____	_____
Social	_____	_____
Other	_____	_____

Are you comfortable with this distribution? How would you spend your energy if you found a way to redirect it?

4. What are your beliefs? What is the meaning of life for you? How would you describe your moral/ethical point of view? Do you believe in the essential goodness of man or in man as essentially bad? Can you identify the foundation of your beliefs—i.e., religious training, reading, life experiences, parental programming or some combination? Can you identify conflicts between your belief structure and those of any institutions or groups with which you associate (i.e., clubs, work groups)?

5. What is your value structure? What aspect of life has the greatest, and what has the lowest, position in that structure? How have you shaped your values; that is, what have been the dominant influences in arriving at this set of values? A way of revealing values is to complete the phrase: It is important to me to . . . (i.e., influence others, make lots of money, see my children succeed, leave a mark on earth).

6. Are you a good communicator? An important part of you is your ability to communicate. Both sending and receiving are important, since learning, growth, and goal achievement are closely allied with contacts with others. Do you see yourself as a good listener? What affects your ability to listen? Are you a conclusion jumper—that is, do you let the sender finish? Do you enjoy explaining things to others? How do people react to listening to you? Do you adjust your rate and style to the conditions?

7. How do you adjust to the "slings and arrows of outrageous fortune"? One way of looking at life style is to look at how we adjust to difficulties and our view of life. For example, what is your technique of adjusting to roadblocks? Do you turn back, jump over, accept and build on them, or what? Do you live each day for its own sake? Do you enjoy life? Did you enjoy today? How do you feel about the past? Does it look better than the here and now? How about the future? Are you living for tomorrow? What is your balance of sense of history, sense of today and feeling of future?

8. Is your career sympathetic (compatible) with your total self or is it a drag or a demanding taskmaster? Has your work left enough time, space and energy for caring for your total self? Where does work fit in your total picture of life?

Summary of Self-Concept
• The role I play and who I am represent who I (really want) (sort of want) (don't want) to be.

• Finding out more about myself, my hang-ups, my strengths and weaknesses is (of no real interest) (not very important) (important) (very important) to me at this time.

• I consider myself (well) (relatively well) (not so well) adjusted to my role and life.

• I feel I (do not gain) (gain) a sense of identity through my work.

Vitality

Vitality is the desire and the ability, capacity, or power to perform effectively and vigorously in life and at work, and to gain personal growth and satisfactions from life and work. Vitality is winning at the game of life and doing it in the context of work. Vitality is being up to date. Vitality is being alive and receptive to new experience.

Vitality is demonstrated through maturity and realism about goals and abilities, is the result of good health and high energy, and is evidenced by high motivation for learning and growth. A nonvital person is, in today's jargon, "turned off." Vitality is not equally displayed in all our activities. For example, it is possible for a person to be turned off at work and turned on in some outside activity which has captured interest. Vitality changes from day to day and with each phase of life.

1. Is your image one of being turned on and tuned in? At work? At home? Do people see you as responsive and interested? Are you consulted as one who knows and can help?

2. What is your physical/psychological energy level? Has it changed recently? What do you know about how it changes and why? Are there health, family or psychological reasons for your energy level being high or low now? Is your energy level what you want it to be? If not, what are you doing about it?

3. How vital is your knowledge of self? What do you know about your motivations? How are your motivations changing? Do you want to change? How? What are you doing about a plan and activities for change?

4. *What is your rate of change?* What are you doing differently today from a year ago, or five years ago? Is change fun or are you fearful about it? What changes do you anticipate in the near future? Can you predict your reaction to these expected changes?

5. *How would you rate your ability to accept and use new ideas, concepts or methods?* Do people see you as one who is searching for new approaches or one who is satisfied and comfortable with the way it's been done before?

6. *Do you have a regular program of physical exercise?* Have you found some form of physical exercise that is fun for you? Do you do this best alone, or with the support of a group? Do you allocate appropriate time to care for your body? Does this effort make you feel on top of the world or like you are borrowing from the world bank?

7. *Do you have a program for exercises of your senses and of the mind?* Are you observant? What about your senses of touch, smell, hearing, taste and sight—are they tuned up or dull? What about relaxation, reflection and contemplation? Do you have a program of "cooling it" as well as a program of activity?

8. *How independent do you feel?* Do you lean on your work, your job, your company, your family and friends? How would you feel if your job ended tomorrow—scared or free? What contributes to your sense of independence or dependence?

Summary of Vitality
- I feel I am a person of (low) (moderate) (high) vitality.
- I see myself as vital in the (work) (home) (hobby) environment.
- I (feel) (do not feel) that rate of change in my interests and abilities relates to my sense of vitality.
- I consider that I adapt to change (slowly) (moderately well) (with relish).

Satisfactions

Understanding satisfactions is a key to developing your personal concept of success. Our needs, the fulfillment of which we call satisfactions, result from our beliefs, goals, and experiences. What we expect relates closely to our concept of ourselves, of what is meaningful, and of where we fit in the world. Needs and expectations form the base for our motivations. The ways in which we gain a sense of accomplishment, a sense of meaningful-ness, and a feeling of impact are many. Some people expect to get their satisfactions from work and some don't. Understanding where and how we get our positive reinforcement is an important aspect of career man-agement, personal growth, and success. It is also necessary to know what frustrates us, our tolerance for frustrations and how our threshold of frus-tration varies with time and conditions.

Satisfactions from life and work are your personal payout.

1. What was the one activity, at work or play, of all things you have ever done, which gave you the greatest sense of accomplishment or well being? When was it? What were the conditions which helped to bring about the feeling of satisfaction? Have you been able to repeat this by setting up similar kinds of endeavor and appropriate conditions?

2. What was the one activity, at work or play, of all the things you have done, which was the most frustrating? Why was it frustrating? Are there personal patterns of frustration you have identified? Have you worked at modifying these?

If all the year were playing holidays
To sport would be as tedious as to work.
　　　　　　　　　　　　　—William Shakespeare, *Henry IV*

---

3. Do the rewards and recognition which result from your work activity meet your expectations? Do they seem in proportion to the effort you expend? Do you usually have a sense of accomplishment when you go home at night? Do you feel it made any difference to the enterprise that you came to work today?

4. How do you impact the business? Can you see ways of improving the type of feedback (recognition) for your activity which will provide in-creased satisfactions for you?

5. How much influence does destiny (the unforeseen) have in your life? Do you expect the unexpected? How has the unexpected affected your satis-factions or choices of your life?

6. Social science researchers have listed satisfactions they feel should be part of the recognition for work. No list is definitive and your ranking of importance of these items varies with time, experience and the environ-ment. Here is a list. Rating their importance to you may help you under-stand what satisfactions you expect and whether your job provides them.

229

	What I Want	What the Job Provides
	Very Important (1) **Somewhat Important (3)** **Not Too Important (5)**	**Most of What I Want (1)** **Some of What I Want (3)** **Little of What I Want (5)**
Challenge and demanding work	☐	☐
Good working conditions and environment	☐	☐
A chance to contribute to the improvement of society and life for man	☐	☐
The opportunity to make decisions about my work—i.e., manage myself	☐	☐
The chance to learn and continue learning on the job	☐	☐
A future beyond this job	☐	☐
Support from my fellow workers including respect, esteem and congeniality	☐	☐
A sense of contribution to the goals of the organization with feedback that tells of my impact	☐	☐
Money, both for its real and symbolic value	☐	☐
A feeling of belonging	☐	☐

7. *Do you feel that you achieve excellence in what you do?* Where does your activity stand with respect to work in your field outside the company? Do you know about activities outside the company? Are you pushing on the frontier or just following? Does it make a difference to you in your sense of satisfaction? Do you get a sense of contribution to something greater than the job?

Summary of Satisfactions

• I (work to live) (work to gain a reasonable proportion of my satisfactions) (live to work).

• I (do) (do not) expect my current job to provide rewards in proper proportions to the effort I expend.

• My job provides (too few) (some) (a lot) of those activities which give me a sense of satisfaction.

• My job provides (too few) (some) (a lot) of those activities which frustrate me.

• What proportion of satisfactions do you feel anyone can reasonably expect from a job (10) (20) (30) (40) (50) (60) (70) (80) (90) (100) percent?

Motivation for Change

Humans have great capability for change. Change usually contains both elements of excitement and anxiety. Most look back on change as a period of learning and growth. Openness to change is a key aspect of vitality. Change in the individual results usually from the individual deciding that he or she wants to change, not from some external force. We tend to resist change which we perceive as being externally forced. Change requires taking personal responsibility.

1. What is your desire to change? Are you reasonably satisfied with yourself, your job and your status? If not, what kind of change do you want? How badly do you want to change—i.e., what price will you pay in hours, dollars, loss of position, etc.?

2. What was the last major change in your life? How did it come about? Did it happen to you or did you do something to bring it about? Was it a change for the better? Did it relate to work or did it occur outside work?

3. What's your change history? Do you make frequent changes or do you make them infrequently and with problems? Are you comfortable in change? Do you enjoy the anticipation of change? Do you feel changes are generally good? Why?

4. Are your family, friends, and management supportive of change in you? Do you feel boxed in and limited by pressures from others? How would you go about effecting improvement in their support of change in you?

5. What can you do to improve your prospects for positive change?

6. What is your urge for change in the normal routine of life? How often do you get fed up with eating lunch in the same place? Do you change your route to or from work occasionally? Is your morning routine of shower, exercise, dressing, breakfast very fixed?

7. Would you enjoy going somewhere where you could freely be different— such as to a Mardi Gras in costume?

8. How locked in are you to your career or job? What conditions would cause you to accept a recycle job—one with lower prestige? Do you perceive your environment as permitting this without personal destruction? Do you see value in recycling people?

9. Do you feel secure enough to risk change of job outside the organization? Do you feel secure enough to make change in your life style? In your appearance? Are you secure in who you are in relation to other people?

Summary of Motivation for Change

• I feel change is (generally good) (neither good nor bad) (generally bad).

• I feel that I (adapt well) (adapt as well as most) (adapt poorly) to change.

• I am currently (motivated to change) (motivated to change myself) (motivated to change my job) (motivated to change myself and my job) (generally satisfied and not motivated to change) (limited in my ability to change myself or my job).

Life and Career Direction

There is extensive literature on life and career planning. Most writing strongly supports the idea of establishing personal goals and plans to give life meaning and direction and increase the sense of growth and accomplishment. Conscious rational planning is important, but it should be done with the knowledge that subconscious and emotional input is important and chance can be a factor.

1. Have you established goals and objectives in the past? What's your track record? Do you usually achieve your goals? Do you feel establishing a plan was important in achieving these goals?

2. What is your current (one year, five year) plan? Or don't you have one, and if not, why? When was it revised? Was the process of planning fun? What actions are you taking to support any plan you may have, however formal or informal?

3. Do you know how to make a plan for your life and establish a career goal? Whom do you consult? What help or information do you need as input to your planning activity?

4. How has your perspective relative to plans changed over the last five years? Does your current plan express different objectives in different terms? Has there been a change resulting from a change in your perspective about learning, growth, or vitality? Have you achieved a level or an age where you no longer consider it desirable to establish a plan?

5. Do you have someone you can really talk to about your career? Is there someone you feel cares about your development in contrast to playing the game? Is there someone to whom it's safe to talk about personal and private desires and goals? Do you know when to break off from your counselor and take personal responsibility?

6. Where are you in your total life cycle? What is most influential in your perspective about your position on this life line? Do you see this position as primarily a position with respect to career or with respect to age, with respect to ability or self-realization, or some other criteria such as family life? How do you feel about your age? Would you like to be younger? If so, why?

Summary on Life and Career Direction

• I believe it (is) (is not) important to establish a career or life plan at this time.

• What has happened to me has been the result of (luck) (subconscious direction) (a rational plan and specific goals) (outside counsel or help at the crucial point) (other).

• My general experience with establishing personal plans is that it (is worthwhile) (is not worthwhile).

WOMEN AND WORK

The women's liberation movement, many observers would argue, has been the major social change of this century. Although the revolution is far from over, in the space of less than a decade, four thousand years of male dominance in Western society has been challenged. Even though, in practice, men still hold most positions of power at work, their *right* to do so is no longer held to be legitimate. By the time the current twenty-to-thirty-year-olds reach retirement age, it would seem a better than even bet that practice will conform with the new social values, and women will be commonly found in the professions, in high government positions, and as managers of large corporations.

Because there is no measurable difference between the intelligence of men and women, and because the educational attainment of the sexes is approaching equality, there has been less *economic* difficulty with the integration of women into the workforce than there has been *social* difficulty. That is, as Rosie the Riveter proved long ago (see Chapter 3), women can do the work men do at least as effectively, efficiently, productively, and imaginatively. When it comes to the bottom line, women are winners at work.

Nevertheless, women are still not fully accepted in some occupations. When millennia of social norms are being quickly overturned, it is hardly surprising that not all aspects of change are going smoothly. As Rosabeth Moss Kanter points out in Chapter 8, "Women and Work in the 1980s," many men still tend to treat women secretaries as inferior helpmates. In addition, no code of appropriate sexual conduct at work has evolved: sexual harassment is all too frequent; and when men and women co-workers do find themselves mutually attracted, it all too often leads to disruption of corporate decorum.

The facts are that over 50 percent of women are still in clerical and service occupations, which tend to be poorly paid (see Howe, Chapter 8). More than anything else, this job segregation explains why the median salary of women who work full-time, year round is only 60 percent of that earned by the average male worker. But these numbers mask the enormous changes that are occurring in higher level jobs, particularly in the professions. In 1972, only 8 percent of all U.S. physicians were women; in 1979, 23 percent of all physicians graduating from medical school were women. In 1970, only 8 percent of all U.S. lawyers were women; but 35 percent of the graduating law school class of 1979 was female. In 1970, there were 1.5 million more men than women enrolled in college full- or part-time. By 1979, women college students *outnumbered* men by nearly half a million! These recent figures portend radical changes that are not yet reflected in occupational statistics. There is little doubt that women now are receiving the training that will help them gain top managerial, technical, and professional jobs in the future.

The Family

Perhaps the most significant recent change in the labor force has involved working mothers. The labor force participation rate of women with children under age six more than tripled in the past decade. Today, 41.6 percent of such women hold paid jobs.

In part, this figure reflects our rising divorce rate: many working women with young children are single parents who must work to support themselves and their families. But for married women who hold jobs because of economic necessity or because they want to (or both), working can create tensions of its own that in some circumstances can increase the likelihood of divorce. Nancy Seifer, for example, points out that working-class men find it particularly difficult to accept their wives taking paid jobs— especially if the wives earn more than they do.

Nor are the tensions limited to blue-collar families. As other articles in Chapter 9, "Work and the Family," make clear, a major problem for working women is conflict with the men in their lives over the division of domestic labor. Women want to work *and* have families. Men want to work *and* have families. But *somebody* has to wash the dishes and take care of the kids. When both the husband and wife in dual career marriages come home exhausted after a miserable day at the office, who should cook the dinner, clean up, and go to the P.T.A. meeting? And who should stay home when junior gets sick? According to authors Rivers, Barnett, and Baruch, few men and women seem able to work out an agreeable fifty-fifty split of job and household tasks.

None of our authors offers a realistic solution to the tensions inherent in dual career marriages. But Rosabeth Moss Kanter has an intriguing suggestion: let's put more emphasis on changing work than on changing the family. A working mother herself, she argues that if employers were to provide better day care facilities, allow for freer paternal and maternal leaves, provide part-time work, flextime and other forms of flexible work schedules (see Chapter 10), and cut down on mandatory (and, often, unnecessary) travel and cross-country job transfers, a great deal of tension could be removed from the lives of mothers and fathers who wish to work. That just might be the best idea in this book.

8

》《

WOMEN
AND WORK
IN THE 1980s

》《

Lin Jakary

» *Louise Kapp Howe* «

Sales Worker

» «

Did you ever wonder why so many salespeople in department stores are rude? Why they can't tell you if the item you want is in stock? Why they always seem to be watching the clock? Writer and journalist Louise Kapp Howe gives plenty of good reasons for such behavior in this selection from her book, Pink Collar Workers. *Perhaps the best clue to understanding their behavior is the realization that sales workers treat customers the way their employers treat them.*

Fifty women and men are standing in line in the basement of one of Manhattan's most popular discount department stores. Filling out forms, fidgeting, waiting for their turn. Yesterday and today there were help-wanted ads for Christmas jobs here and at other stores in the *Times* and *Daily News*. *Earn extra cash . . . Be in the center of things for Christmas . . . Come meet the nicest people . . . Apply now.*

The line moves slowly, or feels that way at least. "Two hours now I've been waiting," says a tiny woman with delicate features in a high soprano voice. "You'd think they'd have the courtesy to provide us some chairs."

"Why should they?" a basso profundo behind her rejoins. "You don't get to sit when you're on the job." . . .

In front of the line a door marked PERSONNEL. Every three or so minutes it flashes open, an applicant departs (did she or he get it?) and the next is ushered in. Meantime, for those still waiting, there is an arithmetic test to complete in addition to the ritual (name-address-age-education-experience-references) application form. A two page test. Add up a column of figures, then another a little longer. Subtract the following. Now multiply and divide. What's seven percent of $5,794.89?

Nervous or simply restless, many on the line go over and over and over their answers. Including me. I am here to learn firsthand, if I can, what it is like to work at a large store such as this, and although I ostensibly mastered simple arithmetic a thousand years ago, now for some reason I find myself hesitating too, checking and rechecking as the line inches up. Perhaps I'm really concerned about all the blank spaces I left in the application form under "experience." In any case, I'm working on $5,794.89 for the third time when a young man comes out of the office and nods, "You next."

Inside, a thin blonde woman sits behind a desk overflowing with applications and arithmetic tests. She indicates a chair by her side. Glances quickly at me, my filled out papers (too rapidly to evaluate the answers *or* the blank spaces), looks up and asks what I'd prefer, sales or cashiering.

"Sales."

"Any special department?"

"Yes, coats. Or suits. Dresses. Something like that."

Then she gets to the questions about my previous selling experience (I have none, I admit, as the application shows; I would like to find out what it's like). She consults a chart on her desk. Makes a large check in one of the boxes. "I think coats and suits will be okay."

"And the pay?" I ask, relieved that it was all this easy.

"Two fifteen an hour."

Which is even lower than the low wages I had supposed. No wonder it was so easy. "Any commission above that?"

"No, two dollars and fifteen cents straight for the Christmas help. Of course you also get ten percent off on most of our merchandise."

She smiles a take it or leave it smile. I ask her when I can begin. She says in two weeks and that being that I leave the office to be immediately replaced by the next person on the still growing line of applicants hoping for the opportunity to earn $86 a week before taxes, about $70 after, in one of the most expensive cities in the world. Did someone say people don't want to work anymore?

True, many on the line appear to be students on Christmas vacations. But there are also many—particularly among the women—who are in their forties, fifties and even sixties. Are they here because they enjoy this kind of work, even though it pays so little? Or because it is the only work they can find? Or are they mainly here, as the help-wanted ads suggested, to "earn extra cash for Christmas" and "be in the center of things"—a few weeks of diversion with pay for the housewife and then happily back to life as usual. In two weeks I should start to find out.

Birth of a Saleswoman

Standing in line again, two weeks later, fifty or more of us as before.

"Do you know what department you're going to?" the woman on my right asks. She is a short plump woman with fluffy red hair. Late fifties, or so.

"Coats and suits," I say.

"Oh, then you'll be with Peggy," she says, tapping the back of the large black woman standing in front of her. "I'm Lillian," she continues. "Dresses."

Then my new co-worker, Peggy, turns around and introduces herself, too. Seems she and Lillian met earlier in the lunchroom where we all had to go first to pick up our "Kit for Employees." (Contents of kit: One large blue and white badge reading TRAINEE, one employee discount card, one locker room key, one brochure about the store, one plastic see-through case for I don't know what.) Unlike me, Peggy and Lillian are both old

239

hands at department store selling, but Peggy turns out to be the one with the particular information we are all avid for now: she worked in *this* store once before, only six months ago in fact.

So how is it? we both ask, what's it like?

"Well, you know, like everywhere else it all depends on which department you're in," Peggy answers, keeping her voice low. "Naturally it's how your manager and the other people you work with treat you, and that's different all over the store."

"Which manager is—" Lillian starts to ask but she is interrupted by a voice from the front of the line: "PLEASE FOLLOW ME UP THE STAIRS INTO THE MAIN FLOOR AND THEN UP THE ESCALATOR TO THE TOP OF THE STORE WHERE THE TRAINING ROOM IS."

The voice is that of the blonde woman from Personnel and we follow her now. Out of the dim basement into the bright main floor, a typical department store main floor—*cosmetics, blouses, jewelry, perfume, scarves, gloves.* Up the escalator . . . [to] the seventh [floor] and finally up a flight of stairs into the attic, the main stock area for the store. At the end of a long corridor full of cartons of all sizes is the training room, a tiny room with a blackboard, a desk, wooden chairs lined up in rows.

The woman from personnel is sitting behind the desk when we arrive waiting for us to be seated too. Peggy, Lillian and I find three chairs together.

The woman rises, a thick looseleaf manual in her hand. Tells us her name (Andrea), her title (assistant to the manager of personnel) and apologizes for the long wait we had downstairs.

"But it's a crazy day as you can all see. We have over 150 people starting today alone, 350 in all for the Christmas season. So it's quite hectic to say the least. But what I have to say now shouldn't take that long."

Sits down again, placing the manual on the desk in front of her. Flips slowly through the pages, stopping at certain places to inform us of company regulations. About:

Time: "Naturally it's important not to forget to punch in or out. If you want to get paid, that is. The company gives you a ten-minute leeway for lateness in the morning, anything above that you're docked. The usual system. Since it's the Christmas rush, you'll all be working some nights and most Saturdays. Your manager will let you know by the preceding Thursday what your schedule the next week will be."

Breaks: "You get a half hour each day, usually divided fifteen in the morning and afternoon, but some take it all at once."

Lunch: "You get an hour each day, although by state law the company doesn't have to give you more than 45 minutes when you work an eight-hour day. Only thing we require is you don't take lunch between twelve and two, since that's the busiest time of our day."

Dress: "Women are allowed to wear pants if they're selling, so long as it's not dungarees or anything that doesn't look proper. We don't ask you to wear only dark colors or only dresses like some stores. Try to look decent, is all we ask."

Shoplifting: "It happens all the time, you wouldn't believe how often. If you catch someone, you get an award, fifteen or twenty dollars. But don't ever try to apprehend a shoplifter yourself. The secret is: Be alert. If you see someone suspicious, call the security officer on the phone in your department right away, describe the suspect and let the officer take it from there. You'll get the award if the person is caught. And another thing. I know this sounds like a terrible thing to say. I know it sounds insulting. But I have to. *Don't shoplift yourself.* . . . Another thing. If you catch a fellow employee in your department stealing, you'll get an award of twenty-five dollars or more if you report it."

Lockers: "You must check your coats and other street clothes in your locker before punching in. Women must check their handbags, too. Take your wallet out and anything else you'll be needing during the day and put it in that plastic case we gave you in the employee kit." (So that's what the see-through case is for: to make sure we're not stealing anything.)

With that, Andrea closes the manual. "Unless you have any questions, that's all for now. Those of you who will be cashiers, keep your seats, you'll be getting special training this week. The rest of you line up and proceed downstairs back into the basement where someone from your department will come to pick you up."

Coats

Back in the basement Peggy and I stand together, waiting to start work. Very soon our names are called and we're introduced to a middle-aged woman named Alice, who has come to escort us to coats and suits. Short gray hair, stern expression.

On the escalator, Alice gives us a bit of advice. "It's a nice department, coats, but one thing, you really have to *worrrrkk.*"

"Oh, is that what we're here for—to work?" I joke to break the tension. Bad joke, bad start.

Alice stares straight ahead, silently, as the escalator carries us up . . .

Arrive safely at coats. Meet Ed, our manager, early forties, curly brown hair, Bugs Bunny smile. Seems surprised to be getting two full-timers, only expected one. Also seems preoccupied (it's the noon rush hour by now) but amiable enough in a distracted sort of way.

"Well, I guess I should show you girls around." (Yes, sisters, I know he should call us women, but this is *not* the time to argue.) Peggy and I follow him to the middle of the department, a huge department really, taking up at least half the entire fourth floor.

"See over there," Ed says, pointing a Glen Plaid arm in the direction of some racks near the wall twenty feet away. "Those are our bike jackets, and next to them are our car coats." He moves his arm a fraction to the right. "And those, see there in the corner, those are our half-sizes." Moving across the floor now, with us following, he points to . . . coats with fake fur collars and coats with real fur collars, to plain cloth coats at regular lengths, at midi lengths, at lengths for the petite, to raincoats with no lining, with detachable linings, with sewed-in linings, to coats on clearance and jackets on *final* clearance, to ski jackets and bike jackets—and then finally we are back where we came in. . . .

"Starting to get the pattern?" Ed asks, obviously impatient to get the whole thing over with.

Starting to get nothing but confused, I wait for Peggy to answer first, since she is the more experienced. "Mmm hmm," she says.

"Mmm," I say, wondering if she could possibly have meant it.

"Good," Ed says, "now let me show you the stockroom." Still in a rush, he leads us to a small room off the floor, with coats and jackets lined up on a long single rack facing one wall, an old wooden desk and chair facing the other. "I suppose you know," he says, "that all of our sales people at this store must also do stock work, so you're going to have to do it, too. What you see here, today, are mainly layaways, that's one of the biggest kinds of business we do at this store. People who don't have all the money and pay us in installments. Come on out, I'll show you how to do the form."

Out of the stock room and over to the cashier booth—a kind of circular cage near the front of the department. Peggy and I are introduced to two cashiers standing inside the booth, both about nineteen or twenty. One works full-time, the other 12 to 4. We also meet two other saleswomen in the department, again one full- and one part-time and they are in their late fifties. So we come in many categories here, I'm learning. Sales and cashiers. Full-time and part-time. Permanent and Christmas.

Ed shows us how to write out a layaway form, which looks simple enough, and our training period is pronounced over. Took, figuring generously, about eleven minutes.

"Now why don't you go and help the customers?" Ed says. Can he be serious? I think. There are about a dozen customers roaming around, all of whom must know the department better than I. Peggy goes to one side of the floor and I to the other.

I approach a woman in a black and white checked coat. "May I help you?"

"No, thank you."

On to the next. "May I help you?"

"Just looking."

A woman in green. "May I help you find something?"

"Not right now, thanks."

A woman of ample proportions. "May I help you?"

"Yes, miss, do you have any cashmere coats in black, size eighteen?"

Look vacantly around the room. Racks and racks and racks and racks of mysterious garments. "Black cashmere? Well, let's see. Over there are our fur-trimmed coats I believe and . . ."

"Not fur-trimmed. Cashmere. Plain black cashmere."

"Right, but next to the fur-trimmed I think are the plain coats. Shall we walk over?"

We do. The coats I saw turn out to be midi lengths, but next to *them* are the real untrimmed regular lengths. Relieved at finding them, I start to look through the rack.

"You don't call those cashmere, do you, miss? Cardboard would be more like it."

"Something the matter over here?" says a voice behind me. It is Alice, our escalator escort.

I turn to her. "Black cashmere. Size eighteen."

"Cashmere? Are you kidding? Someone told you we had black cashmere? Here? Sorry for wasting your time, madam," she says and stalks away.

Next: "May I help you?"

"No, just looking."

"May I help you?" A stunning black woman in a brown wool suit.

"Yes, I'm looking for a plain camel colored coat, size six or eight."

Scan the floor again, then remember. In front, near the cashier's booth. Walk decisively over. Finger through the racks, find three for her to try on. The last looks wonderful, and at $48 is a good buy. She takes it, looking immensely pleased. I'm a bit surprised to find I'm feeling pleased myself.

Lunch

At 3:30 Ed says go to lunch. He's apologetic; usually we are to eat earlier, but today, because of all the training (sic) and confusion we're behind schedule. After punching out, I wander outside the store, find a coffee shop across the street. As I enter a woman waves to me from the counter. It is Lillian, the redheaded woman in dresses I met earlier, sitting with another woman also on her first day. I take the stool next to them, order a hamburger and coffee.

Lillian wants to know how I like it so far and I tell her, I don't know, it seems okay, but it's probably too soon to tell. . . .

Lillian looks at me closely. "I bet you'd rather work in an office, wouldn't you? I know I would. But at my age they almost never hire you. They want younger girls." She takes a sip of her coffee. "Or if they do give you a chance, the few places that do, they make you take a typing test, and that I could never never pass. I don't know why, I can type fine, really. But if there's a test my fingers start to freeze."

"Why do you think office work is so much better than selling?" I ask.

"Well, for one thing, the hours. You don't have to work nights or Saturdays. And the pay is better usually, and the conditions in general, and the way people act toward you." . . .

Coats

In the brief amount of time left in the day after I return from lunch at 4:30, our department is very quiet, and Peggy and I are given our first stock assignment. We are to put all raincoats with price tags reading $16.66 on a special rack marked $16.66 SPECIAL. The raincoats are in different places on different racks and it takes us almost an hour to get them together, a very pleasant hour it turns out since we are able to talk with each other while we work. We talk about the east versus the west—I mention I recently relocated from California and Peggy tells me she once lived in Texas. We talk about children—Peggy has five, ranging from a son of twenty-three to twin girls of five. We talk about this and that, and the hour goes quickly. Then with all the $16.66 raincoats in one place, it's time to help a few customers, take our allotted break, help still a few more, and then finally it's 6:30, time to punch out. Our feet burn, but we made it.

» *Joan E. Crowley, Teresa E. Levitin, and Robert P. Quinn* «

Seven Deadly Half-Truths About Women

» «

The following selection examines some of the myths that employers have used to justify second-class employment for women. The authors present data that, they claim, overturn such stereotypes as "women work just to make pin money," "women would not work if economic reasons did not force them into the labor market," and "women are more content than men with intellectually undemanding jobs." Clearly, the facts show that women vary among themselves as much as men do; there is no "typical" woman. Thus, knowing that a worker is a woman does not help in predicting what she wants from her job. That news should be a blow to both male chauvinists and radical feminists, both of whom tend to present women as monolithic in their work desires.

The American man works to support his family, to contribute to society, to find his place under the sun. He wants a job that challenges him intellectually. Above all in our achievement-oriented society, he wants to get ahead. The American woman works for pin money. She does that only when she has to. She is indifferent to intellectual challenge, not interested in finding work that contributes to her identity. What concerns her are friendly coworkers and whether or not she gets home in time to fix dinner.

These stereotypical views of working men and working women in our society may at first seem innocuous. But they become dangerous when used to relegate women to second-class employment, to justify low salaries and poor working conditions. Such stereotypes can wreak psychological destruction as well: if a woman incorporates them into her self-image she may accept discrimination without complaint and limit the development of her abilities.

If this stereotype of the American working woman is valid, we may assume that occupational segregation by sex is the result of a natural or

245

self-selection. If, on the other hand, the stereotype is inaccurate, this would suggest that occupational segregation is the result of discrimination by employers.

We took the stereotype apart and identified seven central beliefs about women on the job. Then, to check the accuracy of those beliefs, we analyzed the data from a nationwide probability sample of 539 working women and 933 working men.

To understand sex differences in work attitudes, we considered both early childhood socialization and adult experiences. To test the stereotypes, we first determined if in fact women and men differ in their attitude. When we found a significant difference, we controlled on the factor—such as job demands or marital status—that we felt was most likely to affect that job attitude, to see whether the sex difference persisted.

1. American Women Work Just for Pin Money.

This belief is a cornerstone of the stereotype of the American working woman. It presupposes that men in the U.S. support women economically. It suggests that a husband's income provides the basics for family life—housing, transportation, clothing, food, medical expenses—while a wife's income, when there is any, provides such extras as a second car or new curtains for the living room. Employers acting on this belief thus justify assigning men to better, higher-paying jobs and bypassing women employees. The earnings of men, they reason, are more critical to the essentials of their families.

Our data indicated that about two in every five U.S. working women are economically independent of men. A third of the women in our sample were the sole wage earners in their households. An additional eight percent—not sole wage earners—reported that they earned the bulk of their families' incomes

We also found evidence that the wages of working women provided the necessities rather than the frills of family living. Among the high-income working families we interviewed, the percentage of women workers was low. But among families whose annual incomes fell under $5,000, 57 percent of the workers were women.

2. Women Would Not Work if Economic Reasons Did Not Force Them into the Labor Market.

This belief about the motivation of working women would seem to follow from the evidence just presented. The thought is that since economic necessity does force some women to work, those who do work do so only for the money. Neither personal involvement, nor the desire to do a good job for its own sake nor any other intrinsic satisfaction motivates women on the job, according to this stereotype, and they are not interested in performing above minimally acceptable standards.

This belief makes as little sense for women as it does for men. Both sexes can be motivated to work for many reasons that are not mutually exclusive. Demonstrating that someone works for economic reasons in no way rules out the possibility that other motives also influence his or her choice of whether to work or not.

To test this stereotype, we asked: "If you were to get enough money to live as comfortably as you would like for the rest of your life, would you continue to work?" Seventy-four percent of the men indicated that they would continue to work, while 57 percent of the women said they would. Most of this sex difference resulted from responses by married women. Single women did not differ significantly from men in the percentage who said they would continue to work in the absence of economic need.

Why the low frequency of *yes* answers from married women? We suggest that married women in our society have well-defined, socially approved alternatives to work—the roles of wife and mother, which provide great psychological rewards. Men and single women do not have such alternatives. Even so, we consider it remarkable that half of the wives in this sample would work without economic need, thereby rejecting the pressures to be wives and mothers only.

3. Women Are More Concerned than Men with the Socioemotional Aspects of Their Jobs.

The usual implication here is that women let emotional ties with coworkers interfere with their performance on the job. According to the stereotype, women are more concerned with making friends and general socializing on the job than they are with getting their work done.

To find what factual basis there was for this belief, we asked men and women workers to rate the importance to them of four facets of their jobs: "My coworkers are friendly and helpful"; "I am given a lot of chances to make friends"; "My supervisor is very concerned about the welfare of those under him"; and "My supervisor is competent in doing his job." (The male researchers who wrote these items have promised never again to assume that only men are supervisors.)

We found only one significant sex difference. More women (68 percent) than men (61 percent) indicated that it was very important to them that their coworkers be friendly and helpful.

We also note here that women, like men, attached more importance to having a competent supervisor than they attached to having a nice supervisor who was concerned with the welfare of subordinates.

4. Women Are More Concerned than Men with the Hygienic Aspects of Their Jobs.

Women are supposed to be fastidious and less tolerant of dirt and uncomfortable surroundings than men. They are also supposed to be less tolerant of inconvenience on the job. Women—especially those who work for pin money—can afford to be fussy in their job requirements and can shop

247

around for jobs that meet their criteria. This self-selection would account in part for the over-representation of women in office jobs and for their scarcity in skilled labor, factory shift-work, and other dirty, off-hours work. Legislation and union agreements that prohibit women from lifting things over a certain weight, or from working certain hours, for example, reinforce this tendency.

Underlying this belief is the general assumption that women are more interested than men in what Frederick Herzberg, Bernard Mausner, and Barbara Snyderman have called the "hygienic" aspects of work. Data from our study provided some support for this assertion. When we measured the desire for a hygienic job by the importance workers attached to good hours, pleasant physical surroundings, and convenient travel to and from work, we found that women attached significantly more importance to each of these facets than did men. Moreover, when we compared men and women in terms of their actual physical surroundings, hours, etc., the initial sex differences remained. Thus we cannot conclude that women value these commodities more because they do not have them.

5. Women Are Less Concerned than Men that Their Work Be Self-Actualizing.

This belief, like some of the others that shape the stereotype of the American working woman, suggests that women are less involved in their work than men are—that they view their work as just a job, rather than as a career. The idea is that women have no particular desire for meaningful work because their other social roles provide abundant opportunities for self-actualization and personal gratification.

We asked workers to rate the importance of the opportunity to develop one's special abilities through work, the importance of interesting work, and the importance of opportunities to do the things that one does best. Men and women in our sample indicated approximately equal concern about meaningful work.

6. Women Are More Content than Men with Intellectually Undemanding Jobs.

Here we have the rationale for placing women in routine, repetitive, uninspiring jobs. According to the stereotype, women are more likely than men to be satisfied with these jobs. After all, the logic goes, women invest their energies in the roles of wife and mother, and hence aren't interested in challenging work.

Our data completely failed to support this belief. We determined which persons in our sample actually held intellectually demanding positions, by asking them to rate their jobs according to such criteria as "requires that you keep having to learn new things," "requires that you do a lot of planning," and "allows you a lot of freedom and creativity." Women, we found, were underrepresented in intellectually demanding jobs. Only

37 percent of the women indicated that they held such jobs, in contrast to 55 percent of the men.

We next asked workers how satisfied they were with their jobs, and, again, women were less satisfied than men. But this sex difference disappeared when we controlled for the intellectual requirements of the work. Unstimulating jobs are equally disagreeable for both sexes.

7. Women Are Less Concerned than Men with Getting Ahead on the Job.

The lure of promotion, with its attendant increases in pay, status and responsibility, is supposed to encourage hard work and extra effort. A person who is not interested in promotion—a woman, for instance, according to this stereotype—will put forth only the minimum effort acceptable to his or her employer. As a result, the employer will justifiably restrict this person to a poorer job. Neat reasoning, perhaps, but we found little evidence to support it.

How Workers Rate Each Job Facet

		Very important	Somewhat important	Not important
Socioemotional Aspects of Job				
My co-workers are friendly and	men	61	28	11
helpful.*	women	68	22	10
I am given a lot of chances to	men	45	29	26
make friends.	women	43	32	26
My supervisor is very concerned	men	48	28	24
about the welfare of those	women	54	27	19
under him.				
My supervisor is competent in doing	men	59	25	16
his job.	women	65	20	15
Hygienic Aspects of Job				
The hours are good.*	men	46	25	29
	women	61	25	15
The physical surroundings are	men	38	35	27
pleasant.*	women	43	36	21
Travel to and from work is	men	42	30	29
convenient.*	women	55	28	17
Self-Actualization and Job				
I have an opportunity to develop my	men	65	20	15
own special abilities.	women	60	21	19
The work is interesting.	men	73	17	10
	women	73	17	10
I am given a chance to do the things	men	56	29	16
I do best.	women	52	28	20

The "not too important" and "not at all important" categories have been collapsed.

*Sex differences on starred items are statistically significant.

Initially, a significant difference appeared between men and women in whether they ever wanted to be promoted (64 percent of the men versus 48 percent of the women). But desire for promotion turned out to be largely a result of *expectation* of promotion. When we took the current job situation into account, women want promotions as much as men do—*when they think they have a realistic chance of being promoted.* Their apparent lack of ambition is not a personality trait, but a result of their restriction to dead-end jobs (two thirds of all the women never expected to be promoted). We would guess that to avoid frustration, women, like men in the same situations, scale down their ambitions.

Thus, we end up with a picture of American working women that is more complex than the stereotypes warrant. We found that American women do *not* work for pin money even though married women would be somewhat less inclined to work if economics did not force them to. We found that women are not more satisfied with intellectually dreary jobs although they are over-represented in such positions.

Women do appear to be more concerned with the hygienic aspects of work and with the friendliness and helpfulness of their coworkers. But women are not less interested in self-actualizing work than men are, nor are they less interested in being promoted. The belief that women—or men—would trade challenging jobs for cleaner offices is simply not true. The same person can value both social and intellectual activities.

Overall, we found more on-the-job similarities between men and women than differences. It would be easy to explain more differences since the socialization processes that separate men and women from childhood on are bound to lead to typical differences in personality makeups. But socialization does not stop in adulthood. Individuals continue to learn and to react, and their attitudes and motives change in response to new experiences and demands.

The "average women" is a statistical creation, a fiction. She has been used to defend the status quo of the labor market, on the assumption that knowing the sex of an employee reliably predicts his or her job attitudes. This assumption is false. Knowing that a worker is female allows us to predict that she will hold a job in a "woman's field," and that she will be substantially underpaid for a person of her qualifications. But knowing that a worker is female does not help us much to predict what she wants from her job.

Although the stereotypes of the American working woman are not completely false, they are false more often than not and their application to a particular woman in disregard of her personal qualifications is discriminatory. Employers can no longer justifiably hide behind the skirts of ill-founded stereotypes.

» Carl Hoffmann and John Shelton Reed «

Sex Discrimination? The XYZ Affair

» «

Carl Hoffman and John Shelton Reed are researchers who have investigated the question of why there are still differences in the occupational success of men and women after nearly two decades of equal rights legislation. Do such persistent imbalances result, as some people maintain, from continuing biases and discrimination on the part of employers, and from such practices as the use of seniority systems or irrelevant requirements of prior experience and education? Or do these imbalances persist, as others argue, because a significant portion of women workers do not share the career aspirations of the majority of men or the minority of women? The answers to these questions are important, for they largely determine whether or not employers can—or should—be held responsible for existing imbalances. Hoffman and Reed conclude from the case presented here that, in this instance at least, the observed differences in promotions among men and women can be attributed more to the choices women voluntarily make than to discrimination on the part of employers.

In August 1978, the XYZ Corporation,* a Fortune 500 company, approached Hoffmann Research Associates,** a North Carolina consulting firm, to conduct a study of its personnel practices. The company's motive was not altrustic: A sex discrimination suit had been filed in one of its divisions, and it stood to lose a lot of money. The division of XYZ in question was one with considerable sales and clerical responsibility. It employed roughly 6,000 persons, of whom 5,500 were in entry-level clerical positions, and 500 in supervisory and management positions, ranging from assistant supervisor to senior vice-president.

---

*The company has asked that it not be identified. Otherwise, no restrictions have been placed on our analysis or our reporting on it.

**Carl Hoffmann is the president of Hoffmann Research Associates. John Shelton Reed served as a consultant to HRA during the later stages of data analysis and in the writing of the report. They gratefully acknowledge the various contributions of Rachael Tayar, Hunter Hughes, and Herbert Hyman.

The charges of discrimination had been filed by several female clerks who pointed to the fact that, while 82 percent of the entry-level jobs were filled by women between 1971 and 1978, female clerks were only 74 percent of those promoted in 1978 and only 61 percent of those promoted in earlier years. Promotion at XYZ was always from one level to the next. Men were obviously much more likely than women to be promoted at this first level (although at higher levels in the company there was no difference in the promotion rates of men and women).

XYZ made no attempt to dispute these figures, but its management could not explain them. Discrimination was forbidden; an entire district supervisory staff had once been dismissed for such practices; XYZ's management was sure employees were treated fairly. There were no differences in education, training, or experience that could explain the differences, and seniority was not a factor. Management insisted that only knowledge of the job, performance, and leadership played a part in promotion, but never asserted that there were differences between men and women in these respects. The president of the company had started in an entry-level job in this particular division. The management of XYZ was genuinely puzzled. . . .

The research task was to determine the reasons for the lower rate of promotion for female than for male clerks, and to study another pattern that management had noticed, that of women being less likely than men to apply for lateral transfer within the company . . . .

Promotion-Seeking Behavior

Somewhat to the [HRA] researchers' surprise, data analysis quickly made it clear that male and female clerks at XYZ were promoted in almost exactly the same proportions as they expressed interest in promotion. On the face of it, the difference in promotion rates for men and for women did not result from practices and policies that discriminated against women, but from a pattern of behaviors and attitudes that led male clerks more often than female clerks to seek and to accept promotion.

In the year prior to the survey, twice as many men as women (28 percent compared to 14 percent) had asked to be promoted, and the company's response was, if anything, more positive toward the women who asked than toward the men [see Table 1]. Similarly, equal proportions of men and women had been asked if they were interested in promotion, but among those asked, men were nearly twice as likely as women to have indicated that they were interested. Altogether, 39 percent of the male clerks had indicated, in one way or another, that they would like to be promoted; only 21 percent of the female clerks had done so. . . .

It seems reasonable to suppose that promotions will be offered more often to those who have indicated their availability, or at least not indicated that they are not interested. In fact, those who reported that they had sought promotion were twice as likely as the others to report that they had

Table 1. Self-Reported Promotion-Seeking Behavior, 1978 and Before[1]

| | 1978 | | 1977 or before[2] | |
	Men	Women	Men	Women
Percent who requested promotion	28%	14%	30%	11%
Of those, percent reporting positive response	55	70	51	55
Percent asked whether interested in promotion	36	34	41	33
Of those, percent who expressed interest	74	43	69	35
Percent who indicated interest either way	39	21	46	19
(N)	(283)	(363)	(218)	(226)

[1]Source: Hoffman Research Associates survey of XYZ employees.
[2]Asked only of respondents employed before 1978.

actually been offered promotion at some point.

We have one other indication of the behavior patterns that led to the observed differences in promotion. Ambitious clerks might stay well-informed about opportunities for lateral transfers, some of which offer more pay, responsibility, or opportunity. At XYZ, notices of openings are posted, and employees encouraged to "bid" on those that interested them. Twenty-five percent of the male clerks, compared to 10 percent of the female clerks, indicated that they followed the posted openings closely. . . .

It appears, then, that male clerks at XYZ were promoted more often than female clerks to the same extent that they more often exhibited interest in promotion and engaged in promotion-seeking behavior.

Perceptions of discrimination can, of course, vary independently of actual practices. It would not be unprecedented to find a situation where some category of workers was subjected to systematic discrimination without being aware of it. Nor, in the present case, would it be surprising to find a widespread belief that female clerks were being discriminated against, particularly given the undeniable and striking differences in promotion rates and the present litigious climate.

But, as Table 2 . . . shows, although a good many respondents of both sexes were dissatisfied with various aspects of their jobs, only a negligible proportion complained about discrimination of any sort—sex, race, religious, or age—and males were more likely than females to complain. Female clerks were less likely than males to indicate that their own individual chances for promotion were "excellent" or "good," but when asked why they had not in fact been offered promotion, they were much more likely than males to indicate that they were known to be uninterested or that they were not qualified.

These data do not in themselves establish the absence of discrimination—any more than would widespread perceptions of discrimination establish its existence. But they do reinforce the evidence in the earlier analysis of even-handed treatment.

Table 2. Ratings of XYZ Promotion Policies and Perceived Reasons For Not Being Offered Promotion, By Sex[1]

	Men	Women
Percent saying "good" or "excellent"		
Transfer policy	72%	80%
Policy of promoting from within	68	70
"An individual's" promotion chances	43	42
Own promotion chances	34	29
(N)	(281)	(360)
Reasons for not being offered promotion		
Discrimination	3%	1%
Known not to be interested	27	41
Personality, personal history	19	10
Not qualified	14	25
(N)[2]	(230)	(300)

[1]Source: Hoffmann Research Associates survey of XYZ employees.
[2]Asked only of those not offered promotion in 1978.

Aspirations and Motivation

If, as we believe we have demonstrated, the difference in promotion rates between male and female clerks was not due to company policy or practice, the differences in behavior which did produce it remain to be explained. The explanation appears to lie in the fact that female clerks were likely to have lower aspirations than male clerks, less likely to have had the time or to have felt they had the ability for higher-level positions, more likely to have seen their employment as a "job" rather than as a stage in a career, and more likely to have sought better working conditions rather than advancement. . . .

Female clerks, it appears, were more likely than male clerks to have sought a clerical job specifically. Men were more likely to report that they were ready to accept any position that was open, evidently viewing their first position as simply an entree to the company. . . .

When we asked what these clerks' ultimate ambitions were, we found that women were twice as likely as men to be content with their present positions, and those who did aspire to higher positions set their sights lower than men: Only 14 percent sought positions above the level of supervisor, compared to nearly half the men.

In short, the women's ambitions, both for immediate advancement and long-term success, were more limited than the men's. This difference was present when they were hired; it was not something the company created.

Resource Commitment and Career

For most clerks, the first step up is promotion to assistant supervisor, a position which carries a modest increase in salary ($65.00 a month at the time of the survey), longer hours, rotating shifts, and a considerable increase in responsibility. Male and female clerks agreed . . . such a promotion would impose a number of burdens that they did not have to carry in their present positions. . . .

Male clerks were willing or able to give up more, in general, to obtain promotion. They would have been more likely to accept a transfer, more likely to give up an optimal shift assignment. They were more likely to indicate that they had the time to devote to the job. While nearly half of the women said they would prefer to work only part-time, if that were possible, only 18 percent of the men shared that view; male agents were more likely to have worked substantial amounts of overtime. . . .

For many more female than male clerks, the question of promotion was of little importance, because they did not intend to remain employed. . . .

Women, more than men, were unwilling or unable to make a number of sacrifices which, they recognized, career advancement requires. Moreover, a pattern of discontinuous employment, reflecting commitments other than to one's career, was more common among women than among men. Finally, women were substantially more likely than men to believe they lacked the ability to fill higher-level positions. . . . While the perceptions of female clerks—or, for that matter, those of male clerks—may be inaccurate, they can have the same effects as a real difference in abilities. . . .

Those who reported that they aspire to higher-level management, that they would give up a preferred shift schedule for promotion, and that they have the time and ability to be a chief supervisor are labelled "highly motivated." Men fell in this category twice as often as women; 61 percent compared to 31 percent. This difference in motivation goes a long way toward explaining the observed difference in promotion-seeking behavior. . . .

Effects of Marriage and Parenthood

But why were women who were apparently motivated to seek promotion less likely than men actually to have done so? . . .

The breakdowns by marital status [see Table 3] suggest an answer. The differences between unmotivated men and women were relatively small, as were those between highly-motivated, *unmarried* men and women. *The largest difference between men and women [at XYZ] is that between highly-motivated married men and highly-motivated married women. Marriage appears to increase promotion-seeking among highly-motivated men and to decrease it among highly-motivated women.* . . .

For nearly all of our measures of motivation, commitment, promotion-seeking, and perceived ability to meet the demands of a new position, the effect of marriage—marriage *per se*, without the added complications of child-rearing—was to reduce the likelihood of promotion for women, on the average, and to increase that for men. . . .

Table 3. Promotion-Seeking Behavior By Motivation, For Male and Female Clerks, Married and Unmarried.[1]

	Percent Seeking Promotion (N)	
	Men	Women
Low motivation	16%	16%
	(114)	(249)
Unmarried	14%	20%
	(65)	(127)
Married	20%	12%
	(46)	(122)
High motivation	53%	33%
	(172)	(111)
Unmarried	47%	36%
	(88)	(61)
Married	60%	30%
	(84)	(63)

[1]Source: Hoffmann Research Associates survey of XYZ employees.

One implication of this analysis is that married male clerks were more likely than married female clerks to come from households where their job was seen as the principal career within the family [see Table 4]. The demands of male clerks' jobs were usually seen as determining; female clerks had more often to compromise between the demands of their jobs, on the one hand, and those of their husbands' jobs and their own household responsibilities, on the other. These women were most often economic equals with their husbands, while their male colleagues usually had *the* economically important jobs in their families.

Table 4. Indicators of Occupational Primacy Within Family, By Sex (Married Respondents Only)[1]

	Men	Women
Would give up XYZ job if spouse's job required a move	45%	53%
Spouse would give up job if respondent's job required a move	92	55
Respondent's job more important to family than spouse's	90	34
Spouse's job more important	4	50

[1]Source: Hoffmann Research Associates survey of XYZ employees.

Thus, though practically none of the male clerks would have given up his job with XYZ if his spouse's career required a move, roughly half of the female clerks would have done so (but not all, by any means). Similarly, nearly all of the male clerks would expect their wives to follow them, if their XYZ jobs required a move; about half of the female clerks would expect their husbands to move with them. While nine out of ten male clerks said that their job was the most important in the family, female clerks were more evenly divided, and frequently volunteered that their jobs and their husband's jobs were equally important. . . .

Marriage means different things for male and female clerks. Most often, a married male clerk finds himself with a household primarily or even completely dependent on his present and future earnings. He usually expects that his family will adjust to the demands of his career. Those demands are in a strong position in the competition for his time and attention, and he faces no choice between his family role and his job: To a large extent, his family role is his job. But female clerks showed no consistent pattern of either primacy or subordination in the economic lives of their families. Their career decisions often required compromises, which need not go against their career interests, but would not necessarily favor them either. . . .

The effects of parenthood were like those of marriage, only more so. It increased men's desire for promotion and their efforts to achieve it, and decreased both among women. . . .

While parenthood, like marriage, means added responsibilities for both men and women, the responsibilities of wives and mothers conflict with their on-the-job behavior in ways that those of husbands and fathers do not. In this case, it limited women's ability to devote extra time, perhaps at unusual hours, to their jobs—an ability which these clerks recognized is required of supervisors.

Female Supervisors

Many female clerks resolve the conflict between their household responsibilities and their husbands' careers, on the one hand, and their own careers, on the other, by lowering their levels of aspiration and by avoiding the added responsibilities that would accompany promotion. Another possibility, of course, would be to remain single, or childless, as had many female supervisors who sought, were offered, and accepted promotion. . . .

In nearly every respect, supervisors differed from clerks of the same sex in those characteristics that we have identified as important for promotion—characteristics that male clerks were more likely than female clerks to display [see Table 5]. . . . In the first place, male clerks by and large thought and behaved more like supervisors than did female clerks. In the second place, and importantly, female supervisors differed relatively little from

257

male supervisors. They displayed comparable levels of motivation, similar attitudes, and similar behaviors—and they had been rewarded for that with promotion.

Table 5. Promotion-Related Characteristics, By Sex, Among Agents and Supervisors[1]

	Agents		Supervisors	
	Men	Women	Men	Women
Prefer promotion to desired shift	67%	54%	88%	86%
Aspire to higher management	79	60	88	82
Summary index of motivation "high"	61	31	75	75
Would not prefer part-time job	82	56	75	78
Household responsibilities do not restrict hours available	96	92	95	98
Worked overtime in past year	91	86	91	93
Have expressed interest in promotion	39	21	63	61
Follow postings of transfers	25	10	21	6
Would accept promotion to assistant supervisor	66	52	•	•

[1]Source: Hoffmann Research Associates survey of XYZ employees.
• Not applicable, since supervisors have already accepted a promotion.

Some . . . did this by avoiding marriage and parenthood, others by entering into marriages where the principal economic responsibility was theirs. In general, our data showed that the effects of marriage on the attitudes and behaviors of female supervisors were usually negligible, and as often in the direction of increasing motivation and promotion-seeking behavior as of decreasing it—a striking contrast to the situation for female clerks.

In short, those women who sought and accepted promotion at XYZ were disproportionately women who, whether willingly or through force of circumstances, had avoided the pattern of aspirations, values, and behavior which led many of their female co-workers to choose not to compete for promotion. They displayed characteristics which resembled those of male clerks and supervisors, and which set them off from many female clerks. In part, this is because many had remained unmarried, and few of the married women had small children. But even those who had married showed high levels of the promotion-related characteristics we have been examining: Marriage simply appears to have had less of an inhibiting effect on their aspirations and behaviors than on those of female clerks generally. The reason seems to be that they were more likely to have a household division of labor like that of their male co-workers, in which their occupational success played an important, even a primary, part.

Discrimination?

Did the relatively low proportion of women among those promoted reflect discrimination? Clearly the answer is no. It reflected differences in the behaviors and attitudes of male and female clerks—differences the company and its policies had no part in producing. These differences decrease as one moves up the organizational ladder, reflecting self-selection at each step: Those women who are prepared to seek and to accept responsibility are as likely to be promoted as men who do so.

Even at the supervisory level, though, some of the differences persisted, as we have seen. It should come as no surprise to learn, then, that XYZ's records show a much higher rate of voluntary self-demotion among female supervisors than among their male colleagues, and that the reasons given by women usually involve family demands or moves to a new locale required by their husbands' jobs. . . .

[In summary] equality of opportunity and equality of result appear to be antithetical at the XYZ Corporation. Those who argue for the latter rather than the former are eager to tamper with a complex, competitive system, and their search for simple solutions to complex problems may upset the engine of our prosperity—which relies on individual initiative and competition for rewards. In the long run, family structure, sex-role socialization, and child-rearing practices may change to accommodate women's participation as equals in the paid labor force. If so, they may attain equality of position, power, and reward in the economy. But while the family, socialization, and child-rearing may change, scarcity and competition and the need for economic growth and increased productivity will not.

We are not arguing against the application of the Civil Rights Act where discrimination truly exists. . . . [But] a criterion of parity, the insistence that a category of individuals is entitled to rewards proportionate to its numbers and not to its members' performances, does not serve the common good. It is, in fact, antithetical to the social contract, implicit in the American tradition: An individual is entitled to the fruits of his labor, and group membership—whether in a hereditary nobility or a "protected group"—does not entitle him to benefits. . . .

What is a company's obligation to its female employees? It is obliged to offer them the same opportunities as men and to reward them in proportion to their productivity. No more. . . . The inequities (if such they are) of early socialization or of the division of labor in the American household are not the responsibility nor the business, in any sense of that word, of an employer.

If a company is so moved, however, it might reasonably seek to rationalize both its internal labor market and its relations to the external market—examining its seniority systems, lines of progression, training programs, and so forth. In these areas, employers may find that they can serve the interests of their employees from "protected groups" while serving their own as well, by expanding the range of opportunities for *individuals,* and rewarding those who seize them.

» Isabel V. Sawhill «

Perspectives on Women and Work in America

» «

Isabel V. Sawhill, an economist who is currently directing a major research project on women and work for the Urban Institute, is also concerned with why women are clustered in the lower-paying jobs. She discusses two possible explanations: more limited opportunities for women and cultural attitudes toward women's traditional roles. Because of these and other factors, women suffer inequities, and the economy suffers a waste in human resources. In this selection Sawhill reminds us that most women work, whether in the market for pay, in the home, or both. She reviews trends in the participation of women in the labor force, the differences in pay between men and women, and some preliminary implications for family life (which she discusses more fully in another article in Chapter 9).

American women have always worked—it is only the nature of their productive contribution that has changed. During the colonial period, most of their work was carried on at home. Women did the spinning, weaving, sewing, and related work not only for their own families but also as part of the domestic system of industry which prevailed until the beginning of the nineteenth century. In addition, many were employed as servants. In the late eighteenth and early nineteenth centuries women began moving from home to factory to become operatives in the new textile mills, and they were increasingly utilized as teachers. By the end of the nineteenth century, they were finding employment as office workers and salesclerks. During the twentieth century, census statistics document a tremendous expansion in the employment of women, especially in the growing number of white-collar occupations. The result has been a dramatic increase in the proportion of the labor force that is female. Whereas in the early nineteenth century probably no more than one out of every twenty workers was female, by 1890, one out of every six was female, and by 1960 one out of every three.*

---

*Ed. note: By 1980 women constituted approximately 40 percent of the work force.

The increases in female labor force participation have been particularly large since 1940. . . . Any explanation of these trends must therefore deal with the *acceleration* in participation rates in the postwar period and the changing composition of the female labor force that has made this tremendous expansion possible.

At the turn of the century, the typical female worker was young and single. As late as 1940, only 30 percent of working women were married and living with their husbands, whereas [in 1974] about 60 percent [fell] in this category. In short, most of the growth of the female labor force in the postwar period is due to the increased employment of mature married women, many of whom enter or reenter the labor force once their children are grown or in school. More recently, there has also been a rapid increase in the participation rates of younger married women, including those with children under six or in school. . . .

Causes of Increased Participation

While the long-run historical data show increasing labor force rates for women, they show decreasing rates for males (chiefly younger and older males) and, on balance, little variation in the total proportion of the population at work. In attempting to explain these trends, social scientists have turned to an analysis of demographic, economic, and cultural variables.

Demographic Variables Changes in the composition of the population (by sex, age, race, nativity, marital status, residence, and family size) can have an effect on labor force participation. . . . The empirical evidence suggests that none of these factors has been of great importance in explaining changes in the sex composition of the labor force, however. In other words, changes in participation rates within demographic categories have been much more significant in explaining the observed trends than changes in demographic composition.

Economic Variables Economists postulate that as income rises people respond either by working more or by working less. They may work more because higher wages make each hour of leisure more expensive, or they may work less because a higher income permits them to "afford" more hours of leisure. Most empirical evidence has indicated that the latter effect is the stronger one: as incomes have risen over time, the workweek and the workday have been shortened, retirement has been earlier, and schooling has been prolonged. In addition, cross-sectional studies reveal an inverse relationship between the work rates of married women and husbands' incomes. The major piece of evidence to the contrary is the increased labor force participation of women over time in the face of continually improving standards of living.

A major step in resolving this paradox was taken by Jacob Mincer in his analysis of the determinants of the labor force participation of married women. Mincer's contribution was to suggest that women who seek employment are not necessarily foregoing leisure as much as they are substituting work in the market for work in the home. His empirical study showed that women's market work is negatively correlated with husband's income but that it is even more strongly related (positively) to their own earnings. As the earnings opportunities of married women have improved, these women have responded by entering the labor force in large numbers. It is simply too "expensive" for them to stay home. . . .

[Other] studies . . . show that (1) the labor force participation of women is highest in the areas where employment opportunities for women are greatest (such as Washington, D.C.); and (2) the labor force participation of women is highly responsive to wartime demand and the ebb and flow of the business cycle.

Finally, it is well known that better-educated women are much more likely to seek employment than the less well educated. . . . This could be partly because the jobs open to well-educated women provide not only better pay but also better working conditions and higher status than that of a housewife, whereas jobs open to less well-educated women have the opposite characteristics. In other words, women prefer semiskilled work at home to unskilled work in the market, but they prefer skilled work in the market to either of these alternatives.

The implication is that if women are provided with more challenging and higher-paid job opportunities, many more will opt to leave the home. In the process of doing so, they will not be foregoing leisure as much as they will be changing jobs—that is, substituting work in the market for work in the home or possibly leisure consumed on the job for leisure consumed at home.

Cultural Variables   Although economic variables appear to be strategic in understanding the greater employment of women outside the home, they undoubtedly interact with a variety of social or cultural variables in a rather complex fashion. Certainly the attitudes of women themselves (as well as those of their husbands, relatives, and friends) and the willingness of employers to hire women should not be neglected. Although it is difficult to interpret what little hard evidence there is on this question, one is left with the impression that attitudes adjust to changes in the facts rather than that they are the underlying cause of such changes. Nevertheless, once change is initiated, the gradual shift in attitudes that follows helps to create secondary waves of activity which sustain or build on the initial momentum.

Most of the public opinion polls of the thirties and forties showed that the great majority of men and women disapproved of married women working (except to support the war effort). More surprising perhaps is the fact that as late as 1960, a poll conducted by the University of Michigan's

Survey Research Center indicated that only 34 percent of the husbands polled had favorable or qualifiedly favorable attitudes toward working wives in spite of the fact that 38 percent of the wives in the study were working at least part-time. Another survey, carried out by Leland Axelson in 1961, found that the husband's attitude depended very strongly on whether his wife was working or not. Although it is impossible to say whether the husband's feelings are cause or consequence of his wife's employment, the latter interpretation seems more consistent with the relatively small change in attitude in spite of a radical change in the facts.

The polls also show that the major reason for people's disapproval of employment for married women revolves around the family responsibilities of these women—but a significant minority also believes that women who do not need to support themselves should not compete with men for scarce jobs.

Home Work

Although more and more women are seeking paid employment, the majority of the female population of working age is still engaged in keeping house. It has been estimated that married women spend an average of forty hours per week on housework while their husbands spend about four hours per week. When aggregate hours of work in the home are added to aggregate hours of market work, we find that women end up doing a slightly higher proportion of society's total work (paid and unpaid) during a given year than men. . . .

Juanita Kreps suggest[s] that our failure to include the value of housewives' services in the national income may have important consequences for the social status attached to this occupation: "Despite our protests that growth in income is not to be equated with improvements in welfare; that society places a high value on the services of wives in the home and in the community; that the absence of a price tag on a particular service does not render it valueless—despite these caveats, the tendency to identify one's worth with the salary he earns is a persistent one. This tendency is not peculiar to men who earn salaries; it pervades as well the thinking of women who work at unpaid jobs."

Although the increased availability of laborsaving devices and commercial goods for use within the home would appear to have "automated" the housewife out of a job—or at least out of a full-time job—what little evidence there is suggests that there has been surprisingly little reduction in the hours devoted to work in the home. . . .

The Earnings Differential

The differences in the earnings of men and women are astonishingly large. In [1980], among year-round, full-time workers, men earned [about $17,000], while women earned [$10,000] (or only 60 percent as much).

One cannot conclude from the existence of an earnings gap that there is unequal pay for equal work (where the latter is defined as performing the same duties on the same job in the same establishment). The fact is that women workers are concentrated in the lowest-paying jobs and are rarely found doing the same work as men. What we see instead is separate labor markets, where jobs are socially labeled for "men only" or "women only."

The resulting sexual division of labor is pervasive. . . . Women become secretaries, nurses, schoolteachers, waitresses, and department-store saleswomen. Men become plumbers, doctors, engineers, school administrators, and automobile salesmen. Once such a division of labor becomes established, it tends to be self-perpetuating, since each sex is socialized, trained, and counseled into certain jobs and not into others. . . .

What is responsible . . . for the occupational segregation and, ultimately, the lower earnings of women? Are women in some way less qualified for the better-paid positions? . . .Studies have shown that there are no important differences between working men and women where schooling, age, race, and geographical distribution are concerned. Such factors as unionism and excessive absenteeism play a very minor role, if any, in explaining the lower earnings of women. It is true that many married women work intermittently and thus fail to accumulate the on-the-job experience that men have, but several studies have shown that women who do work continuously are not much better off than those who don't. It is the *quality* rather than the *quantity* of their work experience that holds their earnings down. They seldom work in the kinds of occupations that would enable them to acquire valuable skills and advance to more responsible positions.

In short, there appears to be at least a 30 percent gap in the earnings of men and women even after adjustments have been made for differences in educational background, years of experience, and similar factors. The only way in which one can "explain" this gap is to adjust for differences in occupational composition by sex. But this does not settle the question of why women are relegated to the lower-paying, less demanding jobs, why their actual contribution to the economy is far below what they could reasonably be expected to produce on the basis of their education, ability, and work experience. In other words, the occupational status of women is not consistent with their capabilities; it represents the major symptom of an opportunity structure that is much more limiting for women than for men.

> *There is perhaps one human being in a thousand who is passionately interested in his job for the job's sake. The difference is that if that one person in a thousand is a man, we say, simply, that he is passionately keen on his job; if she is a woman, we say she is a freak.*
> —Dorothy L. Sayers, *Gaudy Night*

In a further probe into the causes of existing occupational segregation by sex, two factors appear to be of some importance. First, because of the intermittent nature of their employment, women are often assigned to occupations in which there is virtually no on-the-job training or "learning while earning" which so often provides career progression for men. As a result, their earnings do not increase as they gain additional experience; the male-female earnings gap widens with age. . . .

The second, more important factor confining women to low-paying occupations is cultural in origin and is related to deeply held views about "women's sphere" and the functions that they have traditionally performed. Many of the occupations in which women are found are closely linked to their homemaking role; others to their socialization as male helpmates. Conversely, occupations from which women are excluded tend to be those that involve "nonfeminine" pursuits or that necessitate supervision of other employees. The result of this cultural discrimination is to crowd women into a limited number of jobs, and the pressure of excess supply lowers wages below the level that would otherwise prevail.

Public Policy on Sex Discrimination

The principal laws and executive orders dealing with sex discrimination in employment include (1) the Equal Pay Act of 1963, requiring equal pay for equal work on the same job in the same establishment; (2) Title VII of the Civil Rights Act of 1964, prohibiting discrimination in hiring, promotion, and all other aspects of employment; (3) Executive Order 11246, as amended by 11375 (1968), prohibiting discrimination by federal contractors and requiring that affirmative action programs be developed and carried out under the threat of contract cancellation; and (4) Executive Order 11478 (1969), prohibiting discrimination in covered positions in the federal government. These laws and executive orders are supplemented by additional legislation at the state and local levels.

The potential usefulness of these measures depends, of course, upon the way they are enforced, but even with maximum utilization and enforcement they may not be fully effective, for the reasons that follow.

Equal pay laws do not get at the root of the problem and may actually have adverse consequences. As the evidence above shows, discrimination usually leads to job segregation, not to unequal pay. Even before passage of the Equal Pay Act, there were few cases of women being paid less than men on the same job, and such practices explained only a very minor proportion of the total earnings differential. Moreover, equal pay laws may actually increase job segregation and crowd women into dead-end jobs because they prevent employers from creating a wage differential to offset the added risks of hiring women in more responsible jobs. Young women are being penalized not so much from being *underpaid* as from being *underutilized*. . . .

Equal employment opportunity legislation is clearly of much greater significance, especially when it involves affirmative action programs requiring employers to take the initiative in recruiting and promoting women for all types of work, prohibits sex-segregated want ads, and concentrates on discriminatory patterns and practices. These measures help to break down some of the cultural barriers to equal opportunity. Additional programs should be designed to cope with *institutional* sexism, not just *individual* prejudice. Many of our present laws and court procedures help to protect women and minorities from overt acts of exclusion but are of little use in eliminating customary patterns of behavior and cultural stereotypes which limit opportunities for all but the most aggressive members of these groups.

In the meantime, those faced with enforcing existing laws have the choice of increasing the probability of apprehension or of increasing the cost to those apprehended, since the "expected cost" of ignoring the law is the product of these two factors. Given the difficulties (and costs) of detecting the prohibited behavior, the latter route seems somewhat more promising.

Education is also important. The role of work in the lives of women is expanding enormously, yet employers and women alike continue to behave as if it is not a permanent feature of American life. The increase in the life expectancy of women from forty-eight years in 1900 to seventy-three years today, combined with earlier marriage and childbearing, means that today's young women must find new activities to fill out their later years and that they must be made aware of the need to plan for new life-styles in their adult years.

As women's commitment to work becomes greater, employers will be more willing to provide them with on-the-job training and to advance them to more responsible, higher-paying positions. This, in turn, will encourage female workers to stay in the labor force longer. Employers need to be made aware of the way in which job opportunities affect a woman's commitment to the labor market [since] the excessive turnover of female employees and their more tenuous attachment to the labor force are in part a function of the kind of work they typically do.

Family Life

No assessment of the consequences of women's working would be complete without some mention of the implications for home and family life. More market work for women *could* lead to such outcomes as

• Less total home work (smaller families, smaller houses, greater substitution of commercial goods and services for home-produced items)

• Less leisure for women (or other family members)

• More home work on the part of men or other family members (and less market work)

• Deterioration in the quality of home work (lower housekeeping standards, "neglected" children)

Although from present trends it would seem that the first two alternatives are more likely, it is difficult to predict these outcomes at the present time. We do know that studies of the impact of maternal employment on the welfare of children have not found any significant effects. Similarly, women who work report that they spend less time on housework and that much of what they did when they were full-time housewives was not essential. As Betty Friedan has suggested, "housewifery" tends to expand to fill the time available. Finally, there appears to be some evidence that the domestic role has a negative effect on women's mental health. For all of these reasons, fuller participation of women in the world outside the home can probably be encouraged without fear of adverse consequences.

Perhaps the more interesting question is what will happen to the division of labor between the sexes. Is the outcome of "more home work on the part of men" a realistic alternative? Many of those who are committed to women's liberation believe that it is an essential condition for real equality. . . .

If society were to move in this direction, there would be important ramifications for the working world. Hours of work would need to be modified. Moreover, the single-minded devotion of time and energy to a career that men are currently able to make might not be possible in a society where women did not provide the domestic and social infrastructure for such activities.

But perhaps the overriding issue that must be faced is the extent to which present arrangements provide real freedom of choice. Can women freely choose to work? Can men freely choose *not* to work? Clearly, cultural expectations rather than economic necessity have a way of predetermining the answers to such questions.

Leading Occupations of Women

The Leading 10 Occupations of Women Workers 1870–1970
(in order of size, and as reported in each census regardless of changes in definition)*

	1870	1880	1890	1900	1910
1	Domestic servants	Domestic servants	Servants	Servants	Other servants
2	Agricultural laborers	Agricultural laborers	Agricultural laborers	Farm laborers (members of family)	Farm laborers (home farm)
3	Tailoresses and seamstresses	Milliners, dressmakers, and seamstresses	Dressmakers	Dressmakers	Laundresses (not in laundry)
4	Milliners, dress, and mantua makers	Teachers and scientific persons	Teachers	Teachers	Teachers (school)
5	Teachers (not specified)	Laundresses	Farmers, planters, and overseers	Laundry work (hand)	Dressmakers and seamstresses (not in factory)
6	Cotton-mill operatives	Cotton-mill operatives	Laundresses	Farmers and planters	Farm laborers (working out)
7	Laundresses	Farmers and planters	Seamstresses	Farm and plantation laborers	Cooks
8	Woolen-mill operatives	Tailoresses	Cotton-mill operatives	Saleswomen	Stenographers and typewriters
9	Farmers and planters	Woolen-mill operatives	Housekeepers and stewards	Housekeepers and stewards	Farmers
10	Nurses	Employees of hotels and restaurants (not clerks)	Clerks and copyists	Seamstresses	Saleswomen (stores)

* Compiled by Rosalyn Baxandall, Linda Gordon, and Susan Reverby.

1920	1930	1940	1950	1960	1970
Other servants	Other servants, other domestic, and personal service	Servants (private family)	Stenographers, typists, and secretaries	Stenographers, typists, and secretaries	Secretaries
Teachers (school)	Teachers (school)	Stenographers, typists, and secretaries	Other clerical workers	Other clerical workers	Sales clerks (retail trade)
Farm laborers (home farm)	Stenographers and typists	Teachers (not elsewhere classified)	Saleswomen	Private household workers	Bookkeepers
Stenographers and typists	Other clerks (except clerks in stores)	Clerical and kindred workers (not elsewhere classified)	Private household workers	Saleswomen	Teachers (elementary school)
Other clerks (except clerks in stores)	Saleswomen	Saleswomen (not elsewhere classified)	Teachers (elementary school)	Teachers (elementary school)	Typists
Laundresses (not in laundry)	Farm laborers (unpaid family workers)	Operatives and kindred workers, apparel, and accessories	Waitresses	Bookkeepers	Waitresses
Saleswomen (stores)	Bookkeepers and cashiers	Bookkeepers, accountants, and cashiers	Bookkeepers	Waitresses	Sewers and stitchers
Bookkeepers and cashiers	Laundresses (not in laundry)	Waitresses (except private family)	Sewers and stitchers, manufacturing	Miscellaneous and not specified operatives	Nurses, registered
Cooks	Trained nurses	Housekeepers (private family)	Nurses, registered	Nurses, registered	Cashiers
Farmers (general farms)	Other cooks	Trained nurses and student nurses	Telephone operators	Other service workers (except private household)	Private household cleaners and servants

Sources: Decennial Census, 1870–1940; Janet M. Hooks, *Women's Occupations Through Seven Decades* (Women's Bureau Bulletin #218, U.S. Department of Labor); U.S. Dept. of Commerce, Bureau of the Census: Census of Population, 1960, Detailed Characteristics, U.S. Summary, Table 202; U.S. Dept. of Commerce, Bureau of the Census: Census of Population, 1970, Detailed Characteristics, U.S. Summary, PC (1)D 1; U.S. Women's Bureau, "Occupations of Women, 1950, 1960 and 1970, Tables Reprinted from the Economic Report of the President 1973," 1973.

» Rosabeth Moss Kanter «

Secretaries

»«

Rosabeth Moss Kanter, a Yale sociologist, is also a well-known consultant to large corporations on the problems women encounter in the workforce. In this article, she addresses the job of secretary, the salaried occupation that a woman is most likely to hold. Kanter argues that the status of a secretary is determined more by the status of her boss than by her own merit, a fact that is characteristic of the uniquely personal nature of this job. Unlike almost any other job, the tasks of the secretary are not clearly spelled out; they run the gamut from typing to making coffee to giving alibis for errant or truant bosses. Above all, Kanter argues that a secretary is expected to be loyal to her boss. These over-personalized aspects of the job make it uniquely dissatisfying to many secretaries, according to Kanter. Indeed, some women have gone to court to fight what they consider to be unfair and unprofessional demands, and many organizations are now clearly defining job expectations and criteria for promotion.

> *Skewered through and through with office-pens, and bound hand and foot with red tape.*
>
> —Charles Dickens, *David Copperfield*

> *If a man has an office with a desk on which there is a buzzer, and if he can press that buzzer and have somebody come dashing in response—then he's an executive.*
>
> —Elmer Frank Andrews, Address to the Trade Association
> Executives' Forum of Chicago, 1938

Secretaries added a personal touch to Industrial Supply Corporation work places. Professional and managerial offices tended to be austere: generally uniform in size and coloring, and unadorned except for a few family snapshots or discrete artworks. ("Welcome to my beige box," a rising young executive was fond of saying to visitors.) But secretaries' desks were surrounded by splashes of color, displays of special events, signs of the individuality and taste of the residents: postcards from friends' or bosses' travels pasted on walls, newspaper cartoons, large posters with funny captions, huge computer printouts that formed the names of the secretaries in gothic letters. It was secretaries who remembered birthdays and whose birthdays were celebrated, lending a

[handwritten margin note: Secretaries remember birthdays events functions and other things of their bosses]

legitimate air of occasional festivity to otherwise task-oriented days. Secretaries could engage in conversations about the latest movies, and managers often stopped by their desks to join momentarily in a discussion that
was a break from the more serious business at hand. It was secretaries who
were expected to look out for the personal things, to see to the comfort and
welfare of guests, to show them around and make sure that they had what
they needed. And it was around secretaries that people at higher levels in
the corporation could stop to remember the personal things about themselves and each other (appearance, dress, daily mood), could trade the
small compliments and acknowledgments that differentiated them from
the mass of others and from their formal role. In many ways—visually,
socially, and organizationally—the presence of secretaries represented a
reserve of the human inside the bureaucratic.

Nowhere were the contradictions and unresolved dilemmas of modern
bureaucratic life more apparent than in the secretarial function. The job,
made necessary by the growth of modern organizations, lay at the very
core of bureaucratic administration; yet, it often was the least bureaucra-
tized segment of corporate life. . . .

The Secretarial Ladder at Indsco

The first fact about the several thousand secretaries at Indsco was that they
were all women, except for two men at headquarters who were classified as
typists. If they entered at the bottom, Indsco secretaries were generally
hired out of high school or a secretarial finishing school like Katharine
Gibbs. There was a tendency in corporate headquarters to recruit from
parochial schools, which meant that a very high proportion of secretaries
were white and accustomed to hierarchical discipline. . . . After a several-
day orientation, covering the cafeteria, library, medical department,
policies and benefits, and classes in Industrial Supply style for letters and
telephone calls, new stenographers entered a "pool." . . .

[handwritten margin notes: All women; mostly white]

After six months, they were promoted to Secretary I and given a permanent assignment, typically working for more than one boss. . . .

"Bosses" were not only managers but anyone in the exempt ranks whose
work required secretarial services: professionals, sales workers, and staff
officials as well as people formally labeled managers, directors, or officers.
One of the striking things about secretaries, then, was that their presence
made nearly everyone in the exempt ranks a "boss," generating a shared
managerial orientation among exempt personnel and further drawing the
caste lines between exempt and nonexempt groups.

The secretarial ladder was short, and rank was determined by bosses'
statuses. A secretary with three to four years' experience was eligible for
promotion to Secretary II, working for a PRO (person-reporting-to-officer).
Secretary IIIs had seven to twelve years' experience and worked for divisional vice-presidents. Secretary IVs worked for division presidents and
executive vice-presidents. At the top were executive secretaries of corpo-

rate officers. Sometimes these women took on some supervisory responsibility for the secretaries of lower-level managers, distributing extra work or discussing personnel problems. . . . An old hand recalled: "A person used to be forty-five before becoming an executive secretary and stayed there for fifteen to twenty years. Now they move much faster. They get there at twenty-nine and have no place else to go." Salaries were also not high. Over half of the nonexempt women earned less than $11,000 a year, despite so many with long service.

The executive secretarial position was the peak for nonexempt women at Indsco, . . . in dramatic contrast to the situation for nonexempt men, who, as accounting clerks, could easily move by a standard route into the exempt ranks. The ceiling for secretaries was set by how high a boss they could snare. . . . So secretaries learned to count on a relationship with a boss for their rewards. . . .

Patrimony in Bureaucracy

. . . The secretary-boss relationship is the most striking instance of the retention of patrimony within the bureaucracy. Fewer bureaucratic "safeguards" apply here than in any other part of the system. When bosses make demands at their own discretion and arbitrarily; choose secretaries on grounds that enhance their own personal status rather than meeting organizational efficiency tests; expect personal service with limits negotiated privately; exact loyalty; and make the secretary a part of their private retinue, moving when they move—then the relationship has elements of patrimony. . . .

Status Contingency

Reflected status was part of the primary definition of the secretarial position. Secretaries derived their formal rank and level of reward not from the skills they utilized and the tasks they performed but *from the formal rank of their bosses*. A promotion for secretaries meant that they had acquired a higher-status boss, not that their own work was more skilled or valuable. Most often, above the early grades, secretaries were not actually promoted at all on their own; they just remained with a boss who himself received a promotion. It was common practice at Indsco for secretaries to move with their bosses within the same geographic area, as though they were part of the private retinue of a patrimonial dignitary.

Before Indsco created a centralized personnel administration for nonexempt positions, there was no way to determine secretarial salaries other than status contingency. . . .

Even more important was the fact that the boss's status determined the power of the secretary. . . . Secretaries' power derived from control of bosses' calendars. They could make it easy or difficult to see a top executive. They could affect what managers read first, setting priorities for them without their knowing it. They could help or hurt someone's career by the ease with which they allowed that person access.

If the secretary reflected the status of the boss, she also contributed in minor ways to his status. Some people have argued that secretaries function as "status symbols" for executives, holding that the traditional secretarial role is developed and preserved because of its impact on managerial egos, not its contribution to organizational efficiency. . . . For this reason, personal appearance—attractiveness and social skills—was a factor in the career prospects of secretaries, with task-related skills again playing a smaller role as secretaries moved up the ranks. . . .

Indsco personnel administrators also found that bosses tended to want highly skilled, highly educated secretaries, whether or not the work load demanded it, as a way of inflating their own importance and deriving status from a secretary. . . .

Derived status between secretaries and bosses spilled over in informal as well as formal ways. The parties became fused in the awareness of other organization members. Secretaries became identified with bosses in a number of personal and informal ways. Secretaries could get respect from their peers because of feelings about their bosses, but they could also be disliked and avoided if their bosses were disliked. . . .

Despite the fact that bosses could derive some informal status from characteristics of their secretaries, status contingency operated in largely nonreciprocal ways. It was the boss's *formal* position that gave the secretary formal rank; he, in turn, wanted to choose someone whose *personal* attributes made her suitable for the status he would be conferring. As in the patrimonial official's private ownership of his servants, the secretary was seen by the boss as "my girl." . . .

The secretaries' position in the organization, then—their reward level, privileges, prospects for advancement, and even treatment by others—was contingent upon relationships to particular bosses, much more than on the formal tasks associated with the job itself.

Principled Arbitrariness

The second patrimonial feature of secretarial role relations was the *absence of limits on managerial discretion,* except those limits dictated by custom or by abstract principles of fair treatment. Within the general constraints of Indsco tradition and the practice of other managers, bosses had enormous personal latitude around secretaries. The absence of job descriptions, before the new personnel administration began to generate them, meant that there was no way to insure some uniformity of demands across jobs with the same general outlines. There was no way for personnel staff to help match secretaries' skills to the job, or to compare positions so as to determine whether and how a secretary could be moved. Thus, it was left to bosses to determine what secretaries did, how they spent their time, and whether they were to be given opportunities for movement. There was no such thing as career reviews for secretaries, or for nonexempt personnel in general. A secretary's fortunes, especially in finding other work in the corporation, were in the hands of the boss. . . .

Managerial discretion in job demands combined with another feature of secretarial work to contribute to the sense of personal dependence on arbitrary authority. It was a job with low routinization in terms of time planning, characterized instead by a constant flow of orders. Unlike other parts of the bureaucracy, where the direct exercise of authority and the making of demands could be minimized through understood routines and schedules of expectations, secretarial work might involve only the general skeleton of a routine, onto which was grafted a continual set of specific requests and specific instructions. . . .

Arbitrariness was embedded in the personal services expected of secretaries. . . . Some secretaries included personal services in the core definition of their job, giving them equal importance with the communication functions (like typing and telephones) for which Indsco had hired them. One secretary included among her major responsibilities: "office household duties: watering plants, cleaning cups, sharpening pencils, straightening desks, etc." (A personnel administrator commented about such items, "Does she think that's what the company is paying her for?") And despite media publicity for the controversy over whether or not secretaries should make and serve coffee, Indsco secretaries still performed this service, especially for visitors to their bosses' offices.

The domestic career is no more natural to most women than the military career is natural to all men. . . . If we have come to think that the nursery and the kitchen are the natural sphere of a woman, we have done so exactly as English children come to think that a cage is the natural sphere of a parrot—because they have never seen one anywhere else.
—George Bernard Shaw

Journalists have found good material for their criticisms in the range of personal services secretaries perform: cutting the boss's hair, dog-sitting while he and his wife are on vacation, returning his wife's mail order shoes, and providing homemade (by the secretary) coffee cake at board meetings. One secretary told a writer: "His wife does everything for him at home; I do everything for him here. The only thing he does for himself is well, you know." Many Indsco secretaries seemed to feel the same way. Resentment over personal work was the biggest single issue raised by secretaries when Industrial Supply brought an experimental group of them together with their bosses for "expectation exchanges." The secretaries felt that the official definition of their jobs was fuzzy enough that they were concerned about refusing to do personal things for their bosses even when they would have preferred not to. . . .

There was another kind of personal service that was even more difficult

(handwritten margin note: secretaries serve as a buffer, screen calls, lie)

for secretaries to talk about, since it tread the fine line between official and unofficial, legitimate and illegitimate. This was the secretaries' involvement as critical ingredients in their bosses' presentation of a "front." . . . They served as a buffer between the boss and rest of the world, controlling access and protecting him from callers. And on occasion, they were asked to collude in lies on behalf of this front, from such routine lies as "Mr. Jones is not in just now" when Mr. Jones wanted to sit at his desk undisturbed, to more major lies such as Rose Mary Wood's alleged erasure of a portion of the Nixon tapes. At the managers' discretion, then, secretaries could be implicated in major and minor moral dilemmas. . . .

#3 Loyalty and Devotion

The third patrimonial feature of secretarial role relations had to do with the social psychological tone of the relationship: an expectation of personal loyalty, that secretaries should derive their primary rewards from the relationship with their particular bosses. This arose, in part, as a consequence of the first two features of social organization of the job. Because of characteristics of the organization of the work itself, bosses developed a stake in seeing that secretaries: (1) identify their interests with that of their bosses, subordinating any desires for their own career advancement; (2) suppress resentments of the differential material privileges of bosses and clerical workers by valuing instead the symbolic and emotional rewards of the secretarial job; and (3) develop attitudes that made it easy for bosses to exercise their authority. . . .

Secretaries were rewarded for loyalty and devotion to their bosses. They were expected to value non-utilitarian, symbolic rewards—which did not include individual career advancement—and to take on the emotional tasks of the relationship. Secretaries were rewarded for their attitudes rather than for their skills, for their loyalty rather than their talent. Given the low skill required by the actual tasks they were given to do, and the replaceability of personnel with basic secretarial skills, secretaries found it to their advantage to accept fealty as their route to recognition and reward.

Expectations of loyalty were bound up with the sense on the part of bosses that they were making secretaries part of their personal estate. . . .

If secretaries were evaluated on non-utilitarian grounds, they were also expected to accept non-utilitarian rewards. In many cases, secretaries willingly did so. . . . Clerical workers traditionally viewed themselves as "privileged" in comparison with blue-collar workers, and this sense of privilege was often considered sufficient reward in itself. . . .

"Love" was one non-material reward secretaries were supposed to appreciate. Some Indsco secretaries reported that their bosses managed to turn their complaints about salary or working conditions into expressions of concern about whether or not they were "loved," assuming that women at work were motivated by such noneconomic, emotional factors. . . . When secretaries' rights organizations began to agitate for "raises, not

275

roses," they were challenging this notion of what motivated women.

Yet many Indsco secretaries *were* content to settle for symbolic rewards, for prestige and daily flattery rather than higher pay, job control, and independent recognition. There was a shared feeling on the part of some secretaries that women did better in the higher-level executive secretarial positions than they did in the lower exempt jobs, even taking into account the pay differential. . . . The gifts of knowledge, the invitations to special events, the bits of power secretaries picked up from their bosses' status— all this made it hard for some secretaries to see any other options for themselves. . . .

The symbolic rewards of identification were related to another aspect of the secretary-boss relationship. A tone of emotional intensity may come to pervade it. A "division of emotional labor" may be developed, in which the secretary comes to "feel for" the boss in both senses: to care deeply about what happens to him and to do his feeling for him. Secretaries represented a reserve of permissible emotional expression in the office. Executives unwound to their secretaries, according to an Indsco informant. "They say things they would not say anywhere else. If something goes wrong at a meeting, they will tell their secretary more than their wife." . . .

In return for the secretary's devotion and emotional support, the boss may take on the traditional patrimonial ruler's attitude of caretaking toward his underlings. . . .

The Permissible Personal

Because the secretarial function in Indsco represented a repository of the personal inside the bureaucratic, the last relic of *Gemeinschaft** emotion-laden relations of individual loyalty within a *Gesellschaft*** system of contractual, limited, interchangeable, instrumental involvements, many people were reluctant to tamper with it. If it was the last place where people could be personal beings, they were reluctant to risk losing this reserve of personal territory.

In the first place, since secretaries were largely defined out of the mobility game, they could afford to carry the human side of the office. The reward system and authority structures in their jobs, as we have seen, encouraged secretaries to be leading actors in many forms of personal and emotional communication.

For bosses, the traditional secretarial system offered something many of them found nowhere else in their work. It was a pocket of personal privilege in a setting where few areas of completely individual discretion and control were allowed. Secretaries offered an arena of power and control—and sometimes adoration—for bosses who were otherwise rendered powerless and not very important by the routinization of their own

---

Ed. Note: A spontaneous social relationship characterized by strong reciprocal bonds.
**Ed. Note:* A rational, mechanistic social relationship characterized by impersonal, contracted associations.

job or the numerous constraints upon bureaucratic action. . . .

For the secretaries themselves, there were tradeoffs involved in their position. Although they were subject to the personal whim of their bosses rather than to impersonal rules and orders scrutinized for fairness, they also retained a direct and special relationship to a person they could influence and manipulate. They had only one or two people to please, rather than being enmeshed in the larger bureaucratic tangle, where they would have to manage multiple relationships to get ahead. Although they were rewarded for someone else's achievements and status rather than directly for their own talents and skills, they also could derive much closer contact with power and privilege than they could ever attain on their own. So for many secretaries, too, the personal, non-rationalized residue in their position made life in the corporate bureaucracy easier to live.

Private secretarial setups, or even the small pool attached to a small group of bosses, thus provided more advantageous work conditions than those most clerical workers faced. The present personalized arrangements looked good especially in contrast to an alternative: mechanized systems in which secretaries, like other clerks, became wedded to their machines and to their routine tasks. It was such mechanization of the office that struck C. Wright Mills when he wrote *White Collar* just after World War II. And it is the continuation of trends towards rationalization through mechanization that has led other analysts to write of the "proletarianization" of the clerical labor force and to encourage unionization as the solution to the problems of women clericals. Indeed, nonexempt personnel staff at Indsco were investigating the use of "Word Processing" systems in other companies. Word Processing is a system that, in effect, replaces the private secretary with the assembly line. All communication is sent to a single department that takes dictation over the phone, transcribes tapes, types documents, sends out mail, and performs other "secretarial" tasks, using the latest computerized equipment. In some cases, an "administrative assistant" remains with a unit to handle organizational tasks, but the great bulk of employees are by and large removed from access to the traditional secretarial privileges. But if Word Processing is the only alternative, rather than a genuine upgrading of the secretarial or clerical job so that it has autonomy, pay, status, and mobility opportunity associated with it, then many secretaries prefer the old system.

Resistance to change in this function can be seen as resistance to further bureaucratic encroachment. Inequities in the situation of secretaries seem to demand change, but any change must also acknowledge the reluctance of people to give up preserves of the personal. There needs to be some such relationship in the organization, but it should not be a "hereditary" or "patrimonial" one. Indsco secretaries were locked into self-perpetuating, self-defeating cycles in which job and opportunity structure encouraged personal orientations that reinforced low pay and low mobility and perpetuated the original job structure. The fact that such jobs were held almost

[handwritten margin note: people sometimes do not like or want to change]

entirely by women also reinforced limited and stereotypical views of the "nature" of women at work.

How to restructure the job to enhance opportunity and eliminate patrimonial inequities, but how to simultaneously provide outlets for the needs of human beings for personalized relationships and personal territory—this is the dilemma of the corporate bureaucracy.

9

»«
WORK
AND THE
FAMILY
»«

Nancy Scanlan

» Caryl Rivers, Rosalind Barnett, and Grace Baruch «

He Works, She Works, Does the Marriage Work?

» «

The authors, all psychologists, argue that traditional marriages had a ready-made set of blueprints for ideal marital roles. But couples with dual-career marriages are having to draw up their own plans, from scratch. Agreement between husband and wife is particularly difficult to reach concerning housework. For example, men tend to overestimate the percentage of the total family housework that they actually do—and many do none at all. In addition, the problems in finding good child care frequently place a special strain on parental relationships. In general, few couples seem to have arrived at a mutually acceptable division of housework and child care, according to these authors.

Anew kind of marriage, the two-career couple, is gaining more acceptance, particularly among young and educated urban dwellers. This isn't surprising when you look at the attitudes of young women who are attending college now or have graduated fairly recently.

The College Research Bureau (affiliated with the Educational Testing Service of Princeton, New Jersey) has been studying the attitudes of college women over the past ten years. The findings indicate that young women today want smaller families, are more serious about careers and have a more liberal view about women's role in society than students did in the past.

These facts are going to upset some tidy little models that social scientists have used to explain the way families ought to behave. For a long time, the "lens" for looking at marriages and deciding whether they were or were not working was the theory of Talcott Parsons, a "functional sociologist" (that is, a person who looks at different social systems and figures out how they work).

According to Parsons, marriage calls for a clear-cut division of labor between husband and wife. The husband serves as the family's link to the world of work; he is the breadwinner, and the status and prestige of the family are determined by *his* status and prestige. The woman is in charge of

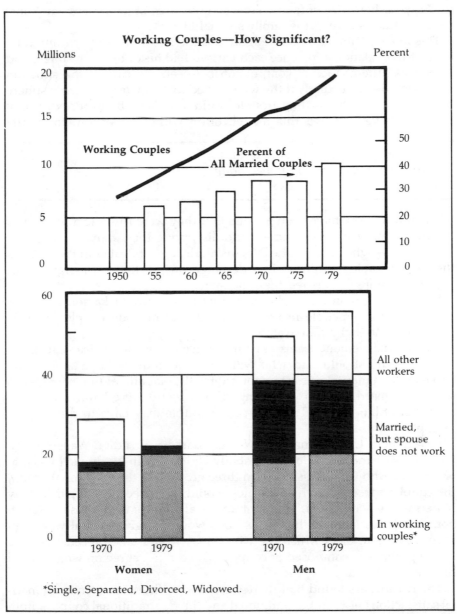

Working Couples—How Significant?

*Single, Separated, Divorced, Widowed.

The significance of working couples: Of the 48 million married couples in the United States today, 20 million—or more than 40 percent—can be classified as working couples. This is close to three times as many as there were in 1950, and represents a doubling of their proportion among all married couples during that time. Families in which the husbands are the sole providers are now about half as numerous as those with working spouses. As recently as the mid-1960s, these two types of families were about equally important in number. (Analysis by Helen Axel, an economist with The Conference Board, a business-research organization.)

the "expressive" side of family life—she nurtures others, eases emotional crises and takes care of the family's social life.

This model, Parsons suggested, offered the maximum opportunity for a conflict-free relationship, since each partner had his or her own sphere and there was little chance of competition between the two. If the situation were altered—particularly if the wife started to compete in the male sphere of work and prestige—then trouble could very well be expected. Social scientists have accepted this model, often without question, for years.

Man may work from sun to sun
But woman's work is never done.

—Anon.

Women who work have been warned that they were running a severe risk of causing marital maladjustment and disrupting the family.

The people who stuck to the Parsons model didn't deal with the fact that the woman's role was the socially devalued one, or that her assigned area was much more constricted than the man's.

By now, common sense should tell us that the rigid Parsonian model doesn't fit many people in today's world, but how do couples actually navigate these tricky new waters?

One crucial element seems to be necessary to success: a clear-cut agreement on who should and who will do what. Studies have shown that agreement on marital roles is important for the stability of the marriage. In traditional marriages, the occupants of that world were handed a ready-made set of blueprints. The dual-career couple may have to draw up its own plans, from scratch.

Researchers Lynn Simonsen Walker, Barbara Strudler Wallston and Howard M. Sandler of George Peabody University in Nashville looked at 57 couples who were classified into three groups. In the traditional group, the couples agreed that the man's job would take precedence, particularly in deciding where to live. The nontraditional couples were those in which both the wives' and the husbands' jobs would be given equal weight in such a decision, or in which the wives' jobs would take precedence. The mixed group was composed of couples who did not agree on what should be done.

The researchers found that there were *no* significant differences in marital satisfaction between the traditional and the nontraditional couples. Both agreed on their roles. But the mixed group, which had not reached such agreement, was significantly lower in marital satisfaction.

Logistics will continue to be a problem to everyone with young children at home, but they can be worked out if both parties can agree to share goals and responsibilities.

Agreement isn't always easy, especially given the sex-role stereotypes so deeply rooted in our culture and our consciousness. There are hundreds of

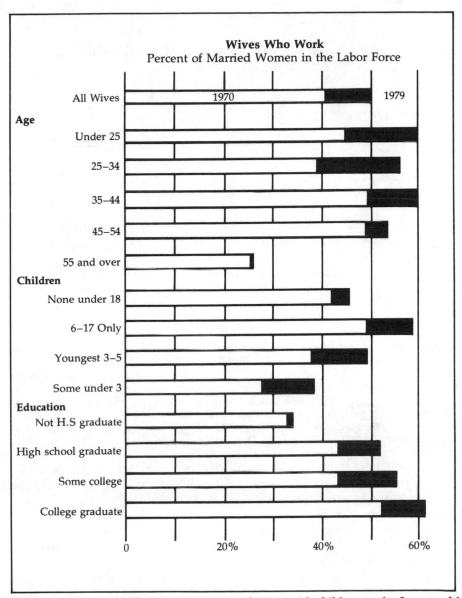

Wives Who Work
Percent of Married Women in the Labor Force

Working wives: In 1979 about 40 percent of wives with children under 3 years old were in the labor force. Less than ten years ago the rate was only 26 percent. Today's female labor force consists of a high proportion of college graduates. Since further education usually means a better chance of employment, the most significant gains in the labor-force participation of married women have occurred among the highly educated. At the same time, attitudes toward family responsibilities have been modified. Wives in their prime childbearing years no longer withdraw automatically from the work force, and when (or if) they do have children, the time spent away from the job market is much shorter. (Sources: US Bureau of the Census and Bureau of Labor Statistics)

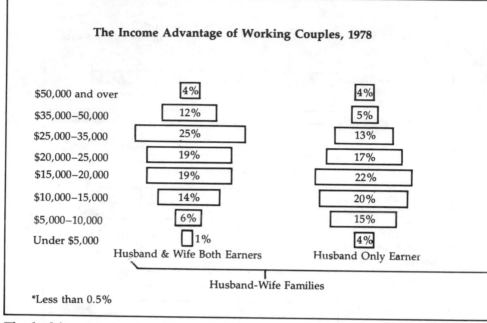

The Income Advantage of Working Couples, 1978

Income	Husband & Wife Both Earners	Husband Only Earner
$50,000 and over	4%	4%
$35,000–50,000	12%	5%
$25,000–35,000	25%	13%
$20,000–25,000	19%	17%
$15,000–20,000	19%	22%
$10,000–15,000	14%	20%
$5,000–10,000	6%	15%
Under $5,000	1%	4%

Husband-Wife Families

*Less than 0.5%

The dual-income advantage: The median income of a working couple, estimated in 1978 to be about $22,700, is 30 percent higher than the median for families that rely only on the husband's salary. On average, a wife who works contributes about a fourth of the family's income.

Working couples constitute a much higher proportion of families in the high-earning brackets than in the low ones. Only 12 percent of husband-wife families in the under-$5,000 bracket have working spouses; 68 percent of those with incomes ranging from $25,000 to $50,000 do. The incidence drops off somewhat above the

little time bombs hidden in the small chores we do each day, chores divided up into "his" or "her" jobs. The "her" jobs usually include the grubby or most menial, and doing them is part of being a "good" wife, mother, homemaker.

The layer of emotional values and social approval that has been slathered over such grungy—and not inherently sex-related—jobs as cleaning a collar or washing a floor makes renegotiating job duties tricky. A woman simply does not say, "I don't want to wash the floor" if she was raised to believe that washing the floor is a labor of love. And her husband may not be hearing, "I don't want to wash the floor." Having been schooled in the same social values as she, he may be hearing, "I don't love you," or he may feel demeaned by having to do a chore identified in his head as irrevocably female.

In fact, one emotion that seems to surface in many couples who are trying to change marital roles today is a sense that they have been somehow "betrayed," that things aren't supposed to be like this! In a study by Jessica Segrè of Boston University and the Somerville Mental Health Clinic,

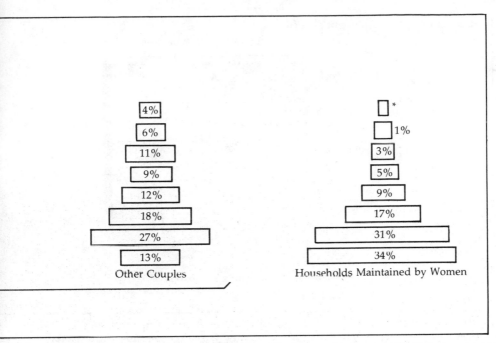

Other Couples	Households Maintained by Women
4%	*
6%	1%
11%	3%
9%	5%
12%	9%
18%	17%
27%	31%
13%	34%

$50,000 level, but dual-earner couples still account for over half of the married couples in that bracket. When a wife has an up-scale job and good salary, it is likely her husband is doing as well.

Women maintaining their own households are at a considerable financial disadvantage. A large proportion of these women, it is true, are elderly and do not work. But even those with jobs are likely to have earnings that fall far short of the resources available to other households.

women who went back to work because of family finances were clearly suffering from such feelings. They felt they were "supposed" to be taken care of. A man putting a load of laundry into the dryer—if his father never did and if he believes this to be women's work—can be in for a heavy dose of feelings of betrayal.

Change may be particularly hard for a man who finds himself taking on household responsibilities. The man who always has had these services performed for him hardly can be expected to leap with joy when he has to do some of them himself. The costs of the change to him are immediate and obvious. The benefits—more economic security, his wife's feelings of usefulness and challenge, less tension and resentment on her part—are subtle and long range.

Even people who are trying to achieve a more equitable share of responsibilities often find that the emotional weight of old roles burdens them with feelings and resentments they really want no part of. They also may find that their separate perceptions about how much they each *do* are at odds. In a questionnaire filled in by readers of *Psychology Today*, husbands

Working Couples: Composite Profiles

By Occupations in 1979

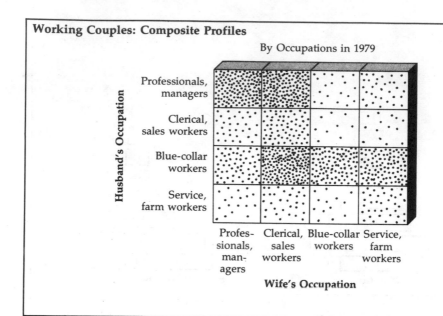

Husband's Occupation

- Professionals, managers
- Clerical, sales workers
- Blue-collar workers
- Service, farm workers

Profes- sionals, man- agers | Clerical, sales workers | Blue-collar workers | Service, farm workers

Wife's Occupation

Profiles of working couples: Conditions that are leading to improvements in the fortunes of working women also are affecting working couples. Professional/ managerial couples are becoming more visible, although they still make up only 14 percent of all employed couples. In one of three couples, for example, the husband

tended to overestimate the percentage of the housework they performed compared to their wives' estimates of what they did. As one man who has custody of his three children said, "When I was married I thought I was doing 50 percent of the work. Now that I have to do it all, I realize I was doing only about 30 percent."

The couple that has lived in a traditional pattern faces perhaps the most difficult task of all when the wife returns to work. One major problem may be that women don't have much experience in negotiating, in coming right out and asking for things. A woman who has been in a caring role at home develops sensitive antennae toward the needs of her husband and children, often sensing their worries and problems before they ask. It's easy for a woman to expect her husband to do the same for her once she's out in the job market. Why doesn't he *offer* to do the dishes; can't he see she's tired? Why doesn't he pick up the junk in the hallway instead of letting her do it?

If housework is a major stumbling block in the path to egalitarian marriage, the real crunch often comes over the issue of child care. Care of children has been a female domain in our society—as in most societies—and women have been given little support when they looked for help.

The hassle of finding good child care so that both husband and wife can lead independent lives can put a real strain on a relationship. Journalist Caryl Rivers remembers a period when she was working part time and

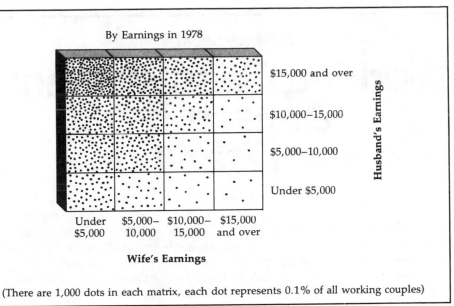

By Earnings in 1978

(There are 1,000 dots in each matrix, each dot represents 0.1% of all working couples)

is employed as a professional, a manager or a skilled blue-collar worker while his wife holds an office job or works as a retail sales clerk. The earnings picture is even bleaker: In only one couple in 20 do both spouses earn $15,000 or more. Over 45 percent of all working wives earn less than $5,000.

doing a constant search for baby sitters. It drained much of her energy, and there were many times she resented the fact that her husband could sail out the door leaving all the planning to her.

Later on, at another period, things were partly reversed: Her husband was writing a book, and Rivers's teaching salary and writing jobs paid the freight. He was home every morning to take care of their daughter, give her lunch and drive the car pool to kindergarten at noon. Rivers noticed after that time that a gleam of sympathy would appear in his eyes when anyone talked about the problems of women who feel trapped at home.

Is this the wave of the future? Only time will tell. In the past, man's work was supposed to come first; and if he provided economically for his family, his duty was done. When Dwight Eisenhower married Mamie, he told her point-blank, "You will always be second. My country comes first." Priorities are not so clear-cut today for most people.

With two careers and children in a family, priorities simply have to change. To make a nontraditional marriage work, both parents have to recognize the career sacrifices necessary. It's not that you have to give up ambitions or chances for advancement, but you achieve them more slowly. You have to learn to pace yourself with the family timetable.

» Nancy Seifer «

Working Class Women: Departure from Tradition

» «

In this selection Nancy Seifer, Director of Community Relations for the National Project on Ethnic America, focuses on the tensions created in blue-collar marriages when wives take paying jobs. Seifer claims that "having a wife who works has long been considered one of the worst possible blows to the self-esteem of many working-class men." Deprived of status in his work, the blue-collar worker derives his status in his home, and his sense of self-respect from his role as bread winner. It is particularly shattering to a blue-collar worker's ego to have a white-collar wife who earns more than he does. In general, Seifer asserts, a wife's independence is more likely to contribute to divorce in blue-collar marriages than in those of other social classes.

Traditional family and neighborhood ties, though sometimes limiting to individual growth and development, generally provide a kind of comfort and security which is now absent from the lives of many working class couples. As wives gain some independence, many husbands grow more unsure of their own roles and marriages begin to flounder. The younger and more affluent families who leave their roots in the old ethnic neighborhood for a better home for their kids in a modest suburb often miss the familiarity and warmth of close relations and neighborhood life. Traditional life patterns are being eroded, and old values are in limbo, but many working class families have as yet found little that is satisfactory to replace them.

A Shifting Balance in Marriage

In the past, the working class wife was unusually dependent on her mate—perhaps more so than the poor woman who was often compelled to fend for herself, or the middle class woman who often had either the means or the skills to support herself. Women looked to men for authority, security, and protection against the outside world. But with paychecks of their own, and greater experience and self-confidence outside the bounds of the neighborhood, the ties of working class women's dependency are weakening and upsetting a delicate balance in many of their lives.

To understand the present struggles of working class women, it is important to understand their husbands. A job, membership in a labor union, involvement in local politics, participation in women's groups, wider contacts with different kinds of people, all serve to lessen the wife's dependence and undermine her husband's once unchallenged dominance in the home. And if blue collar workers or low level white collar workers have no status in their own home, chances are they have it nowhere.

Having a wife who works has long been considered one of the worst possible blows to the self-esteem of many working class men. While there are some signs of a shift in this feeling, studies have in fact shown that despite the extra income that can significantly help to ease financial strain, there was greater discontent among male workers whose wives worked than among those who were the sole wage earners.

In "Discontented Blue Collar Workers—A Case Study," Harold L. Sheppard wrote in 1971 that "machismo" may be as strong among white ethnic males as it is among Latin Americans and blacks, and that "blue collar males do not feel that they have really succeeded if they cannot, all by themselves, provide their families with the necessary income to pay for the level of living they aspire to."

For men must work, and women must weep, And there's little to earn and many to keep. Though the harbor bar be moaning.
—Charles Kingsley, *The Three Fishers*

A philosophical exploration of the extent to which our society deprives the low wage male worker of self-respect is offered by Richard Sennett and Jonathan Cobb in *The Hidden Injuries of Class*. Governed from a young age by outside authorities which make him feel like "he doesn't count" and allow him little autonomy, working at unchallenging jobs which have little social value, the working class man comes to feel that he is "worth something" only to the extent that he is sacrificing for his family. It is working long hours and saving for a house in the suburbs or a college education for his children, and the little authority he has in his home, which give his life some meaning and some dignity. But in viewing the significance of his life as total sacrifice, the freedom of his wife is often sharply curtailed. When she becomes a breadwinner too, she chips away at his small sense of self-worth. . . .

Still, a high proportion of working class women hold jobs and their husbands are obviously not all equally antagonistic to their doing so. There appears, however, to be a direct correlation between the husband's own job and income and his attitude toward his wife working—the higher his income and prestige on the job, the less averse he is to his wife having a job of her own. Clearly, as Yankelovich and others have pointed out, it is tougher to accept for a blue collar worker whose white collar wife may earn more than he does. But many of the wives who work do so at the risk of generating instability in their marriages.

A working class wife's involvement in community affairs, labor union activities, or women's groups poses still another threat to her husband's authority. . . .

While examples are still relatively few, housewives who a few years ago never dreamed they would take part in any kind of demonstration, have recently blocked expressways during rush hour traffic, picketed the homes of city officials, and protested the destruction and neglect of their neighborhoods in a variety of other dramatic ways. For the most part, their husbands are not involved—a question which needs to be further explored. When a wife comes home after testifying at a City Council hearing, from a meeting of the local school or hospital board, or from helping to out-maneuver a local politician or win a vote for day care in her union, she is changing the balance of power in her marriage in the most fundamental way, often without realizing it. . . .

Unless she is willing to defy her husband's wishes, it is still often difficult for a working wife to take part in community affairs. In some neighborhoods it has been noted that relatively more single, widowed and divorced women are engaged in such activities than are married women. However, while the latter are still the exception to the rule, the number who are joining the ranks is slowly growing.

Interestingly, working class women who have adopted a more independent life style usually claim, when asked, that their relationship with their husband and children has not changed at all, and that a job or community work does not interfere in any way with their primary responsibilities. Clearly, the vast majority still define themselves in terms of their families, and the traditional ideas about marriage and motherhood almost always take precedence over all else in life.

Yet observers in white ethnic communities report growing tensions and a rapidly rising separation and divorce rate. . . . It may well be that the self-image of many working class women has not kept pace with their own changing reality. A New York City Irish woman, who said that her marriage hadn't suffered at all from the increasing hours she spent on neighborhood projects, recently explained that she kept peace by letting her husband feel he was still "the boss." "I let him spout off at the mouth," she said, "and then I go ahead and do what I want." Obviously, a wife's independence does not necessarily lead to divorce. But it is perhaps a more important factor in working class marriages than in those of other social classes, since it represents a far more dramatic departure from accepted conventional roles. . . .

More Signs of Departure from Tradition: Daughters

The slow erosion of the conventional role of working class women, . . . is most apparent in the changing attitudes of their daughters. In many ways, particularly when it comes to inequality and strong social barriers between the sexes, it will probably never be quite the same. Young girls are increasingly obtaining education beyond the high school level, and those who do not finish high school are now the exception to the rule. More girls than in the past are planning for full-time employment, long-term careers, and small families.

Even among working class girls who say they identify strongly with tradition and expect their lives to be much the same as their mothers' were, there are perceptible differences (even if only slight) in some of their values and aspirations. Nevertheless, low self-esteem, low expectations and relatively few options still impose limitations on their lives, much as they constricted their mothers', and to a far greater degree than they impede their middle class counterparts in the 1970s.

Low Expectations at School   Traditionally, education for working class girls was given little priority. It may have been useful for getting a job at a decent salary during the years before marriage and childbirth, but otherwise was viewed as having little relevance to later life.

In 1959, *Workingman's Wife* reported that many mothers, recalling school as a hostile and sometimes terrifying environment, sympathized with their children about the years of homework and exams they had to endure. The average mother was "more concerned with hoping that her child will not be unhappy while he (she) is in school." Further, there was little concern, in contrast to middle class mothers, with the potential of education for upward mobility.

> Most working class mothers . . . do not feel there is anything basically wrong or undesirable with working class life for their children . . . Most of them raise their children to the life they themselves know and in the ways that seem natural to them. . . . The reward the working class mother seeks for her efforts is reciprocated love; reflected glory is the secret hope and vanity of the middle class mother.

The limited educational goals of many working class youngsters often lead to limited interest, and low achievement. A kind of vicious cycle is established, described by writer Peter Schrag in "Growing Up On Mechanic Street": "From class to class, from school to home and back, there is a sort of passing through. What is learned is to defer—to time, to authority, to events."

Low expectations are often reinforced by the school itself. In lower middle income areas, some schools routinely "track" many of their students into vocational or commercial programs. Until recently, college was not presented as a serious possibility except to a select few. A poignant description of the fate of many working class girls was offered in "Drowning in the Stew Pool" by Madeline Belkin, a feminist who came from a working class background ". . . guaranteed to provide few expectations in life," but who managed to escape what becomes a self-fulfilling prophecy for the majority.

> It was with some degree of pain, but mainly a feeling of resignation, that I accepted my guidance counselor's advice to take a commercial course in high school. (This was standard advice for the majority of girls in my class.) I know now that the programming or "channeling" of . . . girls of the poor into subservient job training is no accident. It is the very core of our educational system.

Not surprisingly, finding a satisfying job after leaving school becomes a matter of chance—and a long shot at that—for most working class youngsters, especially for girls. A 1964 study done by Ethelyn Davis at the University of Texas found that only one-fourth of the girls from blue collar families expected to find the kind of job they most desired; three-fourths felt they had not been adequately informed about job choices or opportunities.

The thwarting of higher aspirations by the schools serves to reinforce the poor self-image of girls who, for the most part, arrive at school with the belief that a woman's role is to serve her family rather than to pursue her own ambitions. The kind of self-doubt common to working class girls— that they will not be able to do more than just "get by" in the world outside their home—is reconfirmed by the educational system. Thus, many are left with intensified feelings of powerlessness and insecurity even with a high school diploma and a better paying job.

Beyond High School   Compared to students from families with higher incomes, a relatively small proportion of working class boys and girls stay in school beyond high school even today, although the number is increasing markedly. In 1970, when 70 percent of the sons and daughters of families with incomes over $15,000 a year were attending college, over 60 percent of the children of families with incomes between $5,000 and $10,000 were not.

Moreover, when working class youth go to college, they do not as a rule arrive at professional careers. A large percentage attend two-year or community colleges to prepare for a higher skilled and better paying job. As in elementary and high school, most do not expect to excel. As one observer noted, with obvious exaggeration, it seems that the primary goal is simply to get through and out.

For their part, many of the colleges attended by a high proportion of working class youth have often failed to inspire their students with higher aims. In "When Blue Collar Students Go to College," writer and Professor Leonard Kriegel, who taught at Long Island University (attended by many working class students), described the extent to which some colleges reflect attitudes in American society that leave so many blue collar students "imprisoned in a sense of worthlessness." Having been "stamped and categorized" by schools all their lives, Kriegel wrote, and having become accustomed to being told how much they did and did not know, they are pressured and harassed to become "proper Americans," and "denied the right to define the world for themselves."

"Programmed to accept their difficulties," Kriegel continued, "conditioned to think of themselves as unintellectual, incapable, they had little to fall back on." Like most working class children, his students had been "told that the territory they occupied was narrow. And they believed it."

Summarizing his view of the way in which many municipal colleges continue to relate to these students, he said:

> The blue collar student is still taught to distrust both his instincts and his talents, to view with suspicion whatever claims can be made in his name, to believe that he is, in the long run, not really worth the trouble of a college education.

Despite the pyschological hardships endured by many, college education has become more valued by and accessible to working class students over the past decade. An excellent illustration is the Open Admissions Program instituted by the tuition-free City University of New York in 1970. Under this program, every New York City high school graduate is entitled to a higher education, regardless of grade averages, at either a two-year or a four-year college. While it was expected that black and Puerto Rican students would benefit the most from the program, it happened that children from white ethnic working class families took advantage of it to a proportionately far greater degree.

Much of the new enrollment has been in two-year colleges. The student body at La Guardia Community College in working class Queens, is perhaps representative of many such colleges in the city's university system. The majority of students' fathers had blue collar jobs: foreman, truck driver, mechanic, laborer. A much smaller number of fathers had white collar jobs like civil service worker, office worker, or salesman. The largest number of mothers were housewives, followed by clerks, factory workers, office workers and salesladies.

When asked about their own plans for the future, not many of La Guardia's students, men *or* women (separate breakdowns by sex were not available), foresaw any schooling beyond the two years. Only 10 percent aspired to professional careers of any kind, including teaching and nursing. By contrast, nearly 17 percent of all students—probably one-third of all the girls—planned to become secretaries. Thus, where their mothers and fathers are file clerks and truckdrivers, many daughters hope to be executive secretaries or keypunch operators. For the majority, it seems that college comes too late in life to broaden horizons that were narrowed early, or to raise stunted ambitions.

The need for curriculum reform at community colleges is well-known and long-overdue. Far too few resources are expended on motivating students to explore the limits of their potential. But even if broad reforms are undertaken, two-year colleges will continue to be faced with tremendous obstacles, as long as high schools send them girls and boys who are preconditioned to assume that they are destined for little more than the sales counter, the factory or the typewriter.

Marriage, Motherhood and Career   While it appears that the life expectations of the majority of working class girls—those who do not attend college at all and those who go to two-year colleges—remain somewhat limited, some far-reaching changes in aspirations and attitudes about the proper role for women can be seen among the small but slowly growing minority of girls from ethnic working class backgrounds who are now able to go to four-year colleges. As these young girls are increasingly exposed to higher education, they are coming to adopt standards which combine marriage and motherhood with careers of their own. . . .

The idea of combining marriage, motherhood and a full-time career or job probably appeals far less to working class girls who attend two-year schools, or to those who do not go to college at all, since the kinds of jobs available to them are generally less rewarding. But as families continue to shrink in size, it seems likely that this trend will grow, quite apart from questions of financial need.

The average number of children in white ethnic working class families, many of whom are Catholic, has decreased sharply over the past few years. In the opinion of many experts, the Church's influence, particularly on younger Catholics, has been steadily declining. Only a short time ago, the use of birth control devices, disapproved by the Church, was unthinkable for many. Recently, however, an increasing number of Catholic women—including many who consider themselves devout in most other respects—have begun to practice contraception. The trend is particularly strong among younger women. . . .

All over the world, the experience of women in modern societies has been that as their families become smaller and take fewer years to raise, they become more interested in careers and civic concerns. For working class women as for all American women, widespread use of contraception will increase the probability of longer years in the workplace, greater interest in education, more concern with the kind of job they hold, improved chances of advancement, and more time and energy for union and community affairs. And inevitably, younger women will be able to exercise a degree of control over their own lives that their mothers never had.

» Rosabeth Moss Kanter «

Jobs and Families: Impact of Working Roles on Family Life

» «

If the tensions between work and family are to be resolved, it may be more satisfactory for all concerned in the long run to alter work rather than to alter the family (for example, by trading in the nuclear family for communal, homosexual, or single parent families, as some radicals suggest). Kanter argues that greater corporate use of flextime, paternal and maternal leaves of absence, greater availability of day care, and the curtailment of mandatory travel and cross-country transfers are appropriate responses to many of the difficult issues raised in this chapter.

I come at the issue of families from a roundabout direction: the factory, the office, the boardroom, the hospital, the shop. It is in these work settings that, to a large, virtually unexamined and often unacknowledged extent, the quality of American family life is decided. If this assertion was true for the past, for the somewhat mythical pairing of breadwinner-husbands and secondary-worker wives, it will be even more apropos in the future, as ever larger numbers of young women enter the labor force with the expectation of successfully combining marriage and a career. Thus, an understanding of work settings and occupations, of organizations and public policies may offer as much insight into the stresses, strains and challenges that families of the future will face as all the private decisions made by individuals about their relationships and households.

This is a particularly appropriate time to be looking at the dynamic intersections of work and family life, for many converging trends call attention to the nature of work and work organizations as determinants of the quality of life for individuals and families. . . .

The women's movement and the increase of women in the paid labor force (especially married women with children) have focused policy attention on the work-family link for women and on the extent to which work systems make it possible to maintain effective participation in both worlds. A rise in the number of single-parent families has similarly directed attention to the question of bridging the two worlds of work and family. And these issues, of course, are of critical interest to those individuals who find themselves bearing major responsibilities in both domains—working mothers or single parent fathers. . . .

Growth in the numbers of people employed in white-collar jobs and service institutions and other changes signalling the "post-industrial society" have led such scholars as Daniel Bell to conclude that future economic enterprises will pay more attention to their "sociologizing" (human welfare) functions than to their "economizing" (profit-making) functions. But, of course, people come to work in organizations not just as individuals but also as members of private systems, such as families, that are themselves constrained by the policies and practices of organizations.

It may be that organizations of the future will have to pay attention to their effects on people other than those who work for them—on spouses and children of employees—and allow the needs of families to influence the decisions and shape the policies of the organization. Questions about day care, part-time work, maternity and paternity leave, executive transfers, spousal involvement in career planning and treatment of family dysfunctions—all difficult to raise at present—may become primary considerations for organizations in the future.

How Work Constrains Families

One set of themes relating to the constraints work places on families revolves around time and timing—the scheduling of work and the timing of major demands. Especially in highly absorptive occupations, such as upper-level management, politics or certain professions, which make time demands well beyond the 40-hour week and even draw other family members in as vital players in the occupational world, the limited amount of time left for personal or familial pursuits is a source of strain. Indeed, recent literature has focused on the corporate or political wife as "victim"—drawn into the public arena in a visible way but left to handle family affairs as virtually alone as a single parent.

But even in less absorptive pursuits, the timing of work events can have profound impact on families. The most egalitarian or "companionate" marriages seem to be found among lower-middle-class, white-collar workers, perhaps as a function of the greater temporal availability of husbands to share chores and act as companions to their wives. In other occupational groups, such as professors or executives, the spillover of work into leisure time can generate irritability and lack of attention at home.

Shift workers have other work-family issues to contend with, due to the way their hours affect the expected synchrony between work and non-work events. One study discovered that each shift carried its own characteristic family problems. There was more friction between husband and wife for night-shift workers and more trouble with the father role for afternoon-shift workers. Shift work, in a study of a large midwestern company, produced added psychological burdens, in that workers could not establish regular eating and sleeping patterns. But for those preferring isolation, shift work relieved them of community and family responsibilities.

Night workers have not been carefully researched, but journalistic accounts and recent research suggest some of the family issues they face. For one night manager of a grocery store, for example, the major cost was the stress engendered by the limited time the family had to spend together and problems with his wife because of their limited social life, especially on Saturday nights when her friends were all going out. On the other hand, night workers may also be able to help with housework, errands and greeting the children when they come home from school. But when night work fosters a strong occupational community, as among craft printers, the family may lose importance as a focus of primary ties. In any case, such families have to organize their lives around the schedule of the night worker.

The examples of shift and night workers make clear that it is not only the *amount* of time available for family and leisure that is an issue but its *timing*. Since other family members have their own priorities and schedules, and since society makes certain events possible only at certain times, timing becomes important in determining the effects of working hours. Two-worker families, especially, must work out their scheduling issues. Husbands who are home during the day can more easily help with child care, even though wives who do the housework may feel they lose their "job autonomy." In one study, fathers with preschool children were reported to prefer the night shift, hoping to change to a day shift when their children began to attend school.

One striking example of issues created by schedule problems is the failure of some experiments with a 4-day week. In 1958 an aircraft parts plant in California provided workers with one 3-day weekend a month, without a reduction in the total hours worked—once a month the workers had a free Monday. Despite initial enthusiasm, the workers voted to discontinue the system after less than a year. Some of their complaints make clear how much the *timing* of free time may have been at fault: the time was used for home chores that could as easily have been done on Saturdays, it was lonely at home on Mondays with everyone else at work or at school, and daytime television was designed for women and children. In other words, a lump of free time out of synchrony with the rhythms of the rest of the family and society may not improve the quality of family life at all. As David Riesman suggested after reporting a 1957 Roper poll indicating some negative feelings about the 4-day week, housewives may not be eager to have their husbands underfoot on one of *their* working days.

A different kind of time experiment, however, also makes apparent the intertwining of work hours and family life, but with more positive effects. The practice of flexible working hours or *flextime* (a word coined by Willi Haller in Germany) is now in widespread operation throughout Europe and is gradually being introduced in some United States companies. Within specified limits, employees choose their own hours. There is already evidence of its positive effects. (Among other benefits, when enough organizations in a community institute flextime, it lessens traffic congestion and cuts down on commuting time.)

In one survey of workers in a Swiss company, 35 percent (including more men than women) used the flextime hours for spending more time with their families. Married women tended to use their flextime hours to provide more time for domestic chores (in keeping with the highly traditional sex role allocation in Switzerland). Almost 95 percent of the 1,500 employees surveyed were in favor of flextime—45 percent because of the way it improved the organization of private life. Not surprisingly, married women with children were the most enthusiastic of all groups.

For working women in traditional kinds of families, single parents with sole responsibility for children, or men who expect to share family tasks, flextime seems to permit a more comfortable synchrony of work and family responsibilities. Social policy as well as scientific knowledge would benefit from further research on the use and effects of flextime.

Work-related travel poses another time issue for families. If executive husbands and fathers have little time left over after their very long working days to be helpers to wives and companions to children, they are available *none* of the time when they travel. One researcher studied 128 managers and wives in a large multinational corporation for which extensive travel was a job requirement. All felt burdened and stressed by the travel except two people—a single female manager and a man who used travel to escape from his family. The problems of the others included disconnected social relations, especially for the men; increasing responsibility for the wives, since virtually no areas of family life could be assigned to the husbands who were away so frequently; guilt on the part of the husbands for "deserting" their families; fatigue stemming from the travel itself; wives' fears of being alone; and extra worry for one another while the spouses were apart.

Other scholars have mentioned additional travel-related problems: infidelity and a growing gap in the knowledge and life experiences of husbands and wives. If fathers are often absent, the family system may begin to close itself off to them, making re-entry difficult. Important events may occur without them, and the person who has been family leader in their absence may not want to give up the role.

One solution to the travel problem would be to increase the work-family connection and find ways for traveling workers to bring their families along.

Another theme involving work and families relates to jobs as sources of reward—material and/or psychic. The rhythm and setting of work may affect its rewardingness, but these are not the variables considered important in linking work to family life. Instead, the important variables have to do with the prestige, money or exchangeable resources generated by the job. This line of reasoning lies behind the large number of studies of income or, even more frequently, of occupational prestige as correlates of lifestyle and family patterns. It is clear, for example, that income levels and unemployment affect marital stability.

Many social class analyses assign a rank or level to the husband-father's occupation and indicate what proportion of people or families in each group exhibit the predicted private behavior and attitudes. (While the groupings tend to be called "classes," the assignment of ranks in prestige as determinants of consumption style is actually closer to the Weberian definition of "status" than the Marxist notion of class as stemming from relationship to the means of production.) Research in this area remains compelling because of the large number of variables that show predictable patterning when gross occupational and income levels are differentiated, even though there is also a striking amount of variation within income classes.

In a dynamic extension of the reward framework, John Scanzoni has developed and tested an exchange theory of the effects on family cohesiveness of income and general location in the economic structure. He argued that economic and psychic income from a job affects the presence or absence of marital tension. The more a man is integrated into the economic opportunity structure (as measured objectively by his occupational status, education and income and subjectively by his alienation or lack of alienation) the greater the cohesiveness of the family and of satisfaction with the husband-wife relationship, since the husband brings status and income into the family to exchange for services and positive feelings. Lack of integration, however, may cause the displacement of economic discontents onto personal relations.

A third way to approach work-family linkages concerns the cultures within occupations, cultures that are brought home to varying degrees. The assumption here is that jobs shape one's outlook on the world and orientation to self and others, that jobs are important socializers and teachers of values. For example, Melvin Kohn differentiated the nature of white-collar and blue-collar work as it might affect one's world view. White-collar work involves the manipulation of ideas, symbols and interpersonal relations and blue-collar work, the manipulation of physical objects, which requires less interpersonal skill. White-collar work may be

299

more complex and require greater flexibility, thought and judgment, with less supervision, while blue-collar work may be more standardized and supervised.

Kohn then predicted that these differences would be associated with childrearing values and practices—that is, white-collar parents would value creativity, self-direction and initiative in children while blue-collar parents would stress conformity and obedience. Many of Kohn's findings have been replicated, although class-based differences in socialization seem to have diminished during the last decades. The difference between fathers in the white- and blue-collar categories seems greater, in some research reports, than the difference between mothers.

The degree to which the gap between blue-collar and white-collar parents is closing is a function of changes in work, with much white-collar work becoming more routinized and machine-oriented, while blue-collar workers are growing into an affluent working class. Other influences outside of working conditions, such as those of the media, also play a role in closing this gap.

How parental values are influenced by jobs is only one question that can be raised about occupational cultures. How people change as they are exposed to occupational outlooks, and what happens when that change is not congruent with those undergone by other family members are others. What happens when occupational cultures are esoteric or mysterious and so help exclude family members from important parts of each other's experiences? Here work organizations play a part in determining the quality and ease of communication in the family, according to the extent to which companies close their doors against the family or attempt to create bridges between the language, technology and culture of work and that of the home.

The extent to which jobs and work form a culture, cultural outlook—and vocabulary—is seldom recognized. When a group of executives' wives at a workshop were asked to list words which their husbands used, and which they did not understand, more than 100 words were cited by the 12 wives present.

A fourth theme is related: the emotional climate of work. This is the way workers come to feel about themselves and their day, the degree of self-esteem or self-doubt they feel and the sense of well-being or tension which they bring home. There is some evidence, for example, that workers in low autonomy jobs are more severe and hostile as parents. There is also evidence of variation in preferences for leisure "release" among men in different occupations: advertising men, for example, need to "blow off steam" from their high pressure, competitive work. Yet, other people also argue that the emotional climate of work is *not* brought home, that people can behave very differently in the two settings.

Clearly, the nature of the links between work experience and family life still needs to be explored. Many important questions remain. Does the family world serve *compensatory* functions for emotional deprivations suffered at work, or *displacement-of-aggression* functions? Does the family get the best parts of a working member's energy or commitment when these are not called for at work, as some research hints, or does it get only the parts left over from an emotionally draining job? Do people orient themselves to the family emotionally in the same way they come to approach their work?

The overwhelming tendency in social theory has been to assume that experiences of alienation at work result in negative consequences in personal life. Melvin Seeman has recently challenged this perspective, presenting Swedish data indicating that work alienation has few of the unpleasant, personal consequences imagined. Yet other evidence does make a case for the spillover from the emotional connection with work to other areas of life. People with boring work tend to have boring leisure, and people with involving work tend to have higher levels of both leisure and family involvement, even though the latter may work longer hours and bring home more work than the former. Blue-collar workers in similar occupations at the same pay level tend to be more democratic in their politics and more creative in their leisure when their jobs permit more control, participation and self-direction.

Too often in the past we have viewed families in a vacuum, as a realm unto themselves. Only now are we beginning to consider how public policy and such institutions as employing organizations may be responsible for what happens, or does not happen, in private life.

Structural rearrangements that provide people with more flexibility and options may be a first step in helping families. These would include the use of flextime; more flexible leaves and sabbaticals; greater availability of day care; income supports; explicit focus on communication about work events and work culture to workers' families; and reduction in the number of low autonomy, low opportunity jobs that create emotional tensions at home. Major changes in the world of work and the structure of work organizations may, indeed, turn out to have more profound effects on the quality of family life than all the attempts to influence individual behavior.

» *Betty Friedan* «

Feminism Takes a New Turn

» «

Betty Friedan is the Grand Old Woman of the women's liberation movement. Her 1963 book, The Feminine Mystique, *challenged the notion that women were content with only their roles as wives and mothers. In this brief excerpt from a 1979 article, she adds support to Kanter's argument and goes a step further by predicting that working women will bring pressures that will humanize the workplace, which will have positive ramifications for all workers.*

To some it may sound strange for a feminist like myself to be arguing so passionately for the importance of families. Such arguments have been dismissed by some radical feminists as "reactionary family chauvinism." But it may very well be that the family, which has always been considered the bastion of conservatism, is already somehow being transformed by women's equality into a progressive political force. For when men start assigning a higher priority to their families and self-fulfillment, and women a higher priority to independence and active participation in "man's world," what happens to the supremacy of the corporate, bureaucratic system?

Some recent management studies, for instance, indicate that the corporate policy of frequently transferring executives and demanding that they work nights and weekends is not really necessary for the work of the corporation, but that, by estranging them from their communities and families, it serves to make executives corporate creatures, "company men." Will women renounce their bonds and their power within the family in order to become "company women?" Some already have, but in most instances, women's equality, in the home and in the workplace, strengthens the family and enables it better to resist dehumanization.

IV

» «

THE ORGANIZATION OF WORK

» «

Among the changes in American workers—and in their values and attitudes toward work—that we explored in Parts One and Two are the following:

• Demographic changes in the 1970s that brought into the workforce a generation of young workers—the largest age cohort in the nation's history—whose affluence, education, and social experience differentiate them from their parents' generation.

• An alteration in the relationship of men and women that has brought millions of women into the workforce with heightened expectations.

• Changes in society as a whole concerning what is acceptable authority in all institutions, particularly workplaces.

• A growing sense that workers are *entitled* to such things as cost-of-living allowances, generous pensions, and interesting jobs.

• A demand to extend Bill of Rights guarantees into the workplace.

• A growing desire for more leisure time.

• A questioning of the segmentation of our lives into education for youth, work for the middle-aged, and retirement for the elderly.

• Growing interest in mid-career change.

It all adds up to a brave new world of work, one that Samuel Lipson and Agnes Nestor wouldn't recognize, and one in which Russell Sage and Frederick Winslow Taylor would no doubt be uncomfortable. Indeed, many Americans are discomfited by the rapid changes that have occurred in the last twenty years. The Vietnam War era protests, the women's liberation movement, black power demonstrations, the environmental movement, the energy crisis, stagflation, the decline of productivity and the dollar, and the increasing inability of the United States to compete in world markets are just some of the social and economic developments that turned the comfortable America of 1950–1965 topsy-turvy in the 1970s. Significantly, each of those events and trends permeated the walls of workplaces and confronted American managers with a series of difficult but unavoidable choices:

• Should they respond to the new work values by altering working conditions, or should they attempt to "police" the behavior of young workers through redoubled rules, regulations, and supervision?

• Should they respond to the new economic challenges with renewed efforts to increase efficiency through traditional, Tayloristic methods, or should they experiment with new, unproven ways of increasing productivity through fuller utilization of human resources?

New medical findings about environmental hazards, such as toxic fumes and carcinogenic chemicals, and about the adverse effects of stress on both physical and mental health have added to the problems confronting managers. Many managers believe that they now face terrible dilemmas. How should they make the trade-off between the quality of work life and economic efficiency? At what point does flexibility at work come into conflict with the need for order and productivity?

There are no easy solutions to such problems. The tasks of management are hard work, and change always involves considerable downside risks. Managers have responsibilities to shareholders, customers, workers, and society that must be carefully balanced, and there are no simple formulas that permit these disparate interests to be satisfied simultaneously.

However, the following three chapters explore some innovative ways in which a small number of managers are attempting to achieve *both* high productivity *and* a high quality of working life. Since there are various ways to approach the problem, these cases should not be seen as either the *only*, or necessarily the *best*, ways in which to organize work. There are at least a million American workplaces, each with peculiar tasks, missions, machinery, and managerial and ownership characteristics. Clearly, then, there can be no one best way to design jobs or organize work any more than there is a universal set of worker needs and aspirations. Thus, the articles that follow are not prescriptive; rather, they are included to start us thinking about *alternatives* to prevailing modes of work organization.

In Chapter 10, "Alternative Work Patterns," we explore various ways of breaking up the times of our lives. Fred Best looks at flextime, flexweek, flexyear, even flexcareer! Best, Cohen and Gadon, and Olmsted evaluate sabbaticals, part-time jobs, and work sharing as possible programmatic responses to the problems of "life boxing" identified by Bolles in Chapter 7, and to the pressures on working parents identified in Chapter 9.

Chapter 11 explores "The Quality of Work Life." Whereas some companies have concentrated on redesigning the workplace by adding such amenities as recreational facilities, others, such as those discussed here, have redesigned the structure of work itself to increase productivity and the quality of work life. These articles describe plants in Topeka, Kansas, Tarrytown, New York, and Soedertaelje, Sweden, where workers have been organized into small, self-managing teams and given responsibility for such matters as quality control and machine maintenance, tasks formerly handled by supervisors or engineers. As Robert Schrank explains, the results of these redesign efforts are mixed. Often they fail to alter the nature of what is, basically, boring work. And, as Goldmann points out, not all workers want more variety or responsibility if it means more pressure on the job. Nonetheless, Mike LeFevre, Samuel Lipson, or Agnes Nestor would probably have gladly changed jobs with the workers of Topeka, Tarrytown, or Soedertaelje at the drop of a hard hat—although, as Ted Mills explains, their unions might not have pushed for such work reorganization.

The workplaces in Cleveland, Ohio, Holland, Michigan, Washington, D.C., and the Pacific Northwest described in Chapter 12, "Democracy in the Workplace," are organized on an even more radical reformulation of the relationship of workers to their jobs. In these workplaces, workers have full responsibility for the quantity and quality of their work. They participate fully in decision making and in the profits of their companies. Indeed, these are *their* companies. The workers are either major shareholders in the companies in which they work or they are the cooperative owners of their own businesses. Because these companies are governed democratically, the problems (raised in Part One) of authoritarianism, the lack of rights, and invidious class distinctions between blue- and white-collar workers do not arise. Productivity is particularly high in most of these firms, as is the quality of working life. Workers in these plants, like Japanese workers, have lifetime job security. But even these workplaces are not utopias: each has its special problems, and none is a model that could or should be directly copied across the board by all American industries. In particular, it is difficult to see how the sense of community that is so essential to the success of each of these small companies could be transported to giant corporations like General Electric or General Motors.

Nonetheless, it might be argued that the managerial challenge of the future is to take the best from the experiences of these small, innovative firms, and adapt them for the corporate giants that dominate our economy. The good news is that managers will have a wide range of alternatives from which to choose. As these three chapters illustrate, there appear to be many options for achieving high productivity and a high quality of working life simultaneously.

10

»«

ALTERNATIVE WORK PATTERNS

»«

Betty Medsger

» Fred Best «
Flexible Life Scheduling
»«

In Chapter 7, Richard Bolles introduced us to the boxes into which we have compartmentalized our lives. Here, Fred Best, an official in the State of California Employment Development Department, suggests some ways of "unboxing" our work lives. Best argues that the typical forty-hour, 9:00 to 5:00, Monday through Friday work week with two or three weeks off every year for vacation is no more a "natural" way of organizing work than designating ages five through twenty-one for school, twenty-two through sixty-five for work, and sixty-five till death for leisure, is a "natural" way of dividing up our lives. There are dozens of other ways of slicing up the time of our lives. In this selection, he describes experiments with flexible work scheduling, including flextime, voluntary part-time work, job splitting, compressed work weeks, sabbaticals, leisure-sharing, flexiyear contracts, and other imaginative ways to help solve the career problems and work-family conflicts identified in Chapters 6, 7, and 9. Such measures are essential, Best maintains, if we are to meet the needs of individuals for personal growth and self-fulfillment.

While there is, at this time, no systematic overview of the adaptability of work organizations and unions to flexible life patterns, there are a number of indications that widespread work-scheduling flexibility may be possible. Indeed, there appears to be a deluge of varied worktime experiments taking place nationally and internationally. These innovations are tampering with every dimension of worktime from the workday to the worklife. The diversity of these efforts bears testimony to the likelihood that the social forces of our times are not moving us toward some monolithic worktime reduction such as a "standard 35-hour workweek" but to a vast array of worktime reforms that will add up to overall worklife flexibility.

One of the major thrusts of current worktime innovations has been growing interest in part-time work. Not only has the portion of the work force employed in "voluntary" part-time work increased from 10.6 to 18.7 percent between 1954 and 1977, but there has been a growing movement to

307

remove part-time employment from the stigmatism of "second rate" jobs. Up to very recent times, most part-time jobs were low paying, tended to entail menial tasks, offered virtually nothing in the way of security or fringe benefits, and presented little opportunity for career advancement. Today, a growing coalition of women, youth, and older workers are advocating the creation of "permanent part-time jobs" offering fringe benefits such as health insurance and the potential for career advancement. Most gains in these areas have occurred within the public sector. The federal government, many states, as well as some localities have embarked upon formal programs to increase and upgrade part-time jobs. As a result, the number of permanent part-time employees in the federal civil service is reported to have increased a remarkable 20 percent in the one-year period from the end of 1976 to the end of 1977. Other initiatives have sought to increase part-time work among public service jobs funded by the federal government. Within the private sector, there has been less concern with the quality of part-time jobs, but there are some indications that interest is growing.

Another growing worktime reform that is somewhat akin to part-time employment has been "job splitting." This innovation entails the performance of one full-time job by two or more persons. The idea first made its appearance in California during the mid-1960s. There are no figures providing a concrete indication of the incidence of job splitting, but numerous accounts suggest that the practice has grown and spread across the country. This worktime reform seems applicable to many occupations. For example, there have been reports of two or more persons successfully sharing positions such as high school principal, city planner, college professor, secretarial receptionist, and many other types of work. There is no question that "job splitting" requires special effort and unusual cooperation by participants, but when the match of employees is appropriate, employers have found that this practice offers many unexpected benefits. Additionally, job splitting has often served the purpose of allowing persons in professional fields to maintain career attachment when they are unable to work full time or inadequate career opportunities limit chances for full-time employment in chosen fields of work.

One of the most heralded types of worktime reform has been flexitime. This practice has been primarily applied to daily work hours and allows employees to arrive for work and depart at any time during the day as long as they are in attendance during specified "core hours," such as 10 A.M. to 3 P.M., and work a full workday. While there are no overall figures on the incidence of flexitime, it has been estimated that 13 percent of all firms and 6 percent of all employees within the United States were participating in flexitime programs in 1977. Flexitime began during the mid-1960s in Europe and made its first American debut in the early 1970s. Since that time, the practice has evolved from a rare novelty to a common idea that appears to be spreading rapidly within both the public and private sector. In the "big picture" of lifetime scheduling, daily flexitime does not offer the promise of altering overall life patterns. However, the emergence and rapid assimilation of this idea has accomplished a great deal in the way of provoking thought about other forms of work-scheduling flexibility, as well as demonstrating to employers that departures from the standard "8-hour-a-day workweek" need not engender organizational anarchy. Indeed, the notion of flexitime has proven itself so manageable that some firms are beginning to experiment with the notion of "flexiweeks" and "fleximonths."

Beyond the scope of the workday, there have been a number of innovations in the workweek and workmonth. Within the United States, popular attention was first drawn to workweek innovations by the wave of experiments with the "compressed workweek" that surfaced around 1970. The major thrust here was the "4-day, 40-hour workweek" in which employees continued to work 40 hours a week, but put in 10 hours a day in order to gain three-day weekends. While this innovation was orginally hailed as a "revolution in worktime," its growth seems to have leveled in the late 1970s. However, as in the case of flexitime, attention given to the compressed workweek seems to have paved the way for a number of work-scheduling experiments within the context of weeks and months. For example, there have been reports of 3- or 3.5-day workweeks with 11- to 13-hour workdays. One recent reform instigated with union cooperation at DuPont created a system of rotation between regular and night shifts in which employees work four 12-hour days between two-day weekends and receives seven days' extended leave a month. This plan has been in operation since 1974 and is considered an "all-around success" because it provides workers with free time they can use and allows plants to maintain continuous 24-hour operation.

While it is often noted that the American workweek has not declined notably since the mid-1940s, it is important to realize that national averages disguise growing diversity in worktime arrangements. Indeed, analysis of worktime data shows that the small reductions in the workweek that have occurred over the last few decades have largely been the result of increased part-time work and reductions of excessively long hours. More importantly, a good deal of the gains in free time during the "work years of life" have come in the form of longer vacations and paid days off. Indeed, extended vacations have become an increasingly frequent goal of collective bargaining efforts, and vacations of over six weeks' length are becoming increasingly common. Of particular importance has been the recent initiative of the United Auto Workers to bargain for successive stages of paid days off with the ultimate goal of obtaining a 4-day, 32-hour workweek. Such movement toward days off indicates a renewed interest on the part of organized labor toward using bargaining influence on behalf of free time.

Further, such practical adjustment to days off, longer weekends, and most particularly extended vacations underscores the adaptability of work organizations to a variety of discontinuities in employee work attendance.

Some of the most interesting worktime reforms have entailed flexible mechanisms to allow individual employees the choice of foregoing income for more free time within the context of the workmonth and workyear. A much-heralded program set up by Santa Clara County in California allows employees the choice of voluntarily foregoing 5 percent of their annual income for 10.5 days' added paid vacation, 10 percent for 21 days' vacation, or as much as 20 percent for 42 days' added vacation (the level of pay is reduced proportionally for all work and vacation days). During the first year of operation, some 17 percent of all county employees requested one of these options. Participation in subsequent years has declined due to increased work loads and resistance of mid-level supervisors, but these voluntary tradeoff options have become a permanent program supported by the public employee unions and top county management. Other local governments are developing similar programs. One of the most notable of these is a voluntary three-month leave of absence program in which lawyers employed by a number of counties are allowed to exchange 25 percent of their annual earnings for a three-month leave each year. This program has been judged a success because it has allowed attorneys to recover from stressful work during the rest of the year, as well as provide funds for the hiring of additional lawyers. Voluntary tradeoff programs of a less dramatic nature have also been developed within the private sector and federal government.*

Perhaps the most impressive move toward flexible worklives has been the development of "flexiyear contracts" by a number of private firms in Europe. The general idea of this innovation is that employer and employee negotiate on an annual basis an overall worktime agreement for a year's period. Such negotiations have opened the possibility of novel arrangements such as six months on and six months off, part-time work for part of the year (such as summer when children are home), and all manner of other options. It is claimed that such yearly negotiations improve worker morale and productivity and allow employers the predictability to plan a number of worktime arrangements that creatively meet the needs of both firm and workers.

The idea of sabbaticals has also been extended beyond the academic environment in recent years. Despite some criticisms, the well-known U.S. Steel Worker sabbatical negotiated in 1967 was renewed in 1974 and is still firmly intact. This program allows up to 13 weeks' paid vacation every four years for senior workers. A similar sabbatical program was negotiated for cannery workers in 1966. Sabbatical leaves of up to one year have been

---

*For example, the New York Telephone and Telegraph Company allows telephone operators to take one day off each week without pay if the arrangement is made in advance. Personnel officials for the company report that most operators tend to request the day-off option.

implemented among a small number of firms. For example, the Rolm Corporation in California provides a one-year leave with pay to employees who have worked six continuous years with the firm. Additionally, a number of major corporations have instigated programs allowing their executives one- to two-year "sabbaticals" for approved public service projects.

These and other innovations provide evidence that the adaptability of work organizations and unions to flexible worklives is still largely untapped. Certainly, there are problems to overcome and tradeoffs to be made. However, new technologies and models of operation are being developed that allow adaptability to worktime innovations that might have been thought impossible only a few years ago. For example, the rise of flexitime has already stimulated the production of a wide array of time-keeping devices that allow supervisors an efficient and uncostly means of overseeing employee worktime. Similarly, a number of large corporations are beginning to recognize that the vast computer facilities now used for computing payrolls and overtime can be applied to the task of adapting organizational operations to varied work schedules and adjusting fringe benefits to variations of individual worktime arrangements. As an illustration, computer technologies might allow more individualized worktime arrangements (even for highly interdependent assembly-line workers) through staggering each worker's schedule in the same way that the use of classrooms is planned in universities. Yet another innovation supportive of worktime reforms has been "cafeteria benefit plans" in which individual employees can choose between options such as a pay raise, $10 worth of life insurance, or added vacation. Unions have been reserved about such cafeteria plans but are now finding that such approaches can facilitate member solidarity by allowing the development of a dollar-value bargaining agenda rather than internal conflicts over the priority given to life insurance as opposed to more time off.

These innovations are but a few of the mechanisms that are being developed to allow the practical implementation of increased worklife flexibility. While the task of adjusting to widespread worktime flexibility is certainly not to be underestimated, it is also important that it not be viewed as impossible. There is no law written by the hand of God that the standard workweek must be 40 hours and that employees will have two to four weeks' vacation each year. Different types of organizations and occupations will certainly confront varied obstacles to increased flexibility, but there is good reason to believe that a great deal can be done to increase the options available to all types of workers.

Social Policy and Life-cycle Planning

While the interaction among workers, unions, and employers is likely to foster important steps toward more flexible life scheduling, it is important to recognize that the government, as the custodian of common well-being, is also likely to become involved with the issue. As nonwork years become more prolonged at the extremes of the life cycle, there will be increasing social and economic costs in the form of tax burdens to those who are working and impoverishment for those who are not working. Simultaneously, the problems of extended schooling, the demand for jobs, and the desire for more free time in mid-life will cause mounting pressures for government policies to allow more flexible scheduling of education, work, and leisure over a total lifetime.

There are a number of policies and programs that governments will likely consider as mechanisms to foster more flexible life scheduling. Most of these ideas are still in their embryonic stages of development. . . .

Some represent bold strokes of "social engineering" and others less dramatic efforts. Each have their own unique problems and limitations, and all of them are relatively new and untried. . . . Current and yet-to-be presented proposals are still very much in need of further refinement and rigorous assessment, and the process of developing social policies to encourage more flexible life schedules is very much in the initial stages.

Recycling People

In large measure this [selection] has focused on facts and figures documenting social trends that may foster flexible life scheduling. Such an approach tends to downplay the less measurable humanistic issues of personal growth and fulfillment. Yet these concerns are also important, if not preeminent, and it is fitting [to consider] the importance of life scheduling to the inner meanings of human existence.

There is a story concerning a certain Mr. Creech, who allegedly wrote in the margins of his painstaking translation of Lucretius, "Memo—when I have finished my book, I must kill myself." Reportedly, he carried out his resolution, a testimony to the beliefs of past ages in which life without work was held to be meaningless. Values and life styles have changed greatly since that dour Mr. Creech wrote his dismal memo. Nonetheless, most industrial nations must still be viewed as "work societies." Further, this is not likely to change. Despite the advances of technology and evolution of human values, work will certainly remain the essential and focal activity of human life. Yet it is a dismal thought that we have come to view our lives primarily in terms of preparing for work, performance of work, and finally deliverance from work. Perhaps more pertinent, it is more saddening from the standpoint of human fulfillment and growth that the virtues of learning, working, and leisure should be unduly cramped into segregated compartments of life.

It is near idiocy to believe that youth is principally for school and learning, middle age for applying what we learned in youth, and old age for reaping the rewards of a life of work. Life simply is not that way. The learning process continues to our last days. The world changes constantly around us and different stages of life impose new lessons every bit as vital as the "basics" we learn in childhood. Work is a process of self-expression and sacrifice that cannot be restricted to one portion of life without dire results. There are many faces of work, and many seem uniquely fitted to different ages. Physical toil is an experience all of us should taste, and there is no more suitable time than youth. Similarly, work requiring discipline, fully developed skills, and wisdom tends to have its natural place in the life cycle. Increasingly, it appears that those who do not confront work in youth are ill prepared—despite the best of educations—for the demands and opportunities of mid-life; and those who flee their jobs in their early sixties are all too often stranded upon an island of empty time from which there are no bridges to return. Finally, leisure seems to have become at once our most precious and wasted commodity. If anything, our time free of constraints represents the potential to renew and rebuild our spirits; and to pull the fabric of our lives together in a way that balances the meaning that comes from learning, the purposes that drive us to work, and the personal pleasures that somehow make these efforts worthwhile. All too often, it seems that "leisure " is forced upon us in ways we cannot appreciate, or made unduly harried by the pressures of mid-life.

The riders in a race do not stop short when they reach the goal. There is a little finishing canter before coming to a standstill. There is time to hear the kind voice of friends and to say to one's self: "The work is done." But just as one says that, the answer comes: "The race is over, but the work never is done while the power to work remains." The canter that brings you to a standstill need not be only coming to rest. It cannot be, while you still live. For to live is to function. That is all there is in living.

—Oliver Wendell Holmes, Jr.

More flexible life patterns would loosen the time binds that often prevent the natural flow of human activities, as well as nurture and renew our spirits through change and opportunities to actualize personal dreams. Of course, many life changes and dreams can be attained within the realm of work. However, others require time away from the job. Every individual has some desire to explore new experiences and possibly try fundamentally different ways of life. We all have a deeply felt yearning for what we might have been and may yet become: a desire to more freely explore things like playing the guitar, writing a book, building a house, or raising a child. Such dreams take time, and one promise of more flexible life patterns is that each individual might arrange life's activities in ways that broaden the exploration of the countless possibilities of human existence.

With due recognition for the diversity of the human species, it seems that the fullest and most productive lives are those in which individuals

313

fluctuate through periods of action and accomplishment—which expand our awareness and solidify our sense of self—and rest and reflection—which integrate our sense of self and the world. In this way, action becomes more than reaction to an endless treadmill of unchosen challenges, and reflection more than stultifying repetition of old thoughts and experiences. The actualization of this cyclic relationship between action and renewal is essential to human growth and fulfillment, and it requires that there be a better balance of learning, work, and leisure through all stages of our lives.

In the course of history, a time appears to be upon us in which there is an opportunity to realign our values and institutions so that every person has a better opportunity to adjust the rhythm of life's experience to their own needs and temperaments. This is an opportunity that should not be cast aside lightly.

» Allan R. Cohen and Herman Gadon «

Flexible Working Hours

» «

In 1977, about 13 percent of nongovernmental employers with more than fifty workers offered flextime. Although flextime can be managed in many ways, typically all workers in an office will be required to be on their jobs during specified "core" hours (for example 9:00–11:30 in the morning, and 1:00–4:00 in the afternoon), but they can arrive at work any time between 7:00 and 9:00 A.M., and go home whenever they please between 4:00 and 6:00 P.M., as long as they work the total number of hours to which they have agreed. As University of New Hampshire business school professors Allan Cohen and Herman Gadon illustrate, the system has many benefits to organizations, individuals, and society, including increased productivity and morale, and decongested traffic at normal rush hours. On the other hand, flextime makes managers work harder—which is probably a greater factor in restricting its spread than the more obvious problem of applying it to industrial situations that must be fully "manned" twenty-four hours a day.

We *use flexible working hours because it is consistent with our philosophy of giving employees the maximum amount of choice. They choose their hours just as they can choose their vacation time or the color to paint their machine–within constraints, with as much individual choice as possible.*

> —Roger Hetherman, Director of Employee and
> Community Relations, Kingsbury Machine Tool

I'm divorced with one child, ten years old. Flextime lets me come in early so I can be home when my daughter gets out of school. Before I would fight traffic to get home late in the afternoon. Then I would rush through dinner. By the time we were cleaned up I was pooped, couldn't listen or talk to my daughter, was often irritable, couldn't relax, couldn't help her with her school work. Now she's happier, I'm happier and her grades have improved tremendously.

> —File Clerk, Social Security Administration,
> Washington, D.C.

Flexible working hours is essentially a work schedule that gives employees daily choice in the timing between work and nonwork activities. Thus, more than other organizational arrangements, it treats an individual as a whole person, with a life outside work as well as in the organization. It is this characteristic of choice that distinguishes flexible working hours from all other work schedules. Because choice is its essence, it is not mutually exclusive of but can be combined with the other alternatives. . . .

How It Works

Under flexible working hours, special consideration is given to *band width*, or maximum length of the working day. In order to provide opportunities for flexibility, the band is usually extended, perhaps to twelve or sixteen hours per day rather than the customary eight or ten. This extended band is generally divided into *core time* and *flexible time*. Core time represents those hours when everyone has to be in attendance. Flexible time, sometimes called *flexitime* or *flextime*, represents the hours within which employees can decide for themselves when to be present. Employees who come and go during flexible time periods are often said to be *flexing*.

Though common core times are 10:00 A.M. to 12:00 noon and 1:30 to 3:30 P.M., they may be minimal, as little as one hour in a day, or not even required. Each working unit in an organization must have its own designation, based on an evaluation of its own needs and the needs of the organization. In general, the less interdependence among persons, and the more persons there are in a working unit, the less need there is for core times.

Figure 1 illustrates two of the many possible eight-hour workday patterns for a company with core and flexible times distributed as shown over a band width extending from 6:30 A.M. to 5:30 P.M.

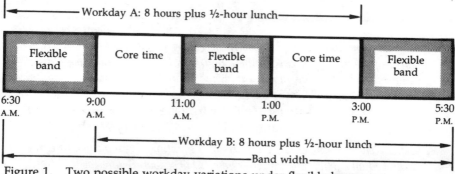

Figure 1. Two possible workday variations under flexible hours.

Flexibility is limited by the number of *contracted hours*, which must be worked in a *reporting period*. Although reporting periods theoretically may be quite lengthy, they are commonly a day, a week, or a month. In the United States, contracted hours are usually seven to eight in one day or thirty-five to forty in one week. In Europe, where pay by the month is common, workers may contract for 160 to 180 hours in a month. An employee who contracts for forty hours in a week, with a core time of four hours in any one day, may vary his or her starting hours and leaving hours each day within the flexible time periods as he or she chooses, so long as forty hours are worked by the end of the week. Thus that person might work four hours on one day, and twelve on another, so long as the longer hours in one day can be accommodated within the band width.

Some organizations allow a *carry-forward* of *debit hours* or *credit hours*. Credit hours are hours worked in excess of the contracted hours in the reporting period. Debit hours are contracted hours in the reporting period that have not been worked. A person in an organization with a carry-forward allowance of 2½ hours, plus or minus, for 37½ contracted hours in a one-week reporting period, might therefore owe the organization 2½ hours, or be owed them. The common experience is for workers to carry credit balances. Despite the fears of many supervisors, most people seem to prefer to work now, play later. . . .

Time Recording

Time recording for pay purposes and for the purpose of assuring punctuality is generally required by most organizations. Usually provided by time clocks, it is often a hated symbol of authoritarian control. Experience with flexible working hours reveals the use of a variety of devices, ranging from traditional time clocks, to manual records maintained by the individual employee, to time-accumulating equipment that records total hours but not times of arrival or departure. . . .

Variations

The degree of choice allowed distinguishes the varieties of arrangements of flexible working hours from each other. Many have acquired names. One variation is the *floating day*, adopted by the Nestle Company in White Plains, and Hewlett-Packard.

The floating day provides a very limited degree of flexibility. Decisions on daily time of arrival are made in advance, usually changeable only on one or more week's notice. Since there is no carryover, times of arrival automatically determine times of departure. Thus a person on an eight-hour day who arrives at 9:00 A.M. leaves eight hours later.

A variation suggested by Willi Haller, an early proponent of flexible working hours and President of Interflex Datensysteme GmbH, a manufacturer of time-accumulating equipment, is *variable hours*. Under variable hours individuals would work according to demands of the job, varying work hours according to load on a daily, weekly, monthly, or seasonal basis. Although not formally working under such a system, farmers the world over and academics can be said to labor on variable hours.

Staggered hours, commonly associated with flexibility, is not really a flexible working hours variant, though it is often assumed to be. It is instead a form of fixed hours, which involves assigning to blocks of workers, usually without their participation or choice, starting and stopping times that will even out peak loads. Companies have used this arrangement to avoid congestion at elevators. Cities, including New York and Ottawa, have encouraged companies to go on staggered hours to ease loads on subways, city streets, and highways. Though staggered hours can ease congestion and is a better system than fixed hours for everyone, it is not flexible and has few of the other benefits listed later.

Systems based on flexibility can emphasize company or individual control, ranging from very little choice, as with the floating day, to total flexibility, as with variable hours.

Estimates of Users

There is no completely accurate measure of the number of companies and individuals using flexible working hours and its variations, but informed estimates range between seven and ten million people. . . . Since the first flexible working hours program in the United States began only in 1973, these numbers represent extremely rapid growth. . . . Applications tend to be made first with white-collar workers in banks, insurance companies, pharmaceutical companies, engineering companies, and government agencies.

Because of the extensive interdependence of manufacturing work and the tendency of employers to be less trusting of blue-collar workers, applications to blue-collar work are still relatively uncommon. However, there is interest in application to manufacturing. . . . Organizations that have adopted flexible working hours have almost never given them up. . . .

Advantages of the Method to Organizations

There are many reasons why the idea has spread so rapidly, and the list of advantages is long. Flexible working hours appears to be one of those rare innovations valued highly by both employers and employees.

Flexible working hours seems to have important effects on short-term absenteeism. Under fixed hours, many individuals who face the prospect of being late decide it is too embarrassing to come in an hour or so after everyone else has arrived, so stay away for the day and say that they were sick. Especially for those variations of flexible working hours in which there is no necessary starting time each day, short-term absenteeism decreases dramatically as employees get used to the idea of flexibility. At Berol Corporation, for example, absenteeism decreased 50 percent. Surprisingly, in some organizations there are even decreases in long-term absenteeism. Since long-term absenteeism is presumably related to sickness, it may be that allowing individuals more choice about how to balance nonwork with work activities leads to greater feelings of autonomy and either less illness or greater commitment to the job.

Tardiness, of course, is virtually eliminated in those systems where daily starting times may vary. . . .

Another reported difference is in the area of employee turnover. It is believed that turnover drops for most employees because they stick with an organization in order to enjoy the benefits of flexible working hours. This advantage, of course, will gradually disappear once the practice is more widespread. For others, the opportunity to adjust personal work schedule with personal life may make it possible to work with less aggravation and therefore to develop greater commitment to the job and to the employing organization. Implementation of flexible working hours may also indicate a general interest in employees that they appreciate and associate with other commitment-building practices.

The organizational outcome in which there is the greatest interest is, of course, productivity. Unfortunately, because most installations have been in the white-collar area, hard measures of productivity are difficult to obtain. A very high percentage of organizations trying flexible working hours report impressionistically that at the least there is greater enthusiasm for work, though no change in productivity. In addition, employees seem more physically ready to get to work when they have been able to adjust their schedule to take care of personal matters or avoid heavy traffic. . . .

In a number of instances, productivity increases of 4–8 percent have been documented where employees work on products that have relatively long start-up times or lengthy processing periods. For example, . . . employees [studied] in a large American pharmaceutical company would not hesitate to start an extra batch toward the end of the day if they could stay until the batch was completed. . . . Pacific Gas and Electric calculated savings of $300,000 from its flexible-working-hours installation in an engineering department after an expenditure of some $50,000 for time-accumulating equipment, and cited a variety of reasons for the savings, including lower absenteeism, higher efficiency, and so forth. . . .

Productivity can also be affected if the change to flexible working hours leads to improved work methods or managerial practices. We studied a large urban bank with severe problems in its typing pool:

> The typing pool was run by a female former military officer. . . .
> The supervisor's military experience had conditioned her to believe that she could not possibly trust any employee whom she wasn't watching continuously. Therefore, she had utilized strict and close supervision. Under flexible working hours, it was not possible for her to be present during the entire working day, so that she was forced to let some work go on without watching it directly. As she gradually discovered that employees were doing their work, even when she was not present, she began to spend less time watching and more time in the office planning. As a result of this change in management style, productivity in the typing pool increased 9½ percent over seven months, as measured by the number of lines typed. This amounted to a saving of approximately $2200 per

319

month, and "saving" of another kind—the "untrainable" supervisor had been "trained." . . .

Advantages to the Individual

In numerous surveys, people on flexible working hours report a number of personal advantages. Flexible working hours was originally invented to deal with traffic problems at a plant in Germany. Since then, reduced commuting time has frequently been mentioned as an individual benefit; it not only offers the individual extra time for pursuing personal interests, but also may facilitate a reduction in aggravation due to traffic jams.

The time saved in commuting or the ability to shift working hours to suit personal needs leads to other personal benefits. Individuals can, and do, use the time to pursue educational goals, spend more time with families, follow leisure interests, do necessary shopping and other errands, arrange for child care, and so on. In some cases a shift in times of work can result in dramatic life changes. Here is an example from our research:

> Charlie is a supervisor in an urban bank. He worked from 9:00 to 5:00 for twenty years; it had never occurred to him that the complexities of his family life could be other than they were. At the end of each working day he would fight the traffic to get home, and then sink into a chair to read the newspaper in the brief time before dinner. With only a short time before dinner, he could somehow never get around to work on the boat he was building in his basement. After dinner, he often had to take his wife shopping, since she didn't drive and they only had the one car. This schedule meant that Charlie was often irritable when he was at home. He never seemed to be able to interest his children in the boat building he so much loved whenever he could find the time for it. After the implementation of flexible working hours in his bank, he . . . began to come in at 7:30 in the morning in order to leave at 3:30 in the afternoon. Because he got home earlier, the family's one car was available to his daughter, who volunteered to take his wife shopping. Within a short time his boys, out of curiosity, joined him after work in building the boat. Because he would get a running start before dinner, he found that he often was quite willing and able to get back to it after dinner, where his boys would once again join him. The greater interaction around boat building with his sons led to more free and easy communication with them that, in turn, made him feel better about himself. Because his wife could get the shopping done before dinner in the evenings she was more relaxed and often either joined in the boat building or socialized with the men. Thus a simple change in working hours had profound and far-reaching effects on family relationships and communications.

While this example is more dramatic than most, it is illustrative of how the option for being flexible can provide opportunities for the individual to make appropriate trade-offs between work and nonwork concerns. . . . Women or men with small children needing care can adjust their work schedule to see their children off in the morning and/or be home to greet them at night. Young, single men and women may extend their lunch hour in order to do shopping while downtown or to meet friends. . . .

Repeatedly in our interviews and in the work of others, individuals say that it makes them feel really good to be allowed to make choices for themselves about worktime. They feel more trusted by the company and feel treated more as adults. This results, we believe, in a generalized enhancement of self-concept. Whether or not this greater feeling of adult autonomy leads to greater productivity, we believe it is worthwhile in and of itself. Independence and autonomy are worthy characteristics for adult individuals.

Advantages to Society

If flexible working hours indeed leads to greater feelings of autonomy and enhanced self-concept, that alone has value in a democratic society. But even if the stock of healthy, adult individuals is not actually increased, there are other social benefits from flexible working hours. The smoothing out of traffic flows can result in significant savings of gasoline, capital equipment, and accidents. . . . As more people use flexible working hours or other variations of the standard workweek, peak demands for recreational facilities are likely to be smoothed out. This can result in much greater use of existing capacity and a reduction of the need for major capital expenditures.

Disadvantages of Flexible Working Hours

For a few companies there may be disadvantages. Flexible working hours is likely to be hardest on first-line supervisors. Often they do not have highly developed managerial skills and rely on first-hand presence and observation to see that work is done. Flexible working hours, with its extension of the hours during which some employees may be present, forces supervisors to do more planning. It requires them to assess what an individual can be expected to accomplish during a day or week, to plan work in advance so that those who come in early or stay late will have something constructive to do, to plan for and arrange ample coverage for those hours of the day or week when employees are less inclined to choose to be present, and so on. Thus, for many supervisors, new skills are necessary. Unless they are provided, supervisors are likely to feel threatened and insecure. . . . Thus organizations wishing to go on flexible working hours need to work closely with the supervisors that will have to implement it. It should be mentioned, however, that even supervisors who are uncomfortable with supervising employees on flexible hours usually like the personal opportunity to flex their own hours.

A second disadvantage for organizations concerns communications. It may be harder to find times to hold meetings that require everyone's presence. Thus more consideration again must be given to planning.

Like any change, flexible working hours calls for careful analysis of the way things are done. Though ultimately such analysis is likely to benefit any organization, working out all the details of hours, coverage, allowance for absences, sick leave, and so on can be costly and time consuming. Though flexible working hours has been extremely popular, there have been a few cases where improper preparation has led to tension and fewer benefits than could have been realized.

The need for some kind of record-keeping system may be a disadvantage. When all hours are fixed, elaborate systems are not necessary for keeping track of employees' coming and going, though those who have to line up to punch a time clock would probably feel otherwise. But with flexible working hours it is desirable to develop a system, whether paper and pencil or mechanical, for recording accumulating hours. . . .

We have seen in some organizations that flexible working hours can make overt, subtle differences in status or contribute to defective decision-making processes, as employees dispute the method for how Friday afternoon coverage will be determined. . . . [There is a] need for conflict-resolving skills that supervisors may not have and probably did not require before.

Another disadvantage for companies is that with flexible working hours buildings must be open longer and therefore bills for lighting and heating may increase. This can be offset by providing longer service hours to customers. It also may be offset by other energy savings, such as lower gasoline consumption because of reduced traffic jams, but these offsetting savings may go to individuals rather than to the company.

Disadvantages to the Individual

It is hard to see what disadvantages there are for individuals except for those who might be disturbed by fellow workers coming and going throughout the morning and afternoon. Some employees may be uncomfortable about the idea of having to make choices about issues such as arrival and departure time, which were fixed in the past, but those employees can usually continue to work the same hours as they always have.

We have seen that those in organizations who already have informally sanctioned flexibility—usually professionals such as engineers—can resent a formal system that makes them strictly accountable. Where they formerly could bend hours a bit as needed, without adding up hours worked, the recording requirements of a formally adopted system can create a *loss* of freedom. Similarly, higher status individuals or groups may feel a relative loss of status when others also have the privileges of flexibility available to them.

Disadvantages to Society

Insofar as keeping buildings open longer requires increased use of energy for light and heat, there may be an overall cost to the society (if not offset by energy saved through improved traffic flow). It is hard to see what other disadvantages there might be.

The Life Stages for Which Flexible Working Hours Is Best Adapted

Because flexible working hours is a system that gives individuals a measure of control over their working hours, the range of those who can benefit from it is great.

For example, the system of flexible working hours also enhances other alternatives to the standard workweek. Combined with part-time work, schedules may be individually arranged to provide opportunities for work for people in school, for mothers with young children, and for older people who want to slow down or partially retire. Used with job sharing, it provides the working pair with the possibility of dividing the worktime in many different combinations. Combined with the compressed workweek, it gives persons more options in distributing their worktime over a long workday so that they can take care of personal needs that are otherwise neglected or take rest periods in order to reduce fatigue.

For working mothers, flexible working hours is a particular boon. It gives them the possibility of arranging child care, staying home to see children off in the morning, or getting home in time to greet them from school. Many mothers who might not otherwise be willing to take jobs can be and have been attracted to the labor force. . . .

Single individuals who lead an active night life may appreciate flexible working hours because it gives them the opportunity to sleep late.

Executives or those in managerial positions, in the stage of their careers where they are establishing themselves and are upwardly mobile, may see little benefit from flexible working hours in its formal implementation because they already enjoy a kind of flexibility—though it usually means flexibility to work much longer hours than the standard forty per week.

Workers heading toward retirement may appreciate flexible working hours as it allows them to adjust their schedules so that they can become involved in volunteer activities or hobbies that will carry them into retirement. For them, however, the ability to reduce the number of hours worked per week may be a more important variation of the standard workweek than flexible working hours.

Single parents would certainly be major beneficiaries, whether male or female, as flexible working hours would allow them to make necessary

323

arrangements for children. And, of course, those who have no special need to flex working hours can continue to work on a regular, fixed schedule, as do many already under flexible working hours. It is a potent method with wide application to those at various stages in their life cycle.

» Barney Olmsted «

Job Sharing— A New Way to Work

» «

The deputy director of the State of California Employment Development Department in charge of legislative liaison is two people: one "owns" two-fifths of the $28,880 job, and the other holds down the remaining three-fifths. One of the women who shares this job does so to spend more time with her family; the other woman is a playwright who uses her three days off a week to pursue her "real" vocation. In Santa Barbara, California, seven men and women share five full-time medical technologist positions. The scheme gives everyone more leisure time. As Barney Olmsted, co-director of an organization called New Ways to Work, argues, job-sharing has evolved in response to various individual needs, including those of women in child-rearing years and older workers who are not ready for retirement.

Few concepts are more entrenched in our thinking than the dictum that serious, career-minded employees always work 40 or more hours a week. Recent employment trends have begun to question that premise and have shown that permanent part-time work is an attractive option for some employees. The older worker who rejects early retirement but wishes for a transition period during the final period of his work life, individuals returning to the educational process or seeking a career change in mid-life, increasing numbers of women who wish to enter or remain in the work force while raising their families, often cite the 40-hour work week as a principal barrier to achieving their goals. Opportunities for responsible, career-oriented part-time work have been sparse, however, since most jobs are designed on the 40-hour-a-week model. Recently, a new work arrangement called "job sharing" has emerged as a means of restructuring full-time positions. While rising initially out of the needs of individuals, it is increasingly appealing to forward thinking employers. The purpose of this article is to acquaint the reader with the concept of job sharing, discuss the advantages and disadvantages to employees and employers, examine how widespread the practice is and suggest ways that interested employers can implement this option.

325

Job Sharing: What Is It?

A shared job is a voluntary work arrangement in which two people hold responsibility for what was formerly one full-time position. Salary and fringe benefits are prorated according to time worked.

The initial interest in sharing a job was expressed by women professionals interested in a better balance between their home and career responsibilities. The success and consequent publicity given two experiments in job sharing in the mid 1960s . . . one with teachers, the other with social workers . . . resulted in the spread of interest in this new work arrangement to the point where some of the jobs being shared now include those of facilities engineer, program director, receptionist, organizational development specialist and employment counselor. Also, in increasing numbers of instances, men are now attracted by this new option. Several of the positions cited above are being shared by male/female teams.

As the practice grows, it is important to distinguish between terms. The restructuring of a full-time job by employing two people results in two *permanent part-time positions.* (Traditionally, employers have differentiated between their permanent part-time and temporary part-time employees.) Depending on how much cooperative interaction the job requires, it can be viewed as having been either *split* or *shared*. For example, a receptionist job that has been restructured so that one woman works from 8:00 to 12:30 and another from 12:30 to 5:00 would presumably be viewed has having been split. Some brief communication might have to take place as the shifts changed, but this would be minimal in most instances. The facilities engineer position, however, requires close communication and cooperation between the two sharers. They are responsible for planning the facilities of the laboratories in a new hospital research unit and truly share the responsibilities and the problems of that job. The distinction—and the element which makes job sharing a really new way to work—lies in the relationship between the sharers.

What Are the Advantages of Job Sharing?

As instances of job sharing have begun to increase, advantages to employers have become apparent. These benefits include:

1. *Increased flexibility.* In many jobs, peak hours of service occur throughout the day, alternating with "dead periods." For example, animal control officers find that their peak hours are in the early morning or during the late afternoon and early evening. When the City of Palo Alto decided to restructure one of these positions and make it a shared job, it extended the hours at either end of the day and reduced the mid-day time. The new schedule resulted in a more effective use of the officers' time, in a way not possible with one full-time person.

Other jobs dealing with the public have similar periods of heavy business during parts of the day and can be restructured in a manner which results in both an extension of service and an increase in productivity, since

326

the employees are working primarily during heavy demand hours.

In addition to "peak hour" flexibility, sharers can substitute for one another in a variety of circumstances. When a serious automobile accident hospitalized his partner during one of the busiest times of the year, Bill Leland, who shares the job of Director of the Action Research Liaison Project at Stanford University, covered the job full time until Edith Eddy could return to work. This type of cooperation in response to more commonplace disruptions leads to a further benefit:

2. *Reduced absenteeism and turnover*. One of the major causes of absenteeism is the need for more personal time than the 40-hour week allows—time for dental appointments, sick children, home repairs, etc. The job sharer has the increased time to deal with many of these responsibilities off the job; in addition, there is the flexibility of "trading off" with his/her partner during times of crisis or illness.

The reduction in turnover rates among job sharers appears to be attributable to the voluntary nature of the sharing. These are people who need or prefer permanent part-time employment. Their low turnover rate reflects, in part, the fact that their needs are being satisfied and that they are aware that such employment is difficult to find. If, however, one of the partners does leave, continuity can be assured by the remaining sharer working full-time until a new partner can be hired.

3. *Increased productivity*. Although there have been very few studies to date on job sharing, the two that are available ("Job Sharing in Municipal Government," ARLO, Stanford University, 1975 and "Part Time Social Workers in Public Welfare," *Catalyst* 1971) both document an increase in productivity. Interviews conducted by New Ways to Work of both job sharers and their supervisors confirm this increase. Reasons cited include shorter work hours, which lead to higher energy levels on the job, improved employee morale, and the opportunity for scheduling during peak hours, already mentioned.

4. *Affirmative action tool*. Since one result of job sharing is the freeing of job hours (if two current employees decide to share one position, a full-time job is opened), it follows that it also creates more opportunity for affirmative action hiring.

Working with someone else (sharing) also offers an opportunity for informal on the job training. One shared job was arranged because a chemist at a food processing plant wanted to return to school part-time to work towards an advanced degree. She arranged to share her job with a minority woman on the assembly line and trained the other woman as her technician.

For women in their child bearing years, the opportunity for permanent part-time employment often means the difference between their being able to continue in their professions. Retention of these women—especially those in middle management or non-traditional job categories—can be very important both in terms of employer recruiting and training costs, and in their overall affirmative action profile.

5. *New options for older workers*. A trend in recent years has been to encourage increasing numbers of workers to retire "early," i.e., at age 55 instead of 65. A number of factors, however, have diminished the attraction of early retirement: 1 the effect of inflation on the fixed income of the retiree, 2. the problem of coping with full-time leisure, and 3. the difficulty in returning to the work force once you are past 50 and unemployed.

Some period of transition between full-time work and retirement seems increasingly attractive to many people. Reduction in hours, while sharing a job, would provide opportunity for expanding community service work, returning to school, or cultivating other leisure activities for which there is no time while working 40 hours a week.

To date, job sharing has emerged as a working arrangement primarily in response to the needs of people who wish to work this way. What are the benefits that they perceive? The one cited most often is increased time for children; for others it is time for school, community service work or non-lucrative careers.

The improved quality of the permanent part-time work is another benefit noted by job sharers. As was mentioned earlier, it is often difficult to find responsible, professional part-time opportunities. Sharing a previously full-time position can be a means of creating part-time opportunities at levels where they did not formerly exist.

The most enthusiastic job sharers work as if they have an unwritten contract to cooperate extensively and to become interchangeable wherever possible. This provides opportunities for substituting for each other when personal emergencies arise, in addition to talking over problems and strategizing solutions. For many people this sharing appears to enrich their work environment; for others, however, it is not a desirable arrangement. Expectations about how much interaction will take place should be clarified before two people decide to work together or an advantage can turn into a disadvantage.

In several instances, job sharing has improved access to job categories. The student sharing a naturalist position, the woman who works with a man as part of an organizational development team, the Ph.D. biologist who was unable to find part-time work in her own field and is now working with an electrical engineer to plan new hospital facilities, are employed in positions where either their inadequate overall experience or the intense competition for openings would have made their hiring highly improbable without the mechanism of job sharing.

In addition to the older employees mentioned earlier, there are other special categories of workers for whom job sharing is an important new option. These include career oriented workers with young children and those with health limitations and handicaps. The Enablers Program at DeAnza College in Cupertino, California, is shared by a man and woman who are both confined to a wheelchair. Unable to work a full 40-hour week, they have, nevertheless, expanded the number of students in the program from 62 to 750 in one and one-half years.

Finally, through proration, the splitting or sharing of full-time positions is resulting in a better salary scale for these permanent part-time employees, as well as encouraging their inclusion in fringe benefit plans.

Disadvantages: Projected and Real

To the employer, having additional people on the payroll is often perceived as a disadvantage; a number have expressed the concern that "everyone will want to do it" if sharing a job is offered as an employee option. In reality, most people either do not want part-time work or cannot afford the reduction in salary.

There are also questions about doubling the problems of supervisors. Again, these worries do not seem to materialize in practice. In some instances, where a person who has held the job full-time has been allowed to share the position, supervisory time for the new employee has been less than normal. On the whole, job sharers appear to be task-oriented and feel responsibility towards the job as a whole as well as to each other.

Often expressed concerns about the commitment of sharers to their work have proved without foundation. To date, the reverse appears to be true. Most supervisors of job sharers are quick to state that "We're getting more mileage and they're certainly doing beyond their 50%."

Finding an equitable way of handling fringe benefits often poses the most complicated problem. It is important to extend benefits to permanent part-time employees in order to encourage their personal identification as full members of the company's community. In order that this not incur an inordinate expense, many employers have arranged to prorate benefits, i.e., the company pays half the cost for each half-time job sharer that it would pay for a full-time employee. The employees can then pay the additional amount for full coverage or not as their need demands. . . .

Since compensatory benefits, including health coverage, differ widely from organization to organization, these must be considered on an individual company basis. Although there is obviously some increase in cost involved in extending even prorated fringe benefit participation to job sharers, those employers who have pioneered in this area seem to feel that it can be minimized. Further, they believe it is offset by other factors such as reduced absenteeism, increased productivity and improved employee morale.

What do the employees perceive as disadvantages? The clearest, of course, is the reduction in salary. This factor alone will limit the number of people willing and able to work fewer hours. Whether or not an individual can afford to earn only a half-time salary, however, should be decided by the employee or job seeker out of their own particular set of circumstances. For many people, the increased flexibility is a compelling reason to seek a shared job, in spite of a lower income.

The necessary increase in communication time is another problem area for job sharers. How to construct a system that is efficient and does not bury the workers under a mountain of scrawled notes is a challenge. Overlap time, conversation logs, and information boxes have all been used. The amount of time necessary depends on the quantity and complexity of the information that needs to be exchanged. An example of the ingenuity that such problems inspire is the pair who worked out a method in which one partner taped the significant information from her day's work on her way home from the office and dropped the tape off at her partner's house. The partner did the same thing the next day. . . .

How Can an Interested Employer Implement Job Sharing in His Company?

The methods used to date have included:

1. Offer the possibility of job sharing to any full-time employees who would prefer to work part-time. An information meeting or a questionnaire sent to the employees outlining pros and cons of sharing has been a good technique to identify those who might be interested.

2. Allow new applicants to interview for regular full-time listings as a pair.

3. Advertise openings as being available for "one full-time or two part-time people."

4. Identify a number of openings as potentially shared positions.

Whether an organization tries a one-job-at-a-time approach or opens the option on a broader basis, there are three ingredients that are necessary for successful sharing.

1. Employee interest—someone who would really prefer to work full-time will not make a good job sharer.

2. Supervisor acceptance.

3. Institutional support in the sense that the job sharers be treated in the same way as other responsible, career oriented workers. . . .

In his . . . book, *The Future of the Workplace* (1976), Paul Dickson comments that "While few aspects of work seem as deadening as the way time is handled, few are so easy to challenge, experiment with and change. And few offer such easy potential for quick employee and employer rewards." There appear to be growing numbers of job sharers and their supervisors who agree with him.

» John L. Zalusky «

Alternative Work Schedules

» «

Not everyone is sanguine about the prospects of alternative work schedules. In this selection, John Zalusky, assistant director of research for the AFL-CIO, argues that it is unlikely that unions will endorse compressed work weeks or job-sharing, but that they remain open-minded on the issue of flextime. Basically, Zalusky believes that flexible work scheduling benefits employers more than workers, and that these alternatives do little or nothing to create jobs or increase wages. Zalusky thinks that unions are better off directing their efforts toward achieving their traditional goal: a thirty-five hour work week with no reduction in wages.

When we talk about The Compressed Work Week, we in the labor movement prefer to view it in a much broader context than has recently been the practice. The Compressed Work Week to us means shorter hours per day, per week, per year, and indeed a shorter working career at no loss in pay. But, most in the media have been talking about fewer days of work with little or no reduction in the hours worked each week.

Our view of less time on the job achieves three worthwhile objectives. First, it creates more jobs in a country that desperately needs to reduce high unemployment. Second, it creates more leisure which we believe almost everyone enjoys. And third, by maintaining wages and purchasing power, we maintain the demand for the products we produce. The idea of five seven-hour days (the thirty-five hour work week) or four eight-hour days (the four-day work week) is our objective and we are getting very close to it.

The forty-hour week for all intents and purposes is dead. We just haven't taken the time to say the last rites. Over ten million full-time workers have a scheduled work week of less than forty hours, and the number keeps growing year by year.

The recent United Auto Workers settlement added twelve additional

331

holidays by the end of the third year. The average union member already enjoys eleven holidays a year.

When we look at vacations and consider this as time off the job, and the growth of "Thirty and Out" retirement plans, we must realize that the American worker is again opting for more leisure. I think Bertrand Russell put it very well in his 1920 Treatise, *In Praise of Idleness:* "Modern methods of production have given us the possibility of ease and security for all; we have chosen instead to have over work for some and starvation for others. Hitherto, we have continued to be as energetic as we were before there were machines; and in this we have been foolish, but there is no reason for going on being foolish forever."

The American worker stopped being foolish years ago. Indeed, he was never being very foolish. During the 20's and 30's a full eight hours work per day at a living wage was his first priority. During World War II, with jobs plentiful and limits on wages, the movement for holidays and vacations caught on. By the end of World War II, the pattern of one week of vacation after one year of service and two weeks after five years was generally widely accepted.

Today, the industrial workers in steel can look forward to thirteen weeks sabbatical vacation once every five years, and six to ten weeks of vacation is now becoming available to certain long-term employees every year. The American has opted for more leisure.

However, to many outside the labor movement, the compressed work week and alternative work schedules mean something else: Four ten-hour days, or in one case three twelve-hour days. This isn't more leisure; it is merely the same amount of time on the job packaged differently for marketing. With these programs we have serious problems. The four-day, forty-hour week merely juggles the work schedule around. No additional time off the job is created; no new jobs are created; and there is, in fact, no reduction in the work week. Our opposition to this is not a slavish adherence to the eight-hour day concept, but a protection of the laws that see over it. We don't want to modify laws that presently protect the eight-hour day to benefit a few employers finding a possible increase in productivity to the injury of thousands of workers who would lose the protection of the eight-hour day. Further, to change these laws to accommodate the ten-hour day, four-day week would make the Department of Labor's enforcement of these worker standards virtually impossible.

Additionally, the ten-hour day does not fit into the social fabric of our country, unless the worker is childless and big on camping. Although workers have an additional day off to enjoy their leisure, in most cases their children or spouse do not enjoy the same free time. The worker, in fact, is away from home twelve to thirteen hours a day rather than ten or eleven. Social functions they may otherwise engage in such as church activities, scouting, PTA, and others are well under way before they finish their evening meal. The end result would be the phenomenon sociologists describe as social isolation. Social relationships are largely limited to those they work with.

Flexitime

Flexitime is a concept that presents far fewer problems. Although it creates no new jobs or leisure time, and may even decrease take-home pay, Flexitime allows workers an expanded degree of control over their own working lives heretofore enjoyed by executives and professionals.

However, we have certain concerns and conditions that we must associate with these programs. First, the workers, through their union, must be actively involved in its development and implementation. In most cases the employer has a legal obligation to do this, but equally important, it is essential to the success of the program.

Great care must be taken with the treatment of groups that cannot enjoy the benefits of Flexitime. Workers on rigid work schedules or tight manning requirements are often excluded from the Flexitime program. They may even want more money because their relative work conditions have changed—something like a shift premium. Any productivity gains, lower absenteeism or turnover the employer may enjoy could well be offset by feelings of alienation in the group that is unable to have Flexitime.

When flexible working time was enjoyed by the higher levels of the hierarchy and the professionals, the presumption was that they were trusted to not only put in an eight-hour day but, in fact, it was assumed they worked much more. However, when employers consider Flexitime for the nonexempt workers, one of their first reactions is installation of time clocks. The underlying presumption is that these workers cannot be trusted. In sort, when Flexitime is being made available to workers, don't give the benefit with one hand and spoil it with the other.

No union is going to welcome Flexitime without a good hard look at the concept and all of its ramifications. There will be concerns about the employer attempting to induce split shifts, reduce overtime opportunities and earnings, and about the impact of Flexitime on shift differentials. There will also be a need for contract language to ensure that the Flexitime schedule is at the employee's option rather than his immediate supervisor's need. In addition, the union will also want some means of dealing with the conflicting rights of workers to exercise the Flexitime option, and some assurance that core time will be fixed.

It's somewhat out of character for me, but I am concerned for front-line supervisors when Flexitime is used. One thing I have noticed in literature on Flexitime is that personnel departments and higher levels of management generally warmly endorse Flexitime and that many workers enjoy it. But, I also notice a lack of comment on the attitudes of first-line supervisors. It would seem to me that they absorb the scheduling problems associated with these systems, which is clearly added work and compounds the problems of work flow. There are also bound to be added pressures from upstairs and from workers as to who gets what schedule. Additionally, these exempt employees probably feel as though they have to be on the job when the first worker appears and until the last leaves. If these first-line supervisors are feeling put upon by this groovy new concept, then all the subordinates will probably pay a part of the price.

In summary, I think most unions will take a hard look at Flexitime, but with interest. It is going to be a critical analysis, and they certainly are not going to endorse it until they are confident that it is in the best interest of their membership. This will involve some hard bargaining. Additionally, I cannot imagine a union endorsing Flexitime to the extent that it has an adverse effect on the eight-hour day concept as it presently exists in most contracts or as a matter of statute. The reasons are essentially the same as I described earlier. That is, labor is not going to weaken statutes that protect many workers for the benefit of relatively few, or weaken the statutes to the point where they become unenforceable. Thus, where we have contractual provisions or statutes that provide for an eight-hour day, we will be talking about Flexitime in terms of a floating day rather than a flexible work week.

Job Sharing

Job Sharing is the third concept, and another hard piece of bread in this dry sandwich of alternate work schedules. In essence, Job Sharing involves the elimination of a full-time job opportunity to create two part-time jobs. The social purpose is to create jobs for those who are not now interested in full-time employment. I find this particularly distasteful when we have approximately ten million people out of work looking for full-time positions. The only one who really seems to benefit from Job Sharing is the employer looking for workers as cheaply as he can get them regardless of the needs of the community. If we had a labor shortage, the use of Job Sharing would make a lot more sense.

I know there are those who say that this allows women who are dissatisfied with staying at home an opportunity to work, but on the other hand there are over three million women who are actively seeking full-time employment who cannot afford to support their families on a part-time job. It is a perversion to try to clothe this concept with a wrapping of equal employment opportunity. I don't believe the three million women who are looking for work in any substantial numbers want part-time jobs. I am confident that it was not the intent of the equal employment opportunity guidelines that the employer meet his obligations through the part-time employment of women and other minority groups.

Disadvantaged workers who are looking for full-time employment will become second-class citizens if the only employment they can find is part-time work with reduced fringe benefits and lesser promotional opportunities. The only beneficiary behind Work Sharing in an economy at far less than full employment is the employer.

Because of the structure of social security taxes, people hired into these categories as job sharers must come in at a wage yielding less than a combined income of $16,000 per year. Thus, we are not really talking about the lawyer who is bored with raising children at home. To hire people in income brackets above a combined value of $16,000 per year adds a 6 percent cost to the employer over a full-time employee. Thus, we are really talking about the lower level jobs.

There are employer cost savings due to the probable higher turnover and lower pension costs and other seniority-related benefits, such as vacation. Even when these benefits are prorated, cost savings to the employer will still exist.

In short, I can't imagine a union supporting the concept of eliminating full-time job opportunities to create part-time employment. . . .

Don't misunderstand me, labor unions and their members will welcome the opportunity to look at almost any alternate work schedule proposal. Flexitime appears to be the most promising concept we have dealt with so far. The ten-hour, four-day, forty-hour week offers very little. Job Sharing offers even less. What we are looking for is the national recognition of the demise of the forty-hour work week. The American worker today is not the foolish consumer of productivity that Russell worried about in the 1920's. Today's workers have been and are allocating more of their increased productivity to leisure time. Leisure time really humanizes the workplace. Leisure time is not equal to idleness—it is free time to do with as they want. More free time also allows others who are looking for decent jobs an opportunity to share in a life of reasonable quality and freedom.

11

»«

THE
QUALITY
OF WORK LIFE

»«

Betty Medsger

» Richard E. Walton «

Teaching an Old Dog Food New Tricks

» «

In 1971, General Foods opened a Gaines dog food plant in Topeka, Kansas, which was designed to overcome the demeaning and unchallenging nature of most blue-collar work (as described in Chapters 2 and 3). To build the sense of community that blue-collar workers seek, all workers at the new plant were organized into self-managing teams, and the plant was designed to encourage informal gatherings of team members during working hours. Activities usually performed by separate units—maintenance, quality control, industrial engineering, and personnel—were the responsibility of each team. There were no foremen, only elected team leaders. At the beginning, the workers experienced high levels of participation in decision making, freedom of communication, a strong sense of dignity, and high self-esteem. Moreover, the plant was highly productive and profitable. Harvard Business School professor Richard Walton describes how these outcomes were achieved—and, sadly, how management then let this promising beginning fritter away.

This . . . article reports in detail on a pioneering manufacturing plant which employs an innovative and potentially influential new work structure. Important as this plant's success is for the people who work in it and manage it, the experience is equally important as an illustration of what is taking place in a small but increasing number of work organizations in the United States.

The plant produces pet foods for General Foods and is located in Topeka, Kansas. Its seven-year history is part of a quiet transformation which may alter the standard practices in design, management, and operation of not only factories, but all kinds of work places. This report deals with successes and failures, enthusiasm and frustration, fantasy and reality. It is not the story of an ideal situation; it is the story of men and an idea. . . .

General Foods' radically innovative dry dog food plant in Topeka was conceived in 1968 and started up in January 1971. In designing the new plant, the original project team, led by GF managers Lyman Ketchum and Ed Dulworth, was determined to avoid the negative worker attitudes in the existing pet food facilities in Illinois. They were inspired by the possibility of engaging unusual human involvement in the new plant.

Self-managing teams assumed responsibility for large segments of the production process. The teams were composed of from seven to 14 members, large enough to embrace a set of interrelated tasks and small enough to permit face-to-face meetings for making decisions and for coordination. Activities usually performed by separate units—maintenance, quality control, custodianship, industrial engineering, and personnel—were built into the responsibilities of each team. For example, team members screened job applicants for replacements on their own team.

An attempt was made to design every set of team tasks to include both manual skills and mental functions such as diagnosing mechanical problems and planning. The aim was to make all sets of team tasks equally challenging, although each set would require unique demands.

Consistent with this aim was a *single job classification* for all operators. Pay increases depended on the mastery of an increasing number of jobs. Since there were no limits on how many members of a team could qualify for higher pay brackets, employees were encouraged to teach each other their skills.

In lieu of the "foreman," a "team leader" position was created. Operators were provided with the data and guidelines that enabled them to make production decisions ordinarily made by higher level supervisors. The team leader had the responsibility for facilitating the team's decision making. As for plant rules, management refrained from specifying any in advance. Rules evolved over time from collective experience.

The technology and architecture were designed to facilitate rather than discourage informal gatherings of team members during working hours. Status symbols were minimized—for example, a single entrance leads into both the administrative office and the plant.

The new work system achieved highly positive results in both human and economic terms. A study by Robert Schrank of the Ford Foundation conducted in 1973 found high levels of worker participation in decisions, freedom to communicate, expressions of warmth amongst the workers, a minimum of status distinction, a strong sense of human dignity, commitment to the job, and individual self-esteem. Schrank gave less credit for this to certain new design features than I do, arguing, for example, that the self-managing team structure, the challenging job contrast, and the skill-based pay system were much less important than the fact that employees had the freedom to move around and socialize during working hours.

Another study of the plant was conducted in June 1974. It used the

338

survey methodology of the University of Michigan and confirmed the Topeka work force's positive attitudes. According to Edward Lawler, of the Institute for Social Research, "Our data . . . show high levels of satisfaction and involvement in all parts of the organization. In fact they show the highest levels we have found in any organization we have sampled. I specifically compared it with other small organizations and still found it superior."

Furthermore, there is no doubt about the economic superiority of the plant. Recent studies by corporate analysts outside Topeka have indicated that the savings attributable to the work innovations in the dog food plant were in the neighborhood of a million dollars annually, a significant figure in a plant with about 100 personnel and involving a capital investment in the range of $10–15 million. . . .

In order to understand some of the innovations at Topeka, here is a chronology of key developments.

Phase I (1968–1970)—Pre-Start Up

Long before start up, team leaders were hired and included in the planning, training, and team building. Lead time was allowed for new concepts to be articulated, debated, and translated into work procedures and structures. Managers had time to develop insights into human behavior and to coalesce as a group. Team leaders screened operators, drawing 63 from more than 600 applicants to form a relatively talented and receptive work force.

Certain events helped establish the new work culture. The screening process used to select team leaders included role playing and group discussion—providing a unique, involving, and even anxiety-provoking initiation. According to one observer, this initial experience created a sense of hardiness, uniqueness, and elitism. The team leaders in turn, utilized similar methods in screening workers, thereby transmitting these same feelings to the work force.

While healthy skepticism about the project existed within the new work force, these initial experiences created a readiness to give the innovations a fair trial.

Phase II (1971)—Technical and Social Start Up

The first year of operation was marked by a variety of minor "tests" of the system; and by the development of potent group phenomena. . . .

After a number of weeks, the operators felt they were ready for their first pay increase, based on mastery of their first job. Management, however, did not anticipate this event. Their initial disagreement both reinforced the doubt of the skeptics and weakened the confidence of the believers. When management ultimately agreed to review the qualifications of operators for increases, they also reaffirmed the responsiveness of the system. . . .

Developments within each of the six work teams largely determined how

339

a person viewed the work system. At times team leaders provided too much structure, seeming to contradict the stated philosophy. At other times, they provided too little structure and seemed to dramatize the impracticality of worker participation. Nevertheless, sooner or later the groups coalesced. They became the most potent factor in forming and enforcing the system's norms about cooperation, openness, involvement, and responsibility.

In brief, 1971 was a period of building technical and social skills and of testing the credibility of the system. Those who were initially receptive had their commitment strengthened and, except for a small minority, many of those who were negative or skeptical decided to "buy in."

Phase III (1972)—Pushing the Technology

In 1972, the *social capital* (skills, knowledge, attitudes, and relationships) was put to work in a demanding way. Demand for production volume, resisted during 1971, now had to be met.

The maximum production effort had several important side-effects: first, quality sometimes suffered, undermining one source of pride. Second, with the plant now "humming" there was less immediate need for group problem-solving and less opportunity for meetings. This reduced the amount of ongoing social maintenance within groups. Third, teams often yielded to the temptation to improve their own performance at the expense of the next shift.

A management change at a higher level also troubled Topeka managers. The man who had initiated the innovations and who had held an umbrella over the fledgling system during the past year, was replaced by a person who was seen as philosophically unsympathetic to Topeka. . . .

Still, the plant was performing well, reaching capacity output with about 70 people (compared with the 110 originally estimated on the basis of standard industrial engineering principles). Substantial savings from lower overhead, fewer quality rejects, and other factors were attributed to the innovative human organization. Participants were proud.

The plant had become perhaps the most publicized U.S. example of a solution to what the media called the "blue-collar blues." . . .

Phase IV (1973)—Turmoil, Decline, and Reversal

During my visit in October 1973, I found a consensus that a trough had been reached during the summer in various indexes of the system's health. This trough was followed by a steady improvement during the fall.

During the first half of 1973, the emphasis on production volume continued, along with long hours, few team meetings, and inter-shift rivalry. The negative effects were cumulative, depleting the social capital to a point that started to weaken basic commitments. Without meetings, trust and openness were declining.

The prolonged push for maximum production also deferred the movement of workers from one team to another, a movement which could occur after an operator had earned "team rate." This delay in opportunity to learn jobs on other teams postponed the date at which an employee could earn "plant rate." The delay tended to undermine commitment.

When interteam movement was finally okayed, a large number of transfers occurred between packaging and processing. At about the same time, 13 team members and two team leaders chose to form the nucleus for a newly-constructed canned food plant. The wholesale movement alleviated some problems but created others. The original teams often had identified closely with their team leaders, whose personal styles varied widely. Now team leaders were faced with new teams and vice versa. . . .

The absence of team meetings now had a dramatically negative effect. Members needed to cooperate hourly in their tasks and weekly in learning exchanges, but had not developed the necessary mutual confidence. Moreover, the recently-hired employees were not learning about their rights and obligations in the system, and many were not developing commitment during the critical first few months.

Also, the new canned food plant helped generate negativism in the dry food plant. Many members felt they had been "deserted" by those who opted to go to a "more advanced rival." . . .

By summer of 1973, the site manager, previously preoccupied with his strained relations in the corporation, started attending to the issues that troubled the Topeka organization. People became aware that they had neglected the acculturation of new members and the development of the newly-formed teams; they resolved to rebuild the social capital. Openness, trust, and commitment were definitely trending up in the fall of 1973. . . .

Notwithstanding the restored commitment and other favorable developments reported above, I detected some weaknesses during my visit in October, 1973.

First, the system had not developed problem-solving mechanisms for the whole plant that were nearly as effective as those in the face-to-face teams.

Second, although there was unusual frankness, there was also concern whether the openness and objectivity were adequate given the stringent requirements of the plant design. For the system to work, an individual had to be candid in contributing to problem solving, conscientious in judging an idea on its merits, not its source, and objective in evaluating the qualifications of peers for higher pay rates. . . .

There is no quantifiable, stable, automatic basis for a person's security, such as seniority. One worker explained that the tenuous basis of his security makes him continuously concerned about his relations with many people who could help or hurt him in the future. Another worker said, "The match in the gasoline is pay!", explaining that decisions about the worth and pay of members are starkly real.

The result was a moderate tendency to ease up on standards, e.g.,

341

shrinking from hard, exacting evaluation of a worker's mastery of all tasks in the plant before awarding him the plant rate. Thus, reciprocation tended toward each giving the other the benefit of the doubt.

More impressive to me than the moderate gap between ideal and actual behavior were the high ideals themselves. The system had idealized influence based on *expertise* (information and skills), rather than either *positional power* (based on formal authority, rules and procedures) or *political power* (e.g., cliques). The managers and workers felt guilty whenever they did not live up to the ideals of openness and objectivity. I found myself wondering at the time: were these people expecting too much of themselves?

Third, among the team leaders there was a striking gap between ideals of high mutual support and trust and their actual behavior. Also, team leaders had a norm of self-sacrifice—most would concern themselves with improving work life for team members but not seek needed changes in their own situations. . . .

Phase V (1974–1976)—Steady State with Traces of Erosion

When I returned in November, 1976, after three years, a number of elements in the positive work culture had declined. Not a steep decline, rather a moderate erosion.

By general agreement it was still a very productive plant and a superior place to work, but the "quality of work life" had slipped. And while the majority still supported—by their own behavior—the unique strengths of the "Topeka work system," an increasing minority did not. Slippage occurred across a broad front of attributes: openness and candor; helping among team members; identification with plant management; confidence in General Foods; perceived upward influence; effective leadership within teams; and cooperation between shifts. In addition, there continued to be serious doubt about the ability of teams to make objective judgments about members' qualifications for pay increases.

 Two major changes since 1973 had occurred: team members now accepted the fact-of-life of subjectivity and other imperfections, and the clique behavior was more pronounced. . . .

Three factors had had depressing effects on the dry plant work system during this period.

First, during 1973–1976, three of the four managers most responsible for the Topeka system had left General Foods and the fourth had moved from the dry food plant to the can plant. . . .

Second . . . management deferred the introduction of many aspects of the new work structure from the dry plant [into the neighboring can plant]. This was interpreted by dry plant members as weakened management commitment to the new philosophy.

Third, there were no new challenges of significance in the dry plant during 1973–76. . . . So some complacency developed.

These three factors help explain the negative drift of the work culture.

However, more significant for me was the absence of potent corrective devices, of a capacity for self-renewal.

As noted earlier, the work system has not dealt effectively with plant-wide issues. Committees that cut across units and levels of the plant have treated a few specific issues, but seldom, if ever, have they gained the full confidence of the employees. Moreover, there have been no regular plant-wide forums in which issues can be discussed.

In the absence of a plant-wide mechanism to which management could respond, management would have had to take the initiative to assess the health of the system, to diagnose problems, to identify opportunities, to review the adequacy of existing procedures and roles, to set goals for organization development, to propose innovative solutions. They have done little of this since 1973 except in relation to a proposed bonus scheme.

Equally important, though, the plant community sometimes lost its appreciation of the idea that the work system would need to evolve continually. Such evolution could only be derived from experience, with a widely-shared responsibility for promoting this evolution. Within the work force there is a widely shared and deeply felt responsibility to *protect*, to preserve the work system. While this is an enormous asset, it could be an even greater asset if the commitment were less defensively oriented and initiatives were taken. . . .

Despite the slippage, the very positive culture has proven to be extremely robust. . . .

The following explanations of the plant's robustness are offered tentatively and without any pretense of being exhaustive.

• First, the original design concepts have proven sound in this situation. None have been abandoned, although, of course, some design ideals have been achieved only in relative terms.

• Second, the implementation of the pre-start up and the start up stages was handled especially skillfully, a judgment I can now make after observing the start ups of several similar work innovations.

• Third, the system was enduring because the underlying philosophy itself was more important than personalities. Although each manager in the dry plant was respected, none aspired to become a charismatic leader. The commitment to certain philosophical principles was reinforced by the publicity given the "Topeka system." I found that many workers wanted to live up to their external image.

• Fourth, pay clearly has been a pivotal element of the work system. One important factor is that it pays for skills acquired and there are no quotas to limit an individual's advancement. . . .

The Topeka organization has produced gains in the quality of work life and productivity and has remained viable over an extended period.

» Robert H. Guest «

Quality of Work Life— Learning from Tarrytown

» «

In 1970, the General Motors plant at Tarrytown, New York, suffered from so much labor unrest and so little productivity that the corporation considered closing the plant permanently. At times, there were as many as 2,000 labor grievances on file, and a 7 percent daily rate of absenteeism was the norm. The young workers in the plant questioned the authority of management and refused to cooperate in efforts to increase productivity. Then, the company and the union had a bright idea: why not cooperate to accomplish two ends simultaneously, high productivity and a high quality of working life? It took time to overcome the workers' mistrust of management, but a process of involving workers in the decisions affecting their work gradually changed their attitudes. Today, worker participation is a way of life for more than 3,000 workers at Tarrytown, according to Dartmouth business professor Robert Guest. Productivity is up, absenteeism is in the 2 to 3 percent range, and in 1978 only thirty-two grievances were on the docket.

This is the story of the General Motors car assembly plant at Tarrytown, New York. In 1970, the plant was known as having one of the poorest labor relations and production records in GM. In seven years, the plant turned around to become one of the company's better run sites.

Born out of frustration and desperation, but with a mutual commitment by management and the union to change old ways of dealing with the workers on the shop floor, a quality of work life (QWL) program developed at Tarrytown. "Quality of work life" is a generic phrase that covers a person's feelings about every dimension of work including economic rewards and benefits, security, working conditions, organizational and interpersonal relationships, and its intrinsic meaning in a person's life.

For the moment, I will define QWL more specifically as a *process* by which an organization attempts to unlock the creative potential of its

344

people by involving them in decisions affecting their work lives. A distinguishing characteristic of the process is that its goals are not simply extrinsic, focusing on the improvement of productivity and efficiency per se; they are also intrinsic, regarding what the worker sees as self-fulfilling and self-enhancing ends in themselves.

In recent years, the QWL movement has generated wide-scale interest. . . . Scores of industrial enterprises throughout the United States are conducting experiments, usually on a small scale . . .

So what is special about the Tarrytown story? First, it has the earmarks of success. Second, it illustrates some underlying principles of successful organizational change that can be applied in a variety of work environments. Third, although a number of promising experiments are going on in many General Motors plants and in other companies, this QWL program has involved more human beings—more than 3,800—than any other I know of. Finally, and this is speculative, I believe that Tarrytown represents in microcosm the beginnings of what may become commonplace in the future—a new collaborative approach on the part of management, unions, and workers to improve the quality of life at work in its broadest sense.

Tarrytown—The Bad Old Days

In the late 1960s and early 1970s, the Tarrytown plant suffered from much absenteeism and labor turnover. Operating costs were high. Frustration, fear, and mistrust characterized the relationship between management and labor. At certain times, as many as 2,000 labor grievances were on the docket. . . .

Workers were mad at everyone. They disliked the job itself and the inexorable movement of the high-speed line—56 cars per hour, a minute and a half per operation per defined space. One worker remembers it well, "Finish one job, and you always had another stare you in the face." Conditions were dirty, crowded, and often noisy. Employees saw their foremen as insensitive dictators, whose operating principle was "If you can't do the job like I tell you, get out."

Warnings, disciplinary layoffs, and firings were commonplace. . . .

In the words of both union and management representatives, during this period "Tarrytown was a mess."

Beginnings of Change   What turned Tarrytown around? How did it start? Who started it and why?

Because of the high labor turnover, the plant was hiring a large number of young people. The late 1960s was the time of the youth counterculture revolution. It was a time when respect for authority was being questioned. According to the plant manager, "It was during this time that the young people in the plant were demanding some kind of change. . . ."

In April 1971, Tarrytown faced a serious threat. The plant manager saw the need for change, and also an opportunity. He approached some of the key union officers who, though traditionally suspicious of management overtures, listened to him. . . .

The plant manager suggested that if the union was willing to do its part, he would put pressure on his own management people to change their ways. . . .

The company decided to stop assembling trucks at Tarrytown and to shuffle the entire layout around. Two departments, Hard Trim and Soft Trim, were to be moved to a renovated area of the former truck line. . . .

Two of the production supervisors in Hard Trim, sensing that top plant management was looking for new approaches, asked a question that was to have a profound effect on events to follow: "Why not ask the workers themselves to get involved in the move? They are experts in their own right. They know as much about trim operations as anyone else."

The consensus of the Hard Trim management group was that they would involve the workers. The Soft Trim Department followed suit. The union was brought in on the planning and told that management wanted to ask the workers' advice. Old timers in the union report "wondering about management's motives. . . ." Many supervisors in other departments also doubted the wisdom of fully disclosing the plans.

Nevertheless, the supervisors of the two trim departments insisted not only that plans *not* be hidden from the workers but also that the latter would have a say in the setup of jobs. Charts and diagrams of the facilities, conveyors, benches, and materials storage areas were drawn up for the workers to look at. Lists were made of the work stations and the personnel to man them. The supervisors were impressed by the outpouring of ideas: "We found they did know a lot about their own operations. They made hundreds of suggestions and we adopted many of them."

Here was a new concept. The training director observes, "Although it affected only one area of the plant, this was the first time management was communicating with the union and the workers on a challenge for solving *future* problems and not the usual situation of doing something, waiting for a reaction, then putting out the fires later." . . .

Moving the two departments was carried out successfully with remarkably few grievances. The plant easily made its production schedule deadlines. The next year saw the involvement of employees in the complete rearrangement of another major area of the plant, the Chassis Department. The following year a new car model was introduced at Tarrytown.

Labor-Management Agreement   In 1972, Irving Bluestone, the vice president for the General Motors Department of the United Automobile Workers Union (UAW), made what many consider to be the kick-off speech for the future of the quality of work life movement. Repeated later in different forms, he declared:

"Traditionally management has called upon labor to cooperate in increasing productivity and improving the quality of the product. My view of the other side of the coin is more appropriate; namely, that management should cooperate with the worker to find ways to enhance the dignity of labor and to tap the creative resources in each human being in developing a more satisfying work life, with emphasis on worker participation in the decision-making process."

In 1973, the UAW and GM negotiated a national agreement. In the contract was a brief "letter of agreement" signed by Bluestone and George Morris, head of industrial relations for GM. Both parties committed themselves to establishing formal mechanisms, at least at top levels, for exploring new ways of dealing with the quality of work life. *This was the first time QWL was explicitly addressed in any major U.S. labor-management contract.* . . .

Local issues and grievances, however, faced both parties. . . .

The union president's observation about that period is extremely significant in explaining the process of change that followed:

"We as a union knew that our primary job was to protect the worker and improve his economic life. But times had changed and we began to realize we had a broader obligation, which was to help the workers become more involved in decisions affecting their own jobs, to get their ideas, and to help them to improve the whole quality of life at work beyond the paycheck." . . .

A new atmosphere of trust between the union and the plant manager was beginning to emerge. Local negotiations were settled without a strike.

I'm not interested in classes. . . . Far be it from me to foster inferiority complexes among the workers by trying to make them think they belong to some special class. That has happened in Europe but it hasn't happened here yet.
—John L. Lewis

There was at least a spark of hope that the Tarrytown mess could be cleaned up. Thus the informal efforts at Tarrytown to improve union-management relations and to seek greater involvement of workers in problem solving became "legitimatized" through the national agreement and top level support. Other plants would follow.

The Testing Period

In April 1974, a professional consultant was brought in to involve supervisors and workers in joint training programs for problem solving. Management paid his fees. He talked at length with most of the union officers and committeemen, who report that "we were skeptical at first but we came to trust him. We realized that if we were going to break through the communications barrier on a large scale, we needed a third party." . . .

Management and the union each selected a coordinator to work with the consultant and with the supervisors, the union, and the workers. The consultant, with the union and the management coordinators, proposed a series of problem-solving training sessions to be held on Saturdays, for eight hours each day. . . .

Top management was very impressed by the ideas being generated from the sessions and by the cooperation from the union. The regular repairmen were especially helpful. Not long after the program began, the workers began developing solutions to problems of water leaks, glass breakage, and molding damage.

In November 1974, at the height of the OPEC oil crisis, disaster struck. General Motors shut down Tarrytown's second shift, and laid off half the work force—2,000 workers. . . .

However, the newly developing trust between management and the union had its effects. As the union president puts it, "Everyone got a decent transfer and there were surprisingly few grievances. We didn't get behind. We didn't have to catch up on a huge backlog." . . .

In spite of the disruption of plant operations, the quality of work life team, the plant manager, and the union officials were determined not to give up. . . .

At this time everyone agreed that if this program were to be expanded on a larger scale, it would require more careful planning. In 1975, a policy group made up of the plant manager, the production manager, the personnel manager, the union's top officers, and the two QWL coordinators was formed. . . .

Brave New World

Early [in] 1977, Tarrytown made the "big commitment." The QWL effort was to be launched on a plant-wide scale involving approximately 3,800 workers and supervisors. Charles Katko, vice president for the division and UAW's top official, Irving Bluestone, gave strong signals of support. . . .

The policy committee and the quality of work life coordinators went to work. In the spring of 1977, all the top staff personnel, department heads, and production superintendents went through a series of orientation sessions with the coordinators. By June, all middle managers and first-line supervisors (general foreman and foremen) were involved. Thus by the summer of 1977 more than 300 members of Tarrytown management knew about the QWL approach and about the plans for including 3,500 hourly employees. All union committeemen also went through the orientation sessions.

Also, during mid-1977, plans were under way to select and train those people who would eventually conduct the training sessions for the hourly employees. More than 250 workers expressed an interest in becoming trainers. After careful screening and interviewing, 11 were chosen. A similar process was carried out for supervisors, 11 of whom were subsequently selected as trainers, mostly from among foremen.

The two coordinators brought the 22 designated trainers together and exposed them to a variety of materials they would use in the training itself. The trainers conducted mock practice sessions which were videotaped so they could discuss their performance. The trainers also shared ideas on how to present information to the workers and on how to get workers to open up with their own ideas for changing their work environment. The latter is at the heart of the quality of work life concept.

The trainers themselves found excitement and challenge in the experience. People from the shop floor worked side by side with members of supervision as equals. . . .

Plant-wide Program   On September 13, 1977 the program was launched. Each week, 25 different workers (or 50 in all from both shifts) reported to the training rooms on Tuesdays, Wednesdays, and Thursdays, for nine hours a day. Those taking the sessions had to be replaced at their work stations by substitutes. Given an average hourly wage rate of more than $7 per attendee and per replacement (for over 3,000 persons), one can begin to get an idea of the magnitude of the costs. Also, for the extra hour above eight hours, the trainees were paid overtime wages.

What was the substance of the sessions themselves? The trainee's time was allocated to learning three things: first, about the concept of QWL; second, about the plant and the functions of management and the union; third, about problem-solving skills important in effective involvement. . . .

Continuing Effort   The program continued through 1978, and by mid-December more than 3,300 workers had taken part.

When all the employees had completed their sessions, the union and management immediately agreed to keep the system on a continuing basis. . . .

Other regular activities to keep management and the union informed about new developments parallel the training sessions. Currently, following the plant manager's regular staff meetings, the personnel director passes on critical information to the shop committee. The safety director meets weekly with each zone committeeman. Top union officials have monthly "rap sessions" with top management staff to discuss future developments, facility alterations, schedule changes, model changes, and other matters requiring advance planning. The chairman of Local 664 and his zone committeemen check in with the personnel director each morning at 7:00 A.M. and go over current or anticipated problems.

After the Dust Settles

What are the measurable results of quality of work life at Tarrytown? Neither the managers nor union representatives want to say much. They argue that to focus on production records or grievance counts "gets to be a numbers game" and is contrary to the original purpose or philosophy of the quality of work life efforts. After all, in launching the program, the

349

Tarrytown plant made no firm promises of "bottom line" results to division executives or anyone else. *Getting the process of worker involvement going was a primary goal with its own intrinsic rewards. The organizational benefits followed.*

There are, however, some substantial results from the $1.6 million QWL program. The production manager says, for example, "From a strictly production point of view—efficiency and costs—this entire experience has been absolutely positive, and we can't begin to measure the savings that have taken place because of the hundreds of small problems that were solved on the shop floor before they accumulated into big problems."

Although not confirmed by management, the union claims that Tarrytown went from one of the poorest plants in its quality performance (inspection counts or dealer complaints) to one of the best among the 18 plants in the division. It reports that absenteeism went from 7¼% to between 2% and 3%. In December 1978, at the end of the training sessions, there were only 32 grievances on the docket. Seven years earlier there had been upward of 2,000 grievances filed. Such substantial changes can hardly be explained by chance. . . .

By May 1979 the Tarrytown plant, with the production of a radically new line of cars, had come through one of the most difficult times in its history. Considering all the complex technical difficulties, the changeover was successful. Production was up to projected line speed. The relationship among management, union, and the workers remained positive in spite of unusual stress conditions generated by such a change.

As the production manager puts it, "Under these conditions, we used to fight the union, the worker, and the car itself. Now we've all joined together to fight the car." Not only were the hourly employees substantially involved in working out thousands of "bugs" in the operations, but plans were already under way to start up QWL orientation sessions with more than 400 new workers hired to meet increased production requirements.

Tarrytown, in short, has proved to itself at least that QWL works.

Learning from Tarrytown

. . . Bringing about change—any kind of change—is extraordinarily difficult in our modern organizations. It is challenge enough to introduce new machines, computers, management information systems, new organizational structures, and all the bureaucratic paraphernalia required to support our complex production systems. It is even more difficult to organize and stimulate people to accept innovations directed at greater efficiency. Perhaps most difficult of all, as one looks at the quality of work life process and Tarrytown as an example, is for managers, union officials, and even workers themselves to adjust to the idea that certain kinds of changes should be directed toward making life at work more meaningful and not necessarily toward some immediate objective measures of results. . . .

In changing the way Americans work, we have, as the chairman of Local 664 said, "barely scratched the surface." What went on at Tarrytown was only a beginning. The intrinsic nature of repetitive conveyor-paced jobs has not substantially changed . . . .

The Tarrytown story may, however, reflect something important about quality of work life efforts springing up in many other places in the United States. Studies are showing that workers in our large, rationalized industries and businesses are seeking more control over and involvement in the forces affecting their work lives. Due in part to the rising levels of education, changing aspirations, and shifts in values, especially among young people, I believe we are witnessing a quiet revolution in what people expect from work, an expectation that goes beyond the economic and job security issues that led to labor unrest in an earlier day.

In parts of Europe, the response to this quiet revolution is manifest in broad-scale political efforts on the part of labor and government to gain greater control over the management of the enterprise itself. In the United States, the response is different. Workers or their unions have given no indications that they wish to take over basic management prerogatives. As the Tarrytown story illustrates, what they want is more pragmatic, more immediate, more localized—but no less important.

The challenge to those in positions of power is to become aware of the quiet revolution at the workplace and to find the means to respond intelligently to these forces for change. What management did at Tarrytown is but one example of the beginnings of an intelligent response.

Quality of Work Life 27 Years Ago!

If a man spends at least a third of his life in direct contact with a mass production environment, why shouldn't we consider as important (to him and to society) the hours of living time he spends inside the factory—as important and valuable, for example, as the product he produces which is consumed outside the factory? We talk of a high standard of living, but frequently mean a high standard of consumption. Man consumes in his leisure, but fulfills himself not only in his leisure but in his work. Is our mass production work environment making such fulfillment impossible?

We suggest that the sense of becoming *de*-personalized, of becoming anonymous as against remaining one's self, is for those who feel it a psychologically more disturbing result of the work environment than either the boredom or tension that arise from repetitive or mechanically paced work.

If it were recognized by both groups (management and labor) that they had much of a mutual interest to tell each other about the assembly of automobiles and about Plant X as a production team, something of great value to human relations might accrue.

Excerpts from Charles R. Walker and Robert H. Guest, *The Man on the Assembly Line* (Cambridge: Harvard University Press, 1952, republished by Arno Press, Inc., New York, 1979).

» Robert Schrank «

How to Relieve Worker Boredom

» «

Robert Schrank has worked as a mechanic and machinist in furniture, printing, and auto-assembly factories. He has been a union organizer, a corporate manager, a government bureaucrat, and, in his late fifties, a doctoral student in sociology. He currently works for the Ford Foundation. Schrank is a skeptic about the quality of work life projects at Topeka and Tarrytown, described in the preceding selections. He argues that the changes that managers made were basically cosmetic—no participation or job enrichment programs can change the fact that blue-collar factory work is basically dull and unchallenging. The best way to increase job satisfaction, according to Schrank, is to give blue-collar workers the same privilieges that white-collar workers currently enjoy: more freedom to do things unrelated to their tasks, such as chatting on the telephone or "schmoozing" with co-workers. Such measures, Schrank believes, would make assembly-line workers a lot happier, even if their tasks remained the same.

Forty years of work in factories and offices have convinced me that many of the problems that industrial psychologists are now trying to alleviate are simply inherent in mass production. I am skeptical of people who tell factory workers their jobs can become creative, autonomous, challenging, and self-actualizing.

The modern production line requires an operation that is predesigned, preengineered, and preplanned to the smallest detail. Schedules and specifications must be strictly adhered to. Given these necessary requirements, how much opportunity can there be for the worker to think for himself or make decisions? There may be some opportunities for creativity and self-actualization in crap games and washroom graffiti, but a production-line worker simply cannot decide on his own that the engine coming down the line should have four cylinders instead of eight, or that a car body should be red instead of blue.

I've been a machinist, assembly-line worker, union organizer, and shop steward; in recent years, my own research and observation have kept me in close touch with so-called job-enrichment and quality-of-work programs. In my visits to factories and in talks with workers, I have learned that most of them tend to view programs imposed from above to improve efficiency with great suspicion.

Yet they often accept these attempts as well meaning. In some cases, they are even grateful for small breaks in their routine. They also consider it an expression of interest in them by their supervisors.

I believe that most factory workers understand quite well—certainly better than industrial psychologists—the limitations of life on the assembly line. They are aware of both the magic and the curse of mass-production technology. They know the magic of seeing raw material start in at one end of a plant and come out as a working thingamajig at the other. They know the curse of having to do the same little task over and over, but they also know that is the secret of the magic.

Recent experiments show little promise of bringing about any real, fundamental change. One of the most publicized programs was undertaken at the Gaines pet-food plant in Topeka, Kansas, where the processing line was built to be run by autonomous work groups operating under little or no supervision. After six years, the plant is reverting to a traditional model: orders coming down the pyramid and groans going up.

Another program that is receiving considerable attention is the Harmon auto-mirror plant in Bolivar, Tennessee, where the workers did have some input into the work redesign. They devised a system that permits them to earn "idle time" by completing an agreed-upon amount of work. They can use this earned time to attend a variety of courses offered by the company to upgrade their status, or they can simply leave the plant and go home. Given the choice, many choose to just leave.

General Motors recently launched an employee communications program at its Tarrytown, New York, assembly plant, where low productivity, efficiency, and morale had nearly led to a plant shutdown (a motivator for workers and managers both!). The company brought in a new manager, who worked closely with the union to turn the plant around. Through small-group training sessions, assembly-line workers and managers were encouraged to "communicate" with one another. Both management and union officials claim the program has been successful so far. Foremen have become more polite to the hourly workers (they say "Good morning" now); union reps have become more concerned with quality control; fewer cars come off the line with leaky windshields. As one GM official put it, "The team spirit has replaced 'them against us.' "

For employees at Tarrytown, communication with their supervisors may be a real step forward, and that's good. But in terms of industrial psychology, the program there hardly represents a major innovation. It merely demonstrates the obvious lesson that people are likely to be more motivated when they are treated as participants in a process rather than as robots who carry out orders. That is a welcome change.

But the habit of subordination is hard to break. Much of our learning about institutions, from childhood through young adulthood, is based on the acceptance of hierarchy—in our homes, in school, in the military. We therefore arrive at a job prepared more for subordination than participation.

Then along come some behavioral scientists who suggest that work might be more fulfilling or satisfying if employees could somehow be given the chance to be more creative or to participate in decision-making. An experiment is launched, often with a lot of public-relations flimflam. It runs into problems, the experimenters leave, and things settle back into the old pyramid. If we really want to increase the level of creativity and participation in working life, we need to consider alternatives to the traditional hierarchical organization. Most companies aren't ready for that.

The schemes proposed by management psychologists usually tend to diversify or rearrange the tasks carried out by each worker. But the tasks themselves remain basically just as dull and repetitive as before. Clearly, if workers prefer multiple tasks, and find the new arrangement better than the old ones, they should be given such options. But rearrangement should not be sold as autonomy, creativity, and self-actualization, because that creates new expectations that cannot be fulfilled, and results in just another feeling of letdown, leading to more frustration and discouragement. For the same reason, psychologists should not claim that the worker will necessarily be happier, healthier, or better adjusted as a result. I know of one instance in which women assembling steam irons in a General Electric plant, each putting on a small part, had their jobs "enriched." As a result, each had to assemble the whole iron, to test it, and so forth. The result—they could no longer talk about TV, movies, sports, lovers, gossip; in a word, "schmooze." They were so unhappy they filed a grievance complaint asking the company if they could go back to the old assembly line.

Industrial psychologists use terms like "autonomy," "satisfaction," "creativity," and "quality-of-work life" so commonly these days that I'm not sure the words have a distinct meaning anymore. One must always ask, "Compared with what?"

Most factory work—and much office work as well—is repetitious and dull. As long as it is, job satisfaction for workers will depend to a great extent on the freedom they have on the job to do things unrelated to their assigned work. I think such freedom offers far more potential for increased autonomy than any rearrangement of the work itself.

Assuming that decent wages and benefits exist, I would urge factory managers concerned about employee dissatisfaction to find ways to increase such nonwork freedom, starting with some of the same privileges enjoyed by white-collar workers. Many people who work in offices, when bored with their work, can reach for the telephone or take a break, or do any number of things to relieve the monotony. They take those privileges for granted. Most factory workers, however, are limited to the same daily schedules, including the same coffee breaks, as provided in their union contracts. They must be productive almost every minute, for the assembly line never stops.

The telephone is but one small example of the inequalities between blue- and white-collar workers. White-collar workers are accustomed to weekly salaries regardless of the number of hours they actually work. Many managerial and professional employees can breeze into the office "some time after nine," take a two-hour lunch break, and stroll out before five. During the workday, they can leave the office for brief periods to socialize with others.

Blue-collar workers, on the other hand, must show up promptly before their shift starts, and stay on the line until it stops. They must punch a time clock four times a day. They get a half-hour break for lunch, but have to ask permission from the supervisor or foreman to leave the line at other times. They work each day under tight production quotas.

If I were to design a manufacturing plant, I would ask the workers to help design it in ways that would permit four to five of them to talk, fool around, use the telephone—in a word, to "schmooze." There is no reason why they can't complete their assigned tasks while schmoozing. Anyone who is familiar with factory life knows that workers find informal ways of doing this anyway, by having their "buddies" cover for them. Why not recognize this basic human need to socialize, and build it into the work structure? Given the same level of freedom, a community of workers could organize this informal buddy system to make their work life more congenial and humane, and still complete the amount of work expected of them, as they presently do.

All the talk of autonomy raises expectations and suggests that somehow individual workers can really have a say in the running of a plant. Yet I know of no place where workers have really participated in management decisions effectively, except, perhaps, through their unions. While they may agree that everyone cannot take part in production decisions, they could have more say in decisions affecting their own welfare. It is odd that people in management and psychologists who talk about the need for more worker control on the job are not similarly moved to having them participate in decisions about improving the conditions of working life. The elitism in this kind of neglect may be unconscious, but it is strikingly clear to the workers. Yet planning how the work will be organized is the very aspect of work from which workers have been excluded. By the time the automobiles start coming down the production line, it's too late for participation in the decision-making process. Until workers are committed to changes they themselves have helped create, they will, most likely, remain bored and alienated.

» Robert Goldmann «

Six Automobile Workers in Sweden

» «

In 1974, Robert Schrank decided to put his skepticism about quality of worklife programs to the test. Supported by the Ford Foundation, he arranged for six American auto workers from Detroit to work for four weeks in an automobile plant in Sweden that had gone further than any other workplace in promoting the quality of worklife. If nothing else, this report by Robert Goldmann, who accompanied the workers to Sweden, casts doubt on the wisdom of trying to transplant foreign experiments into the American work culture. The workers' reactions to the Swedish experiment were mixed. But they were all surprised at how hard the Swedes worked compared to American auto workers. As one of the Americans said in summing up his experience, "If I've got to bust my ass to be meaningful, forget it; I'd rather be monotonous."

Y

ou are like musicians playing in a hall they haven't played in before. They can tell better than anybody why they prefer one hall over another, why they like the acoustics or the "feel" in one place better than in another. That's what we want you to tell us about, two different ways of assembling motors. You can tell quickly what the supervisors are like, how noise levels compare, how you feel about more or less responsibility, how the workers get along with each other, and so on.

With this final explanation from Robert Schrank at their orientation session, six American auto workers from Detroit took off for Sweden on November 15, 1974. They were to spend four weeks working in the engine assembly plant for Saab cars at Soedertaelje, near Stockholm, where they would experience and assess one example of Scandinavian experiments in work reorganization.

Some Issues and Assumptions

Alienation became a byword in the United States during the 1960s. It was used to describe the distress of young people who no longer felt comfortable at home, at work, in school or college; . . . and it stuck as a label for restiveness in the workplace, particularly in mass-production industries—a restiveness that expressed itself in high rates of absenteeism, turnover, and a noticeable irritability in many workers, particularly younger ones.

The same symptoms observed among American workers became apparent in other industrial countries, especially in Scandinavia. Mounting disquiet among the workers was interpreted as a demand for a more humane workplace. This demand seemed to focus on three major needs: better physical conditions (less noise, less heat, better safety and health facilities), job enlargement (more varied tasks, particularly in the monotonous assembly line plants), and job enrichment (a voice in the decisions that govern the workplace, especially on how production is performed and organized). . . .

Scandinavia began experiments in work satisfaction—principally reorganization—in the mid-1960s, and the variety and duration of these experiments have provided much of the data used by researchers and proponents of work redesign. . . .

Saab-Scania, with 34,000 people on its payroll, is Sweden's third largest industrial employer. . . . Scania Division . . . employs about 14,000 people; slightly less than half of those work in the Soedertaelje complex, which does truck assembly, diesel engine and gasoline engine production, gear box production, and is the foundry. The gasoline engine plant, where the six Americans trained and worked, employs 350 people in two shifts of 175 each.

Work reorganization at Scania Division began in the late sixties. . . . They came up with a two-part idea to boost worker involvement. They would organize production groups of ten to twelve members each, in which workers would try to arrive at more effective and satisfying methods of working. Then development groups would be established to bring representatives from two or more production groups together with their foremen, planners, and other specialists, as needed. . . .

The second phase of work reform was introduced in 1972 in the new Saab gasoline engine plant. . . . The Soedertaelje plant . . . has a floor area of 12,000 square meters (about 133,000 square feet) and a capacity of 110,000 engines a year. When we were there, it was producing about half of that number. . . .

The major new work reform at the gasoline engine plant was the introduction of group assembly for part of the assembly process. Groups of three or four workers would get engines with preassembled blocks and heads. The groups would then assemble carburetors, flywheels, injection units, distributors, sparkplugs, camshaft chains, and so forth. Each group decided how to divide the work load among its members. Each worker could handle one engine by himself for a maximum work cycle of thirty minutes, or the work could be divided into cycles of ten minutes each, or a variety of combinations could be used that added up to thirty minutes per motor.

Seven assembly groups were set up with from three to four members at the engine plant. Not all of the groups work at all times. One of the seven stations, where our workers spent two weeks and where newly hired local people spend from four to six weeks, trains new workers for the group method. . . .

The Six Auto Workers

Back in Detroit, the United Auto Workers circulated applications to its members. The criteria used to select the six participants included an interest in the project and the work-related issues it raised, the facility to articulate issues and concerns, a diversity of backgrounds, and a sensitivity to workplace relationships. . . .

William Cox, a thirty-three-year-old shop steward of Irish-English background, works at Chrysler's Mound Road plant in Detroit. An automobile worker for eleven years, he spent most of the time in crankshaft machining. . . . Bill is perceptive, sensitive, and especially interested in union-related issues.

William Gardner is a forty-one-year-old black man who has been an auto worker for twenty-one years. Working on the assembly line for Pontiac, he has done nickel plating, a variety of other jobs on engine assembly, and has served as a union committeeman. He is carrying a heavy course load at the University of Michigan, where he is working at night toward his degree in business administration. His career plans range far beyond the confines of the Pontiac engine plant. He wants to understand social and economic issues, especially how different economic systems work and the complicated problems that underlie mass production.

Herman Lommerse, at fifty-three, was the oldest in the group. Born in the Netherlands, he came to the United States in 1949. He has been working at Cadillac's engine plant in a variety of jobs for fifteen years. . . . If he can't enjoy himself outright, he finds a way to minimize or shrug off annoyances. He hadn't found life too bad or bothersome at Cadillac.

Joseph Rodriguez, thirty-six, a Mexican-American who came to Detroit from San Antonio as a child . . . has been an auto worker for a decade. . . . As a utility man at Ford's Dearborn engine plant, he relieves people on the line. This gives him a variety of tasks to do from day-to-day. He sees the job as a good source of income, believes in doing an honest day's work for his pay, but finds the job incidental to his satisfactions in life. For the good things he looks to his family and his books. . . .

Ruth Russell, thirty-one, has been working at Cadillac's engine plant for six and a half years putting head bolts on the engines. [She is] of German-English extraction. . . . More annoyed than any of the others by her job in Detroit, Ruth took her responsibilities seriously and criticism hit her hard. The foreman's hovering presence "bugged" her. The noise, the monotony, the dirt in the plant, and the narrow work space made her job unpleasant, if not miserable. While other members of the group discovered ways to put some variety into their work or at least to reduce annoyances, she saw no way out of the routine. Her resentments of her job in Detroit were the key to her reaction in Soedertaelje.

Lynette Stewart is twenty-one and was the youngest in the group. About six feet tall, this black woman does part-time modeling, studies toward a nursing degree at Highland Park College, works part-time in a laboratory, takes care of her one-and-a-half-year-old son, and works a full shift on the Cadillac engine assembly line. She had been employed in automobile work for only eight months before she came on the trip and did not intend to make her career there. She has found ways to, as she put it, "create a challenge for myself in my job by making up stock ahead and so getting time to do some studying at work." . . .

Introduction to Work

The gasoline engine plant . . . had been converted and completely re-equipped two years before and for all practical purposes was a new plant. Here the Americans made comparisons on first sight. After all, it was closest to their experience. They found the plant cleaner, far less noisy, and better lit. The working pace seemed more relaxed than at home. The engine blocks were incredibly small in comparison with Detroit's motors. (The Saab motor has four cylinders and the block is less than half as large as that of an American V-8.) "Erector sets" and "toy engines" were characterizations that formed spontaneously.

The next discovery we made was that only a small part of the plant was engaged in group assembly. . . . Most of the workers (about 250 out of 300) were engaged either in machining blocks, heads, and parts, or in the preassembly of blocks and heads along traditional assembly line principles. Only after these operations did the engines reach the relatively small section of the factory where the group assemblers worked. The break from convention was not as radical or plant-wide as the Americans had been led to expect. . . .

First Impressions and Emerging Issues

First impressions that remained high on the workers' list of concerns throughout our stay included cleanliness, noise levels, shifts, boredom and monotony, and the scale and speed of production. . . .

All of the American workers felt that all of Scania Division's plants are cleaner and more attractive than any of the Detroit plants. Most important, stock and parts at Scania Division were kept rigidly behind yellow lines, which reduced accident chances. . . .

All agreed that throughout the Soedertaelje plant noise levels seemed lower than in Detroit. This was particularly striking in testing areas, where the muffling of motor noises was far more effective and where heavy glass shielding did away with excessive heat. The Americans felt that the importance of reducing noise levels could not be overstressed. High noise is not only a strain on the nerves but also makes conversation at work difficult and in some cases impossible, adding to assembly line monotony and frustration. . . .

All six workers disliked the weekly shift alternating (one week on mornings, the next week on evenings) required of everyone in the Scania plant. It killed chances for school or other regularly scheduled activities. The local workers told the Americans they also disliked it. According to the company, the alternating system is traditional in Sweden and is part of the contract between the company and the union. It allows married couples to carry equal loads in the household and gives them an equal opportunity to be with their children. . . .

According to Bill Cox, several local workers also complained a little about monotony, even though they had somewhat more variety in their jobs than there is in Detroit. In the end, said Bill, they have the same motive for work that American auto workers do: The money is good. . . .

In that first week there was also some puzzlement about the role of the foremen. In the United States the foreman was clearly a management representative, but at Soedertaelje he seemed more concerned about the workers and their feelings. Above all, he was much less conspicuous and they felt less pressure from him, something Ruth Russell particularly appreciated after her experience in Detroit.

That Sunday morning one of the most significant discussions of the four-week experience developed in response to this question: "How important is the job to you in your life and would it make a lot of difference to you if the job were reorganized to be more satisfying?"

Bill Cox said that he spends a third of his life at work, so it is important to him how he feels on the job; it affects how he feels and acts at home. "If they could change, back in the States, to better lighting like we've got over here, or change the noise level, or give me a variety of things to do . . . I think it would tend to make me feel more satisfied with my job. . . ." Ruth Russell felt strongly that some variety in her job would make her feel a lot better.

To Lynette Stewart, changes in job design would not mean much. For one thing, she will go into nursing as a profession. Also, "I have three jobs now, and take care of the kid," she said, "and I find pride in myself." Joe Rodriguez also did not expect to spend the rest of his life on engine assembly, hoping to move into different kinds of work at the Ford Motor Company. But he did not think that changing the job would make too much difference. He had noticed that Saab-Scania workers, with much more job variety than workers in Detroit, are still "bored stiff."

Asked to describe the feeling of his coworkers in Detroit on the issue, Bill Cox believed that most of them would enjoy improvements in their job setup but that did not mean that most workers were actively dissatisfied.

360

Bill Gardner, like Bill Cox, Joe Rodriguez, and Herman Lommerse, gets to move around a good deal in his Detroit plant and, like Lynette, he studies at night and finds that a major source of satisfaction.

The relatively relaxed tone of the workers' discussion about job satisfaction contrasted sharply with the urgency in the literature of work reorganization. In effect, the Americans said that they had to make a living and auto work was good money. They did not expect the job to give them all or most of their satisfactions in life, although less monotony and more interesting ways of working would be helpful. With the exception of Ruth Russell, the workers seemed to be saying or implying that more variety in the job would be welcome but wouldn't make all that much difference.

Perhaps we overemphasize the potential of changes in work organization and job design when we try to tackle alienation, restiveness, and dissatisfaction in the work force, especially among young people where it seems to be the highest. Such problems have roots in many spheres of life. Therefore, we can legitimately ask how much difference redesigning work will make or to what extent the limited number of movements or tasks a worker can at best be given in a mass production industry can alleviate some of the psychological problems workers share with many people outside the blue collar population. . . .

The Second Week

In the second week of the Swedish assignment, the six workers began training and work in group assembly. This put them into the heart of work reorganization at Scania Division. . . .

After their first day of learning to put on flywheels, timing chains, and various other parts that go on the outside of a motor block, they came back happy. "It's fun," "it keeps you busy doing different things" were some initial comments. . . .

Herman thought it was like "building little toys" but he still liked it better at Cadillac because the time went faster. He thought that even with this group system, doing motors might get boring in the long run. But then, he added, in any event he couldn't get into group assembly if he worked at Saab-Scania. "They don't like any men there," he said, "it's all women."

This observation—that only women worked on group assembly—developed into a major issue directly related to the broader implications of group assembly at Saab-Scania. . . .

After a few more days of experience, the group tackled the question of whether and how one could transfer group assembly to American plants. The answer was unanimous: It would be difficult because of the size of American motors and the scale of production. Several parts that workers at Saab-Scania can pick up by hand need hoists in Detroit because the American counterparts are so much heavier and larger. Also, much more space would be needed to operate and to store parts. It would take a vastly larger plant area to accommodate all the groups that would be needed to turn out large American motors. At one point in the discussion of likely technical problems, Lynette Stewart said with a smile, "By the time you get through (adapting group assembly), you have another assembly line!"

Joe Rodriguez said the United States could never adopt the group assembly method because it could not meet the needs of American-style mass production. He did think, however, that auto plants in the United States could give workers more of a chance to move around, cut down monotony, and make such improvements as reducing noise, making plants cleaner, and providing better lighting. None of these innovations would require radical changes in production standards or methods. . . .

Joe Rodriguez noted that the union was far less conspicuous on the floor in Sweden than in Detroit where all questions about safety, problems with machinery, stock, and the like could be taken up with the union steward or committeeman. Here in Sweden, Joe remarked, the foreman seemed to do everything and act like "a good father." . . .

But the main topic that Friday night and next morning was the work pace and its implications. Bill Cox noted that most of the people in the plant "wouldn't touch that group assembly" because of the heavy pace. . . . Joe Rodriguez added: "Nobody's saying this is a great place. It boils down to one thing. A job is a job." . . . He said he had talked to one group of women—one Finnish, one Italian, and one Swedish—who had told him that hard work one day gave them a chance to work less hard the next day and that group assembly made part-time work possible. But above all, the motivation was pride in their ability to work hard—harder than the men.

This issue overshadowed such questions as how many tasks a worker should perform, how much say he should have about dividing up the work, and other features of group assembly. Monotony versus variety became almost immaterial. Bill Cox put it this way:

> If you went over to America and took an American assembly-line worker off the most boring job there, brought him over here and let him work over here in group assembly a little while and you tell him: "Now, you've got your choice; which way would you have it? The boring job where you work at a normal pace or the job that isn't so boring because they change around, but you have to work at a faster pace to get your production, which would you have?" And I'm willing to place money on it that he would take the boring job.

And Joe Rodriguez said, "If I've got to bust my ass to be meaningful, forget it; I'd rather be monotonous."

The work cycle in group assembly is thirty minutes per engine. A three-member group turns out six engines an hour, while a four-member group produces eight units an hour. When five groups (omitting the training section) are operating—three with four members and two with three—this means an hourly production of 36 engines. In Detroit, Pontiac turns out 240 engines an hour and Cadillac, 88 with correspondingly larger numbers of workers on the assembly line from beginning to end.

Joe said that group assembly would be all right if the worker could govern his own pace. . . . However, in a group such individual decisions are not possible. The system is planned to require either heavily paced work or a day off. There seems to be little room for flexibility during the workday. . . .

The Third Week

At the third group session on Saturday, December 7, . . . a new subject was raised by the Americans: the relations among workers and opportunities to socialize at work. Everyone objected to the short lunch break (twenty-four minutes on the day shift, eighteen on the afternoon shift). It did not allow time to go to the restaurant—a five-minute walk—and eat there in peace. At Saab-Scania there was a fixed time and an assigned place for everything—including relaxation. In Detroit workers could play cards during a break without having to walk over to a designated area or could sit down on boxes for a talk near their spots on the line. In Detroit there were more opportunities to make individual arrangements for socializing and relaxing during breaks.

I asked the workers to add to the group assembly criteria all the other workplace factors such as safety and facilities and to . . . choose between Soedertaelje and Detroit. The responses to this broader question soon focused on the union's role and the workers' relationship to the foremen. This might be expanded to the issue, "Who am I in the workplace society?"

In order that people may be happy in their work, these three things are needed: They must be fit for it. They must not do too much of it. And they must have a sense of success in it.
—John Ruskin, *Pre-Raphaelitism*

The passion and eloquence of the responses subordinated the concrete factors usually associated with meaningful work—how tasks are organized, membership on committees—to the atmosphere in the workplace.

Bill Gardner started the discussion: "I've often wondered what they meant when they said 'democratic shop,' and I find . . . personally that there's a greater deal of exercise of freedom socially and economically, discourse with the foreman, and all these factors in the States than I have here. . . ."

For Bill Cox, who still picked the States over Sweden, the atmosphere was decisive:

In the States you have your boredom, but you still have your more outward-going, more happy-go-lucky worker. We the workers make the workplace happy while we are there because we have to be there and we make the best of it while we are doing the work. But here it seems they come in and they do it and they leave. . . .

Herman Lommerse chose Detroit for similar reasons: "Things are more open [in Detroit] and you have better counsel with your foreman. The workers associate better too. They're more a part of it. Here, it's separate. . . ."
Ruth Russell was undecided.
Joe Rodriguez went more deeply into the matter:

Somehow I have the feeling, and I don't like the feeling, "you're being had." . . . In the States, even though it's dirty and even though it's noisy, there you don't have to swallow anything. I mean you just come back and say, "Hey, I know where you're coming from; I don't like it; get off my back." And you have the freedom . . . you don't have to be afraid of any consequences . . .

In the States when you step out of line, you know that you're going to get backed up. . . . You feel so free in the States . . . you have an opportunity to exercise your options at will. . . . You can say right now, "That's it . . . get me the committeeman right now.". . .

I asked Lynette Stewart, as the youngest of the group, whether the things Joe had said were important to her. Lynette replied: "Very important, especially for me, because of my having less seniority. I am not afraid anyway to tell my general foreman anything." . . . Lynette [added]:

This familiar attitude, the family, the union, the unit . . . and it's not just the union, it's in the shop . . . the foreman I used to have, I could talk to him about anything . . . it's a family.

Then Joe Rodriguez countered:

It's a family here [too] . . . [but] it's the type of family where the father will provide for all the comforts of his children to see that they have everything they need, but they have no freedom, really, to go against his wishes. . . . Here, it seems that the people haven't reached that point where they will say, "Hey, I am my own person."

Reflections

Quite obviously . . . each of the six is very much an individual. The reactions reported here say much about each worker's values and aspirations, as well as something about engine assembly in Sweden and America.

The Detroit workers' exchange underscored the importance of planning and assessing changes in work design and industrial organization in the context of the total cultural environment. The cultural differences between Sweden and the United States tended to overshadow differences in the way the workplace was organized. What the American workers commented on time and again were features of a society that in their perception inhibits self-expression. They were more interested in the relationships among the worker, his peers, and supervisors, the role of the union, and the worker's position vis-à-vis the employer than in the tasks involved in group assembly. The American workers' rights, their sense of "being their own person," as Joe Rodriguez put it, their freedom to object to what they don't like and to press their needs without fear of the consequences seemed far more important to them than how their task is organized, how changes relieve boredom or create a better atmosphere at work, or whether they are represented on a council or committee.

Much of the information that American work analysts receive from Scandinavia underplays this aspect. . . .

In Detroit [at a reunion meeting] the point was stressed again that there are limits to what can be done about alienation in the workplace since work accounts for only a portion of what is good and bad in life. This would be a platitude were it not that some of the literature and the reporting on work reorganization has tended to overplay what can be expected from reforms on the job. . . .

With the exception of Ruth Russell, the Americans had reservations about the system at Saab-Scania's gasoline engine plant. They appreciated the sense of accomplishment that comes with performing more than one single operation but thought that assembling many parts on a motor also might become boring after it was learned.

The men all objected to the pace and the high degree of concentration demanded of group assemblers. There is a tradeoff between doing a day's work that allows for thought about studies, home, hobbies, or other personal interests and having to pour every ounce of energy and thought into the job. Group assembly at Saab-Scania seems to attract only the most highly motivated workers who are prepared to give the job everything. But it was originally designed to appeal to a variety of people, particularly those who had become alienated and to whom something more than the boredom of the assembly line had to be offered. Judging by the composition of the groups and of workers on the conventional line at Saab-Scania, group assembly has not kept this original promise. What was missing was worker autonomy and initiative in the day-to-day planning and performance of group work.

Asked about the possibilities of transferring group assembly to the United States, the workers saw major problems arising out of the differences in scale of production, the size of motors and parts, and the different social and economic systems. Work reform in America can proceed only in the context of American life and culture. . . .

Finally, the conversation in Detroit again centered on the issue, "Who am I in the workplace?" Several of the six workers noted that everything in Sweden seemed planned with nothing left to chance. Even job enrichment efforts were tightly organized. The works council, production, and development group meetings were held as scheduled, but there was only mild interest in their proceedings. The normal activity of an American industrial union seemed to be a more effective manifestation of worker needs and demands with a more direct impact on day-to-day life in the plant than the innovations in worker participation at Saab-Scania.

Bill Gardner put it this way:

> Even given all these situations where workers have participation in what's going on the floor, it's still a situation of benevolence by the corporation . . . something that is done *for* you . . . we are taking care of your problems, which tends to demean you as a man. . . . A man needs to feel that he is doing something about his own destiny instead of people laying it out to him.

And Joe Rodriguez said: "When it comes to this feeling of freedom, when it comes to having to make a choice between everything they have under their type of system or being here under our type of system, I've still got to say I take this system . . . because of this one issue."

>> *Ted Mills* <<

Human Resources and the Unions

>> <<

One of the ironies of the quality of working life movement has been the relative lack of participation by those organizations historically most concerned with worker welfare: unions. Until recently, most unions have been neutral or downright hostile to what Ted Mills, director of the National Quality of Work Center, calls Human Resources Development—the whole field that is concerned with the human factor in producing our goods and services. Why? Mills gives several reasons, the most important of which is that unions see little role for themselves in situations where management and workers cooperate. Unions historically have made their contribution in adversarial relationships between companies and workers, and they cannot visualize a need for their services where management voluntarily offers security, grievance and arbitration procedures, and authentic worker participation. Yet, as the Tarrytown case illustrates, unions are now carving out meaningful roles for themselves. Since 1975, when this article was written, at least ten U.S. unions have participated in work quality programs. Their prime role: to make the changes introduced in work quality programs contractual, thus eliminating the possibility of arbitrary reneging on the part of management.

Until recently, a . . . common characteristic [of companies moving into human resources development (HRD)] has been the surprising absence of organized labor in HRD advocacy, planning, and implementation. Despite HRD's primary focus on work, workers, and work conditions, available information indicates that, until recently, most HRD activity in the United States has been in nonunion plants and offices, and with a few notable exceptions has been without active union participation in the few organized workplaces where it has appeared. It is probably correct to draw conclusions (which are almost never explicitly stated) that many managements use HRD efforts either to weaken union strength through more satisifed employees or to keep the unions out. In 1973, two well-known HRD practitioners even conducted a seminar called "Making Unions Unnecessary."

Although curiously undeveloped up to now, in the years ahead trade union presence may be crucial to facilitating and accelerating HRD efforts.

From its inception, trade unionism has struggled to provide a better quality of work life for its membership. Cleaner and safer workplaces, with jobs geared to reasonable human limits, have been as important to unions and their memberships as adequate security and rewards from work. The entire grievance machinery of union-management relations is built on conditions of work. It is odd, therefore, that until now management, and not unions, has been the almost exclusive driving force behind the HRD movement.

Union leaders have expressed publicly and to me personally a variety of reasons why most unions have thus far viewed the movement with attitudes ranging from suspicion and hostility to apathy. There seem to be five common concerns:

1. More efficient, "advanced" work organizations such as Procter & Gamble's (nonunion) Lima, Ohio plant or General Foods' famous (nonunion) Topeka, Kansas dogfood plant considerably reduce the size of work forces required.

2. In organized companies, most managements refuse to invite union participation in HRD planning.

3. The intellectual sounds made by "bleeding heart" HRD ideologues about the "poor worker" alienate union leaders and members alike.

4. A "happy" work force might diminish labor militance, grievances, and other forces contributing to allegiance to unions.

5. There is an unexpected, but central, absence of signals upward from rank and file workers indicating that improved quality of work life is an important worker concern—one worth going to the mat for.

In just the past year, despite rising union preoccupation with growing unemployment, such negative (win-lose) attitudes toward HRD activities have shown signs of change in many levels of the labor movement. In fact, the growing interest in and, in some cases, insistence by union leadership on active union participation in HRD activities is an important part of the emerging HRD phenomenon in the United States. (In Europe, and particularly Scandinavia, unions have long been involved in pressing for HRD experiments and practices.)

Two historic turning points in the labor position toward HRD have occurred in the last three years. One is the remarkable agreement between the Steelworkers, under I.W. Abel, and the steel industry to form new labor-management bodies now called "employment security and productivity committees." These committees are now in operation in every workplace in the basic industry's "big ten" companies. Using the threat of dangerous foreign competition as powerful glue, the committees substitute a new win-win collaborative effort for the classic win-lose adversary one between management and workers. Today, both the USWA and the industry point with pride to the achievements of these committees in improving work and work life, and to a soaring productivity rate in the steel industry.

The other turning point in labor history occurred in the 1973 negotiations between the Automobile Workers under Leonard Woodcock and the "big three" automakers for a new contract. Long an advocate of union leadership and participation in HRD activity in the industry, the UAW demanded that the new contract provide for establishment of a joint labor-management "quality of work life committee" in each company. Some of the managements fought the notion as an incursion into management's right to manage. The UAW's victory and the establishment of functioning joint committees in General Motors, Ford, and Chrysler was big labor's first bargained-for commitment to active participation in HRD determinations. Today, as in the steel industry, both the managements and the unions express satisfaction with the beginning achievements of these committees.

Some labor watchers have noticed a correlation between these developments (both of them in industries with histories of achievements by labor) and what the Steelworkers' Philip Murray predicted 35 years ago would be the fourth, or win-win, stage of development of the matured labor movement:

> . . . the beginning of labor-management collaboration for greater gross productivity, in which both may share, thereby affording organized labor with the fullest status and widest hearing, consistent with unified direction and control of the enterprise.

In addition to these two unions, at least a dozen major international service and manufacturing unions have agreed to participate actively and jointly with management in industry and government in the demonstration projects organized by the National Quality of Work Center. In each pilot project, labor-management committees like the USWA's and the UAW's are formed to improve performance and the quality of work life in various kinds of workplaces through collaborative union-management HRD participation.

Unions have started to become an important dimension of today's HRD phenomenon.

12

»«

DEMOCRACY IN THE WORKPLACE

»«

Diana Walker/I am a Camera

» Robert Zager «

Managing Guaranteed Employment

» «

The Lincoln Electric Company of Cleveland, Ohio, is the world's largest manufacturer of arc welding machines and electrodes. But another claim to fame is based on its unusual "no-fire" guarantee to its workers. Like Japanese workers, Lincoln's 2,400 employees do not have to worry about the cyclical layoffs that punctuate the work years of employees in most heavy industry in the United States. In addition, the company offers workers an extensive system of productivity incentives, a large profit-sharing plan, generous bonuses that encourage creativity and entrepreneurship, and an opportunity to participate in an elected, plant-wide advisory board. About 40 percent of the shares of the company are owned by employees. The company has high morale, low turnover, high productivity, and lower production costs than its competitors. In 1979, the average Lincoln employee earned $20,000 and, in addition, a $19,000 bonus! In the following selection, Robert Zager, a management consultant and vice president of the Work in America Institute, analyzes how the company has guaranteed continuous employment without sacrificing profits.

A key belief on which the Lincoln Electric Company was founded was that employees make their fullest contribution to a company only if they feel confident that their higher productivity will not diminish the amount or continuity of their annual income. That principle is embodied in a guarantee of continuous employment, which the company has honored unequivocally.

At the same time, Lincoln Electric has achieved extraordinary levels of productivity and of productivity growth. Regardless of any causal relation between the guarantee and the productivity, Lincoln Electric's experience shows that in a well-managed company the two can coexist without impairing profitability. . . .

Company Background

The Lincoln Electric Company began in 1895 as a manufacturer of electric motors, later expanded into electric welding, and took its present corporate

371

form in 1934. The Lincoln family still owns or controls about 50% of the stock, but active management has been out of the hands of the family since 1965. . . .

The company produces and sells a broad range of electric arc welding equipment and related products, as well as a line of integral horsepower industrial electric motors. It is indisputably the world's largest manufacturer of arc welding machines and electrodes. . . .

At the end of 1977 the company employed about 2,400 people in the United States, mainly at the Cleveland plant. Its U.S. revenues for the year were $256 million.

Lincoln Electric has never had a union. Employees elect representatives to a plant-wide advisory board which consults with management on all kinds of personnel, operational, and financial matters but does not negotiate in the formal sense.

The company is widely recognized for its productivity, its counter-inflationary marketing policy, and its "incentive management" system. The principal elements of the system include: job-evaluated base rates that are average for the industry and area; extensive use of individual piece-work incentives; a very large quasi-profit-sharing bonus; encouragement of creativity and entrepreneurship at every level; promotion almost entirely from within; merit ratings; a well-developed program of fringe benefits; and guaranteed continuous employment.

In addition, all managers work their way up in the company, and they have identical perquisites and fringe benefits with the hourly workers, including the same cafeteria facilities, entrances and exits, and competition for parking spaces in the company lot. . . .

Some 50% of the employees own about 40% of the company's shares. An employee may purchase a limited number of shares a year through an employee stock purchase plan. Shares purchased under the plan must be offered to the company when employment ends (by retirement or otherwise). . . .

In 1958 Lincoln Electric issued a formal guarantee of continuous employment for all of its regular employees. The commitment still stands. . . .

The Basic Commitment

The 1958 commitment promises employees 49 working weeks, of at least 30 hours a week, each year. The remaining three weeks are a paid vacation. The company does not guarantee an employee any particular assignment or wage rate.

The commitment covers all full-time employees (not part-time or special, who are few) having two years' continuous service with the company. . . .

The evidence indicates that the workers accept the guarantee at face value, with good reason. For the past 25 years no Lincoln Electric employee, even one having less than two years of service, has been laid off. Since 1958, working hours have averaged about 2,000 a year, as against the 1,470 hours guaranteed. . . .

Meeting Management Problems

Since the objective of continuous employment at Lincoln Electric has equal status with low prices, high quality, fulfillment of delivery promises, and profitable operation, the company cannot subordinate to other considerations, as most companies do, the problem of avoiding layoffs and lost wages. The typical employer formulates sales and production plans and then tries to figure out how to mitigate adverse effects on the work force. At Lincoln Electric the focus is different: it is on fulfilling the commitment to employees with least inconvenience to customers and least cost to the company. . . .

The commitment means that management must contend with two main problems: (1) how to stabilize and optimize the overall size of the work force; and (2) how to move workers about in order to cope with inevitable fluctuations in production volume.

Growth of Work Force   If a guarantee of continuous employment is to be self-financing, the number of employees whose jobs become surplus as a result of productivity growth must be matched or exceeded by the number of jobs that open up through attrition, quitting, and higher volume of business. Business volume in constant dollars has grown at an average rate of about 5.5% a year, compounded. . . .

Information about changes in the size of the company's work force is sketchy, but the available data indicate that between 1958 and 1971 the work force increased at an average of 3% a year, compounded. . . .

Hiring Practices   The guarantee of continuous employment and the steady growth of the work force prompt Lincoln Electric to be ultracareful about hiring. Orders to add new employees emanate directly from the president and the CEO.

Every recruit is regarded as someone who—subject to probation—will become an employee for life and share in bonus distribution. Therefore, the company makes it a point to wait "too long" before hiring. That is, it waits until the pressure of foreseeable production demand is greater than can be met by stretching the existing work force to reasonable limits of effort and overtime. . . .

One cost of this policy is that, when the industry as a whole experiences a sudden spurt of orders, other companies can beat Lincoln Electric on delivery because they are free to hire extra workers for the occasion.

Besides being slow to take on new employees, management also carefully screens recruits and tracks their progress through the probationary period [of two years]. A committee of three company officers interviews every applicant selected by the personnel department. This committee tries to ascertain whether he or she will fit into the company's culture and become a permanent employee. . . .

Fluctuations in Production   Within the limits set by the overall size of the work force, management has to deploy and redeploy workers to meet fluctuating production demand at the lowest possible cost and least inconvenience. Fluctuations are caused mainly by intraplant imbalances, interruptions of external supplies, and varying sales volume. . . .

The most difficult fluctuations stem from ups and downs in sales—especially downs. Almost universally a slump in sales and production justifies an employer in reducing hours and/or laying people off. Work-sharing programs may be invoked, and in a few industries supplemental unemployment benefits may lighten the burdens of laid-off workers (partially at taxpayers' expense). Lincoln Electric's guarantee allows a limited reduction of hours but bars layoffs. . . .

Flexible Deployment   In order to reconcile continuous employment with economy, customer interests, and the inevitable fluctuations of production volume and mix, the company must have utmost flexibility in deploying workers. The latter, accepting the validity of this need, concede to management the unregulated authority to transfer them and to vary the length of the workweek.

Workers can and do question the wisdom of particular decisions, but not management's right to make them. If management should act arbitrarily, that would destroy the mutual trust on which the entire structure is built.

The freedom to move workers facilitates the foreman's job in the following ways:

• Workers are willing to learn new jobs. When a machine breaks down, the worker gladly trains on a different machine until his own is ready again.

• Workers are willing, when necessary, to work half the day on one machine and half the day on another.

• A notice on the board suffices to gain consent for a swing from overtime to short time, to meet changing demands.

• Workers cooperate to cover stations left open by late or absent colleagues.

Variations in the Workweek.   Although Lincoln Electric employees, like most others, have adjusted their lives to the 40-hour week, variations of a few hours up or down are taken in stride. Workers like a few hours of overtime each week, but anything more elicits strong objections. Nonetheless, during the summer rush the company may run a series of 6-day, 50-hour weeks, or even longer ones, and the overtime is not voluntary. Occasional 50-hour weeks are worked at other times of the year also, though the company tries as hard as it can to avoid overlong as well as short weeks.

When a four-day week becomes necessary, people do not get upset. They enjoy having an extra day at home, knowing that it will not happen often.

Variations in the length of the workweek are usually not across the board, but follow product lines. . . .

Transfer Guidelines. Frequently, the company resorts to involuntary transfers as a means of adjusting the work force to changing production demands. Its guidelines are highly efficient but would probably be unworkable outside the context of continuous employment. For example:

• There is no bumping procedure. An employee who has run out of work is transferred to work that is not currently being done. For the sake of both the company and the individual, management tries to place transferees in jobs that best employ their skills and experience. . . .

• The transferee's pay rate is not protected. As soon as he is moved, he receives either the base rate or the incentive rate of the new job, whether it is higher or lower than the rate of the one he left. In normal times, however, a worker is transferred involuntarily to a lower-rated job only if his own work has run short, or in the case of a disciplinary offense.

• Every effort is made to transfer pieceworkers to piecework jobs.

Factors in Success

What has enabled Lincoln Electric to persevere with the policy of more and more for less and less in good years and in bad? Several factors have contributed:

• Management has stuck to the products and services in which its expertise is greatest. Within that field it has continually added to its range, while rejecting all temptation to diversify into other fields.

• Economy is designed into the company's products. . . .

• Management has pared overhead costs to the bone: nothing is done for show. . . .

• Spurred by the incentive system, employees apply a high (not backbreaking) degree of physical effort and an even higher degree of mental effort toward the objective of speeding output while maintaining quality.

• The company introduces new methods, machines, equipment, and organization structures whenever and wherever these can be shown to improve overall economic performance. Workers cooperate actively, from the start, to get the most out of such changes. . . .

Worker Competition

It is in the nature of individual incentives to promote competition among employees and between employees and company. Lincoln Electric deliberately plays up the competition but averts harmful side effects in two ways:

1. The competition produces only winners, no losers. Some workers do better than others, but everyone does well. The company has no interest in outsmarting any of its employees.

2. The company-wide bonus, which effectively doubles earnings, gives teamwork equal status with individual striving. The ability to keep competition and cooperation hitched in the same harness distinguishes the Lincoln Electric approach from the Scanlon Plan. . . .

Finally, Lincoln Electric workers' earnings run 30% to 40% above those for comparable jobs in similar-sized manufacturing companies, and the same is true for the company managers' earnings (except for the very top jobs, where no clear comparisons can be made).

Basic Questions

The case of Lincoln Electric raises a number of basic considerations. In the first place, as this report illustrates, there is a difficulty of determining, between continuous employment and productivity growth, which is cause and which is effect. In fact, the relationship is reciprocal. The guarantee stimulates workers to cooperate with management in raising productivity. Cooperation contributes to high productivity growth, which enables the company to increase business and profits, which in turn help pay for continuous employment.

In the second place, Lincoln Electric would never claim that its productivity achievements, remarkable as they are, represent the final word. . . .

A third point concerns the absence of a union, often cited by outsiders to explain away Lincoln Electric's success in managing without layoffs. This explanation in turn raises two questions.

First, out of the great number of nonunion employers in the United States—a majority of all employers, in fact—how many provide guarantees of continuous employment? Second, which aspects of Lincoln Electric's management-employee relations that are essential to continuous employment would not be countenanced by a strong union? Presumably critics have in mind (a) nonrecognition of seniority and (b) involuntary overtime and transfer.

The prime purpose of seniority rights is to prevent management from arbitrary action in layoff, recall, promotion, and demotion. Where continuous employment is guaranteed, the order of layoff and recall is irrelevant.

As for promotion and demotion, the difference between Lincoln Electric and unionized companies may be more of degree than of essence. . . .

Involuntary overtime is standard in many unionized plants. Perhaps the most controversial point, however, is involuntary transfer without formal rules. . . .

Involuntary transfer to lower-rated jobs sounds threatening. Yet, when it is called "bumping," unions not only accept it, they demand it, as a means of protecting more senior at the expense of less senior workers.

Why should they not also accept it as a means of protecting the entire work force against layoffs? . . .

The absence of formal rules may be less essential than it seems. Lincoln Electric places a high premium on freedom from rigidities of any kind. But if a management and its union trust each other, they can stitch together some loose-fitting rules that give management the right to transfer employees as the situation requires, subject to later review for alleged inequities.

The fourth basic question is that if continuous employment works so well for Lincoln Electric, and neither unionization nor widespread ownership is a necessary bar, why have so few companies adopted it? Only a broad survey can answer the question reliably, but one may venture some hypotheses.

The force of unexamined custom is strong, and U.S. employers have traditionally held it to be self-evident that in a slump the best way to cut costs fast is to chop the work force. . . .

Business leaders have yet to be persuaded of the vital link between productivity growth and job security; namely, that sustained, rapid growth of productivity requires the active cooperation of the work force, and that cooperation is given only when workers feel confident that management will not benefit at their expense. At present, employees rarely have security even against the direct impact of productivity improvements introduced by their employer, let alone the impact of external forces.

Union leaders have understood the productivity-security nexus for many years. . . .

However, most union leaders regard productivity growth as something primarily in the employer's interest. . . .

If unions could go the next step and acknowledge that productivity growth is as vital to workers as it is to employers, they would make it infinitely easier for employers to see that real job security is likewise in the best interest of both sides.

» David W. Ewing and Pamela Banks «

Participative Management at Work: An Interview with John F. Donnelly

» «

Donnelly Mirrors, a Michigan firm that manufactures approximately 70 percent of the auto mirrors in the United States, has enjoyed considerable success with its experiments in "participative management." At Donnelly Mirrors, all 500 employees participate in both managerial decisions and the firm's profits. The entire workforce is organized into interlocking teams of eight to twelve workers. Each team has access to all the information it needs to be self-managing, and it has full responsibility for making all decisions directly affecting its work: how fast to run the production line; when to shut it down for maintenance; and when and how to implement a schedule increase, a product variation, or a change in method. The highest work team is the executive or management team. There is also a company-wide Representative Committee that deals with grievances, salaries, fringe benefits, promotions, and all other personnel policies and problems. Every month a bonus is paid to the workers based on all increases resulting from innovations, productivity gains, and savings in labor, materials, and operating supplies. The following interview with the company's president, John F. Donnelly, was conducted by David W. Ewing, managing editor of the Harvard Business Review, *and Pamela Banks, editorial assistant.*

People often like the sound of **industrial democracy, and yet it hasn't taken hold very fast in the United States. Why do you think people are skeptical about approaches like Donnelly's?**
Mr. Donnelly: They're afraid of losing authority.

Why do you think they believe authority works better?
Because that's the way it's been done, and that's the way organizations are

structured. They're mostly modeled after the military, and it's difficult for people to conceive of any other system working. I would be the last one to say that we don't use authority in this company. We do. But, . . . if you are not in the position to get people to accept ideas because they're sound and if you are not willing to accept an idea because it's sound, then you're really not a good manager.

So it's not a matter of throwing positions of authority out but of playing them down. That's difficult for people to do. . . . More and more companies are finding that to continue to operate they have to have better contact with all their people. You have to stop the alienation. And you don't stop that except by getting at the root causes of alienation.

How did your company start dealing with alienation, with alternatives to the authoritarian type of management?
In 1952, an associate of Joseph Scanlon from the Massachusetts Institute of Technology—Carl Frost—introduced us to the principles of the Scanlon Plan. Scanlon believed that everybody in a company not only *could* be more productive but *wanted* to be. He set out to prove that it was so.

His idea was born out of efforts he initiated to involve the staff and rank-and-file members of the United Steel Workers to keep a small struggling steel company afloat in the waning years of the Great Depression. He convinced the company president that the men would help him with his crippling burdens if the president would do two things—(1) let the workers know what the problems were in terms they could understand and (2) demonstrate to them that they would share equitably in any improvement made.

How does the Scanlon Plan apply those two ideas?
While there are dozens of variations on the original approach, two major characteristics persist in the great majority of successful applications. Management people and representatives elected by nonmanagement people join in committees that disseminate information on the problems facing the company and solicit suggestions. In addition, there is a monthly company or division-wide bonus based on savings in cost over some agreed-on historical floor. . . . It's intended to get people to realize that you don't have success until the whole company is successful. We're continually working to get people to appreciate what others do. . . .

Donnelly Mirrors [had its] own innovations. . . . What specifically did you do?
The first refinements consisted of putting all savings in labor, materials, and operating supplies into a common pool and splitting this between the people and the company on the basis of a fixed percentage of allowable expenses that remained stable. . . .

What happens when employees work out a series of small improvements,

379

or perhaps one dramatic improvement, that result in the loss of a job?
Each success seems to create a new problem. As far as I know, no bonus
and no need for self-actualization will motivate ordinary working people or
ordinary managers, for that matter, to work themselves out of jobs. We
saw a potentially serious problem here and did something about it.

First, we tried to time our purchases to coincide with upswings in our
employment. This helped, but not enough. Then we added a guarantee
against technological layoff. A person whose job was eliminated by
technology or any kind of work rationalization would be kept for six
months at his old pay. He could be asked to do any suitable work during
that time and would have first bid on job openings that would pay at least
as much as his old rate. Later, we added a guarantee of annual income, and
that increased our people's sense of security. Our guaranteed annual wage
policy provides that any employee with five or more years of seniority will
be guaranteed 90% of current job rate for the next twelve-month period in
the event of job elimination. If you have a climate where people feel secure,
they can do things.

Of course, many companies may give their people similar benefits. The
innovative feature of our action is that, by granting these guarantees in the
context of our total management plan, we can get a return to the company
in human trust. That's an asset not to be taken lightly. We felt this return of
trust the first time an employee felt safe in suggesting how his job could be
eliminated. . . .

*Many observers have been impressed by the amount of teamwork and
communication that goes on between the different groups and departments
of Donnelly Mirrors. Has there been a management technique for
encouraging this?*
We are indebted to Rensis Likert of the Institute for Social Research at the
University of Michigan for the concept of interlocking work teams. It has
been very useful. To show you how the teams work, let's first contrast
them with the usual organization setup. Here's a traditional organization
chart [see the first drawing]. You see these groups of men all responsible to
a single boss. There are many potential teams on this chart, but in spite of
much management rhetoric, few of these groups operate as teams. Even
when a group meets with its boss, there is a tendency to have a series of
one-to-one dialogues with him. Likert found that some groups in companies do act as teams and consequently show consistently higher performance. There's good teamwork when the head of one team is also part of a
successfully working team at the next higher level and becomes a sort of
"linking pin" between the two teams.

Could you draw us a scheme of teams with such links?
Here's the way it looks [see the second drawing]. The one-to-one lines of
reporting are gone. If the peer members of the team support one another,

A Climate of Participation

HBR: How do you represent your people as a member of the Donnelly Committee?

Jo Ann Czerkies, employee in molded products who has completed two terms on the Donnelly Committee: I'll go around and inform my people about the issues that are on the agenda for a meeting. Sometimes I'll take a vote so I know exactly how they stand. But at the meeting, I may hear some new facts we didn't know about beforehand. So I'll have to decide with that information how to vote. What I vote is not always agreeable to the people I represent, so I'll have to go back to them and explain the reasons why I voted as I did. I've been on the Donnelly Committee for four years—I just got off—and for me it's the heart of the company. That's where a lot of very big decisions are made and where we've got management people, production people, office people—everyone—represented. The company *is* everybody, you know.

HBR: What does an employee do when he or she has an idea for improving operations?

Bill Melton, material control supervisor: Generally, the quickest route is for the person to go to his supervisor. But if he doesn't choose to do that, he can get a suggestion form—they're all over the place. He writes up his suggestion and turns it in to the Suggestion Processing Committee. Its function is to make damn sure the suggestion gets assigned to someone who can do something constructive about it. Now, if the idea is totally unworkable, this committee wants to make sure the suggesting person understands why it's unfeasible—what the reasons are. We don't want to just throw the idea into File 13 or someplace like that.

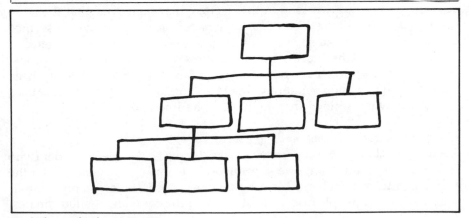

Typical organization pattern

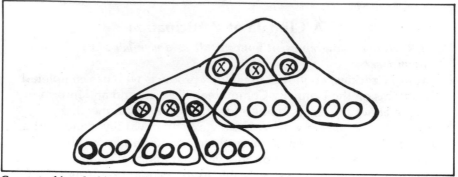

Concept of interlocking work teams

they can deal more realistically with the boss. He can, in fact must, become a leader to remain effective.

The key to the communication of ideas between work teams is the linking pin person. His presence and influence on the "home team" *and* in the team at the next level provide a steady flow of information and understanding of people's needs and of company policies in both directions. The concept is one of participation. Each person manages his own task with participation in the entire company's concerns through his linking pin.

With this approach, we try to achieve consensus among team members, and very often we do. When a team cannot decide an issue, the team leader, using the members' input, makes the decision. Thus there is no abdication of management responsibility, while there is a maximum of participation by those the decision affects.

Could you give us an example of work teams making decisions?
Yes, we had an interesting thing happen recently. During the course of a decision-making process, one supervisor fell ill and an assistant took over for him. Somehow a rumor got into his department, the night shift, that his was the only group working in that factory that night and that the company had decided on a 2% or 3% wage boost for the year, which seemed utterly out of line. And so people decided to have a meeting right then and there. They had the meeting, and the assistant foreman got the proper information and got them back to understanding what had really been said—that no decision about raises had been made. And they all went back to work, having decided that no injustice had been done. . . .

How are the work teams made up?
Each team is built around particular tasks. It consists of a team leader (who is a manager, a foreman, or a supervisor), a team secretary elected by the team, and team members. Team leaders are chosen by selection committees made up of people from several layers in the company—subordinates,

supervisors, and peers. An ideal size for a work team is eight to twelve members.

Reorganizing in this way must have taken quite a bit of effort and concentration. How long was it before it paid off?
Almost immediately—and the rise in productivity was dramatic. Between 1964 and 1969, our productivity (production per unit of direct labor) rose fairly steadily, but when work teams came in, productivity rose dramatically during the next three years—by about one third. Not all of that increase was due to the work teams; some improvements in machinery were made too.

What other steps did you take to carry out your philosophy?
We began conducting regular surveys of employee attitudes, with special emphasis on employees' relations with teams—another of Rensis Likert's ideas. The step that attracted most attention perhaps began with a proposal at one of the work team meetings. The proposal was to eliminate time clocks and put all people on salary. After this idea had been debated at length in work team meetings, we put it to an employee vote, and it was voted in. . . .

Do the work teams and linking pin people deal exclusively with production and cost control?
No, they deal with all phases of the business operation—pricing, marketing, research and development—as well as manufacturing. The phases a team deals with depends on its function. Just about everyone at every level is on a work team. The president of the company is head of the management team, which adopts plans and passes on most of the recommendations that go to the board. The management team monitors progress against plans and coordinates the necessary adjustments that have to be made. One of our tasks is to decide on annual goals for the company.

What about matters of employee morale, grievance, promotion, and compensation? How are they handled?
What we call the Donnelly Committee deals with them. You see, we have what some people call two systems—an *executive* system and a *representative* system. The executive team does the work of the company. The representative system deals with the frictions that normally develop in the course of work. The executive system consists of the work committees linked together. The representative system is the Donnelly Committee, which represents all levels of the company. This committee deals with grievances; establishes pay policies; takes up questions of holidays, fringe benefits, and pay; considers exceptions from policy on promotion; and handles other matters of that kind. . . .

How does the Donnelly Committee operate? It must function differently than the work teams do.
For every 35 or so employees, there is one representative on the committee. The representative is elected for a two-year term, and the terms are staggered, so that every six months some elections are held. However, a representative can be recalled by his or her constituents if they don't like what he or she is doing. The representatives are not paid extra for this work, even though it is time-consuming.

They may be reelected, of course, and some have been, but because the job takes time, they are not likely to serve on and on. . . .

What about the power of committee members?
Every vote is equal, regardless of whom the member represents—whether maintenance teams, grinders, management, or someone else. Unanimous agreement is required for passing a recommendation. If a representative votes no on any issue, it doesn't pass. So a representative cannot pass the buck when he or she goes back to the teams represented and they ask how come such and such was voted. If the committee passed it, the representative must either have voted in favor or not voted at all. . . .

Is cooperative effort hard to teach?
We do get a lot of people in business who are motivated to be individual achievers. When they come to me with an "I can do it all myself" attitude, one of the examples I like to use is this: I say, "Okay, we'll fire all the payroll clerks. How long will you keep on doing your thing and not getting paid?" That usually brings them up short. They agree that, yes, the payroll clerks are needed, and then they start looking around, and the more they look, the more they see the need for other people. . . .

You've indicated that alienation in an organization is destructive. What does your executive team do to deal with it?
Well, it doesn't operate any differently from any other management team. They'll exchange information or sometimes they'll solve a problem; sometimes they'll try to decide what course of action to take. If we're not getting good decisions, we do spend time asking what's blocking us. Is it that we're getting bad information or that people are not speaking their minds or something else?

Is the executive team the highest team?
Yes, except for the board of directors.

It's a different sort of a thing from the work teams?
It's the highest work team in the company.

How do you like the board of directors to function?

384

Boards usually pass whatever management recommends. Unless there's a real fight going on, they very seldom have any serious impact on what management decides. Now I don't think that the board should be in the position to change management decisions all the time, but I do believe that they should be in a position to make recommendations at a formative stage in the decision-making process so that they can keep management tracking toward its long-range goals. . . .

Are you saying that the hierarchy hasn't disappeared but that the lines are getting pretty blurry?
Well, yes. I don't see how a company can operate without levels of responsibility, because problems come in a variety of sizes, kinds, and complexities. But there has to be a free flow of information back and forth, and there has to be a consideration of ideas coming up from other areas. While there are levels of responsibility, it isn't compartmentalized. . . .

A Sense of Achievement

HBR: Does the Donnelly approach to management work?
Bill Melton: It's clearly understood by all of us. When something comes along—something like a schedule increase, a product variation, a method change—we try to decide how we can do that with the least amount of trauma and expense to the individual people. The people who are doing the routine manufacturing every day can be very helpful in developing a common-sense way to do it. In fact, even if they can't, it's worth involving them in it to the point that they understand completely what's going on. We don't get change orders that say, "You used to do that, but now you must do this." We minimize the number of failures on anything new we try by deciding ourselves. You'd be surprised how often people take pride of authorship in what they think up and what kind of effort they put in to make it work.

Jo Ann Czerkies: I think the system works. I think for a while we were leaning toward what I consider permissiveness. Everybody thought that if they wanted a specific thing, it was supposed to be that way. Instead of looking at the overall picture and saying, "O.K., you know this is what we *need* to do" and "What are your ideas?" and then taking that input and then someone making a decision, if we didn't like it, you know, we weren't going to have it. I think now we're getting back closer to what we really need to do with participative management.

Other companies that have experimented with participative management have run into what's called a Hawthorne Effect—that is, when you're paying special attention to an innovation and what the people in the plant are doing, sometimes there can be an increase in productivity and a decrease in absenteeism simply because everybody is interested in what they are doing. Now that the novelty has worn off, are you getting back to what you were beforehand?

No, our absenteeism is low still and our tardiness too. If you pay attention to people, they perform better. At Western Electric Company during the famous Hawthorne Experiment, researchers found that even if you turn off the lights, employees perform better. And what we're trying to do is pay attention to people on a constant basis. So, in a way, what we're trying to do is have a continuous Hawthorne Effect.

» Paul Bernstein «

Advanced Democratization in the American Plywood Industry

» «

In this selection, Boston College business professor Paul Bernstein describes eighteen plywood firms in the Pacific Northwest that are not only managed, in large part, by their workers, but fully owned by them. The typical company in this group has a president and board of directors elected from among the worker-owners. The worker-owners hire a professional manager to run the daily operations of the company, but all important policy decisions are made by the elected board or by a vote of all the workers. All workers have equal voting power, share equally in the profits, and receive identical wages. These worker-capitalists are fiercely independent and amazingly productive. On all common measures of profitability and efficiency, the worker-owned mills outperform nearby conventionally owned mills. The secret of the mills' success was revealed by one worker-owner. "When the mill is your own, you really work hard to make a go of it."

Eighteen plywood manufacturing firms in Oregon and Washington are fully owned by their employees and to varying degrees, are also managed by them.*

These companies make up about one-eighth of the American plywood industry. They range in size from 80 to 450 owner-workers and in gross annual earnings from $3 million to $15 million. They range from nineteen to thirty-three years of continuous operation. . . .

---

*In Washington these companies are (name in italics equals the company and the town): Buffelen Woodworking Company in Tacoma; *Elma* Plywood Corporation; *Everett* Plywood Corporation; *Fort Vancouver* Plywood Company; Hardell Mutual Plywood Corporation in Olympia; *Hoquiam* Plywood Company; *Lacey* Plywood Company; Mt. Baker Plywood, Inc. in Bellingham; North Pacific Plywood, Inc. in Tacoma; *Stevenson* Co-Ply, Inc.; and Puget Sound Plywood, Inc. in Tacoma. In Oregon: *Astoria* Plywood Corporation; *Brookings* Plywood Corporation; Linnton Plywood Association in Portland; *Medford* Veneer and Plywood Corporation; *Milwaukie* Plywood Corporation; Multnomah Plywood Corporation, in Portland; and Western States Plywood Cooperative in Port Orford.

The idea that to make a man work you've got to hold gold in front of his eyes is a growth, not an axiom. We've done that for so long that we've forgotten there's any other way.
—F. Scott Fitzgerald, *This Side of Paradise*

Founding of Worker-owned Firms

The first such company, Olympia Plywood, was founded in 1921. . . . A group of lumbermen, carpenters, and mechanics pooled their resources and built a plant by their own labor in Olympia, Washington. Most of the workers were heirs to a Scandinavian tradition of cooperative enterprise, common to that immigrant population of the Pacific Northwest. To assemble the materials and to purchase a site, the 125 workmen had to contribute $1,000 each, which they raised by cashing in savings bonds, borrowing from friends, pledging future wages, or mortgaging personal property. In return for their individual contribution each worker received by contract a share in the new company entitling him to employment, an equal share in the profits, and an equal vote in directing all company affairs. . . . After the initial sacrifice, the company prospered. Plywood was then a relatively new industry with a steadily increasing demand, and Olympia quickly developed a reputation for high-quality products. Three other worker-owned companies were established just before World War II in much the same way. . . . They, too, found a ready market for plywood, which was being further boosted by wartime demand.

A few years after the war a private plywood company became the first to convert to worker-ownership. As the market price of plywood was then declining and there were problems getting logs, the owner of Oregon-Washington Plywood Co. in Tacoma decided to sell his business. A few workers in this firm were aware of the four successful worker-owned mills and began a campaign to convince their fellow employees to buy the company. Though raising the money would be a hardship and the project itself risky, about three-fifths of the firm's employees pledged their support. The original owner not only agreed to the arrangement but even offered to stay on as sales broker for the first six months. . . .

The ability of worker-owned mills to survive the severe price swings characteristic of the plywood market helped lead to the creation of over twenty worker-owned companies by the mid-fifties. . . .

System of Self-government

The organization of the plants varies from one to another, but all reflect the same general process. Employee-shareholders meet annually to elect from their own number a board of directors (which could just as accurately be termed a workers' council). The board makes most policy decisions, but its power is checked by the whole group: for example, expenditures over $25,000 must be approved by the entire membership of the company. Similarly, any major decision to invest, build a subsidiary plant, borrow a large sum of money, open a sales contract, or sell a sizable asset must be voted on by all the workers. In some companies the rank-and-file can challenge a board decision by collecting a petition of 10 to 20 percent of the membership and calling a special shareholders' meeting to decide the issue.

A president, vice-president, and secretary-treasurer are also elected yearly. In several mills, the president is the worker who received the most votes in the board election. The elections themselves seem to be partly a popularity contest, partly the selection of genuine business-leadership talent, and partly an expression of task-group friendships. This last factor means there are representatives on the board from different parts of the productive process. . . .

The board of directors appoints a general manager to coordinate day-to-day affairs. He is the company's expert on business matters and usually comes from outside the firm. The rest of the administrative staff consists of a plant supervisor, sales manager, logs purchaser, accountant, shipping expediter, and their assistants, usually all shareowners.

The governing process in the mills is based on a circular pattern of authority (see Figure 1). The workers hire the manager, set his salary, and make all major decisions on company expansion, modernization, diversification, and so forth. Yet on a day-to-day basis they work under the manager's direction. The directors, elected by their fellow workers, receive neither deference nor extra pay, and continue to work in the plant while serving on the board. Thus it becomes impossible for them to avoid suggestions from other workers. . . .

Of course, some workers are more involved than others. These workers feel a strong responsibility to make the company succeed; they learn all they can about the company's problems; and they run for director. Others who are known to be talented refuse to take on leadership responsibility: "Why bother? It's too much of a hassle," is their attitude. A good number of workers feel incapable of being leaders and offer only a suggestion or two. Almost all, however, feel willing to complain to any director or officer. Finally, there are some worker-owners who do not participate at all. They consider their company to be like any other mill except that it provides more take-home pay. . . .

To supplement the informal communication network where worker-directors talk with their friends back on the production line, company issues are presented to shareowners in more formal ways. In the most concerned companies, monthly reports are sent to each worker's home. . . . In less diligent worker-owned firms, a shorter statement is prepared quarterly and left in a stack on a table for interested workers to

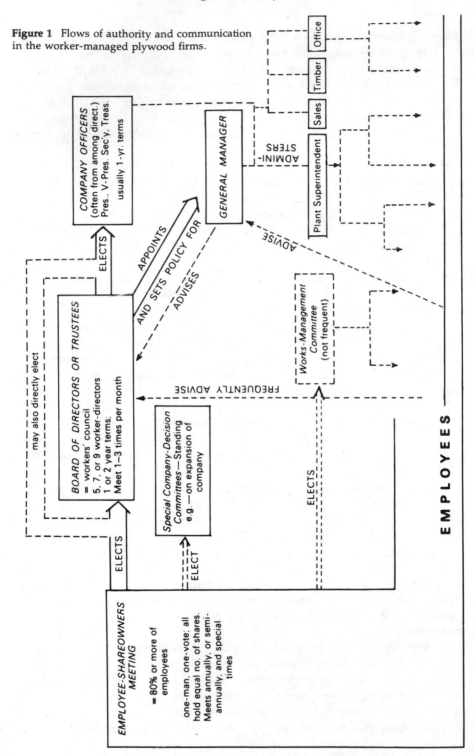

Figure 1 Flows of authority and communication in the worker-managed plywood firms.

pick up. Reports from the twice-monthly board meetings are posted in most companies. At year's end the company financial statement is circulated to all worker-owners, and in at least one firm, a complete audit is mailed to each member, revealing exactly what has been paid to every other member of the firm. . . .

Much of the success or failure of the worker-owned mill depends upon the general manager. He needs both sound business sense and the ability to present his viewpoint convincingly to the directors. His relationship with the members affects their motivation in the mill as workers. It also affects their flexibility and wisdom in making long-run business decisions as owners.

Many a manager has found himself caught between the workers' wants and his own judgment of what is best for the firm. He must deal with a basic tension between the workers' interests as wage-earners and their interests as owners. The first interest focuses on the short-run: "Give me my income now—as big a share of this year's surplus as possible." The other interest is long-term; for example: "We must reserve fifty to sixty percent of this year's surplus to purchase timberland so we'll have an assured supply of raw material in years to come."

Another tension exists between the workers' expertise about their specific jobs in the plant and their minimal knowledge about outside factors to be considered in collective decisions. . . .

Productivity

In spite of such difficulties the firms prosper. Evidently, considerable forces of productivity are released by the self-management process which can outweigh the inefficiencies of semi-amateur management. Worker-owned mills have demonstrated their higher productivity compared to conventionally owned firms in the following ways:

1. Workers' collectives have many times taken bankrupt or losing private plywood firms and converted them into successful enterprises.

2. Worker-owned firms' output averaged 115–120 square feet of plywood per man-hour in contrast to conventional firms 80–95 square feet, during the 1950s. During the 1960s, they were producing 170 square feet per man-hour compared to 130 square feet for conventional firms.

3. In general, worker-owner mills operate at a higher percentage of capacity than do conventional mills.

4. Whenever the entire industry has suffered from a slump in demand and private firms have thus had to lay off workers, worker-owned firms have been able to keep their men on the job. . . .

Motivations behind this greater productivity are apparent in the attitudes of members, as expressed in these comments:

> "When the mill is your own, you really work hard to make a go of it."

"Everyone digs right in—and wants the others to do the same. If they see anybody trying to get a free ride, they get on his back right quick."

"Group pressure here is more powerful than any foreman could be."

"If a guy held back, he didn't feel right. Actually, he was stealing from the others."

Thus pride of ownership motivates the majority to produce more than hired workers, and mutual supervision keeps potential laggards from lowering the standard.

Earnings

Because their roots are in a cooperative, egalitarian philosophy, the plywood mills pay all members an equal wage: floorsweeper, skilled panel-finisher, and accountant alike. Since certain jobs may take longer than others, or a machine may be shut down for repairs and put someone off work for a few hours, a sophisticated system of record-keeping has evolved to equalize the final take-home pay. Every week or month a person's hours at work are totaled and whoever has less than the standard is given first bid for weekend work to bring his total pay up to equality. He need not actually work then if he prefers not to, but he must be offered the opportunity. Likewise, those whose weekly or monthly totals exceed that period's standard must reduce their hours during the next period to the level which allows for equal income.

Highly skilled workers sometimes resent not receiving more pay than men who do the simplest jobs in the firm. And some members regard equal wages as unrealistic, especially because in low-profit years a few workers may leave the company for higher paying jobs elsewhere. . . . In order not to lose men in bad years from certain crucial jobs such as electrician or mechanic, some firms have made these into nonowner positions. Men are hired for those posts at higher salaries than the egalitarian pay. However, most worker-owners are reluctant to create hired, salaried jobs, so the practice is strictly limited to a few positions, most often the general manager.

During all but the worst market times, average pay is almost always higher in worker-owned plywood companies than in other firms, not only on an hourly basis (which usually averages twenty-five percent higher) but also because of the year-end division of profits. . . .

Cooperation in these firms includes the freedom to take time off when needed. From one day to three months can be requested in addition to the worker's paid vacation. . . . The only restriction is that he not use his time off for moonlighting because then he would be violating one basic obligation of his stock-ownership: to contribute equal labor to the common enterprise.

One complaint in the firms is that the older workers do not, in effect, live up to this obligation because they are kept on beyond their usefulness to the company. Retirement is not compulsory, and the employment of older members who are less efficient is criticized by some as a form of feather-bedding. Of course, one might regard the employment of older workers who want to continue working to be far more humane than the forced retirement characteristic of conventional companies. Workers in the plywood firms can continue their life-long trade among close friends during their last years instead of being forced into involuntary idleness.

The Nonowning Worker

In addition to using one or two highly paid, nonowning, skilled workers, many mills employ ordinary production workers on a much larger scale. This practice seems contrary to their egalitarian philosophy. . . .

The most basic reason nonowning workers are not brought in as equal partners is that shareowners fear their own stock must be devalued in order to add more shareowners to the fixed asset-value of the firm. . . .

Nonowning employees at the plywood companies do not receive the same fixed, egalitarian wage as shareowners; they are paid according to the prevailing industry-wide union scale. . . . The other workers are their bosses, not partners, and usually they are not protected by a union.

Unions

Nonowning workers do benefit indirectly from union gains achieved in conventional plants, for the rule of thumb seems to be to give them at least what the industry-wide union contract requires. . . .

The attitude of most worker-owners towards the unions is dormantly sympathetic. They had been union members before they founded their own companies and many keep up their union membership. But they are not active in a local union chapter because the main function of their union,

---

To protect the workers in their inalienable rights to a higher and better life; to protect them, not only as equals before the law, but also in their health, their homes, their firesides, their liberties as men, as workers, and as citizens; to overcome and conquer prejudices and antagonism; to secure to them the right to life, and the opportunity to maintain that life; the right to be full sharers in the abundance which is the result of their brain and brawn, and the civilization of which they are the founders and the mainstay; to this the workers are entitled. . . . The attainment of these is the glorious mission of the trade unions.

—Samuel Gompers

---

negotiating for higher wages and better working conditions, is something they take care of themselves.

The situation is fundamentally anomalous. But the anomaly is resolved once we understand worker-owned mills as a *third system*; neither capitalist ownership, nor its counterforce, the union-organized labor pool. . . .

Implications

The unique experience of these worker-managed firms in America has made evident valuable possibilities for advanced democratization of the workplace:

1. The invention of the "working share," which secures for each person the rights of ownership, labor, and self-government, and does so on an egalitarian basis.

2. The existence already within the present legal environment of a space for workers' self-management; within state law through incorporation either as a cooperative or as a jointly held corporation, and within federal law, after a series of battles with the Internal Revenue Service to define a mutually acceptable status under the tax laws.

3. The creation of a "workers' council" structure and process in the United States without the prelude of a socialist revolution and without waiting for a supportive change in labor union ideology.

4. Development of a mechanism to equalize the distribution of incomes between managing and working classes, again without waiting for government compulsion.

5. At the same time, the equalization of income was not gained at expense of lessening employee motivation or productivity, as other incentives were generated which yielded equal or greater output.

» Daniel Zwerdling «

IPG: Democracy at Work

»«

Although the democratic system of worker ownership functions relatively smoothly at the Oregon and Washington plywood mills, efforts to reproduce this success in other companies have seldom gone as well. Journalist Daniel Zwerdling's case study of International Group Plans (IGP) is a candid account of the perils and pitfalls that can be expected when a radically innovative system of management is attempted. Like the workers at Donnelly Mirrors, IGP employees are organized into self-managing teams. In addition, IGP workers own half of the stock in their company and elect half the members of the board of directors. An insurance corporation, IGP stands out among the many experiments in workplace democratization because its workforce is primarily white collar. The company has also been unusually willing to let its "dirty laundry" be aired in public: democracy doesn't always work at IGP; workers often abuse their powers and privileges; the company is very bureaucratic; and employee discontent and conflict are prevalent. Nevertheless, this experiment is a remarkable and deliberate effort to make life at work conform with the democratic ideology of the nation.

Consumers United—usually called International Group Plans, or IGP—is the $60 million, worker-managed insurance corporation just ten blocks from the White House in the financial heart of Washington D.C. The 340 secretaries, accountants, file clerks, salespeople, and other employees own half the corporation and elect by popular vote half the board of directors. . . .

In just five years this insurance corporation has developed perhaps the most extensive experiment in worker self-management in North America. . . .

More than any other enterprise represented at the Third International Conference on Self-Management, IGP offered a model suggesting that worker self-management—not just worker ownership or worker participation—can work in a contemporary, sophisticated U.S. corporation. IGP is a modern white-collar company in a competitive market using advanced computer technologies. It's a successful corporation that earns close to $1 million profit a year. Workers at IGP aren't left-leaning college graduates like workers are in so many collectives, but are instead a typical assortment of middle and lower income office workers—46 percent white, 43 percent black, two-thirds female, and only a third with college degrees.

Most important, IGP is a firm where rank and file employees really do exert fundamental powers. For example, 85 percent of the workers turned out for the board of directors election, an enviable turnout in any political campaign. "Look, just say we are completely in charge of our own jobs from day-to-day," a claims clerk told me. "I mean that individuals like myself, making close to [IGP's] minimum wage, make decisions on our own that could affect a whole insurance plan, such as whether certain people are eligible to receive claims or not—decisions which only a manager could make at any traditional insurance company."

And the workers at IGP have used their powers to fashion benefits which most U.S. workers can only dream about. In a city where many white-collar clerks start at $6,000 per year, IGP employees have voted a minimum wage over $10,000, plus a share of the corporate profits. In a nation where most workers get a few days paid sick leave, the IGP worker-owners have voted paid sick leave for three months.

The lessons IGP offers are not all about success, however. The company faces some serious problems and has made some serious tactical mistakes from which workers and students of workplace democracy can also learn.

The self-management system at IGP remains wobbly and sometimes embattled, plagued by managers who resist giving up their traditional powers and by production clerks who don't know how to assert their newly obtained powers. Some employees at IGP say they could not care less about making important decisions which shape their work lives.

"I would love to go back to a traditional company, punching time clocks and being told exactly what to do, when and how to do it," one clerical worker said. "I just can't stand the confusion anymore."

The experience at IGP suggests that the journey to self-management in a company is difficult and painful—but rewarding. But then, so is any social change. "If I were at a traditional company I'd still be just a clerk," says a college dropout who started as a clerk at IGP. "But here I've been elected to committees where I've learned skills I never could have learned in school—how to work with people and how to run a multimillion dollar business."

From Insurance to Revolution

James P. Gibbons, the current president, founded IGP in 1964 with three partners and an IBM 1401 computer. . . . In five years Gibbons had 100 employees handling $10 million in premiums. . . .

"I became consciously committed to making this company a self-sustaining, living model of social change," [Gibbons says].

"What I've done," he says, "is to create the first corporate power structure in this country which the employees have the power to change as they want. I'm not talking about anything short of a total revolution."

The birth of democracy at IGP was a paradox. Gibbons imposed self-management on the workers as the enlightened monarch of a tiny nation might liberate the masses by beneficent dictate. One day in spring 1972 he announced he was transferring half the company ownership to the employees in a nonsalable, profit sharing trust. Six months later he announced that employees would begin electing half the board of directors (Gibbons appoints the other half). And then he began creating a network of employee committees which, he decreed, would gradually make the corporate decisions traditionally reserved for the executives. . . .

Gibbons never pursued self-management for self-management's sake. "Hell no, self-management isn't the end objective, the end objective is maximizing humanness," Gibbons says, "creating an environment of justice, equity, equality, beauty, truth—an environment where each member of the community has the opportunity to grow and develop in his or her own unique way, to self-actualize."

The main reason for self-management, Gibbons says, "is to give workers the power to protect themselves against arbitrary uses of power by management. But if we achieve self-management without achieving these other goals, I'll consider the experiment a failure."

Many companies around the country that have instituted some form of worker participation have used it as a tool for making the business more successful. But in Gibbons' revolution, the business itself has become the tool—the tool for creating a radical society, "a utopian community," as Gibbons puts it. He has proclaimed his goals in a credo, emblazoned on a silver poster and taught to new employees on their first day on the job:

• Goal I: To build a lasting economic institution which helps satisfy the real needs of our client organizations . . . and to provide quality service . . . [while] making enough profit to keep the corporation in existence. . . .

• Goal II: To build this institution on a foundation which maximizes the humanness of everyone involved, and which creates a new ethic for economic institutions—an alternative model for business.

"The very idea of creating a humane society within a business institution," Gibbons acknowledges, "is an enormous paradox."

IGP Government

. . . In early 1978 the basic structure at IGP [looked] like this:

• The *worker teams* are autonomous work groups throughout the company, each with about six to a dozen employees who perform the same job. Clerks who pay claims to military clients, for instance, work on the military claims team. Although team power has never been defined on paper, in practice the teams are virtually responsible for organizing and managing

the company's day-to-day work, and handling staff hiring and firing.
 • Each *department* is composed of several teams. Department-level decisions, such as staffing levels and budgets, long-range objectives, and coordinating the work of the teams, are made democratically by a *department operating committee*. The committee includes the *team leaders* (a worker representative elected from each team) and a *department coordinator* whom the team leaders help select. . . .
 • Each *division* includes several departments. Division-level policies are made by the *division operating committee*, which includes the department coordinators, a representative elected by the workers, and a division coordinator elected by the department coordinators. The division coordinator—called a "center forward" in IGP's lingo—is supposed to carry out the decisions of the committee, not give orders like a boss.

Benefits of Self-management

Worker-owners at IGP enjoy the kinds of benefits that most of America's 86 million workers only dream about. Formulated and passed by the employee-elected congress, the CRA, and then approved by the board, benefits include:
 • minimum annual wage: $10,600 plus profits.
 • flexible hours: set your own hours between 7 a.m. and 7 p.m. Some employees work four days a week.
 • no attendance records: everyone leaves a few hours early or takes a whole day off from time to time. As long as you get your work done, no one minds.
 • vacations: no less than two weeks a year, and "no more than the job responsibilities, team, and team leader will agree to." Some clerical workers take a month off.
 • unlimited sick leave: the company pays your full salary for 90 continuous days, then you go on disability. You're guaranteed a job with the same salary whenever you come back.
 • maternity leave: three months at full pay.
 • tuition paid: take a course at a local university that relates somehow to your work, and the company will pay you back. "I'm taking psychology and philosophy," a files team-leader says, "so I can better understand the 'girls.' "
 • first crack at job openings: all vacancies are offered to IGP employees first.
 If your team votes to fire you, you're not yet out in the cold. You can appeal to the employee court while receiving full pay. If you do leave, you can start over at a new company with good will and a clean slate. IGP won't put any negative information in your personnel file.

• The *corporate operating committee* is made up of the handful of top managers who run the corporate business from week to week. It's the least representative committee of all. Except for one member directly elected by the workers, the members are hired by the board. The corporate operating committee reviews all major policies and corporate operating strategies devised by the lower committees before sending them for approval to the board.

• The *board of directors* is half chosen by Gibbons and half elected. The board is supposed to be the ultimate decision-making body, the final vote on major policies from investments to sick leave to wage scales.

• Two of the most important committees operate somewhat outside this chain of responsibility. The first is the seven member *personal justice committee,* the worker-elected court. Official IGP policy guarantees its workers "full protection of your individual rights as a citizen of these United States, in particular freedoms articulated in the Constitution and known as the Bill of Rights." . . .

• The committee that created the worker court is the *community relations assembly,* or CRA, the worker congress. Its 20 representatives are elected by popular vote, each by "constituencies" of about 15 employees. At least one CRA representative sits and votes on virtually every major committee in IGP, which ensures that at least one direct representative of "the people" votes on every decision.

But the guts of the CRA's job is to formulate all the workplace policies that directly affect employees, from vacation rights to production standards, from hiring guidelines to wages. The CRA doesn't have final say, according to corporate policy; it sends its recommendations for "review" by the corporate operating committee and "approval" by the board.

Does It Work?

. . . When it comes to the day-to-day life in this "economic community," as Gibbons calls it, the rank and file employees have enormous power available—and they use it. File clerks making under $11,000 a year hold an impromptu meeting one morning and vote to revamp the entire central files system, the guts of the corporation. Clerks churning out new insurance policies take a break to decide who should answer the telephone; they vote to rotate the hated task. . . .

The worker teams also wield effective control over firing fellow employees, although the power is slightly ambiguous since team leaders and department coordinators also have the power to fire; the company has never firmly resolved just whose power should take precedent. In practice though, the rank and file employees have made firing a rare event in this company. . . .

The clerks paying insurance claims and peering in the microfilm machines don't exert direct power over department and division-level policies, since they don't have a direct vote on the operating committees. But most employees say they aren't interested in worrying about long-term planning and budgeting.

They can, however, exert considerable informal power over department and division decisions when they feel the issues touch them directly. For one thing, there's a company commandment called the "IGP Decision-Making Model": It declares that no decisions may be made until all the workers directly affected have been consulted first. But more important, the workers exert power because there is an assumption that leaders are supposed to act on behalf of the employees and are to watch out for the employees' interests. . . .

No Paper Tiger

IGP employees also wield considerable power over the broad policies that govern their work life, through their Community Relations Assembly. On paper, the CRA seems like a glorified employee sounding board, one that has the empty "power" to *recommend* policies, which managers then can toss in the waste basket—since all CRA policies must be submitted for "review" and "approval" to the corporate operating committee and the board. . . .

But . . . recent members on the CRA have revised all the major workplace policies and started the disciplinary system working. As IGP employees later told participants at the Third International Conference on Self-Management, it was largely the CRA which drafted the company production standards. . . .

Describing IGP through the CRA, the teams, and other committees misses the spirit of employee power and freedom there, especially compared to employee feelings at traditional white-collar firms. . . .

At IGP, clumps of workers sit on their desks, drinking coffee and chatting about a recent CRA vote to reimburse workers for meals, transportation, and even babysitting fees if they work after hours or on the weekends. . . . There's no morning bell at IGP. "I've been coming to work at noon lately because I'm training some horses every morning at a stable," a researcher in the life insurance department says, "I stay and work until 8 o'clock." . . .

When Voices Subside

There's a sharp dichotomy at IGP between the daily world of work and the world of business. When it comes to making decisions about what insurance packages to market, what strategies to use and what investments to make, the rank and file employees have little voice.

The theory behind the structure at IGP has been that "employees don't have any business making decisions about finances if they don't have financial expertise," one researcher explains. Instead, representatives accountable to the rank and file are supposed to make such decisions. . . .

Most of the power to make financial and marketing decisions rests with the corporate operating committee, far from the rank and file. . . .

When really crucial financial policies come up, the board turns over the decision to the entire work force for a vote. It was the rank and file who voted to establish the remarkable, constantly rising minimum wage—now $10,600 per year—and it was the workers who decided how to divvy the profits. . . .

Now the Caveat

Despite the many successes at IGP, the self-management system does not work as well as it might. For every team that asserts its autonomy and power, employees point to a team that shrinks from responsibility. For every decision that a committee reaches by democratic vote, workers point to a committee that waffles and submits to the decision of a self-styled boss. . . .

And the contradictions are nourishing worker discontent. The corporation preaches trust, maximization of humanness, and quality work, yet the absentee rate is increasing, turnover is high (up to 20% during the last few years), and some departments are mired in chronic backlogs and sloppy work. . . .

Workers at many companies, according to social surveys, are discontent with the status quo—their lack of power, their isolation, their alienating role as a cog in a vast corporate machine. But at IGP the workers' discontent stems from change; normal corporate power relationships have been turned upside down. Self-management at IGP . . . has put power and responsibility up for grabs, and neither the managers nor the rank and file have ever been trained to handle it. . . .

"The fact is," says a file clerk who used to work at the post office, "a lot of people need a boss standing over them, telling them exactly what to do." . . .

The Committee Curse

And if committees are the cornerstone of decision-making—there are so many committees at IGP that one can scarcely count them—employees must master the art of listening to others, sharing opinions openly and hammering out a consensus acceptable to the whole group. Yet too many committees flounder at IGP because workers lack successful committee experience. . . . .

No wonder two-thirds of the workers told the 1975 survey they think most committees are a waste of time. . . .

While many employees feel overwhelmed and confused at their sudden rise to power, managers at IGP feel uncertain with their lack of it. "Damn it, don't think of yourselves as managers, think of yourselves as leaders," Gibbons fumes at an operating committee meeting. "*Manager* implies control; *leader* implies government with equal rights." As self-management advocates emphasize, a good leader shares information with the rank and file employees, delegates power as much as possible, inspires and motivates workers rather than gives orders, and, most important, sees his or her role as working on behalf of the workers, not over them.

"Now you tell me," Gibbons says with a sigh one day, "where you can find leaders who have administrative and insurance experience who also believe in these democratic values? Right—nowhere." . . .

Perils of Democracy

Most leaders at IGP complain that group decision-making takes too much time in a business that demands quick action; and unless all the members of a committee are doing their required part, workers with committee experience agree, they're right. Some leaders have become so afraid of crossing the line between providing leadership and imposing dictatorship that they shrink from exercising any initiative at all. "And then," one division center forward says, "inertia sets in." . . .

Workers have watched Gibbons undercut his own carefully nurtured democratic structure many times, pleading "This is a business, we've got to go on." He solves the immediate crisis, employees argue, but contributes to a more profound crisis in the long run: cynicism. . . .

Education in democracy, many employees argue, is one area where IGP stumbles. The transition to self-management should be expected to be difficult, they say, but Gibbons neglected to make the transition smoother by creating long-term training programs to teach employees self-management values and skills. . . .

[But according to Gibbons] "People don't understand that we don't have the luxury of time for all this training. We're not an educational institution, we're a business, and we have economic problems that have to be solved." . . .

The Pendulum Swings Back

The recent events at IGP—the widespread conservatism, culminating in the unsuccessful effort by top managers to toss out fundamental worker powers and freedoms—suggests that IGP confronts a difficult paradox. As the workplace democracy grows stronger and employees feel more assertive, the workplace democracy itself may come under increasing attack. For until recently, most employees, including top managers, went along with Gibbons' visions even if they grumbled under their breath. "Nobody in this company comes right out and says to Jim's face, 'democracy sucks,' " a former board member said. But as more and more employees feel assertive, those who oppose Gibbons' goals are boldly speaking out. And the strongest opposition is among some of the leaders, who feel they have the most to lose. . . .

A former member of the corporate operating committee said, . . . "There are no stock options for us; a guy making $25,000 a year will leave with the same money after 20 years as a mailroom clerk making less than half as much. We don't get power, or prestige—most of us don't even have a private office. Democracy is nice," he said, "but I'm not sure I want it at my business." A few months later, he quit.

Ironically, one of the major obstacles to full self-management at IGP, employees say, will continue to be its most dynamic force—Jim Gibbons himself. The employees at IGP never asked for self-management. Gibbons alone dreamed the self-management vision, imposed it on the employees, and with his charisma made it work. But now employees say Gibbons' role is starting to stunt self-management's growth, for the employees can't quite shake the notion of Gibbons as the beneficent monarch and themselves as grateful subjects. . . .

Questions for the Future

IGP employees are asking difficult questions that every self-managed enterprise must ask and answer. Can a workplace democracy survive if some of the employees don't care to participate? According to the extensive but unscientific 1975 survey, less than half the employees who responded wanted "a lot of say" over selecting management, and not even one-third said they wanted "a lot of say" over hiring and firing fellow workers and deciding how corporate funds should be spent. The statistics coincide with workers' own perceptions. . . .

The company confronts serious problems because not enough workers take an active part in company affairs, yet some employees argue that demanding worker participation is itself an "antidemocratic" rule. . . .

And IGP employees are asking other questions. Can a workplace democracy survive if some employees, including some key leaders, oppose it? Should the company hire only job applicants who swear they're committed to Gibbons' goals? Must every employee share the same values for the humanitarian structure to survive? . . .

Despite its flaws, the system at IGP does work. Along with their griping, most employees acknowledge the company is the best place they have ever worked. "I've been offered far more money at other jobs, and sometimes I've been tempted enough to go for an interview," one employee says. "But the moment I walked in and saw all those rows of robots I knew a conventional job wasn't for me." . . .

The 340 rank and file workers and managers are operating this $60 million corporation, and making a profit, with a degree of freedom, democracy and equality never before achieved by a major U.S. corporation. If they're facing problems, every corporation faces problems. The difference is that workers at IGP can shout their complaints and problems if they want, without fear of getting fired. More important, they've got the power to change their corporation.

V

» «

WORK, PUBLIC POLICY, AND THE FUTURE

» «

Former President Calvin Coolidge once remarked: "When more and more people are thrown out of work, unemployment results." Average unemployment in peacetime has hovered around 4 to 5 percent for most of this century. In the 1970s, the average was 6.2 percent, and it is 7.5 percent in mid-1981. Ironically, more new jobs were created during the last decade than during any time in the nation's history. The economy was expanding, but it could not keep up with the entry of the "Boom Babies" and the increased participation by women in the labor force. The more the economy grew, the further behind it seemed to get.

However, as the authors of the selections in the next two chapters explain, the economy, ultimately, does create enough jobs for most middle-class women and young people who are finished with school. (They just have to wait a while.) But nothing short of war ever creates enough jobs for the "structurally" unemployed, who seldom work even when the rate of unemployment dips to a cyclical low of 4 percent. Many of these people suffer from physical handicaps or are the target of racial discrimination; others lack education or the transportation necessary to find jobs. Their problem, as Feldstein and Liebow explain, is that they lack the skills and incentives needed to hold down good, regular jobs. To the extent that they do work, they work less than full-time, full-year, and for less than the minimum wage. Not only do their jobs offer little in the way of dignity, they are characterized by harsh and arbitrary discipline, unhealthy and unsafe working conditions, and no career path: a dishwasher's job leads only to dishpan hands.

When heads of households are stuck in this so-called secondary labor market, the consequences are serious for the lifestyles and life chances of families. As Liebow illustrates, men who find no dignity in their work and who cannot earn enough to support their families will often desert their families and take up the "easy life" on the streets. The wives and children of these men end up dependent on welfare.

As Moynihan and Liebow argue, when millions of people are dependent on the state for their livelihoods, it is an unhealthy situation for both the individuals and for the larger society. Society pays the cost of dependence not only in such subsidies as welfare payments and food stamps, but in the much higher cost of crime and other social problems. As Liebow says, the urban poor need only one thing: jobs that pay a decent wage so they can break the frightful cycle of dependence that creates generations of people who not only make no contribution to society but are, in fact, counter-productive.

But the policy question is not merely one of providing more jobs—it would be easier if it were. Quality is as important as quantity if society is to reduce or end the deplorable dependency on welfare. Unemployed youths do not just need jobs; specifically, as Wirtz writes, they need *part-time* jobs so they can also attend school. Minority men do not just need jobs; specifically, they need jobs that are competitive with welfare, and jobs that pay enough to support a family.

A few ideas are offered. To provide a greater number of appropriate work opportunities for youth, Wirtz suggests the creation of more work/study programs and federally subsidized jobs in the private sector. Feldstein discusses the possibilities not only for federally subsidized wages for youth and the handicapped, but for upgrading jobs in the secondary labor market to the quality and pay levels of jobs in the primary market. (He doesn't tell us how this could be done, however.) Feldstein also discusses ways in which unemployment compensation could be reformed to end the existing incentives for employers to lay workers off on a seasonal and cyclical basis, and for employees to take long "paid" vacations. He envisions a system similar to that in Japan, where employers plan for full employment by scheduling their production to avoid peaks and valleys. In addition, Feldstein calls for a dual minimum wage: a lower one for unmarried youth, and a higher one for people with families to support.

Other experts have offered a range of proposals to reduce unemployment: improved labor market information, reduction of racial discrimination, tighter control of immigration, public service jobs, job training, and a general expansion of the economy to stimulate growth and create new jobs in the private sector. In Chapter 10, Best offers a work/leisure sharing plan to avoid layoffs. In Chapter 12, Zager describes how the Lincoln Electric company plans for full employment. But no one seems able to offer a comprehensive plan for the many types of unemployment and the differing job needs of the unemployed.

Indeed, uncertainty about what should be done is probably the overriding characteristic of the on-going debate about employment policy. Moreover, at this stage in the book, the reader may even be ready to conclude that uncertainty is the overriding characteristic of every major issue in the work world! Not only do we not know what *should* be done with respect to careers, job design, and public policy, but we particularly do not know what *will* be done in the future. Is there nothing that we can conclude with certainty about the future of work?

Work and the Future

Only one thing is certain about the future: It cannot be predicted. No matter how clever, clairvoyant, or farsighted one might be, there are sure to be significant surprises in the future. With this caveat in mind, it is useful, nonetheless, to explore what work might be like in the years ahead. A careful analysis of many alternatives would allow us to direct our efforts toward the realization of desirable ends, or to work against trends that seem particularly undesirable (but avoidable with a little planning). At the least, we can avoid "future shock" by preparing ourselves for various contingencies.

Futurists have identified a range of alternative workplace futures. Some are utopian. For example, it is commonly predicted that workers will have many exciting jobs in the course of their lives, punctuated intermittently with educational "stop-outs" during which they will be retooled for entirely different careers. They will work flextime, flexweek, flexcareer—most of the time at home, interacting with CRT/computer terminals linking them to offices around the globe. Since robots will do all the grunt work as well as delicate but repetitive tasks, there will be abundant leisure and affluence for everybody. And, when the time comes, people will not want to retire because their latest part-time job will be the most fulfilling and self-actualizing yet.

In contrast, some labor economists have a bleaker view of the future. They say that the best future college graduates can look forward to is a job as a secretary or bank teller at a much lower salary than that earned by high school drop-outs in unionized trades. Because of unfortunate demographic realities, young workers should not count on much upward mobility or on retiring with a nice nest egg. There will be no egg, no nest, and perhaps not even a branch to perch on. Americans will have to work as hard as ever, in dreary jobs, until the day they die.

And some technologists have identified futures that are positively alarming. For example, in his selection on automation in Chapter 15, Colin Norman explores the prospect of mass unemployment, as machines come to do almost all the work of civilization, eliminating not only dirty jobs, but most good ones as well.

Which forecast is right—one of the above or some other possibility? Before answering, consider this. There are three elements that will determine the future: continuity, change, and choice. Since all three factors need to be considered in any forecast about the future of work, it is worth taking a moment to explore each.

Continuity   The future is always influenced by the past and present. Thus the seeds of the future of work are nurturing in today's workplaces. Indeed, the roots of many alternative futures are already growing today in one American company or another. This might be an important hint about the future: If pluralism is the mode of work in America, can we think of any plausible reason to assume that this diversity would be lost in the future, abandoned in favor of a monolithic workplace paradigm? In fact, were we to trace the trend, we would find that American workplaces are becoming even more varied in the conditions of work they offer than they were twenty years ago. Nonetheless, the fact that a trend has been going in one direction for a long time is no guarantee it will continue indefinitely in the same direction. (That is, after all, the error made regularly in economic forecasts.) To understand deviations from continuity we must understand the process of change.

Change   The future is always influenced by unexpected events—developments that break the continuity of history. In the workplace, the Depression of the 1930s broke the long trend of laissez-faire and led to the introduction of government programs designed to increase employee security. In the late 1960s, the youth, environmental, and anti-war movements paved the way for the minor inroads that humanism has recently made in some American corporations. What could happen in the 1980s to alter drastically the current trends? Would a severe energy crisis foster the need for efficiency-minded Taylorism in order to save our standard of living? Would a decade of stagflation lead to a "hunkering down" on the part of workers, and a return to 1930s-type unionism and entitlementarianism? Economic, technological, and political change will no doubt lead to readjustments in the world of work, but how far can we expect these changes to go? Futurists often assume that environmental changes will lead to a flip-flop in values, creating "new" men and women who completely reject all aspects of continuity. But it just is not so. To understand the effects of change on historical patterns we must understand the process of choice.

Choice   The future is always influenced by the choices people make when confronted with a new development. For example, managers often respond to a recession by substituting machines for workers in the hope of increasing efficiency; politicians often respond by creating public service jobs or by using economic policy to stimulate the economy. Individual workers might respond to changing environmental conditions by choosing one job over another, choosing to invest or to spend, or choosing to return to school for further training. Importantly, such choices cannot be predicted solely on the basis of a "rational" response to technological, economic, and other environmental events. What people *want*—their values—is an important determinant of their future actions.

If we look at past behavior, futurists would seem wrong to assume that most workers can, will, or would want to throw out the old and ring in the new. People resist change, and sometimes with good reason. For example, futurists and economists predict that American workers will substitute the long, increasingly expensive commute to work with the convenience of computer terminals in their homes. Rationally, that is what they should do (if we limit rationality to the logic of economics). But workers have other values besides economics and convenience. For most adults, most friendships are formed at work. Without these peers, most of us would have few friends.

In the final analysis, workers will decide whether the continuity of commuting to central workplaces or the change of decentralized working in homes will prevail in the future. It seems reasonable to conclude that some will choose the convenience of working at home, some will choose the pleasures of socializing with co-workers, and some will mix the two. The individual's choice will depend on age, family responsibilities, experiences, personal values, and the nature of the job to be done. Choice—what people want—is thus a central determinant of the future of work. Again, this points toward a pluralistic future of work and away from the monolithic forecasts of the popularizing futurists.

Still frustrated by the blurred image in the crystal ball? There is only one way to clear it up: Make your own forecasts. Begin by identifying the elements of continuity and change that you believe will influence the work world of the future, then analyze how you think these facts will interact with the choices of key players, and you will have a forecast you can trust more than that of any expert. To give you a little help getting started, below are some elements of continuity that you might want to consider.

Elements of Continuity

Each of the following trends could have a profound impact on the number, kinds, and quality of jobs Americans will have in the future.

Economic Growth   Although growth can have some harmful side effects, it nonetheless provides the resources for new jobs, better jobs, and improved working conditions. The absence of growth leads to social and political conflict as groups struggle over the allocation of diminishing work opportunities and social entitlements. Because the entire post-World War II organization of work in America has been predicated on growth, high growth in the 1980s promises a continuation of historical work trends, whereas low growth would bring major discontinuities.

Productivity   This measure of the efficiency of the economy is currently static, if not on the decline, for several reasons: 1) because industry has failed to invest in new plants and machines; 2) because of the shift from a manufacturing-based economy, in which it is easy to increase productivity, to a service-based economy, in which such possibilities are fewer; and 3) because Americans now want to be paid more for working less. Declining growth and sagging productivity have led to a drop in our standard of living. The United States—not long ago the paragon of industrialism—has slipped to ninth in the world in per capita income.

Inflation The impact of inflation on work includes: the unwillingness of citizens to save and businesses to invest; the demands of workers for ever-higher salaries; and the tendency for people to buy gold, antiques, and other nonproductive items. None of these leads to the creation of new jobs.

International Competition Although America has always been part of an interdependent world economy, in recent years it has begun to import large quantities of manufactured goods. Between 1967 and 1979, imports of iron and steel increased by 313 percent, autos by 341 percent, machinery by 501 percent, chemicals by 508 percent. In 1960, the United States produced 25 percent of all world manufacturing exports; today it produces less than 17 percent. The bottom line: the import of cars, clothes, stereos, and televisions equals the export of American jobs.

Innovation Successful new product ideas translate into new, good jobs. But with the exception of the microprocessor and genetic industries, the American well of innovation seems to be drying up. In 1966, 13 percent of all United States patents were awarded to foreigners; in 1975 the number had risen to 28 percent. But job creation depends as much on development as research, and here, again, America is hurting. In the late 1950s, 82 percent of all products brought to market were developed in the United States. Ten years later, the number had dropped to 55 percent. For example, the United States invented video-tape technology—but the Japanese produce 100 percent of all the video-tape recorders sold here.

Underemployment Growth in the number of new professional, technical, and managerial jobs has not kept pace with the rapid rise in levels of educational attainment. As a consequence, many college graduates now take such jobs as bank teller and secretary that were formerly held by high school graduates. When job expectations are not fulfilled, bitterness often results.

These are examples of the types of trends that labor economists include in their forecasts. If these trends continue in their current direction—precipitously downhill—then the prospects for American workers in the 1980s are gloomy. But will these trends continue? That is the 64 trillion dollar question. The trends could turn around, perhaps as O.P.E.C. collapses as the result of new energy developments, as major technological breakthroughs revitalize American industry, as new corporate practices or new national economic policies are adopted. Unfortunately, economists seldom take such probabilities into account when making their forecasts. Doubly unfortunate is the failure of popular futurists to take adequate account of the realities of economic continuity. Clearly, if we are to prepare more valid forecasts, we will have to consider not only continuity but also the following kinds of workplace changes—changes that could influence or be influenced by the continuities described above.

Elements of Change

Significantly, these changes are not the fantasies of wild-eyed stargazers; rather, they are programs that are currently used in a few American companies and *could* become the corporate norm in the 1980s. Some of these have been discussed in earlier chapters of this book.

Permanent, Part-time Jobs　At the Control Data Corporation, jobs are available at "mother's hours," 9:00 to 3:00, or "students' hours," 3:00 to 6:00. The jobs offer medical and other benefits usually associated only with jobs at "regular hours."

Task System　At Harman International, workers negotiate a level of daily production and are free to go home when that level is reached—at 5:00, 4:00, 3:00, or whenever.

Well Pay/Safety Pay　At the Parsons Pine Company, workers with good attendance and safety records get generous bonuses.

Peer-Set Salaries and Raises　At Romac Industries, all workers vote on how much their peers should be paid and on whether or not their contributions merit a raise.

Sabbaticals　At the Xerox Corporation, a Los Angeles law firm, and an Oregon plywood company, workers have access to systems of paid leave to engage in public service and, in some instances, continuing education.

Work Sharing　In Santa Barbara, seven men and women split five full-time medical technician jobs among them. In several California cities, public employees volunteer to work less-than-full-time at less-than-full-pay in order to create jobs for others.

Quality Control Circles　At over five hundred United States corporations—including General Motors—blue-collar workers have accepted full responsibility for the quality of goods they produce. At GM, workers now even negotiate quality standards with suppliers.

Industrial Democracy At several dozen firms, supervisors have been eliminated and work teams have become entirely self-managing. Donnelly Mirrors is governed democratically by joint worker/manager committees. At Chrysler, a union representative sits on the board of directors.

Worker Ownership Over three thousand United States firms now have employee stock ownership plans. In perhaps fifty of these, workers own enough shares to be fully self-managing.

College Degrees Dozens of United States companies now provide the opportunity to earn degrees for local colleges for classwork at plant or office locations. RAND and Arthur D. Little are even accredited to offer on-the-job PhDs.

Phased Retirement A few American companies are said to be experimenting with the European option of letting older workers "glide out." That is, employees between sixty and sixty-five work four-day weeks, those sixty-five to sixty-seven work three days, and those sixty-seven to seventy work two days.

Flexible Scheduling Most people today know that under flextime a worker might come to work between 6:30 and 10:00 A.M. and go home between 3:30 and 7:00 P.M., as long as he or she puts in an eight-hour day. But more radical flexibility may be in the offing. Within broad guidelines, firefighters and flight attendants with sufficient seniority are allowed to arrange their monthly or yearly work schedules in any patterns they desire—clustering work for purposes of travel or education, or spreading it out for purposes of child care.

Automation Machines are changing the work environment in the auto industry, where robots do the welding once done by people, and in offices where electronic mail, word processors, and "intelligent" terminals have altered the tasks of clerks, secretaries, and managers. ARCO has interconnected its hundreds of far-flung operations with two-way video communications in order to reduce costly travel.

This abbreviated list merely illustrates the kinds of changes in working conditions that are not only possible but—in some cases—probable. The forecaster must analyze how such changes might affect and be affected by the continuing trends of inflation, productivity, growth, and underemployment described above. For example, most of these changes would seem to give workers a larger say and stake in the organizations that employ them. This could build loyalty, commitment, and effort, thus, possibly, reducing the negative affects of some of the continuing trends. Once you start thinking about the interactions of continuity and change, you're devising better forecasts than those produced by most economists and futurists. But if you want to graduate to the rank of "Forecaster Firstclass," you will also have to consider the interactions of choice.

Elements of Choice

As continuity and change come to interact in the workplace of the 1980s, politicians, managers, unionists, and workers will all respond to those developments in various and unpredictable (but *not* unimaginable) ways. These actions—including changes in national economic policy and corporate strategies and practices—will, of course, alter the trends and events discussed above. Let's look at only two ways in which workers have reacted during the last decade, and ask if a continuation of such behavior is likely in the future, and how it might interact with the developments we have considered.

Demands for Leisure During the 1970s, the most intense change in worker values was the demand for more time away from work. Managers and workers in blue, white, and pink collars all expressed a desire for more time for family, friends, recreation, and education.

Demands for Entitlements During the 1970s there was a dramatic increase in demands for more "rights," including economic rights (cost-of-living allowance, pensions, dental care), constitutional rights (privacy of personnel files, whistle blowing), organizational rights (voting on plant relocations, rejecting cross-country transfers), and personal rights (freedom to wear hippie beads and jeans in bank teller cages).

Significantly, the demands for leisure and rights in the workplace have continued into the 1980s, even while discretionary incomes and standards of living were eroding. But if such negative economic trends continue for a lengthy period, how will workers react: with continued demands for more leisure time, self-actualization, and psychological rights; or with demands for white-collar unionization, guaranteed job security, and restrictions on plant closings and labor-saving technology? Your ideas about the choices workers might make are as good as anyone's—as long as you also take into account interactions with the factors of continuity and change!

The last selection of the book is a futures exercise in which you can pull the entire course together by exploring some of the changes and choices that are likely to shape tomorrow's world of work.

13

»«

THE
URBAN
UNEMPLOYED

»«

Leroy Woodson/Woodfin Camp, Inc.

» Harry Maurer «

Not Working

» «

For most people, being unemployed is far more damaging to their self-esteem than holding the most demeaning job. Biographies of the unemployed are filled with self-hate, listlessness, futility, and what journalist Harry Maurer, author of this selection, calls "the sense of violence and invasion, the feelings of fear and loss and helplessness." The four case studies presented below from Maurer's oral history of the unemployed, Not Working, *tell of the price individuals and society pay for unemployment. Far better than any statistics or official account ever could, these interviews bring home the reality of a commonly experienced personal crisis. Jim Hughes is a thirty-five-year-old ex-marine whose marriage suffered as he turned to alcohol, self-recrimination, and bitterness during long periods of unemployment. Robin Landau, a twenty-four-year-old daughter of wealthy parents, thought, for a time, at least, that an $85 weekly unemployment check was better than $125 from an unrewarding job. But lacking career goals, she is a drifter who lives "in a fantasy-type world." Karen Lewis is a twenty-two-year-old black woman with two children, no husband, and so little education that her job and life prospects are bleak—a fact she bitterly recognizes. Eddie Vargas is a twenty-four-year-old Chicano who was cheated by the educational system and fooled by the American myth of easy success. Their statements are testimony to the devastating effects of unemployment, regardless of one's race, age, or sex.*

There are many people in this [country] whose living rooms have turned into prisons without bars, and others who gleefully feel they have escaped jobs that were jails. There are people who have been broken by years of idleness, and others who have discovered emotional resources that allow them to endure—even, in a way, to triumph . . .

Unemployed people have been robbed of something, and they know it. The bewilderment they often express is like that of the homeowner who returns to find rooms ransacked, valuable and beloved objects missing. The sense of violence and invasion, the feelings of fear and loss and helplessness descend with the same stunning force when a worker is deprived of work. And the loss is much greater, because work, if the longing of the unemployed is any indication, remains a fundamental human

414

need—even in the crushing form it has increasingly assumed in the modern world. It provides not simply a livelihood, but an essential passage into the human community. It makes us less alone. . . .

How people respond to unemployment is ruled by the interplay between their personality, the objective situation, and a third important factor: ideology. The way they *think* about being unemployed—which really means the tangle of ideas, observations, myths, and precepts they have woven into a vision of their place in the social structure—profoundly affects their ability to endure it. This ideological aspect boils down to one basic question: Who is to blame? And here the unemployed tend to be of two minds. For the record, they usually give an explanation for their joblessness that places the onus elsewhere—on a foreman who's a bastard, or discrimination of some sort, on a heartless company, on the economic downturn. But [to a great] degree . . . unemployed people blame themselves.

* * *

Jim Hughes

A green house surrounded by cornfields on the outskirts of a small town in Indiana. The house is so close to the road that passing cars almost drown out conversation. It is a sweltering July day. Jim comes to the door shirtless, a paunchy man of thirty-five with longish sandy hair and mustache. Except for his years in the Marines he has lived his whole life within ten miles of this house. He is a welder. At night he takes classes in X-ray technology. "My education will be completed in August of next year. Unless I decide to go further, but I don't think I will. Then I feel I'll be able to find work without any problem."

He chain-smokes. His wife sits down to listen in between chores. His five-year-old daughter peeks out from the kitchen. . . .

The whole thing started back when I was fired without just cause. I was working until last July in a tool and engineering shop. And the foreman for some reason—now this is my personal opinion, but a lot of the other fellows I worked with felt the same way—just picked me out and put lots of pressure on me and fired me. . . .

I had some anger, really, because I had never been fired before. I felt my work performance was good. Excellent, really. But he kept putting pressure on me for more and more work. I was doing three times the work they normally wanted on the day he fired me. And he fired me for poor work performance. There was a parking violation, other little things. Like tardiness. I was buying this house at the time, and I think on three different occasions I notified him that I would have to be late. And he still used that

415

as an excuse. So it had to be a personal thing. I liked the job. I liked the people working there. I hated to lose it.

So I went to the unemployment office. That kinda hurt my pride a little. More than a little. I didn't really want to go, but I felt that I had to in this situation. I felt that I wanted to get them for all I could. I wanted a little bit of revenge. But even though I paid that money in, I still didn't like to go. I guess it was from the way I was brought up. Do things for yourself. Reward yourself. Nobody gives you anything for nothing. This is the attitude I had at that time. Still have that attitude somewhat. But I've had to swallow that pride.

When I first applied, the unemployment office turned me down. So I had to get a lawyer, go to hearings, subpoena witnesses. It was April when I got fired, and it wasn't until the next December that the unemployment office finally decided in my favor, that I had been fired without just cause. So I didn't get any unemployment all that time. Only welfare.

It was rough. Of course, I went out almost every day at first and tried to find work, but it was in the middle of the recession. There was just no work available. . . .

Then slowly it got to where the money situation only allowed me to go out looking for work maybe once a week. Then it got to once every two weeks. I couldn't put gas in my car. I had like $400 worth of monthly bills. I was used to making $600 and I was cut to zero. I had money put away, enough to live on. A few dollars, not too many. It wasn't bad the first month. Well, the first two months. But after that the money depleted.

After the first thirty days it was beginning to run out. I knew in the next few weeks I was gonna be at zero. So I went to welfare. Then I *really* had to swallow my pride. The first day at welfare was quite a day. I've tried to push it out of my mind because they really kind of step on you. I got the feeling that they have an iron hand over you, and you're nothing. I got the feeling they didn't care. . . .

It wasn't long before everything was gone. I had swallowed my pride and I was upset about everything. Welfare started giving us $224 a month; but they always gave you a hard time, and you had to go there almost every month for something. The fact of being off work and just laying around with no money. No money to put in the gas tank of the car to go look for work. There was the threat of the utility companies turning the electricity off. The telephone. Furnace running out of fuel all the time. They turned the phone off during that time, but I always managed to borrow some money someplace to keep the electricity from being turned off. I average around $36-a-month electricity, and I think at one time I had an electric bill of $200 and some. It got awful tough. Sometimes we'd be completely flat zero broke. We ran out of food a couple of times. No money to buy food stamps. Wasn't nothing we could do. We just went without. We didn't eat. That's true. Sometimes for three and four days at a time.

And pretty soon you start creating your own problems. I drank a little heavy. Started drinking when there was nothing to do. When the money ran out I couldn't afford it, but any chance I got I did. And I had too much time on my hands. Too much of being home. I think it hurts your relationship, your marriage and so forth. I know in some cases of welfare the father has to leave the home to be able to survive. I wasn't gonna let that happen. I had that gnawing at me. And the wife and I had problems. We started to have little arguments. It wouldn't have happened if I'd been working. They were senseless. They were over little or nothing. . . .

There wasn't nothing to do but just lay around. Try to borrow some money. By that time you'd borrowed from everybody, and they wasn't gonna give you any more, because they knew they weren't gonna get any back. If your electricity was working, you watched the TV. Or listened to the radio. And just get up in the morning and wait for bedtime. . . .

I had a little bit of money. Less than $100. I made that last me all month, and somehow I managed to keep booze around pretty much of the time. I don't know how I did it. I guess by stretching a dollar. And I had no idea what was going to happen to me. No idea, no hopes, no nothing. Everything had went down the tubes. I knew things had to get better because they couldn't get worse. That's the attitude I had. It's the wrong attitude to have, I guess, but sometimes you get to a point of wanting to give up. You know you can't give up. But when you can't do anything, you have a feeling of total worthlessness. You're just worthless.

In September, after six months out of work, he found a job for $2.50 an hour. "That was only $5 more take-home than I would have got on unemployment. On $2.50 an hour in this area you don't make it too good. But it was a stepping-stone." He worked there three months, then found another job as a welder at higher pay. After two months he was laid off for lack of work.

All I know is I went in one morning. There was a pink slip, and I just packed up my tool box and left. Didn't ask any questions. Went to the unemployment office. No hassles this time.

When I came home, I went out looking for work that next morning. I've had a couple of possibilities since then, thinking I was going to get a job here and there. It's taking them a little longer to say no. At least this time it's not just "Well, we're not taking applications." This time they're giving a few interviews. And giving me a little better chance. Everything is better this time. The unemployment check is coming through. No waiting period. There's enough money to cover the bills. Just barely, but there's enough to get by on. We're not starving this time. We don't run out of food like we did. And we don't have the problem of utilities. Being on unemployment isn't all that bad, compared to being on welfare.

But it's starting up again. I've been off about four months now, and it's starting again. I *got* to find work, even if it's digging ditches, because there's no way I'm going to go through that again. I'm foreseeing these things coming. Trying to do something about 'em before they happen this time.

But I have a different attitude now. I know my pride isn't as big as it used to be. It's made me a little short-tempered, short-fused. It's changed the relationship with my family. It's changed the whole surrounding. Before, things always rolled along real smooth. Now I've seen the rough part of life. I know what it's like now. Before, I didn't know what the rough part was. I've seen combat in Vietnam, but as far as how it is out in the world, I know what it's like. Maybe not as rough as what it was during the thirties. But I'm always gonna look back on this and say, "Hey, I've been through it. I know what it's like." It's been rough. Human damage, you might say. . . .

Robin Landau

She grew up in Stamford, Connecticut. "My mother does nothing, and my father is in real estate from his father. He owns shopping centers and apartment buildings." She lives on the East Side of Manhattan and studies child psychology part time. She has been collecting unemployment for nearly a year. Before that she worked for a company in the garment center ("I just hated the people there—they were loud; they were obnoxious") and a film production company. "I was a gal Friday and assistant film editor. I couldn't take the typing and answering phones, and I found out that editing is supertechnical. You can't be creative because the producer and director always tell you what to do." She left there for a job in publishing. She is twenty-four.

I had a friend at a big publishing company. I forget what she was, but she had a pretty important position. She told me a good job was opening up and she would help me get it. So I went there. I was happy about it and real excited about getting a new job which I could train for and maybe enjoy because I love books and I love reading. But I'm just not a business person. I can't take it. It drives me nuts. The job was in the trade sales department. And the company is like this huge publishing house on the thirty-ninth floor of this office building. You've got to zoom up at 8:30 every morning and zoom down at 5:30 [*laughs*]. . . .

I hated it the first day; I couldn't stand it. . . . In the business world I just can't make it unless it's fun and people are nice. But people are not nice in business that much.

I didn't collect unemployment until three months after I quit. 'Cause I'm scared to ask people for favors. I was scared to go back to the place I worked before the publishing company and say, "Could you please say that you laid me off instead of I quit?" And I left there on very good terms. I still see the people. So finally one of my friends said, "You're a stupid idiot; why don't you just go and ask?" After three months I got up enough courage to go. Otherwise I wasn't going to get unemployment. Now that I look back on it, it was so stupid of me. Why not ask? So you get a rejection? It's just that I can't take rejection either [*laughs*].

How did you feel about taking the unemployment money?
Great! Oh, it was the best thing that ever happened to me. It was like a free $85 a week. Just to enjoy myself and fool around with, for doing nothing. For doing *nothing*. I mean when I was working, I was taking home maybe $40 more. Busting my ass. Well, not busting my ass, but just being very depressed and wasting a lot of time for $40 more a week. And here I was collecting $85, doing nothing. It was the best thing that ever happened to me. It was like a gift from heaven. Pennies from heaven. Dollars. It's terrific.

The fact is that I hate working. See, I would be good at volunteer work with children or something. But the thing I really hate about work is getting up so early. Such an ungodly hour. And it's just too much. You work, you come home, you eat dinner, you're so tired, and you have to wake up the next day. And your weekends are the big thing. Weekends are such a drag because they're just so crowded with all these crazy people who do the working and go out to unwind. You can't enjoy yourself on weekends. I would rather go out on a weekday night. So I'm a lot happier when I'm not working.

And I certainly feel no guilt whatsoever about taking the $85. I think this government and the whole world is crazy and war-happy, and that I wasted a large part of my life by working for these people, doing nutty jobs. That's not what life is about, sitting in an office nine hours on your ass, typing or taking orders from somebody. So I feel they owed it to me.

So during the summer I went to the pool and I played tennis and I got skinny and I got a suntan. I was living here, but my parents belong to a club and my friends have tennis courts and pools and I have a car, so I took the car with me and my friends to the Hamptons. I'd bop around there, and I was really relaxing and getting mellow and nice again. What my parents don't understand—but I think now they do—and what people don't believe is that . . . well, a lot of people want to be famous or they want to do something constructive in their life. But I was so happy for six months. I was doing nothing, and I think I could be happy doing nothing for the rest of my life. I have friends and I like to read and I like to go to museums and I like to paint and I like to sculpt and I like to do crafts and I like to go to theater and I like to go to movies and I like to go to parties and I like to dance and I like to have a good time and I like to travel and I also like to be serious. But I think my whole life I could do that without getting a job. People just do not understand that. . . .

I guess I went back to school because of what my father said. One day he

said, "Well, Robin, what's going to happen if I'm not around anymore?"
When he said that, I started to cry hysterically. My father's an idol to me. I
think he's wonderful, a terrific human being and wonderful about everything. I just started to cry and said, "Don't you ever say that to me again,"
and he goes, "It's true. What's going to happen if you don't marry somebody wealthy? What's going to happen if you never get married?" See, my
whole life is dependent on a man to get married and to make sure he's
wealthy. But I would never marry just for money because I couldn't do
that. I would get sick to my stomach if somebody touched me who I didn't
love. So like I need both. I need love and money. And it's pretty hard to
find. So I said to myself, "Let's get your life together." So I bopped into
school, and I'll be happy being a child psychologist every now and then.

I can't live on $85 a week. I don't pay the rent. My parents pay the rent. I
pay everything else and I still have to take money from them. It happens to
be very difficult for me to live on $85 a week. I feel horrible about taking
their money. But I've gotten past the point of feeling horrible; I feel one
step worse than horrible: I feel like I don't care. Like the part about being
horrible is already over because I know that I'm horrible and awful. I'll
never make anything out of my life, so I like to live off of other people. So I
feel like the only attitude to have is to not care and be thankful that they
can do it. I do appreciate it and I don't really take advantage. It's also . . .
you know, in a certain way they never taught me responsibility with
money. All of a sudden I got out of school and there was this great pressure. Now be responsible! But during my whole life there wasn't even a
gradual buildup. I got everything I wanted, everything. And all of a sudden I got out of college and I was so shocked. "OK, now do it yourself."
But I was never *taught*. You don't do that to a person. I blame them for
doing that. I'm not placing the guilt on them. The thing's on me. It's my
fault. But they should've taught me. They should have been more responsible in that respect.

I mean, some people function best when they work. A lot of people need
work, the responsibility, something to occupy their time. Because they
don't have that many outside interests, and it does take up a large part of
your life. But I'm very unliberated because I think men should still support
women. Unless the woman finds something that interests her and she
wants to work. But she shouldn't have to. That's not really my point of
view on men and women, but on men and me. I don't really believe that
about women. That was wrong to say. I just think that for *me* it's right. I
don't want to be liberated in that way.

Basically I'm happy with myself. I think Robin's a good, together, nice
person. But as far as ever having a goal or as far as ever having a future, I
don't think I'll ever have one. It does get depressing at times and I think
that maybe I should. But I'm just not made that way and it never seems
to work for me. Like I probably would be happy just getting married and

420

having a family and being rich and having a good time. I mean, not screwing around because I'm pretty straight sex-wise. I'm pretty monogamous. I just like to fall in love and get married and be very happy. I guess I sort of live in a fantasy-type world [*laughs*]. . . .

Karen Lewis

We're on the front porch of an aging wooden house in a southern Mississippi village. She is twenty-two, a small black woman with two children, no husband, and few prospects other than training in business skills that she receives at a trade school in the county seat, twenty-five miles away. Her schooling is paid for by the Comprehensive Employment Training Act (CETA).

Her voice at first is neutral, guarded. It changes as she talks about the village—still ruled by age-old racial codes—in a bitterly matter-of-fact tone. It's the tone of someone trapped but not yet resigned.

When I got out of high school, I started work at Talvert Industrial. I quit that because it was too far away from home, and I got a job at Alltree Fashion. It was sewing and making shirts. You have to make so many a day, and I couldn't keep up. I worked there for eight months. You're only supposed to stay there for a three-month trial period, and then if you can't meet their qualifications, they're supposed to let you go. But they were gonna let me stay because the work I was doing was good. The head boss said I could stay. But they got a lady at this job, and if she say she don't like you and she don't want you to work, you don't work. We had got into an argument one weekend, and the next week I got laid off. They said it was because I couldn't keep up, but I knew it was because this lady wanted me to go. So I went.

Oh, why don't you work
Like other men do?
How the hell can I work
When there's no work to do?

—Anon., *Hallelujah, I'm a Bum*

Besides Alltree and Froeling Electronics, there's hardly anyplace to work around here. They got this gravel pit, and they got this rock place where they make little rocks that go in goldfish bowls. I tried there and they told me they wasn't hirin' right then but they would be later on. They told me to come back in a week, and I went back in a week and they had hired this white girl. If you don't know the white people here, you don't get no job.

So I was out of work about six months. Drawin' $35-a-week unemploy-ment. Then it started to run down, and I decided the onliest way I could get a job was to take a trade. I decided to go to the trade school.

What do most blacks here do when they get out of high school?
If they have children, they go on welfare; if they don't, they have to go out of town to get a job. Most men work on the railroad or offshore. They got a few at Froeling 'cause Froeling knows they're gonna do whatever they tell 'em to do. And the hard job is at the sawmill. That's mostly black 'cause white people don't want no hard job.

Why didn't you go on welfare?
Well, when my unemployment ran out, I went to get welfare. It took from March to July to get my first check. And then they told me to go back and check my unemployment. I didn't know I could re-sign and get an exten-sion. The man told me I could re-sign, so I just got that one check from welfare and went back on unemployment. 'Cause the unemployment was more money. On welfare they give you $86 a month if you're alone and $112 if you have a child. Well, $35 a week is more than $112 a month. And even after the unemployment started to run out again and I was getting $17 a week, I decided to let welfare alone. I didn't want to go through it. You got to tell who your boyfriend is, and they come to your house and check on you. Nobody wants to go through that 'lessen you're extremely lazy. Lazy people will do it. But I just didn't want to, and Momma told me, "Don't worry about it."

So I finally figured school would be my best out. See, this is a small town. And everything here is run by white people. . . .

The white people have to know your family. If somebody hadda known my mother and father real good, I coulda got a job. But by them not knowing them, it was hard. Somebody else black could come along, and if the personnel lady knew her family real well, she coulda got a job right then. The personnel lady is the most important. 'Cause mostly the boss is gonna say to her, "Well, do you know her? Do you think she'll do?" And if she says, "Yeah," you're hired. . . .

Right now I'm studying to be a clerk-typist. I got seven months to go. We take record keeping, filing, English, math, typing, office procedure, ac-counting, and personality development. Personality development tells how you should act around people. How to groom yourself, stuff like that. I like it 'cause whether or not you get a job when you get out, you've still been and learned something. Even if you can't get a job in what you majored in. Most government jobs, like the post office, you have to have the civil service test. And you have to leave Mississippi in most cases. 'Cause in Mississippi you won't get a black person in the post office or a black person in the bank. No way. You don't get no job in the post office, not black. Oh, you might get a job carryin' mail to the houses, but if you want a job in the office, you don't get that. Working behind the window, you don't get that. Black people not qualified for it, so they say.

I want to be a clerk-typist, but if I can't be a clerk-typist and I pass the civil service test, I want to be a state trooper. Which I doubt they'll let me be. At least I'm gonna try. I'll have to go farther than Mississippi. Up north or west, somewhere like that. Not in the South. These people in Mississippi are not right, I'm tellin' you. Not on the job thing, not on gettin' money. No kinda way. Everybody here know that no black faces ain't gonna get behind no desks. . . .

Eddie Vargas

He lives in the Chicano ghetto of Los Angeles. He grew up in the streets, a gang member from an early age. "Then I met Dorothy, my wife. She was different. Other girls I just picked up to throw away, picked up to throw away. But I seen something different in her. She started talking to me, changing my ways. Even though I came from a Christian family, I was still bad. So it's not inherited. I listened to her and started changing. I went from an F to a B average student."

He is twenty-four and has a child of school age. A visitor to his living room soon notices a huge aquarium against one wall and a dog-eared Bible, the only item on the coffee table. He is a recent convert to fundamentalist religion, describing his past with the phrase, "When I was in the world. . . ."

When I graduated from high school, I got a scholarship to go to college. They knew I came from a Mexican background, so they wanted to help me. I went to a technical college for two years. I was taking a full load and working nights. It was a real ambitious time for me. I was thinking, "Wow, I'm going to college." I graduated after two years with something like seventy units and my qualification in machine shop work. After I graduated, I got married, and then I went to another school for more training, to finish my apprenticeship program. When I did that, I thought I really had it made. I figured, "Wow, I graduated, I had a good average, I've got my apprenticeship credentials." I thought I had a lot behind me. Then I went out there in the streets and started looking for a job. That's where I started getting hurt.

The first place I got work was at Fudd Engineering Associates. They told me, "We can only start you out at $3 an hour." Well, one of my teachers in school used to tell me, "Never settle for anything small. Always aim high." That's what he got into my head: Always aim high. So I told them I wanted more than $3. I was aiming high. But he said, "I'll start you off at $3 and see how you are." I finally said OK. I started doing machine shop work, and there was one job I didn't thread right. He told me, "I gotta lay you off."

Then I went to another company. They wanted to pay me $3 an hour,

423

too, and I said no. I was still aiming high. So I lost out on that job, and the same thing happened at another place. I lost out on two jobs. I was asking for $3.50 an hour and they wouldn't pay it.

Then later on it started getting rough, and I had to settle for whatever I could get. I'd be looking for a job, and they'd be telling me they need ten years' experience or five years' experience. I told them, "Look, I don't have the experience. I have the knowledge and the know-how on up-to-date machines. I got my tools. I know what to do." They'd say, "I'm sorry." So after looking all over the place I got kind of disgusted. Everybody wanted ten years' experience, and I was twenty years old [*laughs*]. Finally I came to a company called Winston Corp. They wanted ten or fifteen years' experience. I was so disgusted and run down by this point that I said, "Give me any job." So I started working on the assembly line. I did that for three years. I put aside my knowledge and my skill because I had to work. I had a little girl, and I had to feed her.

After three years they closed down and went back east, so I got laid off again. Then I started working for another company driving a forklift. After a while they put me on cutting metals, and then I started running the machines. The lathes and mills. It was machine shop work, the first I'd had since I got out of school. I was pretty happy with it. For a while there was a lot of work. But then the work went down, and they laid me off for two weeks. They called me back because there was work again. I worked a week. They laid me off again. And now I've been off for eight months. I'm looking for a job, but not in machine shop. I figure I'll go back into shipping and receiving. Working with the trucks. Plain labor work, in other words. Because I have some experience in shipping and receiving. And I've been looking at the unemployment office for whatever odds-and-ends type jobs they have. . . . So that's the situation I'm in right now.

It gets to me. There are times when I cry about it. I knew it was gonna be hard, but I wasn't expecting it to be this hard. . . .

How come I didn't take advantage when it was there? There were times when I had it in my hand and turned it down. Now if they offer me a job for $3 an hour, I'm gonna take it. Regardless of what the job is. I'm not gonna make that mistake again. I know I can't make it on $2.50. That's not a mistake, me turning that down. But if I turn down a job for $3 again, that's a mistake. So when I pray at night, I pray I don't make a mistake like that again. Take it! Three dollars an hour, take it!

» Elliot Liebow «

Tally's Corner

» «

In 1965, in a black area of south central Los Angeles called Watts, a riot broke out that lasted for several days and nights and led to the deaths of thirty-five people. It was only the first in a series of "long hot summers" in America's ghettos, during which rioting blacks called the nation's attention to their economic plight. At the time of the Watts riot, about 40 percent of the men of this ghetto were either unemployed, or employed only part-time or in jobs that paid less than the minimum wage. Fathers were absent from 39 percent of Watts' families. Sadly, the situation in Watts was representative of the urban ghettos of Detroit, Atlanta, Cleveland, New York, Newark, and even the nation's capital, as Elliot Liebow describes in this selection about unemployed black men in Washington, D.C.

In 1967, anthropologist Liebow's Tally's Corner *struck a sympathetic chord with thousands of Americans who were shocked to learn of the conditions of inner-city blacks. His eloquent explanation of why so many black men failed to enter the primary labor market—and failed to support their families—focused on the relationship between these men and their jobs. The men came to their jobs with a history of being unable to support themselves or their families; their experiences had convinced them of their own incompetence. The only jobs available to them—dishwasher, day laborer, unskilled construction worker—were low-paying and unsteady, offering no benefits, career ladder, or self-esteem. Liebow argues that the streetcorner men put no lower value on these jobs than did the larger society. But given the alternative between a dead end job that paid less than they needed to live, and standing on the street corner drinking beer and engaging in the ego-boosting banter and braggadocio that at least provided a sense of community, many of these men chose the latter. Shamefully, fifteen years after the Watts riots, the job prospects of urban blacks from Los Angeles to Washington are substantially the same as those Liebow describes below.*

The New Deal Carry-out shop is on a corner in downtown Washington, D.C. It would be within walking distance of the White House, the Smithsonian Institution, and other major public buildings of the nation's capital, if anyone cared to walk there, but no one ever does. Across the street from the Carry-out is a liquor store. The other two corners of the intersection are occupied by a dry cleaning and

425

shoe repair store and a wholesale plumbing supplies showroom and warehouse.

Walking north from the Carry-out shop for three blocks or more, one passes a fairly even mixture of dwelling units (generally old, three-story, red-brick row houses, most of them long since converted to rooming and tenement houses), an occasional apartment house, and small-business establishments such as liquor stores, grocery stores, barber shops, cleaners, launderettes, beauty parlors, poolrooms, beer joints, carry-out shops, pawnbrokers, and others. . . .

The residents in the Carry-out neighborhood are almost all Negroes. From census reports and other public sources the casual observer could easily confirm his impression that this is an area with a high incidence of crowded living quarters, poverty, crime, child neglect, and dependence. . . .

Not everyone, however, is poor, dependent, delinquent, nor are all men in the area to be found, at one time or another, hanging out on the corner or in a beer joint, poolroom or hallway. The man who lives up the street from the Carry-out and works two or three jobs to keep his home and family together may divide all his waking time between home and job. Such a man may be unknown at the Carry-out and at other public places in the area. . . .

In this setting, . . . some twenty men who live in the area regularly come together for "effortless sociability." They are not, in any strict sense, a group. No more than eight or ten, and usually fewer, are there at any one time. There is nothing to join, no obligations, no one to say whether you belong or do not belong. Some of the men have never spoken to some of the others beyond exchanging a casual greeting. Some are close friends, some do not like others, and still others consider themselves enemies. But each man comes here mainly because he knows others will be here too. He comes to eat and drink, to enjoy easy talk, to learn what has been going on, to horse around, to look at women and banter with them, to see "what's happening" and to pass the time.

Tally   Tally is a brown-skinned man, thirty-one years old. . . . Tally never went to school. When he was eleven years old, he began working regularly for wages at such jobs as cleaning up a doctor's office and as a dishwasher in a restaurant. Tally spent most of his teen years in Atlanta, and then, despite his inability to read or write, went into the army.

Tally came to Washington, D.C. in 1954. His first job here was as a cook in a hospital, but he later got a job as a laborer in construction work. Since 1959 he has been a semiskilled construction worker averaging about one hundred dollars a week in take-home pay for the six or seven months of the year in which he works regularly.

Tally moved into a room in the Carry-out area in the winter of 1961. In the eight years he has been in Washington, he has married and separated and fathered eight children, three with his wife and five others with five different women.

Sea Cat Sea Cat is twenty-seven years old. He was born and raised in the Carry-out neighborhood and except for his army service has lived all his life in that area. Sea Cat quit school in the tenth grade. He got married when he was twenty but he has long been separated from his wife and children. . . .

Sea Cat disdains the ordinary, frequently choosing to see a special quality, talent or property in ordinary people and ordinary events. He looks at the world much like the caricaturist or the expressionist painter. By a carefully controlled distortion of reality as it is perceived by others—by hyperbole or fancy—he seeks out the individuality, the special character, of the men, women, and events around him.

Richard Richard is twenty-four years old. He is about 5'10", thin and muscular. Richard was born and raised in a small town in the Carolinas. He graduated from high school and married a girl who had lived across the street from him since childhood. In 1960 Richard had to leave his hometown suddenly, in the middle of the night, after assaulting (with provocation, according to his own and his family's account) a local white policeman. His pregnant wife and their small son joined him in Washington a few days later.

Richard worked primarily at janitorial jobs but occasionally tried other kinds of work as well. In his first several months in the Carry-out area, Richard built a reputation for himself as a hard-working man who tried to do his best for his family and as an all-around nice guy. But as time wore on, things changed. Richard got into several fights. In one, he killed a man. People grew afraid of Richard and began to avoid him. Richard dated his troubles from the killing, but they had, in fact, started long, long before.

Leroy Leroy is twenty-three years old. He is tall and thin, even thinner than Richard, and somewhat lighter skinned than most of the men in the area. . . .

Most of Leroy's jobs had to do with hotels and parking lots. Most men and women liked Leroy well enough but he was generally considered weak and immature, a "boy" who "talked big" and who, when competing with men, women, or a job, would probably back down before the confrontation or be the loser after it.

Work is love made visible. And if you cannot work with love but only with distaste, it is better that you should leave your work and sit at the gate of the temple and take alms of those who work with joy.

—Kahlil Gibran, *On Work*

427

Name	Age	Usual Employment
Arthur	28	laborer
Boley	21	janitor
Budder	45	laborer
Clarence	30	laborer
Earl	22	laborer
John	29	counterman
Lonny	26	stock clerk—delivery
Preston	38	laborer
Robert	27	janitor
Stanton	44	truck driver
Stoopy	27	busboy—dishwasher
Sweets	26	busboy—dishwasher
Tonk	23	parking-lot attendant
Wee Tom	37	laborer
Wesley	21	retail delivery
William	31	truck driver

Some of the Other Men

Men and Jobs

A pickup truck drives slowly down the street. The truck stops as it comes abreast of a man sitting on a cast-iron porch and the white driver calls out, asking if the man wants a day's work. The man shakes his head and the truck moves on up the block, stopping again whenever idling men come within calling distance of the driver. At the Carry-out corner, five men debate the question briefly and shake their heads no to the truck. The truck turns the corner and repeats the same performance up the next street. In the distance, one can see one man, then another, climb into the back of the truck and sit down. In starts and stops, the truck finally disappears.

What is it we have witnessed here? A labor scavenger rebuffed by his would-be prey? Lazy, irresponsible men turning down an honest day's pay for an honest day's work? Or a more complex phenomenon marking the intersection of economic forces, social values and individual states of mind and body?

Let us look again at the driver of the truck. He has been able to recruit only two or three men from each twenty or fifty he contacts. To him, it is clear that the others simply do not choose to work. Singly or in groups, belly-empty or belly-full, sullen or gregarious, drunk or sober, they confirm what he has read, heard and knows from his own experience: these men wouldn't take a job if it were handed to them on a platter.

Quite apart from the question of whether or not this is true of some of the men he sees on the street, it is clearly not true of all of them. If it were, he would not have come here in the first place; or having come, he would have left with an empty truck. It is not even true of most of them, for most of the men he sees on the street this weekday morning do, in fact, have jobs. But since, at the moment, they are neither working nor sleeping, and

428

since they hate the depressing room or apartment they live in, or because there is nothing to do there, or because they want to get away from their wives or anyone else living there, they are out on the street, indistinguishable from those who do not have jobs or do not want them. Some, like Boley, a member of a trash-collection crew in a suburban housing development, work Saturdays and are off on this weekday. Some, like Sweets, work nights cleaning up middle-class trash, dirt, dishes and garbage, and mopping the floors of the office buildings, hotels, restaurants, toilets and other public places dirtied during the day. Some men work for retail businesses such as liquor stores which do not begin the day until ten o'clock. Some laborers, like Tally, have already come back from the job because the ground was too wet for pick and shovel or because the weather was too cold for pouring concrete. Other employed men stayed off the job today for personal reasons: Clarence to go to a funeral at eleven this morning and Sea Cat to answer a subpoena as a witness in a criminal proceeding.

Also on the street, unwitting contributors to the impression taken away by the truck driver, are the halt and the lame. . . .

Others, having had jobs and been laid off, are drawing unemployment compensation (up to $44 per week) and have nothing to gain by accepting work which pays little more than this and frequently less. . . .

Only a handful remains unaccounted for. There is Tonk, who cannot bring himself to take a job away from the corner, because, according to the other men, he suspects his wife will be unfaithful if given the opportunity. There is Stanton, who has not reported to work for four days now, not since Bernice disappeared. . . .

And finally, there are those like Arthur, able-bodied men who have no visible means of support, legal or illegal, who neither have jobs nor want them. The truck driver, among others, believes the Arthurs to be representative of all the men he sees idling on the street during his own working hours. They are not, but they cannot be dismissed simply because they are a small minority. It is not enough to explain them away as being lazy or irresponsible or both because an able-bodied man with responsibilities who refuses work is, by the truck driver's definition, lazy and irresponsible. Such an answer begs the question. It is descriptive of the facts; it does not explain them.

Moreover, despite their small numbers, the don't-work-and-don't-want-to-work minority is especially significant because they represent the strongest and clearest expression of those values and attitudes associated with making a living which, to varying degrees, are found throughout the streetcorner world. These men differ from the others in degree rather than in kind, the principal difference being that they are carrying out the implications of their values and experiences to their logical, inevitable conclusions. In this sense, the others have yet to come to terms with themselves and the world they live in.

Putting aside, for the moment, what the men say and feel, and looking at what they actually do and the choices they make, getting a job, keeping a job, and doing well at it is clearly of low priority. . . .

The reasons are many. Some are objective and reside principally in the job; some are subjective and reside principally in the man. The line between them, however, is not a clear one. Behind the man's refusal to take a job or his decision to quit one is not a simple impulse or value choice but a complex combination of assessments of objective reality on the one hand, and values, attitudes and beliefs drawn from different levels of his experience on the other.

Objective economic considerations are frequently a controlling factor in a man's refusal to take a job. How much the job pays is a crucial question but seldom asked. He knows how much it pays. Working as a stock clerk, a delivery boy, or even behind the counter of liquor stores, drug stores and other retail businesses pays one dollar an hour. So, too, do most busboy, car-wash, janitorial and other jobs available to him. Some jobs, such as dishwasher, may dip as low as eighty cents an hour and others, such as elevator operator or work in a junk yard, may offer $1.15 or $1.25. Take-home pay for jobs such as these ranges from $35 to $50 a week, but a take-home pay of over $45 for a five-day week is the exception rather than the rule.

One of the principal advantages of these kinds of jobs is that they offer fairly regular work. Most of them involve essential services and are therefore somewhat less responsive to business conditions than are some higher paying, less menial jobs. Most of them are also inside jobs not dependent on the weather, as are construction jobs and other higher-paying outside work.

Another seemingly important advantage of working in hotels, restaurants, office and apartment buildings and retail establishments is that they frequently offer an opportunity for stealing on the job. But stealing can be a two-edged sword. Apart from increasing the cost of the goods or services to the general public, a less obvious result is that the practice usually acts as a depressant on the employee's own wage level. Owners of small retail establishments and other employers frequently anticipate employee stealing and adjust the wage rate accordingly. . . .

Other consequences of the wage-theft system are even more damaging to the employee. . . . He cannot draw on what he steals to build his self-respect or to measure his self-worth. For this, he can draw only on his earnings—the amount given him publicly and voluntarily in exchange for his labor.

With or without stealing, and quite apart from any interior processes going on in the man who refuses such a job or quits it casually and without apparent reason, the objective fact is that menial jobs in retailing or in the service trades simply do not pay enough to support a man and his family. This is not to say that the worker is underpaid; this may or may not be true.

430

Whether he is or not, the plain fact is that, in such a job, he cannot make a living. Nor can he take much comfort in the fact that these jobs tend to offer more regular, steadier work. If he cannot live on the $45 or $50 he makes in one week, the longer he works, the longer he cannot live on what he makes. Construction work, even for unskilled laborers, usually pays better. . . .

Construction work, however, has its own objective disadvantages. It is, first of all, seasonal work for the great bulk of the laborers, beginning early in the spring and tapering off as winter weather sets in. And even during the season the work is frequently irregular. . . .

Both getting the construction job and getting to it are also relatively more difficult than is the case for the menial jobs in retailing and the service trades. Job competition is always fierce. In the city, the large construction projects are unionized. One has to have ready cash to get into the union to become eligible to work. . . .

Still another objective factor is the work itself. For some men, whether the job be digging, mixing mortar, pushing a wheelbarrow, unloading materials, carrying and placing steel rods for reinforcing concrete, or building or laying concrete forms, the work is simply too hard. . . .

Men who have been running an elevator, washing dishes, or "pulling trash" cannot easily move into laboring jobs. They lack the basic skills for "unskilled" construction labor, familiarity with tools and materials, and tricks of the trade without which hard jobs are made harder. Previously unused or untrained muscles rebel in pain against the new and insistent demands made upon them, seriously compromising the man's performance and testing his willingness to see the job through. . . .

Logan was a tall, two-hundred-pound man in his late twenties. His back used to hurt him only on the job, he said, but now he can't straighten up for increasingly longer periods of time. He said he had traced this to the awkward walk he was forced to adopt by the loaded wheelbarrows which pull him down into a half-stoop. He's going to quit, he said, as soon as he can find another job. If he can't find one real soon, he guesses he'll quit anyway. It's not worth it, having to walk bent over and leaning to one side. . . .

In summary of objective job considerations, then, the most important fact is that a man who is able and willing to work cannot earn enough money to support himself, his wife, and one or more children. A man's chances for working regularly are good only if he is willing to work for less than he can live on, and sometimes not even then. On some jobs, the wage rate is deceptively higher than on others, but the higher the wage rate, the more difficult it is to get the job, and the less the job security. Higher-paying construction work tends to be seasonal and, during the season, the amount of work available is highly sensitive to business and weather conditions and to the changing requirements of individual projects. Moreover, high-paying construction jobs are frequently beyond the physical capacity of

431

some of the men, and some of the low-paying jobs are scaled down even lower in accordance with the self-fulfilling assumption that the man will steal part of his wages on the job. . . .

When we look at what the men bring to the job rather than at what the job offers the men, it is essential to keep in mind that . . . each man comes to the job with a long job history characterized by his not being able to support himself and his family. Each man carries this knowledge, born of his experience, with him. He comes to the job flat and stale, wearied by the sameness of it all, convinced of his own incompetence, terrified of responsibility—of being tested still again and found wanting. . . .

Thus, the man's low self-esteem generates a fear of being tested and prevents him from accepting a job with responsibilities or, once on a job, from staying with it if responsibilities are thrust on him, even if the wages are commensurately higher. Richard refuses such a job, Leroy leaves one, and another man, given more responsibility and more pay, knows he will fail and proceeds to do so, proving he was right about himself all along. The self-fulfilling prophecy is everywhere at work. . . .

Lethargy, disinterest and general apathy on the job, so often reported by employers, has its streetcorner counterpart. The men do not ordinarily talk about their jobs or ask one another about them. Although most of the men know who is or is not working at any given time, they may or may not know what particular job an individual man has. There is no overt interest in job specifics as they relate to this or that person, in large part perhaps because the specifics are not especially relevant. . . . In large part, the job market consists of a narrow range of nondescript chores calling for nondistinctive, undifferentiated, unskilled labor. "A job is a job."

A crucial factor in the streetcorner man's lack of job commitment is the overall value he places on the job. *For his part, the streetcorner man puts no lower value on the job than does the larger society around him.* He knows the social value of the job by the amount of money the employer is willing to pay him for doing it. In a real sense, every pay day, he counts in dollars and cents the value placed on the job by society at large. He is no more (and frequently less) ready to quit and look for another job than his employer is ready to fire him and look for another man. Neither the streetcorner man who performs these jobs nor the society which requires him to perform them assesses the job as one "worth doing and worth doing well." Both employee and employer are contemptuous of the job. The employee shows his contempt by his reluctance to accept it or keep it, the employer by paying less than is required to support a family.[1] Nor does the low-wage job offer prestige, respect, interesting work, opportunity for learning

---

1. It is important to remember that the employer is not entirely a free agent. Subject to the constraints of the larger society, he acts for the larger society as well as for himself. Child labor laws, safety and sanitation regulations, minimum wage scales in some employment areas, and other constraints, are already on the books; other control mechanisms, such as a guaranteed annual wage, are to be had for the voting.

or advancement, or any other compensation. With few exceptions, jobs filled by the streetcorner men are at the bottom of the employment ladder in every respect, from wage level to prestige. Typically, they are hard, dirty, uninteresting and underpaid. The rest of society (whatever its ideal values regarding the dignity of labor) holds the job of the dishwasher or janitor or unskilled laborer in low esteem if not outright contempt. So does the streetcorner man. He cannot do otherwise. He cannot draw from a job those social values which other people do not put into it. . . .

The streetcorner man wants to be a person in his own right, to be noticed, to be taken account of, but in this respect, as well as in meeting his money needs, his job fails him. The job and the man are even. The job fails the man and the man fails the job.

Furthermore, the man does not have any reasonable expectation that, however bad it is, his job will lead to better things. . . . The busboy or dishwasher who works hard becomes, simply, a hard-working busboy or dishwasher. Neither hard work nor perseverance can conceivably carry the janitor to a sit-down job in the office building he cleans up. And it is the apprentice who becomes the journeyman electrician, plumber, steam fitter or bricklayer, not the common unskilled Negro laborer.

Thus, the job is not a stepping stone to something better. It is a dead end. It promises to deliver no more tomorrow, next month or next year than it does today. . . .

As for the future, the young streetcorner man has a fairly good picture of it. In Richard or Sea Cat or Arthur he can see himself in his middle twenties; he can look at Tally to see himself at thirty, at Wee Tom to see himself in his middle thirties, and at Budder and Stanton to see himself in his forties. It is a future in which everything is uncertain except the ultimate destruction of his hopes and the eventual realization of his fears. The most he can reasonably look forward to is that these things do not come too soon. Thus, when Richard squanders a week's pay in two days it is not because, like an animal or a child, he is "present-time oriented," unaware of or unconcerned with his future. He does so precisely because he is aware of the future and the hopelessness of it all. . . .

In many instances, it is precisely the streetcorner man's orientation to the future—but to a future loaded with "trouble"—which not only leads to a greater emphasis on present concerns ("I want mine right now") but also contributes importantly to the instability of employment, family and friend relationships, and to the general transient quality of daily life.

Let me give some concrete examples. One day, after Tally had gotten paid, he gave me four twenty-dollar bills and asked me to keep them for him. Three days later he asked me for the money. I returned it and asked why he did not put his money in a bank. He said that the banks close at two o'clock. I argued that there were four or more banks within a two-block radius of where he was working at the time and that he could easily get to any one of them on his lunch hour. "No, man," he said, "you don't understand. They close at two o'clock and they closed Saturday and Sunday. Suppose I get into trouble and I got to make it [leave]. Me get out of town, and everything I got in the world layin' up in that bank? No good! No good!"

In another instance, Leroy and his girl friend were discussing "trouble." Leroy was trying to decide how best to go about getting his hands on some "long green" (a lot of money), and his girl friend cautioned him about "trouble." Leroy sneered at this, saying he had had "trouble" all his life and wasn't afraid of a little more. "Anyway," he said, "I'm famous for leaving town."

Thus, the constant awareness of a future loaded with "trouble" results in a constant readiness to leave, to "make it," to "get out of town," and discourages the man from sinking roots into the world he lives in. Just as it discourages him from putting money in the bank, so it discourages him from committing himself to a job, especially one whose payoff lies in the promise of future rewards rather than in the present. In the same way, it discourages him from deep and lasting commitments to family and friends or to any other persons, places or things, since such commitments could hold him hostage, limiting his freedom of movement and thereby compromising his security which lies in that freedom.

What lies behind the response to the driver of the pickup truck, then, is a complex combination of attitudes and assessments. The streetcorner man is under continuous assault by his job experiences and job fears. His experiences and fears feed on one another. The kind of job he can get—and frequently only after fighting for it, if then—steadily confirms his fears, depresses his self-confidence and self-esteem until finally, terrified of an opportunity even if one presents itself, he stands defeated by his experiences, his belief in his own self-worth destroyed, and his fears a confirmed reality.

» Willard Wirtz «

No Man's — or Woman's — Land

» «

When this selection by former Secretary of Labor Willard Wirtz was written in 1974, the famous "boom babies" were teenagers just about to enter the labor force. They are all in the labor force now, but, significantly, rates of teenage unemployment have not fallen even though there are now fewer teenagers. Why? For the very reasons Wirtz describes: Teenage unemployment is different in nature from adult unemployment in that most young people are looking for part-time jobs while they attend school. The demand for part-time jobs has, in fact, increased over the last half-dozen years, but supply (though growing) has not kept pace. In addition, the kinds of work that teenagers could do best are exactly the kinds of jobs that are being eliminated through automation or taken by adult women entering the labor force or by immigrants who, because of their maturity, are more attractive to employers than are teenagers. As Wirtz points out, the solution to the teenage unemployment problem is not more jobs, but more jobs with the characteristics needed by student workers. As yet, no one has figured out how to create such jobs in sufficient numbers.

Every American over fourteen and going on twenty-one moves through a maze of legal markers and mores reflecting prevailing, often contradictory, views about the relationship of age to capacity: to drive a car, to vote, to marry, to fight a war, to have a credit card, to be or not to be an adult. "Just tell me," your sixteen-year-old interrupts, "how old do I have to be to get into the human race?" You are glad and a little surprised at this continuing interest, and you wish you knew the answer.

This general ambivalence about coming of age shows up in its sharpest form when the time comes to leave school and go to work. Suddenly, after years of acclimation to a compulsory and highly structured school system, young people find themselves almost entirely on their own.

Unhappily, this abrupt change is only a particularly critical incident in a pervasive confusion about how the education and work chapters in people's lives are supposed to fit together. In a great many cases they don't fit at all.

Statistics are boring. They are also dangerous. We use them as mirrors in which to look at ourselves, without realizing that they reflect only those features of the human circumstance that can be quantified. Most of them report only conditions, not causes. If they seem to call for action we start looking for shortcuts, even across quicksand.

There are, though, some figures that—if shaken well before using—tell quite a lot about how badly these education and work processes have gotten out of kilter and about the difficulty and waste this is causing.

The youth unemployment rate in this country is a startling 20 percent, a statistic that is truly meaningful, however, only by comparison.

It is almost three times as high as the rate for adults. It is twice as high as it was when these figures were first collected in 1947. It is up from 12 percent [in 1965].Unemployment among teenagers (sixteen to nineteen) was 15 percent in February 1974 and 19.9 percent in February 1975.

The unemployment rate is twice as high among those who are both young and black or of Mexican, Puerto Rican, or American Indian descent. Among these, the rate now exceeds 40 percent.

In any particular month between a million and a half and 2 million teenagers are looking for work and unable to find it—which is the only circumstance that the current measurement system defines as "unemployed." This means that in the course of a year between 4 and 5 million young people will go through this experience. This is just about half of all of those who look for work during the course of a year.

These youth figures get buried in the monthly reports of the country's *overall* situation. In the minds of most people the picture of unemployment is of a head of a family who loses his or her job; and this indeed is generally the more serious situation. But almost a quarter of all unemployment in the United States is among teenagers. Over a third is among those under twenty-two, although they make up only one seventh of the work force. . . .

The conditioned response [these statistics] evoke—that the answer here is just "more jobs"—is dangerously wrong.

A few for instances:

John A and Mary B are high school graduates who have had all the school they want for right now, are willing and able to work, and are looking for jobs but can't find them. Their situations may leave questions about what their abilities and desires and prospects would be if they had had different schooling or different backgrounds, and there is the question too, of the likelihood—now that machines have virtually the equivalent of high school educations—of young A and B "ever amounting to much." These though, at least in current terminology, are properly classified as cases of "unemployment." Yet less than a quarter of that reported 20 percent involves the John As and Mary Bs.

436

Henry C and Robert D are seniors in high school, both doing well, and looking forward to college. They try to get work after school, on weekends, or during holidays. C wants money to keep up his car; with D it is a matter of being able or unable to stay in school. But there are no part-time jobs to be found. Are C and D properly reported among the country's "unemployed"—along with forty-year-old heads of households? Are the C and D cases enough alike to be measured together? In any event, about half those officially reported as unemployed among sixteen-to-nineteen-year-olds are in school and looking only for part-time employment.

Helen E and William F dropped out after two years of high school, have had three or four jobs they couldn't or at least didn't hold, and are looking again. Unemployed? Yes, but with the obviously serious question of whether "more jobs" is the answer to their problem. And theirs is the situation that prevails for most of the rest of that 20 percent.

Susan G and Robert H have finished high school and are in their first year at college. They despise every minute of it and are only going through the motions of learning. They want very much to get out, and probably will. The only figures they show up in are those for college enrollments, the rise in which we cheer, no questions asked.

Finally, Philip I, Frances J, and Eileen K have all left school—one without a high school diploma and by economic necessity, another on graduating and by choice, the third when she failed college in her freshman year. They all looked for work, found it, and are staying with it. But they are in jobs that, in themselves, lead nowhere. These three—and unnumbered hundreds of thousands like them—are presently carried on the credit side of the ledger, as employed.

In short, these youth "unemployment rate" figures—based on concepts developed essentially to measure the adult work situation—reflect poorly what is, in fact, only one aspect of a basic change in the ways young people are spending their transitional years: They are now both in school *and* working.

The two parts of this picture are closely interrelated. To see the whole, it is essential to look at some of the education [patterns] for these same youth, to consider their enrollment and unenrollment as well as their employment and unemployment. . . .

Large numbers of young people remain unenrolled. A recent astonishing report, still neither explained nor fully verified, is that 2 million boys and girls between seven and seventeen are, for one reason or another, not in school. One out of every ten in the sixteen-to-seventeen-year-old age group has dropped out or been pushed out. Under today's circumstance, this spells trouble, both for the individual and for the rest of us. If a high school diploma is no longer a significant job credential—and it isn't—and if a surprising number of high school age youth aren't even in school, it hardly seems to be grounds for optimism that half of all high school graduates now go on to college.

So there is going to have to be continuing attention to the fact that a lot of young people are still leaving school without passports to any place. Who are they? Why are they leaving? What happens to them?

Only beginning efforts have been made to get at the information that will answer these questions. The answers will come only from longitudinal studies—which go into the backgrounds of particular groups of young people of the same age and then follow them not only through their school years but their subsequent experience. One such study, initiated at the University of Michigan in 1966, has already yielded significant enlightenment: Dropping out of high school is better recognized not as a problem in itself but as a symptom of *other* problems rooted in family and economic background, ability limitations, and difficulties in school. As much of this often traces to institutional shortcomings as to individual fault.

One significant element in the recent record of changing school enrollments at various levels is that previous racial differences have been notably reduced and almost eliminated. This is true, at the postsecondary level, to a considerable but lesser extent of sex differences. . . .

By their apparent consistency, enrollment statistics contribute on the whole to an illusion that the pattern of education is now set in this country. It obviously is not. The figures reflect too little the impact during the [sixties] of the postwar baby boom as its reverberations have moved through the educational system. Moreover, they show only the beginning effects of the country's acceptance, in principle, of the equal-opportunities standard for both women and minority groups. And these are all only head-count figures. This much, though, is clear: More and more young people are going to be staying longer and longer in one form of institutionalized education or another.

Why, then, with educational enrollment figures going up so dramatically, is there at the same time such a sharp increase in the unemployment rates among the same group of people? More in school, more out of work. It doesn't seem to make sense.

And it doesn't. There is an imperative need to be met here. The apparent anomaly develops from looking at the education and work figures separately. Both to clear it up and, much more significantly, to get on with meeting this imperative need, the two pictures must be put together.

The Bureau of Labor Statistics now reports that almost 40 percent of sixteen-to-nineteen-year-old boys and girls who are in school are also either working or looking for work, in most cases part-time jobs. This report is based on monthly interviews with parents drawn from a national sample of household surveys. Interestingly, a survey based on interviews with young people themselves shows even more work activity among those in school—at percentages between 50 percent and 60 percent, depending largely on age and race.

These current, or very recent, figures are markedly higher, especially for girls, than they were ten and fifteen years ago. . . .

438

This increased "starlighting"—going to school and working (or trying to) at the same time—is significant in several respects. It is part of the reason the youth unemployment rate is as high as it is. The larger number of marginally qualified workers—those who move in and out of the "labor market" as holidays and vacations and school pressures come and go, who look for part-time work that can be fitted into what are primarily school schedules—is bound to create more situations in which the work being looked for can't be found.

In this connection serious question arises whether the sixteen-to-nineteen-year age group should be included at all in the overall national employment and unemployment figures. These figures used to include fourteen- and fifteen-year-olds as well, but they were removed with publication of data for 1967, and there would appear to be as much reason today for excluding at least the sixteen-to-seventeen-year-old group. The adult unemployment situation is so essentially different from the typical youth unemployment situation—especially in the case of students in schools—that the records should probably be segregated. This would concentrate *separate* attention on the youth unemployment situation, with its much higher figures, thus better illuminating the essentially different problems it presents and facilitating efforts to work out the different answers it requires.

The more basic implication of this increased "starlighting" is that there is already in place a broad base for the development of the work-study and experiential learning programs that are now the subject of so much increased attention among educators. It is time to recognize this subject, and to approach it, as a matter of *both* education and work. What these young people are telling us, by what they are already doing, is that we are making a serious mistake in keeping two separate sets of books and virtually ignoring this now substantial area of dual activity simply because the two parts of it come under the different institutional jurisdictions.

Looked at all together with both eyes instead of separately with one eye on each, these statistics show some other things—four in particular—that must be taken into account before the education and work gears can be properly meshed:

1. A substantial number of these high school and college students who are looking for work *are* finding it. Their difficulties in finding work are often substantial enough to get them into the unemployment statistics as now collected; but in one way or another, at one time or another, a lot of them are getting work experience of some kind or other. This does *not* make the work-study and experiential learning initiatives less important. On the contrary. What it indicates is that with perhaps only minimal collaborative administration, this catch-as-catch-can starlighting could probably be made into a much more effective, and certainly more efficient, school-to-work operation.

Youth *employment* is increasing significantly—that is, it was, until the

439

recent worsening of the economy. . . .

In October 1973, when this situation was . . . surveyed, the number of teenagers (sixteen-to-nineteen-year-olds) *in school and employed* was 3.8 million. This is only about one third of them. But this is during a single school month. When the fact of larger youth employment during the summer months and certain holiday months is taken into account, along with the fact that different young people are employed at different times during the year, it appears that about half of all sixteen-to-nineteen-year-olds who are in school are also getting *some* outside employment during the course of the year.

Some other incomplete figures tend to confirm what these BLS reports suggest: *that in the course of what is primarily their school experience, three out of every four young people are getting some kind of actual work experience in the competitive labor market.* This does *not* satisfy the necessity of including a broad experiential learning component in the educational curriculum; what it *does* suggest strongly is that unless whatever is going on now in the economy disrupts this so far encouraging development, the makings of such a component are available.

2. The work young people are doing—both those who are still students and those who have left school—is taking on a distinctive character of its own.

There is increasing talk and evidence of the emergence of still undefined youth-type jobs. This does *not*, however, mean dead-end jobs.

Teenage employment today is concentrated in a band of unskilled jobs. The relative importance of this fact is shown clearly when compared to the proportion of similar jobs held by older males with the *same education*. . . . Although this occupational concentration of youth employment is nothing new, it is showing up more and more sharply.

It is increasingly evident, beyond this, that private employers, particularly the larger corporations, are hiring fewer and fewer males under age twenty for what are normally considered "entry-type jobs with a prospect of upward mobility." This is true even with respect to jobs traditionally considered as requiring no more than a high school education to perform. (The surveys made so far include hotel clerks, arc welders, bank tellers, hospital orderlies, and so on.) No distinction is being made between those with and those without high school diplomas.

On the other hand, the available statistics disclose striking differences in the kinds of jobs female high school graduates are able to get. Both graduates and nongrads are heavily concentrated in traditional "female" occupations. . . . So far as this "transitional" period is concerned, young women entering employment directly out of high school, unlike young men following the same route, get jobs of a similar nature to those held by adult women who have been in the labor force for some time. This is a reflection of the limited range of employment opportunities available for women in general—regardless of age or educational and experiential backgrounds. The short of it is that women are put in their place sooner rather than later.

3. It is in a sense only a different aspect of the preceding point that there is a critical change going on in the ratio between the number of young people getting more education and the number of jobs presumed to require higher levels of education.

In 1970 about one in six members of the adult labor force had only an elementary education or less. This will decline precipitiously to *one in sixteen* by 1990. At the other end, one in eight had four years of college or more in 1970; by 1990 college education is projected to spread to the point where about one out of every four citizens will be a degree holder. Optimism for the educational requirements of jobs keeping pace has little basis in the trends of the past several decades. . . .

4. It is *apparently* true that more and more young people are orienting their education and training toward *particular* occupational and career prospects, but that fewer of them are finding, when they are through, the jobs they had prepared for. . . .

Young people with unquestionable qualifications in a variety of areas look futilely for jobs today—while the help-wanted columns in the newspapers list more and more needs for computer programmers.

This subject warrants further development. It is by no means clear that more sharply oriented education is less valuable than a general course of study, even if the particular opportunity prepared for turns out not to be available. There are some other things to be considered.

It is, however, critically important that the development of skills be better matched with society's needs for these skills. So far we lack the facts necessary either to understand the seeming mismatch or to correct it.

Give me, Richelieu boasted, six sentences from the words of the most innocent of men, and I will hang him with them. So it is, too, of statistics, which can serve opposite conclusions equally well, depending on who makes the selection from among them. These seem, however, to be the facts in the education-work records that are the closest allies to the truth:

• Whatever may be its various interpretations, the 20 percent youth unemployment rate—40 percent for those doubly disadvantaged by age and descent—*demands* attention to this youth problem.

• The education and work elements in the youth situation cannot responsibly be considered separately; most of these young people at and approaching this critical transition point are both in school and in the work force.

• More and more of them are getting more and more education and mixing it with more and more work experience.

• There *is* work to be done by youth; it is emerging increasingly as work with particular characteristics—distinguishing it in material respects from the work that most adults do.

• The rising "educational attainment level of the work force" has a significant impact on what an education-work policy should be.

• There is evidence of an increasing mismatch between the development of particular competencies and the need for them, but the evidence regarding this is inadequate and the analysis incomplete.

• The answer is not just more school and more jobs for everybody under twenty, if what this means is simply staying longer in the same old classrooms and then looking for some work to relieve the extended monotony of it.

The prevailing mood today is a compound of national exasperation with somebody else and frustration at our own failures. Much of public commentary seems to have become a more-apocalyptic-than-thou kind of sweepstakes. We are down in the mouth and inclined to be perhaps overly self-critical.

But we don't like it this way, and there is no point or reason in approaching this education work situation in negative, overly critical terms.

The shock that most youth unquestionably experience during the critical initiation rite they go through as they move from learning to earning a living is a result neither of neglect nor of any deliberate intent to toughen up the young. It is the consequence, rather, of a giant society's always lumbering and awkward movement in reshaping its traditional processes and its established institutional structures to the impetuous imperatives of change.

It would be worse error to suggest or imply that the passage from youth to adulthood used to be something that was either easily or satisfactorily accomplished, and that this has now some way gone wrong. No boy or girl in this country today, knowing even a little of history, would trade present circumstances or prospects for those any earlier time afforded—or for those currently available any place else in the world.

That, though, isn't the question. The essential quality of this country's remarkable progress in the past decade and a half is that we no longer measure where we are by where we used to be, but rather by where we now know we can go. Part of this current sense of frustration is from our own revolution of increased expectations—and from a new realization that the improvement of the human condition is so much more within the human competence than we used to think. So we look today from a higher vantage point—in a wider perspective of larger purpose—at the manifest evidence of serious losses and costs being incurred at the transfer point between education and work.

14

»«

CREATING
TOTAL
EMPLOYMENT

»«

United Press International

» *Elliot Liebow* «

The Human Costs of Unemployment

» «

This article, written in 1970, again points up the persistence *of the problems of unemployment. At the time, Liebow was worried about an unemployment rate of 5 percent (or, four million Americans unemployed). In mid-1981, the figure is 7.5 percent and growing (about eight million unemployed), and the prospects for a solution are no better than they were a decade before. Liebow argues that income maintenance (welfare) is not the answer to America's problems of poverty. For all the many reasons cited throughout this book, people need* jobs. *But jobs alone won't do. People need steady jobs that pay enough for them to support their families. In short, jobs and money must be linked to break the frightful cycle of dependence. Liebow, therefore, proposes that every American should have a legal right to a socially useful job that pays a decent wage.*

Now that we have, in effect, seized upon unemployment as a weapon of choice in the battle against inflation, we face the prospect of an unemployment rate of 5 percent (4 million persons) or more. And as the unemployment rate goes up, economists and public policy makers debate the question: How much unemployment can the country stand?

Strictly speaking, it is not "the country" that is being asked to "stand unemployment." Unemployment does not, like air pollution or God's gentle rain, fall uniformly upon everyone, nor does it strike randomly at our labor force of 80 million. Unemployment is directional and selective; it strikes from underneath, and it strikes particularly at those at the bottom of our society. . . the day worker, the unskilled and semiskilled laborer, the Job Corps and the on-the-job trainee, those with little or no seniority in the labor unions and those making their first try at breaking into the labor force.

Since there is little unemployment at the upper and middle occupational level, a 5 percent *average* rate means unemployment rates of 10 percent and 20 percent in our ghettos and other hard-core areas. And among certain groups, such as black and other minority-group youths and women, it means an unemployment rate as high as 25 or 30 percent. Increased unemployment, then, means not only more people out of work, it means mainly more black people, more young people, and more poor people out of work. The question is not simply how much more unemployment we can stand, but whether we can stand, through deepening unemployment, a deepening of the race and class divisions that are already threatening to tear our society apart.

We could, of course, deal with the newcomers to the ranks of the unemployed and the poor in the same way that we deal with those who are already there, but this would be to make believe that we don't know the destructive and self-defeating consequences of our public-welfare programs, whose positive effects are largely limited to the simple maintenance of life at bare subsistence levels. . . .

From the very beginning of human history, it has been through work that man has provided himself with the necessities of life. So closely is work tied in with the social and psychological development of man that it is almost impossible to think of what it means to be human without thinking of work. Indeed, the connection is so strong, so close, and so obvious that attempts to talk about the importance of work often sound banal. "Work is the fundamental condition of human existence," said Karl Marx; "work is man's strongest tie to reality," said Freud.

It is also through work, as a producer of socially useful goods or services, that the individual—especially the adult male—carries out those social roles (husband, father, family head) that define him as a full and valued member of his society. That work becomes, in effect, a kind of admission ticket to society is not something invented by white middle-class Americans, although many of us often act as if it is. . . .

In subsistence economies, the entire population has to work to produce the goods and services necessary to survival, and there is always work to be done. In such societies, people are not recognizable as being in or out of the work force—the work force is synonymous with the total population.

In industrial societies, unemployment strikes deep at the man, as well as at the way he fits into his family, his community, and the larger society. It can put a man "out of it," and can turn him into a caricature of himself, giving him the appearance of being stupid and lazy with no concern for the future. . . .

We can see the general problem most clearly by narrowing our focus to black people and other racial minorities in our society, for they are the principal victims. Black people suffer more from unemployment not only because more of them, proportionately, are unemployed, but because they are more likely than their white counterparts to have been unemployed in the past and to remain unemployed or underemployed in the future. This circumstance of life—a major thread in the collective history and present experience of black people as a group—shapes the way the black man sees himself and is seen by others as fitting into the larger community. It also gives meaning to the assertion that we are a racist society, a racism that is intimately bound up with work and productivity and individual worth.

445

Let me give an example. The six-year-old son of a woman on welfare was struck and killed by an automobile as he tried to run across the street. The insurance company's initial offer of $800 to settle out of court was rejected. In consultation with her lawyer, the mother accepted the second and final offer of $2,000. When I learned of the settlement, I called the lawyer to protest, arguing that the sum was far less than what I assumed to be the usual settlement in such cases, even if the child was mainly at fault. "You've got to face the facts," he said. "Insurance companies and juries just don't pay as much for a Negro child." Especially, he might have added, a Negro child on welfare.

If the relative worth of human life must be measured in dollars and cents, why should the cash surrender value of a black child's life be less than that for a white child's life? . . . On what basis do they make lowered projections of earnings for a six-year-old child, before he has acquired or rejected an education, before he has demonstrated any talents or lack of them, before he has selected an occupation, or, indeed, before he has made a single life choice of his own?

There can be only one answer. The answer is, simply, on the basis of skin color and social class. And what is most important for us to know and admit is this: the insurance company was *absolutely right.* Anthony was more likely than his white, middle-class counterpart to go to an inferior school, to get an inferior education, to be sick, to get an inferior job, to be last hired and first fired, to be passed over for promotion, and to live a shorter life. In all probability, then, Anthony *would* be less productive over his lifetime than his white middle-class counterpart. And we are a racist society because we know this to be true before the fact, when Anthony is only six years old.

Typically, we admit the problem, but we place the cause in the Negro (Puerto Rican, Mexican-American, American Indian, Appalachian white) himself. We say that because of their history, or their subculture, or their family structure, these minorities are lazy, irresponsible, and don't want to work. Then, in the midst of an affluence never before achieved by any society, we offer them the most menial, the dullest, the poorest paid jobs in our society, and, sure enough, some of them don't want to work.

But the one most important fact is often overlooked. Most Negroes (Puerto Ricans, etc.), like everyone else in our society, do want to work. Indeed, most of them have been working all along. In Washington, for example, the garbage does get picked up, the streets get swept, hotel beds are made, school and office-building floors and halls get mopped and polished, cars and restaurant dishes get washed, ditches get dug, deliveries are made, orderlies attend the aged, the sick, the mentally ill, and so on. And most of the people whose job it is to do those things are black.

But if most Negroes do have jobs, what is the problem? It is mainly that most of those jobs pay from $50 to $80 or $90 a week. . . . The man with a wife and one or two children who takes such a job can be certain he will live in poverty as long as he keeps it. The longer he works, the longer he cannot live on what he makes.

This situation makes for a curious paradox: the man who works hard may be little or no better off than the man who does not look for a job at all. In a sense, he may even be worse off. The man who works hard but cannot earn a living has put himself on the scales and been found wanting. He says to society, "I have done what needed doing. Now, what am I worth?" and society answers, "Not much, not even enough to support yourself and your dependents." But the man who does not seek out or accept such a job may, for a while at least, fool himself or his fellows into thinking that he has not climbed onto the scales at all. . . .

From this perspective, the problem is how can we change our society so that all who belong to it can become full and valued participants in it?

For a beginning, we must make the poor less poor. We must get money into their hands. We must choose one or a combination of the many income-supplement programs that have been proposed and put them into practice. Another beginning step might be to focus our concerns on the low-paying, menial jobs that have to be done in every society. Since these jobs have to be done by someone, it makes little sense to keep insisting that we must always and only upgrade the person. At some point we are going to have to upgrade the job.

For systematically upgrading jobs such as these, we might use the airline stewardess as a model. Casual observation suggests that, for the most part, her job is that of a waitress. But the airlines, through adroit public relations, through the use of smartly designed uniforms, by setting performance standards, and by paying a decent salary, have upgraded the job of the airborne waitress to a much higher level of respectability and desirability than that enjoyed by her ground-based counterpart.

Not all menial jobs can be upgraded so easily and so far. Many menial jobs are dirty jobs, and there is not a lot we can do at this time to make them less dirty. But that is not the only reason they are despised and among the lowest status jobs in our society. They are also among the lowest paying jobs. . . .

There is little that is intrinsically bad about being a janitor or trash collector. What is so bad about them is that in such jobs you cannot earn a living. Where the pay for garbage and trash collectors approaches a living wage, as in New York City, there is intense competition for the work that is elsewhere shunned and accepted only as a last resort.

That these jobs tend also to be dead-end jobs is probably true, but perhaps we make too much of this also. The job of the lathe operator, the assembly-line worker, the truck driver, the secretary, these tend to be dead-end jobs too, but they are not bad jobs because of it. Not everyone in our society is career-oriented. We have a large and relatively stable working-class population which does not aspire to moving up a career ladder. The working man who earns a living and supports his family by doing work that everyone agrees is socially useful does not necessarily want to become a foreman, or plant manager, or office executive. If he is dissatisfied, it is probably because he wants more of what he has and wants to be more certain of keeping what he has, not because he wants something different. So would it be, perhaps, with jobs that are presently considered menial, dead-end jobs. If a man could earn a living at these jobs, they would not be dead-end. They would be much like other jobs—a job.

I do not mean to suggest that all unemployed and underemployed men and youths want nothing more than jobs that pay a living wage. Many do want careers and an opportunity to use their brains and their strengths to take them as high and as far as they can go, and they must have these opportunities. The point here is that not everyone wants to scratch his way to the top of something. Most people, black and white, want the creature comforts and the psychic rewards that come with having jobs that enable them and their families to live like most other people in our society.

This brings us to my final proposal. It has been suggested many times by many people, but because it has been labeled unrealistic or too expensive or destructive of free enterprise, it does not seem to be getting the serious attention I think it deserves. . . . If having a job and earning a living is, as I believe it is, the linchpin of full and valued participation in our society, then every able-bodied man must have a right—a legal, statutory right—to a job doing socially useful work which pays a decent wage. To do this would probably require that government—federal, state and local— already the largest employer, become also the employer of last resort. At the federal level, there are many different employment models to choose from: Civil Service, the Tennessee Valley Authority, the Public Health Service, contract, grant and draft mechanisms, the old WPA, and CCC, etc.

The crucial thing here is not the mechanism but the avoidance of contemptible make-work by matching a wide range of job skills and aspirations to tasks that are clearly of a high order of social usefulness, such as construction of public and low-cost housing, restoration of cities, expansion and improvement of mail service, and host of other programs and projects directed at the unmet public need in the areas of health education, child care, urban mass transit, conservation, pollution, and so on. Where appropriate the federal government could subcontract such projects, or parts of them, to state and local governments through a revenue-sharing system, thereby insuring that national programs and policies were matched to local needs.

We have already seen that, by themselves, neither money nor a job is sufficient to guarantee full and valued participation. The two must be linked together. A man must have the right to a job that pays a decent wage. Thus, though income-assistance plans are needed for the immediate future, and indeed always will be needed for those persons—the aged, the sick, the handicapped, and women with dependent children—who cannot or should not work, such plans should be viewed for the working poor as stopgap emergency measures rather than long-range solutions.

In general, income-assistance plans for the man who works but does not earn a living wage are focused on the wrong end of the employer-employee relationship. We are probably all agreed that, given a wage-labor system, a man who does an honest day's work, whether it be sweeping the floor or simply guarding a gate, is entitled to an honest day's pay. An honest day's pay must mean, at the minimum, enough for the man to support himself and an average number of dependents. If it means anything less, it means nothing at all.

If a business or industry cannot afford to pay the worker enough to live on, the failure lies with the company, not the employee, and it is the employer who needs welfare, not the worker. Enterprises which through inefficiency or other reasons cannot afford to pay their workers enough to live on must leave the field or, if they are deemed socially useful and necessary, must be subsidized by the government—let's call it cost-sharing—so they can pay their workers a living wage. In this way, the stigma, the badge of dependency that goes with being a recipient of public assistance, is removed from the worker (where it did not really belong in the first place) and placed on the employer (where it does belong). . . .

Acknowledgment of every citizen's uncompromised right to earn a living is not proposed as a solution to all of our social problems. It would, however, be an important first step toward dealing with many of them: behind much of what presents itself to us as family instability, dependent women and children, violence, crime, and retreatist life styles, stand men and women, black and white, who cannot support themselves and their families. In addition, raising the social and economic status of its members is the surest and safest way for a society to reduce its rate of population growth. Most immediately and directly, however, the right to a job at a decent wage would go a long way toward removing simple, brutal poverty from our national life. And unlike variations on the welfare theme, it would do this in a way that would help reorder the relationship between citizen and society so that everyone could enjoy that minimum sense of security and self-respect without which talk of freedom, equality, and opportunity does not mean very much.

A society in which everyone works is not necessarily a free society and may indeed be a slave society; on the other hand, a society in which there is widespread economic insecurity can turn freedom into a barren and vapid right for millions of people.
—Eleanor Roosevelt, "The Struggle for Human Rights"

» Daniel P. Moynihan «

The Problem of Dependency

» «

In this selection Daniel Patrick Moynihan, formerly a Harvard professor and now a U.S. Senator, picks up the theme of dependency introduced by Liebow in the preceding article. Moynihan calls our attention to the fact that dependency is an unhealthy state for adults, but that an unintended consequence of public policy is literally to "hook" millions of black Americans on welfare dependency. As many as two out of three black children reaching maturity in the late 1960s had been supported at some time by welfare. But as Moynihan points out, conservatives who focus on the dollar costs of welfare miss the real point of this statistic: being dependent is a terrible stigma and humiliation, and "it cannot too often be stated that the issue of welfare is not what it costs those who provide it, but what it costs those who receive it."

The issue of welfare is the issue of dependency. It is different from poverty. To be poor is an objective condition; to be dependent, a subjective one as well. That the two circumstances interact is evident enough, and it is no secret that they are frequently combined. Yet a distinction must be made. Being poor is often associated with considerable personal qualities; being dependent rarely so. This is not to say that dependent people are not brave, resourceful, admirable, but simply that their situation is never enviable, and rarely admired. It is an incomplete state in life: normal in the child, abnormal in the adult. In a world where completed men and women stand on their own feet, persons who are dependent—as the buried imagery of the word denotes—hang. . . .

When such persons are very young or very old, allowances are made. But when they are of the age when other persons work to earn their way and, further, if they are dependent during periods when work is to be had, dependency becomes a stigma.

This is the heart of it. The issue of welfare involves a stigmatized class of persons. The recipients know this. Or rather they share this judgment. Of late, perhaps, some do not. And yet the manner and the tactics of those who assert that welfare is a right that certain citizens are entitled to are somehow unconvincing. Over and again what occurs is an effort to humiliate or intimidate others who are not dependent, especially if they are in some symbolic or functional way those depended upon. It cannot too often be stated that the issue of welfare is not what it costs those who provide it, but what it costs those who receive it. . . .

Early social welfare efforts in the United States tended to locate the sources of dependency in the habits of the poor. There was a case to be made for this view. Drink, to cite an example, was and is a formidable source of poverty and dependency. It was and is especially destructive to families. The temperance movement was onto something real. The family of the sober working man was far better off than that of the drunken one. And yet there is a sense in which social conditions create drunkenness, and that too is real. . . .

Regardless of the evidence, however, opposition to the moralistic tone of welfare assistance appeared early, and by the beginning of the twentieth century had become the mark of "advanced" thinking in the field. An individual might be seen as having traits which caused him difficulty, but these tended to be ascribed to social or, later, psychopathic, conditions over which he had little control.

The Great Depression made the proposition that the unemployed are somehow not looking for work seem absurd, as indeed it was at the time, while, in general, advances in economics have increasingly portrayed joblessness as the consequence of national decisions that have nothing whatever to do with the character traits of the jobless. Again, this may not be wholly the case, but it is not to be doubted that the sensibilities of American social reformers have grown increasingly offended by definitions of social problems which seem to locate the source of difficulty in the behavior of the individual in trouble rather than in some abstraction made up of persons not in trouble. This concern is hardly unique to American social attitudes, but it is felt with special intensity here. Dependency amounts to failure, a fate seemingly more dreaded among us than others. Americans feel the need to deny failure, or to ascribe it to the most generalized sources. If there is a pattern among us it is that of denying the existence of a problem as long as possible, and thereafter quickly ascribing it to some generalized failing of society at large.

This instinctive avoidance is never more powerful than when the matter at issue touches on sexual behavior—which family matters necessarily do. As far back as social records go, poverty, especially urban poverty, has been associated with illegitimacy, desertion, and failure to provide, subjects so painful to humanitarians that many seemed able to confront the reality only by denying that it was in any way a failure of those who experience it, as in the formulation that family patterns of the poor represent an admirable, even enviable, rejection of bourgeois repression. Others contrived to know only as much about such matters as was absolutely necessary. This pattern became chronic within government. Where the tendency of most bureaucracies is to exaggerate the gravity of problems with which they deal, the tendency of welfare bureaucracies has been rather the opposite. One Secretary of Health, Education, and Welfare concluded toward the end of his tenure that his officials were so extremely reluctant to face the realities of dependency that they persistently underestimated prospective rises in the welfare rolls. A tradition of being "color blind" enabled those in the Federal bureaucracy who so wished to conceal from themselves the degree to which dependency had become associated with race, while a tradition of liberal-minded tolerance caused them to deny that problems such as illegitimacy existed.

As with most patterns of self-deception, this ended as self-defeating. The time came when the question of a generalized failure of the social system had to be confronted, but when it did the task fell to others. Welfare dependency became a "crisis" in the mid-1960s *not* because it was consuming large amounts of money, or involved large numbers of people. The amounts of money were trivial, and the numbers not that large. Welfare had to be defined as a crisis because of the rate at which the rolls commenced to grow. "The heart of it," Robert L. Bartley writes, "is that such growth has powerful overtones of social disintegration." Here surely was an opportunity to argue that the individual caught up in the system was not to blame, but the habit of analysis had been lost (or never acquired) among those nominally closest to the subject. The whole matter had become just too painful.

It was thus that American society was peculiarly unprepared to respond to the rise of welfare dependency that occurred with such suddenness in the mid-1960s. The difficulty was not primarily or even significantly an unwillingness to *do* anything about the problem. Rather, it was an inability to *think* about it to any purpose. Nathan E. Cohen and Maurice F. Connery have described this as "a schism in our thought in which some processes of our society are perceived as subject to understanding and control and others subject only to some vague, unknowable dynamics to which we can only hope to respond." The cost of this schism was, and continues to be, considerable. It involved, for one thing, the intellectual denial of a primary social reality, namely that family structure and functioning have consequences for children, and that, by and large, families function best in traditional arrangements. (Persons who have benefited from such arrangements sometimes find it easy to disparage them. A Southern saying goes, "A dollar ain't much if you got one.") Just as significantly, among social activists the presumption was reinforced that family matters were not to become public questions. Thus, when the United States Supreme Court early in 1971 upheld the constitutionality of a New York State law providing for periodic home visits to welfare recipients, there was an audible response that another blow had been struck against civil liberties. *The Times*, in its news columns, described the decision as evidence of an emerging "conservative" majority on the court. A *Times* editorial resisted this view, pointing out that the welfare worker in the case was seeking to visit a child that had at various times suffered a skull fracture, a dent in the head, and a "possible" rat bite. Justice Harry A. Blackmun had ruled that "the dependent child's needs are paramount, and only with hesitancy would we relegate those needs, in the scale of comparative values, to a position secondary to what the mother claims as her rights." The *Times* editorial defended this judgment, but the more general opinion was revealed in the news story. The "liberal" decision would have been to bar the social worker, as "government has no business interfering with family life." In this there was to be seen an odd continuity between the laissez-faire liberalism of the nineteenth century and the far more interventionist liberalism of the twentieth. . . .

The War on Poverty of the 1960s was officially announced in the Economic Report of the President of January 1964. The Council of Economic Advisers defined as poor any family of two or more persons with income for the year less than $3,000. . . .

This was a period of great concern about poverty, especially black poverty. A profusion of programs came forth from Washington, some of which had measurable consequences. Some may even have contributed to the decline of poverty, but almost certainly the most important influence in this respect was a long, sustained period of economic expansion which phased into a wartime boom. . . .

The number of persons classified as poor in the span 1959 to 1968 decreased by 36 percent. The number of public-assistance recipients rose 41 percent. . . .

Race, family size, family structure: all these were correlates of poverty. But none was nearly so powerful in aggregate terms as the mere fact of geographic region. All in all, by the end of the 1960s half of all the nation's poor families—two in five of the poor whites, and two in three of the poor blacks—lived in the sixteen states plus the District of Columbia which Federal statistics define as the South. . . .

As the 1960s progressed, poverty came to be better understood. It was seen to be a dynamic rather than static condition. In a given year as many as a third of poor families were "new arrivals," which is to say families that had not been poor the previous years. Correspondingly, as the overall numbers declined, an even larger number of families would have "left" poverty in such a year. The population "at risk" was significantly larger than the number of poor at any given moment. Families cycled in and out: something like that. No one knew for certain. During intervals of personal hard times welfare became a prime or sole source of income. Studies of AFDC families showed that half received assistance for less than two years. Something led into dependency and then led out of it. For some, presumably, the pattern repeated itself. No one could say for how many, but one fact did emerge most powerfully from the studies of this period: the AFDC program was far and away the most significant antipoverty effort of the Federal government, and was the core element of a national family policy.

453

One child in five reaching maturity at the end of the 1960s had at one time been supported by AFDC. Among black youth the proportion may have been as high as two-thirds. Again, using nonwhite data as a surrogate for low-income and poor persons generally, there could be no doubt of the immense, if unintended, influence of this singular form of income maintenance.

I believe in the dignity of labor, whether with head or hand; that the world owes no man a living but that it owes every man an opportunity to make a living.

—John D. Rockefeller

» Martin Feldstein «

The Economics of the New Unemployment

» «

Harvard economist Martin Feldstein argues that there is no reason why the high average rates of unemployment that have prevailed over the last thirty-five years need to continue. It is unlikely, however, that the rates can be greatly reduced below 5 percent simply by stimulating the economy to create more jobs. Not only would such a policy create unacceptably high levels of inflation, but it would also do little for the "structurally" unemployed—minority, handicapped, teenage, and other workers who never seem to find jobs even when unemployment rates are extremely low. For young workers, Feldstein advocates a special, lower minimum wage than for adults, and federal supplements to private employers who will hire and train them. For the hard-core of minority unemployed workers, he suggests an upgrading of low level jobs to make this work more attractive than welfare. For the handicapped, he proposes that the government either supplement their wages or integrate the minimum wage law with general income maintenance. For workers in seasonal and cyclical work, he advocates changing the current unemployment compensation rules to encourage unemployed workers to seek jobs sooner and to encourage employers to spread their production more evenly throughout the seasons and over the business cycle.

A high level of unemployment is a persistent problem of the American economy. . . . High unemployment rates imply substantial personal and aggregate losses. Moreover, as I shall emphasize below, the American pattern of unemployment is a symptom of a more serious failure in the development and use of our nation's manpower.

Unfortunately, there is no reason to expect that the next 20 years will be better than the last. Without substantial new policy initiatives, American unemployment rates will remain significantly higher than those that prevail in Western Europe and in most other industrial nations. Now that unemployment has fallen from the very high rates of 1970 and 1971, it is important to ask whether there is anything that can be done to lower permanently the average rate of unemployment to three percent or below.

I . . . examined this question in a study prepared for the Joint Economic Committee of the U.S. Congress. Although my conclusions and proposals should be regarded as tentative, I believe that it is important to stimulate discussion about these issues at the current time. The basic conclusions of my study can be summarized briefly:

First, I believe that we probably can lower the permanent unemployment rate to a level substantially below the average of the post-War period. An average unemployment rate significantly less than three percent, and possibly close to two percent, for those seeking steady full-time employment is a realistic goal for the next decade.

Second, the economy is not likely to achieve such a goal, or indeed to perform any better than it did in the past two decades, without significant changes in employment policy.

Third, expansionary macroeconomic policy cannot be relied upon to achieve the desired reduction in unemployment. Any possible increase in aggregate demand that does not have unacceptable effects on the rate of inflation would leave a high residue of unemployment. I believe that this is true even if one is very optimistic about the effect of increases in aggregate demand on inflation. The structure of unemployment and the current functioning of our labor markets imply a high overall rate of unemployment even when certain key unemployment rates are extremely low. Better management of aggregate demand has a role to play, but it cannot do the entire job.

Work expands so as to fill the time available for its completion. General recognition of this fact is shown in the proverbial phrase "It is the busiest man who has time to spare."

The rise in the total of those employed is governed by Parkinson's Law and would be much the same whether the volume of work were to increase, diminish or even disappear.
—C. Northcote Parkinson, *Parkinson's Law*

Fourth, lowering the overall rate of unemployment will require new types of policies aimed at increasing the stability of employment among young workers, at eliminating unnecessary seasonal and cyclical fluctuations in labor demand, and at increasing the speed with which the unemployed return to work. . . .

The Limited Efficacy of Increasing Demand

Most macroeconomic analyses of unemployment are based on ideas about the causes and structure of unemployment that are inappropriate and out of date. The basic framework of Keynesian economics, conditioned by the experience of the 1930's, has always emphasized the inadequacy of aggregate demand as the source of unemployment. The conventional view of post-War unemployment might be described as follows: "The growth of demand for goods and services does not always keep pace with the expansion of the labor force and the rise in output per man. Firms therefore lay off employees and fail to hire new members of the labor force at a sufficient rate. The result is a pool of potential workers who are unable to find jobs. Only policies to increase the growth of demand can create the jobs needed to absorb the unemployed."

This picture of a hard core of unemployed workers who are not able to find jobs is an inaccurate description of our economy and a misleading basis for policy. A more accurate description is an active labor market in which almost everyone who is out of work can find his usual type of job in a relatively short time. *The problem is not that these jobs are unavailable but that they are often unattractive.* Much of the unemployment and even more of the lost manpower occurs among individuals who find that the available jobs are neither appealing in themselves nor rewarding as pathways to better jobs in the future. For such individuals, job attachment is weak, quitting is common, and periods without work or active job seeking are frequent. *The major problem to be dealt with is not a chronic aggregate shortage of jobs but the instability of individual employment.* Decreasing the overall rate of unemployment requires not merely more jobs, but new incentives to encourage those who are out of work to seek employment more actively and those who are employed to remain at work. . . . An important part of these incentives is a change in the kinds of jobs that are available.

It is difficult to replace our old notions about demand-determined unemployment by this new view. Let me therefore describe . . . some of the characteristics of American unemployment during the past decade.

First, the duration of unemployment is quite short. Even in a year like 1971 with a very high unemployment rate, 45 percent of those unemployed had been out of work for less than five weeks. In 1969, this proportion was almost 58 percent. Similarly, very few are without jobs for as long as 27 weeks; in 1969 this was 4.7 percent and in 1971 it was 10.4 percent of all the unemployed.

Second, loss of jobs accounts for less than half of total unemployment. In 1971, only 46 percent of the unemployed had lost their previous jobs. In the more favorable market conditions of 1969, this proportion was only 36 percent. The remainder are those who voluntarily left their last jobs, are reentering the labor force, or never worked before. In 1969, with an overall unemployment rate of 3.5 percent, losing one's job contributed only 1.2 percent to this figure.

Third, the turnover of jobs is extremely high. Data collected from manufacturing establishments show that total hirings and separations have each exceeded four percent of the labor force per month since 1960. Moreover, the number of quits has consistently exceeded layoffs during the past five years. Even with the high unemployment of 1971, more workers quit manufacturing jobs than were laid off. . . .

Demographic Differences

Perhaps the most important characteristic of our current unemployment problem is the differences in unemployment experience among demographic groups. The unemployment rates in certain groups are not only very high but are also quite unresponsive to changes in the aggregate demand for labor. This implies that fiscal and monetary policies that drastically cut the unemployment rate of mature men would still leave a high overall unemployment rate. . . .

Finally, non-white unemployment rates are higher in every category, but again job loss accounts for less than half of total unemployment. Even though non-whites have more difficulty in finding employment, unemployment due to voluntary separations and withdrawals from the labor force is approximately twice the level for whites. . . .

The current structure of unemployment in the American economy is not compatible with the traditional view of a hard core of unemployed who are unable to find jobs. Even with the high unemployment rate of 1971, the durations of unemployment were short, job losers accounted for less than half of unemployment, and quit rates generally exceeded layoffs. An examination of the past experience of individual demographic groups indicates very substantial variation in the response of unemployment rates to aggregate demand and implies that even an extremely tight labor market would leave some groups with high unemployment rates. . . .

Unemployment Among Young Workers

Unemployment rates for young persons seem outrageously high. . . . Youth unemployment is not primarily due to inadequate demand. The statistic[s] . . . indicate that the unemployment rate of young persons would remain high even in a very tight labor market. There are two main sources of the chronic high unemployment in this age range: (1) unnecessarily slow absorption of new entrants and (2) low job attachment among those at work. Because of the slow absorption, a very significant part of the unemployment of young workers is among new entrants to the labor force and others who are seeking their first full-time job. . . .

I would favor a federal program that reimbursed states for the cost of operating a Youth Employment Service that met certain federal standards. The Service should be separate from the regular Employment Service and should deal only with persons below 21 years of age. Although available to those who have already left school, it should focus mainly on an active program of advising and placing those who are about to leave. A participant state should require each student to be interviewed by the Youth

Employment Service before he graduates from high school or is allowed to leave school legally. Making a Youth Employment Service an integral part of the educational system should facilitate the transition from school to job. The knowledge that everyone entering the labor force is seen by the Youth Employment Service would encourage employers to list jobs that are not now given to the regular Employment Service. If those leaving school are more aware of the options open to them, they are more likely to find a job with which they will be satisfied. They will not only find a better job in this way, but will also be less likely to leave that job in an illusory hope of improving their position.

The Instability of Teenage Employment

The second source of unemployment—the high rate at which young men and women lose jobs, quit jobs, and drop out of the labor force—is both a more serious problem and a more difficult one to solve. Much of the unemployment among experienced young workers occurs not because jobs are unavailable but because they are unattractive. For many young workers, the available entry-level jobs are also dead-end jobs. They offer neither valuable training nor opportunities for significant advancement within the firm. Since employers have made no investment in these workers, they do not hesitate to lay them off whenever demand falls. Since comparable jobs are easy to find, these young workers do not hesitate to quit. The growth of our economy during the past few decades now permits relatively high wages even for those with entry-level jobs. Among the young and single, these high wages encourage an increased demand for leisure. If the content of the job and the structure of the firm's employment policy do not outweigh this, job attachment will be weak and quit rates high.

All of the evidence points to this highly unstable character of employment, rather than to any long-term difficulty in finding jobs, as the primary source of unemployment among experienced young workers. First, the mean duration of unemployment is much lower for this group than for the rest of the labor force. . . . Second, unemployment among job leavers and those reentering the labor force is much more important for younger workers than unemployment among job losers. . . . Third, these high reentrant rates appear to be associated with relatively high rates of being outside the labor force. . . .

Students and Non-students

Why is employment so unstable and labor force attachment so weak in this age range? . . . I believe that a fundamental reason is the types of jobs that are available and the lack of adequate reward for stable employment. . . .

Part of the high quit rates and rates of leaving the labor force merely reflects the impact of our educational system and the seasonal character of the labor force activity of students. Those who have not stopped their formal education seek full-time employment when schools are closed and may also seek different part-time jobs during the school year. . . . Moreover, many of those who leave school and take jobs later return to being full-time students. High unemployment among young Americans is therefore in part a reflection of our commitment to providing many more years of schooling than is common in other countries, and is a price we pay for a very fluid educational system which encourages people to move back and forth between full-time work and full-time education.

In considering the gap between the unemployment rates of young persons and of more mature workers, it is important not to lose sight of their differences in motivation and attitudes. Most young workers have no family responsibilities and many continue to live with their parents. . . . Many young persons want more leisure than is consistent with full-time employment and a permanent attachment to a particular firm. They prefer to alternate between working and other activities rather than to seek and hold permanent employment. . . . For those in higher education, the daily routine is varied and the individual is generally free to choose his own activities and pace of work. Perhaps much of the high turnover and voluntary labor force withdrawal among young non-students reflects an attempt to enjoy the same freedom and occupational irresponsibility that we take for granted in our student population of the same age.

The extremely high unemployment rates are therefore not quite what they seem. They reflect the peculiar labor force behavior of students and the temporary and voluntary unemployment that young people can afford in an affluent society. Despite this, I believe that there does exist a real and serious problem. The high turnover rates and voluntary unemployment are also a response to the unsatisfactory type of job that is available to many young workers. These are often dead-end jobs with neither opportunity for advancement within the firm nor training and experience that would be useful elsewhere. The young worker's incentive to stay at work is often further reduced by a seniority system that implies that the newest employees are most likely to be laid off during the next small business downturn. Moreover, the lack of sufficient opportunities to begin careers leading to high-paying jobs or to obtain valuable on-the-job training in industry and business is no doubt responsible for an excessive reliance on formal education. I shall not venture to guess how many of our college students might be served better by working than by going to school if more adequate jobs were available.

The Minimum Wage and Opportunities for Training

At the root of this problem is the hard economic reality that firms cannot afford to offer useful on-the-job training to a broad class of young employees. A firm can generally provide the opportunity to acquire new marketable skills—by on-the-job training, detailed supervision, or even just learning by experience—only to a worker whose net product *during the period of training* is at least equal to his wage. Unfortunately, the current minimum wage law prevents many young people from accepting jobs with low pay but valuable experience. Those who come to the labor market with substantial skills and education need not be affected by the minimum wage. They are productive enough to permit employers to pay at least the minimum wage while also providing further training and opportunities for advancement. But for the disadvantaged young worker, with few skills and below-average education, producing enough to earn the minimum wage is incompatible with the opportunity for adequate on-the-job learning. For this group, the minimum wage implies high short-run unemployment and the chronic poverty of a life of low-wage jobs. . . .

The problem then is to remove the barrier to better on-the-job experience and training that is currently posed for some young workers by the minimum wage law. There are a variety of ways to do this. The method that one prefers depends in part on whom one wants to bear the cost of these better job opportunities. One obvious solution would be to modify the minimum wage law so that its full force does not apply to young workers. This would put the full cost of the better training on the young workers themselves. Although there is strong opposition to changing our current minimum wage system, the case for a minimum wage is clearly the weakest when applied to young workers. At best, the minimum wage is an administratively simple way of providing a minimum annual income for every family with a full-time working member. It suffers even in this context from its failure to relate that income to family size. This is particularly relevant to young workers who are single and who often live with their parents. . . .

A wide variety of alternative programs, differing in the degree of control that the government exercises over the individual's training, could be designed. *Central to all such programs would be a Youth Employment Scholarship paid to young workers as a supplement to their wage income.* . . .

Four Sources of Adult Unemployment

Unemployment among mature workers reflects several distinct problems. . . .

Some unemployment is, of course, the inevitable consequence of a healthy and dynamic economy. The changing mix of output and the process of technological advance displaces workers who generally become temporarily unemployed. Women often return to the labor force as their children grow older; in 1971, reentrants accounted for 40 percent of the unemployment among women 20 years old and over. Families occasionally migrate to new areas in order to find better employment opportunities and then spend time searching for work. All of these sources of unemployment produce important gains for the economy and often for the unemployed themselves. It is clear that they should not be discouraged. In particular, it is important to avoid the temptation—to which other countries have sometimes succumbed—to prevent temporary unemployment by permanent

461

subsidies for unwanted output and inefficient technology.

Although some unemployment among adults is appropriate, the actual unemployment rates among experienced men clearly represent an undesirable and unnecessary waste of resources. . . .

Although better management of aggregate demand has a more important role to play in lowering the adult unemployment rate than in improving the teenage employment situation, macroeconomic policies cannot do the job alone. . . . It is now time to consider the more specific reasons why a variety of policies are needed to achieve a more desirable level of unemployment among adult workers. To do so, it is useful to distinguish . . . the implications of four different sources of adult unemployment: (1) the cyclical and seasonal volatility of the demand for labor; (2) the weak labor force attachment of some groups of workers; (3) the particular difficulty in finding permanent employment for persons with very low skills or other employment disabilities; and (4) the average of several months of unemployment among job losers.

Cyclical and Seasonal Variation in Demand

The American unemployment rate is not only higher than the rates observed in foreign countries but also much more cyclically volatile. During the 1960's, the total U.S. unemployment rate varied from 3.5 percent to 6.7 percent. The cyclical variation in unemployment—the gap between peak and trough—was 3.2 percent. The unemployment rate was nearly twice as high in the worst year as in the best. . . .

A variety of special schemes might be developed in the United States to encourage firms to reduce the sensitivity of employment to changes in aggregate demand: required minimum notice before employees are laid off, large compulsory severance payments, a guaranteed annual wage, substantial tax penalties (or rewards) for volatile (or stable) employment, and the like. Similar policies have already been adopted by some European countries; however, such actions can only lower the volatility of unemployment by reducing the efficiency of the labor market and therefore lowering real wages. There is no reason for the government to impose a lower wage and correspondingly greater employment security than the employees themselves actually want. Collective bargaining agreements can achieve any desired degree of employment security through the same techniques of minimum notice, supplementary unemployment benefits, and so on. The outcome of collective bargaining, moreover, can reflect the employee preferences and the real opportunity costs of lost earnings. The government should only provide inducements to disguised unemployment to the extent that these are considered a more efficient form of deficit spending or that they provide tangible benefits to persons other than the individual employees and employers. It should go without saying that the government should also avoid policies that artificially stimulate the responsiveness of unemployment to changes in aggregate demand. . . .

Weak Labor Force Attachment

Unemployment caused by weak labor force attachment is generally a smaller but more serious problem among adults than among young workers. While some of the unemployed adults who are not seeking permanent employment are still students or are mothers with young children, the social problems are associated with the group with low skills and little education. These adults suffer from the same limited opportunities as some of the young workers described in the last section. Because they have low skills, little education, and generally bad work habits, they never enter the mainstream of employment opportunities. The only jobs open to them are the dead-end jobs with low pay and no future.

High unemployment among the men and women in this "secondary labor market" reflects their rejection of the jobs that are available. Many of those with very limited job opportunities prefer to remain unemployed rather than accept what they consider undesirable jobs. Many others who take these jobs soon quit.

Boston's experience with trying to secure employment for a large group of such low-skill workers dramatically illustrates that the problem is not providing jobs but making these jobs acceptable to the unemployed. During the eight months beginning in September 1966, Boston's ABCD program referred some 15,000 disadvantaged workers to jobs. Seventy percent were actually offered jobs. Nearly half of the job offers—45 percent—were rejected. Of those who did accept work, less than half remained on the job for one month. A very high proportion of these separations were voluntary. Even among those over age 25 who were being paid more than $1.75 per hour in 1967, the separation rate in the first month was 33 percent.

What can be done to reduce unemployment among low-skilled adult workers? It is clear that the problem cannot be solved by increasing aggregate demand in order to create more jobs. There is no evidence of a shortage of jobs for this group. The Boston experience shows that jobs can be found but that they will not be accepted. *Lowering the rate of unemployment requires steps to bring the characteristics of the actual jobs and the standards of the acceptable jobs closer together....*

The Current Unemployables

In addition to those who are cyclically unemployed or voluntarily out of work, there is a substantial residue of unemployables who would be unable to find steady employment even in a very tight labor market. Permanent physical disability, subnormal intelligence, or psychological problems severely limit the productivity of these men and women. The problem is most serious among those with both a physical impairment and limited education. Law and custom prevent firms from lowering wages to the levels at which it would pay to hire handicapped individuals.

Although vocational rehabilitation could improve the prospects for some of them, in many cases—especially among those who are older and less educated—the costs of additional training would exceed the benefits. *Two forms of job creation for these permanently disadvantaged workers have been suggested: subsidies to firms and direct permanent public employment. A third option, integrating the minimum wage law with general income maintenance, is also possible. . . .*

Duration of Unemployment

A worker who is laid off often does not accept the first job offer in his own line of work but investigates several job possibilities over a period of weeks before accepting new employment. Part of this process of searching is information gathering. The worker who has not recently been unemployed generally does not know what wage and working conditions his own skills and experience will command in the market. He spends time locating relevant jobs and learning about them. Part of the search also consists of delaying in the expectation that the next job offer may be better. The greater the individual's uncertainty and the greater the variance of wage rates and working conditions in his relevant market, the longer he will tend to search.

Not all unemployment can be interpreted as conscious or unconscious search. Some skilled workers and union members know just what the local market wage is in their occupation and prefer to wait until such work becomes available rather than accept alternative work at lower pay. Some workers are waiting to be rehired into the same job from which they were temporarily laid off because of a seasonal or cyclical fall in demand or because of scheduling problems. Some workers, especially those with severe handicaps, are not able to find any employment. At the other extreme, some of those who report themselves as unemployed and looking for work are actually temporarily out of the labor force and not interested in finding employment.

The average duration of unemployment during the post-War period has been about three months. This varies cyclically: In 1971, it was 11 weeks; in 1969, it briefly dropped below eight weeks, and in 1961, it rose to over 16 weeks. These mean durations reflect a very skewed distribution. Although the mean in 1971 was 11 weeks, more than two thirds of the unemployed had durations of less than 11 weeks and 45 percent were out of work for less than five weeks.

Any reduction in the mean duration of unemployment would lower the average unemployment rate. *A fall of one month in the average duration of unemployment would lower the unemployment rate from 4.5 percent to less than 3.0 percent. Even a two-week reduction would reduce the unemployment rate by 0.75 percent.* Those who stress the importance of search activity suggest that the duration of unemployment could be reduced by improving the flow of job market information. The computerized "job banks" recently developed by the Department of Labor are a primary example of how this might be done.

The duration of unemployment also depends on the cost to the unemployed of remaining out of work. Our current system of unemployment compensation substantially reduces—indeed often almost completely eliminates—the cost of temporary unemployment. . . .

The Effects of Unemployment Compensation

For more than 30 years, unemployment compensation has provided valuable support for millions of unemployed workers and has been an important source of security to millions more who are employed. It is important to reexamine and strengthen this system by adapting it to the changing nature of unemployment.

All of the basic features of our current unemployment system were designed and adopted in the depths of the Depression. The modern Keynesian principles of income determination were neither understood nor accepted. Now we are all Keynesians. We have come to accept the government's general responsibility for maintaining a high level of demand through variations in spending, taxation, and monetary policy. The structure of unemployment has changed accordingly. The large pool of long-term unemployed workers has been replaced by a much smaller relative number whose durations of unemployment are also much shorter. Almost every unemployed person can now find a job in a very short time. But despite the changing nature of unemployment, the system of unemployment compensation continues essentially in its original form.

Under the economic conditions that have prevailed in the post-War period, our current system of unemployment compensation is likely to have increased the average rate of unemployment. The usual presumption, that unemployment compensation reduces unemployment because it automatically increases government spending when unemployment rises, is really irrelevant. The same fiscal stimulus would now be provided through other expenditure increases or tax cuts by a government committed to maintaining aggregate demand. The primary effect on aggregate unemployment of our current system of unemployment compensation is not its contribution to aggregate demand but its adverse impact on the incentives of employers and employees. As a result, unemployment compensation is likely to increase nearly all sources of adult unemployment: seasonal and cyclical variations in the demand for labor, weak labor force attachment, and unnecessarily long durations of unemployment.

Our current system of unemployment has two distinct but related bad incentive effects. First, for those who are already unemployed it greatly reduces and often almost eliminates the cost of increasing the period of unemployment. Second, and more generally, for all types of unsteady work—seasonal, cyclical, and casual—it raises the net wage to the employee relative to the cost to the employer. The first of these effects provides an incentive to inappropriately long durations of unemployment. The second provides both employers and employees with the incentive to organize production in a way that increases the level of unemployment by making the seasonal and cyclical variation in unemployment too large and by making casual and temporary jobs too common. . . .

Improving the Current System

The challenge at this time is to restructure the unemployment compensation system in a way that strengthens its good features while reducing the harmful disincentive effects. The virtue of our system is that it permits the family of a lower-income or middle-income worker who is temporarily unemployed to maintain approximately its previous level of spending. Although the fall in net income is relatively greater among higher-income workers, almost all insured families are protected against a substantial change in net income. The disadvantage of our current system is that it raises the rate of unemployment and imposes a loss of economic welfare. This welfare loss occurs because the unemployment compensation system encourages each individual employee to act in a way that is in conflict with the interests of all employees as a group. More specifically, although most of the cost of the unemployment benefits and the reduced federal and state tax collections falls ultimately on employees as a whole, each individual employee is induced to behave in ways that increase this cost. It is rational for the unemployed individual to delay returning to work and for the job seeker to give less than the correct weight to the risk of future unemployment. For the group as a whole, however, such behavior incurs costs that far outweigh the benefits. This is the essence of the loss of economic welfare.

What could be done to reduce the harmful disincentives without losing the valuable features of unemployment compensation? Some gains could be achieved by removing the ceiling on the employer's rate of contribution and by lowering the minimum rate to zero. Employers would then pay the full price of the unemployment insurance benefits. The change in the rates of contribution would encourage employers to stabilize production and employment. It would also tend to increase prices for goods produced in firms with unstable employment. This would have the effect of shifting production to firms and industries with more stable employment.

Further improvement could be achieved if unemployment insurance benefits were taxed in the same way as other earnings. This would eliminate the anomalous situations in which a family's net income is actually reduced when an unemployed member returns to work. More generally, it would significantly reduce the very high implicit marginal tax rates that an unemployed person faces when he considers returning to work. It would also end the distorting situation in which, for the same total cost to the employer, a worker with some unemployment during the year receives more net income than a fully employed worker. Since the lowest-income families pay no income tax, the taxation of unemployment benefits would not be a burden to the poor. Even at higher incomes, the total effect on family income of taxing benefits would be small even though the marginal effect is sizable. In any case, the current system is inequitable in imposing a higher tax on an employed person than a person *with the same net income* and family circumstances who does not work steadily throughout the entire year.

An Individual Experience Plan

A much more important reform could be achieved by shifting the basis of experience rating from the firm to the individual. This would have the advantage of making the individual consider properly the costs of a longer duration of unemployment and of a job with a greater risk of unemployment. One possible way of shifting the experience rating would be to calculate a reserve ratio for each individual. The individual reserve ratio would be defined in the same way that it now is for employers: the difference between the cumulative contributions made and the cumulative benefits received by that individual, divided by the individual's recent covered earnings. Each individual would have a prescribed contribution level based on his current reserve ratio. With individual experience rating it would be necessary to have a maximum rate of contribution.

There are a variety of possible ways to finance these contributions. One possibility would be to require that employers pay the maximum rate of contribution for each employee with the provision that the employee receives, as a wage supplement, the difference between the maximum tax and the contribution that is required on the basis of his own reserve ratio. A wage supplement based on the individual's past experience would have the effect of rewarding workers who have had shorter durations of unemployment and encouraging individuals to seek more stable employment.

Under this individual experience plan, an unemployed worker would receive benefits just as he does now. However, the longer he remains unemployed, the more his own reserve position would fall. When he returns to work, he would receive no wage supplement or a reduced supplement until his reserve ratio reached the appropriate level. The individual experience plan in effect provides an opportunity for an unemployed person to borrow against his future earnings (at a zero rate of interest). Because the individual will repay these benefits, it should be possible to raise the benefit rate in each income class and to increase the maximum benefit. Other special features, such as allowing workers to withdraw a lump-sum amount to pay for moving expenses or to cover the costs of tuition in a private training program or educational institution, should also be possible. In short, by introducing individual experience rating into our current system, unemployment compensation can provide greater security without the current harmful disincentives.

There are, of course, a number of problems that would have to be solved in the design of a practical individual experience plan. Benefits would have to continue even after an individual's reserve is exhausted. Moreover, he must not be permitted to have such a large negative reserve ratio that there is no incentive for him to try to raise his reserve position. Some provision must also be made to reward retiring workers who have accumulated positive reserves. But these and other problems could be solved by balancing the objectives of income security and improved incentives. The result of doing so can be a more efficient economy and a much lower rate of unemployment.

Reducing the Rate of Unemployment

All the analysis in the current study supports the conclusion that our permanent rate of unemployment can be lowered substantially without inducing an unacceptable rate of inflation. It is important to recognize, however, that macroeconomic policy is unlikely to lower the permanent rate of unemployment much below the 4.5 percent that has prevailed during the post-War period. Nevertheless, a series of specific policies could reduce the unemployment rate for those seeking permanent full-time employment to a level significantly below three percent and perhaps closer to two percent.

Speeding the absorption of young workers into employment and stabilizing their employment through better on-the-job training could lower the overall unemployment rate by at least 0.5 percent. The current minimum wage law prevents many young people from obtaining jobs with low pay but valuable experience. Reducing the minimum wage for young workers might be useful but it would not be sufficient. A more effective policy would emphasize Youth Employment Scholarships that temporarily supplement earnings and allow young workers to "buy" better on-the-job training.

Better management of aggregate demand has a more important role to play in lowering adult unemployment than in improving the teenage employment situation. Nevertheless, even here macroeconomic policy can only achieve a small part of the total possible reduction in unemployment. The current system of unemployment compensation encourages excessive delays in returning to work. It also provides both employers and employees with the incentive to organize production in a way that increases the level of unemployment by making the seasonal and cyclical variation in unemployment too large and by making temporary jobs too common. A restructuring of the unemployment compensation system could reduce the unemployment resulting from cyclical and seasonal instability and from unnecessarily long durations between jobs by an additional 1.25 percent or more. Further desirable reductions in unemployment could be achieved by subsidizing wages or incomes for handicapped workers and others with very low skills. There is, in short, no reason to allow the high average rate of unemployment that has prevailed in the post-War period to continue in the future.

Work helps to preserve us from three great evils—weariness, vice and want.

—Voltaire, *Candide*

—15—

»«

WORK
AND THE
FUTURE

»«

David Franklin/TIME Magazine

» Bernard E. Anderson «

Minorities and Work: The Decade Ahead

» «

In the two preceding chapters, it was shown that poor, urban blacks have made little economic or job progress during the last two decades. However, during the same period, a sizable number of middle-class blacks made enormous strides. As Bernard Anderson of the University of Pennsylvania's Wharton School illustrates in this selection, the black community has become highly skewed compared to the nation as a whole. Whereas income inequality among whites has been declining, there has been a pattern of growing inequality of income distribution within the black community. Millions of black professional, managerial, technical, and clerical workers have moved rapidly toward the median family income of similarly employed whites, leaving the black urban "underclass" far behind. Anderson expects that future gains for the poor urban blacks will be determined by the overall rate of growth of the economy (which experts expect to be low), and by the level of national commitment to root out employment discrimination.

During the past several decades, minorities have experienced uneven gains in the labor market. The labor force participation rate, a measure of a group's attachment to the world of work, has steadily declined among black men, while the rate among black women has remained stable. All age groups showed a similar trend, but black men of middle age and above dropped out of the labor force at rates significantly greater than whites of similar age.

Recent Trends in Labor Force, Employment, and Income

Black women have long shown higher rates of labor force participation than white women, but the gap between the two groups has narrowed in recent years as larger numbers of married white women have entered the job market. Indeed, the increased labor force participation of white women has been perhaps the single most significant development in the labor force since 1960. Expanding female participation has increased job competition

471

and contributed to the difficulties of reducing unemployment rates to satis-factory levels. . . .

Trends in unemployment reveal most clearly the difficulties faced by the black work force. . . . Since late 1976 the black unemployment rate has remained in the neighborhood of 13.0 percent, while the unemployment rate among whites declined from 7.1 to 5.6 percent.

Black youth have been especially disadvantaged in the labor market. During each of the past twenty years, the unemployment rate among black teenagers has exceeded 25 percent, while that among whites of similar age never rose above 15 percent. Further, an increasing number of black youth, especially young black men, have dropped out of the labor force. As a result, the measured rate of unemployment among black youth, 37.0 per-cent in January 1978, understates the full extent of joblessness within this group.

The unfavorable position of black youth is explained in part by general economic conditions, but also by serious structural imbalances in labor markets. A disproportionate number of black youth are concentrated in low-income sections of urban areas where job opportunities have declined markedly in the past several decades. Such areas also display neighbor-hood deterioration reflecting high crime rates, poor social services, and inadequate public schools. The pathology of the inner city is reflected in the flight of many small business and other commercial establishments that in the past comprised a major source of jobs for youth, including part-time jobs for youth attending school. Black youth unemployment is tied closely to the urban crisis, and a solution to one depends upon efforts to deal with the other.

Occupational Trends The occupational distribution of the black work force improved somewhat during the 1960 decade, but the magnitude of change was insufficient to equalize the job status of blacks and others in the labor market (Table 1). Blacks have shown employment gains among white-collar workers, especially professional, technical, and clerical work-ers. At the same time, blacks have also experienced upgrading in the blue-collar fields, moving out of the unskilled labor and domestic service fields into semi-skilled operative and skilled occupations.

Within the broad occupational categories, however, blacks tend to be concentrated in the least prestigious and most poorly paid jobs. Among professionals, for example, blacks are disproportionately concentrated in the teaching and social service fields and have made only marginal gains in fields such as engineering, sciences, and management. Moreover, black occupational gains in the white-collar fields, especially management, have been concentrated in the public sector rather than in the private sector.

Income Status There are substantial differences between the incomes of black and white Americans that are based largely on differences in their

Table 1. Employed Persons 16 Years and Over by Occupation Group and Color: 1959, 1969, and 1974

	1959 Total		1959 Black			1969 Total		1969 Black			1974 Total		1974 Black		
OCCUPATION	No.	% dist.	No.	% Dist.	% of Total	No.	% dist.	No.	% dist.	% of total	No.	% dist.	No.	% dist.	% of total
TOTAL EMPLOYED	64,627	100.0	6,621	100.0	10.2	77,902	100.0	8,383	100.0	10.8	85,936	100.0	9,316	100.0	10.8
WHITE-COLLAR WORKERS (total)	27,593	42.7	954	14.4	3.5	36,845	47.3	2,198	26.2	6.0	41,739	48.6	2,977	32.0	7.1
Prof. & Tech.	7,140	11.1	304	4.6	4.3	10,769	13.8	695	8.3	6.5	12,338	14.4	970	10.4	7.9
Managers & Adm. (ex. farm)	6,936	10.7	163	2.4	2.4	7,987	10.3	254	3.0	3.2	8,941	10.4	379	4.1	4.2
Sales Workers	4,210	6.5	83	1.3	2.0	4,692	6.0	166	2.0	3.5	5,417	6.3	214	2.3	4.0
Clerical Workers	9,307	14.4	404	6.1	4.3	13,397	17.2	1,083	12.9	8.1	15,043	17.5	1,414	15.2	9.4
BLUE-COLLAR WORKERS (total)	23,993	37.1	2,728	41.2	11.4	28,237	36.2	3,590	42.9	12.7	29,776	34.7	3,748	40.2	12.6
Craftsmen	8,554	13.2	389	5.9	4.5	10,193	13.1	709	8.5	7.0	11,477	13.4	874	9.4	7.6
Operatives	11,816	18.3	1,321	20.0	11.2	14,372	18.4	2,004	23.9	13.9	13,919	16.2	2,041	21.9	14.7
Nonfarm Laborers	3,623	5.6	1,018	15.3	28.1	3,672	4.7	877	10.5	23.9	4,380	5.1	833	8.9	19.0
SERVICE WORKERS (total)	7,697	11.9	2,109	31.9	27.4	9,528	12.2	2,239	26.7	23.5	11,373	13.2	2,337	25.1	20.5
Private Household	1,948	3.0	973	14.7	49.9	1,631	2.1	714	8.5	43.8	1,228	1.4	474	5.1	38.6
Other Service Workers	5,749	8.9	1,136	17.2	19.8	7,897	10.1	1,525	18.2	19.3	10,145	11.8	1,863	20.0	18.4
FARM WORKERS (total)	5,344	8.3	830	12.5	15.5	3,292	4.3	356	4.2	10.8	3,048	3.5	254	2.7	8.3
Farmers & Farm Mgrs.	3,013	4.7	232	3.5	7.7	1,844	2.4	84	1.0	4.6	1,643	1.9	64	0.7	3.9
Farm Laborers and Supervs.	2,331	3.6	598	9.0	25.7	1,448	1.9	272	3.2	18.8	1,405	1.6	190	2.0	13.5

Source: U.S. Department of Labor, Bureau of Labor Statistics, Manpower Report of the President, 1975, Table A-15, p. 225, and Table A-16, p. 227.

labor market positions. In 1975, the median income of black families was $8,779, and that of white families, $14,268 (Table 2). The ratio of black median income to white median income was thus 0.615. Further, more than 27 percent of black families were below the poverty income level in 1975, compared to less than 8 percent of white families.

Table 2. Changes in Ratios of Nonwhite-to-White and Black-to-White Median Family Income, 1947 Through 1975

Year	Median Family Income (Dollars)			Ratio of Nonwhite-to-White	Ratio of Black-to-White
	Nonwhite	Black	White		
1947	1,614	N/A	3,157	0.511	N/A
1949	1,650	N/A	3,232	0.511	N/A
1954	2,416	N/A	4,338	0.557	N/A
1959	2,915	N/A/	5,643	0.517	N/A
1964	3,838	N/A	6,858	0.560	N/A
1969	6,191	5,999	9,794	0.632	0.613
1974[a]	8,265	7,808	13,356	0.619	0.585
1974[b]	8,577	8,005	13,408	0.640	0.597
1975	9,321	8,779	14,268	0.653	0.615

Source: U.S. Bureau of the Census, "Money Income in 1975 of Families and Persons in the United States," *Current Population Reports,* Series P-60, No. 105 (1977), Table 10.

N/A = Not available.

[a]Unrevised 1974. This estimate should be compared to the earlier years.

[b]Revised 1974. Because of change in estimation procedures by Current Population Survey, the revised 1974 estimate should be compared to later years.

Black family income has increased relative to white family income during the past several decades, but the gains have been uneven. From the early 1960s through 1969, the ratio of black median family income to white median family income rose from about 52 percent to 61 percent. Since that time, however, there has been virtually no change in the relative income position of blacks.

The aggregate trends conceal some important developments among specific sectors of the black community. For example, the rate of income gain since 1965 has been more rapid among blacks in the South than in other sections of the nation. Also, much of the gain in income over the long term can be explained by the migration of low income blacks from rural areas of the South to higher-wage industrial employment in the North and the West.

In addition, a close examination of income patterns shows a growing inequality of income distribution within the black community, while income inequality among whites has declined. This divergent trend may be due in part to the increasing inequality of earnings in general, and the fact that a larger share of black income than white consists of wage and salary earnings. The divergent trend may also reflect the greater gains of black professionals and others in better occupational positions relative to those in low income jobs.

Factors Affecting Past Trends

Among the many factors influencing the trends described above, three seem most important: general economic conditions, improvements in education, and protection of equal job opportunity.

General Economic Conditions   A wealth of evidence accumulated over a long period of time shows clearly that black economic well-being is heavily dependent upon the state of the economy. When economic activity is high, and labor markets are tight, blacks find far more jobs at better wages than when labor markets are loose and unemployment is high. This observation, simple as it may seem, is one of the most reliable predictors of the relative position of blacks under alternative economic conditions. . . .

Economic policies designed to hasten the reduction in unemployment by accelerating economic growth are especially beneficial to minorities. Conversely, policies that retard growth, perhaps to minimize the fear of inflation or to accomplish other objectives, tend to perpetuate racial inequality in economic life. The position of minority groups in the labor market can thrive only in an environment of expanding opportunity for all. Economic policies that sacrifice full employment for other goals are harmful to the economic interest of minorities.

Improvements in Education   Improvements in schooling among blacks have contributed to modest gains observed during the past decade. Increased high school enrollment by black teenagers, coupled with higher retention rates, has resulted in increased educational attainment as measured by the number of years of education completed. . . .

But, although larger numbers of blacks are now enrolled in school, less progress has been made in improving the quality of education. In many urban public schools in which large numbers of blacks are enrolled, the quality of education is less than desirable. In some cases, achievement levels are several years below the average nationwide. The disparities in the quality of education reduce, but do not completely erase, the contribution increased schooling has made toward an improvement in the labor market position of blacks.

Also important are gains blacks have registered in higher education. Between 1966 and 1976, college enrollment of blacks increased from 4.6 percent to 10.7 percent of total enrollment. Slightly more than one million blacks were enrolled in post-secondary schools during 1977, and 40 percent of that number were in four-year degree-granting institutions.

Data on career preparation in higher education show that black college students have broadened their occupational interests. More are now entering the sciences, engineering, architecture, and other fields that relatively few black students entered in the past. Increased numbers have also selected law, medicine, and business management in recent years, although the proportion of blacks in such fields continues to be very low. These trends undoubtedly reflect the perception among black students that labor market prospects will be more favorable than in the past.

Protection of Equal Job Opportunity Efforts to promote equal job opportunity have influenced the labor market status of minorities, but it is difficult to assign a specific value to this factor. Black employment in firms reporting to the Equal Employment Opportunity Commission (EEOC) rose much faster than employment in the economy as a whole between 1966 and 1974. But the EEOC-reporting firms showed greater gains among black clerical and sales workers than among other white-collar employees. Indeed, among professional, technical, and managerial workers, the EEOC-reporting firms lagged behind the economy at large in expanding jobs for blacks.

Nonetheless, much anecdotal data suggest that because of EEOC, blacks and other minorities have obtained jobs they might not have obtained otherwise. Increased pressures from the Commission, as well as enforcement efforts by the Office of Federal Contract Compliance and the Department of Justice, have created a climate of sensitivity to racial employment practices. It is hard to believe these pressures have not resulted in job gains for minorities, even if proof of the relationship cannot be verified with precision.

A major contributing factor has been the changing concept of discrimination during the past decade. Prior to the mid-1960s, when the courts began to adjudicate disputes under Title VII of the Civil Rights Act of 1964, "discrimination" was viewed as overt acts by employers (and employment-related institutions such as trade unions and the U.S. Employment Service) to deny jobs to members of minority groups. But the judicial perception of discrimination that emerged during the past decade turned the focus from overt acts to the consequences of seemingly neutral employment systems that had the effect of restricting the job opportunities of minorities. Increasingly, the courts drew a comparison between the proportion of minorities employed in a specific firm and their relative number in the population, and when a gross disparity was found, attributed the difference to discrimination. The remedies imposed by the courts to correct such "statistical discrimination" focused on placing minorities in jobs where relatively few had been employed before. . . . It may be difficult to measure the impact of . . . changes in hiring policies on minority employment, but the emphasis on numbers employed rather than conscious intent to discriminate has no doubt been highly significant.

Factors Affecting the Decade Ahead

A review of past trends can be very useful for discussing the labor market prospects for minorities in the decade ahead. Because the basic structure of the economy and attitudes and values concerning intergroup relations are not likely to change rapidly, the forces affecting opportunities for minorities in the 1980s may be very similar to those observed in the recent past. Opportunity, as reflected in the demand for labor, preparation for employment, and access to better jobs will be as important during the next decade as before. But there are several developments on the horizon that may influence the way these factors interact to affect minority employment. Specifically, an evaluation of the prospects for minorities in the decade ahead requires an assessment of likely trends in economic growth, the structure of labor markets, and government efforts to protect equal job opportunity.

Long-Term Economic Growth The Joint Economic Committee of the U.S. Congress recently released a report on economic growth prospects, representing a summary of the views of some of the nation's leading experts in the field. The projection is for a slower rate of growth of the nation's potential GNP from its present rate of about 4 percent, to about 3 percent by the late 1980s, and to an even lower rate in the 1990s. Productivity gains, which since 1966 have proceeded more slowly than during the first twenty postwar years, are expected to accelerate again. Sources of mineral raw materials are expected to be adequate for demand, and investment funds should be readily available, barring a sustained investment boom extending into the 1980s. Most importantly, the experts believe that "social limits to growth" such as changing attitudes toward work and the growth ethic may be more important than the earth's physical limits in curbing the economy's development over the next several decades.

Labor Market Projections Due to the steady decline in the U.S. birth rates since 1960, annual labor force growth is expected to fall to less than one percent by the late 1980s. The proportion of women who work is expected to continue its gradual rise, and the reduction in labor force growth may be moderated somewhat by a rise in illegal immigration. . . .

The minority group labor force is expected to grow more rapidly than the white labor force. From 1970 to 1980, for example, the black labor force is projected to increase by 26.9 percent compared to an increase of 16.0 percent among whites. The widest gap in growth rates between the two groups, however, is observed among youth aged sixteen to twenty-four. . . .

The changing structure of employment observed in the recent past is expected to continue into the next decade with some modifications. Employment in manufacturing, transportation, and public utilities will grow more slowly than in trade, services, and the finance-related industries. Similarly, among occupations, laborers, semi-skilled workers, and farm workers will experience modest growth, or even a reduction in employment, while professional and technical, clerical, and service workers grow at rates exceeding the growth of the labor force at large. . . .

Black Occupational Change   The projections for 1980 and 1985 show employment levels for 56 separate occupational groups. According to this projection, blacks will improve their position most significantly among professional and technical workers, managers and officials, clerical workers, and skilled craftsmen. The black participation rate is projected to decline among service workers and nonfarm laborers. . . .

The pattern of projected change to 1980 is expected to continue through 1985. But the degree of change, as measured by black participation rates in various occupations, may decline in comparison with the change projected for 1970 to 1980. Advancement into professional, technical, managerial, and craft jobs will increase the black participation rate in those fields. Similarly, the attrition of blacks in agriculture, nonfarm labor, and service work is expected to continue.

The projections show little penetration into the higher paid job classifications by 1985 in comparison with the gains achieved by blacks through 1980. . . .

On balance, the evidence on projected occupational progress for blacks leads to a modestly optimistic prognosis. Occupational upgrading observed in the past will continue, and further gains in the higher paid, more prestigious occupations will occur. Yet, no acceleration of upgrading is projected. In fact, in some of the skilled craft occupations, there is virtually no change in the proportion of blacks between 1980 and 1985. This means that while the occupational field is expected to grow during the five-year period, blacks at best might hold their own in competing for expanding job opportunities.

Summary and Conclusion

The prospects for minorities in the world of work in the next decade will be determined by much the same forces that have influenced minority status in past years. A vigorous and balanced economic growth environment is a necessary backdrop for minority labor market gains. But in addition to economic growth, minority progress also must depend on special efforts to reduce economic inequality in American life. Determined efforts to root out employment discrimination will be necessary for the status of blacks and other minorities to improve.

All indications suggest that minorities will continue to obtain more schooling, with increased numbers holding academic degrees in a variety of professional and technical fields. But labor force projections also suggest an increasing degree of competition among college graduates for a relatively smaller number of jobs that this group typically holds. If the projections are correct, improvement in the relative position of minorities will not be assured.

In the past, labor market gains among minorities have been uneven and unstable, although halting progress has been made. Based on a projection of the most likely conditions in the national economy and the most likely set of attitudes and preferences among the population, it is difficult to conclude that the decade ahead will be very different from the past.

Table 3. **Employment Projections Under a National Energy Policy, by Occupational Group and Race, 1980 and 1985 (numbers in thousands)**

| | 1980 | | | 1985 | | |
| | | Black | | | Black | |
	Total	Number	Percent	Total	Number	Percent
PROFESSIONAL, TECHNICAL	14,318	1,216.6	8.5	15,967	1,434.0	9.0
Engineers	1,327	45.3	3.4	1,460	57.6	3.9
Chemical	57	2.7	4.7	62	3.9	6.3
Civil	199	9.2	4.6	225	11.2	5.0
Electrical	334	13.5	4.0	374	18.7	5.0
Mechanical	211	3.9	1.8	234	4.6	2.0
Registered nurses	1,008	79.4	7.9	1,190	100.3	8.4
Health technicians	499	78.3	15.7	614	99.3	16.2
Social scientists	209	20.6	9.9	242	25.7	10.6
Teachers	3,666	340.8	9.3	3,769	351.0	9.3
Accountants	911	59.4	6.5	995	70.5	7.1
MANAGERS, OFFICIALS	9,993	494.7	5.0	10,871	598.1	5.5
SALES WORKERS	5,881	115.8	2.0	6,268	107.2	1.7
CLERICAL WORKERS	17,813	1,825.7	10.2	20,112	2,220.7	11.0
Typists, stenographers	5,385	406.3	7.5	6,264	503.6	8.0
Office machine operators	697	101.1	14.5	725	108.0	14.9
Telephone operators	387	31.6	8.2	385	31.0	8.1
CRAFT AND KINDRED WORKERS	12,722	1,156.7	9.1	13,760	1,342.7	9.8
Carpenters	1,210	71.8	5.9	1,314	78.0	5.9
Brick, stone masons	193	24.5	12.7	211	31.4	14.9
Cement finishers	106	43.8	41.3	120	51.4	42.8
Electricians	653	33.0	5.1	731	40.4	5.5
Grading machine operators	355	22.6	6.4	420	26.6	6.3
Painters	486	35.2	7.2	502	35.1	7.0
Plumbers, pipe fitters	487	20.6	4.2	558	23.4	4.2
Boiler makers	52	6.4	12.3	62	8.4	13.5
Foremen	1,627	89.3	5.5	1,770	111.4	6.3
Machinists	470	16.1	3.4	487	18.7	3.8
Millwrights	106	5.4	5.1	115	6.4	5.6
Molders, metal	61	8.8	14.4	63	7.9	12.5
Rollers, finishers, metal	24	6.3	26.3	24	6.2	25.8
Sheetmetal workers	177	8.1	4.6	190	9.6	5.1
Crane operators	193	51.3	26.6	199	55.0	27.6

Table 3. *(cont.)*

	1980 Total	1980 Black Number	1980 Black Percent	1985 Total	1985 Black Number	1985 Black Percent
OPERATIVES	14,606	2,123.8	14.5	15,178	2,287.7	15.1
Furnace tenders	83	20.9	25.1	86	21.5	25.0
Welders	738	79.2	10.7	814	89.8	11.0
Weavers	36	3.8	10.6	32	4.3	13.4
Checkers, examiners	874	125.2	14.3	172	153.4	15.8
Packers (except meat)	700	114.7	16.4	720	119.9	16.7
Asbestos workers	41	1.4	3.4	50	1.8	3.6
Assemblers	1,254	251.6	20.1	1,350	283.2	21.0
Mine operatives	176	8.8	5.0	178	8.9	5.0
Painters, mfg. articles	185	29.4	15.6	187	30.1	16.1
Sawyers	137	29.7	21.7	140	30.3	21.6
Stationery firemen	87	10.2	11.7	85	10.1	11.9
Bus drivers	298	45.6	15.3	325	51.5	15.8
Conductors, urban transit	10	2.7	27.0	11	2.9	26.4
Delivery, route workers	622	65.3	10.5	645	68.9	10.7
Taxi cab drivers	156	34.0	21.8	142	35.7	25.1
Truck drivers	1,832	258.3	14.1	1,900	268.1	14.1
SERVICE WORKERS	13,112	1,941.1	14.8	14,562	2,062.4	14.2
NONFARM LABORERS	4,591	491.1	10.7	4,767	415.8	8.7
Carpenters helpers	104	29.9	28.8	104	29.8	28.7
Longshore workers	52	22.9	44.0	50	21.6	43.2
Logging workers	73	17.3	23.7	63	12.9	20.5
FARM WORKERS	1,100	144.5	13.1	848	53.5	6.3

Source: U.S. Department of Labor, Bureau of Labor Statistics.

>> **Colin Norman** <<

The New Industrial Revolution: How Microelectronics May Change the Workplace

>> <<

Computer "chips" half the size of postage stamps that can do as much work as the room-sized computers of a generation ago are just part of the extraordinary progress in microelectronic technology that has touched off a "Second Industrial Revolution." According to Colin Norman, a senior researcher at the Worldwatch Institute, the new technology can automate countless jobs previously done by human workers. Although such automation promises great increases in productivity, Norman warns that it also threatens to eliminate thousands of jobs and radically alter the nature of thousands of others.

It is time to sit up and take notice when a committee of the National Academy of Sciences states that "the modern era of electronics has ushered in a second industrial revolution . . . its impact on society could be even greater than that of the original industrial revolution." Academy committees are not usually noted for hyperbole.

The Academy is not alone in suggesting that recent advances in electronic technology are harbingers of sweeping social changes. In the past decade, when most industries experienced sluggish growth and flagging innovation, the electronics industry saw its sales boom and its products change dramatically. The key to these developments is the ability to imprint tens of thousands of electronic components and complex circuits on chips of silicon one-fourth the size of a postage stamp. This technological feat has shrunk the size of electronic equipment, increased the power and flexibility of small computers, and slashed the cost of storing and manipulating information.

Some of the technological developments that lie at the core of this electronic revolution are less than a decade old. An attempt to assess their social and economic significance is thus akin to forecasting the impact of the automobile on society as the first Model T rolled off the assembly line. Yet one thing is clear: microelectronic technology will have a pervasive and long-lasting influence on international trade, patterns of employment, and industrial productivity.

Chips and Jobs

Fears of massive unemployment have greeted technological changes ever since the Industrial Revolution. Far from destroying jobs, however, rapid technological advance has generally been accompanied by high rates of job creation. The quarter-century following World War II, for example, saw the industrial economies flooded with new technologies while the number of jobs increased steadily and unemployment shrank to exceptionally low levels. Yet there is a good reason to take seriously the recent outpouring of concern that microelectronic technologies will have a fundamental impact on both the numbers and types of jobs in the industrial world in the coming decades.

Central to these concerns is the pervasiveness of microelectronics. The microelectronic revolution could affect employment in enterprises ranging from steelworks to banks; no technology in history has had such a broad range of potential applications in the workplace. Another source of concern is that products incorporating microelectronic devices generally require significantly less labor to produce than the goods they replace, a fact that extends the employment implications of technology well beyond its direct impacts on automation. And a third reason for apprehension is the speed with which the technology is advancing. Although microelectronic controls will not sweep through the industrial world overnight, most experts expect them to be firmly established in production processes, products, and daily activities over the next two decades.

"Jobless Growth" in Industry

As is well known, a combination of technological changes and economic and social pressures led to a sharp reduction in the agricultural work force in the developed world over the past half-century. In every major Western industrial country, the agricultural labor force now represents less than 10% of the working population; in the United States and Britain, the proportion is below 4%. While the number of agricultural workers has decreased, however, output has generally risen substantially—a phenomenon that has been dubbed "jobless growth." Now there are indications that in many parts of the world jobless growth is occurring in manufacturing industries as well.

"People don't look for kinds of work any more, ma'am," he answered impassively. *"They just look for work."*

—Ayn Rand, *Atlas Shrugged*

The spread of microelectronic technology will be a mixed blessing. Its impact on levels and patterns of employment could be enormous. The labor-saving potential of microelectronics is such that many jobs could disappear as employers take advantage of the increased productivity offered by computer-controlled equipment. Indeed, it is this potential that provides much of the driving force behind the rapid adoption of the technology. Concern about the employment implications of microelectronics is heightened by the fact that the technology is coming to fruition at a time when the prospects for overall economic growth—and hence job creation—seem particularly grim.

It is this gloomy economic environment that makes the technology at once promising and threatening. On the one hand, it offers the prospect of enhanced productivity and the chance to revitalize some economic activities. But on the other hand, it threatens to aggravate unemployment in some industries and to reinforce the structural divisions that have been growing in the industrial countries during the past few years, as youth unemployment has climbed to epidemic levels and joblessness among blue-collar workers in heavy industries has risen sharply.

The Four Sectors of the U.S. Labor Force by Percent 1860–1980
(using median estimates of information workers)

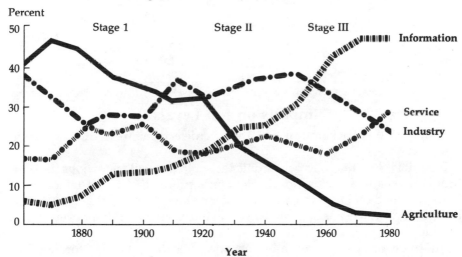

Most people in the United States worked on farms less than 100 years ago, but now fewer than 4% of the American people work in that sector, largely because of advances in agricultural technology. Recently, automation in the manufacturing sector of the economy has reduced employment there, too, and more people are working in the service and information sectors. Employment patterns in these areas may soon change as microelectronic intelligence automates these jobs. *Source:* Marc Porat, *The Information Economy: Definition and Measurement.* Office of Telecommunications Special Publication 77-12(1), May 1977.

Set against these concerns, however, is the fact that microelectronic technologies hold the promise of increased productivity over a broad range of industrial enterprises. In theory, this should lead to enhanced economic growth, which in turn will translate into new jobs. That, in essence, is how technological change in the past has operated to increase employment in the industrial world—at least until the mid-seventies. Put crudely, the extra production made possible by technological changes coincided with rising wealth and increased demand for manufactured goods and services, a combination that led to high rates of economic growth and near-full employment. But there are good reasons why those historical trends may not provide a reliable guide to the future. Both the hopes and the concerns surrounding microelectronics must be seen in the light of other economic forces and in the context of the deep structural changes that have been taking place in the industrial labor force over the past few decades. . . .

The transition from agriculture to industry, and more recently to tertiary [service] sector employment, has not been smooth or even. Some industries have continued to expand their employment, while others, such as steel and textiles, have contracted. . . .

A return to high levels of demand for the products of some labor-intensive industries, such as steel and shipbuilding, is considered unlikely even if inflationary pressures moderate, as the market for these products is reaching saturation.

Average Annual Growth in Employment in OECD Countries, 1965–75

Sector	1965–70	1970–75
Agriculture	−0.5%	−0.5%
Industry	0.4	−0.1
Tertiary	1.2	1.3
Total Civilian Employment	1.1	0.8

Source: Organization for Economic Cooperation and Development, *Medium Term Strategy*

Impacts on Job Levels

It is against this background that the microelectronic revolution must be assessed. . . .

First, it is clear that microelectronic technologies will create jobs in those industries manufacturing novel, electronic products. The $4 billion now being lavished on electronic watches, calculators, games, and other microelectronic products has spawned a whole industry that did not even exist a decade ago. . . .

But these jobs will not represent net additions to work force, for they will be offset to some extent by job losses in the manufacture of goods with which the new microelectronics-based products are competing. The Swiss watch industry, for example, lost 46,000 jobs in the seventies as customers switched in droves from mechanical timepieces to electronic watches made in the United States and Japan. Seventeen Swiss watch manufacturers went bankrupt in this period.

Moreover, as manufacturers incorporate microelectronic devices into their products in place of mechanical or electromechanical parts, their labor requirements often plummet. The reason is that one tiny piece of micro-electronic circuitry can substitute for hundreds of moving parts, which eliminates the labor required to make those parts as well as the labor involved in assembling them. . . .

A committee of the Organization for Economic Cooperation and Development, studying the relationship between technological change and economic growth, has . . . surveyed the plans of major electronics corporations and found that few of them expected to increase employment over the next few years. "Electronics has dramatic growth prospects ahead in the next decade. If this industry expects to achieve such growth with little or no increase in employment," the committee noted, "then the question may be asked where in the manufacturing sector is . . . growth in employment to come?"

More Robots Employed

Many of the industries that have traditionally been leading employers, such as those producing automobiles, chemicals, appliances, and so on, are likely to incorporate microprocessors and small computers into production processes to improve efficiency and productivity. Already, the introduction of robot welders in automobile assembly has resulted in sharp reductions in jobs and consequent increases in productivity in a few plants. . . .

It is not just in car production that robots are making major inroads. General Electric, for example, planned to spend $5.1 million in 1980 for 47 robots that will carry out such tasks as spraying the coatings on refrigerators, and over the next 10 years it plans to have as many as 1,000 robots conducting a range of assembly operations in its appliance plants. The reason? Last year's outlay will save $2.6 million a year in labor costs, and the company ultimately expects to replace half its 37,000 assembly workers with robots.

Increased Automation

A well-publicized area in which electronic technologies have decimated jobs is the printing industry. In West Germany, for example, employment among printers dropped by 21.3% between 1970 and 1977, while productivity per hour rose by 43.5%. Many American newspapers have also gone over to computerized typesetting in the past few years and have seen sharp boosts in the productivity of their print workers. . . .

The use of microelectronics in the production of television sets has had a two-pronged effect on employment. First, integrated circuits have replaced many individual components in recent years, thereby reducing assembly operations. And second, computerized assembly lines have been developed. . . .

The automation of textile manufacturing is proceeding rapidly in the United States. The industry there is expected to spend about $2 billion a year during the eighties on new equipment, some of which will be computer-controlled. As a result, as many as 300,000 relatively low-paid jobs could disappear in American textile plants by 1990 while the United States preserves or even increases its share of world textile production. . . .

The manufacture of garments has always been a labor-intensive business in which developing countries have enjoyed a comparative advantage. But new technologies are cutting into labor requirements there as well. A computerized system for laying out patterns on material, combined with electronically controlled laser cutting, has reduced skilled labor requirements in one British plant from 200 to 20 people. And similar technological advances have taken place in sewing clothes together, with the development of microprocessor-controlled sewing machines. Although fully automated garment production is still a long way off, these technological changes are laying the foundation for a much less labor-intensive process that will erode the comparative advantage of cheap labor in developing countries.

This level of job loss will not be felt in every manufacturing industry, but the potential range of microprocessor-based automation is very broad. A study by the National Electronics Council in Britain, for example, has suggested that the industries most ripe for automation by computers include metal and plastic fabrication, instrument engineering, electrical engineering, shipbuilding and marine engineering, vehicles, electronic components and assembly, office machinery, aircraft, and printing and publishing.

The use of microprocessors in manufacturing industries will essentially intensify the jobless growth that has been taking place in industrial countries in recent years. The key question, therefore, is whether the number of jobs in the tertiary sector will continue to expand to absorb the projected growth in the labor force. There are two chief reasons why the answer could be negative. First, the number of jobs in government offices—an area of substantial employment growth in recent years—may not expand much more because of demands in virtually every country to reduce public expenditure and to cut government payrolls. Second, most observers have predicted that the most far-reaching impacts of microprocessors will be felt in offices and in such service activities as retailing and maintenance.

The use of computers and other intelligent machines will lead to increased employment in some areas, it should be noted. Computer programming, for example, is a labor-intensive activity that is a likely source of many thousands of new jobs in the eighties. Demand for programmers is already outstripping supply, and some analysts have even suggested that this shortage could constrain the growth in the use of computers in the coming years. But in most other areas of the tertiary sector, microelectronics is likely to lead to slower rates of employment growth or even to job losses.

486

White-Collar Automation

In areas such as insurance and banking, which are labor-intensive occupations that rely primarily on printed paper for their transactions, the application of electronic technology could have a major impact. Already, growth in employment in these industries in Europe has begun to tail off, while their business carries on expanding. (See table.) Some observers are therefore suggesting that the jobless growth apparent in agriculture and manufacturing is now occurring in this sector.

Annual Change in Employment in Banking and Insurance in Five European Countries, 1964–77

Country	1964–74	1974–77
Belgium	10.2%	0.7%
Denmark	6.1	0.7
France	6.3	3.1
United Kingdom	3.3	0.6
West Germany	3.7	−1.9

Source: European Economic Commission

The most widely publicized of such projections was made in a report to the president of France, which warned that 30% of the jobs in the French banking and insurance industries could disappear during the eighties as more and more work is consigned to computers. Such projections should not be treated lightly. . . .

The introduction of word processors, computers, and other intelligent business machines will not always cause job losses. In many offices, the machines will be used to improve quality and upgrade services without displacing people. But several studies have suggested that the widespread use of these machines will ultimately lead to small job losses in large numbers of offices. . . .

Outside the office, microelectronics is likely to affect employment in service occupations ranging from stock handling to mail delivery. The ability to link cash registers to a central computer that monitors stock levels and automatically initiates reordering, for example, will reduce labor requirements in retail operations. As more and more messages are relayed electronically between word processors and computers, a reduction in the amount of paper-based mail can be expected, and hence in the number of people needed to deliver it. The increasing use of microelectronic controls in products such as automobiles could change not only the types of maintenance jobs, but also the tools needed to carry them out. A garage lacking highly sophisticated computerized diagnostic equipment, for example, is unlikely to be able to service a computer-controlled automobile. . . .

487

Microelectronics will affect not only the number of jobs in industrial countries, but also the types of jobs available. The early use of robots on assembly lines has largely been in dangerous, dirty, and difficult occupations that few people are lining up for. But as automation extends into design shops and machine rooms, highly skilled occupations could be affected. And, at the other end of the scale, the use of intelligent office machines and electronic information storage is likely to eliminate many filing and routine clerical jobs. Microelectronics thus has the potential to decrease skill requirements in some jobs and increase them in others.

The types of jobs most likely to be affected, according to a study conducted for the British government, are "proofreaders, library assistants, mail carriers, telegraph operators, draftsmen, programmers, accountants, financial analysts, administrators, secretaries, billing clerks, keypunchers, cashiers, filing clerks, meter readers, shipping clerks, TV repairmen, plateprinters, telephone repairmen, light electricians, machinists, mechanics, inspectors, material handlers, warehousemen, sales clerks, compositors." Moreover, if, as most experts are predicting, the chief impact of microelectronic technologies is felt in offices, women workers are the ones who will bear the brunt of the new technology.

In addition to its effect on levels and types of jobs, the use of computers and microprocessors to control production lines and office work will lead to increased control over the work force itself and the reorganization of jobs around the dictates of the new technology. Computers not only control machines, but in many cases they are used to control the speed of production lines and the routing of work in factories and offices. Harley Shaiken, a consultant to the United Auto Workers Union in the United States, describes an automobile plant in which a computer-controlled assembly line had been installed: "The system links a large central computer to a microprocessor on a machine. When the machine cycles, it is recorded in [the] central computer. When a machine doesn't produce a part in its allotted time, it is immediately obvious to more than the computer: that information is displayed in the foreman's office and recorded on a computer printout." Under this system, Shaiken says, "the foreman no longer decides to discipline the workers. He merely carries out the 'automatic' decisions of the system."

Productivity versus Displacement

It is easy to point to the advantages of raising productivity with new technologies, but if those advantages are won at the expense of displaced workers, the fruits of technological change will be bitter indeed. And, as already outlined, the pervasive nature of microelectronics, coupled with its potential for introducing labor-saving change in both blue-collar and white-collar industries, will heighten the problems of adjustment.

The transition to the electronic age will thus require policies designed to deal with technological unemployment in addition to those that support high-technology industries. Simply hoping that the unemployment problem will disappear in the white heat of technological revolution does not constitute a viable employment policy in a period of relatively slow growth and rapid technological change. Most of the needed programs—industrial retraining, the creation of jobs in depressed areas, support for community development, and labor-intensive programs such as energy conservation and the development of solar energy—are already the topics of intense debate. But the special problems posed by the widespread use of microelectronics also call for some special responses. . . .

If the widespread use of microelectronics does usher in a period of "jobless growth," attention must be given to new ways to distribute the benefits of this growth. Increased productivity can mean higher living standards for many. The benefits from economic growth have traditionally trickled down through higher wages, expansion in the number of jobs, and the use of tax revenues to support unemployment benefits, pensions, and other social programs. The time may have come to consider how to share work in a high-productivity economy. Proposals to reduce the number of work hours, through a shortened workweek, longer vacations, sabbaticals, and similar steps, have been raised in negotiations by several European trade unions. A few American unions, which have long resisted such notions, have begun to follow suit. Industry groups have, however, generally opposed these proposals.

The microelectronic revolution is thus likely to have major impacts on the numbers and types of jobs available in the industrial world over the next few decades. But every expert who has studied the potential employment impact of microelectronics has reached the same conclusion: more jobs will be lost in those countries that do not pursue the technology vigorously than in those that do. The reason is that microelectronics will enhance productivity to such an extent that the industries that move swiftly to adopt the technology will have a competitive advantage in international markets.

Microelectronic technologies promise an array of benefits, and the electronic age is already well under way. As it progresses during the last two decades of the twentieth century, it will lead to improvements in productivity in factories and offices, changes in the way information is processed, stored, and communicated, and alterations in the content of many jobs. Like all major technological changes, the transition to microelectronics will raise difficult political issues, among which the impact on jobs and employment is the most prominent. A combination of revitalized employment policies, greater industrial democracy, and new ways of distributing both the hours of work and the fruits of technological change will be needed to ensure that the benefits of the microelectronics revolution are equitably shared.

≫ *Warren Bennis* ≪

Beyond Bureaucracy: Organizations of the Future

≫ ≪

In Chapter 5, John DeLorean described life in an organization that he characterized as developing conformity and "group think," strangling innovation, and stifling entrepreneurial drive. We have a word for General Motors and the other large, highly structured organizations in which most white-collar Americans labor: bureaucracy. These pyramidal structures, with authority centralized in a few hands, were suitable arrangements for routine tasks. But according to Warren Bennis, professor of research at the Graduate Business School of the University of Southern California, the environment of business has changed. Organizations of today (and of the future) must be adaptable structures, capable of coping with turbulence and flux. Consequently, we need adaptive, learning organizations in which ad hoc teams of workers come together for a short time to solve a problem, then separate and reconfigure with others to work on the next problem. The future of work, then, will be dominated by what Bennis calls "temporary systems," in which the scope of individual choice is enlarged—most likely with concomitant increases in strain and tension.

Most of us spend all of our working day and a great deal of our nonworking day in a unique and extremely durable social arrangement called "bureaucracy." I use the term "bureaucracy" descriptively, not as an epithet about "those guys in Washington" or as a metaphor *à la* [Franz] Kafka's *Castle,* which conjures up an image of red tape, faceless masses standing in needless lines, and despair. Bureaucracy, as I shall use the term here, is a social invention, perfected during the Industrial Revolution to organize and direct the activities of the firm. . . .

490

Bureaucracy and Its Discontents

. . . Max Weber, the German sociologist who conceptualized the idea of bureaucracy around the turn of the century, once likened the bureaucratic mechanism to a judge qua computer: "Bureaucracy is like a modern judge who is a vending machine into which the pleadings are inserted together with the fee and which then disgorges the judgment together with its reasons mechanically derived from the code."

The bureaucratic "machine model" Weber outlined was developed as a reaction against the personal subjugation, nepotism, cruelty, emotional vicissitudes, and subjective judgment which passed for managerial practices in the early days of the Industrial Revolution. Man's true hope, it was thought, was his ability to rationalize and calculate—to use his head as well as his hands and heart. Thus, in this system roles are institutionalized and reinforced by legal tradition rather than by the "cult of personality"; rationality and predictability were sought for in order to eliminate chaos and unanticipated consequences; technical competence rather than arbitrary or "iron" whims was emphasized. These are oversimplifications, to be sure, but contemporary students of organizations would tend to agree with them. In fact, there is a general consensus that bureaucracy can be dimensionalized in the following way:

1. A division of labor based on functional specialization
2. A well-defined hierarchy of authority
3. A system of rules covering the rights and duties of employees
4. A system of procedures for dealing with work situations
5. Impersonality of interpersonal relations
6. Promotion and selection based on technical competence

These six dimensions describe the basic underpinnings of bureaucracy, the pyramidal organization which dominates so much of our thinking and planning related to organizational behavior.

It does not take a great critical imagination to detect the flaws and problems in the bureaucratic model. We have all *experienced* them: bosses without technical competence and underlings with it; arbitrary and zany rules; an underworld (or informal) organization which subverts or even replaces the formal apparatus; confusion and conflict among roles; and cruel treatment of subordinates, based not upon rational or legal grounds, but upon inhumane grounds. Unanticipated consequences abound and provide a mine of material for those comics, like Chaplin or Tati, who can capture with a smile or a shrug the absurdity of authority systems based on pseudologic and inappropriate rules.

Almost everybody, including many students of organizational behavior, approaches bureaucracy with a chip on his shoulder. It has been criticized for its theoretical confusion and contradictions, for moral and ethical reasons, on practical grounds such as its inefficiency, for its methodological weaknesses, and for containing too many implicit values or for containing too few. I have recently cataloged the criticisms of bureaucracy, and they outnumber and outdo the Ninety-five Theses tacked on the church door at Wittenberg in attacking another bureaucracy. For example:

1. Bureaucracy does not adequately allow for personal growth and the development of mature personalities.

2. It develops conformity and "group-think."

3. It does not take into account the "informal organization" and the emergent and unanticipated problems.

4. Its systems of control and authority are hopelessly outdated.

5. It has no adequate juridical process.

6. It does not possess adequate means for resolving differences and conflicts among ranks and, most particularly, among functional groups.

7. Communication (and innovative ideas) are thwarted or distorted because of hierarchical divisions.

8. The full human resources of bureaucracy are not being utilized because of mistrust, fear of reprisals, etc.

9. It cannot assimilate the influx of new technology or scientists entering the organization.

10. It will modify the personality structure such that man will become and reflect the dull, gray, conditioned "organization man."

Max Weber himself, the developer of the theory of bureaucracy, came around to condemning the apparatus he helped immortalize. While he felt that bureaucracy was inescapable, he also thought it might strangle the spirit of capitalism or the entrepreneurial attitude. . . . And in a debate on bureaucracy he once said, more in sorrow than in anger:

> It is horrible to think that the world could one day be filled with nothing but those little cogs, little men clinging to little jobs and striving toward bigger ones—a state of affairs which is to be seen once more, as in the Egyptian records, playing an ever-increasing part in the spirit of our present administrative system, and especially of its offspring, the students. This passion for bureaucracy . . . is enough to drive one to despair. It is as if in politics . . . we were deliberately to become men who need "order" and nothing but order, who become nervous and cowardly if for one moment this order wavers, and helpless if they are torn away from their total incorporation in it. That the world should know no men but these: it is such an evolution that we are already caught up in, and the great question is therefore not how we can promote and hasten it, but what can we oppose to this machinery in order to keep a portion of mankind free from this parcelling-out of the soul from this supreme mastery of the bureaucratic way of life.

I think it would be fair to say that a good deal of the work on organizational behavior over the past two decades has been a footnote to the bureaucratic "backlash" which aroused Weber's passion: saving mankind's soul "from the supreme mastery of the bureaucratic way of life." At least, very few of us have been i different to the fact that the bureaucratic mechanism is a social instrument in the service of repression; that it treats man's ego and social needs as a constant, or as nonexistent or inert; that these confined and constricted needs insinuate themselves into the social processes of organizations in strange, unintended ways; and that those very matters which Weber claimed escaped calculation—love, power, hate—not only are calculable and powerful in their effects but must be reckoned with.

Modifications of Bureaucracy

In what ways has the system of bureaucracy been modified in order that it may cope more successfully with the problems that beset it? Before answering that, we have to say something about the nature of organizations, *all* organizations, from mass-production leviathans all the way to service industries such as the university or hospital. Organizations are primarily complex goal-seeking units. In order to survive, they must also accomplish the secondary tasks of (1) maintaining the internal system and coordinating the "human side of enterprise"—a process of mutual compliance here called "reciprocity"—and (2) adapting to and shaping the external environment—here called "adaptability." These two organizational dilemmas can help us organize the pivotal ways the bureaucratic mechanism has been altered—and found wanting.

Resolutions of the Reciprocity Dilemma Reciprocity has to do primarily with the processes which can mediate conflict between the goals of management and the individual goals of the workers. Over the past several decades, a number of interesting theoretical and practical resolutions have been made which truly allow for conflict and mediation of interest. They revise, if not transform, the very nature of the bureaucratic mechanism by explicit recognition of the inescapable tension between individual and organizational goals. These theories can be called, variously, "exchange," "group," "value," "structural," or "situational," depending on what variable of the situation one wishes to modify.

The exchange theories postulate that wages, incomes, and services are given to the individual for an equal payment to the organization in work. If the inducements are not adequate, the individual may withdraw and work elsewhere. This concept may be elaborated by increasing the payments to include motivational units. That is to say, the organization provides a psychological anchor in times of rapid social change and a hedge against personal loss, as well as position, growth and mastery, success experience, and so forth, in exchange for energy, work, and commitment.

I shall discuss this idea of payment in motivational units further, as it is a rather recent one to gain acceptance. Management tends to interpret motivation by economic theory. Man is logical; man acts in the manner which serves his self-interest; man is competitive. Elton Mayo and his associates were among the first to see human affiliation as a motivating force, to consider industrial organization a social system as well as an economic-technical system. They judge a manager in terms of his ability to sustain cooperation. In fact, once a cohesive, primary work group is seen as a motivating force, a managerial elite may become obsolete, and the work group itself become the decision maker. This allows decisions to be made at the most relevant point of the organizational social space, where the data are most available.

Before this is possible, some believe that the impersonal value system of bureaucracy must be modified. In this case the manager plays an important role as the instrument of change, as an interpersonal specialist. He must instill values which permit and reinforce expression of feeling, experimentalism and norms of individuality, trust, and concern. Management, according to Blake, is successful as it maximizes "concern for people"—along with "concern for production."

Others believe that a new conception of the structure of bureaucracy will create more relevant attitudes toward the function of management than formal role specifications do. If the systems are seen as organic rather than mechanistic, as adapting spontaneously to the needs of the system, then decisions will be made at the critical point, and roles and jobs will devolve to the "natural" incumbent. The shift would probably be from the individual to cooperative group effort, from delegated to shared responsibility, from centralized to decentralized authority, from obedience to confidence, and from antagonistic arbitration to problem solving. Management which is centered around problem solving, which assumes or relaxes authority according to task demands, has most concerned some theorists. They are as concerned with organizational success and productivity as with the social system.

However, on all sides we find a growing belief that the effectiveness of bureaucracy should be evaluated on human as well as economic criteria. Social satisfaction and personal growth of employees must be considered, as well as the productivity and profit of the organization.

The criticisms and revisions of the *status quo* tend to concentrate on the internal system and its human components. But although it appears on the surface that the case against bureaucracy has to do with its ethical-moral posture and the social fabric, the real *coup de grâce* has come from the environment. While various proponents of "good human relations" have been fighting bureaucracy on humanistic grounds and for Christian values, bureaucracy seems most likely to founder on its inability to adapt to rapid change in the environment.

The Problem of Adaptability Bureaucracy thrives in a highly competitive, undifferentiated, and stable environment, such as the climate of its youth, the Industrial Revolution. A pyramidal structure of authority, with power concentrated in the hands of few with the knowledge and resources to control an entire enterprise was, and is, an eminently suitable social arrangement for routinized tasks.

However, the environment has changed in just those ways which make the mechanism most problematical. Stability has vanished. As Ellis Johnson said: ". . . the once-reliable constants have now become 'galloping' variables . . ." One factor accelerating change is the growth of science, research and development activities, and intellectual technology. Another is the increase of transactions with social institutions and the importance of the latter in conducting the enterprise—including government, distributors and consumers, shareholders, competitors, raw-material and power suppliers, sources of employees (particularly managers), trade unions, and groups within the firms. There is, as well, more interdependence between the economic and other facets of society, resulting in complications of legislation and public regulation. Thirdly, and significantly, competition between firms diminishes as their fates intertwine and become positively correlated.

My argument so far, to summarize quickly, is that the first assault on bureaucracy arose from its incapacity to manage the tension between individual and management goals. However, this conflict is somewhat mediated by the growth of an ethic of productivity which includes personal growth and/or satisfaction. The second and more major shock to bureaucracy has been caused by the scientific and technological revolution. It is the requirement of adaptability to the environment which leads to the predicted demise of bureaucracy and to the collapse of management as we know it now.

A Forecast for the Future A forecast falls somewhere between a prediction and a prophecy. It lacks the divine guidance of the latter and the empirical foundation of the former. On thin empirical ice, I want to set forth some of the conditions that will dictate organizational life in the next twenty-five to fifty years.

1. *The environment.* Those factors already mentioned will continue in force and will increase. That is, rapid technological change and diversification will lead to interpenetration of the government and legal and economic policies in business. Partnerships between industry and government . . . will be typical, and because of the immensity and expense of the projects, there will be fewer identical units competing for the same buyers and sellers. Or, in reverse, imperfect competition leads to an oligopolistic and government-business-controlled economy. The three main features of the environment will be interdependence rather than competition, turbulence rather than stability, and large rather than small enterprises.

2. *Aggregate population characteristics.* We are living in what Peter Drucker

calls the "educated society," and I think this is the most distinctive characteristic of our times. Within fifteen years, two-thirds of our population (living in metropolitan areas) will attend college. Adult education programs, especially the management development courses of such universities as M.I.T., Harvard, and Stanford, are expanding and adding intellectual breadth. All this, of course, is not just "nice," but necessary. As Secretary of Labor Wirtz recently pointed out, computers can do the work of most high school graduates—more cheaply and effectively. Fifty years ago, education was called "nonwork," and intellectuals on the payroll (and many staff) were considered "overhead." Today, the survival of the firm depends, more than ever before, on the proper exploitation of brainpower.

One other characteristic of the population which will aid our understanding of organizations of the future is increasing job mobility. The lowered expense and ease of transportation, coupled with the real needs of a dynamic environment, will change drastically the idea of "owning" a job—and of "having roots," for that matter. Participants will be shifted from job to job, even from employer to employer with much less fuss than we are accustomed to.

3. *Work-relevant values.* The increased level of education and mobility will change the values we hold vis-á-vis work. People will be more intellectually committed to their jobs and will probably require more involvement, participation, and autonomy in their work. [This turn of events is due to a composite of the following factors: (1) There is a positive correlation between education and need for autonomy; (2) job mobility places workers in a position of greater influence in the system; and (3) job requirements call for more responsibility and discretion.]

Also, people will tend to be more "other-directed" in their dealings with others . . . so we will tend to rely more heavily than we do even now on temporary social arrangements, on our immediate and constantly changing colleagues.

4. *Tasks and goals of the firm.* The tasks of the firm will be more technical, complicated, and unprogrammed. They will rely more on intellect than on muscles. And they will be too complicated for one person to handle or for individual supervision. Essentially, they will call for the collaboration of specialists in a project form of organization.

Similarly there will be a complication of goals. "Increased profits" and "raised productivity" will sound like oversimplifications and clichés. Business will concern itself with its adaptive or innovative-creative capacity. In addition, *meta*-goals will have to be articulated and developed; that is, supra-goals which shape and provide the foundation for the goal structure. For example, one *meta*-goal might be a system for detecting new and changing goals; another could be a system for deciding priorities among goals.

Finally, there will be more conflict, more contradiction among effectiveness criteria, just as in hospitals and universities today there is conflict between teaching and research. The reason for this is the number of professionals involved, who tend to identify as much with the supra-goals of their profession as with those of their immediate employer. University professors are a case in point. More and more of their income comes from outside sources, such as private or public foundations and consultant work. They tend not to make good "company men" because they are divided in their loyalty to professional values and organizational demands. Role conflict and ambiguity are both causes and consequences of goal conflict.

5. *Organizational structure.* The social structure in organizations of the future will have some unique characteristics. The key word will be "temporary"; there will be adaptive, rapidly changing *temporary systems*. These will be organized around *problems-to-be-solved*. The problems will be solved by groups of relative *strangers* who represent a set of diverse professional skills. The groups will be conducted on *organic* rather than mechanical models; they will evolve in response to the problem rather than programmed role expectations. The function of the "executive" thus becomes *coordinator,* or "linking pin" between various project groups. He must be a man who can speak the diverse languages of research and who can relay information and mediate among the groups. *People will be differentiated not vertically according to rank and role but flexibly according to skill and professional training.*

Adaptive, temporary systems of diverse specialists, solving problems, linked together by coordinating and task-evaluative specialists, in organic flux, will gradually replace bureaucracy as we know it. As no catchy phrase comes to mind, let us call this an "organic-adaptive" structure.

As an aside, what will happen to the rest of society, to the manual laborers, to the less educated, to those who desire to work in conditions of high authority, and so forth? Many such jobs will disappear; automatic jobs will be automated. However, there will be a corresponding growth in the service-type of occupation, such as the "War on Poverty" and the Peace Corps programs. In times of change, where there is a discrepancy between cultures, industrialization, and especially urbanization, society becomes the client for skill in human interaction. Let us hypothesize that approximately 40 percent of the population would be involved in jobs of this nature and 40 percent in technological jobs, making an *organic-adaptive* majority, with, say, a 20 percent bureaucratic minority.

6. *Motivation in organic-adaptive structures.* . . . The organic-adaptive structure should increase [employee] motivation and thereby effectiveness because of the satisfactions intrinsic to the task. There is a congruence between the educated individual's need for meaningful, satisfactory, and creative tasks and flexible structure or autonomy. . . .

There will be, as well, reduced commitment to work groups. These groups . . . will be transient and changing. While skills in human interaction will become more important because of the necessity of collaboration in complex tasks, there will be a concomitant reduction in group cohesiveness. I would predict that in the organic-adaptive system, people will have to learn to develop quick and intense relationships on the job and to endure their loss. . . .

Jobs in the next century should become *more*, rather than less, involving; man is a problem-solving animal, and the tasks of the future guarantee a full agenda of problems. In addition, the adaptive process itself may become captivating to many. At the same time, I think the future I describe is far from a utopian or a necessarily "happy" one. Coping with rapid change, living in temporary systems, and setting up (in quickstep time) meaningful relations—and then breaking them—all augur strains and tensions. Learning how to live with ambiguity and to be self-directing will be the task of education and the goal of maturity.

New Structures of Freedom

In these new organizations, participants will be called on to use their minds more than at any other time in history. Fantasy and imagination will be legitimized in ways that today seem strange. Social structures will no longer be instruments of repression . . . but will exist to promote play and freedom on behalf of curiosity and thought.

Not only will the problem of adaptability be overcome through the organic-adaptive structure, but the problem we started with, reciprocity, will be resolved. Bureaucracy, with its "surplus repression," was a monumental discovery for harnessing muscle power via guilt and instinctual renunciation. In today's world, it is a prosthetic device, no longer useful. For we now require organic-adaptive systems as structures of freedom to permit the expression of play and imagination and to exploit the new pleasure of work.

» *James O'Toole and August Ralston* «

Exploring Trends and Events That Might Mold the Future of Work

» «

This concluding selection contains two futuristic exercises to sharpen your thinking about where workers and work in America are headed in the decades to come.

In the first exercise, seventeen trends are traced from 1960 to 1978, then extrapolated on a straight line to the year 1995. Because the future is unlikely to be a simple extension of past trends, you might want to make your own estimates of where you think these trends will be in 1985 and 1995. Before you make your estimates, think of factors that might cause the trend to be either higher or lower than the simple-minded extrapolations that are plotted. Looking at trend 1, for example, you might not believe that only 1.2 percent of the total workforce in the year 1995 will be people over age 65. You might reason that the historical downtrend will be reversed, and that more people will work after age 65 because of one or more of the following: mandatory retirement will be eliminated, inflation will erode savings and pensions, people will be bored by retirement, social security eligibility will be postponed until age 70, and biomedical advances will permit longer life.

For each of the following then, give your estimate of where the trend is going, and your reasons for what might lead to a reversal of a projected downtrend, or a reversal of a predicted uptrend.

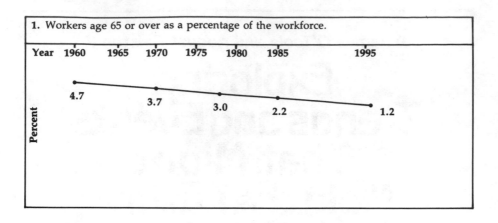

1. Workers age 65 or over as a percentage of the workforce.

Year 1960   1965   1970   1975   1980   1985   1995

Percent

4.7   3.7   3.0   2.2   1.2

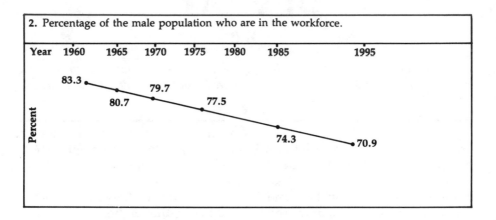

2. Percentage of the male population who are in the workforce.

Year 1960   1965   1970   1975   1980   1985   1995

Percent

83.3   80.7   79.7   77.5   74.3   70.9

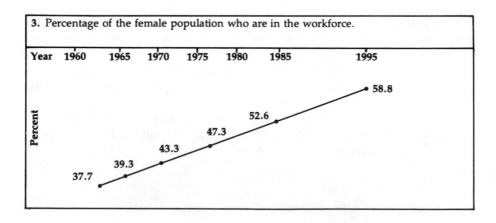

3. Percentage of the female population who are in the workforce.

Year 1960   1965   1970   1975   1980   1985   1995

Percent

58.8   52.6   47.3   43.3   39.3   37.7

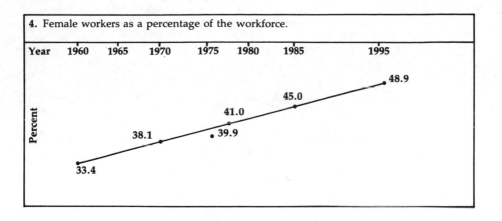

4. Female workers as a percentage of the workforce.

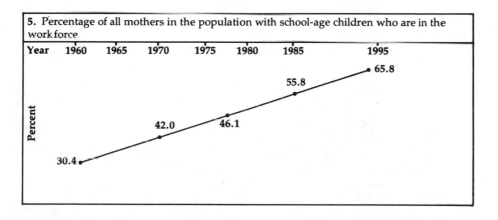

5. Percentage of all mothers in the population with school-age children who are in the workforce.

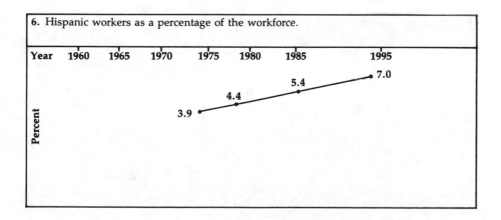

6. Hispanic workers as a percentage of the workforce.

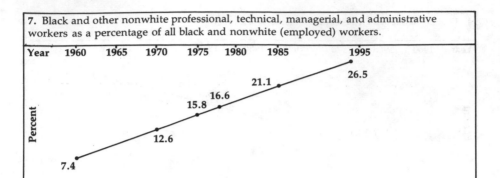

7. Black and other nonwhite professional, technical, managerial, and administrative workers as a percentage of all black and nonwhite (employed) workers.

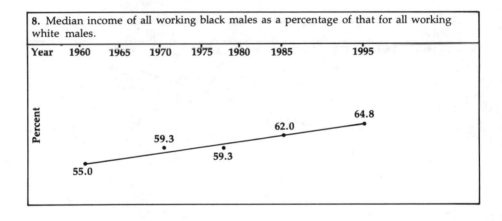

8. Median income of all working black males as a percentage of that for all working white males.

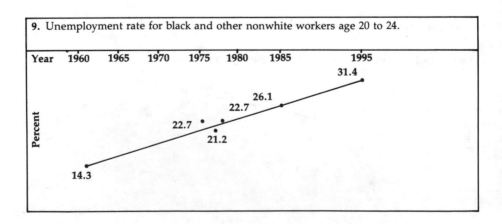

9. Unemployment rate for black and other nonwhite workers age 20 to 24.

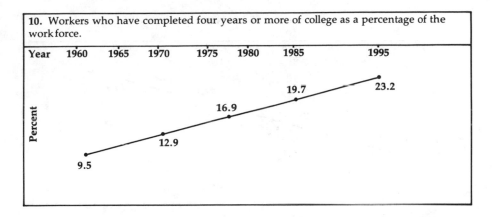

10. Workers who have completed four years or more of college as a percentage of the work force.

| Year | 1960 | 1965 | 1970 | 1975 | 1980 | 1985 | 1995 |

9.5   12.9   16.9   19.7   23.2

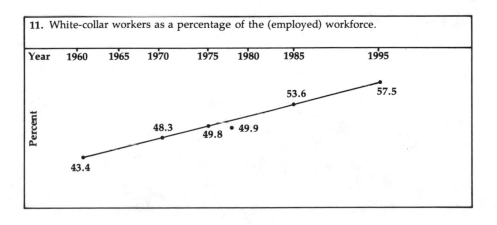

11. White-collar workers as a percentage of the (employed) workforce.

| Year | 1960 | 1965 | 1970 | 1975 | 1980 | 1985 | 1995 |

43.4   48.3   49.8   49.9   53.6   57.5

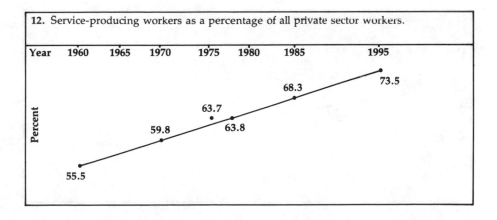

12. Service-producing workers as a percentage of all private sector workers.

| Year | 1960 | 1965 | 1970 | 1975 | 1980 | 1985 | 1995 |

55.5   59.8   63.7   63.8   68.3   73.5

13. Workers employed by government at all levels as a percentage of the workforce.

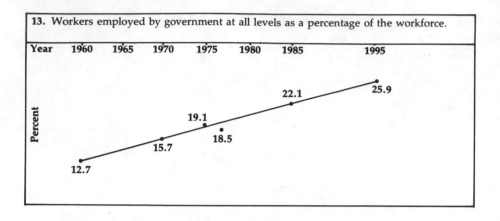

14. Part-time workers as a percentage of the workforce.

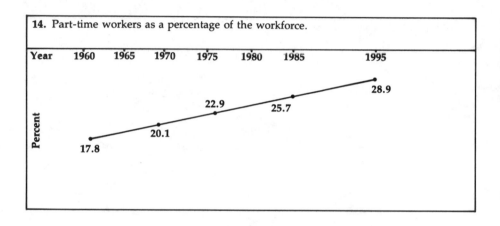

15. Workers who are union members as a percentage of the workforce.

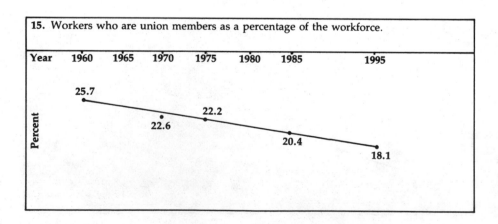

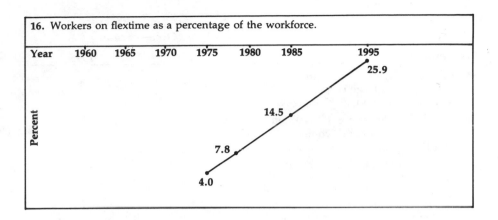

16. Workers on flextime as a percentage of the workforce.

Year	1960	1965	1970	1975	1980	1985	1995

25.9

14.5

7.8

4.0

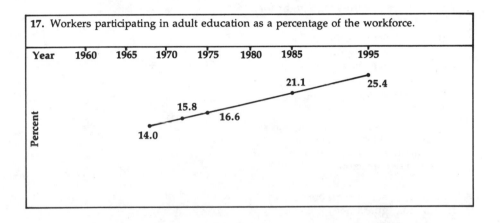

17. Workers participating in adult education as a percentage of the workforce.

Year	1960	1965	1970	1975	1980	1985	1995

21.1

25.4

15.8

16.6

14.0

This second exercise lists seventeen possible events that, *were they to occur*, would greatly alter American worklife. For each possible event, give your own estimate of the likelihood of its occurring by the years 1985 and 1995. For each event, ask yourself what the consequences of its occurrence would be for workers, for corporations, and for society. For each event, ask yourself what could happen that would significantly increase the possibility of it occurring. Looking at event 1, for example, you might feel that there is a 2 percent probability in 1985 and a 25 percent probability in 1995 that Congress would legislate lifetime employment security (such as that in the Lincoln Electric Company, described in Chapter 12) for *all* employees of large corporations. One consequence of such an event might be more productive employees with greater commitment to their jobs. A development that might increase the likelihood of the event occurring would be greatly increased competition from Japan (where many workers already have such a commitment from their employers).

Possible Event	Your Estimate of Likelihood of Occurrence in	
	1985	1995
1. Lifetime employment security for employees of large corporations is legislated by the U.S. Congress.		
2. In most major corporations, equal numbers of men and women are employed in managerial positions.		
3. A National Public Works Program is created in which the federal government, acting as employer of last resort, provides a job to every citizen who wants a job but cannot find one.		
4. Paternity leaves are a legal right for all male employees.		
5. Affirmative action programs are prohibited on the grounds that they are discriminatory.		
6. The majority of major corporations provide the option for spouses or a family to share one job.		
7. In at least one-third of the nation's Fortune 1,000 largest corporations, workers own the majority of shares of stock in the companies in which they work.		
8. Congress enacts a workers "bill of rights" that guarantees full civil liberties on the job.		
9. The federal government abolishes mandatory retirement at any age.		
10. In at least one-third of the major corporations, the middle managers are unionized.		
11. Unions advocate job-sharing among members to avoid layoffs.		
12. Pay raises for workers in major corporations are determined by a vote of employees.		
13. Day-care centers at places of work are mandated by the federal government.		
14. Most major corporations provide lifetime income benefits to workers who lose their jobs as a result of technological advances.		

506

15. Unions embrace the quality of working life as *their* primary issue.

16. Work satisfaction indexes for major corporations and industries are reported along with objective productivity measures.

17. A majority of workers alternate work, education, and leisure activities instead of progressing directly from education to work to retirement activities.

Compare your forecasts with those of your friends, colleagues, or classmates and discuss the reasoning behind your various estimates. Now, are you ready for the future?

The fact is, that civilization requires slaves. The Greeks were quite right there. Unless there are slaves to do the ugly, horrible, uninteresting work, culture and contemplation become almost impossible. Human slavery is wrong, insecure, and demoralizing. On mechanical slavery, on the slavery of the machine, the future of the world depends.
—Oscar Wilde, *The Soul of Man Under Socialism*

About the Authors

Mortimer J. Adler, philosopher and author, taught at the University of Chicago from 1930 to 1952, when he founded the Institute for Philosophical Research in San Francisco. He has edited several massive works, including the 54-volume *Great Books of the Western World,* the 20-volume *Annals of America,* and the 15th edition of the *Encyclopaedia Britannica.* Among the books he has written are *How to Read a Book, The Idea of Freedom,* and *How to Think About War and Peace.*

Bernard Anderson teaches at the Wharton School of the University of Pennsylvania, having formerly been an economist with the U.S. Bureau of Labor Statistics. He is the author of *The Impact of Manpower Programs* and several articles on black employment.

Solomon Arbeiter has been a planning officer with the College Board since 1973. He was previously assistant chancellor for higher education in New Jersey and director of the federal government's program for integrating institutions of higher education.

Rosalind Barnett is a clinical and research psychologist at Brandeis University and at the Wellesley Center for Research on Women. She is coauthor of *The Competent Woman: Perspectives on Socialization.*

Pamela Banks is an editorial assistant at the *Harvard Business Review.*

Grace Baruch is a development psychologist at Brandeis University and at the Wellesley Center for Research on Women. She is coauthor of *The Competent Woman: Perspectives on Socialization.*

Jacques Barzun, a historian and critic, is professor emeritus at Columbia University, where he taught history and served as provost. Among his many books are *Teachers in America, The House of Intellect,* and *Science: The Glorious Entertainment.*

Warren Bennis is a research professor in the School of Business at the University of Southern California. Previously he was an administrator at the State University of New York, Buffalo, and a professor of psychology at the Massachusetts Institute of Technology. His books include *The Leaning Ivory Tower, Management of Change and Conflict,* and *Beyond the Bureaucracy.*

Paul Bernstein is a sociologist at Boston College. He is author of *Workplace Democratization: Its Internal Dynamics.*

Fred Best directs research on work sharing at the California Employment Development Department. A sociologist, he formerly held positions at the National Commission for Employment Policy and various federal agencies. His books include *Flexible Life Scheduling, Work Sharing,* and *The Future of Work.*

Bill Billiter is a writer for the *Los Angeles Times.* Formerly he worked at the *Louisville* (Kentucky) *Times* and was co-winner of a Pulitzer Prize in 1965 for his reporting on strip mining. He has also taught journalism at Ohio State University.

Richard N. Bolles is director of the National Career Development Project, a program of the United Ministries of Education headquartered in Walnut Creek, California. He is author of the best-selling book *What Color Is Your Parachute? A Practical Manual for Job-Hunters and Career-Changers* and *The Three Boxes of Life and How to Get Out of Them* and is coauthor with John C. Crystal of *Where Do I Go from Here with My Life?*

Daniel Boorstin is Librarian of Congress. He was formerly director of the National Museum of History and Technology of the Smithsonian Institution and professor of history at the University of Chicago. His books include *The Genius of American Politics* and the prize-winning multivolume study *The Americans.*

Augusta Clawson was a federal government worker in the 1940s. She decided to go to work in a shipyard in Oregon in order to write about her experiences and encourage other women to join the war effort.

About the Authors

Allan R. Cohen is professor of management at the University of New Hampshire and vice president of Goodmeasure, Inc., a consulting firm. He is coauthor of *Alternative Work Schedules: Integrating Individual and Organizational Needs*.

John R. Coleman, an economist, has been president of Haverford College since 1967. He is author of *The Changing American Economy, Comparative Economic Systems,* and *Blue-Collar Journal: A College President's Sabbatical*.

Joan E. Crowley is a social psychologist at the Human Resources Research Institute at Ohio State University.

Thomas Dublin is associate professor of history at the University of California, San Diego. A former director of the Lowell Museum Project, his book, *Women at Work: The Transformation of Work and Community in Lowell, Massachusetts, 1826–1860,* won the Bancroft Prize and the Merle Curti Award of the Organization of American Historians. He also edited *Farm and Factory: The Mill Experience and Women's Lives in New England, 1830–1860.*

Amitai Etzioni, a sociologist, is now on the faculty of Georgetown University, after teaching for more than twenty years at Columbia University. He was also director of the Institute for War and Peace Studies. His many books include *Genetic Fix* and *Social Changes: Sources, Patterns and Consequences.*

David W. Ewing is managing editor of the *Harvard Business Review* and a member of the Harvard Business School faculty. A graduate of the Harvard Law School, he is the author of *Freedom Inside the Organization, The Human Side of Planning,* and *The Managerial Mind,* in addition to dozens of articles for such magazines as *Fortune, Psychology Today,* and *Saturday Review.*

Martin Feldstein is professor of economics at Harvard University and president of the National Bureau of Economic Research. He has also been a consultant to several government agencies. He is editor of *The Economics of Public Services.*

Betty Friedan was founder of the National Organization for Women (NOW) and organizer of the National Women's Political Caucus. She is the author of *The Feminine Mystique,* the book generally credited with sparking the women's movement, *It Changed My Life,* and numerous magazine articles.

Herman Gadon is a professor in the Whittemore School of Business and Economics at the University of New Hampshire. He is coauthor of *Alternative Work Schedules: Integrating Individual and Organizational Needs.*

Robert Goldmann, a journalist, is news editor of the "Voice of America" radio programs and a program officer at the Ford Foundation. He is author of numerous articles and editor of the recently published book, *Round Table Justice.*

Emily Greenspan is a free-lance author who writes frequently about behavior and health. She has contributed to such magazines as *The New York Times Magazine* and *Seventeen.*

Robert H. Guest is professor of business administration and organizational behavior at the Amos Tuck School of Business at Dartmouth College. He is coauthor of *The Man on the Assembly Line,* a classic study of blue-collar workers' job satisfaction.

J. Richard Hackman is professor of organization and management and of psychology at Yale University. He has published widely in social and organizational psychology and is coauthor of *Behavior in Organizations.*

Carl Hoffmann is president of Hoffmann Research Associates, a consulting firm in North Carolina.

Louise Kapp Howe is a free-lance writer and journalist. Among the books she has edited are *The White Majority, The Future of the Family,* and *Pink Collar Workers.*

Rosabeth Moss Kanter is professor of sociology and of organization and management at Yale University. She is also chief executive officer of Goodmeasure, Inc., a consulting firm. Her books include *Men and Women of the Corporation, Work and Family in the United States,* and *Commitment and Community.*

Teresa E. Levitin is a social psychologist currently at the National Institute of Mental Health.

Elliot Liebow is chief of the Center for Work and Mental Health, National Institute of Mental Health. An anthropologist, he previously headed NIMH's Center for Study of Metropolitan Problems. He is the author of *Tally's Corner.*

509

Samuel Lipson worked in the textile mills in Lawrence, Massachusetts, in the early part of the twentieth century.

Michael Maccoby, a psychoanalyst and social psychologist, directs the Project on Technology, Work and Character. Affiliated with the Kennedy School of Government, Harvard Universizy, the project studies how management and new technology in the workplace affect human development. He also designed the "Bolivar Project," the first American joint union-management program to improve the quality of working life. He is author of *The Gamesman* and the forthcoming *The Leader: Managing the Workplace.*

Harry Maurer, an investigative journalist, is a former editor of *The Nation.* His articles on international affairs, labor, and economics have appeared in such magazines as *The Progressive* and *The New York Review of Books.* He is the author of *Not Working: An Oral History of the Unemployed.*

Donald Britton Miller is executive officer of Vitality Associates, a consultant firm specializing in human resources management. His particular interest is in creating positive work environments for professionals. He is author of *Personal Vitality, Working with People,* and *Careers '80–'81.*

Ted Mills is director of the nonprofit National Quality of Work Center in Washington, D.C. A former broadcast executive and producer at NBC-TV, he was a member of the National Commission on Productivity and Work Quality.

Daniel Patrick Moynihan is U.S. Senator from New York. He formerly directed the Joint Center for Urban Studies at Massachusetts Institute of Technology and Harvard University, where he was professor of education and urban politics. He served in various federal posts under Presidents Kennedy, Johnson, and Nixon. His books include *The Politics of a Guaranteed Income* and *A Dangerous Place.*

Agnes Nestor was a union organizer in the 1920s. She later became vice-president of the International Glove Workers Union and president of the Chicago Women's Trade Union League.

Colin Norman is a journalist for *Science* magazine. He was previously a senior researcher with the Worldwatch Institute. He is author of *Running on Empty: The Future of the Automobile in an Oil-Short World.*

Pamela O'Connor was a member of the staff of the Survey Research Center at the University of Michigan.

Greg R. Oldham is associate professor of business administration and of labor and industrial relations at the University of Illinois. He has published widely on organizational behavior and work design and motivation.

Barney Olmsted is codirector of New Ways to Work, a Palo Alto, California, organization that she cofounded to improve the quality of work life and expand job opportunities through innovative employment practices. She has been a consultant on job sharing to the California government.

James O'Toole is associate professor of management in the Graduate School of Business Administration and director of the Twenty Year Forecast Project in the Center for Futures Research at the University of Southern California. He was chairman of the Secretary of Health, Education and Welfare's Special Task Force on Work in America in 1972 and principal author of its report. His books include *Watts and Woodstock* and *Work, Learning, and the American Future.*

Göran Palm is a Swedish poet and author.

Robert P. Quinn is at the Survey Research Center, the University of Michigan, where he has directed several surveys of working life. He is coauthor of *The 1972–73 Quality of Employment Survey, The 1977 Quality of Employment Survey,* and *The Chosen Few: A Study of Discrimination in Executive Selection.*

August Ralston is associate professor of finance in the Graduate School of Business at the University of Southern California, specializing in insurance issues.

John Shelton Reed is a sociologist at the University of North Carolina, Chapel Hill. He has also served as a consultant with Hoffmann Research Associates.

About the Authors

Caryl Rivers is public affairs commentator for WGBH-TV in Boston and associate professor of journalism at Boston University. A contributor to such magazines as *The Saturday Review, Ms,* and *The New York Times Magazine,* she is the author of *Aphrodite at Mid-century: Growing Up Female and Catholic in Post-War America.*

Daniel T. Rodgers is associate professor of history at Princeton University, having previously taught at the University of Wisconsin. He is author of *The Work Ethic in Industrial America,* which was awarded the Frederick Jackson Turner prize of the Organization of American Historians.

Russell Sage (1816–1906), a financier, amassed a fortune of more than $70 million in the stock market, railroading, and banking. After his death, his wife gave much of his fortune to philanthropic organizations.

Isabel V. Sawhill is program director for employment and labor policy at the Urban Institute, where she was also the first director of a program on women and families. A labor market economist, she has taught at Goucher College and served with the U.S. government as a policy analyst and as director of the National Commission for Employment Policy. She is the author or coauthor of numerous articles and government reports, and of *Time of Transition: The Growth of Families Headed by Women.*

Robert Schrank is a program officer at the Ford Foundation and a consultant to several government agencies and universities. He has held a wide variety of blue-collar and white-collar jobs, including plumber, auto mechanic, machinist, coal miner, plant manager, union official, and city commissioner. He has a doctorate in sociology.

E. F. Schumacher, who died in 1977, was economic adviser to England's National Coal Board from 1950 to 1970. His ideas on technology were set forth in *Small Is Beautiful: Economics as if People Mattered.*

Nancy Seifer is director of the Center on Women and American Diversity sponsored by the American Jewish Committee. She formerly headed the Office of Ethnic Affairs for New York City's Mayor Lindsay. Her books include *Absent from the Majority: Working Class Women in American* and *Nobody Speaks for Me.*

Earl Shorris is a contributing editor of *Harper's* magazine and author of *The Oppressed Middle: Politics of Middle Management.*

Graham L. Staines, a social psychologist, is on the faculty of Rutgers University. He formerly was a staff member for more than ten years of the University of Michigan's Survey Research Center, where he codirected the 1977 Quality of Employment Survey and was assistant study director of the 1969–70 National Survey of Working Conditions. He is the author of several of the reports from these surveys and of many articles on work and work roles.

Studs Terkel has a syndicated daily radio program in Chicago. He has been an actor, disc jockey, sports commentator, and television master-of-ceremonies, and he has traveled around the world doing on-the-spot interviews. His best-selling books include *Working, Hard Times,* and *American Dreams—Lost and Found.*

Katherine A. Terzi was a member of the staff of the Project on Technology, Work and Character. She is coauthor with Michael Maccoby of several articles on work.

Robert Townsend, a management consultant, was president and vice chairman of Avis Corporation and is now publisher of *The Congressional Monitor.* He is the author of *Up the Organization.*

Richard E. Walton is professor of business administration at the Harvard Business School. He has written extensively on work innovation and his books include *A Behavioral Theory of Labor Negotiations* and *Interpersonal Peacemaking.*

Barbara Mayer Wertheimer is a member of the extension faculty of Cornell University's School of Industrial and Labor Relations, where she directs its Working Women's Program for Research and Education. She formerly was an organizer for the Amalgamated Clothing Workers of America and director of its national education department. She is author of *We Were There: The Story of Working Women in America* and *Trade Union Women: A Study of Their Participation in New York City Locals.*

Terry Wetherby, a writer, also works as a shipyard welder in California. She is the author of *Conversations: Working Women Talk About Doing a Man's Job.*

Willard Wirtz was Secretary of Labor from 1962 to 1969. He was previously a professor at Northwestern University and he has been in private law practice.

J. Patrick Wright, a writer and reporter, was formerly Detroit bureau chief for *Business Week.* He is author of *On a Clear Day You Can See General Motors* and numerous articles in such publications as *Atlantic Monthly,* the *Los Angeles Times,* and the *Washington Post.*

Daniel Yankelovich, a psychologist and social researcher, is president and director of the consulting firm of Yankelovich, Skelly and White. He has taught at New York University and the New School for Social Research. His books include *The Changing Values on Campus* and *The New Mortality: A Profile of American Youth in the Seventies.*

Robert Zager, a management consultant, has been affiliated with the National Center for Productivity and Quality of Working Life in Washington, D.C., and is now vice president of the Work in America Institute, Inc., in Scarsdale, New York.

John L. Zalusky is assistant director of research for the American Federation of Labor and Congress of Industrial Organizations.

Daniel Zwerdling is with National Public Radio in Washington, D.C. He was formerly affiliated with the Association for Self-Management, which is devoted to the study and development of self-management and organizational democracy. He is author of *Democracy at Work.*

Suggestions for Further Reading

Chapter 1
Toward a Definition of Work

Adler, Mortimer. "Labor," in Volume I of the "Syntopicon" of the *Great Books of the Western World* (Chicago: Encyclopaedia Britannica, 1952), pp. 921–939. This is the best short review of how the meanings of work have developed from the ancient Greeks through the early Christians to Adam Smith and Karl Marx and finally to Freud. This useful piece contains several hundred references to the major discourses on work written over the last three thousand years.

de Grazia, Sebastian. *Of Time, Work and Leisure* (New York: Twentieth Century Fund, 1962). This is a humanist's account of how people in Western societies divide their lives between work and leisure. Although the book might be slow reading for some, it presents a unique account of the institution of leisure, which is often discussed but seldom understood.

Kranzberg, Melvin. "Organization of Work," in *Encyclopaedia Britannica*, 15th edition (Chicago: Encyclopaedia Britannica, 1974), pp. 932–942. This is an excellent historical account of how work has been organized from primitive through modern industrial societies. The author discusses the social, political, economic, and technological ramifications of the organization of work.

O'Toole, James. *Making America Work: Productivity and Responsibility* (New York: Continuum Publishing, 1981). This is a state-of-the-art review of what social scientists have learned about work. Just published, this broad overview explores why work is such an important topic in the early 1980s and reviews the latest thinking on such diverse subjects as changing work values, productivity, the organization of work, unemployment, education, and women and work.

Schumacher, E. F. *Small Is Beautiful* (New York: Harper & Row, 1973); and *Good Work* (New York: Harper & Row, 1979). These two books by the late British economist offer an optimistic, humanistic alternative to many of the most dissatisfying aspects of modern industrial life.

Terkel, Studs. *Working* (New York: Random House, 1972, 1974). Terkel's interviews with several dozen blue-collar and white-collar workers provide the clearest single assessment of job satisfaction in contemporary America.

Vermilye, Dyckman. *Relating Work and Education* (San Francisco: Jossey-Bass, 1977). The title of this book is somewhat misleading. In fact, its twenty-five articles relate work not only to education but to leisure, the family, mid-career change, and almost every other important issue facing students enrolled in higher education or continuing education.

Chapter 2
What Work Means to a Blue-Collar Worker

Bell, Daniel. *The Coming of the Post-Industrial Society: A Venture in Social Forecasting* (New York: Basic Books, 1973). Traces the history of industrialism from its beginnings up to its present dissolution into what Bell calls the era of "post-industrialism."

Chinoy, Eli. *Automobile Workers and the American Dream* (New York: Random House, 1955). An examination of the American dream—the ideology that success and equal opportunity are accessible to everyone—based on interviews with sixty-two auto workers.

Gutman, Herbert G. *Work, Culture, and Society in Industrializing America* (New York: Knopf, 1976). This history of the American Industrial Revolution, written from a working-class perspective, describes how workers responded to conditions in the factory with resistance, accommodation, and a preservation of their working-class culture.

Kremen, Bennett. "No Pride in This Dust," in Irving Howe, ed., *The World of the Blue-Collar Worker* (New York: Times Books, 1973). Kremen gives a good description of the experience of a young man working in a South Chicago steel plant.

513

Palm, Göran. *The Flight from Work* (Cambridge, Mass.: Cambridge University Press, 1977). Based on his personal experiences as an assembly worker in a large Swedish factory, the author, a poet, offers an important and insightful analysis of the plight of the manual laborer, and outlines a system of employee participation that has received wide recognition.

Sennett, Richard, and Jonathan Lobb. *The Hidden Injuries of Class* (New York: Knopf, 1972). The authors isolate what they call the "hidden signals of class" through which today's blue-collar worker measures his own worth against society's arbitrary scale of achievement. They examine the working-class psyche through a series of intensive interviews with "ordinary" people.

Walker, Charles R., and Robert H. Guest. *Man on the Assembly Line* (Cambridge, Mass.: Harvard University Press, 1952). This book is a classic in its field. It is an analysis of life on an automobile assembly line in Framingham, Massachusetts, that was drawn from a representative sample of 180 workers. Based on in-depth interviews conducted in people's homes, the study debunks the notion that all people on assembly lines have the same kind of reaction to their work. It also points up what could be done to ease some of the boredom and monotony.

Chapter 3
Blue-Collar Women

Abbott, Edith. *Women in Industry* (New York: Arno Press, 1969). Originally published in 1910, this classic book traces the history of women and work from colonial times through the 1800s.

Cantor, Milton, and Bruce Laurie, eds. *Class, Sex, and the Woman Worker* (Westport, Conn.: Greenwood Press, 1977). This collection of essays examines the experiences of women workers in the United States from the early nineteenth century through the mid-twentieth century from several new perspectives, including our current knowledge of labor history, women's studies, and ethnic identity.

Hourwich, Andrea, and Gladys Palmer, eds. *I Am a Woman Worker: A Scrapbook of Autobiographies* (New York: The Affiliated Schools for Workers, 1936). A collection of autobiographical sketches written by women industrial workers in the mid-1930s.

Komarovsky, Mira. *Blue Collar Marriage* (New York: Random House, 1964). This standard work of family sociology is of interest because of what it tells us about the lives of women in blue-collar families.

O'Neill, William. *Women at Work* (New York: Quadrangle Books, 1972). This book presents two classic studies on blue-collar women. The first is Dorothy Richardson's 1905 autobiographical piece, "The Long Day," about a single woman's move from rural Pennsylvania to the sweatshops of New York City at the turn of the century. The second is Elinor Langer's article, "Women in the Telephone Company," in which the author describes her experiences as a phone sales representative during the 1960s.

Rainwater, Lee, *et al. Workingman's Wife* (New York: Arno Press, 1979). This 1950s study of the lives of the wives of workingmen was originally prepared with advertisers and manufacturers in mind who were trying to capture the blue-collar market. Its value lies in the interesting analysis it offers.

Rubin, Lillian. *Worlds of Pain* (New York: Basic Books, 1977). A recent book that explores the lives of contemporary women, comparing working-class women with those of the middle class.

Schreiber, Carol Tropp. *Changing Places: Men and Women in Transitional Occupations* (Cambridge, Mass.: M.I.T. Press, 1979). A scholarly treatment of women in traditionally male occupations and men in traditionally female ones.

Smuts, Robert. *Women and Work in America* (New York: Columbia University Press, 1959). A good statistical treatment of women's employment patterns from 1890 to 1950.

Terkel, Studs. *Working* (New York: Random House, 1972, 1974). This excellent collection of brief autobiographical vignettes includes a number of selections that focus on blue-collar women.

Further Readings

Van Vorst, Bessie, and Marie Van Vorst. *The Woman Who Toils* (New York: Doubleday, 1903). The authors posed as factory girls for two years in order to write this lucid account of the lifestyles and problems of female industrial workers around the turn of the century.

Walshok, Mary Lindenstein. *Blue Collar Women: Pioneers on the Male Frontier* (New York: Anchor/Doubleday 1981). A new study, based on extensive interviews, of the motivations, attitudes, and job experiences of skilled blue-collar women.

Chapter 4
Professionals and Managers Are Workers, Too

Bennett, Leamon J. "When Employees Run the Company," *Harvard Business Review* (January–February 1979), pp. 75–90. Puget Sound Plywood, Inc., a worker-owned company in Tacoma, Washington, has prospered since its founding in 1941. In this article, its worker-elected chairman-president describes how the company is run and recounts his own experiences since gaining office. He also discusses the types of changes he would like to see in the company and offers some opinions on the reasons for its success. In several interviews, three other workers in the company add their insights. Such employee civil liberties as dissent, conscientious objection, and "due process" are emphasized.

Cary, Frank T. "IBM's Guidelines to Employee Privacy," *Harvard Business Review* (September–October 1976), pp. 82–90. Almost all organizations maintain files with personal data on their employees. But just how necessary is some of this information, and how easily can it be used to violate privacy? In this interview, Frank T. Cary, IBM's chief executive, discusses the responsibility his organization feels toward protecting the privacy of its employees, and describes the code that IBM has developed to ensure this right.

Clausen, A. W. "Listening and Responding to Employees' Concerns," *Harvard Business Review* (January–February 1979), pp. 101–114. A. W. Clausen, head of the world's largest bank, discusses the half-dozen programs designed to protect the rights of bank employees to speech, privacy, and "due process." Following the main interview, eight employees talk candidly about their own experiences with these programs.

de Mare, George, and Joanne Summerfield. *Corporate Lives—A Journey into the Corporate World* (New York: Van Nostrand Reinhold, 1976). In this book, ten executives, whose identities are disguised so they can speak freely, talk about their careers—the crises they have faced and the effects of career demands on their personal lives. Covering the worlds of the corporation, education, politics, the professions, and the arts, these personal narratives reveal not only individual careers, but the life styles and patterns that prevail in American life.

Elbing, Alvar O.; Herman Gadon; and John R. M. Gordon. "Flexible Working Hours: It's About Time," *Harvard Business Review* (January–February 1974), pp. 18 ff. The authors maintain that some form of the flexible working-hours system popular in Europe may become the standard for U.S. companies. They describe the benefits of adopting this system and some of the problems involved in implementing it, and suggest that the key issues are mutual trust and the autonomous distribution of one's time.

Ewing, David W. "Civil Liberties in the Corporation," *New York State Bar Journal* (April 1978), pp. 188–229. The author discusses recent court decisions affecting the freedom of speech, conscience, and privacy in corporations. He suggests that the practice of these rights ultimately enhances management's productivity, as shown by the success of employee rights programs at IBM, Delta Airlines, and other high-profit companies.

————. "The Ghosts of the Founding Fathers Haunt the Boardroom," *New Jersey Bell Journal* (Summer 1980), pp. 26–35. The author holds that civil liberties—such as rights to privacy, free speech, conscientious objection, and due process—are American ideals that can and should be elements of the corporate substructure. He explains how these rights apply in the workplace and benefit both the employee and the employer.

————. "What Business Thinks About Employee Rights," *Harvard Business Review* (September–October 1977), pp. 81–94. This article summarizes the results of an HBR survey of business peoples' attitudes about employee rights. It analyzes the responses of the 2,000 HBR subscribers and finds strong support for increased employee rights, despite threats to business stability. The study also suggests that the stereotype of executives as conservative and oppressive does not hold and that social and economic conditions may determine executives' interest in "constitutionalism."

Further Readings

Ginzberg, Eli. "The Professionalization of the U. S. Labor Force," *Scientific American* (March 1979), pp. 48–53. Through a statistical analysis of the U.S. labor force, this article provides an overview of the number of people affected by the professional work experience.

Greiff, Barrie S., and Preston K. Munter. *Tradeoffs* (New York: The New American Library, 1980). Subtitled "Executive, Family and Organizational Life," this book is a guide to practical strategies for achieving a balance to make executive life a harmonious whole rather than a desperate juggling act. It considers some key questions about priorities between work and home life with the purpose of assessing the dilemmas that face executives at all stages of their careers.

Kanter, Rosabeth Moss, and Barry A. Stein, eds. *Life in Organizations: Workplaces as People Experience Them* (New York: Basic Books, 1979). This is a collection of twenty-two articles, each offering a unique perspective on working in organizations. The focus, as the editors state, is on "the decisions people must make, the dilemmas that they must untangle or survive, [and] the preoccupations and concerns that are likely to arise for them." Articles include profiles of both well-known and anonymous people and organizations that have dealt in special ways with the social and psychological implications of work.

Leeman, Cavin P. "Contracting for an Employee Counseling Service," *Harvard Business Review* (March–April 1974), pp. 20 ff. This short article describes and analyzes an unusual counseling service a bank offers its employees. Although often unrelated to work problems, the counseling has had beneficial effects on the work as well as on the personal lives of the employees who participated.

Sarason, Seymour B. *Working, Aging and Social Change* (New York: The Free Press, 1977). The author examines the historical factors and personal attitudes that attract people to the professions, the frustrations they encounter in their practices, and the consequences of their experiences as professionals. He focuses on the medical profession, but applies to other disciplines the finding that many highly educated professionals feel trapped in their jobs. Chapters 4 and 6 are particularly valuable for their personal insights into young and older professionals' attitudes toward their careers.

"The Troubled Professions," *Business Week* (August 16, 1976), pp. 126–130. This article investigates the changing role of three groups of professionals: lawyers, doctors, and accountants. It examines the expectations people hold of such professionals and concludes that as the American public pressures for better services, the autonomy and the mystique of these respected groups will disappear.

Walters, Kenneth D. "Your Employees' Right to Blow the Whistle," *Harvard Business Review* (July–August 1975), pp. 26–28. The author assesses the status of laws applicable to employee dissension in public and private organizations. He suggests that by enabling the employee to express his or her views without compromising public integrity, management can do much to improve employer-employee relationships and thus obviate the need for employee whistle blowing.

Westin, Alan F. and Stephan Salisbury, eds. *Individual Rights in the Corporation* (New York: Pantheon, 1980). This reader compiles fifty-four critical articles on the growing issues of employee rights. Topics include unjust dismissal, whistle blowing and employee loyalty and obedience, protection against sexual harassment, due process for grievances, and participative management. Some articles provide overviews of the issues; others are more in-depth analyses. All raise issues of law that are becoming increasingly important for people who work in and manage American corporations.

Chapter 5
Roots of the American Work Ethic

Bell, Daniel. "Work and Its Discontents: The Cult of Efficiency in America," in *The End of Ideology: On the Exhaustion of Political Ideas in the Fifties* (Glencoe, Ill.: The Free Press, 1960). Bell examines recent transformations in the world of work in terms of the major modern ideologies of management—particularly Taylor's scientific management and Mayo's human relations approach.

Further Readings

Brody, David. *Steelworkers in America: The Nonunion Era* (New York: Harper & Row, 1970). In this account of workers and work in the nation's most important industry during the era of Andrew Carnegie, Brody tells the story of the creation of one of the first major modern corporations, U.S. Steel.

Cawelti, John G. *Apostles of the Self-Made Man: Changing Concepts of Success in America* (Chicago: University of Chicago Press, 1965). An account of how the idea that any hard-working person could make his way to the top became widely accepted in the nineteenth century, and how it has declined in modern times.

de Grazia, Sebastian. *Of Time, Work, and Leisure* (New York: Doubleday/Anchor, 1964). A provocative study of the rise of modern leisure, in which de Grazia argues that we have much less free time than we think we have and no leisure at all—at least nothing that the Greeks, who invented the word "leisure" and cultivated its practice, would have recognized as such.

Gutman, Herbert G. "Work, Culture, and Society in Industrializing America, 1815–1919." *American Historical Review* 78 (1973), pp. 531–87. In this extension of E. P. Thompson's idea of the contest between industrial values and pre-industrial habits, Gutman argues that what makes the history of work in America unique is that the contest—renewed with each new immigrant group—has never ceased.

Hareven, Tamara K., and Randolph Langenbach. *Amoskeag: Life and Work in an American Factory City* (New York: Pantheon, 1978). An excellent collection of interviews with workers, foremen, and owners joined together in one of the biggest mills in New England in the early twentieth century.

Kasson, John F. "The Factory as Republican Community: Lowell, Massachusetts," in *Civilizing the Machine: Technology and Republican Values in America, 1776–1900* (New York: Penguin, 1977). A study of the creation of the textile mill town of Lowell, Massachusetts, in the 1820s and 1830s. Lowell was both a pioneer experiment in industrialization and a brave attempt to create a Utopian factory town that would be free of poverty and exploitation. Although ultimately unsuccessful, Lowell was significant in that it represented the first major attempt to change work without dramatically changing the fabric of society itself.

Rodgers, Daniel T. *The Work Ethic in Industrial America, 1850–1920* (Chicago: University at Chicago Press, 1978). An exploration of the ways in which nineteenth-century Americans quarreled with and ultimately decided what kinds of work should be altered by the industrial transformation of labor.

Taylor, Frederick W. *The Principles of Scientific Management* (New York: W. W. Norton, 1967). A short, vivid description of the work and proposals of the most important modern industrial engineer.

Thompson, E. P. "Time, Work-Discipline, and Industrial Capitalism," *Past and Present*, No. 38 (1967), pp. 56–97. An account of the irregular rhythms of work as they existed before the invasion of the clock, the employer-employee relationship, and the factory; the long resistance of workers to attempts to make their work habits more rational and efficient; and the ways in which a new, modern consciousness of work and time was finally imposed and internalized. Although Thompson's examples are largely English, they are just as applicable to nineteenth-century America.

Walker, Charles R. *Steel: The Diary of a Furnace Worker* (New York: Arno Press, 1977). This book, published in 1922, may be hard to find, but no other account comes closer to describing what life was like in heavy industry during the early twentieth century. It was written by a young college graduate who wanted to see it for himself.

Walkowitz, Daniel J. *Worker City, Company Town: Iron and Cotton-Worker Protest in Troy and Cohoes, New York, 1855–1884* (Urbana, Ill.: University of Illinois Press, 1978). A particularly good example of modern labor history that explores work and life in two neighboring industrial towns—one dominated by small iron-working shops, the other by a few large textile mills—and asks why their stories were so different.

Weber, Max. *The Protestant Ethic and the Spirit of Capitalism* (New York: Scribner, 1958). First published in 1904, this is the classic book on the roots of the modern work ethic, which Weber traced to Calvinism and the Protestant Reformation.

Further Readings

Woodward, C. Vann. "The Southern Ethic in a Puritan World," in *American Counterpoint: Slavery and Racism in the North-South Dialogue* (Boston: Little, Brown, 1971). An exploration of how the South, as Woodward sees it, escaped the work ethic; written by one of the most influential modern Southern historians.

Yellowitz, Irwin, ed. *The Position of the Worker in American Society, 1865–1896* (Englewood Cliffs, N.J.: Prentice-Hall, 1969). An essay and documents on the ways in which American workers adjusted—or failed to adjust—to the prospect of spending their whole lives working for someone else.

Chapter 6
The Work Ethic Today

Alger, Horatio. *Ragged Dick and Mark, the Match Boy* (New York: Codien Books, 1962). Alger expresses in fiction the entrepreneurial ideal that the lowest level worker can reach the top.

Bendix, Reinhard. *Work and Authority in Industry* (Berkeley: University of California, 1974). This book describes the change in workplace ideologies from the entrepreneurial to the career ethic and the changing role of authority.

Chandler, Alfred D., Jr. *The Visible Hand, the Managerial Revolution in American Business* (Cambridge: Harvard University Press, 1977). The rise of the professional manager at the end of the nineteenth century and his role in running large organizations is described and analyzed.

Chinoy, Ely. *Automobile Workers and the American Dream* (Boston: Beacon Press, 1955). This is a description of how auto workers survive dehumanizing work by the dream of becoming their own boss.

Lemisch, Jesse L. *Benjamin Franklin: The Autobiography and Other Writings* (New York: New American Library, 1961). Franklin expresses the craft ethic of individualistic self reliance and integrity.

Maccoby, Michael. *The Gamesman: The New Corporate Leaders* (New York: Simon and Schuster, 1976). Maccoby studied more than 250 corporate managers; he describes four types, including the entrepreneurial gamesman.

————. *The Leader: Managing the Workplace* (New York: Simon and Schuster, to be published fall 1981). In the context of historical change in America, six new-style leaders are shown to improve both productivity and the quality of working life.

Mills, C. Wright. *White Collar* (New York: Oxford University Press, 1951). From the point of view of the craft ethic, Mills maintains that office work de-skills and demoralizes the worker.

Quinn, Robert P., and Graham L. Staines. *The 1977 Quality of Employment Survey* (Ann Arbor, Mich.: Survey Research Center, Institute for Social Research, University of Michigan, 1977). The Michigan survey of working conditions describes what satisfies and dissatisfies workers in America.

Tocqueville, Alexis de. *Democracy in America* (New York: Vintage Books, 1958). This is a classic analysis of the American character in the 1830s, showing how values of individualism and egalitarianism are rooted in a nation of self-employed farmers, craftsmen, and businessmen.

Whyte, William H. *The Organization Man* (Garden City, N.Y.: Doubleday, 1956). From the point of view of the entrepreneurial ethic, Whyte examines the behavior and values of the managerial class.

Chapter 7
Changing Notions of a Career

Bolles, Richard N. *What Color Is Your Parachute?* (Berkeley: Ten Speed Press, 1980). This popular, best-selling book contains a wealth of information and practical advice for people seeking jobs or considering a career change.

Catalyst. *What to Do with the Rest of Your Life* (New York: Simon and Schuster, 1980). Written for women, this is a guide to jobs in career fields expected to offer the greatest opportunities during the 1980s—namely, business, government and law, science and engineering, health, and the skilled trades.

Elkstrom, Ruth B; Abigail M. Harris; and Marlaine E. Lockheed. *How to Get College Credit for What You Have Learned as a Homemaker and Volunteer* (Princeton, N.J.: Educational Testing Service, 1977). Written for women who are contemplating a career change, this is a useful manual for assessing and capitalizing on skills acquired as a homemaker and/or volunteer worker.

Haldane, Bernard. *Career Satisfactions and Success: A Guide to Job Freedom* (New York: Amacom, 1974). The audience for this book is the business and professional world. In it Haldane outlines a system to help readers learn how to maximize their personal career potential and/or increase employee productivity.

Holland, John L. *Making Vocational Choices: A Theory of Careers* (Englewood Cliffs, N.J.: Prentice-Hall, 1973). In this book, the originator of the idea that all careers can be grouped into six basic families describes methods for matching individual stories with specific types of jobs or careers.

O'Neil, Nena, and George O'Neil. *Shifting Gears: Finding Security in a Changing World* (Philadelphia: Lippincott, 1974). This book examines some of the issues involved in making the decision to switch jobs or careers. Approaching the problem from the standpoint of changing societal values and lifestyles, the authors offer some practical suggestions for overcoming fears that often prevent people from acting out their impulses to seek out more rewarding forms of employment.

Schreiber, Carol Tropp. *Changing Places* (Cambridge, Mass.: M.I.T. Press, 1979). The author explores recent changes in the workplace, with particular emphasis on the movement of men and women into new so-called transitional occupational situations.

Chapter 8
Women and Work in the 1980s

Bailyn, Lotte. "Taking Off for the Top—How Much Acceleration for Career Success," *Management Review* (January 1979), 18–23. This insightful article on the traditional fast-burn path to the top and its impact on long-term career progress and work/family responsibilities includes suggestions on how worklife might be restructured to make room for two-career families.

Bem, Sandra L., and Daryl Bem. *Training the Woman to Know Her Place: The Social Antecedents of Women in the World of Work* (Harrisburg, Penn.: Pennsylvania Department of Education, 1973). A concise treatment of such topics as women in the world of work, discrimination, the effects of sex-role conditioning on women's aspirations, and the presumed imcompatibility of family and career. A last section challenges the counselor to awaken young women "to an entire spectrum of new possibilities."

Blaxall, Martha, and Barbara Reagan, eds. *Women and the Workplace: The Implications of Occupational Segregation* (Chicago: University of Chicago Press, 1976). A fine presentation of the proceedings of the Conference on Occupational Segregation, this volume examines the social institution of occupational segregation, its historic roots, and its economic dimensions, then outlines some policies for combating it.

Broverman, I.K., *et al.* "Sex-Role Stereotypes and Clinical Judgments of Mental Health," *Journal of Consulting and Clinical Psychology* 34 (1970), 1–7. A landmark article on clinicians' perceptions of mental health and their association with men's (as opposed to women's) adult qualities.

Daniels, Pamela. "Dream vs. Drift in Women's Careers: The Question of Generativity," in Barbara Goldman and Barbara Forisha, eds., *Outsiders on the Inside: Women and Organizations* (Englewood Cliffs, N.J.: Prentice-Hall, 1980). A beautifully written essay on the impact of women's perceptions of their own role as limiting to their professional lives and aspirations.

Epstein, Cynthia Fuchs. *Women's Place: Options and Limits in Professional Careers* (Berkeley, Calif.: University of California Press, 1970). An examination of the cultural themes and value systems that influence women's decisions about careers, the consequences of the socialization process in career choice, and role conflict. The author also analyzes the structure of the professions and the tendencies of particular professions to change as they relate to the women in them.

Ginzberg, Eli, and Alice M. Yohalem, eds. *Corporate Lib: Women's Challenge To Management* (Baltimore: Johns Hopkins University Press, 1973). A collection of papers presented at a 1971 conference on women at the Columbia Graduate School of Business. The thirteen contributors (representing management, the feminist movement, government, labor, and the academic world) discuss the problems women face and such root causes as discrimination, sex stereotyping, and role conflict. They also offer a variety of conclusions about women's future in corporate management.

Holstrom, Lynda Lytle. *The Two-Career Family* (Cambridge, Mass.: Schenkman Publishing Co., 1972). An analysis of the impact of the two-career family on the rigid structure of the professions, the isolation of the nuclear family, and the equating of masculinity with superiority. Comparisons between "professional" and "traditional" couples highlight the differences in their attitudes toward such issues as child-raising, sharing of tasks, geographic mobility, competition between spouses, and allocation of time, effort, and money.

Kreps, Juanita. *Sex in the Market Place: American Women at Work* (Baltimore: Johns Hopkins University Press, 1971). A review of the literature on women's labor force activity, examining when women work, at what jobs, and under what arrangements. The author discusses the factors influencing the demand for and supply of women workers and how the supply and demand factors differ for men and women, and the possible implications of increased female labor force participation for men's roles, both in the home and in the job market. A section titled "The Future" discusses discrimination and the changes needed.

————, ed. *Women and the American Economy: A Look to the 1980s* (Englewood Cliffs, N.J.: Prentice-Hall, 1976). A collection of essays exploring the ways in which women are re-shaping the economy and society, with a look at major questions for the 1980s.

Miller, Jean Baker. *Toward a New Psychology of Women* (Boston: Beacon Press, 1978). A strongly feminist perspective on women's psychological health and strength for a new society.

Ruddick, Sara, and Pamela Daniels, eds. *Working It Out: 23 Women Writers, Artists, Scientists, and Scholars Talk About Their Lives and Work* (New York: Pantheon, 1978). In this candid account of the dilemmas and challenges faced by creative working women, twenty-three people representing a variety of occupations talk about their careers, their families, and their loves.

Safilio-Rothschild, Constantina. *Sex-Role Socialization and Sex Discrimination: A Synthesis and Critique of the Literature* (Washington, D.C.: Department of Health, Education and Welfare, 1979). A thoroughly researched and clearly annotated survey and critique of the existing literature on socialization and discrimination.

Sheehy, Gail. *Passages: Predictable Crises of Adult Life* (New York: Dutton, 1976). In this best-selling book, Sheehy traces the stages in adult development. The emphasis is more on people in their 20s, 30s, and 40s than on those 50 and older.

U.S. Department of Labor. *Women and Work* (Washington, D.C.: Department of Labor, 1979). This comprehensive review of recent studies on women and work covers such topics as male and female earning gaps, labor market experiences of women, women's employment problems, and strategies for upgrading women's opportunities.

Wilson, Barbara Lazarus, and Nancy Tobin. *Women and the World of Work* (Newton, Mass.: Educational Development Center, 1975). A booklet summarizing data for counselors on the status of women in the work force, the impact of sex-role stereotyping on women's goals and aspirations, nontraditional career opportunities for women, and protective legislation.

Chapter 9
Work and the Family

Coser, Rose Laub, ed. *The Family: Its Structure and Functions* (New York: St. Martin's, 1964). This is an excellent introduction to family life, written from a sociological and anthropological point of view.

Erikson, Erik H. *Childhood and Society* (New York: Norton, 1950). Still the best analysis of the psychological needs of the child and, by implication, of the consequences to the child of excessive familial burdens.

Fraiberg, Selma. *Every Child's Birthright: In Defense of Mothering* (New York: Basic Books, 1977). This powerful and well-documented indictment of day-care centers raises questions that will have to be addressed if American children are not to be the ultimate and tragic "payees" for the kind of family life our social and economic system now seems to encourage if not demand.

Freud, Anna; J. Goldstein; and A. Solnit. *Beyond the Best Interests of the Child* (New York: The Free Press, 1973). Relying on their knowledge of the law, their clinical experience with broken families, and their understanding of child development, the authors define and discuss what they believe to be the real needs of the "wanted child."

Ginzburg, Eli, and Hyman Berman. *The American Worker in the Twentieth Century* (New York: The Free Press, 1963). An important compilation of autobiographical sketches that includes statements by Americans on what work means to them and their families.

Janeway, Elizabeth. *Man's World, Woman's Place* (New York: William Morrow, 1971). A shrewd and powerfully stated analysis of the changing sexual climate in America—its effects both on personal and family life and on the nation's economy.

Moore, Kristin, *et al. Teenage Motherhood: Social and Economic Consequences* (Washington, D.C.: The Urban Institute, 1977). This book provides an in-depth look at a special but increasingly pervasive problem in this country.

Chapter 10
Alternative Work Patterns

Best, Fred. *Flexible Life Scheduling: Breaking the Education-Work-Retirement Lockstep* (New York: Praeger, 1980). A humanistic argument of the benefits that would result to both individuals and society from more freedom to schedule the time of our lives.

Giele, Janet Zollinger. "Changing Sex Roles and Family Structure," *Social Policy* (January–February 1979), 32–43. An insightful and provocative discussion of changing sex and family roles, with particular attention to the expected increase in demand for more flexible work-time.

Hedges, Janice Neipert, and Daniel Taylor. "Recent Trends in Worktime: Hours Edge Downward." *Monthly Labor Review* (March 1980), 3–11. An analysis of recent worktime trends.

Meir, Gertl S. *Job Sharing: A New Pattern for Quality of Work and Life* (Kalamazoo, Mich.: W. E. Upjohn Institute for Employment Research, 1978). A good research report on the impact of job sharing both on people's working lives and on their personal lives.

Nollen, Stanley; Brenda Eddy; and Virginia Martin. *Permanent Part-Time Employment: The Manager's Perspective* (New York: Praeger Special Studies, 1978). A major study of the effects of part-time employment on perceived worker productivity, turnover, and morale; it includes a discussion of the managerial pros and cons of other worktime innovations.

Sheppard, Harold, and Sara Rix. *The Graying of Working America* (New York: The Free Press, 1977). A comprehensive and well-documented discussion of older members of the working population, with particular attention to the problems of financing pensions for the large post-World War II "baby boom" generation.

Vermilye, Dyckman W. *Relating Work and Education* (San Francisco: Jossey-Bass, 1977). A collection of essays dealing with the relationships between work and education.

Wirtz, Willard, and the National Manpower Institute. *The Boundless Resource* (Washington, D.C.: New Republic Book Company, 1975). A recent and major volume on the topic of life scheduling flexibility, written by a consortium of policymakers and academics working under the leadership of former Secretary of Labor, Willard Wirtz.

Work, Time, and Employment. Special Report No. 20. National Commission for Employment Policy, Washington, D.C., October 1978. This report examines issues and policies related to work sharing; it is important because it contains the viewpoints of both proponents and opponents of work sharing.

Chapter 11
The Quality of Work Life

Bluestone, I. "Decision-Making by Workers," *The Personnel Administrator* (July–August 1974), 26–30; and Winpisinger, W. W. "Job Enrichment: A Union View," *Monthly Labor Review* (April 1973), 54–56. Here are the views of two national labor leaders who disagree about what the stance of organized labor should be toward work redesign and quality of work life innovations in the years to come.

Fein, M. "Job Enrichment: A Reevaluation," *Sloan Management Review* (Winter 1974), 69–88. Here is the case *against* work redesign as a strategy for personal and organizational change. The author suggests that few benefits will be obtained by increasing worker autonomy and job challenge in blue-collar settings, in part because such intrinsic aspects of the work as these are of secondary importance to the people who do the work.

Hackman, J. R., and G. R. Oldham. *Work Redesign* (Reading, Mass.: Addison-Wesley, 1980). This book reviews what is required to create conditions for self-motivation and self-management in organizations. Included are strategies for the design of involving work for individuals, for the creation of self-managing work teams, and for designing and carrying out the work restructuring process.

Herzberg, F. *The Managerial Choice* (Homewood, Ill.: Dow Jones-Irwin, 1976). This is the most recent and comprehensive statement of the views of the originator of the "job enrichment" approach to personal and organizational change through work redesign. The book includes an explanation of "motivation-hygiene theory" (the basis for Herzberg's strategy for job enrichment), examples of applications of the theory, and a very readable question-and-answer defense of this approach to work design.

Lawler, E. E., III. "The New Plant Revolution," *Organizational Dynamics* (Winter 1978), 2–12. Is there an impending revolution in how new organizations are designed? Here is a description of how multiple innovations (including reward systems, physical layouts, personnel policies, and designs for work) have been installed simultaneously in new plants. If these experiments are as successful as Lawler thinks they will be, their implications could be substantial.

——. *Pay and Organization Development* (Reading, Mass.: Addison-Wesley, 1981). Overview of the key role that pay and other rewards play in quality of work life projects.

——. "Should the Quality of Work Life Be Legislated?" *The Personnel Administration* (January 1976), 17–21; and Locke, E. A. "The Case Against Legislating the Quality of Work Life," *The Personnel Administrator* (May 1976), 19–21 These two authors lay out the arguments for and against government involvement in improving the quality of work life in organizations through legislative action.

Leavitt, H. J. "Suppose We Took Groups Seriously . . .," in E. L. Cass and F. G. Zimmer, eds. *Man and Work in Society* (New York: Van Nostrand Reinhold, 1975). What if organizations were designed using groups rather than individuals as the basic building blocks? Here is a provocative and optimistic view of what might happen.

O'Toole, J. *Work, Learning, and the American Future* (San Francisco: Jossey-Bass, 1977). This book addresses a number of major questions about the utilization of human resources in U.S. organizations, probes the interdependencies between work and education, and analyzes how changes can be wrought in a technology-dependent capitalist society. It takes up where the classic *Work in America* left off.

Tichy, N. M., and J. N. Nisberg. "When Does Work Restructuring Work?" *Organizational Dynamics* (Summer 1976), 63–80. The authors present a framework for evaluating work redesign and other devices for creating high-involvement organizations, and then use that framework to analyze two quality of work life projects—showing why one succeeded and the other failed.

Walton, R. E. "Successful Strategies for Diffusing Work Innovations," *Journal of Contemporary Business* (1977), 1–22. This paper presents an in-depth analysis of three work restructuring programs. Based on these cases, the author offers some insights into the conditions under which such programs will spread to other organizational units.

Walton, R. E., and L. S. Schlesinger. "Do Supervisors Thrive in Participative Work Systems?" *Organizational Dynamics* (Winter 1979), 24–38. What is to be done with the role of the supervisor when high-involvement work systems are created? Here are some ideas about that, based on studies in a number of organizations where self-managing work has been installed. Some specific suggestions for action are included.

White, B. J. "Innovations in Job Design: The Union Perspective," *Journal of Contemporary Business* (1977), 23–35. The response of U.S. labor unions to the creation of enriched, self-managing work is explored in this essay. Reasons for the views of organized labor on the topic are offered.

Chapter 12
Democracy in the Workplace

Bernstein, Paul. *Workplace Democratization: Its Internal Dynamics* (Kent, Ohio: Kent State University Press, 1976). The best organizational behavior study of the plywood firms of the Pacific Northwest, considered to be the most successful worker cooperatives in the United States.

Blasi, Joseph. *The Communal Future: The Kibbutz and the Utopian Dilemma* (Norwood, Penn.: Norwood Editions, 1978). A participant-observer's study of a kibbutz told in the context of a more general analysis of the kibbutz movement.

Johnson, Ana Gutierrez, and William Foote Whyte. "The Mondragon System of Worker Production Cooperatives," *Industrial and Labor Relations Review* (October 1977). An analysis of the most successful system of worker cooperatives to appear thus far in a private enterprise economy. The Basque case of cooperative development is beginning to be considered by both activists and researchers as the most promising model for building cooperative production firms within private enterprise economies.

Levitan, Uri, and Menachem Rosner, eds. *Work and Organization in Kubbutz Industry* (Norwood, Penn.: Norwood Editions, 1980). Reviews ten years of research on industrial firms in Israeli kibbutzim.

Oakshott, Robert. *The Case for Worker Cooperatives* (Boston and London: Rutledge and Kegan Paul, 1978). A survey of worker cooperatives in western Europe.

Stern, Robert, and Tove Helland Hammer. "Buying Your Job: Factors Affecting the Success or Failure of Employee Acquisition Attempts," *Human Relations* 31 (1978), 1101–1117. An analysis of both successful and unsuccessful cases in which, following a conglomerate divestiture, workers and community people attempted to save jobs by purchasing the plant.

Vanek, Jaroslav, ed. *Self-Management: Economic Liberation of Man* (Hammondsworth, England, and Baltimore: Penguin Books, 1975). A collection of essays on the theory and practice of self-management (worker cooperatives). The cases discussed are primarily European.

Whyte, William F. Statement in *Congressional Record* in support of the Voluntary Job Preservation and Community Stabilization Act (June 19, 1978). Whyte and Joseph Blasi worked together with Congressman Peter H. Kostmayer, Stanley N. Lundine, and Matthew F. McHugh on the bill, which, though not enacted, has served to stimulate a broad range of employee ownership legislation.

———. "In Support of Voluntary Employee Ownership," *Society* 15, No. 6 (September/ October 1978). A much more extensive discussion of the case for the legislation referred to above. Also deals with some of the problems of building employee participation into worker ownership.

Whyte, William F., and Joseph Blasi. "From Research to Legislation on Employee Ownership," *Economic and Industrial Democracy* 1, No. 3 (1980). Examines the process of getting the first employee ownership legislation introduced and enacted.

Whyte, William F., and Donald McCall. "Self-Help Economics," *Society* 17, No. 4 (1980). Shows how worker-ownership fits in with emerging locally based development strategies.

United States Government. Hearings on Small Business Employee Ownership Act in Senate Select Committee on Small Business (1979). Includes case reports and a general statement.

United States Government. Hearings on Employee Ownership before Subcommittee on Economic Stabilization of House of Representatives Committee on Banking, Finance, and Urban Affairs (February 27, 1979). Of special interest are reports on particular cases in testimony of some of the principal actors involved.

Zwerdling, Daniel. *Democracy at Work* (Washington, D.C.: Association for Self-Management, 1978). A wide-ranging review of cases, problems, and potentialities, with special emphasis on the emergence of employee ownership out of conglomerate divestitures in the United States.

Chapter 13
The Urban Unemployed

Bakke, E. Wright. *The Unemployed Worker* (New Haven, Conn.: Yale University Press, 1940); and *Citizens Without Work: A Study of the Effects of Unemployment Upon the Worker's Social Relations and Practices* (Hamden, Conn.: Shoestring Press, 1969, reprint of 1940 ed.). These two books are classic studies of the destructive consequences of unemployment on workers during the Depression. Included is an analysis of how public assistance, although initially effective in helping the unemployed, was ultimately unable to restore their relationships with family, friends, and community.

Ferman, Louis. "After the Shutdown: The Social and Psychological Consequences of Job Displacement," *Industrial and Labor Relations Report*, (Ithaca, N.Y.: Cornell University, Spring 1981) pp. 22–27. A contemporary description of the effects of a plant shutdown, individual workers, and their social relationships.

Jahoda, M.; T. Lazarsfeld; and H. Zeisel. *Marienthal: The Sociography of an Unemployed Community* (Chicago: Aldeen Atherton, 1971). A study of a small Austrian mill town that closed down during the Depression. The millworkers who lost their jobs also lost all sense of time and their ability to plan budgets realistically; they spent money on trinkets rather than on essentials.

Kornblum, William, and Terry Williams. "Youth Unemployment," *Social Policy*, May–June, 1981. A recent study of the problems of young people, particularly members of minority groups, in finding employment in our central cities.

Komarovsky, Mira. *The Unemployed Man and His Family* (New York: Dryden Press, 1940). Like the books by Bakke and Jahoda, *et al.*, this is a classic study of the social and psychological impact of unemployment during the Depression.

Levitan, Sol. *Work Is Here to Stay, Alas* (Salt Lake City: Olympus, 1973). A general book on manpower and the kinds of jobs that are available now and will be available in the future. The author concludes that automation will not eliminate the need to work.

Padfield, Harland, and Roy Williams. *Stay Where You Were: A Study of Unemployables in Industry* (New York: Lippincott, 1973). A study of blacks who have been in government job training programs but are unable to keep steady jobs.

Slote, Alfred. *Termination: A Closing at Baker Plant* (New York: Bobbs-Merrill, 1969; reprinted by University of Michigan Social Research, 1977). A very moving account, written by a journalist, of what happens to employees when a plant closes down. Slote's report is based on a careful academic study by Sidney Cobb and Stanislav Kasl.

Chapter 14
Creating Total Employment

Berg, Ivar. *Education and Jobs: The Great Training Robbery* (Boston: Beacon Press, 1971). This social science classic takes on the common wisdom that vocational training helps people get and keep jobs. Berg shows that success in the labor market is far more complex than many policy makers have assumed.

Ginzberg, Eli, ed. *Employing the Unemployed* (New York: Basic Books, 1980). An analysis of programs designed to convert unemployment into employment.

Okun, Arthur M., ed. *The Battle Against Unemployment* (New York: Norton, 1972). Rev. ed. This collection of articles by such well-known economists as Milton Friedman and Walter Heller discusses the relationships between unemployment, inflation, and fiscal policy.

Osterman, Paul. *Getting Started* (Cambridge, Mass.: The MIT Press, 1980). This book analyzes the problems facing young workers as they break into the labor force. It contains an extensive and useful bibliography.

Palmer, John L., ed. *Creating Jobs* (Washington, D.C.: The Brookings Institution, 1978). An analysis of government programs designed to encourage employment.

"Planning for Full Employment," *The Annals of the American Academy of Political and Social Science*, Vol. 418, March 1975. This entire issue of *The Annals* is devoted to an exploration of policies to create full employment. The authors include politicians (such as Hubert Humphrey) as well as scholars who deal with all aspects of this complex problem.

Thurow, Lester C. *Generating Inequality* (New York: Basic Books, 1975). An analysis of the relationship between jobs and earnings.

U.S. Department of Labor, Bureau of Labor Statistics. *Employment and Earnings* (Washington, D.C.: U.S. Government Printing Office). These monthly reports contain basic data on employment and unemployment.

Wirtz, Willard. *The Boundless Resource* (Washington, D.C.: New Republic Book Company, 1975). Former Secretary of Labor Willard Wirtz argues cogently for a new national education/work policy designed to prepare young people for successful careers and to combat the terrible problems of teenage unemployment.

Chapter 15
Work and the Future

Best, Fred. *Flexible Life Scheduling: Breaking the Education-Work-Retirement Lockstep* (New York: Praeger, 1980). Presents some creative and humanistic ideas about how to arrange and schedule work, education, and leisure in the future. Reviews the existing literature on these issues and provides some interesting new evidence on how people view the tradeoff between more time and more money.

Freeman, Richard B. "The Evolution of the American Labor Market, 1948–80," in Martin Feldstein, ed. *The American Economy in Transition* (Chicago: University of Chicago Press, 1980). A scholarly but not overly technical review of seven labor market trends that have occurred since World War II. It includes a particularly good discussion of declining unionization and the changes in government policy that have altered personnel practices.

Friedrich, Otto. "The Robot Revolution," *Time* (December 8, 1980), 72–83. This readable article examines the current impact of robot technology and automation on the American economy and business world.

Fullerton, Howard N., Jr. "The 1995 Labor Force: A First Look," *Monthly Labor Review* (December 1980). This article contains the most up-to-date official data on labor force projections. Alternative growth paths by age, race, and sex are also discussed.

Rosow, Jerome M., and Clark Kerr, eds. *Work in America: The Decade Ahead* (New York: Van Nostrand Reinhold, 1979). A good collection of articles on the work force of the future and the emerging work environment by a distinguished group of authors. Among the topics discussed are the quality of work life, the impact of technology on the working environment, and emerging trends in collective bargaining.

Smith, Ralph E., ed. *The Subtle Revolution: Women at Work* (Washington, D.C.: The Urban Institute Press, 1979). Excellent collection of articles on the changing labor force status of women and some of the implications of these changes for families and for society.